Writing
for **television,**
radio, and
new media

From the Cengage Series in Broadcast and Production

Writing
for **television, radio,** and **new media**

ELEVENTH EDITION

Robert L. Hilliard
Professor Emeritus, Emerson College

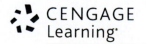
CENGAGE
Learning®

Australia · Brazil · Japan · Korea · Mexico · Singapore · Spain · United Kingdom · United States

CENGAGE
Learning·

Writing for television, radio, and new media, Eleventh Edition
Robert Hilliard

Product Director: Monica Eckman

Product Manager: Kelli Strieby

Content Developer: Rebecca Donahue

Associate Content Developer: Erin Bosco

Media Developer: Jessica Badiner

Marketing Manager: Jillian Borden

Art and Cover Direction, Production
Management, and Composition:
PreMediaGlobal

Manufacturing Planner: Doug Bertke

For product information and technology assistance, contact us at
Cengage Learning Customer & Sales Support, 1-800-354-9706

For permission to use material from this text or product,
submit all requests online at **www.cengage.com/permissions**
Further permissions questions can be emailed to
permissionrequest@cengage.com

Library of Congress Control Number: 2013951173

ISBN-13: 978-1-285-46507-4

ISBN-10: 1-285-46507-5

Cengage Learning
200 First Stamford Place, 4th Floor
Stamford, CT 06902
USA

Cengage Learning is a leading provider of customized learning solutions with office locations around the globe, including Singapore, the United Kingdom, Australia, Mexico, Brazil, and Japan. Locate your local office at **www.cengage.com/global**

Cengage Learning products are represented in Canada by
Nelson Education, Ltd.

To learn more about Cengage Learning, visit **www.cengage.com**

Purchase any of our products at your local college store or at our preferred online store **www.cengagebrain.com**

Printed in the United States of America
2 3 4 5 6   19 18 17 16 15

For
Amy and Roger
&

Ella and Jeff
whose use of the written word has informed, stimulated, and entertained and, above all, raised our consciousness and our consciences

CONTENTS

5   News and Sports / 147

PREFACE

The year 2012 marked the 50th anniversary of the publication of the first edition of this book, then entitled *Writing for Television and Radio*. The technological aspects of media have changed considerably in the past half century, and we have recognized these changes not only with the title of this book, currently *Writing for Television, Radio, and New Media*, but, as available and appropriate, with new sections and examples reflecting the impact of technological advancement. With each new edition we have discovered and reaffirmed something that has continued as a hallmark since the beginning of recorded literature: Even within technological change, the principles of good writing remain virtually the same. They adapt to the requirements of the new form of distribution—for example, new principles of dramaturgy for television when that medium emerged in the first half of the 20th century. Yet, those new principles were based on the same principles that governed stage dramas in western culture since Roman and Greek dramaturgy of 2000 and 5000 years ago. The chapter in this book on "The Play" illustrates that. What changes for the playwright and for the writer in another format in a new media is principally technique. The 10th edition expanded that approach with extended narrative and examples of writing for the Internet.

This edition, the 11th, recognizes a subset of the Internet that has expanded exponentially in the past few years, especially since the last edition of this book: Social Media. Facebook, LinkedIn, Twitter, and other social interchange programs not only have gained millions upon millions of users, but have expanded in content, not the least of which is that of commercials. Just as we have in past editions added techniques of writing commercials for the Internet in general, in this edition we have added material on writing for the social media, including techniques appropriate for effective commercials.

As this edition goes to press, texting is ubiquitous. (Okay, what's the texting shorthand for that word?!) Finding a way to condense an important advisory into 140 characters requires creative thinking—and spelling. In the play, *Inquisition*, one of the characters asks "why would anyone text someone when they can actually talk to them live more effectively and efficiently?" Another character answers that it's mostly teenagers who are texting, their fragile egos hiding behind silent words rather than opening themselves to verbal conversations. The point is that texting is, for whatever reasons, widespread, as is tweeting and notifications on Facebook. Therefore, writing techniques relating to effective use of these programs is important.

In the 10th edition of this book we noted the emergence of a new, powerful factor in communications—convergence. In this edition we carry the concept even further.

Convergence is the melding of different means of audio and video delivery so that they become interdependent and differences among them become blurred. The traditional broadcasting model has moved closer to the Internet model, and the Internet has opened up to accommodating broadcasting procedures. TV stations not only stream onto the Internet, but originate on web sites, as well. Television manufacturers make their products Internet compatible, and Internet developers are adapting to high-quality full screen video. Internet radio has grown. Analog has converted to digital. Internet-based relationships of the media to their audiences have been marked by dramatic increases in mobile, hand-held audio, video, and data receivers, with various applications or apps, for virtually any contentor service available. Individuals can communicate from virtually any place and virtually to the entire world with video, audio, and text. Advances in high definition, video-on-demand, 3-dimensional pictures, video compression, and receiver software mark some of the ongoing changes in technology. Social Internet sites—some with hundreds of millions of active members—have created new psychological- and sociological-related adaptations. These dramatic changes require frequent new editions of textbooks in this field, including this one devoted to writing, if current students and current and future practitioners are to keep up with the requirements of their profession.

Although the basic principles of good writing remain essentially the same, as in any field, concepts, approaches, and techniques must be adapted to fit the advantages and the disadvantages of the new model. This edition, as past editions, is not designed to teach you how to write Internet software programs. That differs from helping you learn to write *for* the Internet, adapting your writing for radio and television, your writing of audio and video. If you want to write software or online programming such as video games, you would do well to take a course specializing in those areas.

USING THIS BOOK

As with previous editions of *Writing for Television, Radio, and New Media*, revisions to this Eleventh Edition are based largely on comments and suggestions from users of the book—professors in colleges and universities and students and professionals. I am aware that many professors who use this book as a text do not include some or many of the chapter subjects in their curriculum. For example, some institutions have separate courses for writing the television drama or sitcom, or for news and sports, or for commercial advertising writing. The inclusion of Internet writing techniques and approaches in most chapter formats may not be germane to those courses that concentrate specifically on broadcast television and/or radio. This book, however, is designed to provide a coverage that is broad and deep enough to offer a selection of formats that will cover the needs of almost any given writing course. Many beginning courses in media writing use virtually the entire book's contents as a comprehensive introduction for the future professional writer. Other courses use this book as a menu, with the user picking and choosing the contents that fit her or his needs and ignoring those chapters that are not relevant to the particular syllabus.

This edition also continues to include suggestions for writing for diverse audiences such as racial and ethnic groups, women, children, and various lifestyles. Hopefully, this material will help students become more aware of the multicultural society in which we all live—an imperative for current and future professionals, who must understand the needs, concerns, and goals of all peoples and nations if they are to function effectively and contribute meaningfully to an increasingly shrinking world.

FORMAT EXAMPLES

During the past few years the reality show format has proliferated in popularity and scheduling, and this edition attempts to reflect that trend adding that genive to other format examples. One of the longest-lasting and most popular of the reality shows is the highly successful "Dancing With The Stars," segments of which are included in this book.

THIS WRITER'S RESPONSIBILITY

I wish to emphasize to the student a key rationale for this book: Creativity and talent cannot be taught, but principles and techniques can. If you are willing to devote time, energy, and hard work to learning the basics of writing, you will be able to write at least an adequate script for any video, audio, or Internet program or project. If you also have writing talent and the determination to combine it with effective principles and techniques, you are on your way to making important contributions to the media industries. With persistence and luck, you may also find yourself with an Emmy on your mantle and a Porsche in your driveway.

But while you are doing all that, do not forget that television, radio, and the Internet are the most powerful forces in the world for affecting the minds, emotions, and even the actions of humankind. Like it or not, as a writer for the media, you are (or will be) in a position of tremendous power to serve either *only* the bottom-line economic self-interest that dominates most of the media, or you can choose to make certain, as well, that you serve the audience's individual and group well-being. In other words, you can use the media's influence to help make a better world for everyone.

FEATURES

A key feature of this textbook is using real-world examples to illustrate applications of writing principles and theories. This approach is used in all chapters, with radio, television, and Internet professional scripts and storyboards. For example, in Chapter 4, "Commercials and Announcements," readers will find straight-sell, drama, humor, testimonials, and other types of spots. Chapter 6, "Features, Documentaries, and Reality Programs," includes scripts such as the rundown for a Macy's Thanksgiving Day Parade and, as noted earlier, for the reality show "Dancing With The Stars." Chapter 10, "The Play," includes a script excerpt from a produced screenplay and, as an example of your power as a writer through the power of the media, a strong presentation of a political view in an excerpt from the 2000's first decade powerful series, "Boston Legal." Chapter 7, "Interview and Talk Programs," includes the script of a broadcast interview of this book's author about another of his books.

The application of video and audio writing continues to be a critical component of this textbook. As with previous editions, new quotes containing advice for would-be professionals from current professionals in the field in various format areas and in various chapters are featured. Reviews of earlier editions of this textbook referred to it as a "bread-and-butter" approach to writing for the media. This new edition attempts to continue to that approach.

PEDAGOGICAL FEATURES

A key pedagogical approach is to present principles to the learner, followed by pertinent explanatory examples, followed by exercises applying the material thus far learned, concluding with evaluation of the student's work. Each chapter in this book attempts to follow this process with, where warranted, application exercises at the ends of chapters. As part of the practical approach of this textbook, many exercises suggest projects beyond the classroom and into the student's real-world environment. For example, reflecting similar approaches in the exercises for other chapters, a sample exercise in Chapter 5, "News and Sports," is "If your college or university has a radio or television station, arrange to write a news story for one of the news programs."

NEW TO THIS EDITION

This edition contains new material on writing for the Internet, specifically that related to social media, the fastest growing area of communications. It continues the emphasis on different program formats found online, stemming from the concept of convergence. The various key writing formats are retained, but references to people and events have been updated, where appropriate and necessary, to reflect significant changes since the publication of the previous edition of this book. Keep in mind, however, that in the year it takes for a book to reach a student after the author has submitted the manuscript to the publisher, the fast-changing nature of the media may make any reference quickly obsolete. While some new examples of scripts, such as political spots reflecting the 2012 national elections, are included, scripts throughout the book considered excellent writing examples are retained. Although the economic recession that prompted some of the new material in the chapter on "Professional Opportunities" in the previous edition is ostensibly over as this is written, the competition for jobs in a changing communication landscape prompts additional suggestions on seeking and obtaining a writing position including the use of social media and additional tips on seeking and handling interviews.

ACKNOWLEDGMENTS

I would like to acknowledge the good work of my publisher, Michael Rosenberg; project manager, Jyotsna Ojha, Sr. Rights Acquisition Specialist, Jennifer Meyer Dare; and other members of the Cengage Learning staff, including Erin Bosco, Kelli Strieby, and Rachel Schowalter. Special thanks to content developer Rebecca Donahue. In addition, I would like to thank the reviewers of this Eleventh edition: Charles Cogar, Metropolitan Community College; Cara Cotellese, Kutztown University; Elizabeth Feldman, Montgomery College; and Barbara Carroll Rogers, Middlesex Community College. I appreciate the patience and encouragement of JoAnn Reece.

ABOUT THE AUTHOR

Robert L Hilliard began his media writing career as a sports reporter and, after service in World War II, became a radio writer-announcer and a writer-director in the fledgling field of television. While working in the media in New York, including a stint as a theater, film, and television critic, he developed the broadcasting curricula at two area colleges. He taught a writing course that became the basis for this book, first published in 1962 and named by *Writer's Market* as one of the 10 best books on writing.

He spent more than 15 years at the Federal Communications Commission (FCC) in Washington, D.C., as Chief of the Public Broadcasting Branch. He also served as Chair of the Federal Interagency Media Committee, linking 25 federal agencies and reporting to the White House, and chaired other federal media and education groups. Hilliard left Washington to become Dean of Graduate Studies, Dean of Continuing Education, a tenured professor of media arts, and currently a professor emeritus at Emerson College in Boston. He has been an officer, board member, and committee or project chair for a number of professional organizations and national, state, and community groups, and has been honored with awards from a number of media, educational, national, and international institutions and organizations.

Hilliard earned a B. A. degree from the University of Delaware, M. A. and M.F A. degrees at Western Reserve University, and a Ph.D. from Columbia University. He has published some 35 volumes on the media, including, with co-author Michael Keith, *The Broadcast Century and Beyond: A History of American Radio and Television; Global Broadcasting Systems; Waves of Rancor: Tuning In the Radical Right; Dirty Discourse: Sex and Indecency in American Broadcasting; and The Quieted Voice: The Rise and Decline of Localism in Radio.* He is also author of *Surviving the Americans: The Continued Struggle of the Jews After Liberation; Media, Education, and America's Counter-Culture Revolution;* and *Hollywood Speaks Out: Pictures That Dared to Protest Real World Issues.* He is author of a number of plays and the recent novels *Phillipa* and *The Greener Trees.* The film documentary, *Displaced: Miracle at St. Ottilien,* deals with his work in helping to save the lives of thousands of Holocaust survivors at the end of World War II in Europe, during which he received the Purple Heart as a U.S. combat infantry soldier.

Dedicating his work in communications to world peace, equal opportunity, and civil justice, Hilliard has been a consultant for government, industry, and education in the United States and abroad, lectured on all continents, published hundreds of magazine and newspaper articles, and made hundreds of speeches on media potentials and responsibilities, including their application to world affairs and education.

CHAPTER 1

The Mass Media

During the process of writing, the writer is usually isolated, alone in a room with whatever instrument she or he uses for writing: pen, pencil, typewriter, computer. Yet every word, every visual image has to be created with the thousands and even millions of people in mind who will be watching or listening. When you write for a mass medium, you are writing for a mass audience. The nature of that audience must constantly be in the forefront of your mind and be the key to what you create.

Although millions may hear or see what you have written, they will experience it individually or in small groups: a family at home in a living room, a few youngsters in a schoolyard, several college students in a dorm's common room, an individual on a bus or subway, a person alone in his or her room, a commuter in a car. Increasingly compact and mobile receiving devices, such as iPod (New) iPods, make it possible for almost any individual, anywhere, to receive what you are communicating. The Internet audience is even more individualized while at the same time being limitless, one person sitting alone at a computer or connected through a hand-held device. Potentially millions of people throughout the world are simultaneously seeing and hearing what you wrote. You are writing for an individual, for a small number of people who have a lot in common, and for a large number of people who may have little in common.

Reaching such an audience effectively is especially difficult because it is not a "captive" audience. Most of what airs over television, radio, and cyberspace is free. Unlike the theater or movie audience, which has paid a fee and is not likely to leave unless seriously bored or offended, the television, radio, or Internet audience can press a button, hit a key, or click on an icon to move to something else if it doesn't like what it sees or hears.

People who go to a play or film usually know something about what they are going to see from reading reviews viewing excerpts, or being influenced by ads. Although some television viewers carefully select shows, most viewers tune in to particular **formats** (evening soaps, family **sitcoms**, police programs, reality shows, movie channels, et al) and to specified continuing series, including local and network newscasts, by force of habit. Many people will switch to another program if the one they are watching does not hold their interest, or they will watch only half-heartedly or intermittently, missing some of the story content and, most regrettably from the viewpoint of the network and station, the commercials. Radio listeners do the same. They may tune in to a particular music or talk-show format, but if the music or discussion subject is not exactly what they want at the moment, it's easy for them to flip the dial to something more interesting. Many viewers and listeners shop around the dial at random until they find something that grabs their attention. Internet users have an even wider choice than do radio and TV users. Although the latter may have hundreds of channels to choose from, the former can browse the World Wide Web and choose from hundreds of thousands of sources.

What does this mean for the writer? You must capture the attention of the audience as soon as possible and hold it. Every picture and every word must be purposeful, directed toward keeping the audience's interest. As a writer you must make certain that no irrelevancies and no extraneous moments are in your script. Write directly, sharply, and simply. The mass media audience is as diverse as the population of wherever the given program reaches—in cyberspace it's the entire world. The opinions and prejudices, the educational, social and political backgrounds, the economic status and the personal creeds of people watching and listening vary from A to Z.

In recent years, radio has changed drastically. Terrestrial radio at one time was highly localized, serving the special needs and interests of each station's specific community. As a result of the vitiating of virtually all anti-monopoly rules by the Telecommunications Act of 1996 and through subsequent Federal Communications Commission (FCC) rulings, radio has become by and large a consolidated industry. Large conglomerates bought up as many stations as they could afford, and by the end of the first decade of the 2000s most small independent radio stations that had been dedicated to providing local service disappeared. In some larger cities as many as eight stations are owned by the same company, which saves money by consolidating personnel and services. Large conglomerates program their owned and operated stations from central sources sometimes hundreds of miles away from the stations, frequently with the exact same programming to distant local areas that may have little in common. Concomitantly, many of these consolidated stations have had drastic personnel reductions—some with no local programmer or on-air personality—thus eliminating any possibility of serious or informed local service. In part because radio listeners in many communities no longer have their special interests in music being served, subscribers to satellite radio have increased, Internet radio has proliferated, and listeners have a choice of many more music genres and greater opportunity to find that which most suits them. Although terrestrial conglomerates and satellite providers have attempted to provide news and weather directed to some regions and cities, local news has faded seriously, especially in small markets. An example: Officials tried to warn the people of a community of a toxic spill from a train accident, but the local radio station, conglomerate-owned and computer-operated, had no one on duty. Local radio service might have prevented the resulting illnesses as and death. (If you are going into radio, you may wish to consult the Hilliard-Keith book, *The Quieted Voice: The Rise and Demise of Localism in American Radio.*)

Because financial rather than artistic or social considerations control programming decisions and content, the producers and advertisers try to reach and hold as large a segment of the viewing or listening population as possible. In television, the easiest and most effective way to do this is to find the broadest common denominator—which frequently turns out to be the lowest. The term *LCD* is used to describe this lowest common denominator programming target. Despite increasing **narrowcasting** programming—programs oriented toward specialized audiences, reflecting the growing number of program and distribution sources such as multi-network and multi-channel cable and satellite systems and Internet sites carrying streamed and original programming—the primary aim of video producers too often still seems to be to present material that will not offend anyone.

The most popular commercial network shows—sitcoms, action adventure, police, hospitals, reality, talent programs—follow that formula. Programs willing to deal in depth with ideas or to present controversial material are in the minority. There are exceptions. The drama series *Boston Legal* invariably included a controversial social or political issue in its scripts, frequently taking an irreverent view. *60 Minutes* from time to time deals with significant issues, although the degree of controversy the program is willing to tackle is usually mild. Its original success prompted a spate of similar shows, such as *Dateline, 48 Hours,* and *20/20*. They sometimes cover key events and touch on serious issues but mostly limit their content to non-controversial human interest features. News and documentary programs that do deal with controversial issues in depth don't last long. Self-censorship of controversial ideas, with the occasional exception of comedy satire such as, *The Daily Show* and *The Colbert Report*, predominates.

Some PBS and NPR news and public affairs programs still challenge the status quo, but government pressure on public broadcasting to reflect or at least not challenge the government's political policies has resulted in timid programming. Perhaps the most controversial programming in the mass media today, aside from the alternative programming that has found a home on the Internet, is on talk shows. However, inasmuch as the mass media (including newspapers and magazines) are owned predominantly by political conservatives, virtually all television and cable network and syndicated radio talk shows—there are some exceptions such as MSNBC's Rachel Maddow and Ed Schultz shows— range from moderate right-wing to radical right-wing, with personalities such as Rush Limbaugh, Sean Hannity, and Bill O'Reilly dominating the airwaves. With alternative news web sites, and bloggers and tweeters their own gatekeepers, the Internet offers a greater variety of information and opinions than do the traditional media.

Although traditionally and consistently politically conservative, the media have become less and less conservative in terms of social behavior. Partial nudity, profane language, undisguised sexual situations, and non-judgmental recognition of the real-world's alternative life styles are staples of early 21st century programming. Although obscene material is banned from the airwaves, indecent and profane material, euphemistically labeled adult programming, is permissible under certain circumstances. The FCC defines indecent program material as "language or material that, in context, depicts or describes, in terms patently offensive as measured by contemporary community standards for the broadcast medium, sexual or excretory activities or organs." Therefore, the writer for the media is cautioned to check with the appropriate legal representative of his or her organization, while at the same time exercising every effort to maintain the integrity of what is being written. A sad commentary on the mores and Psychological sensitivity of viewers is that violence, sometimes deliberately graphic, has became a high-ratings staple of television.

DEMOGRAPHICS

When network radio, which was comparable to network television today, disappeared in the 1950s as television took over the older medium's most attractive programs and stars, radio, to survive, became fragmented into local audiences. Individual stations developed formats that appealed to specifically targeted groups of listeners. As noted earlier, the elimination of most monopoly controls and increased consolidation have resulted in a diminishing of programming specifically designed by a local programmer for a local audience. Nevertheless, ideally, the writer should attempt to prepare material that appeals to and is needed by a specific audience.

The makeup of the potential audience for a given program or station is called **demographics** or **demos**. The principal demographics are age and gender within the given market's locale. Some demographic studies go deeper, into job or profession, income, and education. When the audience's beliefs, attitudes, and behavior are included—such as political affiliation, religion, where the viewer or listener shops, and what brands he or she buys—it is called psychographics. These conditions and interests of the audience determine the kinds of writing that appeal to the given audience, as well as the product or service the audience is most likely to purchase. The demographics of radio audiences sometimes are even more precise than those of television audiences. Because radio is virtually all music—with the exception of some full-service stations, talk, all-news, all-sports, religious, and a few other specialized formats—each station attempts to program to a specified group of loyal listeners who are attracted to a particular music type and format. Radio stations may even break down their potential audiences into which interest groups might be listening in a particular place (home, work, car, on the street) and at a particular time of day or night. Cable audiences are fairly easily targeted because most cable channels are quite narrow in scope, and Internet audiences, with the exception of some browsers, are usually interested in a given site's subject matter. The Internet reaches a more diverse, worldwide audience but still tries to reach the demographics must likely to buy any given product or service.

The basic concept of demographics use is illustrated in the following example: Take the same product and stress in the advertising spot the specific appeal that would be most effective with a given audience.

For an audience in a highly urbanized area: "The new Powerhouse Six is the latest in automobile styling. Its sleek, long look and ample interior, however, belie its length of only 86 inches, short enough to fit into some of the smallest parking spaces."

For an audience in a middle-class suburban area: "The new Powerhouse Six is the latest in automobile styling. Its ample interior is large enough to carry six children and assorted soccer, band, and school picnic equipment."

For an audience in an upscale suburban area: "The new Powerhouse Six is the latest in automobile styling. Its long, sleek look makes it a perfect second car that reflects the superior workmanship and appointments of its interior and exterior."

For an audience in a rural area: "The new Powerhouse Six is the latest in automobile styling. Its rugged exterior and roomy interior match the supercharged engine's remarkable 32 miles per gallon."

Well, you get the idea! Factor in what you know about the audience's age, gender, income, political milieu, religious affiliations, and other available information and you can pinpoint the content that might be most effective. For example, during the economic recession in the latter half of 2000's first decade more and more ads stressed "low price." When you get to the different formats in this book, practice writing your assigned scripts for different demographics. An important part of demographics is the racial and ethnic makeup of the specific market. Station formats reflect the interests of the audience.

Advertisers want to go beyond the basic demographics of age, gender, social and economic class, education, nationality, and religion, to identify the likely customers for their specific goods and services. They want the **psychographics** of the viewers and listeners. Psychographics go more in depth than demographics and try to determine lifestyles, values, attitudes, and even personality. Psychographics attempt to tell the advertiser not only whether the potential customer is likely to want to buy the product, but how they *feel* about it. Finding the feelings and behavior of the buyer in relation to the product or service facilitates more specific targeting. Researchers have developed even further levels of depth in audience analysis. **Geodemographics** combines geography with demographics in researching specific neighborhoods by their zip codes and factoring in housing style and income level with other **demos** to hone in on that narrow target of potential customers. And if that isn't enough to add to your knowledge of the basic demographics approach to audience research, there is also a method called **cohort analysis**. This essentially seeks to find common bonds that prompt a group of people to think and feel the same way about a given item or an issue, based on similar experiences in the same time frame. Marketing campaigns, for example, have been targeted to specific generations, such as Baby Boomers, born between 1946 and 1964; Generation X, 1965 to 1976; and Generation Y, between 1977 and 1995; and Generation Z, frequently called the Internet generation.

In sum, advertisers want to know not only how many people see their show (networks and stations are more interested in the numbers inasmuch as ratings determine the prices they charge for commercial air time), but whether the audiences they reach are likely purchasers of what they are selling and engage themselves with the product or service by continuing to watch during the commercial, record the show, and blog about it.

Because the Internet is interactive, audience research is possible in greater depth and on a broader basis. **Cookies** track every site you log onto. Information is collected on your tastes in content and, through analysis of the ads you click on, your product and service interests. Even your financial and medical information can be tracked and made available; financial and health organizations and companies are among the Internet's biggest advertisers. Invasion of privacy? Of course! In the latter part of the first decade of the 2000s, the Federal Trade Commission (FTC) called for self-regulation. As this is written, however, your medical records, drug prescriptions, financial information, and much more are an open book.

THE ELECTRONIC MEDIA

Thus far we have dealt, principally, with the television and radio media. What about films made for TV? What about **cable**? Is there a difference between a script prepared for a cable pay channel and that written for a local cable access channel? Is a different writing approach needed for material distributed by satellite? Does one write differently for the Internet? What about other systems that make up the panoply of *electronic mass media*? To paraphrase Gertrude Stein, writing is writing is writing. The demographics may differ among people watching. The material permissible on an over-the-air station can differ from that seen on a pay-per-view "adult" channel. The techniques of writing programs for a type of format, whether for broadcast or cable, are essentially the same. But the medium sometimes does affect the message.

No overt distinction is made in this book among writing for broadcast, cable, or satellite transmission except where the demographics or other special considerations mandate different format or technique requirements. This is not true, however, for the Internet. Still developing in these early years of the 21st century, the Internet nevertheless has been moving steadily from using little-changed adaptations of television and radio writing ("streaming" programs from the older media was the most direct way of enlarging broadcasting's audience base) to using its interactive ability as a creative base for entertainment programming. Writing for the Internet's full potentials requires different approaches and techniques. A story headline in *Time* magazine in mid-decade stated: "Spending more time with your computer than with your TV? Then TV's coming to find you." NBC's *The Office* streamed mini-episodes that people at computers could watch when they had a little time to spare. ESPN, Comedy Central, Discovery, MTV, HGTV, and other cable networks implemented broadband channels. NBC and CBS planned on-line-only reality shows. CBS launched an online channel, "innertube," for programming developed solely for the Internet and supported by advertising. In addition, CBS showed episodes of a number of its TV programs on the Internet the day after they appeared on television. One of the network's premiere programs, *CBS Evening News*, was offered free, in full, for Internet streaming. The hit reality show from Fox TV, *American Idol*, went on the Internet, and even Internet radio began using television materials, with a number of channels playing the music of Idol contestants. By the end of the first decade of 2000, online programmers included Cinemax, CNN, CNN International, College sports TV, E-online, Fox News Channel, GSN (game network), HBO, TBS, TCM (Turner Classic Movies), WE (Women's Entertainment), TV Guide, and the Weather Channel. ABC and NBC joined to add to their shows such as *Dancing With the Stars* on the popular video web site Hulu blockbuster programs such as *Desperate Housewives*, with extension of their programming to Hulu's partner sites such as MySpace and AOL.com. With Internet access becoming faster and faster, what started as 2-minute clips of shows are becoming longer and longer, with original programming of 10 and 20 minutes, moving toward full-length presentations. Original online shows are called **Webisodes**.

While most people studying to write for the electronic media concentrate on television and radio, it is important to understand that the Internet is fast becoming the base for both origination and distribution of virtually all media programming. While some critics say that the new media will not replace the older media, but will result in radio and television growing and adapting into new models, **convergence** (the melding of two or more media) thus far suggests otherwise.

Production techniques may seem irrelevant to the writer. But the writer should know at least some of the key production elements to understand what each medium can do. The writer must be able to write for the eye and ear, in addition to mastering the use of words. For example, the film format for television is not the same as the format for a **live-type** show recorded before a studio audience. Within each format, reflecting different aesthetic as well as physical approaches, are varying production techniques made possible by different equipment and technical devices. The writer must understand the production elements just as a painter understands different brushes, canvasses, and paints. The writer's basic tools are covered in Chapter 2.

Although other technologies developed after radio and television, such as cable and satellite, are often referred to as "new media," they are essentially distribution systems. Except for programming in the larger sense—such as narrowcasting, given the multiple channels and fragmented video audiences here in the United States—their aesthetics are essentially the same as the older media. That is, they rarely require special or different writing techniques for their programs. They merely distribute through an additional service the programs that otherwise would be aired over traditional television or radio.

But cyberspace is different. The Internet sets up a number of special technical, aesthetic, and psychological parameters that the writer must understand and use if he or she is to prepare a script that has optimum impact in the newer medium. In this sense, the Internet is to the writer today what television was when it first opened up to programming. For example, the approaches used for writing a drama or documentary for film or a play for the stage or any program for radio had to be adapted to the needs and potentials of television. The same principle applies to writing for the Internet today.

TELEVISION AND THE MASS AUDIENCE

Television can combine the live performance values of theater, the mechanical abilities of film, the sound and audience orientation of radio, and its own electronic capacities. Television can use the best of all previous communication media.

Television combines both subjectivity and objectivity in relation to the audience, fusing two areas frequently thought of as mutually exclusive. With the camera and various electronic devices, the writer and director can subjectively orient the audience's attentions and emotions by directing them to specific stimuli. The television audience cannot choose its focus, as does the stage audience, from among all the aspects of any given presentation. The television audience can be directed, through a **close-up,** a **zoom,** a **split screen,** or other camera or **control board (switcher)** movement, to focus on whatever object or occurrence most effectively achieves the purpose of the specific moment in the script. Attention can be directed to subtle reaction as well as to obvious action.

Objectivity is crucial to lending credibility to non-dramatic programming such as newscasts and documentaries. Creating an objective orientation is accomplished by bringing the performer more openly and directly to the viewer, for example, through the close-up or the zoom, than can be done in the large auditorium or theatre, even with a live performance, or in the expanse of a movie house. Unlike most drama, where the purpose is to create illusion, the performer in the non-dramatic program (television host/hostess, announcer, newscaster) wants to achieve a non-illusionary relationship with the audience. At the same time, the small screen, the limited length of most programs, and the intimacy of the living or bedroom when watching at home or on an iPod anywhere create effects and require techniques different from those of a film shown in a movie theater.

Stemming from the early days of television when all productions were live with continuous action, non-filmed television continues to maintain a continuity of action that differs from the usually frequent changes in sequence that one sees on the movie screen. A few television programs are still done as if they were live: recorded with few breaks in the action. In this respect, television borrows a key aesthetic element from the theater.

Television screen size—even 60 inches or more—restricts the number of characters and the size of the setting (note how poorly large-scale films look on television), and by the limited time available for a given dramatic program (approximately 21 minutes of playing time for a half-hour show and 42 minutes for the hour show, after commercial and **intro** and **outro** time has been subtracted). This is especially true if watching on a small hand-held device. Television uses virtually every mechanical technique of film, adding electronic techniques of its own to give it a special versatility and flexibility. Even so, the most successful shows still reflect a cognizance of the small screen and limited time, concentrating on slice-of-life vignettes of clearly defined characters.

There is a negative side to television's mechanical and electronic expansion. After videotape's advent in 1956 with its editing capabilities, television gradually moved from live to taped and filmed shows, and the center of television production, which had been in New York City with its abundance of experienced theater performers, moved to Hollywood. Soon the Hollywood approach dominated television. Some television critics argue that much of television has become a boxed-in version of the motion picture. Conversely, some film critics believe that television techniques imported to Hollywood have negatively affected films and have made them smaller, busier, and blander.

The writer must always keep in mind that television is visual. Where a visual element can achieve the desired effect, it should take precedence over dialogue; in many instances, dialogue may be superfluous. A story is told about a famous Broadway playwright, noted for his scintillating dialogue, who was hired to write a film script. He wrote a 30-page first act treatment in which a husband and wife on vacation reach their hotel and go to their hotel room. Thirty minutes of witty and sparkling conversation reveal that the wife has become increasingly disturbed over her husband's attention to other women. An experienced movie director went over the treatment and thought it presented a good situation. However, for the 30 pages of dialogue he substituted less than 1 page of visual directions in which the husband and wife enter the hotel, perfunctorily register, walk to the elevator, enter the elevator where the husband looks appraisingly at the female elevator operator, and the wife's face expresses great displeasure as the elevator doors close.

A simple test can show that many television writers have not yet learned the visual essence of their medium. Turn on your television set and turn the brightness down until the picture is gone, leaving only the audio. Note in how many programs, from commercials to dramas, you will "see" just about as much as you would with the video on. Is much of television, as some critics say, still just radio with pictures?

RADIO AND THE MASS AUDIENCE

Radio is not limited by what can get presented visually. By combining sound effects, music, dialogue, and even silence, the writer can develop a picture in the audience's mind that is limited only by the listener's imagination. Radio permits the writer complete freedom of time and place. There is no limitation on the setting or on movement. The writer can create unlimited forms of physical action and bypass in a twinkling of a musical bridge minutes or centuries of time and galaxies of space.

Before the advent of television, when drama was a staple of radio, writers set the stage for what were later to become the science fiction favorites of television, such as *Star Trek* and its clones, and of film, such as *Star Wars*. Writer Howard Koch's and director Orson Wells's *War of the Worlds* is still famous for its many provocative radio productions throughout the world. Radio in America has become virtually all music and talk. Except for commercials and occasional features, artistic writing and directing in commercial radio are virtually dormant. But they are not totally dead, and hopefully there are still some opportunities for those who want to explore the aural medium's potentials.

The radio audience hears only what the writer-director wants it to hear. Audience members "see" pictures in their imaginations. The radio writer can create this mind picture more effectively than can the writer in any other medium because in radio the imagination is not limited by what the eye sees. Radio's subjectivity enables the writer to create places, characters, and events that might be extremely difficult or too costly to show visually.

The writer can place the audience right alongside of or at any chosen distance from a character or performer. Voice distances and relationships to the microphone determine the audience's view of the characters and of the setting. For example, if the audience is listening to two people in conversation and the writer has the first person fade off from the microphone, the audience, in its imagination, stays with the second person and sees the first one moving away. Of course, different listeners may imagine the same sound stimulus in different ways because each person's psychological and experiential background is different. Nevertheless, the good writer finds enough common elements to stimulate common emotions and reactions. No television show, for example, has ever created the mass hysteria of radio's *War of the Worlds*.

A scene must be set in dialogue and sound rather than established through sight. This must not be done too obviously. Radio often uses a narrator or an announcer to set the mood, establish character relationships, give information about program participants, describe the scene, summarize the action, and even comment on the attitude the audience might be expected to have toward the program, participants, or performers. The background material, which sometimes can be shown in its entirety on television through visual action alone, must be given on radio through dialogue, music, sound—and silence.

Because drama has almost totally disappeared from radio, except for some programming on public radio stations and as a key element in many commercials, we tend to ignore the aesthetic potentials of the medium. We sometimes forget that a staple of radio, commercials, can be highly artistic, and often are, in fact, mini-dramas.

You can easily tell the difference between the quality of a commercial expressly written for radio and that of a television commercial whose sound track is used for a radio spot. Bernard Mann, former president of WGLD and other stations in North Carolina, who began as a broadcast writing student in college and whose experience has included serving as the president of the National Radio Broadcasters Association, stated:

> One of my great frustrations is that too little of the writing done for radio is imaginative. We have almost made it part of the indoctrination program for copywriters at our radio stations to listen to some of the old radio shows. During that time, listeners were challenged to use their imagination. Nothing has changed. The medium is still the same. The opportunity for the writer to challenge the listener is still there. It's just not being used very much. Of course, radio today has very little original drama, but every day thousands of pieces of copy are turned out with very little imagination. Often an advertiser will tell a salesperson, "I can't use radio, it must have a picture," but I think that's radio's strength. The picture leaves nothing to the imagination, but a description will be colored by the listener to be more toward what he or she wants or likes.

Radio is indeed the art of the imagination. Technologies such as multi-track and digital recording further enhance this aural medium's potential. The radio writer is restricted only by the breadth and depth of the mind's eye of the audience. A vivid illustration of this potential and, appropriately, an example of good scriptwriting, is Stan Freberg's award-winning promotional spot for radio, "Stretching the Imagination."

MAN: Radio? Why should I advertise on radio? There's nothing to look at . . . no pictures.

GUY: Listen, you can do things on radio you couldn't possibly do on TV.

MAN: That'll be the day.

GUY: Ah huh. All right, watch this. (AHEM) O.K. people, now I give you the cue, I want the 700-foot mountain of whipped cream to roll into Lake Michigan which has been drained and filled with hot chocolate. Then the royal Canadian Air Force will fly overhead towing the 10-ton maraschino cherry which will be dropped into the whipped cream, to the cheering of 25,000 extras. All right . . . cue the mountain . . .

SOUND: GROANING AND CREAKING OF MOUNTAINS INTO BIG SPLASH!

GUY: Cue the air force!

SOUND: DRONE OF MANY PLANES.

GUY: Cue the maraschino cherry . . .

continued

SOUND:	WHISTLE OF BOMB INTO BLOOP! OF CHERRY HITTING WHIPPED CREAM.
GUY:	Okay, twenty-five thousand cheering extras . . .
SOUND:	ROAR OF MIGHTY CROWD. SOUND BUILDS UP AND CUTS OFF SHARP!
GUY:	Now . . . you wanta try that on television?
MAN:	Well . . .
GUY:	You see . . . radio is a very special medium, because it stretches the imagination.
MAN:	Doesn't television stretch the imagination?
GUY:	Up to 21 inches, yes.

Courtesy of Freberg, Ltd.

THE INTERNET AUDIENCE

The Internet audience is quite different from that for other media. It consists of single individuals in a one-on-one communication exchange, even though millions may be logged on to the same site at the same time. Through the Internet's interactive capabilities, each member of the audience may be a participant in the communication process, rather than a passive viewer or listener. The Internet has flexibility as well as control over the material being presented. Internet users have an even wider choice of selections than do radio and TV users. The latter have perhaps hundreds of channels to choose from, but the former can browse the World Wide Web and can choose from literally hundreds of thousands of sources. Further, each individual user is also, if desired, a programmer, with access to distribution sites such as YouTube and with the ability to write individual *blogs* and *tweets*. Most important is that although traditional media are controlled by multi-national corporations and self-serving corporate executives—the gatekeepers who allow only the programming that serves their vested interests—there are few gatekeepers of the Internet—except where some governments attempt to control the Internet service providers (ISPs) and through them the programming. The Internet is open and free to alternative programming from any group or individual source. (Examples of these differences are illustrated in Chapter 5, News and Sports.)

What does this mean for producers, directors, and, for purposes of this book, scriptwriters? A medium interprets what we have written for an audience. Writing for films is different than writing for stage, just as writing for radio is different than writing for film or stage, just as writing for television is different than writing for radio. We write to fit the aesthetic and technical requirements of the given medium.

Although the Web is increasingly a source of distribution for film, video, and audio on a mass scale, and although producers of Hollywood films, television programs, and radio and music audio materials are increasingly meeting Internet requirements and potentials, many are simply using the Internet as a distribution medium without understanding that it is an entirely different creative environment for their productions than traditional film, television, or radio. Note the term "interactive." It is a key to writing for this medium. For example, journalists might assume greater responsibility for accuracy and greater excellence in writing for the Internet, given the viewers' and listeners' opportunity to double-check any news story from an immediately available variety of sources and to compare the art and effect of a story with other reports. Further, the Internet news audience can have instant access to a wider variety of opinions and interpretations of the news and is able to bypass biased news, whether the bias is a result of nationalism or local pride or political or economic—that is, advertiser—pressure. Simply put, with news, as with all other aspects of the Internet relative to programming, the individual audience member is in control and participates actively and interactively, rather than—as with traditional video, audio, and film distribution—passively. The chapters on different formats include discussions on how the writer can take advantage of this interactive independence of the audience.

Although the receptor, or audience, in this medium is given unlimited interactive opportunities, the writer must remember that as the creator, the guide, the influencer, he or she must not lose control of the material. If the writer has a point of view, the writer does not want the audience to wander in cyberspace unguided and to come to just any feeling, thought, or conclusion. The writer has a purpose and must present as many opportunities for interactivity as possible, but for each of those activities the writer must also provide stimuli that, in any combination and from whatever source, can lead the receptor to the thought and feeling that the writer intends to convey. Even with an ostensibly totally objective format—such as hard news—the writer must be certain that all points of view and interpretations are available. If the older media are skewing the news—as they frequently do because of advertiser, owner, or, sometimes, producer-writer control—the Internet offers the possibility of implementing the presentation of alternative viewpoints to popular thought and belief otherwise usually unavailable. The receptor might do extensive Web browsing, but the writer can help orient the audience to sites that offset restricted attitudes and information.

Advertisers—and producers—on the Internet realize that it provides an instant global market. The trend in media generally is toward increasingly large monopolies and toward consolidation of media industries into fewer and fewer mogul gatekeepers, thus restricting creative options and diversity of views. (Writer-critic A.J. Liebling once observed that freedom of the press belonged to the person who owned one.) This, thus far, is less so on the Internet. Although as this is being written, media moguls and other corporate controllers, principally Internet Service Providers (ISPs), are seeking legislation that will eliminate *net neutrality*—that is, Internet freedom—and give the ISPs the power to reject or censor any user or material. The writer needs to be aware that literally the whole multi-cultural, multi-opinion world is watching or listening. This creates different requirements for content and for technique than if the material is to be seen or heard principally in one's own country or in a limited region or locality.

Daniel Roth wrote in *Fortune* magazine that writers for the older media are having a hard time adjusting to the "techie"-culture types who continue to control the Internet. The older media types put content first and tend to look down on the technical emphases. Conversely, the techies are usually impatient with and sometimes even contemptuous of the video-audio people, believing that the latter cannot or will not adjust to the new technical-dominated communications world. Thus far, the techies have dominated, with the tools and processes of Internet communication considered by the new media operators as more important than the material to be disseminated, but the gap is closing. Broadcasters are trying to maximize their proficiency and access. For example the National Association of Broadcasters web site (www.nab.org) has links to new technology, convergence, and Internet information and advice on developments in the new media that affect broadcasters.

The Internet can have a salutary as well as a competitive effect on the more traditional media. In addition to its extension of popular music, the Web has made it possible for some otherwise dormant radio formats to revive. For example, a number of people in many different communities might like to hear science fiction drama or listen to the Library of Congress "books-on-tape" series. With not enough people in any one community to make such programs economically feasible for any given radio station, such programs are rarely presented. On the Internet, however, an otherwise "dead" program could reach enough people nationally and internationally to be successful.

In addition, the Internet's ability to allow any individual anywhere to communicate with other individuals anywhere, unlike the older media that limit access to those who can afford to either own or buy time on a station or channel, has spawned a myriad of so-called social sites with their own writing techniques for presenting and acknowledging material. Some of the writing approaches for Internet social site communication will be discussed later in this book.

SUBJECT MATTER

The writer not only has to exercise talent in producing quality material, but also has to exercise judgment in the specific material used. Television and radio writing particularly are greatly affected by censorship.

Censorship comes from many sources. The production agency, whether an independent producer or a network, usually has guidelines about what materials are acceptable. Advertisers exercise a significant role in determining content, frequently refusing to sponsor a program to which they have some objection. Pressure groups petition and even picket networks, stations, and producers. Television critic Jay Nelson Tuck once wrote, not altogether facetiously, that three dirty postcards from a vacant lot can influence a sponsor to do almost anything.

Owners want their media properties to reflect their personal and social views whenever possible, or at least not present views that disagree with theirs. In as much as most media are owned by conservatives, the media reflect conservative agendas. (Strangely, many people erroneously refer to "the liberal media.") Stations managers, producers, and program directors sometimes get their views included—presuming they do not clash with those of their bosses and thus threaten their jobs.

Censorable Material

Although prevented by the Communications Act of 1934 from censoring program material, the FCC is authorized to levy fines or suspend a station's license for "communications containing profane or obscene words, language, or meaning." "Indecency" clause implementation depends on the FCC commissioners' orientation at any given time. The conservative public attitudes and presidential administrations of recent decades have prompted the FCC to take action against programming the FCC deems offensive. In 1996, despite objections from civil liberties groups and Action for Children's Television, the Supreme Court ruled that the FCC has the right to establish a "safe harbor" for adult programming, ostensibly to protect child viewers. The hours of 10 P.M. to 6 A.M. compose the "safe harbor," based on the assumption that children will not be watching television during that period. Conversely, programming that is deemed "adult" may not be broadcast between 6 A.M. and 10 P.M.

The FCC has cracked down especially on talk show hosts who present materials the Commission deemed offensive. Though not ever specifically defining what it meant by indecency, the FCC relied on what was called the "Miller test"—the 1973 Supreme Court decision in *Miller v. California*, which applied three criteria in judging whether a work was indecent or obscene: (1) that, applying contemporary community standards, the work appeals to the average person's prurient interests; (2) that the work describes sexual conduct in a patently offensive way, as defined by state law; and (3) that the work as a whole lacks literary, artistic, political, or scientific value. Although many critics cannot understand how the FCC can enunciate what contemporary community standards for the average person can possibly be, the Commission nevertheless has levied fines against companies, stations, and performers for indecent programming.

At this writing, the Supreme Court has ruled on only one indecency case pertaining specifically to the application of the First Amendment's freedom of speech clause and the electronic media (not including the Internet): the so-called Seven Dirty Words case in which Pacifica radio station WBAI in New York carried the George Carlin routine as a segment of a program on communication and language. The FCC fine was upheld by the Supreme Court in 1978, but the court did not further define indecency. Thus, the broadcast writer continues to play Russian roulette when writing, knowing for certain only that the Seven Dirty Words routine cannot be aired on a broadcast station. Subsequent complaints brought before the FCC have been judged individually by what the Commissioners at the given time consider to be average community standards. In 2012, in a case involving FCC fining broadcast entities for allegedly broadcasting indecent material, the Supreme Court found the FCC at fault for not giving sufficient notice of changes in its indecency rules. But, as in a case in 2009, the Supreme Court did not address the First Amendment principles.

The Telecommunications Act of 1996 included a provision that requires new television sets to contain a "V-chip" that permits the screening of programs that fall into different rating categories for "violence, sex, and other indecent material." A companion Communications Decency Act also banned the transmission of "indecent" material via computer, ostensibly to protect children. Although the former was implemented, the courts have found the latter and subsequent similar legislation banning certain content from the Internet to be unconstitutional violations of the First Amendment rights of freedom of speech and press.

Broadcasting realized that at least some facts of life cannot be made to disappear by banning them from public discussion or observation or by pretending that they do not exist. Many talk shows, discussion programs, and dramas deal with explicit sexual references and frequently with sexual acts, the latter sometimes simulated even if not fully seen. Language approximates that used in real life, from sitcoms to serious drama, although some of the most common four-letter words have not yet made it to broadcast television. More freedom of language usage is found on cable, particularly on pay channels.

Until 2004, except for large fines for what it deemed to be material that clearly and principally appealed to the prurient interest, the FCC took a selective view of what constituted indecency. For example, a discussion of masturbation on the Howard Stern show, in the context of its presentation, might well be considered indecent. However, a discussion of the same subject on the Oprah Winfrey show, presented in a medical and educational context, would not be considered indecent. (Those were actual findings.) Fleeting or unintentional profanity was not considered a violation. However, in 2004 an incident occurred that most media experts considered relatively mild, but which, in light of and perhaps as a consequence of the growing political, social, and religious conservatism of the time, became a cause celebre. That incident was the "wardrobe malfunction" that resulted in the baring of part of one of Janet Jackson's breasts during the nationally televised half-time presentation at the Super Bowl. While quite mild in comparison to partial nudity on programs such as *NYPD Blue* and sitcoms about 20-somethings with raging hormones, and quite innocuous when compared to the material on virtually all "shock-jock" programs, it resulted in a national uproar. Citizen groups, religious organizations, and even Congress demanded increased FCC crackdowns on any material that might even remotely be considered indecent. The FCC obliged, and at this writing has fined and continues to fine networks, stations, and even personalities amounts totaling millions of dollars. In part because of this crackdown, Howard Stern abandoned his long-time terrestrial radio home and moved to satellite radio, over which the FCC has not yet exercised direct content regulation. The FCC similarly has no rules regarding cable content, but the threat of such regulation and recent congressional legislation raising indecency fines multi-fold has resulted in self-censorship by most media.

Erik Barnouw, discussing movie censorship in his book *Mass Communication*, wrote: "Banning evil example . . . does not ban it from life. It may not strengthen our power to cope with it. It may have the opposite effect. Code rules multiply, but they do not produce morality. They do not stop vulgarity. Trying to banish forbidden impulses, censors may only change the disguises in which they appear. They ban passionate love-making, and excessive violence takes its place."

Controversial Material

Freedom of expression and democratic exchange of ideas in television and radio are endangered because many media executives fear controversy. On the grounds of service to the sponsor and on the basis of good ratings for non-controversial, generally mediocre entertainment, controversial material and performers frequently have been banned. Many companies refuse to sponsor a program with controversial material if they feel it might in any way alienate any potential customers. Erik Barnouw observed that "when a story editor says 'we can't use anything controversial,' and says it with a tone of conscious virtue, then there is danger."

Most broadcasters fought for years to abolish the **Fairness Doctrine,** which authorized the FCC to require stations, in some circumstances, to present more than one side of significant issues in the community, therefore bringing controversy to the fore. Following President Reagan's veto of a congressional bill making the Fairness Doctrine into law, the FCC abolished it in 1987.

The history of censorship of controversial material in broadcasting is a long one, and, unfortunately, one in which both broadcasters and the public never seem to learn the lessons of integrity and democracy. One of the United States's darkest and most shameful periods was the blacklist of the 1950s, during the heyday of McCarthyism, when Senator Joseph McCarthy cowed most of America into supporting his demagoguery of guilt-by-accusation—even false accusation. Broadcasters cooperated with charlatans to deny freedom of speech and the freedom to work to countless performers, directors, producers, and writers who were accused by self-proclaimed groups of super-patriots of being un-American. Broadcasters panicked and threw courage to the winds and ethics out the windows. Many careers and a number of lives were destroyed. Although broadcasters have since apologized for their undemocratic and cowardly behavior, political considerations are still a priority on the censorship list. Following the 9-11, 2001, terrorist attacks, and increasingly since 2009, political pressures and conformity have resulted in the mainstream media by and large reporting inaccurately or not at all on the abrogation of America's cherished civil liberties—and the accompanying nationwide protests—by the Patriot Act, the Foreign Intelligence Surveillance Act, the National Defense Authorization Act, and drone monitoring of American civilians, among other actions. This self-censorship applied as well to massive anti-war protests in the United States during the Iraq and Afghanistan wars, as well. As noted earlier, the media are by and large controlled by conservative individuals and companies. With few exceptions, only alternative media sites on the Internet reported objectively what was happening.

Several classic situations have resulted from censoring material that might put the sponsor's product or service in a poor light or that might suggest a competing product. Among them is a program that dealt with the German concentration camp atrocities of the 1940s from which the sponsoring gas company eliminated all references to gas chambers. Another program deleted references to President Lincoln's name in a civil war drama because it was also the name of a car produced by a competitor of the automobile sponsor. In retrospect such situations are funny, but they were not funny then and would not be now to the writer forced to compromise the integrity of his or her script.

Censorship is sometimes the result of an owner's attitudes toward or conflict with the content of a program. For example, the American Broadcasting Company's highly regarded news program, *20/20*, had a segment prepared on hiring and safety problems at the Walt Disney World entertainment complex. Written assurances were given that there would be no problem with ABC's corporate owner—the Walt Disney Company. The story was killed. It should be noted, however, that *20/20* had previously aired a story critical of another Disney project. Some censorship takes place not because of feared public reaction or even because of a sponsor's vested interest, but because of direct prejudice. One play, the true story of a large department store owner who was Jewish and who gave his entire fortune to fight cancer, was cancelled by the sponsor because the play allegedly would give "Jewish department store owners" an unfair advantage over other department store owners.

Media executives and sponsors alone are not to blame. Writers and other personnel often give up their integrity out of fear for their jobs or to curry favor with their employers. In Boston, for example, after a local station cancelled a program under pressure from a local religious group, a governing board member of the New England Chapter of the National Academy of Television Arts and Sciences (NATAS) introduced the following resolution:

> Freedom of the press, including television, is a cornerstone of American democracy. The United States is one of the few countries in the world where the media legally have freedom from the control of outside forces. To abandon that freedom under pressure from any group, public or private, no matter how laudatory its aims, is to subvert a basic principle of democracy, and to undermine one of our cherished freedoms. As communicators in New England, we urge our broadcasting colleagues here and throughout the nation to stand firm, with courage and conviction, not to succumb, but to maintain the open marketplace of ideas that has marked freedom of speech, thought, and press in our country. We pledge our support to our colleagues in this endeavor.

The other members of the NATAS Board of Directors refused even to consider that resolution. One NATAS officer suggested that the resolution "was perceived by many as a criticism of the actions taken by a member station." Of course it was. Not only, therefore, do outside pressures determine programming decisions and content, but the pressures of management also tend to force individual broadcasters and writers to give up the principle and courage to support freedom of ideas and speech.

The late Sydney W. Head, a leading teacher and writer in the communications field, stated, "Television, as a medium, appears to be highly responsive to the conventional conservative values," and that a danger to society from television is that television will not likely lend its support to the unorthodox, but "it will add to cultural inertia." The media's great impact and television's and radio's ability to affect people's minds and emotions so strongly are clearly recognized by the media controllers or, as they are often called, the gatekeepers, who by and large represent the status quo of established business, industry, social, and political thought and power. In her book *Screened Out: How the Media Control Us and What We Can Do About It*, Carla Brooks Johnston notes the increasing global control of the media by fewer and fewer companies that decide what the public is permitted to see and hear. It is not surprising that the conglomerate-controlled mainstream media have only superficially covered or distorted the growing worldwide protests against corporate globalization. In this instance, as in others, the full stories may be found principally on the Internet.

Commercials *do* sell products and services, and Madison Avenue advertising agencies wield considerable impact. News and public affairs programs and even entertainment shows have had remarkable impact in changing many of our political and social beliefs, policies, and practices. Broadcasting's cooperation with manipulative politicians, spin-doctors, "sound-bites," and other non-substantive and non-issue reportage in covering politics and elections indicates how effectively the media can influence and even control the political process.

At the same time, the media have been responsible, through similar control, for great progress in human endeavors. Television's coverage of the civil rights movement in the 1960s often is credited with motivating many people to insist on congressional action guaranteeing all Americans civil rights. Television's bringing of the Vietnam War into the nation's living rooms is credited with motivating millions of citizens to pressure our government to end the war, resulting in one president ending his political career and another eventually ending the nation's overt military activities in Southeast Asia.

Conversely, the media have from time to time voluntarily cooperated with the government and military in denying information to the American public. Following the media's revelations of the military's lies and deceptions in the Vietnam War, thus strengthening the public's resolution to bring that war to an end, the Pentagon took pains to see that it would not happen again and imposed strict censorship of all news in subsequent conflicts, including the invasion of Grenada, the action in Panama, the Gulf War, and the wars in Afghanistan and Iraq. Although many media organizations later apologized to the American public for deliberately keeping it in the dark about what was really happening in the Persian Gulf in 1991, the media once again showed its lack of integrity and courage by allowing itself to report false and incomplete information during the U.S. involvement in the NATO action in Yugoslavia in 1999 and for accepting the false information that Iraq had weapons of mass destruction, was linked to the 9-11 terrorist attacks in the World Trade Center and the Pentagon, had ties to Al Qaeda, and was a threat to the United States—all proven false by U.N. and U.S. agencies, including the CIA, prior to the invasion of Iraq. The late broadcast news icon Walter Cronkite publicly criticized the government and the military for its censorship and the media for its complicity with that censorship in its reporting of the Kosovo crisis. As noted earlier, the media's abandonment of its traditional freedoms and its obligation to serve the public was exacerbated in its coverage—or, rather lack of coverage—of the government's covert actions, including wiretaps in cooperation with communication companies and warrantless arrests, against its own citizens, including political dissenters, in the "war against terrorism."

Frank Stanton, past president of CBS, said this:

> The effect of broadcasting upon the democratic experience has gone far beyond elections. The monumental events of this [20th] century—depression, wars, uneasy peace, the birth of more new nations in two decades than had occurred before in two centuries, undreamed of scientific breakthroughs, profound social revolution—all these were made immediate, intimate realities to Americans through, first, the ears of radio and, later, the eyes of television. No longer were the decisions of the American people made in an information vacuum, as they witnessed the towering events of their time that were bound to have incisive political repercussions.

Sadly, the media, by and large, too often have appeared to have forgotten their heritage and have become virtual mouthpieces for special government and private interests.

The media writer who prepares material dealing with issues and events has the satisfaction of knowing that he or she can contribute to human progress and thought and is participating directly in changing society and solving problems of humanity. Not many professions allow you to accomplish this on such a broad and grand scale! Theoretically, the writer can help fulfill the mass media's responsibility to serve the public's best interests, to raise and energize the country's cultural and educational standards, and to strengthen the country as a whole. Realistically, the best-intentioned writer is still under the control of the network or station or advertiser, whose first loyalties usually are directed toward its own bottom line and not necessarily to the needs of the public. Occasionally, these interests coincide. The writer who wants to keep a job is pressured to serve the employer's interests. Hopefully, conscience will prompt the writer to serve the public interest as well.

Basic Elements of Production

The media writer must know the tools the director uses to bring the script to life, whether for a six-hour miniseries or a 30-second commercial—or even a piece of cyberspace spam. When you write for a visual or aural medium, you should be familiar with the key production techniques that can facilitate and enhance a script. You should learn what the camera can and cannot do, what sound or visual effects are possible in the control room, how microphones help create mind pictures, what terminology to use in furnishing descriptions and transitions, what a web site consists of, and other technical and production devices and terms that are essential for effective writing.

However, keep in mind that unless you, the writer, are also the director of the given script, the determination of production elements is the prerogative of the director. It is not only unnecessary, but a nuisance to the director for the writer to include camera movements, shots, and control room techniques when writing a script. An exception is where it is absolutely necessary to do so to explain or forward the purpose of the particular sequence. This chapter, therefore, is designed only as a general introductory overview of some of the key elements of production. The wannabe writer would do well to take a production course in one or more of the media areas in which she or he intends to work.

New developments in media technology seem to be never-ending. What was standard a few years ago may be outmoded today. Digital cameras and storage, computer graphics, and other constant changes impact what is produced, how it is produced, and how it is delivered. Computers and iPhones have increasingly taken over the work of traditional facilities and even personnel. The writer may not favor or wish to personally use this technology, but nevertheless needs to be aware of how the technology affects the creative process of writing for the media.

Viewers may regard cable and satellite television as different from the broadcast television service, but the difference is principally in the means of transmission. Although we currently mostly receive our programs on platforms like satellite and cable, which effectively erases the broadcast distinction, we increasingly view programs on a variety of receivers such as computer, tablet, and smart phones. The medium is still television. The writing is still basically the same. But the programming can differ in some respects, requiring a different orientation by the writer. For example, many cable franchises have local origination channels, providing local, frequently live productions. The type and content of these programs usually are of semi-professional quality with dedicated subject matter aimed at and often produced by special interest groups. The writer should have an awareness of the restrictions of live production using limited and sometimes older equipment. Frequently, local origination and especially public access channels provide an opportunity for television exposure for neighborhood, ethnic, minority, and other culturally diverse groups that traditionally have been denied equal access to the media.

Because cable and satellite requires a user fee, and some channels are "pay" television per channel or per view, some cable and satellite viewers may represent a relatively affluent and culturally sophisticated audience. This sometimes means depending on the channel or program, you can write on a higher level than in broadcasting's usual lowest-common-denominator orientation. The Internet's **interactive** capabilities open the door to service-oriented programming and two-way communication. The key word for the current technical state of the art is "digital."

TELEVISION

Although the television writer does not have to know all the elements of production to write a script, he or she should have a basic understanding of the special mechanical and electronic devices of the medium. The writer should be familiar with (1) the studio or shooting location; (2) the camera, with its movements, lenses, and shots; (3) the studio control room, including digital computer-driven editing techniques; (4) special video effects; and (5) sound.

The Studio

Television studios vary greatly in size and equipment. Some have extensive state-of-the-art electronic and mechanical equipment and are as large as a movie sound stage. Others are small and cramped, with barely enough equipment to produce a broadcast-quality show. Although network studios, regional stations, and large independent production houses are likely to have the best studios, one occasionally finds a college or a school system with facilities that rival the best professional situation. The writer should know the size and facilities of the studio: Will it accommodate large sets, many sets, creative camera movement, and lighting? Are field settings necessary? Is the program produced on tape or disc or shot on film with the availability of cranes, outdoor effects, and other special studio devices? Should the script be a combination of studio shooting plus exteriors? In other words, before writing the final draft of the script (and, if possible, even the first draft), the writer should know what technical facilities will be available to produce the script, including what can and cannot be done in the studio likely to be used. Professor and former BBC director Tom Kingdon notes that, increasingly, dramas and sitcoms are being made film-style in the field or on sound stages. Therefore, it is important for the writer to be aware of the potentials of the film camera and film production techniques. Important among the technical facilities, Kingdon states, are the graphic capabilities of the studio control room. He suggests that the writer should consult with the director to determine whether there can be vivid graphic components such as elaborate lower-thirds, moving graphics, fancy digital transitions between shots, among other techniques, or whether the graphic elements should be played down. With greater and greater miniaturization, the studio for some formats can be no larger than the top of a desk. Bloggers and others doing news commentary on their web cams, for example, don't need a full studio to produce streaming video or even to use layered graphics or chroma keys.

The Camera: Movement

Whether the show is being recorded on film, digitally, or on tape, the camera movements and the terminology are basically the same. The principal difference is the style of shooting: short, individual takes for film, longer and sometimes continuous action sequences for video. Instant digital recording and editing has brought the two approaches closer by combining elements of both. Professor Kingdon advises that production has evolved from the videotape-in-the-studio and film-in-the-field approach. "With the development of HDTV and digital camera formats, which rival the quality of 16 mm film," he states, "more and more shows—and independent films—are being shot on video instead of film. This raises the question of what is the difference between having your show shot on film or video. All film has the 'film look,' which is hard to categorize, but is recognizable as pleasingly soft yet containing attractive highlights. Video, comparatively, tends to have greater resolution, but looks very transparent. But as video improves and cameras allow shooting at 24 frames a second, like film, aesthetic distinctions begin to disappear."

The writer should consider the film or video camera as a moving and adjustable proscenium through which the writer and director can direct the audience's attention. Four major areas of audience attention can be changed via the camera: (1) the distance between the audience and the subject, (2) the amount of the subject the audience sees, (3) the audience position in relation to the subject, and (4) the angle at which the viewer sees the subject. The writer must understand

and be prepared to designate any and all of the following six specific movements to direct the audience's attention:

1. *Dolly-in and dolly-out.* The camera is mounted on a "dolly," a movable platform that permits smooth forward or backward movement. This movement to or away from the subject permits a change of orientation to the subject while retaining a continuity of action.

2. *Zoom-in and zoom-out.* Used to accomplish more easily the same purpose as the dolly from mid- and long distances, the zoom can narrow the angle of view and compress depth, making people or objects appear closer. Some writers and directors believe that psychologically the dolly is more effective, moving the audience closer to or further from the subject, whereas the zoom gives the feeling of moving the subject closer to or further from the audience. In other words, as Tom Kingdon puts it, "the dolly gives the audience the sensation of actually moving through space, especially when the camera itself is moving past foreground objects, while the zoom simply alters the size of the frame without adding that special dimension of movement through space."

3. *Tilt up and tilt down.* This means pointing the camera up or down, thus changing the view from the same position to a higher or lower part of the subject.

4. *Pan right and pan left.* The camera moves right or left on its axis. This movement is used to follow a character or a particular action, or to direct the audience's attention to a particular subject.

5. *Follow right and follow left.* This is also called the **travel shot** or **truck shot**. The camera is set at a right angle to the subject and either follows alongside a moving subject or, if the subject is stationary, such as an advertising display, follows down the line of the subject. The audience, through the camera lens pointed sharply to the right or left, sees the items in the display. This shot is not used as frequently as the preceding ones. The follow left or follow right can also be a panning shot, where the camera itself does not move. In the truck shot the camera itself moves right or left on a dolly or on a wheeled pedestal, a lateral-movement version of dolly-in and dolly-out. The truck shot is sometimes referred to as a **crab** shot, with the terminology "crab right" or "crab left."

6. *Boom shot.* Originally familiar equipment in Hollywood filmmaking, the camera boom has also become a standard part of television production practice. A crane, usually attached to a moving dolly, enables the camera to **boom** up or down from its basic position, at various angles—usually high up—to the subject. This is known also as a **crane shot**.

As hardware gets "smarter," controlling the devices to achieve these movements gets easier. For example, web cams can use software to control framing, zooming, panning, tilting, and following of the given individual being recorded.

Newsrooms have cameras with preset positions; with the push of a button the on-air personality delivering the news can be director, camera operator, and technical director for pre-programmed moves.

Note the use of the basic camera positions in the following scripts. The writer should not specify so many camera directions. The director would determine them and write them in the left column of the script. They are included here to indicate to the beginning writer the variety of camera and shot possibilities. This approximates a *shooting script*, with the video directions that the director, rather than the writer, would insert.

VIDEO	AUDIO
ESTABLISHING SHOT.	DETECTIVE BYRON: (AT DESK, IN FRONT OF HIM, ON CHAIRS IN A ROW, ARE FOUR YOUNG MEN IN JEANS AND LEATHER JACKETS, WITH MOTORCYCLE HELMETS NEARBY.) All right. So a store was robbed. So all of you were seen in the store at the time of the robbery. So there was no one else in the store except the clerk. So none of you know anything about the robbery.
DOLLY IN FOR CLOSE-UP OF BYRON.	(GETTING ANGRY) You may be young punks but you're still punks, and you can stand trial whether you're seventeen or seventy. And if you're not going to cooperate now, I'll see that you get the stiffest sentence possible.
DOLLY OUT FOR LONG SHOT OF ENTIRE GROUP. CUT TO CLOSE-UP. PAN RIGHT ACROSS BOYS' FACES, FROM ONE TO THE OTHER, AS BYRON TALKS.	Now, I'm going to ask you again, each one of you. And this is your last chance. If you talk, only the guilty one will be charged with larceny. The others will have only a petty theft charge on them, and I'll see they get a suspended sentence. Otherwise I'll send you all up for five to ten.
FOLLOW SHOT ALONG LINE OF CHAIRS IN FRONT OF BOYS, GETTING FACIAL REACTIONS OF EACH ONE AS THEY RESPOND.	(OFF CAMERA) Joey? JOEY: (STARES STRAIGHT AHEAD, NOT ANSWERING.) BYRON: (OFF CAMERA) Al? AL: I got nothin' to say. BYRON: (OFF CAMERA) Bill? BILL: Me, too. I don't know nothin'. BYRON: (OFF CAMERA) OK, Johnny. It's up to you.
TILT DOWN TO JOHNNY'S BOOT AS HE REACHES FOR HANDLE OF KNIFE. PAN UP WITH HAND AS IT	JOHNNY: (THERE IS NO ANSWER. THEN JOHNNY SLOWLY SHAKES HIS HEAD. IMPERCEPTIBLY, BYRON NOT NOTICING, HE REACHES DOWN

continued

VIDEO	AUDIO
MOVES AWAY FROM THE BOOT INTO AN INSIDE POCKET OF HIS JACKET. CUT TO MEDIUM SHOT ON BOOM CAMERA OF JOHNNY WITHDRAWING HAND FROM POCKET, BOOM DOWN TO OBJECT IN JOHNNY'S HAND.	TO HIS MOTORCYCLE BOOT FOR THE HANDLE OF A KNIFE. SUDDENLY THE HAND STOPS AND MOVES UP TO THE INSIDE POCKET OF HIS JACKET. JOHNNY TAKES AN OBJECT FROM HIS POCKET, SLOWLY OPENS HIS HAND.)
[Ordinarily, a boom shot would not be used here. A zoom lens would be easier to use and at least as effective.]	

The Camera: Lenses

The principal differences in lenses are between the **zoom** lens and the **prime** lens. The latter has only one focal length, not permitting a zoom factor. Almost all TV cameras, whether in the studio or in the field, use zooms. Remote and studio zoom lenses differ in the required light levels and angle width needed. The attention-getting dramatic shots required in commercials necessitate highly sophisticated and flexible lenses. Tom Kingdon notes that "all lenses have specific effects associated with them. Narrow or telephoto lenses tend to compress space and place backgrounds out of focus, while wide-angle lenses tend to open up space in the frame and keep things in focus. For example, news camera operators use wide-angle lenses."

A good lens can save production time. For example, a prime lens requires a pause in the shooting sequence for readjustment or change; a lens that can go smoothly with perfect focus from an extreme close-up to a wide long shot and then back again facilitates continuing, efficient shooting. ENG/EFP lenses focus at a distance as close as three feet to the subject. Some lenses with micro-capability focus from just a few inches away.

The Camera: Shots

In some instances the writer needs to capture a specific subject for the logical continuity of the script or for the proper psychological effect of the moment upon the audience, and feels compelled to at least suggest to the director a specific shot that might not be immediately obvious to the director within the context of the script.

Shot designations range from the close-up to the medium shot to the long shot. Within these categories are gradations, such as the medium long shot and the extreme close-up. The kind of shot usually indicates the specific subject to be encompassed; for example, "XCU [for extreme close-up] Joe's right hand." The terms and their meanings apply to both the television and the film format. Here are the most commonly used shots:

- ◾ *Close-up (CU).* "CU Harry," "CU Harry's fingers as he twists the dials of the safe," or "CU Harry's feet on the pedals of the piano." A **close-up** of a human subject usually consists of just the face, but can include some of the upper body. Unless specifically designated otherwise, the letters **XCU** or **ECU** (*extreme close-up*) usually mean the face alone. Variations of the close shot are the *shoulder shot*, which indicates the area from the shoulders to the top of the head, in addition to *bust shot, waist shot, hip shot,* and *knee shot.*

- ◾ *Medium shot (MS).* In the *medium shot* (**MS**) the camera picks up a good part of the individual, group, or object, usually filling the screen (but not in its entirety), without showing too much of the physical environment.

- ◾ *Long shot (LS).* The *long shot* (**LS**), sometimes called the **establishing shot** or *wide shot* (**WS**), is used primarily to establish the entire setting or as much of it as is necessary to orient the audience properly. From the long shot the camera may go to the medium shot and then to the close-up, creating a dramatic movement from an overall view to the essence of the scene or situation. Conversely, the camera may move from the extreme close-up to the clarifying broadness of the *extreme long shot* (**XLS**). Both approaches are used frequently to open a sequence.

- ◾ *Full shot (FS).* In the *full shot* (**FS**), the subject is put on the screen in its entirety. For example, "FS Harry" means that the audience sees Harry from head to toe. "FS family at dinner table" means that the family seated around the dinner table is seen completely. Some directors use the designation **FF** for *full figure shot.*

- ◾ *Variations.* Many variations of these shots are used when necessary to clarify what is desired. For example, if two people in conversation are to be the focal point of the shot, the term *two-shot* (**2S**) is appropriate. If the two people are to fill the screen, *tight 2S* is the right term, as illustrated in the next script example. Similarly, *medium two-shot* (**M2S**), *three-shot* (**3S**), and other more specific shot designations may be used.

The screen size of the receiving device should be considered in selecting and framing shots. An XCU is not a likely choice for an Imax screen, while it is clearly a better choice for cell phone reception than a WS where the content would be so small that it would be difficult to make out. As this is being written, most production is still prepared for distribution to all receiving formats.

Note the use of different types of shots in the following hypothetical script example. The video directions at the beginning of this script tell the story solely with pictures. The writer usually would include a narrative description without the shot designations. The same approach would apply to the end of the segment. Most of the video directions within the example would, as well, have been omitted by the writer, who would leave that job to the director. Note that in many of the actual scripts used in this book, the writers provide few video directions.

VIDEO	AUDIO
FADE IN ON LONG SHOT OF OUTSIDE OF BAR. ESTABLISH STREET FRONT AND OUTSIDE OF BAR. DOLLY IN TO MEDIUM SHOT, THEN TO CLOSE-UP OF SIGN ON THE WINDOW: "HARRY SMITH, PROP." CUT TO INSIDE OF BAR, CLOSE-UP OF MAN'S HAND DRAWING A GLASS OF BEER FROM THE TAP. FOLLOW MAN'S HAND WITH GLASS TO TOP OF BAR WHERE HE PUTS DOWN GLASS.	
DOLLY OUT SLOWLY TO MEDIUM SHOT OF HARRY, SERVING THE BEER, AND MAC, SITTING AT BAR.	
ZOOM OUT TO WIDE SHOT, ESTABLISHING ENTIRE INSIDE OF BAR, SEVERAL PEOPLE ON STOOLS, AND SMALL TABLE AT RIGHT OF BAR WITH THREE MEN SEATED, PLAYING CARDS.	
	JOE: (AT TABLE) Harry. Bring us another deck. This one's getting too dirty for honest card players.
	HARRY: Okay. (HE REACHES UNDER THE BAR, GETS A DECK OF CARDS, GOES TO THE TABLE.)
TIGHT 2S HARRY AND JOE	JOE: (TAKING THE CARDS, WHISPERS TO HARRY.) Who's the guy at the bar? He looks familiar.
	HARRY: Name of Mac. From Jersey someplace.
CUT TO CU JOE	JOE: Keep him there. Looks like somebody we got business with. (LOOKS AROUND TABLE.)
CUT TO FS TABLE	Right, boys? (THE MEN AT THE TABLE NOD KNOWINGLY TO HARRY.)

continued

VIDEO	**AUDIO**
	HARRY: Okay if I go back to the bar?
	JOE: Go ahead.
PAN WITH HARRY TO BAR. DOLLY INTO BAR, MS HARRY AND MAC AS HARRY POURS HIM ANOTHER DRINK. MCU HARRY AS HE WRITES. CUT TO CU OF WORDS ON PIECE OF PAPER.	HARRY: (WALKS BACK TO BAR, POURS DRINK FOR MAC. SCRIBBLES SOMETHING ON PIECE OF PAPER, PUTS IT ON BAR IN FRONT OF MAC.)

Control Room Techniques and Editing

The technicians in the control room have various electronic devices for modifying the picture and moving from one picture to another, giving television its ability to direct the attention and control the audience's view. The technicians in the film editing room have the same capabilities except that the modifications are done solely during the editing process. In live-type recorded video, some modifications can be done as the program is being recorded, as well as during a subsequent editing process. Where digital equipment is used, editing can be virtually instantaneous.

Tom Kingdon has found that "the use of digital effects in the control room greatly enhances the repertory and sophistication of available effects. Whereas in the past you might simply dissolve between two shots or do a simple transitional wipe (see below), now almost any kind of elaborate visual effect is achievable. Digital editing in the edit suite is usually referred to as **non-linear** editing, which means that any shot can be added almost instantly to the **timeline**—the sequence of shots that an editor constructs—at any point."

- *Fade.* The **fade-in** brings the picture in from a black (or blank) screen. The **fade-out** takes the picture out until a black level is reached. (You've often heard the phrase "fade to black.") The fade is used primarily to indicate a passage of time, and in this function serves much like a curtain or blackout on the stage. The fade also can be used to indicate a change of place. Depending on the action sequence, the fade-in or fade-out can be fast or slow. The writer usually indicates the fade-in and fade-out on the script.

- *Dissolve.* While one picture is being reduced in intensity, the other picture is being raised, one picture smoothly dissolving into the next—replacing or being replaced by the other. The **dissolve** is used primarily to indicate a change of place, but sometimes to indicate a change of time. The dissolve has various modifications. An important one is the *matched dissolve,* in which two similar or identical subjects are placed one over the other, with one fading in and the other fading out, showing a metamorphosis taking place. Dissolving from a newly lit candle to a candle burned down to indicate a passage of time is a matched dissolve. The dissolve can vary in time from a *fast dissolve* (almost a split-second movement) to a *slow dissolve* (as long as five seconds). At no point in the dissolve does the screen go to black.

- ■ *Cut.* The **cut** is the technique most commonly used and consists simply of switching instantaneously from one picture to another. Care must be taken to avoid too much cutting; make certain that the cutting is consistent with the mood, rhythm, pace, and psychological approach of the program as a whole.

- ■ *Superimposition.* The **super** is the placing of one image over another. It is sometimes used in stream-of-consciousness sequences when the memory being recalled is pictured on the screen along with the person doing the recalling. To obtain necessary contrast in the superimposition, one picture must have higher light intensity than the other. The superimposition is sometimes used for non-dramatic effects, such as placing a commercial name or product over a picture. Although the principles of the super continue to be used, the mechanical control room superimposition has been replaced by the more effective *key* or *matte*.

- ■ *Key or matte.* A **key** is a two-source special effect where a foreground image is cut into a background image and filled back in with itself. A **matte** is a similar technique, but can add color to the foreground image. **Character generators** (**chyrons** or **vidifonts**) electronically cut letters into background pictures. Titles and commercial names of products are keyed or matted. **Chroma key** is an electronic effect that cuts a given color out of a picture and replaces it with another visual. Newscasts use this technique; the green matte background behind the newscaster is replaced with a taped, filmed, or digital sequence.

- ■ *Wipe.* One picture wiping another picture off the screen in the manner of a window shade being pulled over a window is known as a **wipe**. The wipe can be from any direction—horizontal, vertical, or diagonal. Wipes can also *blossom out* from the center of a picture or *envelope* it from all sides. Wipes often designate a change of place or time.

- ■ *Split screen.* In the *split screen* the picture on the air is divided, with the shots from two or more cameras or other sources occupying adjoining places on the screen. A common use is for phone conversations, showing the persons speaking on separate halves of the screen. The screen can be split into many parts and into many shapes, as is sometimes done when news correspondents report from different parts of the world. One segment of virtually any size can be split off from the rest of the screen; in baseball broadcasts, for example, one corner of the screen might show the runner taking a lead off first base while the rest of the screen shows the pitcher about to pitch to the batter.

The VIDEO and AUDIO columns in the following script comprise the standard two-column script, presented here to illustrate the uses of control room techniques. The *commentary* column at the left is *not* part of a shooting script but is inserted here as a learning device for understanding how the appropriate terms are designated and used.

COMMENTARY	VIDEO	AUDIO
1. The fade-in is used for the beginning of the sequence.	FADE IN ON SHERIFF'S OFFICE. SHERIFF FEARLESS AND DEPUTY FEARFUL ARE SEATED AT THE DESK IN THE CENTER OF THE ROOM.	FEARLESS: I wonder what Bad Bart is up to. He's been in town since yesterday. I've got to figure out his plan if I'm to prevent bloodshed.
		FEARFUL: I've got faith in you, Fearless. I heard that he's been with Miss Susie in her room.
		FEARLESS: Good. We can trust her. She'll find out for us.
		FEARFUL: But I'm worried about her safety.
		FEARLESS: Yup. I wonder how she is making out. That Bad Bart is a mean one.
2. The dissolve is used here for a change of place without passage of time. This scene takes place simultaneously or immediately following the one in the sheriff's office.	DISSOLVE TO MISS SUSIE'S HOTEL ROOM. BART IS SEATED IN AN EASY CHAIR. SUSIE IS IN A STRAIGHT CHAIR AT THE OTHER END OF THE ROOM.	BART: I ain't really a killer, Miss Susie. It's only my reputation that's hurting me. Only because of one youthful indiscretion.
		SUSIE: What was that, Mr. Bart?

continued

COMMENTARY	VIDEO	AUDIO
3. The superimposition is used here for a memory recall device.	SUPERIMPOSE, OVER CU BART, FACE OF MAN HE KILLED AS HE DESCRIBES SCENE.	BART: I can remember as well as yesterday. I was only a kid then. I thought he drew a gun on me. Maybe he did and maybe he didn't. But I shot him. And I'll remember his face as sure as I'll live—always. SUSIE: I guess you aren't really all bad, Mr. Bart.
4. Here the cut indicates a different view of the character in the same continuous time sequence.	PAN WITH BART TO THE HALL DOOR. CUT TO HALL AS HE ENTERS IT.	BART: You've convinced me, Miss Susie. I've never had a fine woman speak to me so nice before. I'm going to turn over a new leaf. (WALKS INTO THE HALL. AN EARLY MODEL TELEPHONE IS ON THE WALL.) I'm going to call the sheriff. Operator, get me the sheriff's office.
5. The wipe here moves from left to right or right to left. It designates a change of place. The use of the split screen indicates the putting of two different places before the audience at the same time.	HORIZONTAL WIPE INTO SPLIT SCREEN. BART IN ONE HALF, SHERIFF PICKING UP TELEPHONE IN OTHER HALF.	FEARLESS: Sheriff's office. BART: Sheriff. This is Bad Bart. I'm going to give myself up and confess all my crimes. I've turned over a new leaf. FEARLESS: You expect me to believe that, Bart? BART: No, I don't. But all I'm asking is a chance to prove it. FEARLESS: How do you propose to do that?
	WIPE OFF SHERIFF OFFICE SCENE. CU BART'S FACE AS HE MAKES HIS DECISION.	BART: I'm coming over to your office. And I'm not going to be wearing my guns.

continued

COMMENTARY

6. The fade here indicates the passage of time.

VIDEO

FADE OUT. FADE IN ON MISS SUSIE SEATED ON HER BED.

AUDIO

SUSIE: That's all there was to it, Fearless. The more I talked to him, the more I could see that underneath it all he had a good heart.

(SHE WALKS TO THE SMALL TABLE AT THE FOOT OF THE BED, TAKES A GLASS AND BOTTLE, THEN WALKS OVER TO THE EASY CHAIR. WE SEE SHERIFF FEARLESS IN THE EASY CHAIR.)

Here, Fearless, have a sarsaparilla. You deserve one after what you've done today.

FEARLESS: No, Susie. It was you who really did the work. And you deserve the drink. (AFTER A MOMENT) You know, there's only one thing I'm sorry for.

SUSIE: What's that?

FEARLESS: That Bart turned out to be good, deep down inside, and gave himself up.

SUSIE: Why?

FEARLESS: Well, there's this new gun I received this morning from the East that I haven't yet had a chance to use!

---

7. Fade is used to signify the end of a sequence, a passage of time, and a change of place.

THEME MUSIC IN AND UP STRONG. SLOW FADE OUT.

continued

COMMENTARY	VIDEO	AUDIO
8. In studio show, stock film or recorded material may be necessary for the exterior scene, not reproducible in a studio.	FADE IN SOUTH DAKOTA BADLANDS, CUT TO FEARLESS AND SUSIE ON THEIR HORSES ON THE TRAIL WAVING GOODBYE TO BART, WHO RIDES OFF INTO THE DISTANCE.	
9. Key or matte permits the insertion of words onto the picture.	KEY CREDITS OVER THE SCENE AS FEARLESS AND SUSIE CONTINUE TO WAVE.	

Sound

In the technical—not the artistic—sense, video and audio use sound in essentially the same ways, except for some obvious differences. The microphone (**mic**) in the television play is not stationary, but is on a boom and dolly to follow the moving performers. Chest mics, table mics, and cordless mics are used in television, usually for the non-dramatic studio program such as news, panel, and interview shows, and sometimes for dramas in preset positions and situations. In television, the dialogue and sound on the set usually emanate from and are coordinated with the visual action. Off-screen (**OS**) sound effects can be used, but they must clearly represent something happening offscreen; if they represent an action taking place on camera, they must appear to come from that source.

The term "off-camera" (**OC**) is used in the script for the character or sound heard but not seen. Sound can be prerecorded for television or, as is frequently done with filmed productions, added after the action has been shot. Television and radio both use narration, but narration is infrequent in the visual medium. In television the *voice-over* (**VO**) can be a narrator, announcer, or the prerecorded thoughts of the character.

Television uses music as program content, background, and theme. Other uses of sound and music in radio can be adapted to television, but remember that in television the sound or music does not replace visual action but, rather, complements or heightens it.

RADIO

Microphone use, sound effects, and music are the primary technical and production elements the radio writer should be aware of. The writer should further understand how the studio and control room can or cannot implement the purposes of the script. Although the most creative uses of radio's potentials can be realized in the drama, few plays are heard on radio anymore. Nevertheless, these same creative techniques can be applied to commercials, many of which are short dramatic sequences, and to lesser degrees, to other radio formats.

The Microphone

The basic element of radio broadcasting is the microphone, usually abbreviated as *mic,* but sometimes seen in its older abbreviation, *mike*. The number of microphones used in a show is usually limited. For the standard program—a disc jockey or news program—only one is needed. A panel, discussion, or interview program may have a mic for each person or for every two people.

Not all microphones are the same. The audio engineer selects certain types of microphones for their sensitivity and specific effects uses. The writer has only one important responsibility in this area: To understand the performer's relationship to the microphone. This physical relationship determines the listener's orientation. For example, the audience might be with a character riding in a car. The car approaches the edge of a cliff. Should the sound of the character's scream and the noise of the car as it hurtles off the cliff be on mic, thus keeping the audience with the car, or should these sounds be faded into the distance, orienting the audience to a vantage point at the top of the cliff, hearing (and in their minds' eyes, seeing) the character and car going downward?

There are five basic microphone positions. **On mic** is taken for granted when no position is designated next to the line of dialogue. If the performer has been in another position and suddenly speaks from an on mic position, then "on mic" should be noted.

- ◼ *On mic.* The performer speaks from a position right at the microphone. The listener is oriented to the imaginary setting in the same physical spot as the performer.

- ◼ *Off mic.* The performer is some distance away from the microphone. This conveys to the audience the impression that the sound or voice is at a proportionate distance away from the physical orientation point of the listener, which is usually at the center of the scene. This listener orientation can be varied by removing the performer's voice but indicating through the dialogue that the performer has remained in the same physical place. The listener rather than the performer is moved from the central point of action.

- ◼ *Fading on.* The performer slowly moves toward the microphone. To the listener, the performer is approaching the physical center of the action.

- ◼ *Fading off.* The performer moves away from the microphone while speaking, thus moving away from the central orientation point.

- ◼ *Behind obstructions.* The performer sounds as if there were a barrier between him or her and the focal point of the audience's orientation. The writer may indicate that the performer is behind a door, outside a window, or perhaps in the middle of a mosh pit. Special microphones may be needed. The filter mic, for example, creates the impression that a voice or sound is coming over a telephone. The voice at the focal point of the audience's orientation, even though speaking over a telephone, too, would be on mic. The echo chamber, another device, creates various degrees of an echo sound, ranging from an impression that a person is locked in a closet to that of being lost in a boundless cavern. Today most studios can create sounds digitally that can place the performer in virtually any position or setting.

Note how the five basic mic positions are used in the following script example. The *commentary* column on the left is *not* a part of the script, but is used here solely as a learning device. *Note, too, that although the radio scripts in this book are single-spaced for space reasons, ALL radio scripts should be double-spaced.*

COMMENTARY

1. With no mention of position, the character is assumed to be ON MIC.

2. The orientation of the audience stays with George as Myra leaves the focal point of the action.

3. George must give the impression of projecting across the room to Myra, who is now at the front door.

4. Myra's physical position is now clear to the audience through the distance of her voice. As soon as she comes ON MIC, the audience's physical position arbitrarily is oriented to that of Myra at the door.

5. This is an example of the behind-an-obstruction position.

6. The physical orientation of the audience stays with Myra. George is now OFF MIC.

AUDIO

GEORGE: I'm bushed, Myra. Another day like the one today and I'll just . . .
(THE DOORBELL RINGS)

MYRA: Stay where you are, George. I'll answer the door.

GEORGE: Thanks, hon. (DOORBELL RINGS AGAIN)

MYRA: (RECEDING FOOTSTEPS, FADING) I'm coming . . . I'm coming. I wonder who it could be at this hour.

GEORGE: (CALLING) See who it is before you open the door.

MYRA: (OFF) All right, George.

(ON MIC) Who is it?

MESSENGER: (BEHIND DOOR) Special delivery for Mr. George Groo.

MYRA: Just a minute. (CALLING) George, Special delivery envelope for you.

GEORGE: (OFF) Sign for me, will you Myra?

continued

COMMENTARY

AUDIO

MYRA: Yes. (SOUND OF DOOR OPENING) I'll sign for it. (SOUND OF PAPER BEING HANDED OVER AND THE SCRATCH OF PEN ON PAPER)

MESSENGER: Thank you ma'am. (SOUND OF DOOR BEING CLOSED)

MYRA: (SOUND OF ENVELOPE BEING OPENED) I'll open it and … (SILENCE FOR A MOMENT)

7. Note the complete shift of audience orientation. The audience, at the door with Myra, initially hears George from the other end of the room; George, fading on, approaches the spot where the audience and Myra are. Finally, George is at that spot. Note the use of the term ON MIC at the end, when the character comes to that position from another position.

GEORGE: (OFF) Well, Myra, what is it? (STILL SILENCE)
GEORGE: (FADING ON) Myra, in heaven's name, what happened? What does it say? (ON MIC) Myra, let me see it.

Sound Effects

There are three major categories of sound effects: recorded, manual, and digitally created, although there are relatively few facilities that are not now completely digital. Virtually any sound effect desired can be found on disc, record, tape, or computer. For split-second incorporation of sound into the program's action, manual or live effects are sometimes more effective. Manual effects include such sounds as the opening and closing of a door (coming from a miniature door located near the microphone of the sound effects operator) and the rattling of cellophane to simulate the sound of fire. Natural effects are those emanating from their natural sources, such as the sound of walking where a microphone is held near the feet of a sound effects person. Combinations of sounds can be made from an amalgamation of digital, recorded, manual, and natural effects.

Michael Keith, author of *The Radio Station*, notes that virtually all studios today generate sound effects with the aid of a computer and specially designed software, the common practice or method of integrating sounds into a production. Effects taken from tape or vinyl discs virtually no longer exist. Even CD-effects libraries are used less and less, especially at larger stations with state-of-the-art facilities and equipment. In recent years digital devices, such as multi-effects processors, have featured comprehensive menus of sounds for use in studio mixing. Keith points out that this new generation of audio hardware, along with computers and digital workstations, have radically transformed the production room environment and mixing experience.

Inexperienced writers occasionally overdo the use of sound. Sound effects should be used only when necessary, and then only in relation to the principles that determine the listener's orientation. Think of your own orientation to sound when listening to the radio. For example, a high pitch, high volume, or rising pitch generally suggests a climax or some disturbing element, whereas a low pitch, low volume, or descending pitch generally suggests something soothing and calm. Combinations of these sounds and the relationship of the specific sound to the specific context of the script can alter these generalizations. For instance, a low pitch in the proper place can indicate something ominous and foreboding rather than calm; the combination of a low pitch and high volume, as in thunder or an explosion, creates anything but a soothing effect. A high or ascending pitch can, in context, indicate something happy and bright. Sound effects can be used for many purposes, such as the following:

- *Establish locale or setting.* The sound of marching feet, the clanging of metal doors, and the blowing of a whistle suggest a prison. Soft violin music, the occasional clatter of dishes and silverware, the clinking of glasses, and whispered talking suggest a restaurant, perhaps an old-world Hungarian or Russian restaurant.

- *Direct audience attention and emotion.* Emphasis on a distinctive sound can specifically orient the audience. For example, the sudden banging of a gavel in a courtroom scene will immediately orient the audience toward the judge's bench. If the audience is aware that a person alone at home is an intended murder victim, the sound of steps on a sidewalk followed by the sound of knocking on a door, or the more subtle sound of turning a doorknob, will direct the audience's attention toward the front door and orient its emotions toward suspenseful terror and expected violence.

- *Establish time.* A clock striking the hour and a rooster's crow are rather obvious but nevertheless accepted devices. The echo of footsteps along a pavement, with no other sounds heard, designates a quiet street late at night or early in the morning. If an element referred to in the program, such as a passing freight train, has been established as going by at a certain time, every time that sound effect—the passing train—is used, the audience will know the time.

- *Establish mood.* The sounds of laughter, loud music, and much tinkling of glasses establish a different mood for a party than would subdued whispers and the soft music of a string quartet. Sound can be used effectively as counterpoint to an individual character's mood. The attitudes and emotions of a worried, sullen, fretful character may be heightened by placing the person in the midst of sounds of a wild party.

- *Signify entrances and exits.* The sound of footsteps fading off and the opening and closing of a door—or the reverse, the opening and closing of a door and sound of footsteps coming on—unmistakably signify an exit or an entrance. Other sounds can be used to show a character's coming to or leaving a specific place. The departure of a soldier from an enemy-held jungle island after a secret reconnaissance mission can be portrayed by the sounds of boat paddles, the whine of bullets, and the chatter of jungle birds and animals. If the bullet, bird, and animal sounds remain at a steady level and the paddling of the boat fades off, the audience remains on the island and sees the soldier leave. The audience leaves with the soldier if the paddling remains at an on-mic level and the island sounds fade off.

■ *Serve as transition.* If the transition is to cover a change of place, the sounds used can be the means of transportation. The young graduate, about to leave home, says tender farewells. The farewells **cross-fade** into airplane sounds, which in turn cross-fade into the sounds of horns and traffic of a big city. These sounds cross-fade into a dialogue sequence in which the graduate rents an apartment. The change of place has been achieved with sound providing an effective transition.

If the transition is to cover a lapse of time, the sound may be that of a timing device, such as a clock striking three, the clock tick fading out and fading in again, and the clock striking six. The sound indicating the transition need not relate to the specific cause of the transition and can be of a general nature. For example, a **montage** of street sounds covers a change of place and a lapse of time for someone going to a store, in a commercial, to buy the advertised product. Sometimes a montage, which is a blending of a number of sounds, can be especially effective when no single sound fits the specific situation.

In a non-dramatic sequence, such as a transition between program segments, sound relating to the next segment can be used. In some situations the sounds may relate to the program as a whole rather than to a specific circumstance, such as a news ticker sound as a transition or establishing sound for a news program.

■ *Create non-realistic effects.* Note Norman Corwin's description in "The Plot to Overthrow Christmas" of the audience's journey to Hades, "to the regions where legions of the damned go."

> CLANG ON CHINESE GONG. TWO THUNDER PEALS. OSCILLATOR IN A HIGH PITCH BEFORE THUNDER IS ENTIRELY OUT. BRING PITCH DOWN GRADUALLY AND FADE IN ECHO CHAMBER, WHILE HEAVY STATIC FADES IN. THEN OUT TO LEAVE NOTHING BUT OSCILLATOR AT A LOW OMINOUS PITCH. THEN RAISE PITCH SLOWLY, HOLD FOR A FEW SECONDS.

Courtesy of Norman Corwin

Combinations of sound and music can be used to create almost any non-realistic effect, from the simplest to the most complex.

Sound can achieve several purposes at the same time. A classic sound effects sequence—to many the best and most famous in radio history—accompanied comedian Jack Benny's periodic visits to his private vault on his radio show. Older people remember it and younger people who have listened to revivals of old-time radio programs may have heard it. The sounds establish setting and mood, orient the audience's emotions, direct its attention, signify entrances and exits, serve as transitions between places and the passage of time, and create non-realistic effects.

SOUND: FOOTSTEPS . . . DOOR OPENS . . . FOOTSTEPS GOING DOWN . . . TAKING ON HOLLOW SOUND . . . HEAVY IRON DOOR HANDLE TURNING . . . CHAINS CLANKING . . . DOOR CREAKS OPEN . . . SIX MORE HOLLOW FOOTSTEPS . . . SECOND CLANKING OF CHAINS . . . HANDLE TURNS . . . HEAVY IRON DOOR OPENS CREAKING . . . TWO MORE FOOTSTEPS (DIALOGUE BETWEEN THE GUARD AND JACK) . . . LIGHT TURNING SOUND OF VAULT COMBINATION . . . LIGHT TURNING SOUND . . . LIGHT TURNING SOUND . . . LIGHT TURNING SOUND . . . HANDLE TURNS . . . USUAL ALARMS WITH BELLS, AUTO HORNS, WHISTLES, THINGS FALLING . . . ENDING WITH B.O. FOGHORN . . .

Courtesy of the Jack Benny Trust.

Keep in mind that many sounds, no matter how well or accurately done, sometimes are not immediately identifiable to the audience and often can be confused with similar sounds. The writer may have to identify the sounds through the dialogue. For example, the rattling of paper can sound like fire, and the opening and closing of a desk drawer can sound like the opening and closing of almost anything else. The following sequence attempts to make the sounds clear as a natural part of the dialogue.

DICK: (RUFFLING THE PAGES OF A MANUSCRIPT) Just about the worst piece of junk I've ever written in my life.

ANNE: Well, even if you don't like it, I think it can become a bestseller.

DICK: (RUFFLING PAGES AGAIN) Three hundred and forty-two pages of pure unadulterated mediocrity. Listen to them. They even sound off-key. (SOUND OF A DESK DRAWER OPENING) There. That's where it belongs. (SOUND OF MANUSCRIPT BEING THROWN INTO THE DRAWER)

ANNE: Don't lock it up in your desk. I think it's good.

DICK: Nope! That drawer is the place where all bad, dead manuscripts belong. (SOUND OF DESK DRAWER CLOSING) Amen!

Music

Music is radio's principal programming today, but music goes beyond content alone. The writer should also understand how to use music as a bed, program theme, bridge, or sound effect, and for background or mood.

- ■ *Content.* Recorded (record, tape, cartridge, and compact disc have been replaced by digital) music played by disc jockeys dominates radio programming. With few exceptions, all recording used on the air is digital.

■ *Bed.* "Bedding" is the generic term used to describe music used under or as backup of an announcer's sound tracks.

■ *Theme.* From the earliest days of radio, star performers used theme music for personal identification. Listeners who heard the beginning of the song "The Make Believe Ballroom" knew immediately that it was time for Martin Block, one of radio's first and premiere disc jockeys. The first few bars of "Love in Bloom" meant that Jack Benny was about to make his entrance. "A Hard Day's Night" signaled the appearance of the Beatles. "Hello Love" is identified with the American Public Radio Network's *A Prairie Home Companion* show. "Born in the USA" is Bruce Springsteen. "The Material Girl" introduces Madonna. "Billie Jean" means Michael Jackson, "A Beautiful Day" means U2, and "Mo Money, Mo Problems" means rapper Notorious B.I.G. Music can be used as a program theme or to peg a specific event or particular personality. The action or performer is identifiable as soon as the theme music is heard. A theme can be used for the opening, closing, and commercial break transitions in a show. The following script is an example.

MUSIC:	THEME, "ROCK AROUND THE CLOCK," IN, UP, AND UNDER.
DEEJAY:	Welcome to another afternoon session of "The Best of America's Rock Stars," with music, gossip, information, and a special guest, live, interviewed by yours truly, your rocking host, Joe J. Deejay.
MUSIC:	THEME UP AND OUT.
CART:	60 COMMERCIAL
DEEJAY:	First on our agenda is our special guest. One of the greatest stars of all time, in this country and internationally.
MUSIC:	"BORN IN THE USA" IN, UP, AND UNDER.
DEEJAY:	Welcome, Bruce Springsteen, to "The Best of America's Rock Stars."
MUSIC:	OUT
DEEJAY:	Boss, what brings you to our city . . . ?

After the final commercial and Deejay's outro (the announcer's final comments, as differentiated from intro, or introduction), the theme is brought in, up, and out to close the show.

■ *Bridge.* The musical bridge is the most commonly used device to create transitions. Music lasting only a few notes or a few bars can be used to indicate the breaks between segments of the program. The music bridge can also be used to distinguish the commercial inserts from the rest of the programs.

In a dramatic sequence (in a commercial, for example), the music bridge frequently indicates a change of place or a passage of time. Care must be taken that the bridge represents the mood and content of the particular moment. The bridge is usually only a few seconds long. When it is very short, only a second or two, it is called a *stab*. Note the bridge in the next script example.

SOUND:	WATER RUNNING, ECHO IN BATHROOM
MARY:	I hate to say this, John, but if you want to make a good impression to your boss today, you ought to change your brand of toothpaste.
JOHN:	This one tastes good.
MARY:	But it doesn't give you the fresh breath of Angelmint.
JOHN:	I'm glad you told me. I do want that promotion.
MUSIC:	BRIDGE
SOUND:	DRUG STORE NOISES
JOHN:	A tube of Angelmint, please.
CLERK:	Yes, sir. It's our best-selling toothpaste.
SOUND:	CASH REGISTER
MUSIC:	BRIDGE
JOHN:	Mary, Mary, I got the promotion, thanks to you.
MARY:	Thanks to Angelmint, John.
MUSIC:	STAB AND OUT

■ *Sound effect.* Brass and percussion instruments can convey or heighten the feeling of a storm better than sound effects alone. Some effects cannot be presented effectively except through music. How better to convey on radio the sound of a person falling from the top of a tall building than through music moving in a spiral rhythm from a high to a low pitch and ending in a crash?

SOUND:	THUNDER, HEAVY RAIN POUNDING ON CAR ROOF EMPHASIZED AND PUNCTUATED BY MUSIC STABS, CONTINUING UNDER DIALOGUE
ALICE:	Ralph, please pull the car over and stop. It's raining so hard you can't see five feet in front of you.
RALPH:	Aw, Alice, I'm a good driver.

continued

ALICE:	But, Ralph, we're in a whiteout. I'm afraid we'll have an accident.
RALPH:	I know this road. Stop nagging.
ALICE:	If we don't see the turnoff by the bridge, we'll go right off the cliff . . .
SOUND:	SCREECHING OF BRAKES, EMPHASIZED WITH MUSIC SCREECH (e.g., VIOLIN), SPIRALING MUSIC SOUND FADING FROM HIGH TO LOW PITCH ENDING IN A CRASH COMBINING SOUND EFFECTS AND MUSIC (e.g., CYMBALS, DRUMS)

■ *Background or mood.* Music can heighten the content and mood of a sequence. The music must serve as a subtle aid, however; it must not be obvious or, sometimes, even evident.

The listener who is aware of the background music during a commercial sequence has been distracted from the primary purpose of the production. The music should have its effect without the audience consciously realizing it. Background and mood music should not be overdone or used excessively. Well-known compositions should be avoided because they can distract the audience with their familiarity.

If you plan to include music in the script, either as principal content or as incidental or effects background, remember to consult with the producer about what you have in mind. You cannot use any music without the permission of the copyright holder. The producer will have to negotiate with ASCAP (American Society of Composers, Authors and Publishers) or with BMI (Broadcast Music Incorporated) for the rights. If the use is for a network or station, it likely already falls under an agreement between these organizations and the NAB (National Association of Broadcasters).

Sound and Music Techniques and Terms

Several important terms are used by the writer to designate the techniques that manipulate music and sound. These techniques are applied at the control board.

■ *Segue.* **Segue** (pronounced seg-way) is the smooth transition from one sound into the next. This particularly applies to the transitions between musical numbers, when one number is faded out as the next number is faded in. Segues are used in dramatic sequences as well as in music, but in the former the overlapping of sounds makes the technique a cross-fade rather than a segue—as seen in the following music program:

ANNOUNCER:	Our program continues with excerpts from famous musical compositions dealing with the Romeo and Juliet theme. First we hear from Tchaikovsky's <u>Romeo and Juliet</u> overture, followed by Prokofiev's <u>Romeo and Juliet</u> ballet, and finally Gounod's opera <u>Romeo et Juliette</u>.
MUSIC:	TCHAIKOVSKY'S "<u>ROMEO AND JULIET</u>."
	SEGUE TO PROKOFIEV'S "<u>ROMEO AND JULIET</u>."
	SEGUE TO GOUNOD'S "<u>ROMEO ET JULIETTE</u>."
ANNOUNCER:	You have heard . . .

and in this dramatic sequence:

ANNOUNCER:	And now, a word from Millweiser's Light Beer.
MUSIC:	IN AND UP, HOLD FOR FIVE SECONDS AND OUT. SEGUE INTO
SOUND:	TINKLING OF GLASSES, VOICES IN BACKGROUND IN CONVERSATION, MUSIC PLAYING.

■ *Cross-fade.* The *dissolving* from one sound into another, *cross-fade* sometimes is used interchangeably with *segue*. But cross-fade is the crossing of sounds as one fades in and the other fades out, whereas the segue is simply the immediate following of one sound by another. In the following example, the telephone ringing becomes blended for a second or two with the music before the music is entirely faded out, and then only the telephone ringing remains.

MUSIC:	IN AND UP, HOLD FOR FIVE SECONDS. CROSS-FADE INTO THE RINGING OF A TELEPHONE.

■ *Blending.* **Blending** refers to two or more different sounds combined and going out over the air simultaneously. Blending can include combinations of dialogue and music, dialogue and sound effects, sound effects and music, or all three. The example of the tinkling glasses, background voices, and music illustrates the latter.

■ *Cutting or switching.* **Cutting** or **switching**, the sudden cutting off of one sound and the immediate intrusion of another, is a jarring break, sometimes used for a special effect. Cutting can simply designate a sharp change from one microphone to another or to a different sound source. It also can be used for remotes.

ANNOUNCER:	We now switch you to Times Square where Tom Rogers is ready with his "Probing Microphone."
CUT TO ROGERS AT TIMES SQUARE	
ROGERS:	Good afternoon. For our first interview, we have over here . . .

■ *Fade-in and fade-out.* Bringing up the volume or turning it down is a relatively simple operation that is frequently used to fade the music under dialogue, as well as to bring music into and out of the program. Music can *fade in, up* (higher in volume), *under* (lower in volume), or out. The following example illustrates fade-in and fade-out on the disc jockey show.

MUSIC:	THEME, "YOU RAPPED MY RAPPER WITH A RAP." (FADE) IN, UP AND UNDER.
ANNOUNCER:	Welcome to the Rappin' Robert Rap Repertory.
MUSIC:	THEME UP, HOLD FOR FIVE SECONDS, THEN UNDER AND (FADE) OUT.
ANNOUNCER:	This is Rappin' Robert ready to bring you the next full hour right from the top of the charts. And starting with number one on the rack, Kitchen Sink and his new hit . . .
MUSIC:	SNEAK IN AND HOLD UNDER
ANNOUNCER:	. . . that's right, you know it, Kitchen Sink with "Dirty Dishes."
MUSIC:	UP FAST, HOLD TO FINISH, AND OUT.

The Studio

The physical limitations of a radio studio can affect the writer's purposes. Try to determine if the studio is large enough and has the equipment necessary to perform your script properly. Most professional studios are acoustically satisfactory, but some are not, and you need to know whether it is possible to achieve the sensitivity of sound required by your script. Although many music stations do not have a separate studio, performing all of their air work in the control room, some stations have separate studios for panel, interview, and other shows. The studio will contain microphones and other equipment necessary for both recorded and live production.

The Control Room

The control room is the center of operations, where all of the sound—talk, music, effects—are coordinated. All the inputs are carefully mixed by the engineer at the control board and sent out to the listener. The control board regulates the volume of output from all sources and can fade or blend the sound or any one or combination of inputs. The control room needs only a computer containing the station's music library, but some stations may still have CD, tape, and cartridge machines and maybe even an old turntable for playing prerecorded material, plus microphones for the deejays and announcers. Computers access and broadcast an array of programming material, such as jingles, promos, IDs, commercials, and Public Service Announcements (PSAs). With computerized music libraries an operator calls up a scheduled song on the computer monitor and broadcasts it when ready. Other programming elements such as commercial logs and format clocks may also be made readily available to deejays and announcers through a control room computer. The control room also contains equipment for recording material, including entire programs, for later broadcast.

More Radio Terminology

Some key terms the writer should know that frequently appear in the production script (several of those below have been noted earlier): **bed** (a music base), **SFX** (sound effects), **cart** (cartridge, containing the prerecorded material to be played), **ATR** (audio tape recorder, serving the same function as the cart, but less often), **fade** (slowly lower or raise volume), **crossfade** (fade out of one element while introducing another), **ET** (electrical transcription), **live tag** (postscript to recorded music), **out cue** (last words in a line of recorded copy), **punch** (emphasis or stress), **segue** (uninterrupted flow from one element to another), **stinger/button** (music or sound effect finale), **voiceover** (talk over sound), **RT** (reel type), **CD** (compact audio disc), and **mic** (microphone).

As frequently noted in this chapter, records tapes, and other older technology have given way to digital.

Producer, professor, and author of *The Radio Station*, Michael Keith, offers the following advice to radio writers from the vantage point of the production team:

- Understand the unique nature of the medium to create pictures with the mind.
- Be familiar (or get familiar) with the audience you are attempting to address.
- Know, too, what you are talking about: the product.
- Reflect the established mechanics and criteria or copy layout and format.
- Observe proper punctuation, grammar, and spelling.
- Time the copy to fit the production elements.
- Write in plain English and avoid elaborate sentence construction.
- Use phonetic spelling where necessary.
- Avoid excessive numbers and complex directions.
- Be creative.

INTERNET INTERACTIVE TECHNIQUE

A key addition of the Internet to the media mix is its ability to be interactive—between the presenter (writer) and the receptor (the audience). Interactivity suggests an exploitation of the Internet's multimedia potentials, not only a mix of audio and video, but also live action, controlled sound, still photographs, charts and graphs, text, and animation via various channels for input such as telephone, fax, studio audiences, street interviews, and live inserts from field cameras. Until recent years this kind of interactivity required a lot of hardware and technicians. Now the writer can execute these activities by himself or herself or with a small web team simply by clicking on specified items and adding video commentary to a time line or adding links to other content. This not only permits but also requires a new set of writing concepts, approaches, and techniques. Interactivity requires a larger number of variables in writing. The writer presents information, ideas, and emotional stimulation in the form of links; one item is linked to the next according to the desire of the individual members of the audience on an individual basis, but not in a point-by-point logical or, as in previous media, linear fashion.

The writer has to prepare a virtually unlimited series of options for the audience, specific choices that the audience might make that will, in turn, affect the next item in the chain. More than in other media, the writer must both anticipate what individual audience members' reactions and counter reactions will be and design a writing product that will guide the audience toward those choices that the writer thinks will achieve the purpose of the program or script.

Instead of presenting material in the traditional manner of step-by-step logical linear progression, the writer for cyberspace is in the center of a creative universe, able to reach out into an infinity of space and time to integrate a limitless number and variety of ideas, concepts, impressions, information, aural and visual materials, and emotional and intellectual stimuli in any form, placement, and mixture, in an interactive or non-interactive mode.

Both the writer and the receptor must have complete flexibility. The computer or tablet permits the receptor to mix and match, in effect making choices, even at random, from the totality of what has been presented, from any bit of material no matter where and when and how presented. Thus, because the Internet process itself dominates the content, Marshall McLuhan's dictum that "the medium is the message" takes on added meaning.

Approach

The word "hypertext" is frequently associated with creating material—writing—for the Internet. In simple terms, hypertext refers to conveying our thoughts closer to the way we think—many ideas, many viewpoints rushing through our minds almost simultaneously, rather than in the logical linear fashion that we put them down on paper after we have properly organized them to make them understandable through the linear mode of communication. The Internet's hypertext, or interactive, ability means we can present a conglomeration of stimuli virtually at once, with a variety of multimedia providing the receptor—the audience—with a multitude of information and ideas about any and all things. In this respect, the Internet does for audio-visual-print communication what Picasso's cubism did for painting. As some Picasso interpreters have stated, the early 20th century developments in communication and transportation no longer restricted the view of an object to a single plane, but the transcending of space and time made it possible to see an object from many viewpoints virtually at the same time. This is what the Internet has done for communication: Hypertext interactivity enables the receptor to receive and also to originate many varied stimuli from a virtually unrestricted space-time continuum with many varied sources virtually at the same time.

The writer of drama, for example, can provide the receptor with the opportunity to see the unfolding of the plot through the eyes of any or all characters, with the plot concomitantly developing by virtue of the characters' own psyches, backgrounds, and motivations. The audience can pick and choose in any combination. For example, in a history documentary on the 2001 terrorist attacks on the World Trade Center and the Pentagon, the Internet audience could branch off from the linear narrative at any time to obtain information on the al Qaeda papers warning of an attack that the Clinton administration turned over to the Bush administration; photos and narration about the known attackers, including their families and homes; documents revealing what the CIA, FBI, and National Security Agency knew and didn't know; background on Osama bin Laden—in other words, selecting at any moment additional in-depth information on any of the principals, events, or sites, visual information about any of the subjects, explanations of any legal term or procedure, and on and on. The receptor is also the creator, in the center of a universe of available stimuli—or to use an Internet term, in the center of a giant, unending Web—who can reach out anywhere in that Web, either specifically or at random, for whatever stimuli may be desired or available.

Process

This book does not intend to present information on writing a software program, which is essentially what the writer of basic material for the computer does, or for creating a web site. Our concern is essentially the adapting of one's writing techniques in traditional television, radio, and film to writing those formats for cyberspace. It will not be long before almost all programs now delivered via radio or television will be received through one's computer or a computerized mini-receiver, whether it's called a cell phone or iPod or a blueberry, blackberry or boysenberry.

Although different writers use different processes to prepare material for the Internet, one frequently used approach is to create a chart of sequence boxes, like the outline for a term paper. But instead of moving from box to box or step one to step two in a logical linear fashion, as soon as one item is put in a box, all possible links to material pertaining to that item are linked by arrows from that box to appropriate additional boxes. In turn, further possible links are then designated. What develops is a gigantic web, with arrows crisscrossing each other, designating the links (and information or stimuli) needed to create the whole. Each link can be of any combination of traditional media, including print, charts and graphs, visual movement, audio, photographs, talking heads, and drawings. For most writers, these options loom like a large burden, especially for those who can create words, but can't create pictures. But available software permits you to insert any kind of visual materials, music, drawings, audio, and other non-print stimuli, in monochrome or color, at any place in any form. Further, you can provide instructions to the receptor at any stage—go forward, go back, click here for a link, click for a visual, and so on.

Although the creative writer interested in the content of a given format might have difficulty determining the mechanical requirements for full receptor interactivity—that is, directions for using the mouse for clicking, moving, or pointing at designated icons to recall material, pop-up boxes, or sidebars, scroll, rollover items, and other procedures—it is necessary to learn how to incorporate the technical directions as part of the interactive writer-receptor process. This will help you present the different levels of stimuli to the receptor. First, most obviously, is the material that appears forthrightly on the screen. A second level of stimuli appears as the receptor moves the mouse or picture at random or follows your directions to move over the so-called hot areas of the screen that reveal additional stimuli. The third level is reached when the receptor makes a conscious choice of the alternatives you provide, by selecting a specific icon to deliberately seek out interactive stimuli. The writer, by understanding this process, retains control of the receptor's experience, even while providing the receptor with the flexibility of going beyond what appears to be obvious on the screen to seek out stimuli that is of personal interest and importance.

Technique

The special considerations that went into writing for the new television medium over a half century ago, compared with writing for the cinema at that time, are almost the same as those of writing for the new cyberspace medium today. Foremost is the limited viewing area of the computer monitor or tablet or iPhone compared with the average TV screen. The viewing area is small. The term "streaming video" is applied to the carriage of the moving visual images. Lack of bandwidth—and therefore lack of definition—is another key factor. Poor resolution requires an avoidance of wide shots with a number of characters, and of night scenes or scenes in dark or dimly lit settings. Sometimes additional light sources will provide better definition, and electronic adjustment sometimes helps. The still limited bandwidth and the frame rate for Internet transmission suggests a limiting of movement, of the number of people shown, and of the number of sound sources used. A further consideration is the attention span of the person sitting at the computer screen or using a mobile device. It may be much shorter than that of a person sitting in an easy chair in front of a large-screen TV set. Therefore, scenes and the program as a whole sometimes should be shorter than what one would write for television and, most certainly, for films. Conversely, the "do's" as differentiated from the "don'ts" suggest that you should concentrate on close-ups where possible, on sharp, crisp dialogue, on minimal movement of the performers, on conciseness, and on a clear beginning and end.

Video compression causes text with moving images in the background to lose detail. This lack of detail or, as it appears, lack of depth on the computer screen limits the kinds of background action or information and transitions that have become accepted on television. For example, you may have a dramatic scene with a bank guard in the foreground and a bank robber waving a gun at a teller in the background. In films and on television that would easily work. But on the Internet the background figures would appear to be somewhat fuzzy. Technology is improving this situation.

Eric Johnston, president of Pangaea Multimedia Communications Corporation of Boston, Massachusetts, has written comprehensive current essay on the recent developments in the media and their application to online video, "It Isn't Just Television Any More…." It is presented here in its entirety.

"It Isn't Just Television Any More…."

No matter what the technological stage of the medium you are writing for, focus on its positive aspects and use them to the best of your and the medium's ability.

When considering the question regarding strategies and techniques for writing for various forms of media, we can no longer simply focus on the audience and message. The world has changed. Television isn't just television any more. We are no longer crafting messages from one to many. While we continue to have some options regarding whether or not to provide multimedia elements or interactive options, we can no longer choose whether or not to engage in social media. Social media is integrated everywhere, either with intent on the part of the producer and links clearly integrated or indirectly through discussions regarding out content. The way audiences interact with our content has changed. The medium has changed. Whether print, cinemas, broadcast, live or non-synchronous, they are all eventually distributed electronically to audiences which are able to engage the content. Perhaps now more than ever, the new medium is the message or at least a wake-up call that we as a society need to consider the ways in which television, viewing television, and our new technologies are impacting our audiences, our values, our communities, and the very nature of our society.

The role of the audience has changed; viewers are no longer passive recipients. Our role as producers and writers, programmers, even policy makers, must also change. It is all too easy to get caught up in the changes and use technology for technologies sake, frequently because many of us have an overwhelming desire to experiment with the technology; however, in all of the excitement it is important that we step back from it all and consider our goals and objectives of our message. How are we engaging our audience? Are the ideas that we are conveying fostering positive and meaningful discussions? Traditionally, story tellers served a very important purpose, not simply to entertain, but to use hope, excitement, success, fear, even frustration, as a means to fostering the values that make us who we want to be. While there are bigger philosophical and strategic questions underlying our messages, in the end it is no longer a one-to-many message that we are crafting; instead it is an effort to start a conversation, attract others to engage in that conversation, and ideally to present information and situations which spark a desire to explore, experience, pose scenarios, and question concerns, all to help to guide some group or individual inquiry. The integrity of our predecessors, using our abilities as story tellers, reporters, and communicators, all comes together to encourage critical thinking, creativity and the many traits we desire in our kids, our neighbors and ourselves.

Technological developments have had a huge impact on how video is produced, delivered, and consumed. The ways in which content may be viewed, the ways audiences may interact with the content, the producers, sponsors, other viewers, even characters within the stories, all influence how and what we produce. Over the last few decades television has become more interactive, taking on computer-like features, while computer technology has been pushing to take over the qualities and capabilities of television. Television is no longer a steady stream of linear programming interrupted by all too frequent advertisements, viewed on a piece of furniture in our living-rooms. It has evolved. Those who produce and develop content need to consider the broader spectrum of issues related to how we reach and engage various audiences.

As television first got off the ground, there were a number of competing manufacturers, each with a somewhat unique approach and each recognizing that there was a need for a standard technical specification in order to insure compatibility and cross channel viewing. Television would not have grown into the industry that it has if it were not for the joint efforts of manufacturers and a number of shrewd policy makers, intent on insuring both the successful growth of a new industry and protection of public interests. If it were not for the Federal Communications Commission's action to form the National Television Systems Committee and the later adoption of the NTSC standard back in 1940–41, our country and society would be very different today.

The line separating film, cinema, broadcast television, and consumer television has become blurred. While the technical specifications, production components, and approaches to production remain substantially different, to the end user even the basic components such as screen size and aspect ratios are of little concern. Consumer video, cell phone video, and even web cam video are now frequently featured in broadcasts and occasionally even in cinemas. In fact, there are growing numbers of independent films being produced as video, even new industries such as Nollywood's feature films produced on low budgets with a production cycle that is only one week long (www.ted.com/talks/franco sacchi on nollywood.html).

On the delivery side, consumers have virtually seamless access to broadcast content, feature films, and "home movies" on nearly all consumer electronic devices—assuming of course that individuals are willing to invest in the purchase of such devices.

Even the technology used in production is crossing the feature film; broadcasting, professional/consumer (also known as "pro-sumer") and consumer lines are frequently crossed. The latest in image sensing technology is the Complementary Metal-Oxide Semiconductor Active Pixel Sensor (CMOS APS sensor), which has made High Definition (HD) and Ultra High Definition (UHDTV) possible, is replacing the CCD chips in the broadcast video cameras, is making broadcast cameras smaller, lighter and more similar in characteristic to the pro-sumer product lines, and is well suited for miniaturized camera on a chip applications such as those in consumer electronics. There are many reports of changes in the broadcast industry due to the pressure put on established technologies and manufacturers by the successes of low cost competitors. Well established manufactures are attempting to shift strategies, retool, restructure, and redesign finding new ways to "adapt or die." (http://broadcastengineering.com/shows/once-dominant-vendors-nab -show-it-s-now-adapt-or-die). This is not to say that cell phones are going to take over the film industry, but the technology is evolving and opening doors to significant changes in television, video, and content, while impacting the very core of our society, affecting how we communicate, interact, and learn.

In the 1980s, editing a broadcast video generally meant having a room filled with nearly a million dollars worth of equipment, supported by an engineer, tape operator, graphic artist, and an editor. At that time, most of the broadcast news crews were comprised of a two-person crew, a Camera Operator and a Sound Technician—someone who carried and operated the field recorder, field mixer, cables, microphones, extra batteries and a supply of video tapes, each of which would hold 20 minutes of video and was the size of a four-terabyte hard drive today. Now, variations of all of these capabilities may be found on-board a single ENG camcorder. Even the need for the microwave or satellite truck is going away, as it is now possible to mount a HD cellular transmitter on a camera. Even the capabilities of the full broadcast edit suite can be found in software that can be run on a single laptop computer. If you want to consider the consumer options, most people, including children today have cell phones with cameras built in, enabling many to record high definition video. With relatively little experience or training, an elementary school student can edit that video, in some cases right on the phone.

Granted, one cannot truly compare the quality of the video that originates with a broadcast camera with three two-third inch multi-mega-pixel chips vs. a miniaturized single chip fixed lens camera that is only a couple of millimeters thick—including the lens. Nor can a team of professional producers necessarily work efficiently with laptop-based solutions. However, for the consumers the issue of quality is really one of perceived quality, something that for many consumers is difficult to see. The real difference for many consumers is the cost, accessibility, size, weight, and ease of use. As a result, individuals are not limited to making home movies of family activities any more. They are planning, scripting, shooting, editing, and distributing their own programs and launching their own television shows or even their own television channels, without the organization, the overhead or budgets required for our traditional business models, yet catered to by online providers attempting to provide a software as a service (SAAS) which supports this industry and saves these producers the trouble of having to build or even pay for their own infrastructure or delivery platform.

Online video streaming services are attempting to build their own membership base, retain viewers as followers and attract new users. Advertising has not disappeared from the picture. On the contrary, current methods of delivering ads can be even more aggressive than in the broadcast world, with longer targeted ads repeatedly forced on viewers, without any regulated frequency or any best practices regarding ad placement. Viewers of Internet media may be forced to re-watch the same ad or at least the first several seconds of the same ad every time they start, pause or revisit not just a media clip but a web site. While such practices may eventually change based upon loss of viewers, producers or competition, at the moment the redundancy and aggressive placement of advertisements is excessive.

One of the interesting features online video services are providing to producers is a "home page" which can be customized by its owner, enabling the producer to give the perception of a dedicated "channel" for their content. Simply by setting up an account a user can now have a landing page which features his or her content, thereby bypassing the need for a web site. Most users quickly realize they can do much more with a private web site— expanding services and the ways in which they engage viewers or incorporate other social media tools. The Internet, Web-based television, and IP technologies have opened a plethora of additional options which cannot be ignored. Most major broadcast programs and feature films also have web sites which tap into social networking and online promotion, each attempting to engage their audience and the powerful viral aspects of social media.

While it may seem that an ability to deliver video over the Internet without having to involve Broadcast or Cable providers is a wonderful byproduct of the improvements in technology and a significant boost for advocates of free speech, these alternatives may also be seen as something of a threat to the traditional power brokers in the communications industry. Consumers may be slowly making the move away from Cable and Satellite to devices such as AppleTV", Roku", gaming devices like Microsoft" Xbox" and WII", other paid video over Internet services such as Netflix", Hulu, Aereo™, and Amazon", as well as free Internet services such as Vimeo", BlipTV" and, depending upon the publishers choice, YouTube", which at least for the moment still has a free option, instead of a premium for services.

The United States is moving to an environment with many competing delivery methods, many different and not necessarily compatible formats, many different video players, many incompatible paid multichannel delivery systems, most carriers charging users by the amount of data they are receiving, more broadcasting networks specializing in specific content or targeting specific groups of viewers, and a continued weakening of the traditional broadcasting networks. The growing number of specialty channels will likely result in content being limited to specific channels and even specific carriers, where our once intentional design with viewers able to access all content on a single television now requires users to purchase specific devices, subscribe to specific carriers, and pay for specific channels dependent on the type of content they want to be able to access. For viewers interested in content representing different perspectives, it is possible that subscribing to one system will not be enough. Such viewers may not simply be able to switch channels any more; instead they may have to subscribe to different carriers and possibly even purchase different devices.

Television receives today are designed to display signals broadcast over the public airwaves, but they do not include the antenna necessary to receive those signals. Many consumers are unaware that television can still be received over the air. Even in urban areas, the number of channels which a consumer is able to receive depends heavily on the strength of the signal from the local broadcasting station and the ability of the television set to tune in and maintain reception of that signal via a digital antenna, purchased and installed separately. Many deem this unsatisfactory and feel they have no choice but to pay a multi-channel carrier for access to their system. To complicate things further, it is not clear that such multi-channel providers are providing access to all of the local broadcast stations. Access to broadband Internet has begun to change this situation in that households can opt to 'cut the cord' and unplug from the more expensive multi-channel providers.

Despite the expectation that thousands of households were unplugging their cable boxes and switching to online alternatives, 9% of all households dropped cable services in 2011 (http://www.newsobserver.com/2012/06/24/2153676/why-your-cable-tv-bill-will-never.html). Comcast® claims to have lost only about 5% of its subscribers to those "cutting the cord" and is not concerned (http://readwrite.com/2013/03/27/pay-tv-broadcasting-sounds-of-self-denial). On the Internet side of the equation, Netflix® content is growing its customer base and is now responsible for 29% of all Internet data (http://www.engadget.com/2012/11/08/sandvine-netflix-29-percent-of-north-american-internet-traffic/). Recently Netflix® has published a paper (http://files.shareholder.com/downloads/NFLX/2441659654x0x656145/e4410bd8-e5d4-4d31-ad79-84c36c49f77c/IROverviewHomePageLetter 4.24.13 pdf.pdf) stating its belief that traditional TV is dying and it will be replaced by Internet Television (http://broadcastengineering.com/cable-amp-iptv/netflix-unveils-plan-replace-broadcast-television).

Netfilx® caught the attention of many in the industry with its creation of "House of Cards," a subscribers-only television series. In September 2012, it was reported that Microsoft® hired CBS's entertainment president and was in talks with NBC to launch Xbox Studios (http://articles.latimes.com/2012/sep/18/entertainment/la-et-ct-microsoft-tellem-xbox-20120918) and revive the superhero television series "Heroes" and distribute it on Xbox Live (http://tvline.com/2013/04/17/heroes-relaunch-msn-xbox/). Amazon® has more traditionally been distributing recorded media, but may have already come out with a set top box similar to a cable box or the features now built into network ready DVD players, where subscribers will have a box specifically to control and purchase media from Amazon®. This is what Sony® has done with the PlayStation® and Microsoft is doing with Xbox 360. While YouTube® may not yet be getting into the content production side of the business in 2013, it made significant changes in its format, templates and service offerings in early 2013. YouTube changed the deal. The free channels are going away and users are forced to upgrade their channel (http://www.youtube.com/onechannel). In 2013 YouTube® announced a service option for viewers to pay $1.99 per month for each channel subscribed to. While this may work for television providers to get their content in front of a wider audience, it potentially undermines all of the social media aspects of sharing video. It is highly unlikely that someone will pay to continue to subscribe to a channel which does not have a steady stream of new content that is consistently of interest to the viewer. It has been reported that the revenue model will likely be similar to their current model for advertising revenue, where the producer of the content receive 55% and YouTube® 45% (http://www.digitaljournal.com/article/349604). One YouTube® subscriber complained (http://www.youtube.com/watch?v=CseOSUjF05U), that the new format moves away from the social aspects of the service, making it more difficult to leave comments or have discussions around particular videos, favoring instead a channel format which is more like television or the apps provided by other providers, with one segment running immediately into the next and comments and discussions buried on other screens. In this day of social media, many will agree with this subscriber and consider this to have been a poor decision, hoping that YouTube® will supplement their layout options with a discussion-based layout. All of these gaming, cable, fiber, broadband, and wireless options seem to be moving in the same direction, a paid subscription service with as large a share of the viewers as possible, and a growing number of advertisements.

When Cable Television first became available, it was to solve reception issues and insure clear viewing. Cable also became a means of providing specialty programming channels, content which was not available over the air. In 1992 the U.S. Cable Television Protection and Competition Act added a requirement for "retransmission consent" (http://www.fcc.gov/encyclopedia/retransmission-consent). In return for the rights to distribute broadcast programming to paying customers, broadcasters were paid a fee by cable distributors. The move to take television programming, particularly broadcast programming, to the Internet has been slow. Some speculate that the revenues from cable distribution may be an important factor; however, it may simply be the complexities of needing to gain rights to redistribute content via additional outlets that is the issue. Nevertheless, producers of most every type of content have been exploring the best ways to reach the ever growing on-line audience. Online streaming services have stepped in to fulfill some of this need but have been limiting it mostly to older episodes rather than live programs.

To better understand what network broadcast programming is available online one would need to explore the relationship between broadcast networks and their local affiliates as well as their contracts with distributors.

It is likely that the networks have limited rights to the content created and distributed by the local affiliate, just as the local station likely has limited rights to redistribute the programming syndicated by the network. Because Network broadcasters do not control their local affiliates programming they cannot redistribute that programming (http://money.cnn.com/2013/04/25/technology/yahoo-snl-aereo/index.html). American Broadcasting Corporation, ABC, has announced it will soon provide live streaming of their network programming; however, it is going to require the consumer to log-in, verifying that they have an active subscription with a cable company or multi-channel video programming distributor to gain access the stream. To do this, ABC secured the rights to distribute the local newscasts from each of its local affiliates as well as the rights to redistribute syndicated talk shows and national series from their owners (http://www.nytimes.com/2013/05/13/business/media/abc-to-let-app-users-live-stream-local-programming.html? r=0). There are some examples of programs which produce live content for local broadcast and are able to stream their live content in bursts simultaneously to when it is actually fed to the broadcast antenna; for example, WCVB Channel 5, an ABC affiliate in Boston, and WABC Channel 7, the local ABC affiliate in New York City, both stream their live news feeds and have Apps which provide a directory of their content as well as links to their live news feeds. These news broadcasts, while available in short bursts following their live feeds, segment the programming and make it difficult for audiences to select a source and view it as they would an on-going stream of programming. Time will tell if this practice will continue after this programming starts streaming directly from ABC. In considering the streaming of other content, it is also possible that program owner and producers may have deals with current distributors wherein they may not be able to provide their programming directly or via other carriers.

There are new companies coming online in an effort to resolve the problem of providing the live streaming video content from broadcast stations and other programmers over the Internet. Aereo™, a startup online streaming service, has found an interesting way around some of legal ownership and distribution obstacles by "setting up thousands of tiny, old-fashioned by TV-antennas in its data center. It assigns each customer a unique antenna and, using a server farm as the middleman. it streams TV from those antennas to customers via their Internet connections."

(http://money.cnn.com/2013/04/25/technology/yahoo-snl-aereo/index.html) In March 2013, Aereo™ won a high profile appellate court ruling (http://www.hollywoodreporter.com/thr-esq/aereo-beats-broadcasters-big-appellate-431988) in the legal battles over copyright laws and rebroadcasting fees surrounding its services; however, broadcasters continue to argue that Aereo™ is illegal.

Regardless of how content is distributed—Broadcast, Cable, Fiber, Cinema, Internet, as a rental from an on-line provider, a fast download kiosk, or on some medium such as a DVD, CD, or flash memory—most producers and carriers have an on-line presence, maintaining dedicated web sites for supplemental information, references, promotional media, schedules, and related links, not to mention chats, blogs, data, and custom Apps for the array of personal computing devices, all with integrated links and feeds from social media tools.

Twitter", FaceBook" as well as a wide variety of other social media outlets are providing a framework for parallel discussions and are generally integrated into web sites and Apps. New services such as ConnectTV" are taking things a step further. Recently, users needed to navigate to the appropriate Web page or channel to participate in a particular discussion related to content they might be viewing, or the broadcaster provided a link on the page associated with that content to direct viewers to an appropriate chat room or blog. ConnectTV" uses audio recognition to determine what you are watching, then provide the viewer with relevant information and links, integrating chat rooms and Facebook-like features which enable you to voice your opinion and contribute to conversations, synchronizing them to the appropriate content and accessible on your computer or integrated online.

While cell phones, computers, and other social media devices continue to improve and further the use of embed media and online discussions in our society, the cutting edge of technical developments today seems to be focused on the delivery side of the equation. Flat screens are seeing significant improvements. Compression, transmission, and Internet Protocol (IP) devices are transforming the distribution side of the equation, enabling video in a wide variety of new devices. Most DVD players are Internet ready with built in WIFI and presets for Internet-based video content from Internet based providers. The glass screens associated with liquid crystal (LCD) and plasma displays may soon be replaced by flexible, more durable cloth-like material.

One of the biggest advancements in recent years may have been the accidental discovery of a process for making high quality sheets of Graphene (http://en.wikipedia.org/wiki/Graphene), a key element in the production of the next generation of screens. This extremely strong yet flexible carbon material (http://io9.com/5987086/meet-the-scientific-accident-that-could-change-the-world) seems to be capable of storing most anything containing a carbon atom. While the team that discovered this new manufacturing process is working on supercapacitors, the process has implications virtually everywhere, from constructing light weight super strong materials for spacecraft to fuel cells. This technology is what makes the flexible transparent screens possible for the next generation of cell phones (http://www.slideshare.net/nehhalpota/mobile-phones-using -graphene) with transparent and bendable screens possible (http://www .lockergnome.com/mobile/2012/11/05/miracle-metal-graphene-makes -transparent-and-bendable-smartphones-possible/) and may well eliminate batteries in favor of ultra-fast charge supercapacitors (http://www.slate.com /articles/health and science/alternative energy/2013/03/graphene supercapacitors small cheap energy dense replacements for batteries.html).

Apple has filed patents for flexible screen devices including items such as trifold screens (http://www.patentlyapple.com/patently-apple/2013/04/apple -patent-reveals-advanced-idevice-flex-display-features.html). Online there is an endless array of videos depicting flexible, waterproof, and wearable wrist phones (http://www.youtube.com/watch?v=h1m5WMyTC8Q). The flat transparent screens have been demonstrated at consumer electronic shows steadily the past several years. Samsung's flexible screens were featured in 2013 (http://www.youtube.com/watch?v=p3a9WrfzZOM ; http://www.youtube .com/watch?v=dY ADCTBKVE) utilizing an Active Matrix Organic Light Emitting Diodes (AMOLEDs) (http://en.wikipedia.org/wiki/AMOLED). This new technology does not require a back light and can be built into a flexible thin transparent plastic screen eliminating not only the glass, but the majority of the casing from our current technology. This will bring new meaning to wearable technologies not to mention, retractable/roll out screens, transparent displays on windshields, windows, glasses, and a host of other applications and will transform yet again the way in which society consumes and interacts with video.

The potential for eyeglasses with built-in screens has been around for a while. Nokia has been showing this technology since 2009, planning to bring "Gaze tracking eyewear" to the marketplace (http://www.slashgear. com/could-nokia-beat-project-glass-to-the-ar-market-05221730/). Google® is rushing to be the first to bring its version of this technology to market. "Google® Glass™" was available in 2013 in limited quantities to developers and enthusiasts. Glass is essentially a voice activated, 5 mega pixel 720p video camera, a miniature display, a cell phone processor, 16 Gigabytes of storage, a touch pad and a bluetooth radio—all built into what looks like a cross between a pair of eyeglasses and a sleek cyborg head piece. Google® claims this small transparent block that hangs just above your line of sight is a "high resolution display the equivalent of a 25-inch high-definition screen from eight feet away" (https://support.google.com/glass /answer/3064128?hl=en). Both of these technologies will yet again transform the way that technology is integrated into our society. Facial recognition could mean that simply looking at someone could result in a database query and the instant display of background information on that individual visible only to the person wearing the device. The speed and accessibility of this information combined with the potential for this information to be "hacked" was foreseen in a wide range of action adventure/"Mission Impossible"-type movies. One of the questions we should step back and consider as these new technologies become further and further embedded in our lives: is the application of these technologies in the public interest? Will we as a society be able to maintain our individuality while protecting the freedom and privacy we have fought so hard to obtain?

We have moved from a one-to-many broadcast to a one-to-many broadcast that triggers a response; those who start as viewers become empowered not only to comment, but to truly engage and become part of the story, some by offering objective observations, others by offering contrary arguments and linking in credible sources, still others by not impartially reacting to the content. There are a nearly endless number of situations in which the act of observation can impact the results and it should be expected that the untrained consumer, the want-to-be good Samaritan with a cell phone could very easily become not just an accidental reporter but a part of the story.

The news coverage during the hunt for the 2013 Boston Marathon bombers, the role of crowd-sourced media and social media took on a new role. Individuals took on the role of reporters and cell phones and web cams were featured in news updates internationally. While some consumers were tied to their televisions, others were on social media participating in conversations and sharing media. The FBI criticized the media for reporting unconfirmed and inaccurate information, such as reports of an arrest that hadn't happened (http://www.nytimes.com/2013/04/18/business/media/fbi-criticizes -false-reports-of-a-bombing-arrest.html?ref=todayspaper& r=1&).

Social Media can take on a very strong democratic role because it is possible for a mass grass roots response to be organized and articulated almost instantly. A growing number of positive as well as negative results can come from reports generated by crowd-sourced social media, otherwise known as citizens with cell phones. An example is the "Lady Profeco" case in 2013. A woman, the daughter of a senior Mexican official entered a crowded cafe and requested a table. She was reported to have had a tempertantrum when she was not able to get a table. Customers in the restaurant began documenting the event and it quickly went viral. The woman threatened to use her connections to call in a health inspector to shut down the café. It might have happened if not for the customers who recorded the incident and reported it on Twitter® and FaceBook®. Adam Thomson, correspondent for the Financial Times, reported the incident (http://blogs.ft.com /beyond-brics/2013/05/16/lady-profeco-a-mexican-tale-of-power-abuse-and- progress/#axzz2TWfDOH5A), stating:

> . . . *social networks now clearly play a significant and growing role in exposing the excesses of Mexican officials and law-enforcement officers. They force greater responsibility and accountability on those in power, and that is a vast and necessary change from the past.*

New displays, miniature wearable cameras, recorders, and wireless devices will result in new ways to record, view and interact with media as well as new ways for us to interact with each other. The remote sensors in the gaming world, combined with wearable technology and flexible, lightweight and transparent screens are all just the tip of the iceberg. The bottom line for producers and writers is the need to consider when and how to engage audiences while exploring, testing and developing new practices to capture and retain audiences using these tools. We are no longer talking about basic video on screens, ranging from a cell phone to a 200-inch flat screen television. We are talking about a world in which every viewer is a participant, each potentially contributing to the conversation, potentially affecting the storyline or interacting with characters or altering timelines. For the short term, viewers may continue to range from those who will watch a few minutes of a program while waiting in line to those who will sit down and watch every episode in a series from beginning to end, with those truly engaging the content the exception rather than the norm; but the transformation is coming. The world of media is changing quickly and there is an enormous need for quality, engaging interactive multimedia programming which is appropriate to the way in which the viewer is experiencing that specific medium.

The quantity of programming, variety of channels, production process and technology, number and types of carriers, delivery and display methods have all exploded, as have the ways in which we can interact with and around that content. Yet despite all of these choices, the comment that "there's nothing on!" is still echoed throughout many homes, driving some to surf specialty content or consumer generated programming on-line. The need for fresh content across the board is growing. The question is where is the content going to come from, how is it going to be funded, and who will control whether or not consumers are able to access it.

There will likely always be content which exists solely to provide an escape for the audience, but much of this content, intentionally or not, contains messages positioning products, demonstrating philosophies, modeling behavior. The subtlety and power of the media, especially when reinforced by elements of social media, especially input from a wider body of people, should not be dismissed. Hopefully, as we look forward, issues of public interest will be a significant portion of the discussion. As writers and producers we should always strive to do what is right. Not just for a particular company, party, or cause, but to use these powerful tools to pass along the knowledge and understanding necessary for future generations to lead happy, healthy and not just productive but meaningful lives. We should not forget that we have responsibility to our audiences and to our society. As members of the audience we also have a responsibility: to engage in appropriate and responsible behavior; our actions as citizens with cell phones could easily take us from passive observer to commentator to accidental reporter to being part of the story.

Biased news, gate-keeping for the purpose of supporting a particular set of beliefs, marketing campaigns staged as news-making events are certainly not in the public interest. In an increasingly conglomerate market what can be done to insure protection of the public interest by protecting what remains of fair and equal access and equal time?

Are we and will we be using the media, technology, and screen time to help instill appropriate values, lessons and morals, in our society rather than simply chasing a buck and using media mainly for entertainment and escape? We need to use media technology to move society forward, educating, informing, and challenging everyone to engage in life, in democracy, in community, to protect our environment, to make this world a better place.

APPLICATION AND REVIEW

Television

1. Write a short sequence in which you use the following camera movements: dolly-in and dolly-out, pan, follow, boom, and zoom.

2. Write a short sequence in which you indicate the following shots: CU, M2S, LS, FS, XLS, XCU.

3. Write a short sequence in which you designate the following effects: fade-in and fade-out, dissolve, wipe, and key.

Radio

1. Write a short sequence in which you use all five microphone positions: on mic, off mic, fading on, fading off, and behind obstructions.

2. Write one or more short sequences in which you use sound effects to establish locale or setting, direct the audience's attention by emphasizing a particular sound, establish time, establish mood, show an entrance or exit, and create a transition.

3. Write one or more short sequences in which you use music as a bridge, as a sound effect, and to establish background or mood.

4. Write a short script in which you use the following techniques: segue, cross-fade, blending, cutting, or switching, and fade-in or fade-out.

Internet

Take one of the sequences you wrote for the preceding exercises and adapt it for the Internet by including at least one link.

CHAPTER 3

Format and **Style**

Script formats vary among stations, independent studios, and production houses. Some standard conventions and basic script formats are widely used, however, and are acceptable to almost everyone in the field. These formats are presented in this chapter and constitute most of the professional script examples throughout this book. As much as possible, scripts are presented as they were written or produced. The principal difference is that although some television and all radio scripts are double-spaced, to save space most of the scripts in this book are single-spaced.

Several basic script formats are used in television and radio: (1) the single-column format endemic to radio; (2) the single-column format used for screenplays and for single-camera television shows; (3) the two-column television format, with video on the left and audio on the right, used for multi-camera productions; and (4) the film or screenplay format with each sequence consecutively numbered. Final production scripts in radio are sometimes two columns, with the technical sources on the left and the continuity on the right. Television scripts sometimes have the audio on the left and the video on the right. (If you are reading this as part of a course in video, film, or audio writing, your instructor will probably recommend a format, whether one of these or a different one. Be consistent within whatever format you are using.)

The single-column format differs for television and radio. The single-column television script resembles that of the screenplay or stage play, with only essential character movements added to the dialogue, and virtually no video or audio techniques inserted. Because radio is not a visual medium, music, sound effects, and microphone positions are essential parts of the script.

In the two-column television format, the video directions are most often found on the left side and the audio information, including the dialogue, is found on the right. The video column contains all the video directions deemed necessary by the writer. Although the writer cannot be cautioned too often to refrain from intruding on the director's domain—too many writers feel compelled to write in every dissolve, cut, and zoom—the writer frequently uses visual images rather than dialogue to tell the story, and these must be included.

The two-column radio format has all the production information on the left side. On the right side are the directions and dialogue that usually are found in the one-column audio script. Although formats may vary from organization to organization, the two-column format is usually used in multi-camera television productions and in some filmed productions such as documentaries and industrial shows, and for television news. Gene Lavanchy, news anchor on Boston's FOX TV station, stated that "we still do use the left-side, right-side scripts. The left side contains director's cues (take video, SOTS, chyron info, outcues, etc.), the right is the copy for the anchors to read." He noted that although a lot of material is done through the computer and some stations do it differently, the script format used by stations is generally the same.

The dramatic screenplay format, with or without numbered sequences, is used for filmed dramas. Some writers prefer not to actually number the sequences because they feel numbering makes the script look too technical and impedes the flow of the story. Other writers use numbering to provide quicker identification of and access to individual sequences for editing purposes, just as the producer and director require numbering to determine more easily how to plan set, location, and cast time. Films are shot out of sequence; all scenes in a given setting are shot consecutively, no matter where they are chronologically located in the script. Some writers, as well as producers and directors, believe that numbering the sequences provides a better understanding of a given script's production requirements. For example, 150 different sequences may be acceptable for a given budget, but 250 may not be. Stations and production organizations are now digital. Some, however, still use tape. Therefore, you sometimes will see not only past but current scripts with SOT (sound on tape).

Script preparation begins with a **summary** or an **outline**, whether for a 30-second commercial or a two-hour drama special. The outline, or summary, is a short overview of the script, written in narrative form. The **treatment** or **scenario** is a more detailed chronological rundown of the prospective script, giving information on the setting, plot, and characters and, sometimes, examples of the dialogue. For a commercial, the summary or outline might be a few sentences, with the scenario or treatment ranging from a paragraph to a page. For the one-hour drama or documentary, the summary might be two or three pages, with the treatment as long as a fifth of the entire projected script. Developing the treatment for a play is covered in Chapter 10.

In the next section, the following outline and scenario will be shown as scripts representing the different basic formats, to provide a comparison of approaches for one-column television, two-column television, film, and one-column radio. The story used here could be part of a commercial or a segment from a play.

Outline or summary

A man and woman, both about 60, are at the beach and find a kind of beauty in being in love that they did not feel when they were younger. The story shows that romance in older years can sometimes be even more joyful and exciting than in youth.

Treatment or scenario

It is morning. Gladys and Reginald are on a beach, by the water's edge, holding hands and looking lovingly at each other. They are about 60, but their romantic closeness makes them seem much younger. They kiss. They talk about how they are even more in love than when they were younger. Hand in hand, they enter a beach house.

The finished script fleshes out the scenario with the characters' actions and dialogue.

VIDEO	AUDIO
A BEACH AT SUNRISE	GLADYS AND REGINALD ARE BY THE WATER'S EDGE, HOLDING HANDS. THEY ARE ABOUT 60, BUT THEIR BRIGHTNESS OF LOOK AND POSTURE MAKE THEM SEEM YOUNGER. THEY KISS.
	GLADYS: I did not feel so beautiful when I was 20.
	REGINALD: (GRINNING) Me, neither. But we weren't in love like this when we were 20.
ENTRANCE HALL OF BEACH HOUSE—MORNING	THE DOOR OPENS AND GLADYS AND REGINALD WALK IN, HAND IN HAND, LAUGHING.

Television

The writer for television writes visually, showing rather than telling, where appropriate. In the following television formats, the writer has added video directions that convey to the director the exact visual effects the writer deems necessary to tell the story effectively to the viewer.

In the one-column format, as in the two-column format, the character's name is sometimes placed to the left of the dialogue. Most of the time, it is placed above the dialogue, approximately centered.

Television—One-Column

FADE UP:

A BEACH AT SUNRISE, THE WAVES BREAKING ON THE SAND.

TWO PEOPLE ARE IN THE DISTANCE, AT THE WATER'S EDGE, HOLDING HANDS, STARING TOWARD THE SEA. THEY ARE ABOUT 60, BUT THEIR BRIGHTNESS OF LOOK AND POSTURE MAKE THEM SEEM MUCH YOUNGER. THEY SLOWLY TURN THEIR FACES TO EACH OTHER AND KISS.

GLADYS: I did not feel so beautiful when I was 20.

REGINALD: (GRINNING) Me, neither. But we weren't in love like this when we were 20.

DISSOLVE TO ENTRANCE HALL OF A BEACH HOUSE. IT IS MORNING.

(THE DOOR OPENS AND GLADYS AND REGINALD WALK IN, HAND IN HAND, LAUGHING.)

or

Television—Two-Column

VIDEO	AUDIO
FADE IN ON BEACH AT SUNRISE. PAN ALONG SHORE LINE AS WAVES BREAK ON SAND.	(GLADYS AND REGINALD ARE SEEN IN THE DISTANCE, BY THE WATER'S EDGE, HOLDING HANDS, STARING AT THE SEA. THEY ARE ABOUT 60, BUT THEIR BRIGHTNESS OF LOOK AND POSTURE MAKE THEM SEEM MUCH YOUNGER.)
ZOOM IN SLOWLY	(GLADYS AND REGINALD TURN THEIR FACES TO EACH OTHER AND KISS. THEIR FACES REMAIN CLOSE, ALMOST TOUCHING.)
	GLADYS: I did not feel so beautiful when I was 20.
	REGINALD: (GRINNING) Me, neither. But we weren't in love like this when we were 20.
DISSOLVE TO ENTRANCE HALL OF BEACH HOUSE—MORNING	(THE DOOR OPENS AND GLADYS AND REGINALD WALK IN, HAND IN HAND, LAUGHING.)

Film

The numbers in the left column of the following script refer to each shot or sequence. The numbers make it possible to easily designate which sequences will be filmed at a given time or on a given day, such as "TUESDAY, CALL 7:00 A.M., Living Room Set—sequences 42, 45, 46, 78, 79, 82."

FADE IN

1. EXT. BEACH—SUNRISE

2. PAN SHORE LINE AS WAVES BREAK ON SAND

3. EXT. BEACH—SUNRISE

    Two figures are seen in the distance, alone with the vastness of sand and water around them.

4. ZOOM SLOWLY IN UNTIL WE ESTABLISH THAT THE FIGURES ARE A MAN
    AND WOMAN.

5. The man and woman are standing by the water's edge, holding hands, staring toward the sea. They are about 60, but their brightness of look and posture make them seem much younger.

6. They slowly turn their faces to each other and kiss.

7. Their heads and faces are close, still almost touching.

                              GLADYS

                I did not feel so beautiful when I was 20.

                             REGINALD

                             (grinning)

            Me, neither, but we weren't in love like this when we were 20.

8. INT. BEACH HOUSE—ENTRANCE HALL—MORNING

    The door opens and Gladys and Reginald walk in, hand in hand, laughing.

Radio

Note how much more dialogue is necessary to convey the same story in sound alone.

SOUND:	OCEAN WAVES, SEAGULLS, FOOTSTEPS OF TWO PEOPLE ON THE SAND, OCEAN SOUND COMING CLOSER AS THE PEOPLE APPROACH THE WATER.
GLADYS:	(FADING ON) The ocean is so beautiful. I remember first coming to this beach 40 years ago, Reginald. I was 20 years old.
REGINALD:	I remember this beach, too, Gladys.
GLADYS:	I did not feel so beautiful then as I do now.
SOUND:	SOFTLY KISSING
REGINALD:	Me, neither. But we weren't in love like this when we were 20.
GLADYS:	(SUGGESTIVELY) Let's go back to the beach house.
MUSIC:	BRIDGE
SOUND:	GLADYS AND REGINALD'S FOOTSTEPS GOING UP STAIRS. DOOR OPENING.
REGINALD:	(LAUGHTER IN HIS VOICE) What a beautiful morning this is!
GLADYS:	(LAUGHTER IN HER VOICE) It's a glorious day!

SCRIPT GUIDELINES

Radio producer Christopher Outwin has noted that audio script formats frequently have split pages: "The left-hand side of the page usually is reserved for technical instructions and the sources for each channel of sound. The right-hand side of the page usually is reserved for descriptions of actual audio content, incues and out-cues, and the actual narrative or dialogue itself." Outwin stressed that the script information must be complete enough to ensure that all engineering, directorial, and performance members of the team understand precisely what they are supposed to do and when they are supposed to do it—but the script should not be cluttered. "Production personnel need to be able to find their places and execute their duties quickly and without confusion."

Television production teachers as well as producers usually recommend the split two-column format for studio or multi-camera production and the one-column format for single-camera production as well as for the screenplay. As a writer you should have in your mind the pictures you want the audience to see, and you should describe them in your script. But while you tell the director what should be shown on the screen, don't tell him or her how to do it—how to use the cameras, how to move the talent, or what the camera shots should be. Those are the director's responsibilities and prerogatives. Nevertheless, convey clearly what the visual message should be; if there is any question in your mind that the descriptions might not be perceived exactly as intended, then insert and specify video directions as necessary.

An excellent set of professional script guidelines for the *filmed teleplay* is contained in the *Professional Writer's Teleplay/Screenplay Format*, issued by the Writers Guild of America. The following are the basic format directions suggested by the Guild:

1. All camera directions, scene descriptions, and stage directions are typed across each page, from margin to margin.

2. All dialogue is typed within a column approximately 3 inches wide running down the center of the page. The name of the character who speaks is typed just above his line of dialogue. Parenthetical notations as to how the lines should be spoken are typed beneath the character's name and a little to the left.

3. Single spacing is used in all dialogue, camera directions, stage directions, and descriptions of scenes.

4. Double spacing is used between the speech of one character and the speech of another, between a speech and a camera or stage direction, and between one camera shot and another.

5. When a method of scene transition (such as DISSOLVE TO) is indicated between two scenes, it is always set apart from both scenes by double spacing.

6. The following script elements are always typed in capital letters:

CAMERA SHOTS & CAMERA DIRECTIONS

INT. OR EXT. (Interior or Exterior)

INDICATION OF LOCALE (at beginning of scene)

INDICATION OF NIGHT OR DAY (at beginning of scene)

METHOD OF TRANSITION (when specified)

NAMES OF ALL CHARACTERS (when indicated above the dialogue they speak, and the *first time* they appear in descriptive paragraphs)

The Guild booklet provides the following sample script, the first part explaining format approaches and the subsequent pages illustrating how to present actual story material and directions.

ACT ONE

(Act designations are used only in teleplays)

FADE IN:
EXTERIOR OR INTERIOR LOCATION—SPECIFY DAY OR NIGHT CAMERA SHOT—SUBJECT
OF CAMERA SHOT INDICATED HERE

continued

Descriptions of scenes, characters, and action are typed across the page like this. Music and sound effects are typed here too.

CHARACTER

(manner in which the character speaks)

The actual lines of dialogue go here.

2nd CHARACTER

Speaks here.

3rd CHARACTER

Speaks here. Note that all dialogue is typed within a column running down the center of the page.

Additional descriptions and CAMERA MOVEMENTS are typed in this manner whenever they are needed.

TRANSITIONAL INSTRUCTIONS (CUT TO, DISSOLVE TO, etc.)

Note: Transitional instructions are used very sparingly by the professional writer who leaves most such decisions up to the director. It is only when a specific effect is required such as JUMP CUT or SMASH CUT that the manner of transition should be indicated.

NEXT SCENE OR CAMERA SHOT TYPED HERE

FADE IN:

EXT. SUBURBAN RAILROAD STATION—LATE AFTERNOON ESTABLISHING SHOT

It is the end of a hot summer day. A train has just pulled into the station, and COMMUTERS are pouring out—some with jackets thrown over their arms, many with loosened ties. Outside the station, a number of WIVES are waiting in cars for their commuter husbands. Car horns are HONKING in chaotic profusion.

MED. TWO-SHOT—JACK DOBBS AND FRED McALLISTER

They are youngish middle-aged businessmen who have just gotten off the train. JACK is bull-necked, nearly bald, powerfully built; he is a former athlete who keeps himself in excellent shape. FRED has the more typical suburban pot-belly and slouch; a man of dry martinis and electric golf carts.

FRED

Need a lift?

JACK

No, thanks. Joan's picking me up.

(looking around at the cars)

I guess she must have got stuck in traffic.

continued

A horn HONKS raspingly.

> FRED
> (dolefully)
> I'd know that sweet voice anywhere. See you tomorrow.

> JACK

Bring money!

Fred goes off to his waiting wife, as CAMERA MOVES IN CLOSE on Jack. His eyes continue to search the station parking field. Behind him, the train may be seen pulling out of the station.

JACK'S POV—PANNING SHOT—THE STATION PARKING LOT

It is now completely empty of cars. A few scraps of paper are blowing across the parking field, propelled by the hot summer wind.

BACK TO JACK

as he continues to gaze at the empty parking field. He is puzzled, and a little worried. Then making a sudden decision, he turns towards the station hack stand.

> JACK
> (calling)

Taxi!

A moment later; a taxi glides up to where he stands, Jack enters the taxi.

DISSOLVE TO:

EXT. A LOVELY SUBURBAN STREET—LATE AFTERNOON HIGH ANGLE SHOT—STREET AND HOUSES

A taxi pulls up to a white colonial house. Jack gets out, and pays the DRIVER. The taxi ROARS away.

CLOSE-UP—JACK

as he turns towards the house, and stops suddenly—a look of bewilderment on his face.

JACK'S POV—THE HOUSE

The grass is overgrown. A white-haired WORKMAN is nailing wooden boards across a window.

PANNING JACK

He approaches the house, and stops near the Workman.

> JACK

What's going on?

continued

> The Workman ignores him, and continues his hammering.
>
> JACK (Cont'd)
>
> (a pause, then angrily)
>
> Hey, mister! You hard of hearing, or something? I asked you what's going on!

*The preceding format directions and script illustrations are courtesy of Writers Guild of America, East, Inc., from its booklet **Professional Writer's Teleplay/Screenplay Format**, written by Jerome Coopersmith, illustrated by Carol Kardon.*

STYLE

Writing for the Ear and Eye

By the time you take a course in writing for television and radio, you've probably had more than a dozen years worth of courses in writing for print—from the elementary school three-R classes to college studies in writing literature, poetry, and essays. But you've likely had few, if any, courses in writing for the electronic media, even though the overwhelming majority of people in the world spend more of their time communicating and being communicated to visually and aurally than with print.

In broadcast writing, *be brief.* Although your writing for print—whether news, an essay, a novel, a short story, or other form—can be as long or as short as it needs to be for optimum effectiveness, your broadcast writing is constrained by time. A good news story in a newspaper ranges from hundreds to thousands of words. The same story on radio or television may have to fit into 30 seconds—perhaps no more than 100 words—or, if an important story, 90 seconds or 2 minutes. And unless you have reached the stature of writing a miniseries of four, six, or more hours, you have to condense what might in print be the contents of a novel or a play into the equivalent of 42 minutes for the hour show or 21 minutes for the half-hour show.

Retain an informal tone. The listener or viewer does not have the luxury of rereading formal or intellectually challenging passages to better understand what is being presented. On radio or television, a message is heard or seen just once. Although formal language and content structure can be appropriate for some documentaries and news/talk shows, the audience members who miss the next bit of action because they stopped to consider the previously presented material will quickly be lost.

Be specific. Vague, generalized action or information tends to be confusing and might persuade the audience to switch stations. Make sure that whatever is presented, whether visual or aural, is simple and clear. Ambiguity can be intriguing in print, but it usually is dull and boring on the air. This does not suggest that you write down to a low level of intellect or understanding. The content you present can be both significant and sophisticated, but you must write in a way that will reach and affect the audience; otherwise, you've wasted their time and yours.

Remember, too, that although the term "mass media" is used, *the radio-television communication process is essentially one-to-one:* The presenter at the microphone or in front of the camera and the individual receptor at home. The material should be written as if the presenter were sitting informally in the audience's living room making the presentation.

Personalize. Demographics are essential to understanding and reaching a specific audience. Try to relate the style and content of your writing to that audience and, as much as possible, to each individual member of that audience.

Be natural. Young writers frequently confuse flowery language with high style, and simple, uncluttered sentences with low style. It takes time to shed the glamour of ostentation. This is especially true in the electronic media. Remember the comment in Chapter 1 about the playwright whose 30 pages of scintillating, sophisticated dialogue were replaced by 30 seconds of terse visual writing.

Avoid the tendency to write in the following manner:

> Enough timber was consumed by the rampaging fire in the north woods to create 232 thousand square feet of prime building lumber, the embers of these never-to-be-realized residential manors reaching into the heavens above charred, twisted treetops, disappearing into the void like hordes of migrating fireflies.

Learn to write it this way:

> The north woods fire destroyed enough timber to build 100 six-room homes, and the smoke and flames were visible as far as 40 miles away.

As a young sportswriter, this author developed his style of writing by pretending that he was saying the things he was writing to a group of people in a bar or sitting around a living room. Later he adapted the style to the broadcast media by changing the group to a single individual. When you are writing, create in your mind a typical viewer or listener, an imaginary member of the audience to whom you are "speaking" directly, one-to-one. The key: Use informal, concise, active, down-to-earth language.

Simplicity

Ernest Hemingway's style as a journalist and novelist would have adapted very effectively to the electronic media. Hemingway advised young writers to "strip language clean . . . down to the bones." Be simple and direct. Use words of two syllables instead of three. That isn't catering to the lowest common denominator, but to the essence of aural and visual communication. In the electronic media, the language goes by so quickly that one has neither the opportunity nor the luxury of savoring it, thinking about the nuances of a word or sentence, as one does when reading. The action usually cannot be stopped in a television or radio presentation (unless you are viewing it on TIVO or a DVD), as it can when you slow down to reread or pause in the middle of a print story to think about what you have read.

Choose words that are familiar to everyone in the audience. Don't lose your viewers or listeners by being pretentious or by trying to teach them new vocabulary words. The best way to teach is through the contents and purpose of the script as a whole—through the presentation of ideas. The more sharply and clearly the ideas are presented, the more effectively the audience will understand and learn.

Sometimes choosing simple words is hard to do because you must at the same time avoid cliches and trite expressions. Pity the scriptwriter for the disc jockey show featuring a popular pianist. "Meandering on the keyboard"? "Rhythmical fingering of the blacks and whites"? "Carousing on the 88s"? You wouldn't use any of these overused phrases, of course. But how many times can you repeat "playing the piano"?

Look for fresh ways to say the same thing, and if you can't find a new way that isn't dull, pretentious, or inane, then just say it as simply and directly as possible.

Don't use words that might be common in *your* conversation but are not ordinarily used. As a college-trained professional, you have a vocabulary that is at least a cut above that of most of the people you are trying to reach. Someday, perhaps, when you've achieved a reputation that prompts people to listen to you not because of what you say, but because of who you are, you can use language and ideas on a level the audience might otherwise tune out. Again, this is not to say that you shouldn't raise the level of the audience's consciousness, but unless you keep the audience tuned in, there is no consciousness to raise.

Grammar

A character you create for a play can use slang or incorrect grammar as part of that fictional person's characteristics. Slang may be appropriate for a given commercial or in the continuity of a personality. Other than that, however, you should use proper and effective grammar if your ideas are to be communicated and accepted. A news script with grammatical errors not only will embarrass the anchor reading it, but also could result in the writer losing his or her job. If proper grammar, however, creates a stilted sentence or phrase, difficult to read or comprehend, then shortcuts are required. Frequently, a short, incomplete sentence is better than a rambling complete sentence. Just like the sentence you are now reading.

Verbs

Use the present tense and the active voice, with the subjects of the sentences doing or causing the action. It would be grammatically correct to say, "Last night another rebel village was destroyed by the Army, and many women and children were killed," but it would be more effective, as well as grammatically correct, to say, "The Army destroyed another rebel village last night and killed many women and children." In introducing movie idol George Starwars in an interview script, you might say, "The new movie, *Robots of Planet X,* was completed last week by George Starwars." It would be better to say, "Last week George Starwars completed his new movie, *Robots of Planet X.*"

Keep in mind the sports writing analogy offered earlier in this section: Be conversational.

The Right Word

Make sure you use the right word. In English, many words have multiple meanings. Sometimes, even in context, meanings can be mistaken. Be certain that every word you use is the best word to convey what you mean, that it cannot be confused with another meaning, and that it is not so abstract or vague as to make your meaning unclear.

Keep a dictionary handy. Use a thesaurus. Have a basic book on grammar, punctuation, and spelling available. Considering the inconsistency of spelling rules in English, it is hard to resist President Andrew Jackson's admonition that "it's a mighty poor mind that can't think of more than one way to spell a word." Nevertheless, an important sign of professional literacy is the proper use of words. For example, do you know the difference between *its* and *it's, your* and *you're, there* and *their, then* and *than?* Making errors with words such as these when trying to get into the professional field almost guarantees continuation of your amateur status.

If you've ever been in a newsroom and have pulled copy off a wire service machine or an online printout, you'll remember that the wire service puts the phonetic spelling of difficult words in the continuity of the script or at the beginning or end of the stories. If you have any doubt whether the word you are using will be pronounced correctly, do the same thing. For example, "Our special guest on *Meet the Reporters* today is Worcester (WOOSTER) State Representative Joe Cholmondeley (CHUMLEE)." When you've finished your script, read it out loud and proofread your copy. Redo your script if necessary to get a clean copy to submit to the producer or script editor. A sure sign of a careless, unprofessional writer is a sloppy script with many errors.

Punctuation

Punctuation is more functional in broadcast scripts than in other types of writing. Punctuation tells the performer where to start and stop. It indicates whether there is to be a pause (by using an ellipsis: . . .), a shorter pause (dash:—), an emphasis (!), a questioning tone (?), and other time and inflection cues. How would you read each of the following?

- She thinks he is a good actor.
- She thinks he's a good actor!
- She thinks he's a good actor?
- She thinks he's a . . . good actor.

Underlining a word or sentence specifies that it should be emphasized when read aloud.

Abbreviations

With certain exceptions, avoid abbreviations. Remember, you are writing material for a performer to read or to memorize and say aloud. Writing "dep't" and "corp" suggests that you want the performer to pronounce them D-E-E-P-T and K-A-W-R-P. Write out "department" and "corporation." Common terms that cannot be misunderstood or mispronounced, such as *Mr., Prof.,* and *Dr.,* need not be written out. Terms that are usually pronounced in their abbreviated forms, such as *AT&T, YMCA,* and *CIA,* remain so in the script. On the other hand, some common terms that frequently are seen as abbreviations, but always are pronounced in full, should not be abbreviated. Dates are an example. *Mon., Feb. 29,* should be written out as *Monday, February 29th* (or even "twenty-ninth").

Gender

Diane Sawyer of NBC News is no more an *anchorman* than Anderson Cooper of CNN News is an *anchorwoman.* The term "he" or "his" is not acceptable for generic use, certainly not for professional communicators. "In the history of medicine, the doctor hasn't always had his patients' best interests in mind" would be better written, "In the history of medicine, the doctor hasn't always had his or her patients' best interests in mind" or still better, "In the history of medicine, doctors have not always had their patients' best interests in mind."

The elimination of sexist and racist terms sometimes is confronted by old habits of unthinking insensitivity. Diane Sawyer may be an *anchorwoman;* Anderson Cooper may be an *anchorman.* Either may be an *anchorperson* or *anchor.* The gender-describing suffix is disappearing, and the most direct nonsexist way of describing someone is by the position held. *Chairman, chairwoman,* and *chairperson* have given way to *chair,* in the manner that *secretary* became the descriptive word for that position, not *secretaryman, secretarywoman,* or *secretaryperson.* The professional communicator must take the lead in being sensitive to language changes and move the general public toward the elimination of the prejudice and inequality that are fueled by bias in language.

Accuracy and Research

Whether writing a play, documentary, or news story, be sure you have the facts before you write. If you set your play in a northern urban high school, know precisely what the students and faculty are like in that milieu and what the physical, psychological, administrative, academic, and social atmosphere is at such a school. You can then selectively dramatize those elements that fit your play, eliminating those that you don't want but doing it from a sound, accurate base.

If you are doing a feature on clergy raping and sexually abusing children, be sure you are thoroughly familiar not only with the events but also with the people, their backgrounds, the church, and all the other variables necessary for developing an accurate script.

Learn to do thorough research. The success or failure of a script is determined in the preparation period; the actual writing is only one part of the process. Where do you do research? Everywhere. Each format chapter in this book contains information on obtaining materials when you are preparing an outline or script for that particular program genre. Note especially the research section in Chapter 7, which describes the various information sources that should be checked when preparing an interview. In fact, many programs, as well as networks, stations, and production houses, employ people just to do such research. These can be excellent starting positions for young college graduates entering the field.

In general, there are several key sources. Look into your own knowledge and experiences first. You may frequently find information on the topic that you had forgotten you knew. All of us, no matter how long we've been around, have more or less limited backgrounds, and we need to go further than our own selves. Recorded material is important: books, magazines, newspapers, photographs, diaries, letters, and audio and video recording. Individuals who are experts on a given subject or who know a given person are good sources, although it is important to get a cross-section of such individuals to avoid slanted conclusions. Libraries, workplaces, organizations and associations, participants, video and audio archives, relatives, neighbors and friends, event sites, artifacts, museums, and educational institutions are some key sources of information. Through the Internet you can access material on virtually any subject. You can get information from official government sources or from web sites serving specialized and even arcane interests. Google, for example, opens up myriad sources on any given subject. Using the Internet does not obviate the need for doing individual field research, but it can save much time and energy, allowing you to complete research and prepare a script in a shorter time than otherwise would be needed. A warning: Because anyone, regardless of credentials, can set up an Internet web site, it is sometimes difficult to know whether the information you are getting is valid or unreliable. Before you use any material obtained from the Internet, protect your personal reputation by being certain it comes from a reputable site and by double-checking it with proven, knowledgeable, reliable sources. For example, anyone can add to the information found on Wikipedia, making that site frequently unreliable.

Be sure to get all the information you need to be objective. However, suppose you might not want to be objective? Perhaps you want to slant your feature to meet the political views of the station's owner, or create a misleading commercial to meet the sponsor's orders, or self-censor a play or documentary to avoid controversial issues that might displease potential buyers of the advertiser's product. At least put yourself in the position of being able to be honest and objective if you want to be. And have the integrity and courage to be.

Finally, broaden your abilities and expand your skills. The media encompass all the disciplines of the world, and as a writer or in any capacity that gets the program on the air or online, you should have a background in breadth and depth, especially in the arts and humanities, most particularly in history, political science, sociology, and psychology. Read a lot: books, plays, and film, television, and radio scripts. Learn content and writing techniques from them. Good writers are good readers first.

THE COMPUTER

Would *Hamlet* have been a different play if Shakespeare had written it on a typewriter rather than with a quill pen on foolscap? Would Arthur Miller's *Death of a Salesman* have been different if written on a computer or word processor? Take the exact same piece of material: A news report, a commercial, a documentary feature. Would it come out exactly the same if written with a pencil on paper, with a typewriter, or with a computer? You will find clear and distinct differences in writing the same material for different media, and in using the techniques of varying media in preparing material for one medium. Does this principle apply to the use of different tools in writing, as well? Some writers insist that the tools with which they write affect the feeling and rhythm that are used in creating a work. Would there be more and slower character development and more measured pace in a dramatic script—or a sitcom—written by hand than in one attuned to the mechanical rhythms and speed of a computer? Is there a difference in the scene the artist paints if she or he uses oils or charcoal or water colors?

If not content difference, is there an aesthetic difference? Does this have a direct analogy for the writer? No comprehensive studies yet suggest acceptable answers. But the question has been raised. It is important to you, personally, because as a writer you will find yourself in situations where you have to produce scripts using various writing methods. For example, in an ad agency, around a conference table, you may be asked to revise, on the spot, the continuity in a commercial. You may be asked to do a **rewrite** and add material on the set of a newscast just minutes before air time. During the field recording of a documentary, you may have to come up with new and changed questions, answers, and transitions while the crew and the subjects are immediately available.

You'd better be able to think quickly and effectively with a piece of paper in front of you and a pen in your hand, as well as with a laptop.

All good writers will tell you that there is an ambience between them and the tool they use for creative writing. Until the advent of typewriters, writers wrote by hand with whatever pen or pencil or equivalent tool was available. Some writers still write only with a pen or pencil and insist that they cannot write effectively with a mechanical device.

Many writers will tell you that they can think only with a typewriter. An entire generation of writers grew up writing their first creative words on a typewriter and believe that they can't work with a pen or pencil. At the same time, they will tell you that the mechanical steps needed to operate and make corrections on a computer make it impossible for them to maintain a flow of ideas and creative juices when using one for writing.

An "Open Source" program on NPR, discussing the impact of computers on writing, suggested that networked computing is as significant a development as written language and the printing press, and that the computer has led us into social revolution. Whereas written language allowed us to outsource memory, it was stated, computers allow us to outsource thinking itself. Has the computer-as-a-tool for writing now become the computer-as-an-intelligence agent?

Your generation—people of college age—has moved into a new era of writing tool. With schools offering computer courses from the elementary grades up, newly developing writers find the computer the easiest writing tool. Aside from its symbiotic relationship with any given writer, the computer clearly is a highly efficient writing tool. It saves time on editing. It permits instant reproduction. When properly used, it permits a writer to turn out a product much faster than any other way. It enables a team of writers, even from different geographical areas, to work at the same time on the same script. It permits the writer immediately to incorporate information, ideas, and materials from any source anyplace in the script. Laptop computers have, for most writers, replaced the restaurant place-mat as the medium for recording sudden script inspirations.

Newspaper and broadcasting newsrooms use computers. Writers of drama who may question the mechanical effect imposed on their writing by computers nevertheless are eager to take advantage of the transfer of material from computer to computer, enabling them to get instant criticism on any or all of what they've written, giving them wider access to such assistance and greater overall and quicker productivity. Software can provide the basic formats discussed earlier in this chapter for television, film, and radio scripts.

Software Types

Software is available for writing letters, term papers, scripts, and virtually anything and everything else.

The *database* files and retrieves information in any format you want to design. For example, when you have finished your script on your word-processing software, you can use your database software to call up the name and address of your literary agent. Using your software and the database, you can write the agent a letter, prepare a copy of your new script, and type the envelope label for the agent.

Spreadsheet software helps you keep track of your financial information and budgets. You can extend your writing into the production area by figuring out all the finances for production planning. You can keep track of your royalties and, considering the especially burdensome recordkeeping imposed on writers by the tax code, spreadsheets can help you straighten out your tax records and determine your tax liabilities. May you be successful enough as a writer to require that kind of service from your computer!

Communications software takes your script from the confines of the desk. A modem permits script development from a number of sources at once, facilitates critiques of your script at any time in the writing process, provides for changes quickly and easily at any stage of writing, and allows instantaneous editing based on comments from producers, directors, agents, script editors, and others. Software for the one- and two-column formats and, separately, for the dramatic screenplay automatically sets up the proper margins and spacing for the script form you choose, capitalizes the characters' names and any other terms you wish, puts stage directions and other appropriate information in parentheses, numbers sequences in the dramatic screenplay format, and automatically renumbers the sequences correctly if you edit, delete, or add scenes. It also reprints and readjusts pages, and shortens or lengthens them as necessary. It tracks which scenes have been cut or added and designates which is new material and which is old as the script is printed. A screenwriting program can change a script in a one-column format into a two-column format, or into a numbered-sequence column. Software can also draw **storyboard** frames that permit drawings—the kind of material required in the preparation of commercials and public service announcements. You can continuously check the continuity process in your writing from all the material you have written on the project, accepted and rejected, good and bad.

Writing is no longer limited to words on a page. Compact discs, CD-ROMs, flash drives, and sound cards fed into a computer can integrate still pictures, moving pictures, and sound tracks into a writing project. Video, photos, and text can be delivered directly to computers from cell phones and cell phone size *flip* mini-cams. Professor Marcia Peoples Halio of the University of Delaware's writing program stated in the university's alumni journal, "Too often students use computers as very expensive typewriters, and we want them to do much more . . . they should know how to block off a chunk of text and move it around, how to complete on-line revisions and how to work with a split screen, so that they're looking at their notes on one side of the screen while also working on a document." Software changes constantly, becoming increasingly sophisticated with each passing year. When you are ready to use your computer for formatting scripts, check with your local computer software outlet for the latest and most efficient program that will best serve your specific needs. By the time you read this book, being revised in the spring of 2013, all this may be outmoded. This author, wishing to work on media manuscripts while away from home, unsuccessfully sought a tablet or iPhone with word-processing capacity to replace the mini-laptop he was then using. You may now be using your tablet or iPod or new device for scriptwriting.

Computers and the Screenplay

Most screenwriters use what is called "story development software." ScriptZone, for example, offers a sample analysis of a screenplay to help the writer determine whether comparable elements in his or her screenplay need the same kind of critical revision. Scriptdude provides software that will virtually develop a story line and even characters and dialogue. Write a Blockbuster is a program that takes you step by step through the process of writing the kind of screenplay that has been most successful in Hollywood. Final Draft provides writers with the format for the screenplay. Use of such software and Internet web site material tends to create more and more formula writing, and providing these basic approaches does not replace each writer's greatest asset: personal creativity. Many writers use these programs to remind them of key techniques that they might have overlooked when writing their screenplays.

Computers and the News

The computer is used in several major ways in both the newspaper and broadcast newsroom. One way is for the actual writing and editing of a story—composing the content and words and editing those words. The story, completed on one computer, is edited by the editor on another computer. Using a **modem** to transfer material from one computer to another permits a story to be written in Chicago, edited in Los Angeles, and produced in New York. Laptop computers are invaluable for on-the-spot composition, even as the news story is breaking. By plugging the laptop computer into a telephone line or using Wi-Fi, the writer or editor can relay the story to a computer in the newsroom.

Another computer use is for creating **graphics**, including charts, graphs, maps, and other visuals that are used in newspapers and on television. In broadcasting, the graphic can be electronically fed right into the newscast. Radio has used specialized sounds created by computers, in a sense providing an audio "graphic." The computer may store all visuals, including video, for integration with the anchors on a live news show.

A further major computer use in news is accessing information, obtaining databases for material that can be used in writing the story. Getting the text of a just-passed piece of legislation and obtaining "morgue" information on all the stories ever published in a given newspaper on the particular news topic are two types of information retrieval. As noted in other sections of this book, while search engines can facilitate and expand research, you need to make sure that the information you retrieve is valid. Another use, important for newspapers and journals, is laying out the page—designing the format for a particular issue.

Computers in Production

If your role as writer extends into the actual production process, you can find software that facilitates your job immeasurably. The writer-producer or writer-director can convert the content into a breakdown detailing every production item required by the script. This could include every character's costume needs, every special effect, all audio effects, the number of extras required and their costumes, and all props, whether in the field or in the studio, whether large like an automobile or small like a piece of jewelry. Software can also provide a production board, which lists every element in any given scene and which includes boxes that can be checked as each item is accounted for. The computer can be used to work out detailed production schedules, too, based on which characters are required for which scene and on which sets. And a spreadsheet can be used for the production budget.

INTERNET FORMAT AND STYLE

Professor Maurice Methot of Emerson College noted that "a Web site is not normally 'scripted' in the sense of linear drama. The code that lays the content out into the browser is more integral to the user's experience than any linear storyboard, but this code is meaningless unless interpreted by the browser." Methot stated:

> What is needed is a better understanding of interactive media as an emergent social and cultural construct. Online identity and community building may be bringing about a significant transformation of traditional models based on send/receive communication theory. Text, as with all media online, moves laterally in samples and appropriations where distortion becomes an integral component to the message itself. The ongoing explosion of technology, bandwidth and social adaptation ensure that accurate forecasting of the future of the web is a fuzzy proposition at best.
>
> How does the construction of a social identity by a young person on MySpace, YouTube, or Flickr figure into the meaning of writing online? How do text, audio, and video weblogs, instant messaging, multi-player online gaming, and ubiquitous wireless networks shape our participation in and experience of networked interactive media? How can cybernetics—date itself as 'active design agent'—create new content through grammatical engines, algorithmic routines, and the infinitely expanding database of metadata (date about data)?
>
> Web pages can retrieve from an infinitely expanding database of information and display it in an endless variety of visual and sonic means. Text, sound, still and moving images are all hypertextual, meaning that anything can link to anything else. Social interest in cyberspace is driven to a great extent by the

participatory nature of the experience—one may go online to search information, download clips, and order videos, but the popularity of such sites as MySpace, YouTube, and Flickr indicate a significant need for social participation and the construction of personal web identities. The explosion of personal narrative and web logs indicate that people adapt well to reading and writing online. These messages are already seamlessly integrated into the very social fabric of our lives.

While at some level the art of information design is located in a global and fully participatory forum, it is the experience of this expanding sea of data and meta-data which drives the design of the systems which parse and organize it for our consumption and response. Following this line of thought one might argue that the most critical writing online is the very computer that shapes our online experience—code written by programmers.

The task of developing "guidelines" for the effective design and layout of text on the Internet is as broad as the subject of computer/human interface itself. On the net, the text is "content," the design and nature of which is determined by various factors. Among these are:

1. intended audience
2. purpose of display
3. nature of Web project
4. nature of interface design paradigm
5. target technology base

Professor Methot offers "a few guidelines that can be useful in creating web sites that are 'reader-friendly'":

1. Do not use fonts smaller than 12 points in size.
2. At large sizes, almost any font is okay, but at smaller sizes stick to sans-serif fonts.
3. Avoid tight spacing.
4. Leading (space between the lines of text) should be set at one or two points higher than the actual size of the text itself.
5. Keep text organized in small, digestible, bulleted "textbites." Avoid wide columns and long paragraphs.
6. Restrict text color to those hues that allow the text to be as readable as possible against the background color (or image) of the page.
7. Try to limit the amount of text on any single page.

While basic formats apply to all genres, you'll find special adaptations in program types and distribution modes noted in chapters throughout this book.

Used by permission of Maurice Methot.

Commercials and Announcements

It is often said that Madison Avenue has perfected the techniques of persuasion so artistically and effectively that it could sell refrigerators at the North Pole and heaters at the equator. *Madison Avenue,* of course, is a euphemism for the advertising industry in the United States.

Commercials, although changing in form, type, length, and technique, nevertheless have been for many decades the staple of commercial broadcasting and have been perfected to a high art.

Some commercials are good because they are well crafted, sometimes even more aesthetically pleasing than the programs they are in. Others are good because they are educational, providing the consumer with information on available goods and services.

Some commercials, however, insult our logic and intelligence with their biased or misleading content. Others play upon the emotions of people to buy things they can't afford and pressure children to ask for toys and other items their parents may not have money for. All of us, whether we admit it or not, have at one time or another been influenced sufficiently by commercials to buy something that we didn't need or want and that was probably no good for us. Charles "Chuck" Barclay, as director of Creative Services for the Radio Advertising Bureau, observed, "Even the worst commercial, repeated often enough, sometimes produces results."

S. J. Paul, as publisher of *Television/Radio Age,* wrote in one of his editorials, "The commercial makers are themselves the stars of the radio-television structure. For in the short time frame of 20, 30, or 60 seconds a mood is created—a message is transmitted—and a sales point is made. This finished product is the result of many talents. In some cases, as it has often been remarked, the commercials are better than the programs."

Commercial advertising constitutes the principal financial base for the U.S. media industries. One exception is public broadcasting. But with increasing deregulation, public television and radio stations give more than just an underwriting credit. They often give the **logo** or slogan, and even an identifying comment about the underwriter's product or service. Cable television, which some once considered a possible alternative to commercial-cluttered broadcasting, became a bastion of advertising. One commercial-free alternative is *pay-per-view* television. Many observers believe, however, that its operators will not long be willing to forego the lucrative income derived from adding commercials to their programs. Internet advertising continues to increase and the web has become as commercial as broadcasting and cable.

The title of this chapter is "Commercials and Announcements." Although the meaning of "commercial" is clear, the term "announcement" is sometimes confusing. *Announcement* can be used to designate any short non-entertainment, non-news presentation on the air, including a commercial. Usually it refers to the noncommercial announcement, with the word "spot" most often used to mean a commercial.

Announcements have the same structure, form, and length as commercials. They usually are divided into two categories: (1) **promos** and (2) **PSAs,** or *public service announcements.* The commercial is designed to sell a product or service for a profit-making advertiser. The promo most often promotes the station itself: An upcoming program or series, a station personality, a contest for listeners—anything that induces the public to tune in or otherwise support the station.

The PSA is similar to the commercial except that it does not sell a product or service for money, but is made on behalf of a non-profit organization or activity and can include advancing an idea or policy. Principally, the PSA seeks support for activities of non-profit groups: Health organizations such as the American Cancer Society's antismoking campaign, citizen environmental groups' anti-pollution efforts, fund-raising for Christmas toys for indigent families in the community, support of shelters for the homeless, understanding and preventing AIDS, a bake sale at the local high school, or information about public services available from local government offices. At the top of page 85 is an example of a PSA promoting a cause in which the station itself is directly participating.

The writer has a responsibility to the agency, advertiser, and station to create not only the most artistically attractive message possible, but also one that convinces and sells. At the same time, the power of the commercial or announcement charges the writer with the responsibility of being certain that the commercial has a positive effect on public health, ethics, and actions.

(You will note in this chapter a variety of script forms and styles. These reflect the different approaches among advertising agencies, production companies, and stations. Within each organization, however, the form and style tend to be consistent. In addition, many of these examples are "shooting scripts" using the

"Walk for Housing"—20 seconds

VIDEO	AUDIO
Pan people—men, women, children— lined up in front of homeless shelter.	V.O. AND MUSIC THOUSANDS OF PEOPLE IN OUR CITY, PEOPLE YOU MAY EVEN KNOW, HAVE NO PLACE TO LIVE. WE CAN'T STOP HOME FORECLOSURES, BUT WE CAN HELP FIND HOUSING.
Dissolve to graphic.	JOIN THIS STATION, WHLR, AS WE SPONSOR THE WALK FOR HOUSING ON MAY 3. FOR INFORMATION LOG ON TO WWW.WLHR.COM.

two-column approach whereas the writer's original submission may have used the one-column format and with only those video or audio directions necessary for the specific presentation.)

ETHICAL CONSIDERATIONS

Commercial advertising can be used responsibly; it can also be used irresponsibly. In this media area, more than any other, you will be faced throughout your career with hard ethical choices.

Suppose you are employed by an advertising agency and are assigned this commercial campaign: A leading beer company wants to expand its market among new young drinkers of minimum legal drinking age, with an emphasis on increasing its share of on-premises (bars, restaurants) consumption.

Would you give any thought as to whether any ethical considerations are involved in such an assignment? At one of the annual International Radio and Television Society (IRTS) Faculty/Industry Seminars in New York, this assignment was given to the approximately 75 faculty participants from colleges and universities throughout the country. The participants were to work from a real beer company's plans and budget, under the guidance of that company's representatives. This was a practical exercise in which the beer company would, as some participants put it, "pick their brains." As was traditional with IRTS seminars, the exercise was as close to a real working situation as possible. That particular beer company had over the years developed a reputation as an anti-union employer discriminating against minorities and women. Some participants who were given the exercise were among those nationwide who had been boycotting that beer for some years.

One cannot work in the media in a vacuum. A writer in any genre of broadcasting must be knowledgeable about the world around him or her. Some participants in this exercise felt that in good conscience they could not prepare an advertising campaign that might be valuable to a company whose practices they believed were inimical to their personal ethical standards. Most of those objecting to the project did not want to lend their efforts to a campaign that encouraged increased alcohol consumption, especially among young people.

About one-third of the participants publicly objected to the assignment, with many refusing to work on it—in effect, quitting their "jobs." About another third, although not "resigning" from the exercise, stated their reservations about doing the project.

What, if anything, would you have done, and why?

The ethical, responsible ad writer should identify with the anonymous creator of commercials who wrote in *Television/Radio Age* that "accounting to a set of practical, working rules allows a good balance of involvement with the industry and accountability to the consumer public. It's hard to try and dupe, or con, the viewer when you feel 'we are they' . . . and realize that you are only cheating yourself."

LENGTHS AND PLACEMENT OF COMMERCIALS AND ANNOUNCEMENTS

Commercials are usually 30 or 60 seconds long. As commercial time and production costs increased, the "split-30"—two 15-second commercials in a 30-second space—became popular, as did later the 15-second stand-alone announcement. One also finds 10-second, 20-second, 90-second, 2-minute, and even longer spots on non-broadcast media.

Public service announcements, or PSAs, are not paid for, but usually follow the same time lengths, mostly 30 and 60 seconds. They usually are aired only when the station hasn't sold all of its available commercial time segments. For that reason, many PSAs produced by or for the non-profit organization are sent to the station in two or more time-length versions for greater possibility of use.

Station *promos* have similar time lengths. Station **IDs** (station identifications, consisting of the call letters or *logo*, city, and sometimes an identifying or promotional phrase about the station), many of which are highly creative, usually are 10 seconds long for a station break. Sometimes IDs have a commercial attached—two seconds for the station ID and the remaining eight seconds for a paid advertisement.

Many copywriters use a word count scale to determine how many words will go into a given time segment. Although such a count can be fairly accurate for radio, non-aural visual material must be included to get a good approximation for television. In addition, the lengths of individual words, complexity of ideas, need for emphasis through pause and variation in rate, and personality of the performer delivering the announcement also affect the number of words that can be spoken effectively in a given length of time.

In general, however, the 10-second announcement contains about 25 words; the 20-second announcement about 45 words; the 30-second spot about 65 words; the 45-second spot about 100 words; the 60-second announcement about 125 words; the 90-second announcement about 190 words; and the two-minute spot about 250 words.

The ID is given at the station break, usually every half-hour on the hour and half-hour. Other announcements, including commercials, PSAs, and promos, can also be given then, depending on how much time is available between programs. Time availability can vary from literally only a few seconds to several minutes. Program lengths usually are a half or full hour, and sometimes 15 minutes.

Although most announcements are clustered at logical breaks, including the beginning and end of programs, most commercial programs have built-in commercial breaks, some at the halfway mark for half-hour programs, and at the one-third and two-third marks for hour-long shows. Programs with relatively good ratings draw more commercials, of course, and movies, for example, may have interruptions every few minutes. Stations that are network affiliates carry the network commercials, but are given specified times within the network programs for inserting local announcements.

The ID

The station identification, as required by the Federal Communications Commission, must contain the station's call letters and the originating city or, optionally, the name of a larger city that is the principal area of service. Some stations include the station's frequency to help the audience remember the radio or television channel they should tune to. A simple, direct ID would be the following:

You are listening to WNBC, 660, New York.

To make themselves more distinctive, many stations add a qualifying phrase designed to promote the station's format, if a radio station, or the station's image, if television. The ID is a public relations trademark for the station and should be identifying and distinguishing at the same time. For example:

America's number one fine music station, WBBB-FM, New York.

CBS-TV's ID has made the network and its affiliates unmistakable.

VIDEO	AUDIO
Channel 2's "Eye"	Keep your eye on Channel 2, CBS, New York.

Some stations use music or sound effects to promote their stations in the IDs. KFOG, San Francisco, used a foghorn sound. WGLD, High Point, North Carolina, established in its ID an identification between its format, beautiful music, and its key promotional word, "gold." The first of two following IDs reminds new or infrequent listeners of the format; the second ID doesn't have to.

> With beautiful music . . . this is gold at FM-100 . . . WGLD, High Point.
> At FM-100, this is gold . . . WGLD-FM, High Point.

Some IDs include a paid commercial, such as "This is WRLH at 4 P.M., Soporific Watch Time. See the Soporific Wrist Alarm—date and calendar—twenty-one jewels."

The PSA

PSAs frequently are given as part of the ID. For example, "This is WMVH, your election station. If you've been listening to the important campaign issues on WMVH, you'll want to vote on Election Day. Register today so that you can." The sponsoring organizations often issue kits containing the same announcement in various lengths, to maximize the possibility of their use. Following are illustrations from the "register to vote" campaign.

PSAs are written, as well, to fit into particular program types, to relate to holidays or to special occasions—for all and any purposes that may enhance the possibility of their use. Remember that they are not paid advertising and the organization depends upon the station's goodwill and time availability to carry them. The more flexibility the PSA has in content and length, the easier it is for the station to place it. The following are some illustrations:

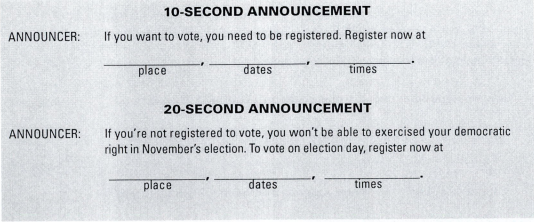

10-SECOND ANNOUNCEMENT

ANNOUNCER: If you want to vote, you need to be registered. Register now at

_____, _____, _____.
      place   dates   times

20-SECOND ANNOUNCEMENT

ANNOUNCER: If you're not registered to vote, you won't be able to exercised your democratic right in November's election. To vote on election day, register now at

_____, _____, _____.
      place   dates   times

Courtesy American Heritage Foundation

TIME SIGNAL

(20 Seconds, Radio)

ANNOUNCER: It's _____ . . . and right now an emotionally disturbed child in
             (time)

_____ needs your help and understanding. This is National Child
(town or area)

Guidance Week. Observe it . . . and attend the special program on emotionally disturbed
children in _____ presented by the _____
             (town or area)

PTA, on _____ at _____ .
        (date)   (place)

DISC JOCKEY PROGRAM

(30 Seconds, Radio)

DISC JOCKEY: _____ . . . a recording that sold a million copies. Easy listening, too.
               (title and artist)

But here's a figure that's not easy to listen to: Over 1,000,000 American children
are seriously emotionally ill. During National Child Guidance Week, the
_____ PTA, in cooperation with the American Child Guidance
Foundation, is holding a special meeting to acquaint you with the problems faced by
children in _____ . It's to your benefit to attend.
             (town or area)

Be there . . . _____ . . . to learn what you can do to help.
              (date and address)

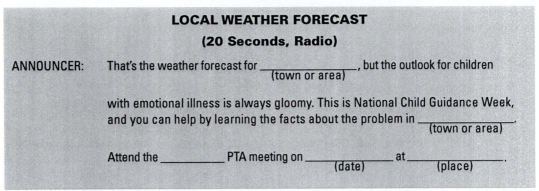

LOCAL WEATHER FORECAST
(20 Seconds, Radio)

ANNOUNCER: That's the weather forecast for _____, but the outlook for children
                                                 (town or area)

with emotional illness is always gloomy. This is National Child Guidance Week,
and you can help by learning the facts about the problem in _____.
                                                              (town or area)

Attend the _____ PTA meeting on _____ at _____.
                                          (date)   (place)

Prepared for American Child Guidance Foundation, Inc. by its agents,
Batten, Barton, Durstine & Osborne, Inc.

Sometimes the PSA can be persuasive like a commercial, not only providing information, but also motivating the audience to take action, such as attending a fund-raising event for a worthy cause, and giving details about place, time, and cost. The PSA can even seek the audience's direct participation in raising funds—similar to selling a product, but for a nonprofit, human service purpose, as in the following:

HEARTS IN BLOOM—LIVE COPY
30 SECONDS

THIS WINTER, GIVE THE GIFT OF LIFE. THE AMERICAN HEART ASSOCIATION'S HEARTS IN BLOOM CAMPAIGN CAN BRING HEARTWARMING BOUQUETS TO YOUR OFFICE, AND HELP FIGHT THIS NATION'S NUMBER ONE KILLER—HEART DISEASE.

YOU CAN HELP BY SIGNING UP THIS JANUARY AS YOUR COMPANY'S HEARTS IN BLOOM COORDINATOR AND TAKING ORDERS FROM YOUR FELLOW EMPLOYEES. TO FIND OUT HOW, CALL THE AHA AT 508-620-1700, AND ASK FOR EXTENSION 3946. IT WILL DO YOUR HEART GOOD!

Courtesy of the American Heart Association

WRITING STYLES

Keep the commercial or PSA in good taste. Although the style of writing can capitalize on visual and audio elements that are exciting to the audience, there are boundaries between what is attractive to the viewer or listener and what becomes repugnant or disturbing. Remember, the sponsor does not want to alienate a single potential customer. Some ads oriented to 17–25-year-olds use a "high-tech" approach—the sometimes frenetic, hyper-produced, high-decibel elements that proved so successful in music videos. These ads can carry the viewer right to the edge of bad taste—sexual innuendo, physical or psychological violence, implications of nudity or partial nudity—but they should not go over the line.

Humor, drama, music, and other techniques can be used to persuade the audience to subscribe to the product or service. Within each format, be direct and simple. If the commercial or PSA is to seem sincere, the performer must have material that is conversational and informal within the context of the situation so that the audience really believes what it sees and hears. In a rap music type of commercial, for example, the performer's language may seem obtuse and complicated, but it is appropriate for the situation and normal for the audience ages it is aimed at. In one popular spot approach, one simply watches or hears a conversation among some people, the kind of conversation one would likely be part of at a gathering of that age group. The audience identifies with the group. Without even verbally identifying the product name in the television version of the ad, the commercial discloses it by directing attention to the labels on the characters' clothing.

In making the characters in the ad identifiable, the writer does not necessarily use ultra-colloquial or slang dialogue. Such dialogue is perfectly acceptable when it fits the situation—just as one develops appropriate dialogue for the characters in a play. On the whole, vocabulary should be dignified, but not colorless; attention-getting, but not trite; simple and direct, but not inane or illiterate.

The writing should be grammatically correct, except, of course, if the performers' characterizations call for non-grammatical dialogue. Action verbs are extremely effective, as are concrete, specific words and ideas. If you want to make an important point, repeat that point, usually in different words or forms. An exception is a slogan or trademark, where word-for-word repetition is important. Keep in mind that there is a distinct difference between the television, radio, and Internet ad, even for the same product or service. Avoid false claims, phony testimonials, and other elements of obvious exaggeration. Aside from ethical considerations, such a commercial could antagonize much of the audience, even while deceiving another part.

Mike Luoma, long-time radio copywriter, offers the following advice:

- Learn all the rules of grammar, but when you're writing ad copy, especially for radio, proper grammar is much less important than capturing the rhythm and flow of conversation. You want your ads to engage the listener, so it has to be a conversation, even if a one-sided one.

- Read your copy out loud. If it doesn't sound conversational, if it doesn't sound the way people talk, try an exercise where you tell a friend about what you're advertising.

- What do you say? How do you say it? This can be tricky, especially when you're dealing with a client advertiser who's convinced that *everything* needs to be in his/her ad. It doesn't and it's a law of diminishing returns. Attention is at a premium and there's a point after which the more information you throw at the listener, the less sticks. You might not be able to convince the client of that, but do your best!

TECHNIQUES

There are no essential differences between writing the commercial and the PSA. The audience analysis, familiarization with the product or service, appeals to the viewers' or listeners' needs and wants, effective organization, and format types are the same. The principal distinction to remember is that the commercial sells a product or service for money whereas the PSA usually sells an idea or action.

Successful announcement writing requires more than technique, talent, and hard work. Roy Grace, a creator of the award-winning Volkswagen ads for the Doyle Dane Bernbach (DDB) advertising agency, asserted that 50% is doing the work and 50% is believing enough in what you create to fight for it and sell it to the account executive. John Noble, co-creator with Grace of the VW ads, warned, "There are account men who can talk young creative people out of a concept very easily. . . . There should be a battle." Robert Levenson, as creative director of DDB, offered guidelines for copywriters:

1. The commercial should be clearly on the product.
2. The discipline of keeping your eye on what you are selling and how clearly you're selling it is half the battle.
3. The commercial still isn't good without the skills, the talents, the instincts, the hard work that the best creative people bring to their jobs.
4. The discipline comes first. Then we get to . . . attention-getting, warm, human, lifelike, funny, and all the rest.
5. Here's the test: If you look at a commercial and fall in love with the brilliance of it, try taking the product out of it. If you still love the commercial, it's no good. Don't make your commercial interesting; make your products interesting.

Audience Analysis

Advertisers seek audiences who are most likely to buy their products or services. A product designed for women between 17 and 39—cosmetics, for example— would not be advertised on a program that reaches a predominantly male audience, such as a sports show. Once the target audience is determined, the commercial is designed to appeal to the specific needs and wants of that audience. Audience analysis is called *demographics*, which may include such information as age, gender, economic level, political orientation, occupation, educational level, ethnic background, geographical concentration, and product knowledge. *Psychographics*, even more detailed audience analysis, includes such elements as lifestyles, primary interests, and attitudes and beliefs. (See the section on demographics in Chapter 1.) The SRI Consulting Business Intelligence web site discusses audience analysis for advertising purposes in terms of primary motivation and resources. It states that "consumers buy products and services and seek experiences that fulfill their characteristic preferences and give shape, substance and satisfaction to their lives." It states that a consumer's actions are determined by several primary motivating factors: self-expression, achievement, and ideals. Self-expression refers to social and physical activity, variety, and risk; achievement relates to products or services that show others one's personal successes—a "keeping up with the Joneses" syndrome; idealism means being guided by principles and knowledge. The web site also indicates that analysis of potential customers should go beyond the basic applications of age, gender, income, and education, but should include areas that go even beyond the general concepts of psychographics: "energy, self-confidence, intellectualism, novelty-seeking, innovativeness, impulsiveness, leadership, and variety."

Although writers attempt to appeal to the largest number of people expected to watch the program and the commercial, you must take care not to spread the message too thin. Television audiences tuned to network programs tend to be disunified demographically. Independent local or regional stations can determine audience demographics more easily because of the smaller number of viewers limited to a smaller area. Local cable systems can determine demographics most accurately, serving a prescribed area and knowing exactly who their subscribers are. Most radio stations have highly structured formats, appealing to specific audiences in their communities, so each station can determine its demographics with relative ease. Consolidation, as noted earlier, has made that more difficult. The Internet literally reaches out to the entire world. Advertisers rely principally on a program-type and on the registered (through Internet tracking) habits of users to match their products or services.

After analyzing as fully as possible the audience likely to view the commercial, the writer consciously includes materials that appeal to that audience. The same audience analysis criteria apply to public service announcements. Audience analysis is then combined with specific needs and wants appeals within the commercial to make the most effective impact. Before this step, however, the writer must be thoroughly familiar with the product or service to be advertised.

Familiarization with the Product

In addition to personal observation or use of the product, the writer should collect as much information about it as possible from those connected with it. A good source of information is the research or promotion department of the advertiser's company. Develop receptive and flexible attitudes toward products and services. Aside from ethical considerations, you may be given the assignment for a product or service that seems totally dull and uninteresting to you. In fact, it may seem the same way to most of the potential customers. Your job is to make it exciting.

If you are given a new digital camera to promote that fits in the palm of one's hand, has a 10-megapixel quality or sharpness, a 12X optical zoom, a 3-inch screen that does not fade out in backlight, a viewfinder, a built-in capacity for 1000 pictures, and that sells for under $200, your job as a copywriter may appear to be easy. However, what if one or more other companies are advertising a similar camera? What is it about your camera that would make it of greater appeal to consumers.

That's what you look for. The ad writers who creatively stressed that the Toyota Corolla, then the Camry and, more recently, the Prius, has a long-lasting engine, large seating capacity and storage space in a compact car, and, as costs of gasoline soared, high gas mileage, made Toyota the best-selling automobile in the United States.

On the other hand, you may have to deal with a more prosaic product or service such as one of the many fast-food chains or one of the many cell-phone companies or one of the many auto insurance companies or even just an athletic shoe or sneaker. If you come up with a slogan that standing alone identifies the product or service in the minds of potential customers, you've got it made as a copywriter. For example: "You're Loving It" (McDonald's), "Can You Hear Me Now" (Verizon), "Even a Cave Man Can Do It" (GEICO), "Just Do It!" (Nike). Visual IDs can have the same impact, such as Nike's check-mark slash and GEICO's gecko.

Appeals

The third important factor in preparing a commercial or PSA is to appeal to the audience's basic needs or wants. All viewers and listeners are motivated by essential psychological and intellectual concerns, some conscious, most subconscious. By playing on these motivations, the copywriter can make almost any audience feel or believe almost anything and, in many cases, even persuade the audience to take some action—such as running right out and buying the product or phoning an 800-number to purchase a service or going online and ordering the product.

Three basic appeals, applied through the ages and based on Aristotle's three key elements of persuasion—ethos, logos, and pathos—translate today as ethical, logical, and emotional appeals.

Ethical Appeal

Aristotle called persuasion by someone recognized as a "good person" an ethical appeal. When a celebrity—a well-known or well-respected person—tells us something, we tend to believe it more than if the same statement had come from a non-celebrity. For example, we not only buy products advertised by entertainment stars, but we even pay attention to political and social comments by a pop singer or a baseball player whose actual knowledge of the subject may be nil. Later in this chapter you will study the *testimonial* as one principal commercial form. The testimonial is based on *ethical appeal*.

A further application of *ethos* or ethical appeal relates the concept of the product or the manner in which the product is presented to the audience's ethical values. Of course, this varies in different sections of the country and even within the same market and is determined by psychographic surveys.

Logical Appeal

The logical appeal is exactly what it says. The persuasion is based on the facts, attempting to convince the potential buyer that the product or service fills a logical, practical need. For example, study the next commercial you see for an automobile. Does it recommend that you buy the car because its shorter length will make it easier for the owner to find a parking space in most cities? Because the car's lower horsepower will save on gasoline? Because its design and construction might save its passengers' lives in an accident? If so, then the ad appeals to logic. Note, however, under *emotional* appeals, what most car ads really appeal to.

How many ads can you remember that have consisted principally of logical appeals? Probably very few, except in times when high gasoline prices and/or a poor economy puts a premium on low operating cost as a logical appeal. Ads for many electronics, such as portable DVD players, high definition large-screen digital TVs, iPods and cell phones usually emphasize styling and size rather than quality, construction, and durability. Some commercials, however, do use logical appeals. Computer hardware and software ads frequently stress the computer's greater capacity and flexibility and the software's multiple uses, although many of the prospective customers don't need the complexity of the product they are being motivated to buy or are not aware that the rapid advances and changes in the computer field may make their expensive new purchase obsolete within months or even weeks.

Many commercials only appear to use logical appeals. Closer examination reveals the appeals are really emotional in content, the most used and most effective type in advertising.

Emotional Appeal

An emotional appeal does not mean one that evokes laughter or tears, but one that appeals to the non-logical, non-intellectual aspects of the viewer's or listener's personality. It is an appeal to the audience's basic needs or wants. Most car ads, for example, have traditionally emphasized size, power, and styling. Even compact cars have been sold with the slogan "big car room." Television ads show cars driving at powerful ultra-high speeds, zooming dangerously around curves on small country roads or over rocky terrain. Minivan commercials stress the logic of family use, even though emphasizing the size to accommodate many people and the power to carry them and, of course, omitting any mention of their poor gas mileage. Most auto ads highlight design and equipment by featuring passengers who look like movie stars, with the implication that people who drive these automobiles associate with beautiful, rich people or that if you own that car you will certainly attract one.

These are emotional appeals: appeals to feelings rather than reason. These auto commercial approaches appeal to basic emotional needs: power, prestige, and good taste. The power to attract love or sex partners, the power to move quickly without any impediment through life, the prestige of associating with prestigious people, the prestige of owning something that draws envy from others, the good taste to more than keep up with the Joneses.

Other emotional appeals that have proven highly motivating in commercials and PSAs are love of family, as evidenced in insurance company commercials; patriotism; reputation; religion; and loyalty to a group. Conformity is effectively used in advertisements for young people's clothes that may be torn, discolored, and even uncomfortable, but promoted as necessary for peer acceptance. The appeal to self-preservation is perhaps the strongest emotional appeal of all. Drug commercials, among others, make good use of this technique.

The following commercial is a good illustration of the appeal to prestige. The implications are that if you serve Libby's foods you have good taste, are a smart shopper, and have more sophistication and intelligence than those who do not serve Libby's. (The implications of emotional appeals may, of course, be quite valid.)

Did you note the appeal to love of family in the statement that "everyone in every family goes for . . ."? Did you note the logical appeal at the end of the commercial, on saving money by using Libby's coupons? If you had written the commercial, would you have included another logical appeal, such as stressing "nutritious food"?

VIDEO	AUDIO
1. MCU ANNOUNCER BESIDE LIBBY'S DISPLAY.	ANNOUNCER: LIBBY's presents a word quiz. What is the meaning of the word "epicure"? Well, according to our dictionary the word means a person who shows good taste in selection of food. And that's a perfect description of the homemaker who makes a habit of serving . . .
2. INDICATES DISPLAY.	LIBBY's famous foods. Yes, everyone in every family goes for
3. INDICATES EACH PRODUCT IN SYNC.	LIBBY's Peaches . . . Fruit Cocktail . . . LIBBY'S Pineapple-Chunks, Crushed or Sliced . . . Pineapple Juice . . . LIBBY's Peas . . . Beets . . . Corn—Whole Kernel or Cream Styled . . . LIBBY's Tomato Juice . . . Corned Beef Hash . . . and LIBBY'S Beef Stew. AND right now, smart shoppers are stocking up
4. HOLDS UP LIBBY'S COUPONS.	on LIBBY'S famous foods . . . because there's still time to cash in those LIBBY'S dollar-saving coupons you received. You can save whole
5. MOVE IN FOR CU LIBBY'S DISPLAY.	dollars on this week's food bill. So stock up now on LIBBY'S famous foods . . . and cash in your LIBBY'S coupons and save! Always make LIBBY'S a "regular" on your shopping list!

Courtesy of Nestlé Foods Corp.

The following announcement is designed for a larger audience, but at the same time contains a personal orientation and a strong "love of family" appeal.

Client ACS   Length: 30
Title: How to Fight Cancer with a Calendar
Adult Cessation TV spot

VIDEO	AUDIO
Open on a women at her kitchen counter writing on a calendar with a red marker. Her marks are very emphatic. She reveals that she has circled a date and written "Anniversary" really big on it with multiple arrows pointing to it.	ANNCR.: (Very matter of fact/instructional) How to improve your marriage with a calendar.
The husband walks by sipping his coffee and does a double take at the calendar.	HUSBAND: Clever. Very clever.
Cut to same woman putting the calendar on the fridge revealing the writing: "Quit Smoking" on a date.	ANNCR.: How to fight cancer with a calendar. Set a date and stick to your decision. It's a lot easier when you have help. The American Cancer Society can double your chances of quitting for good.
ACS Logo cancer.org/GreatAmericans 1.800.ACS.2345	Call or visit us online. This is the American Cancer Society.

Courtesy of the American Cancer Society

The following television PSAs combine logical and emotional appeals to stress the strongest motivation: self-preservation. Note how the same message can be presented in three different ways to appeal to three different audience groups: the general public, parents, and youth.

ANNCR: This is secondhand smoke. It's what you breathe when you're in a room where other people smoke. The same stuff you smell on your clothes goes into your lungs and increases your risk of getting lung cancer by 34%. You know, there's a warning label on cigarette packs for people who smoke. Where do you think the tobacco industry should put the warning for people who breathe?

SUPER: It's time we made smoking history.

LEGAL: A message from the Massachusetts Department of Public Health.

Courtesy of the Massachusetts Department of Public Health

(guy cutting out pictures of his daughter)

FATHER: I know I shouldn't smoke. I've tried to quit a million times. I know about lung cancer, strokes, heart disease . . . all that stuff. I mean, they're listed right on the side of the pack. Still doesn't make quitting any easier. But I'm going to keep at it.

(guy slips picture of his daughter in cellophane of pack)

FATHER: Because the way I see it, if the reasons on the side of the pack don't get to me, the reason on the front will.

SUPER: Call 1-800-TRY-TO-STOP.

SUPER: It's time we made smoking history.

LEGAL: A message from the Massachusetts Department of Public Health.

Courtesy of the Massachusetts Department of Public Health

ANNCR: Couplea kids in Chicopee hang at a mall, lotsa cool stores, lotsa cool food, second hand smoke, not cool. They don't like it, what do they do? They go to the top guy, the head mall honcho. They talk to people, they talk to chickens. Big meetings, small meetings, the big picture, the bottom line, before long, done deal. Hello, smoke free mall. Couple of kids, they had an idea. They took control. They changed the rules, so can you.

SUPER: It's time we made smoking history.

LEGAL: A message from the Massachusetts Department of Public Health.

Courtesy of the Massachusetts Department of Public Health

Organization of the Commercial or Announcement

The purpose of the commercial or announcement is to persuade. Many rhetoric experts have developed systems for persuasion. College students usually are exposed to such systems in elementary communication, business, or philosophy courses. Essentially, five steps of persuasion can be applied to virtually every commercial or PSA.

First, get the audience's attention. This can be accomplished by many means, including humor, a startling statement or visual, a rhetorical question, vivid description, a novel situation, and suspenseful conflict. Sound and digital visual effects attract attention. Keep in mind that the television viewer is prone to use the commercial break to head for a bathroom, a beer, a phone call, or food. If you don't get a viewer's attention in the first few seconds, before he or she leaves the area of the television set, you've lost your viewer. Viewers watching online are subject to the same distractions and are easily tempted to check their e-mail. Those watching on mobile hand-held devices such as Blackberries or cell phones are frequently in environments that can distract them. Viewers and listeners will tune out or switch channels, even if only temporarily, if the spot is not entertaining enough to hold their interest. Internet commercials, often in the form of pop-ups, have to be especially attractive to hold one's attention.

Perhaps one of most ubiquitous yet egregious attention-getters is the pop-up on the Internet. It certainly gets one's attention. At the same time, it can be annoying, interrupting a user's concentration on a different issue or task. Many users have been so annoyed by specific pop-ups that they have deliberately refused to purchase that product or service. Do pop-ups work? If they didn't, would we see so many of them?

Second, after you get the audience's attention, hold its interest. One effective technique is constructing the mini-drama, establishing a conflict that keeps the audience viewing or listening for the climax or resolution. In effect, this approach follows the same plot structure as the play does, except this mini-drama unfolds in 30 or 60 seconds. Anecdotes, testimonials, statistics, examples, and exciting visuals and sound are among the devices that can be used to hold interest.

Third, create an impression that some sort of problem exists, related to the function of the product or service being presented. This can be done subtly by implication, or more directly.

Fourth, plant the idea that the problem can be solved by using the particular product or service. Sometimes, the product or service has not yet been introduced in the spot, but is saved until the final step.

Fifth, finish with a strong emotional and/or logical and/or ethical appeal to motivate the audience to take action on the product or service: Put it on a grocery list, mail in a donation to a charity, or run right out and buy whatever it is. Or, alternatively, come away with such a strong impression that they will remember it the next time they go shopping.

In most cases immediate action is, of course, not obtained, and the audience may not consciously make a written or mental note to do anything about it. But all of us, at one time or another, have bought or done something that we likely would not have, had we not been influenced, even subconsciously, by the ads for that product or service.

Find the persuasion steps in the following Volkswagen commercial. Remember that the five steps are a guide, not a mandate, in structuring a commercial, and sometimes you may not find all five, or you may find a given step very subtly made and barely perceptible. In most commercials and PSAs, however, the first four steps are clearly evident and the fifth one is frequently included.

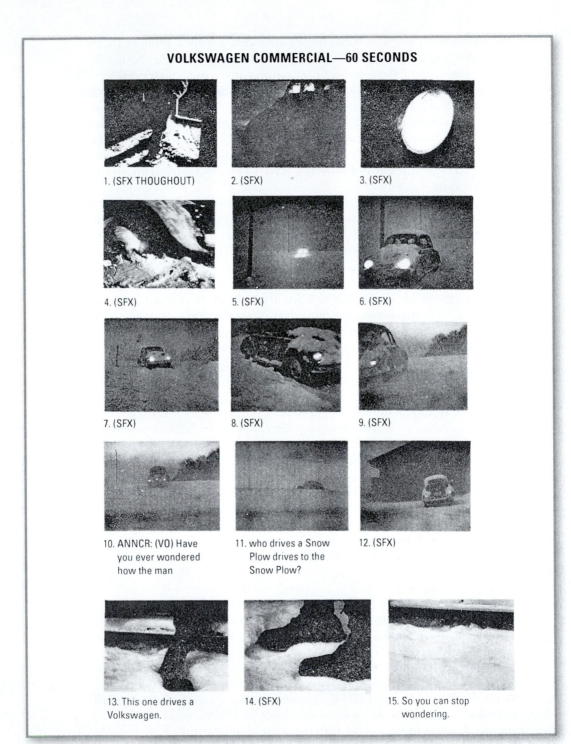

VOLKSWAGEN COMMERCIAL—60 SECONDS

1. (SFX THOUGHOUT)
2. (SFX)
3. (SFX)
4. (SFX)
5. (SFX)
6. (SFX)
7. (SFX)
8. (SFX)
9. (SFX)
10. ANNCR: (VO) Have you ever wondered how the man
11. who drives a Snow Plow drives to the Snow Plow?
12. (SFX)
13. This one drives a Volkswagen.
14. (SFX)
15. So you can stop wondering.

continued

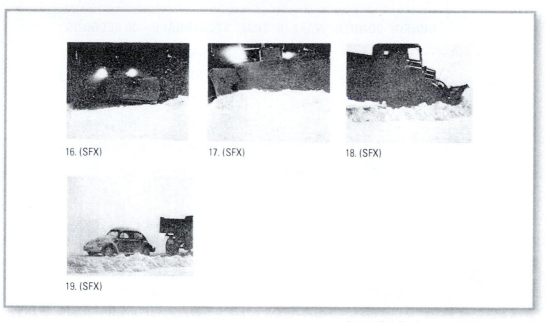

16. (SFX)   17. (SFX)   18. (SFX)

19. (SFX)

Courtesy of Doyle Dane Bernbach Inc. for Volkswagen of America

THE STORYBOARD

Clients, producers, and account executives like to see as early and as fully as possible what the visual contents of the commercial or PSA will look like. After the basic ideas have been formed, producing the actual copy begins with the written word, including verbal descriptions of the script video portion. The next step is producing a series of drawings—a **storyboard**—showing what the described scenes will actually look like. The storyboard shows the sequence of picture action, optical effects, camera angles and distances, and settings. Under each drawing is a caption containing the dialogue and stating the sound and music to be heard.

Some storyboards are prepared for the preliminary presentation, along with the script draft, by the writer. Depending on the writer's art skills, the storyboard can be as simple as a series of stick figures. In large agencies the writer works with an artist, who prepares the initial storyboard. Final storyboards, prepared for client conferences by the agency artist, are sometimes as complete and excellent as the artwork for a high-quality animated film.

The Dunkin' Donuts storyboard shows the drawings prepared at the agency, followed by the same sequences as actually filmed for the finished commercial.

DUNKIN' DONUTS "WAKE UP TIME" STORYBOARD—30 SECONDS

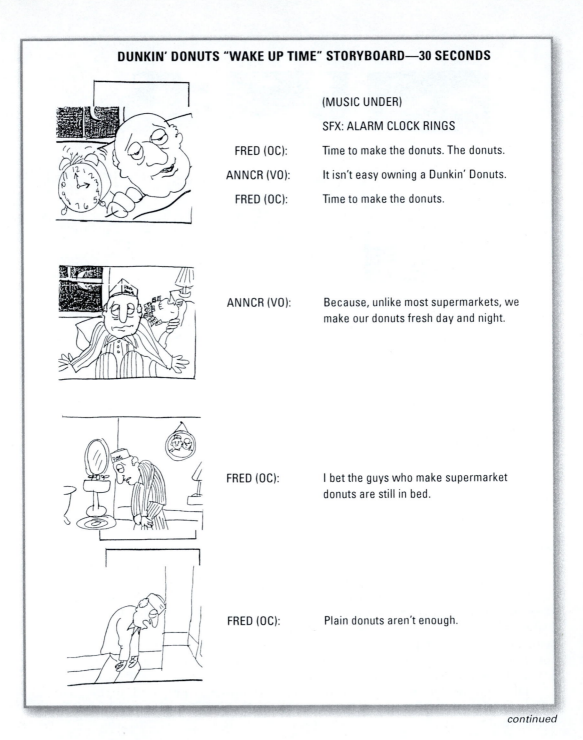

(MUSIC UNDER)

SFX: ALARM CLOCK RINGS

FRED (OC):   Time to make the donuts. The donuts.

ANNCR (VO):   It isn't easy owning a Dunkin' Donuts.

FRED (OC):   Time to make the donuts.

ANNCR (VO):   Because, unlike most supermarkets, we make our donuts fresh day and night.

FRED (OC):   I bet the guys who make supermarket donuts are still in bed.

FRED (OC):   Plain donuts aren't enough.

continued

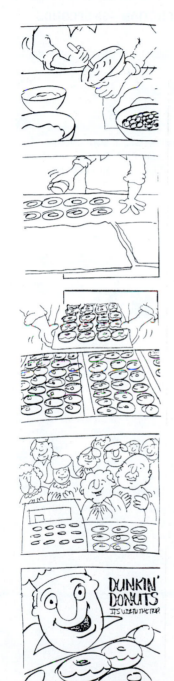

Five kinds . . .

Five kinds of jelly donuts,

creme filled,

honey-dipped . . .

ANNCR (VO): Of course, when you make donuts this good, there is one reward: they taste so great, people buy an awful lot of 'em.

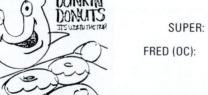

SUPER: DUNKIN' DONUTS IT'S WORTH THE TRIP.

FRED (OC): Good mornin', folks!

DUNKIN' DONUTS "WAKE UP TIME" FINAL PRODUCTION—30 SECONDS

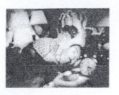

1. (MUSIC UNDER)
(SFX: ALARM CLOCK
RINGS) FRED: (OC)
Time to make the
donuts.

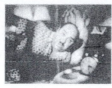

2. The donuts.

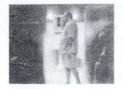

3. ANNCR: (VO) It isn't
easy owning a Dunkin'
Donuts. FRED: (OC)
Time to make the
donuts.

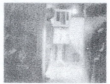

4. ANNCR: (VO)
Because, unlike most
supermarkets,

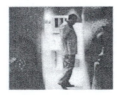

5. we make our
donuts fresh day

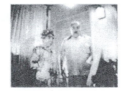

6. and night.

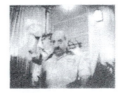

7. FRED: (OC) I bet the
guys who make super-
market donuts are still
in bed.

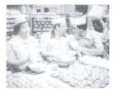

8. Plain donuts aren't
enough.

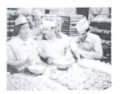

9. Five kinds . . .

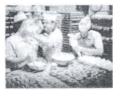

10. VOICE UNDER: Five
kinds of jelly donuts,
creme filled, honey-
dipped . . . ANNCR: (VO)
Of course, when you
make donuts this good,

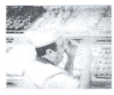

11. there is one reward:
they taste so great.
FRED: (OC) Good
mornin', folks!

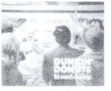

12. ANNCR: (VO) people
buy an awful lot of 'em.

Written and produced by Ally & Gargano, Inc., Advertising; courtesy of Dunkin'
Donuts of America, Inc.

Because television is visual, many critics believe that writers in all formats, including commercials, should use principally the medium's video aspects, rather than present radio with pictures. In effect, the storyboard should be the essence of, if not the complete commercial. This has happened when a product or service has gotten so well known that live or animated action or non-dialogue effects such as music result in an effective commercial without the product's or service's name even necessarily mentioned in the script dialogue or continuity. For many years the musical jingle was a staple of radio and television advertising, from the 1930s "Pepsi-Cola Hits the Spot" (which brought that company into serious competition with Coca-Cola) to the more recent McDonald's "You Deserve a Break Today." In the latter part of the 2000's first decade jingles began to be replaced by pop songs, the product presented in conjunction with a current favorite. You may recall CBS's use of the Black Eyed Peas song "It's Going to Be a Great Night" to promote one of its seasons.

The same general approach—that is, not stating verbally the sponsor's name—sometimes is used in a visual-only commercial. An example is the following Pepsi spot.

PEPSI STORYBOARD DESCRIPTIONS

INNERTUBE:

Open on a Pepsi bottle with a straw in it. Camera pulls back to reveal a cute young kid on a beach with a cute sailor cap on. He's drinking the Pepsi through the straw, and getting quickly to the bottom of the bottle. Camera pulls in closer. We see the young kid sucking on the straw so hard that his face is starting to be sucked in; the sailor cap starts to turn inward. In one quick swoop, the kid gets sucked into the straw, and into the bottle. The camera pulls back to reveal the bottle on the beach.

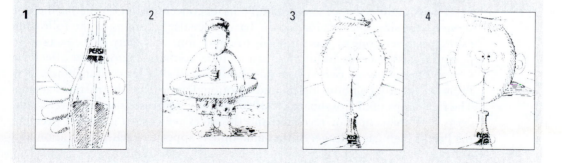

continued

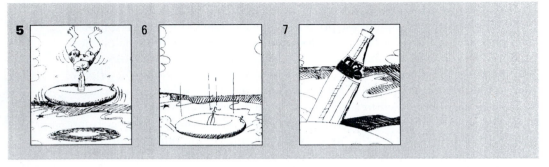

FORMATS

The five major format types for commercials and PSAs are the straight sell, the testimonial, humor, music, and the dramatization. Any single announcement can combine two or more of these approaches.

The Straight Sell

This should be a clear, simple statement about the product or service. Don't involve the announcer or station too closely with what is being sold or promoted, except, of course, when the announcement is a promo for the station itself or a fund-raising or other support spot for a cause or organization with which the station and its personnel want to be publicly associated. Do not say "our product" or "our store" unless a personality is presenting the commercial, where the combination of the straight sell and testimonial can be strengthened by the personality's direct involvement.

Although the straight sell should be direct, it should not hit the audience over the head, nor be so laborious as to antagonize any potential customers. The writing should stress something special about the product or service, real or implied, that makes it different or better than the competition's.

The straight sell spot can be simple in its concentration on the product or service, stressing one or more of the basic appeals. It can, as in the following examples, orient one or more appeals to conditions in society that concern the potential customer. In addition, it can include aesthetic factors that affect the senses. The following two Toyota ads that are part of a series launching a new Prius excellently combine logical and emotional appeals with artistic elements. The first script (and storyboard), "MPG" directly addresses the car buyer's concerns with the economic recession and the excessive cost of gasoline, stressing the Prius's high gas mileage. At the same time it appeals to self-preservation and environmental concerns—lessening smog forming, global warming emissions. The second example, "SOLAR," also deals with self-preservation, comfort, and environmental protection, keeping the driver and passengers cool by using solar power as an alternative to polluting fossil fuel. Both storyboards use music, visual color and movement, abstract images, and pace to effectively attract and hold attention and to create a bright, positive feeling that psychologically becomes associated with the product. The storyboards were designed to present the concepts and the guides for the spots and were used flexibly during the production and editing process. They appear to have enough material for full-minute ads, and selections and changes were made to arrive at 30-second spots.

AS PRODUCED SCRIPT

Job Number	Job Title	Length	ISCI Code	AE	CW	PM	PR	Date/Time	Rev. #
TC0001	PRIUS LAUNCH "MPG"	:30 :26/04 :30HD	TYCP9141 TYCP9142 TYCP9141H	BL		CL	JP	5/14 3pm	

SFX: Music throughout spot.

DISC: Vehicle shown with options. Dramatization

VO: It gives the world fewer smog-forming emissions.

DISC: Compared to the average new vehicle.

VO: It gives you a 50 mile per gallon rating.

DISC: EPA 50 combined (48 hwy/51 city) mpg estimates. Actual mileage will vary.

VO: The 3rd Generation Prius.

VO: It's harmony between man, nature and machine.

LOGO: Prius.

LOGO: Toyota
moving forward

SUPER: toyota.com

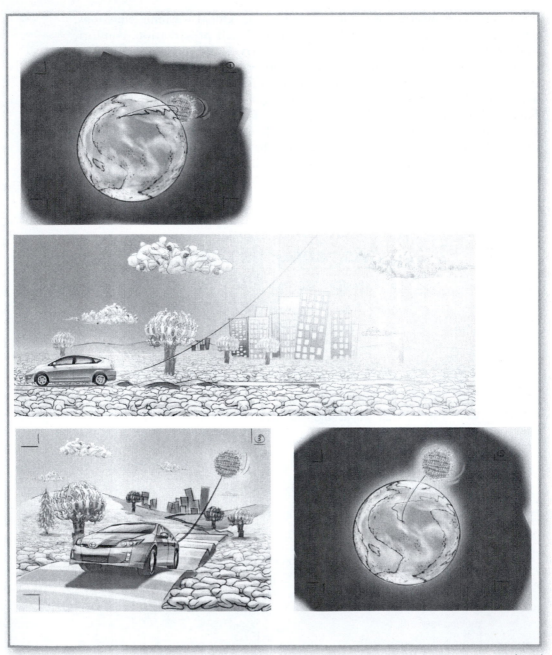

continued

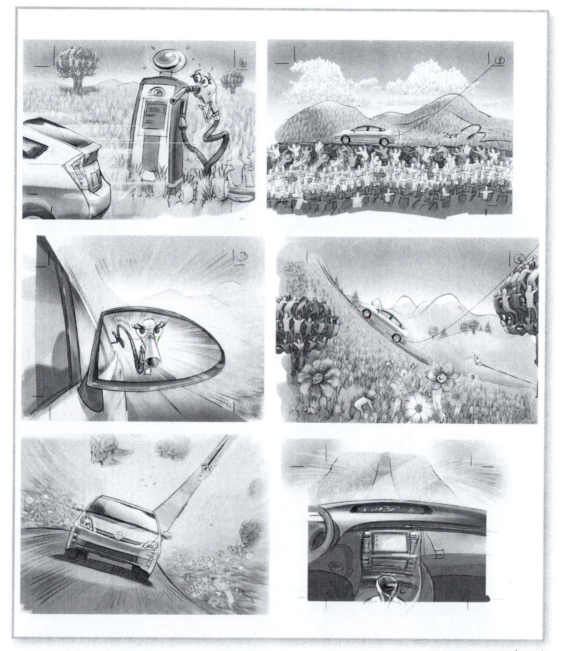

continued

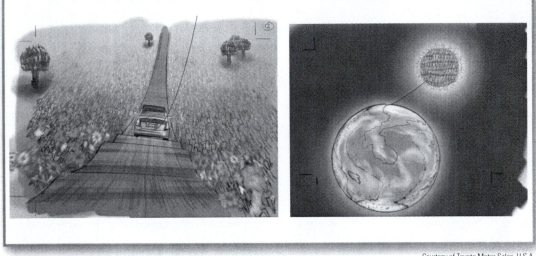

Courtesy of Toyota Motor Sales, U.S.A.

AS PRODUCED SCRIPT

Job Number	Job Title	Length	ISCI Code	AE	CW	PM	PR	Date/Time	Rev. #
TC0001	PRIUS LAUNCH "SOLAR"	:30 :26/04 :30HD	TYCP9102 TYCP9103 TYCP9102H	BL	EB	CL	JP	5/28 3pm	

SFX: Music throughout spot.

DISC: Options shown.

VO: What if we could use the sun, to help keep us cool?

VO: Solar Powered Ventilation to help cool you.

DISC: Solar Roof: When parked in direct sunlight, its fan draws air into cabin. *See Owner's Manual.*

VO: Available on the 3rd Generation Prius.

VO: It's harmony between man, nature and machine.

LOGO: Prius.

LOGO: Toyota
moving forward

SUPER: toyota.com

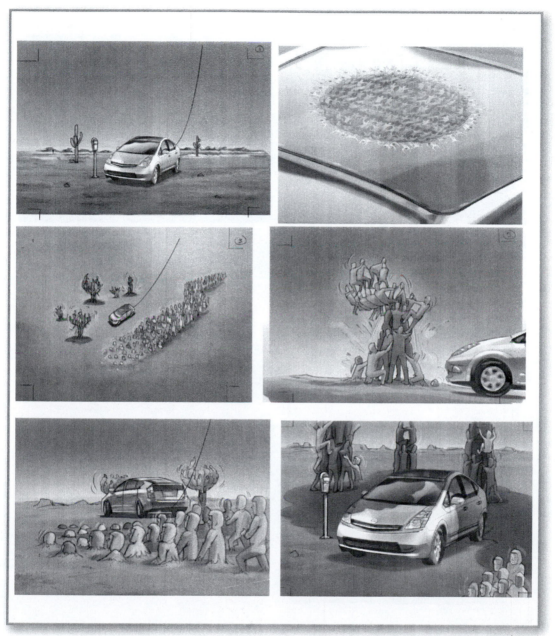

continued

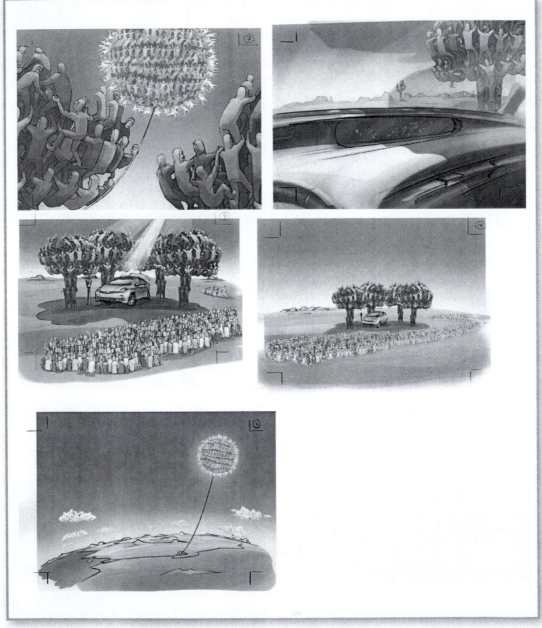

An example of a straight-sell spot for radio:

Sinbad Mediterranean Restaurant

(Greek Music, lapping water fx)

The Mediterranean: the cradle of civilization. It's seen the rise and fall of empires and cultures. It's home to the world's most classic flavors and foods, the favorites of kings, emperors, sultans, and regular folks for centuries.

Now Sinbad brings those classic flavors of the Mediterranean to Johnsville!

Try Lebanese and Greek dishes, like marinated beef wrapped in a Lebanese pita, hamburger skewers, kafta, chicken, and shish-kebabs, schawarma, falafels, meat pies . . . Sinbad has a full menu, with steak, salmon, barbequed chicken breast, and a wide assortment of salads, too.

Fresh, different, and affordable . . . take a trip with your taste buds to the Mediterranean, at Sinbad's in Johnsville: 7362 Independence Drive, Johnsville. Call 555-8312.

Courtesy of Mike Luoma, copywriter

The Testimonial

When the testimonial is given by a celebrity, the emotional appeals of prestige, power, and good taste are primary. What simpler way to reach the status of the celebrity, if only in one respect, than by using the same product or service he or she uses? For the celebrity testimonial to be effective, its content and style, including the setting, action, and type of dialogue, must be consistent with the public image of the personality. The audience must believe that the celebrity really believes what he or she is saying about the product or service.

Important ethical considerations arise for the writer when commercials are aimed at children. Promotion of a product, such as a toy or cereal, by someone admired by youngsters—for instance, the host of the television program on which the commercial is featured—may have an undue and unfair influence. Children are easily susceptible to such promotion.

The first testimonial that follows features the acclaimed actress Meryl Streep in a PSA that seeks support from the public in preventing war. It combines the testimonial with the straight sell.

MERYL STREEP SCRIPT—For TV—30 Seconds

My baby will never have polio, diphtheria, or measles.

We've cured them.

continued

But one of the last major childhood diseases remains. Nuclear War. Deadlier than all the rest combined.

Please join Millions of Moms in sharing information about the prevention of nuclear war.

Send your name and address to MOM, Post Office Box B, Arlington, Massachusetts 02174.

You can help cure a major childhood disease.

Courtesy of Women's Action for Nuclear Disarmament Education Fund

An alternative to the celebrity testimonial is the testimonial from the average man or woman—the worker, the homemaker, the person in the street with whom the viewer or listener at home can directly identify. Through such identification the viewer may more easily accept the existence of the common problem in a commonly experienced physical, economic, or vocational setting and, consequently, more readily accept the solution adopted by the person in the commercial—using the sponsor's product, service, or idea.

The following commercial follows this "everyperson" approach but does not directly sell the sponsor's product. This is an *institutional* announcement, which creates goodwill for the sponsor and in general keeps the company name in the public consciousness in a highly positive setting.

60 SECONDS, RADIO

MAN: I was a drunk driver. I'd give anything in the world if I hadn't been. It was after a party. I had more than a few beers and my friends wanted to take my car keys and drive me home. But I was an experienced drinker and driver. I had never had an accident when drinking. But this night I did. This kid—couldn't have been more than eleven or twelve—stepped off the curb into traffic. The alcohol had slowed down my reactions and I couldn't stop in time. He was dead by the time the ambulance got there. I'll live with that the rest of my life. And today you couldn't pay me to drive even if I've had only one or two beers and think I'm perfectly sober.

ANNOUNCER: This message is brought to you by the Continental Motors Corporation.

The following non-celebrity testimonial is a radio spot appealing from kid-to-kid to promote and sell a product—in this case a particular shop. Note how the emotional appeal, love of family, plays a key role.

Jamie's Creations

1 X :60

Kid read for Mother's Day;

Okay, listen up, I'm gonna tell you how *you* can help make your Dad look good this Mother's Day . . . Get your Dad to bring you to Jamie's Creations in Millerstown.

You'll be able to give your Mom something unique and original, a one of a kind creation made just by you for her for Mother's Day. . . . pretty cool, huh?

Jamie's has tons of polished stones, shells, ceramic and glass beads, and metal beads, cool weird stuff, too, like little animals and bizarre shapes. Jamie's has everything you need to make Mom a one of a kind necklace, bracelet, anklet . . . or whatever . . . including all the wire, clasps and strings.

At Jamie's Creations you can use your imagination to make something cool for your Mom! When you tell her your Dad brought you to Jamie's, you'll make him look good, too.

Mother's day is coming up faster than you think, so get in to Jamie's Creations today and let your imagination take over! That's Jamie's Creations, in the East End Mall in Millerstown, next to Barnes and Noble.

Courtesy of Mike Luoma, copywriter

Humor

Just as public attitudes toward humor change over the years, so do the humorous approaches in commercials. Humor is always an effective attention-getter, but successful humor must reflect current humorous trends. The gag or one-liner was once the staple of advertising humor but has now been largely replaced by satire and parody. Most humor is used in conjunction with dramatization, tied to a story line or to character relationships.

Some humor is bizarre, some gentle, some reaching toward slapstick. Here is an example of a type of humor you've seen frequently with various commercial products.

30 SECONDS	
VIDEO	AUDIO
Child sitting at kitchen table. Mother at stove cooking.	Child: What are you making for dinner, Mom?
Mother puts a plate of broccoli on the table along with an tub of "Mellowbutter."	Mother: Something good for you to eat.
	Child: Ugh. Broccoli. It tastes awful.

continued

MELLOWBUTTER TUB BECOMES ANIMATED, LIFTS ITS LID.

MELLOWBUTTER: Not with me it doesn't.

CHILD: Who said that?

MELLOWBUTTER: Me. Mellowbutter. Try me, you'll like me.

CHILD: Well, I don't know. Okay.

CHILD PUTS SOME MELLOWBUTTER ON THE BROCCOLI TASTES THE BROCCOLI.

CHILD: Hey, that's good.

MOTHER. CHILD, AND MELLOWBUTTER TUB BEAM.

MELLOWBUTTER: And next meal, you'll even like spinach with me on it.

CU SMILING MELLOWBUTTER TUB.

ANNOUNCER: Mellowbutter makes anything and everything taste better.

Music

The musical commercial has always been one of the most effective methods for predisposing an audience to remember a product. Some historians attribute the initial growth of Pepsi-Cola and its success in becoming a competitor to Coca-Cola to its 1930s radio musical jingle, "Pepsi-Cola hits the spot . . . nickel, nickel, nickel . . ." The success of that jingle propelled the growth of that commercial format. Have you ever listened to a song on radio or television, been caught up in its cadence, and then suddenly realized it was a commercial and not a pop tune?

Producer Susan Hamilton observed in *Broadcasting* magazine that

> music is still basically an emotional thing. And the reason we are producing commercials that sound like recordings is to try and grab the listeners. We're always told that when a commercial comes on the radio kids immediately turn the dial. But when you make your spots sound like songs, there's a chance you may be able to reach those kids before they reach those dials.

Not only have many original tunes for commercials become popular hits, but many ads have used on a continuing basis already-known pop songs, the latter, too, becoming associated in the public mind with the products. In fact, original and popular music both have been so effective in creating such associations that many people remember and identify the advertiser, such as Coca-Cola or McDonald's, first with the theme music and only secondarily with a particular sales message. An example of a TV music commercial is the following CLOROX® jingle, "Keep Touching."

VIDEO	AUDIO
OPEN ON CU OF ALARM CLOCK BEING PRESSED.	
CUT TO PARENTS WAKING UP.	
CUT TO LIGHT SWITCH BEING TURNED ON.	MUSIC
CUT TO FAUCET BEING TURNED ON.	Monday, feeling breezy
CUT TO SHOWER TURNING ON.	
CUT TO CHILD WAKING UP.	
CUT TO TOASTER BEING PUSHED DOWN.	Tuesday, feeling new
CUT TO REFRIGERATOR HANDLE BEING PULLED MULTIPLE TIMES.	
CUT TO COFFEE POT BEING PULLED FROM COFFEE MACHINE.	Wednesday, feeling easy
CUT TO CU OF CLOROX® WIPE BEING PULLED FROM CLOROX® WIPE CANISTER.	
CUT TO CU OF WOMAN'S HAND WIPING REFRIGERATOR HANDLE.	Life is sweet when I can touch you
CUT TO MAN'S HAND OPENING CAR DOOR.	
CUT TO CU OF FRONT DOOR BEING CLOSED.	
CUT TO CHILD GRABBING ENTRANCE RAIL OF SCHOOL BUS.	
CUT TO CHILD'S HAND SPINNING GLOBE.	
CUT TO CHILD'S HAND PLAYING WITH TOYS.	Thursday, I'm feeling merry
CUT TO WOMAN'S HAND WIPING A REMOTE CONTROL WITH CLOROX® WIPES.	
CUT TO MULTIPLE HANDS TOUCHING THE UP BUTTON OF AN ELEVATOR.	I cant help smiling when I feel what I do

continued

CUT TO A MAN'S HANDS TYPING ON A KEYBOARD.	VOICEOVER: We touch a lot of things throughout the day.
CUT TO A FRONT DOOR BEING OPENED.	
CUT TO A STOVE BEING TURNED ON.	So, it's nice that
CUT TO BATHTUB FAUCET BEING TURNED ON.	
CUT TO CLOROX® DISINFECTING SPRAY BEING SPRAYED ON THE EDGE OF A BATHTUB.	Clorox® Disinfecting Products
CUT TO A HAND TURNING ON A TELEVISION WITH A REMOTE CONTROL.	help kill the germs
CUT TO A LIGHT SWITCH BEING TURNED OFF.	that can live on surfaces for up to 48 hours.
CUT TO FOUR PRODUCT SHOTS APPEARING ON A SINGLE SCREEN: CLOROX® WIPES, CLOROX® BLEACH, CLOROX® TOILET BOWL CLEANER AND CLOROX® CLEAN-UP® SPRAY.	
HAND REACHES IN AND TOUCHES THE MIDDLE OF THE SCREEN.	
SUPER: CLOROX® LOGO. KEEP TOUCHING.	

CLOROX is a registered trademark of The Clorox Company and is used with permission. © 2015 The Clorox Company, Inc. Reprinted with permission.

The following radio spot, delivered like rap, conveys the advertising message with or without actual music:

For under ten k
You can get a Hyundai
Today . . . any day!
Hyundai's under ten k!

continued

For under ten k
You can get a Hyundai
Today . . . any day!
Hyundai's under ten k!

When you need to buy a car,
Go to where they've raised the bar!

At Robinson's Hyundai
Your car's under ten k!
Pay less, every day!
For your new Hyundai!

Wasting cash on something used?
Don't shell out for what's abused!
Tires, engine, brakes, soon go—
Costing you a bunch of dough!

You can buy a new car!
Warranted to go far . . .

No worries plus warranty
For a hundred K miles . . .

A guaranteed hundred-grand
Road's worth of smiles.

At Robinson's Hyundai
Your car's under ten k!

Courtesy of Mike Luoma, copywriter

The approaches used in music videos have been adapted to commercials aimed at young audiences. MTV scenic, dance, prop, electronic, and sound techniques are staples of many television ads. *Broadcasting & Cable* magazine described these spots as "surrealistic and sex-oriented and distinguished by quick cuts, bands of light, bright colors, loud rock music, optical illusion, and a minimal amount of dialogue." The Levi's commercial on the next page is not the storyboard, but a series of photos of the completed spot. Note the use of angles, close-ups, and quick cuts, all in the rhythm of the contemporary music sound. The multi-faceted technological potentials of the computer have made many Internet ads models of multi-senses razzle-dazzle.

LEVI'S COMMERCIAL—30 SECONDS

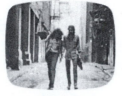

SINGERS:
*Every late night morning I
put on my blues*

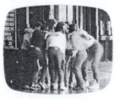

*Ooo bop bop
uh huh . ooo bop.*

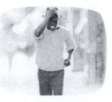

*Levi's button fly
501 blues.*

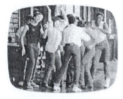

Ooo bop bop oo bop.

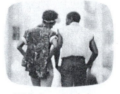

*Well, they shrink down
to fit you and only you.
They . . .*

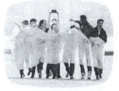

*button fly. Don't it make
you wanna*

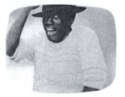

*ooo bop bop ooo bop.
That's the truth.
Ooo bop bop ooo bop.*

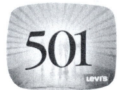

*Levi's 501 Blues.
Ooo bop bop ooo bop.*

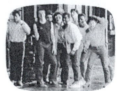

Ooo bop bop.

Courtesy of Levi Strauss & Co.

The Dramatization

The dramatization is, in effect, a short play, presented in 30 or 60 seconds. Most commercial dramatizations follow the standard play form (see Chapter 10) that itself reflects the basic steps of persuasion—exposition, conflict, rising action, climax, and, sometimes, resolution. In other words, the dramatization is a sequence that gets the audience's attention and interest, creates suspense, and solves the problem the character or characters are facing. Some dramatic spots put the characters in a specific setting (as in the Top-Round Restaurant radio ad that follows) and some are solely "dialogue" spots at no particular site.

Top-Round Restaurant

:60

One-sided cell phone conversation with GPS locator accompaniment.

(FX:	car interior driving sound)
VX:	. . . it's hands free, so I'm good. But did you say Alligator Bites?
GPS:	Right turn. Exit Interstate 80 here, at exit 23.
VX:	I'm almost there. Top-Round Restaurant in Winthrop, right? (Pause) Top-Round! Am I breaking up? I said Top-Round! I'm almost there . . .
GPS:	Right turn.
VX:	Yeah, I can't believe I haven't been to Top-Round yet, either. I keep meaning to. The Zeke Martin Quartet plays live there every weekend. I keep meaning to . . . (pause). Yeah, I know.
GPS:	Right turn.
VX:	The place with the big "Surf and Turf" sign, right? Oh, I see the sign: Top-Round! RightnexttotheHolidayInnExpressthere.What'sthat?(pause)You'reoutonTop-Round'snew deck?Sweet!(fx:shutoffcarandopendoor).I'monmywayin!NowIjustgottadecidebetween the prime rib or the barbequed ribs or seafood . . . (fades)
Announcer:	Come to the Top-Round Restaurant for lunch or dinner or just to kick back on their brand new deck! And on weekends, the ZMQ quartet! Top-Round, exit 23 in Winthrop.

Courtesy of Mike Luoma, copywriter

Format Combinations

Commercials and announcements usually combine more than one format, although one may predominate. An award-winning example of such a commercial, IBM "Skates," includes all the basic formats presented here. "Skates" is clearly a dramatization in which the principal character solves a problem. Music is used throughout much of the first part of the ad. The narration describing what the product can do employs straight sell. Humor, found in the Charlie Chaplin "Tramp" character's slapstick actions, prevails throughout. Can you determine the testimonial aspect of the spot? Although no live personality endorses the product, the ad ties the likeness of the great Charlie Chaplin to the product, thus supplying the testimonial "ethical person" aspect.

continued

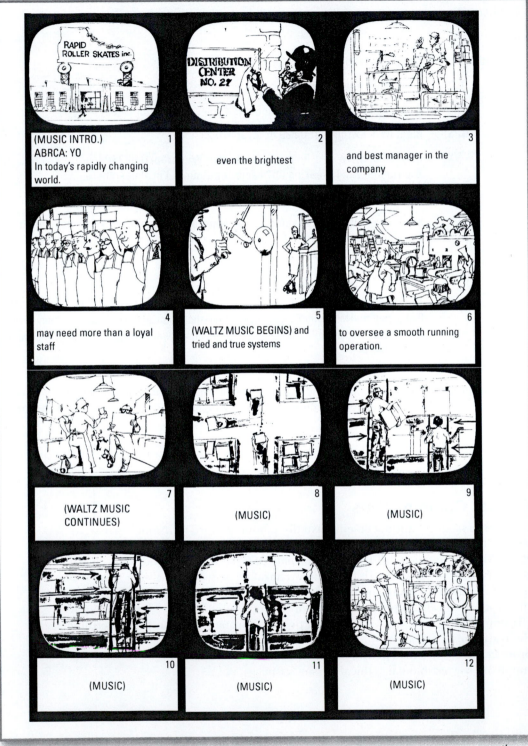

1. (MUSIC INTRO.) ABRCA: YO In today's rapidly changing world.
2. even the brightest
3. and best manager in the company
4. may need more than a loyal staff
5. (WALTZ MUSIC BEGINS) and tried and true systems
6. to oversee a smooth running operation.
7. (WALTZ MUSIC CONTINUES)
8. (MUSIC)
9. (MUSIC)
10. (MUSIC)
11. (MUSIC)
12. (MUSIC)

continued

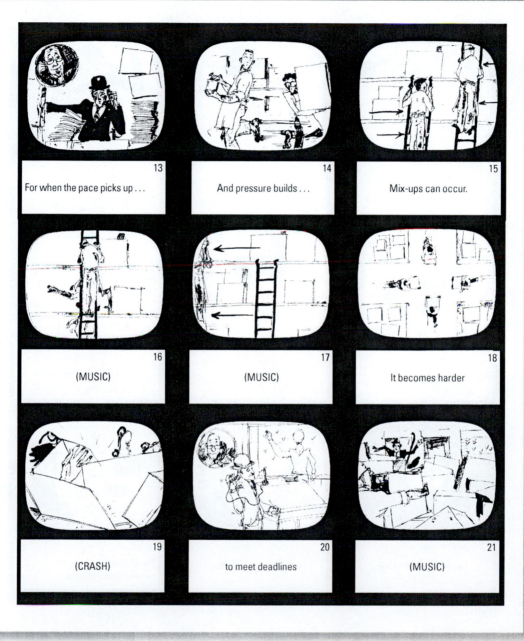

13 — For when the pace picks up . . .

14 — And pressure builds . . .

15 — Mix-ups can occur.

16 — (MUSIC)

17 — (MUSIC)

18 — It becomes harder

19 — (CRASH)

20 — to meet deadlines

21 — (MUSIC)

continued

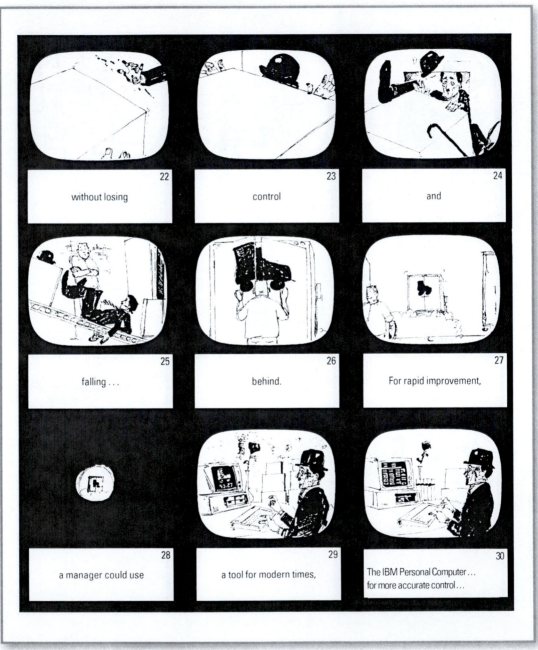

continued

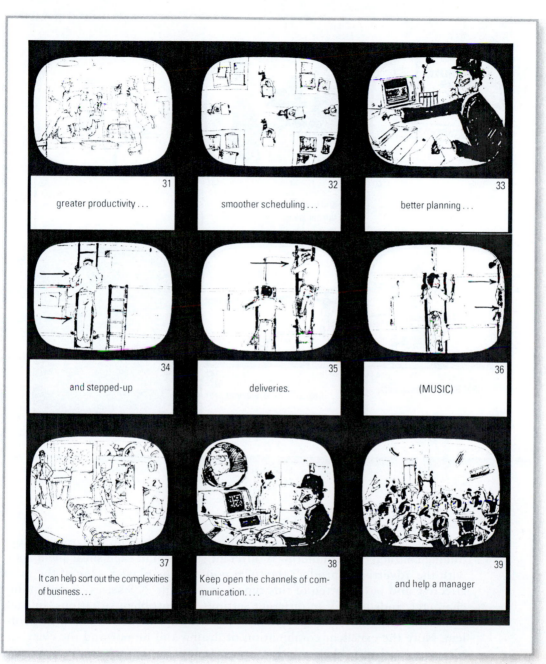

31 greater productivity . . .

32 smoother scheduling . . .

33 better planning . . .

34 and stepped-up

35 deliveries.

36 (MUSIC)

37 It can help sort out the complexities of business . . .

38 Keep open the channels of communication. . . .

39 and help a manager

continued

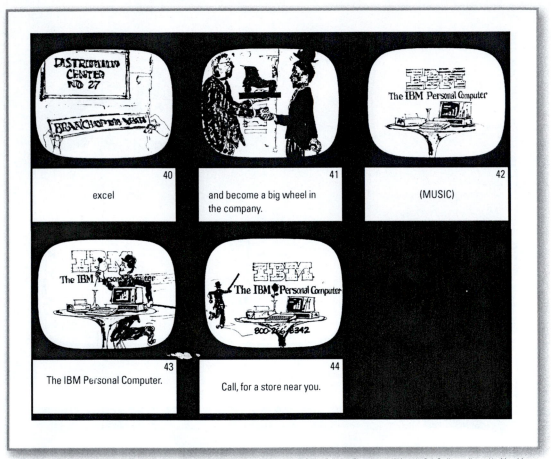

Prepared by Lord, Geller, Federico, Einstein, Inc. Written by Bob Sarlin, art directed by Mary Morant, creative director Thomas Mabley. Courtesy of IBM.

Some commercials are, in effect, mini-drama series, with one or more continuing characters encountering a different situation in each subsequent spot, with the advertiser's product the focal point of the playlet. One of the most effective and best-written of this type was a Sprint PCS series. A continuing character finds himself in different settings and problem situations. In each commercial, he shows the people involved how Sprint PCS solves their problem. Note the excellent combination of drama and humor and the clear application of the problem-solution organizational approach in the following example from this commercial series. The script is followed by photos of the production sequence.

SPRINT: "LEMONS/REV1/MASTER BRAND"

OPEN ON FIVE WOMEN (MID-30s) OUTSIDE ON THE CABIN LAWN PLAYING CARDS, READING MAGAZINES, BRIAN IS WITH THEM. ONE OF THE WOMEN EXPLAINS THE PROBLEM:

WOMAN 1: So I call her and I say, "Bring fresh lemons" . . . and she brings . . .

WE HEAR SOMEONE SAY "COME ON, LET ME IN" FROM A CANOE ON THE LAKE—THAT'S ALL BRIAN NEEDED TO HEAR. HE COCKS HIS HEAD AND RICHARD SIMMONS SAYS:

SIMMONS: I'll be so quiet . . .

BRIAN: Richard Simmons.

WOMAN 2: Give it a rest . . .

NOW WE SEE RICHARD ON A CANOE IN THE LAKE, SINGING A SONG AND DANCING. HE SINGS THROUGHOUT THE COMMERCIAL.

THE WOMAN CAN'T TAKE IT. SHE STANDS UP.

WOMAN 3: You know what . . .

WOMAN 3 STANDS UP, BUT BRIAN GETS BETWEEN HER AND THE LAKE.

BRIAN: It's not his fault. It's the cellular static. Here, Sprint built the largest all-digital, all-PCS nationwide network from the ground up, so calls are clear.

LEGAL: Nationwide network reaches more than 230 million people.

BRIAN HANDS HER A PCS PHONE, AND SHE RELAXES; ALL THE WOMEN THANK BRIAN.

WOMAN 3: Thanks.

WOMAN 2: What about him?

BRIAN: Maybe some people shouldn't be heard.

RICHARD: Hey, I heard that . . .

TITLE CARD: THE PCS FREE & CLEAR PLAN[SM]
4000 MINUTES FOR $39.99
NATIONWIDE LONG DISTANCE INCLUDED

WWW.SPRINTPCS.COM 1 800 480 4PCS

LEGAL: 350 ANYTIME MINUTES + 3,650 NIGHT & WEEKEND MINUTES. REQUIRES 1-YEAR TERM AGREEMENT & CREDIT APPROVAL. ACTIVATION & TERMINATION FEES APPLY.

SUPER: SPRINT PIN DROP.

continued

TITLE CARD:	SPRINT DIAMOND LOGO
	4000 MINUTES FOR $39.99
	NATIONWIDE LONG DISTANCE INCLUDED
	WWW.SPRINTPCS.COM 1 800 480 4PCS
LEGAL:	350 ANYTIME MINUTES + 3,650 NIGHT & WEEKEND MINUTES.
	REQUIRES 1-YEAR TERM AGREEMENT & CREDIT APPROVAL.
	ACTIVATION & TERMINATON FEES APPLY.
VO TAG:	4,000 minutes for $39.99 from Sprint.

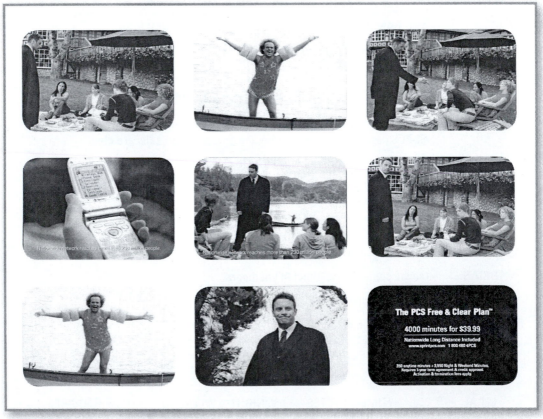

Courtesy of Publicis and Hal Riney, San Francisco

PROMOS

There are non-profit organization promos and profit-oriented company promos. The latter appear not to be commercials and do not directly advertise a product or service, but try to establish goodwill attitudes toward the company. You frequently see such presentations for public broadcasting underwriters and corporate contributors. Their purpose is to make you think of that entity when you need to purchase a particular product or service offered by that entity. The former include the promos you see on public broadcasting stations promoting the station and its programs, frequently during fundraising periods. Somewhere in-between are the spots on commercial stations promoting their upcoming programs and services. If you find yourself working for a station, you may find yourself involved in the writing and production of station promos.

Below are five examples of a public broadcasting station's promos, prepared and aired by WGCU Public Media at Florida Gulf Coast University in southwest Florida. The promos represent good, careful writing regarding key aspects of public broadcasting: promoting a show related to a principal mission of public broadcasting, educating children; developing audience relationships by bringing them to the station's studio for a live broadcast of a popular program; two spots promoting programs that deal with critical issues in the station's coverage area; and a statement by WGCU's Manager, Rick Johnson, regarding the station's services to its community and its need for continued funding in the State's budget. Note that conciseness and clarity are keys to the promos. Note, too, the references to other aspects of the organization's work. Being positive and maintaining goodwill is important. In the last promo, for example, Manager Rick Johnson's statement on financial support does not mention the State's officials apparent reluctance to fund public broadcasting even as the audience understands the need to convince the Governor to provide such support.

WGCU Public Media

Proof of performance

TV script

:60

Educate, entertain, engage

That's the foundation of WGCU's mission.

And the reason we are proud of our

Curious Kids project and our partnership

With the Golisano Children's Museum of Naples.

Our WGCU Curious Kids activity center at C'mon

continued

Is a fun place for young people to learn and grow.

Our WGCU presents day at C'mon give children of

All ages a chance to meet their favorite PBS stars

While learning and doing.

Educating children of all ages . . . what better way to

Build a stronger community.

WGCU is proud to be a part of Southwest Florida's future.

:60

Educating, Entertaining and Engaging

That's the heart of WGCU Public Media's mission.

Our Curious Kids project takes us into the community and

Brings the community to WGCU.

With our Curious Kids Family workshops, WGCU works with

Elementary schools in Lee, Collier and Charlotte counties

To bring learning workshops to moms and dads.

Our curious Kids TV show produced by kids and for kids takes

Local kids to amazing places throughout Southwest Florida and

Teaches kids about the world around them.

Our Curious Kids activity center at the Golisano Children's Museum of

Naples Is a fun place for young people to learn and grow.

Educating children of all ages . . . what better way to

Build a stronger community.

WGCU is proud to be a part of Southwest Florida's future.

:30

Invite to WHYS studio show

Ros Atkins

This is Ros Atkins from the BBC's World Have Your Say inviting our listeners in Southwest Florida to attend our live studio show. We will be at WGCU Public Media on Wednesday, January 13 for a studio show and we want you to be in the audience. You are invited to be a part of our global discussion . . . see how World Have Your Say is produced . . . and share your insights with the world. To reserve a seat, go to wgculive@gmail.com or call 239.590.2507. I look forward to meeting you on January 13 when World Have Your Say comes to Southwest Florida.

WGCU Your Voice 104: Addicted
:26 PROMO

VIDEO	AUDIO
	(upbeat music)
GREEN SCREEN	I'm Rachelle Grossman inviting you to join us as we look inside the realities of addiction. From alcohol to illegal drugs to the fast-growing problem of pain pill addictions, WGCU will discuss the realities and hope of Addicted!
	Join us Thursday night at 8 o'clock on WGCU TV. As experts and recovering addicts talk about addiction and take your calls.
	IT'S YOUR VOICE!
	(END FOR TIME)
	TAG
	THIS THURSDAY NIGHT AT 8 O'CLOCK ON WGCU-TV AND RADIO.
	AND
	IT'S YOUR VOICE . . . TONIGHT AT 8 ON WGCU-TV AND RADIO.

Lucia Promo

Florida is a major destination state for human trafficking—a form of slavery in which mostly young women are lured across borders under false promises.

Now there's an effort to stop it at its roots, by the women themselves to their mothers and their little sisters.

Letter Interpreter: "This is how I arrived in this country. I survive, but my soul is in pieces. Please, Mama, do not ever let my little sisters make that trip."

Lucia's Letter. January 12 at noon and again at 8 P.M. On WGCU—NPR for Southwest Florida.

BILLBOARD

Doug *"One of the things that I felt when I listened to her letter was reminding me what my mission is in terms of prosecuting slavery cases because what happened to her should not happen to any human being."*

Genelle *"A lot of these women came up when they were under 15-years-old, they were treated to terrible abuse, they were raped repeatedly. We did a composite letter describing the experiences leaving their family in Guatemala, coming up through Mexico with the coyote, what happens them when they arrive in Florida. The women who helped prepare the CD about human trafficking were women who have experienced human trafficking here in Southwest Florida."*

continued

Letter interpreter *". . . . and told her not to make noise and to leave slowly. She went with him but she never returned to be with us in the room . . . "*

Amy *"Marta, do you know if you would do it again if you were a 17-year-old in Guatemala?"*

Marta *"NO. Definitely no. I prefer to do housekeeping there all my life but not to come here."*

Amy *"Lucia's Letter to her mother . . . . a plea to stop human trafficking . . . . Next."*

Rick Johnson

General Manager

WGCU Public Media

Hello, I'm Rick Johnson.

As the Florida Governor and Legislature work to finalize our state's budget, I want to let you know the important role WGCU Public Media plays in providing you with news and information about Florida. WGCU TV is part of the statewide delivery system for the Florida Channel providing coverage of the Legislature and the Supreme Court. WGCU Radio is part of the state network of public radio stations bringing you official evacuation route information during emergencies.

WGCU TV is the preschool classroom for Southwest Florida's children with over 60 hours a week of standards-based programs. We also work with dozens of schools each year to provide workshops, presentations, and tours.

Governor Rick Scott

State of Florida

(850) 488-7146

(850) 487-0801 (fax)

Email:

http://www.flgov.com
/contact-gov-scott
/email-the-governor/

Our funding from the state is significantly important. (It allows us to provide these services and bring you all of the great PBS and NPR programs who rely on as well as meaningful locally produced programs.)

More information is available at wgcu dot org. You may contact the Governor's office at the numbers listed on the screen to let him know about the role WGCU plays in the quality of life in Southwest Florida.

The six preceding scripts are courtesy of WGCU Public Media, Fort Myers-Naples, Florida

THE POLITICAL SPOT

In the past few decades the media, especially television, have become determining factors in America's elections. With few exceptions, the candidates in primaries and in general elections finish in the order of how much money they have spent on television advertising. Political spots—there is a reluctance to call them commercials, but that's what they really are on behalf of a given candidate—follow the same formats as commercials.

Many campaign spots feature the accomplishments of a given candidate, stressing how his or her previous contributions will be translated into even great service to the specific constituency. Credentials are lauded in a highly positive way. Some spots feature the candidate's views on a particular hot issue, stressing how those views or plans will translate into action desired by the voting majority. Demographics and the political product are just as important as in the commercial that sells a product or service—and maybe even more so. And, like other commercials, political spots stress emotional as well as ethical appeals. This was established in 1952 when Dwight D. Eisenhower was running for president on the Republican tickets against Democrat Aldai E. Stevenson. Early in the campaign the candidates aired spots and longer time periods presenting the candidates' views on issues. When the Republican party booked a full hour for its candidate, it was expected that it would deal with the issues facing the country. It turned out to be a biography of Eisenhower's life, showing highly positive pictures and events from his boyhood to his service as a General and as a university president. The emotional and ethical appeals were overwhelmingly successful in persuading the audience—the voters. Since then personality, as opposed to issues, have constituted the backbone of political commercials.

Some of the most effective political spots have been in the drama format. In addition, recent political media campaigns have featured attack ads. That is, spots attempting to portray negatively the opposing candidate or candidates. Many of these spots concentrate on some issue or attribute taken out of context. Others specify the lack of certain qualifications of the candidate. Some feature a moral failing or suspicious behavior or even a scandal. Some exaggerate a failed policy or official action. Some are untrue accusations. Some are true accusations. Examples of the drama format attack spots are the following, part of a series written independently for the 2012 presidential campaign, but never aired.

TV spot :60
A diner in Anytown, USA. (Number 1)
(Flo is a waitress behind the counter. Joe is sitting at the counter, a customer with a donut and cup of coffee.)

FLO: Well, Joe, which way you leaning in this election?

JOE: I'll tell you, Flo, I'm not stuck on either guy yet. But I kind of like Romney, even though he seems to say one thing one day and the opposite the next.

FLO: Some politicians do that.

continued

Joe: He does seem like a nice guy, though.

Flo: Really? I'm not sure about that.

Joe: Whaddya mean?

Flo: When he was in school he terrorized a gay classmate. When he was with Bain Capital he put thousands of Americans into foreclosure and poverty by sending thousands of jobs overseas in order to make himself more millions. And putting his dog on his car roof for hundreds of miles until that poor dog almost died.

Joe: Not such a nice guy, I guess. I don't know about voting for the other guy, but I sure don't feel like voting for Romney.

TV spot :60

A diner in Anytown, USA (Number 4)

(Flo, a waitress, is behind the counter. Joe, a customer, is seated with a donut and cup of coffee.)

Flo: What's the latest on the political front, Joe?

Joe: I've been giving more serious thought about who I'm going to vote for.

Flo: Shouldn't we all?

Joe: Too many lying politicians these days. Flo. Hard to believe any of them.

Flo: You don't mean Romney?

Joe: You know that what's bothering me, don't you? He says one thing one day, the opposite the next, one thing to one group and a different thing to another.

Flo: Are you saying he has no principles? Can't be trusted?

Joe: I hate to think so.

Flo: But . . .?

Joe: Well, he says he's against abortion when talking to conservatives, but he supported abortion when he ran for governor and senator in Massachusetts. He now says he's against gay marriage, but only a few years ago was for it when campaigning to liberal voters. And he's been attacking Obamacare, which is almost identical to the Romneycare that he enacted when he was governor to Massachusetts. It's like on that old television show, "will the real Mitt Romney please stand." It really worries me about voting for him.

With the proliferation of increasingly technologically sophisticated commercials, getting audience attention has become paramount. Remarkable technical effects of sound, color, and motion grab our eyes and ears to hold us in front of the screen. Advertising writers and producers vie with each other to prevent the audience from dashing off to the refrigerator or bathroom during the frequent breaks in content in most programs. Get attention and hold it! Sometimes that's all the spot seems to do, not going through the traditional steps of persuasion. Thirty seconds of unending movement, sound, and light effects with the name of the product or service somehow emerging before the audience gets away and the commercial ends. But ask yourself this question: Are you selling the commercial or selling the product? Be careful that your very creative and entertaining spot doesn't leave the audience saying, "I liked that . . . what was it they were advertising?"

INTERNET CONSIDERATIONS

Early in this chapter it was noted that there are differences between writing commercials for the Internet and for television or radio. While the basic purposes, formats, and appeals are the same, the special characteristics of the Internet require special approaches and adaptations. Amy Nicholson, director and creative director of commercial spots for television and the Internet, discusses the differences:

> The world of online advertising is a fairly recent phenomenon. It is only in the last couple of years that broadband access has reached the majority of homes, allowing for commercials and mini-movies of the caliber of more traditional TV spots. There are two major differences in the concept and production of online vs. traditional commercials. For the purpose of this discussion, I am limiting the *type* of online advertising to the moving image. Banner and pop up advertising on the web has come a long way, but there is no parallel in traditional media, and most Internet surfers find them a nuisance.
>
> The first difference that should be kept in mind when concepting advertising for the web is the way in which people receive the message. As opposed to the passive activity of watching TV, the online world is interactive. That doesn't mean that the ad has to get you to do something, although most online "commercials" are designed to drive viewers to a micro site for a certain company where they will happily interact with that company's product for hours and hours. What I find most intriguing is the idea that if the commercial or short film is great and people enjoy it, they will pass it around. This has been come to be known as the YouTube effect. Many advertisers have asked their agencies to make them a "viral video." The funny thing is, a video can't be made to be viral, it just becomes viral from being good. There have been attempts to create things that are so outrageous that people just *have* to pass them on, but most advertisers are not brave enough to risk their reputations for shock value, and it's cheap trick. So the idea that the piece of communication can be made more or less successful by the "voting" of the audience should be a big consideration. Basically that means that your idea has to be great. It has to engage people actually more than traditional

spots, and it has to do it in the clutter of the Internet and on a potentially small screen with "so-so" video quality.

That brings me to production issues. These issues are slowly going away as broadband becomes ubiquitous and more advertising dollars are funneled into online advertising. But for traditional advertisers, online is usually *in addition* to traditional media. So the budgets are usually smaller to begin with. Of course there are advertisers who have embraced new media and have funded some spectacular concepts. Remember BMW films? They were a very progressive set of short films featuring huge stars that appeared only on the Internet (and back when no one was putting films on the net!) The smartest thing about them is that they featured storylines and driving situations that would have probably been banned from traditional TV spots. It was a brilliant way to showcase their cars; it also didn't hurt that they did it before anyone else.

But now that there is so much clutter on the web and the days of pretending that "someone just made this and threw it up on YouTube" have come and gone, I see a bright future for films and spots that are elegant solutions to a client's brief that are based on great conceptual thinking and use limited (or not) resources to their advantage. What I mean is that if you have a certain budget and it happens to be low, you'll have to come up with a solution where the finances of the ad are transparent. There are plenty of examples in traditional media where the creatives came up with amazing concepts even without a lot of money.

I would also study classic advertising and films for their production quality. As convergence happens—and I think it will—computers will function more and more like TV's and visa versa, and there's no hiding bad art direction or poor direction. Eventually I think that the standards of traditional advertising will come to life on the web. They have already, but not quite in critical mass. And pretending that some guy shot the ad in his basement will no longer be a valid concept. People will expect not only a great idea, but also beautiful production value. That brings us back to the beginning: as sites like Hulu bring more TV-like viewing to the Internet, the skills to create an engaging piece of communication will be the same no matter where they end up. But on the Internet, you have no time limits, and the ability to measure exactly how popular that communication is. You just have to figure out a way to do it with a smaller budget.

New forms of advertising may eventually eclipse the moving image as a way to sell people things, but I'm a big believer in the beauty of a great piece of film. Storytelling will never go away and great storytelling is an art form—even when you're trying to get people to buy toothpaste.

Integrated copywriter* Ben Hughes, whose work includes commercials specifically designed for the Internet, offers the following advice for writing online spots:

The most important thing to remember about writing for the web is the context your spot will live in. The vast majority of web media is opt-in, as opposed to opt-out. That means you have to create content that people will actively want

*An "integrated copywriter" combines a number of advertising approaches and processes to create commercials that reflect the epitome and principle attributes of the product or service she or he is promoting.

to see, so much that they'll choose watching it over anything else they could be doing at that moment. This is daunting, but it's also the future—DVRs and ad-skipping technology are quickly doing the same thing to TV. The days when you could count on consumers' rapt, open-mouthed attention are over.

Think of it another way: you are competing against the sum total of the Internet, from cute kitten pix to Hulu. This is not ads vs. ads, it's ads vs. everything. Don't assume the bar is lower because it's not a five million dollar Super Bowl spot. The web frees you, for the most part, from the time constraints of TV. Suddenly, you can create a spot that runs ninety-two seconds, or thirteen or eight and a half minutes. Just remember the golden rule: it has to be consistently engaging and interesting for those eight and a half minutes. The moment it isn't, people will wander off and do something else. There's a reason most successful web spots hew pretty closely to the standard thirty to sixty second formats: because thirty to sixty seconds is a reasonable amount of time to be entertaining without wearing out your welcome.

Avoid long intros or complicated set-ups. People will get bored and move on. This is not the time for long, *Star Wars*-esque preludes.

Production values matter. Just because people will watch poorly shot footage of some poor sucker getting kicked in the jewels does not mean they will watch your poorly short ad. Unless you have a conceptual reason for trying to replicate the shaky, "shot on my cell phone" look (and it better be a great reason, because that look has been done to death), don't do it. There are plenty of simple ways to make a web spot look professional without spending a ton of money. Tripods are a good start.

Web spots are not automatically viral. Viralness is something you earn, not something you declare. And the easiest way to make something go viral is to create something so good it has to be passed on.

An example of the kind of work Nicholson and Hughes do is the following Nokia "GPS" online commercial, "1812 Reenactment." When the script was developed, it did not yet have performers and the R/GA production agency group director, Dave Edwards, used his name in the script as the reenactment group's leader. Performers in the commercial were a real War of 1812 reenactment group from Massachusetts, "The 1812 Marine & Navy Guard," and the leader of the group, historian Mark Hilliard, used his own name in place of that of Edwards when the script was filmed. The reenactment group altered their otherwise always accurate historical costumes for the satirical spot. As occasionally happens, this spot did not have a prepared storyboard. Following the script on the next page, therefore, are "screen grabs" or stills from the finished spot to give you an idea of what it looked like.

Nokia N series

Site Videos "GPS"

Main Theme: GPS

Point of differentiation: Always ready GPS, Maps, geo-tagging

Extras: Phone, photos

Open on a thirtysomething guy. He's dressed in an authentic uniform from the war of 1812. As he talks, we cut to shots of his War of 1812 reenactment society.

DAVE: Uh, hello. My name is Dave Edwards and I hold the rank of Brigadier General in the South Norwalk War of 1812 Reenactment Society.

Cut to DAVE walking across a field looking at his N95.

DAVE: Our society prides itself on authenticity. Boots, hats, clothing . . . we're authentic right down to the buttons. We even eat what they ate.

The small army of about 6 guys continue through the field. Dave is looking at his N95 as they walk. Some are trying to chew on some very tough beef jerky.

DAVE: To find the exact location of the pivotal battles, we use the GPS function on my N95.

Cut to a group of people in historical costume running down a hill.

DAVE: When we go into a new area, I can easily download new maps.

Cut to a shot of the N95 in Dave's hand as a map is downloading.

DAVE: I can even go step further and create a rich map with photos, coordinates, battle plans and troop movement all right from the phone.

Dave takes a picture of his group with the N95 and uploads it.

DAVE: So now, the next generations can literally follow in our footsteps. All this has made the N95 the only post-1812 technology allowed at our little outings.

Dave and his group standing outside a suburban Laundromat. They look a little puzzled.

FRIEND: This is where they surrendered?

DAVE: Actually it's where the soap machine is . . . but . . . Ok guys, let's set up.

They put down their packs and Dave sets the N95 on top of the pack. The camera moves in for a nice natural shot of the phone.

TITLE: THE NOKIA N95. OPEN TO ANYTHING

DAVE: Charge! Wait hold on . . .

Dave answers the N95

DAVE: Hello. Hi sweetie. Yes, I should be home by 5 . . .

Courtesy of R/GA

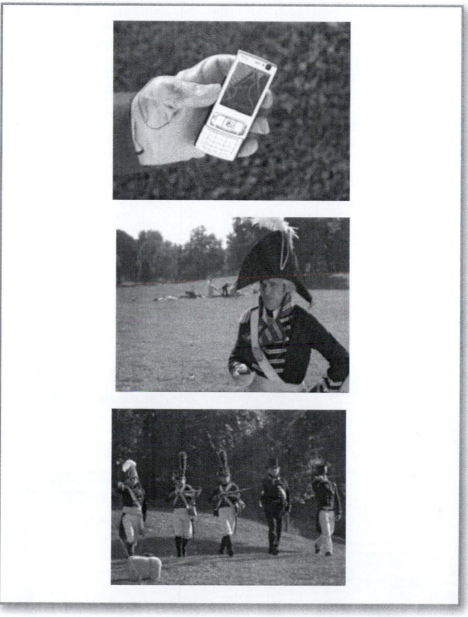

The reenacters are Mark Hilliard, Matthew Brenckle, Jeff Tew, Dana Bogdansky, Zach Woods.

When preparing commercial or promotional material for the Internet, it is very important to remember the links. The initial page must be attractive and, as in any announcement, get and hold the attention of the viewer. As noted by Professor Maurice Methot in Chapter 3, the design must be attractive, with appropriate size and type fonts and colors. Visual moving images and music or other sounds can enhance the home page. But to get the viewer to go further and learn more about the product or service and be convinced to patronize it, the viewer must be enticed to click on one or more links. The links should carry the viewer through the organizational elements of persuasion and end in convincing the viewer to take some kind of action: Buying a product online, supporting a cause, logging onto additional web sites, or, as in the following WBUR example, listening to or viewing another medium.

Matt Ostrower, former web promotions manager for WBUR-FM, Boston University's NPR (National Public Radio) station, stated his approach to WBUR. org online promotions:

> When we are promoting our content, on-air the scripts always end with a specific call-to action. There needs to be a compelling statement that will convince listeners to visit the Web site to learn more. The tone of the writing changes once they reach the site as our content strives to be in-depth and give a unique perspective on a particular topic. The text often includes hyperlinks to supplementary visual components such as photos, videos, and audio. In addition to supporting the radio broadcast, we view the Web as a vehicle that provides the user with an enhanced interactive experience that is only available online.

Here is a WBUR-FM Internet home page. Note the major links at the top: The Forums, About the Show, Archives, Public Radio Store, and Join the Connection. The search option, too, entices the viewer into further exploration into WBUR. The viewer can also find out information about a favorite

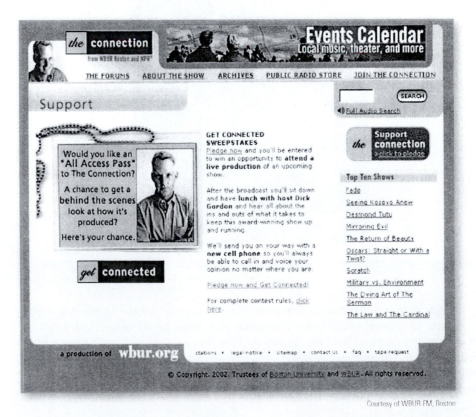

Courtesy of WBUR-FM, Boston

program—note "Top Ten Shows" links at the right. Special emphasis is given to WBUR's premier interview show, "The Connection."

The Internet permits direct participation of the audience in the advertising process. A Pepsi interactive web site during a World Cup soccer tournament that took place in Germany featured a German oom-pah band playing a song while a Pepsi German soccer team squared off against a team of lederhosen-clad dancing players. Those who log on to this site are able to submit their own videos for viewing, set to the oom-pah music. On a web site promoting the Volkswagen Jetta, users can access further information in a "Jetta Report" link and are also encouraged to answer questions for a survey about Volkswagen users.

In 2013 new approaches to Internet offerings expanded the potential writing field in that medium. For years original Internet fare—that is, not from non-Internet media sources such as cable or TV or Netflix—was basically single shot or single camera presentations, including talking heads. The *New York Times* reported a major change: major media companies were presenting "ambitious slates of original programming to advertisers for the first time" and "companies that were already producing web content, like Yahoo and Hulu, also announced greatly expanded offerings." In addition to writing dramas and reality shows for television and cable stations and networks, writers will be originating such shows for the Internet. For example, Hulu will offer a comedic docu-series on sports mascots and Yahoo will present "Your Virginity With John Stamos," with Stamos interviewing celebrities about their first sexual experiences. As the *New York Times* also noted, "advertisers are . . . shifting dollars from traditional display advertising to sites like Facebook that can deliver huge audiences."

Article writing has also increased on the Internet as more and more companies are establishing their own web sites. The writer must keep in mind the purpose of the web site and its owner, including the audience it wishes to reach. The content and language of the writing must be such that it is easy access through search engines. Put yourself in the place of user; what key words would you use to find the particular subject? Make sure you use those key words prominently in what you write. In order to make your writing interesting to the user, who obviously has a special interest in the subject, do sufficient research so that your material comes across as expert information, but in manner that is neither obtuse nor preachy. In other words, don't be boring.

SOCIAL MEDIA

The proliferation in number and use of social networking sites on the Internet has opened a huge new market for commercial advertising. In recent years ads have increased greatly on sites such as Facebook, and LinkedIn, as well as blogging sites such as Twitter. Businesses are plugging their products into social networks not only getting greater exposure for their wares, but achieving a closer, personal connection with their current and potential customers. While large companies such as Dell, Starbucks, and Comcast have been using Twitter, more and more small businesses that cannot afford traditional advertising find sites such as Twitter essential to their success. Even with no budget, a super-small business finds these outlets easily accessible and free, drawing enough attention—and customers—for that small business to remain viable.

With the crackdown on pirated music, social network sites have become important venues for legitimate and lawful music downloads. Sites such as MySpaceMusic and YouTube have millions of songs available free, supported by ads and links to concert tickets and merchandise. Social networking sites offer a significant new frontier for writers, producers, and directors of commercials.

A key mantra for writing on Facebook is not to write too much. Where for personal networking or business purpose such as online marketing, include only the information that supports the reason you are using Facebook. What items do you want to attract people to and are they clear, concise and prominent in your posting? Facebook expert Jim A. Zimmermann has developed a number of key approaches to Facebook writing, including the following:

- Write to a target audience, avoid posting irrelevant material.
- Involve readers by posing questions or creating interactive discussions.
- Use the personal approach by orienting your posts to a specific person or persons, rather than expecting the entire group to be interested and read your information. That applies not only to social networking but to advertising.
- Keep evaluating your posts. If they are not getting the responses you want, try to determine why, whether they are not interesting enough, whether you need a new writing or content approach.
- Keep posting updates so that you don't lose readers.

You not only want to engage your readers, but to get them to do something, whether it's to support an animal rescue organization about which you posted, come to see you act in a community theatre play, vote for a particular candidate, or purchase a product or service you are promoting. That mean including visuals, such as photos, and proving links, if possible for follow-up. Don't turn off readers. Avoid negative posts. Be positive.

One of the ways to attract readers to your post is with a headline. For example, a picture of an abandoned kitten with the headline, "Who Will Save This Kitten?" Or a photo of a well-known "friend" in a wedding dress, headlined "Is This The Right Wedding Dress For Janie?" Or a book cover with the title, "Be A Better Blogger on Facebook." Headlines should directly relate to the content of your posting, should relate to the reader's immediate wants or needs, and should be different enough from other headlines to attract the reader's interest.

If you are marketing a product or service on Facebook, there are already a number of articles and even books on the subject. One of the more concise statements, entitled "Facebook Marketing: Ultimate Guide," originally posted by Tim Suolo and later as a blog on http://www.seomoz.org/blog/facebook-marketing-ultimate-guide. A summary of its major points follows:

■ Keep your personal account and your business account clearly separate. Establish a "brand" if it's a business account and readers will associate whatever is on that posting with your product or service.

■ For a business, create a Facebook page. Your page name should have key words that potential customers are likely to use in a search engine. Develop an attractive profile picture. Users will learn about your business under the "Info" tab, so make it as brief and engaging as you can.

■ Your initial URL may be a series of numbers, hard to remember and not attractive. Once you have 25 fans, you can establish a user name that relates to your business or product or service.

■ Customize your Facebook page to make it attractive and draw fans.

■ Promotion is important and you need to get as many "likes" as possible. Add to your "friends" people who are compatible with what you are presenting and will support it. Use Facebook "Search" to track mentions of your brand and get feedback. When you get direct feedback from anyone, be sure to respond to them.

■ Keep your page fresh and interesting with pictures, videos, and links. Don't post too many, too frequent updates, don't duplicate your web site, don't automate the content.

■ Fill your page with material about your business, such as visuals of your office, your products or services, events that you host, your employees. Use videos to respond to your fans, as former President Bill Clinton has done on his page.

■ Reward your fans/customers: discounts, special offers. One technique is to show or name them on your page, creating a loyal promoter.

■ When you post a community-oriented update, you can ask your fans to share it with their friends.

■ Watch your competitor's Facebook presentations for new ideas that work and what to avoid that doesn't work.

■ Be careful in your use of ads. While most people have no objection to ads, almost ten times as many people dislike them than like them.

■ When you have a Facebook page, list its address wherever you can, with e-mail signatures, in social media, and on business cards.

The vast number of people reached by Facebook has prompted some marketers to call it a "deliciously fertile playground." Where else can one get, so cheaply, so many "likes" for a product or service. As you write ads for Facebook, keep in mind the need for highly focused demographic targeting despite the powerful appeal of being able to reach billions. Organize your presentation as carefully as you would for a traditional television ad: determine your goals and write your headline, text, insert logos and visuals clearly in support of your objectives, constantly being aware of the requirement of brevity. Your headline will have to be strong enough to attract the attention of your target audience amid the plethora of other headlines aimed at the same audience. But don't fool the audience with false or exaggerated claims. For example, don't headline "New type-2 Diabetes Monitor Avoids Lancing" if the test results are really not as accurate. Remember, a disaffected user can reach the same number of potential customers as easily as you can. Use whatever logical, emotional, and/or ethical appeals will best hold the attention of your targets. Concentrate on the word "Like" as you write. You not only want to be, but you need to be "liked." Avoid anything that might be construed as negative. Leave a positive impression with whoever reads your page or post.

Jeff Bullas notes that hours between 8 P.M. and 7 A.M., where there is less competition for attention, generates about 20% more "likes" than other times. Postings on Wednesdays and Sundays appear to get more responses. Don't overdo the number of postings. One or two postings a day appear to get 32% more "likes" and 73% more "comments" than three-to-four postings per day. One to four weekly posts get 71% more comments than five or more weekly posts. Shorter posts get more responses than longer posts. The most effective way to get responses is to ask questions in your post. Posts with a fill-in blank, such as "I like . . ." get about nine times more responses. The more specific sales promotion terms "$ off" and "coupon" get more response than "% off" and "sale." And, above all, keep it simple. Too many words, photos, or links turn people off.

As you read this, you may be thinking that these suggestions smack of too much conformity, not enough cutting edge advertising. You may be right. The company you are representing may wish to take a chance on the notoriety of a posting attracting more customers than the negative aspects turn away. A Kmart video ad on YouTube in 2013 had customers in the ad stating that they would "ship their pants" through a Kmart free shipping program. But the word "ship" sounded like a different word. Many social media users attacked the ad as "gross and vulgar," while many other users thought it displayed a cutting edge sense of humor. The ad went viral, expanding from social media to traditional media.

Conversely, many companies use a subtle approach, such as branding, where a simple slogan or a visual or a snatch of music immediately identifies the product or service. Brand mascots have found a home on social media. The picture of red-haired Wendy Thomas for Wendy's, the photo of Doc Pemberton for Coca-Cola, Mr. Peanut for Planters Peanuts, and the towering, strong Mr. Clean for Mr. Clean Cleaning Products are some examples.

If you are a blogger, social media especially Twitter, Facebook, StumbleUpon, and Pinterest are leading sites for you to get your blogs read. Here, too, there are special techniques to optimize your outreach. Liz Borod Wright, an adjunct professor at the Columbia School of Journalism and prominent blogger, offers 10 principles for successful blogging:

145

- Display your social media icons prominently toward the top of your web site. Simplicity and easy access to your profile are important.
- Give your blog its own space on Facebook.
- StumbleUpon is an alternate browser that can generate excellent traffic.
- Showcase on LinkedIn your blogs that relate to your professional goals and list the web site on your profile.
- Pinterest is the hot new frontier for bloggers. Strong visual content does well.
- Using a link shortener gives you access to metrics and information on how many people clicked and when.
- Using your blog name as your user name makes it easier for people to remember you across different venues.
- Join blogger groups on Facebook. Group orientations vary from regional to subject matter.
- Be generous with other bloggers. Promote their content and they will do the same for you.
- Be on social media even if you're not getting many clicks. It keeps you in the loop.

Blogger Mohammad Mustafa Ahmedzai offers some ideal blogging advice. "Blogging . . . lets you communicate with a multicultural online world of 2.2 billion people, each of them . . . eager to find out what . . . you [have] to share. Blog only to spread knowledge and love. Give more value to quality content, respect copyrights, your readers, and hate blogging for money alone."

SPECIAL CONSIDERATIONS

Although most commercial writers are aware of ethical considerations, such as role stereotyping, many are not sensitive to the special characteristics of many segments of the population that determine those audiences' reactions to specific commercial stimuli. Audience analysis must go beyond the perception that all viewers or listeners of the same age, gender, economic, education, and geographical demographics, for example, will react the same way.

Dr. Cecil Hale, a communications professor and former president of the National Association of Television and Radio Artists, believes there must be a common understanding, a mutual feeling between the writer, announcer, and audience for any broadcast material, including advertising spots, to be optimally effective. Hale states that the writer must find relationships among the character of the product, the character of the audience, and the character of the occasion. Commercials for the same product need to be different for different audiences because the audiences see the product differently. Not all people in a given ethnic or racial group are alike. Hale warns against stereotyping any segment of the audience.

Two African–American-oriented or Latino-oriented stations in the same community may deal with different audiences, just as would two white-oriented stations.

As recently as 2009 General Motors posted on YouTube an online promo for its Chevrolet Camaro, aimed at a gay audience. Over-the-top stereotyping resulted in the ad being pulled. Long-time president of GM Alfred P. Sloan once said that GM wanted to build "a car for every purse and purpose." The Camaro video illustrated the effort—and the difficulty—to market the same product to different audiences. More recently homophobic bigotry has abated and targeted ads would be Accepted. However, is it A Form of bigotry to segregate any designated group as a target audience?

Caroline Jones, as creative director of the Black Creative Group, advising ad agencies dealing with the African-American market, remarked in a Joel Dreyfuss *Washington Post* article, "Blacks and Television," that "they are getting blacks in ads, but they are not doing black ads. It's not black lifestyle." Referring to studies showing that African-American women in general cook foods longer than do white women, and add more spices, stressing taste rather than speed, Jones said that an African-American–oriented commercial, "instead of saying, 'You can cook it in a minute,' should say, 'You will have more time to spend with your family.' I'm talking about why they use a product, why they buy it. They haven't researched it."

The same principles apply to all audiences, and the writer who analyzes the audience's distinct varying attitudes, backgrounds, and lifestyles will more accurately find the common ground between product and audience.

APPLICATION AND REVIEW

1. Choose a product, a television program, and a television station. Write a 30-second commercial script and storyboard for the product you've chosen. Justify what you've prepared by stating (1) your audience analysis, (2) emotional and/or logical and/or ethical appeals, and (3) the steps of persuasion you used.

2. Write the same commercial for radio, considering the differences between the two media.

3. Write the same commercial for the Internet.

4. Using the same considerations, prepare a PSA for television, radio, and the Internet.

5. Write a commercial for one of the social media you are most familiar with.

If your college or university has a television, FM radio, or carrier current station, arrange to do as many of the previous exercises as possible as practical assignments for the stations.

Discuss your completed commercials in class not only according to principles and techniques of ad writing, but especially in terms of ethical considerations, as well.

News and Sports

NEWS

A ny happening that might interest or have an effect on people is news. Anything from a cat up a tree to the outbreak of a war can be worthy of transmission to the mass media audience. The reporter is responsible for determining just what is newsworthy and selecting what to cover and report. The writer is responsible for taking that information and putting it into broadcast form—broadcast in this respect meaning any and all electronic media that reach the public.

The reporter and writer frequently are the same person. Except for network or large station operations, where staff newswriters may be employed to take the reporter's notes and turn them into a script for the on-air anchors, the reporter usually writes his or her own script, providing the segment for the program as prerecorded sound-on-tape (SOT) or in a live remote or live studio presentation or for computerized sound bites. Sometimes the reporter has not had time to prepare a written script and must extemporize.

While laptop reporting and use of other micro means of transmitting news is now old-hat to relatively young or new journalists, these devices created a new reporting life for older journalists. Before stories could be filed on laptops, stories had to be phoned in or sent by fax. And before mobile phones, stories could not reach the news desk until the reporter, relying on notes, found access to a wired phone. Laptops revolutionized the reporting of written stories. Following WiFi development they could be relayed immediately from the field, even as the event was happening. In addition, a story could be edited even as it was unfolding. Today the event and its media dissemination are only as far away as the nearest iPhone. Working as a media journalist today is a far cry from this writer's early experience as a sports reporter covering live contests in the press box on a manual typewriter, writing the story as the game progressed, adding the lead when the game was over, and editing—penciling in changes and corrections—on the way to the newspaper's offices or station's studios to make a deadline. This book frequently notes writer's relationship to new media devices. Take advantage of them.

With the development and growth of compact mobile transmitting devices, such as cell phones, smart phones, and iPhones, and the ubiquitousness of cyberspace connections, a new form of personal journalism has arisen. Through blogging, tweeting, and communicating to sites such as YouTube, any individual anywhere in the world theoretically can instantly send observations of events that might qualify as news to millions of viewers, readers, or listeners. Where banning or censorship of journalists by governments may occur—a frequent happening in many countries—news that may otherwise not get out has been distributed. For example, Iran banned foreign reporters and any reports of the government's crackdown on protesters objecting to what appeared to be a rigged presidential election. Individual tweeters and picture cell phone users reported the brutality and extent of the suppression and, subsequently, the state of civil dissent in the country. Although not a substitute for professional journalist reportage, new technology permits some information where otherwise there would be none. Aside from the use of social media to get news out where professional reporting is banned, professional journalists are increasingly using these connections, with emphasis on Twitter, cell phone text messages, and iPhone visuals to file their reports much quicker than through traditional methods. Given the deaths and arrests of journalists in many places in the world, use of these on-the-spot devices also creates better safety by pinpointing where the journalist is in case of danger.

Sources of News

The principal news source is the reporter-writer. If the reporter is a news-gatherer who collects the information, but does not write it up into final form and never gets on the air, a writer takes the information and prepares it or rewrites it for the on-air personalities. Sometimes on-air personalities, particularly in small stations or on some Internet web sites, do their own reporting and at least some of the writing. Information for local media sometimes comes from a non-station source, such as a citizen phoning in a tip or an observation, the police or fire department reporting a crime or a fire, the promotion or advertising offices of businesses and organizations, or press agents and public relations agencies—any source that officially deals with newsworthy events or that is being paid to make an event seem newsworthy. When you begin to put together the script from such non-reporter sources, you must be extra careful in judging the validity of the material and the trustworthiness of the source.

Of course, if the material comes from a reporter in your own station, network, or news service, you will already know how complete and accurate that reporter usually is in gathering material. If the submission is not scripted (with visuals and audio) or not sufficient to provide a satisfactory story or if you have any question about the material's objectivity and veracity, you or another writer may have to do additional research, verification, and writing. You can obtain additional information through phone calls, texting the Internet, or personal on-the-spot newsgathering if time permits.

To be considered complete, good news stories should inform the audience of the five Ws—who, what, when, where, and why. For example, suppose you know "what" happened, "when," "where," and to "whom"—but you don't yet know the "why" and you should try to dig it out. If you suspect a story has implications that go beyond the information available to you, you may need to do research on the background of the story, including any five Ws of a previous story that might be relevant and any material you can find on the current event's importance for the future.

Another likely source of material is the "morgue" of all past stories that your organization may have. This morgue is similar to the files kept by newspapers, categorized by subject and person. The electronic medium morgue will have audio or video material that can be reused; if none relating to the specifics of the story is available, **stock** footage or audio recording can be helpful. You must make clear that any stock material is not live or current; don't mislead the audience.

Clipping stories from local newspapers has provided newscasts for many radio stations and even for some television stations. If you adapt your news broadcast from the newspaper stories, keep in mind the styles and techniques of broadcast writing discussed later in this chapter that differentiate print from air news.

Have on hand those books that frequently help the newswriter, such as an encyclopedia, a world atlas, and history books—including those dealing with your region, state, and local area. Most cities issue municipal directories that contain information on the city boards and offices. In many cities, the social service agency issues a manual of all social services offices and activities, including a list of non-profit organizations. Many states issue directories or monographs with statistical data on the state, including population demographics. A city's chamber of commerce usually issues a directory that provides information on the area's business organizations, companies, and activities, including financial data such as sales, income, and advertising expenditures. In many instances you can save time and effort by "googling" or "binging" the specific subject. But be aware that a lot of information you find in cyberspace, such as some on Wikipedia, may be inaccurate.

Several news agencies provide services to radio or television stations. These include the **Associated Press (AP); Reuters; British Broadcasting Corporation (BBC); Worldwide Television News (WTN), and Cable News Network (CNN).** The larger networks have their own news divisions. Several organizations provide special news material, especially pictorial matter, for television. Almost all television and radio stations subscribe to at least one wire service. MS and MS-NBC are two of the Internet sources.

Most smaller stations do not have separate news departments, so news broadcasts are prepared by available personnel, usually someone who has some news background, but has a different primary assignment at the station. If there is a continuity department, for example, the writer or writers in that office will be expected to prepare the local news reports. In radio the person on the air at the time of the news presentations—a disc jockey or a general staff announcer—may be required to prepare and present the news, usually in a one- or two-minute break. In some instances a writer with the station writes it; in others, the on-air person simply reads the latest copy from a news service with little or no editing.

In sum, the most desirable news source is the writer/reporter himself or herself. Whenever possible, the writer/reporter should observe the event first-hand. Even if the report is not live, the story should contain the immediacy of the writer/reporter being on the scene. Most often, however, the reporter arrives after the occurrence—unless the event is preplanned or the reporter happens to be at a propitious place when an unexpected event occurs. Such a situation spurred the development of live news coverage in broadcasting. In 1937 Herb Morrison, a reporter for radio station WLS in Chicago, was testing a new disc recording machine at the landing of the German dirigible *Hindenberg* at Lakehurst, New Jersey. Usable portable tape recorders had not been invented yet. Unexpectedly, the *Hindenberg* burst into flames. Morrison's now-famous sobbing words, "This is one of the worst catastrophes in the world . . . oh, the humanity . . ." was carried—from the disc recording—by all three networks the next day and prompted the increased use of recordings and on-the-spot live news.

If the reporter can't be at the scene as the event happens, the next best thing is to get eyewitness first-person accounts and, for video, shots of any continuing activity and any people involved. In some cases in radio—for example, a fire, a bombing, a festival—the continuing sounds at the scene should be recorded as background to enhance the narration and interviews that constitute the news broadcast.

Another source that can make the story more complete, accurate, or interesting is recorded material: aural, visual, and print.

Style

The news writer is first and foremost a reporter whose primary duty is to convey the news. The basic principles of news reporting apply to radio, television, and the Internet as well as to print. But there are distinct differences among them. For example, the traditional five Ws—who, what, when, where, and, if possible, why—always go into the opening, or **lead,** of the newspaper story. Some media newswriters advise doing the same in the opening seconds of the television or radio report; others warn against packing too much into the broadcast lead because an overload of information in a short time can confuse the audience. Yet, the media newswriter must include as many details as possible within a much more limited presentation than that of the newspaper writer. The key focus is *condensation.*

Broadcast journalist Phyllis Haynes suggested several approaches for the writer reporter:

When James Joyce, the famous writer from the Emerald Isle, wrote in a stream of flowing words, the meanings were meant to be gleaned from deep within the writing. The traditions of the great novelists, poets, and mystery writers allow the reader to go on a long and winding journey. But the broadcast journalist has a different responsibility to the audience. He or she must get the listener and the viewer to understand an intricate plot of unfolding news within a matter of seconds. There can be no flighty adjectival clauses that allow the mind to linger. The broadcast journalist must reveal the plot immediately and have the audience understand upon the first run. But within this restriction there is also great art. The good broadcast journalist is a master of first impression. The old adage "less is more" is quite appropriate when writing for broadcast. One might say that a stone sculptor and a news writer come at their art with a similar problem. The sculptor must chip away at the hard rock to reveal the desired image. The sculptor must decide what is extraneous, but be careful not to chip away so much that the final rendering of the statue is faulty. So, too, the broadcast journalist must sort out the extraneous information and choose only the phrases and comments that bring the desired story moving forward in the mind's eye. The journalist, like the sculptor, must decide what is necessary and what is to be chipped away. There is always the danger of chipping away too much, leaving the audience confused or, worse, indifferent. But unlike the sculptor, the broadcast journalist is faced with the additional problem of time. Stories must get on the air by the broadcast deadline, usually leaving the journalist only a few hours, and sometimes much less, to complete the story. Time is not forgiving in this business. A great story can quickly become yesterday's news. No matter how marvelously crafted or well researched, if it's old, it's useless. Broadcast journalists write against the clock.

Further, the media writer must find logical transitions between each segment of the newscast; the newspaper writer's stories are complete in themselves. Clarity, types of leads, use of quotes, objectivity, and verification of information apply to both print and air. The media writer has to consider the additional factors of timing, visual and aural materials, and the personalities of the newscasters who will present the news.

Today, most young journalists have had some 12 years of print writing and literature by the time they graduate from high school, but little or no formal education in writing in or understanding the electronic media. Although young journalists have grown up with extensive informal use of the Internet, few have formal training or experience in writing professional quality online news. Many journalists frequently think of journalistic writing principally in print terms. This book provides several reminders to help you learn the key differences between writing for print and writing for visual and audio reception.

One reminder is that the structure of the stories themselves can differ markedly. For example, newspaper stories usually provide all the five W information at the beginning, in the first or lead paragraph. The need to condense for electronic media may require eliminating one or more of the five Ws in the opening statement or even inverting the order that seems logical for a full report. For instance, a mass media news report, to avoid passive writing, might put the story source first, instead of later in the report. Note the following:

- *Newspaper:* "All the members of the City Council should be impeached for misuse of public funds," the president of a newly formed political activist group stated at the public meeting yesterday.
- *Radio or television:* A new political organization wants the members of the city council impeached for misuse of public funds.

(Sometimes, however, the media story can have more of the five Ws than the print story, even in a shorter time. See the example below.)

Leads

Begin the story with clear, precise information. The opening should be, as much as possible, a summary of the entire story. Be wary, however, of including too many details. Remember that the audience sees or hears the news only once and, unlike newspaper readers, cannot go back for clarification or better understanding of particular points. The audience must be able to grasp the story on the first hearing. Don't overload. Because they usually have to fit into 30, 60, or 90 seconds, broadcast news stories are sometimes little more than the equivalent of newspaper headlines, subheads, and the lead paragraph.

Compare the following openings for the same story, first on the AP news wire and second in *Broadcasting & Cable* magazine:

NBC NEWS, FINDING THE USE OF NEWS RECREATIONS IN ITS "YESTERDAY, TODAY AND TOMORROW" SPECIALS TOO CONFUSING TO VIEWERS, SAID MONDAY IT WON'T USE THE TECHNIQUE ANYMORE. IT WON'T KEEP THE SHOW, EITHER.

(AP)

Recreations—which have been subjected to considerable criticism when used to advance a news story or documentary—no longer figure in NBC News's plans. NBC News President Michael Gartner announced last week not only that the division will discontinue the use of actors portraying real-life characters for the purpose of conveying information, it will abandon the program on which it was used—"Yesterday, Today and Tomorrow." The concept of using recreations is being taken over by NBC's Entertainment division, without the news staff who have worked on the three segments that have been aired.

Both stories present the five Ws—although the print story, which came out some days after the announcement, omitted the "when," while the broadcast story, even condensed severely, got all five Ws in, including the "when" because of its more timely presentation. Although a story in print may have a long lead, in effect summarizing the entire story in the first sentence or two, the broadcast lead must be short. If necessary, save some of the five Ws for a second sentence or a follow-up visual.

Often the print story will have what is called a *second lead*; the second paragraph will contain the essential information that had to be left out of a first paragraph that became too lengthy in presenting only a few of the five Ws most important to the story. The broadcast presentation does the same, but only when the secondary Ws are considered essential to the viewers' or listeners' basic understanding of the story. Where the print story then elaborates on the lead or leads, the broadcast story usually ends. Any elaboration usually is confined to the active Ws—who, what, where, when. Rarely is there any time for the "why." Although many Internet news programs follow the tight time schedules of broadcast and cable, many take advantage of the time flexibility still available on the Internet, and present in-depth reports.

Following is a standard 30-second length television report, containing the essence of the story, including necessary video material.

VIDEO	AUDIO
JOE ON CAM	If you've been worried about the BP oil spill ruining your vacation on southwest Florida's Sanibel and Captiva Islands, you can relax.
VO Sanibel beaches	Although hundreds of thousands of gallons are polluting the seashore in the western Gulf of Mexico, it hasn't and is not predicted to reach the eastern Gulf.
VO Washington, DC, Capitol and White House	While Congress is debating what to do about continued deep-water drilling, President Obama has called a meeting of several federal agencies to determine what can be done to stop the spill.

A similarly important story for which there is at the moment more information and visuals may get three times as much coverage and, if dramatic enough, as many as two or three minutes of the approximately ten minutes of hard news (excluding sports and weather) coverage in the half-hour TV show. The lead may be a **tease** or, as also called, a **soft lead**—a dramatic or human interest bit that will hold the audience's attention into the specific information of the **hard lead**. A second lead may follow, adding more depth, usually through significant visuals or interviews with participants or observers.

The following script is such a story.

VIDEO	AUDIO
VO VTR	Rising tides . . . churning winds . . . boarded up buildings:
BRIAN	The signs of Hurricane Hugo are everywhere as this killer storm zeros in on the coastline from Florida to the Carolinas.
2S/VTR	Good evening. I'm Brian Leary.
SUSAN	And I'm Susan Wornick. Right now Hurricane Hugo is building strength and bearing down on the southeast coast of the United States. It should come ashore a little before midnight tonight.
BRIAN	New England could get a taste of this powerful storm as early as tomorrow night. But for now all attention is focused on the Southeast, where most people have boarded up and headed for higher ground.
	We now have a series of reports. First, our chief correspondent Martha Bradlee looks at preparations in the hurricane warning area.
SOT MARTHA	The mayor of Charleston said it is important that no one underestimate the danger of this hurricane. Mayor Joseph Riley said the storm could be the city's biggest since a 1938 tornado that killed 32 people and injured 100's.
SUSAN	Here in New England we could be feeling the effects of Hurricane Hugo by Saturday night. Let's go right to Dick Albert now for the latest on that.
ALBERT	[Weather report.]
BRIAN	The effects of Hugo are already being felt along the coast of Georgia and the Carolinas. Let's go to Wendy Chee-OH-gee of the Newstar Network . . . live in Savannah. Wendy . . . how's the weather?
LIVE NEWSTAR	[Live Newstar]
VTR CARIB DAMAGE SUSAN/VO	In the Caribbean . . . where Hugo has already left its mark . . . officials are still coping with water shortages . . . homelessness . . . and widespread looting. U.S. troops have arrived in the Virgin Islands. A government official just back from St. Croix says the situation there is out of control.
SOT	[SOT]

continued

VIDEO	AUDIO
MORE V/O	But the governor of the Virgin Islands insists the looting is not as bad as it seems.
SOT MORE V/O	[SOT] In Puerto Rico the biggest worry is a scarcity of fresh water.
SUSAN	As expected, the President declared Puerto Rico a federal disaster area today. He did the same for the Virgin Islands yesterday. We will, of course, continue to monitor the path of Hurricane Hugo and bring you updated information throughout the evening.

Courtesy of WCVB-TV, Boston

In sum, try to get the story into the first lead. If you can't, get it all in the second lead. Then, if the story has been given additional air time, elaborate on the lead or leads.

Hard Lead.   The hard lead contains the most important of the five Ws, succinctly telling the crux of the story. For example, see the following script.

VIDEO	AUDIO
ENG/VO/SOT	Tonight almost one thousand students are under arrest in South Korea.
	Earlier today in Seoul, students on a university campus were demanding to be allowed to visit North Korea. Violence erupted after police stormed the campus with tear gas.

Courtesy of WLVI-TV, Boston

Soft Lead.   The soft lead tries to get drama into the story to attract and hold the audience's attention and follows this with the hard lead. Note the soft lead that opened the BP oil spill newscast cited earlier.

VIDEO	AUDIO
JOE ON CAM	If you've been worried about the BP oil spill ruining your vacation on southwest Florida's Sanibel and Captiva Islands, you can relax.

Dennis White, a writer and producer of television news programs, advise students to forget the styles of writing they've learned in the past, except for writing the basic sentences. He noted that most students were taught to write long, involved sentences, but in broadcasting they must do just the opposite. "We must now recreate spoken language," he said. "It's much like writing a play." White stated,

> Our audience doesn't have the opportunity to go back and review what it has just heard. We only have one chance to grab our audience's attention. If we fail, our audience will be lost. Broadcast news writing has a simple structure but uses a high density of language. We must make every word count since we have a limited amount of time in which to tell our story.

White said that the news writer's first goal is to get the audience to listen:

> We usually top our story with a sentence of five to ten words that gives a general idea of the story. For example: "A five alarm fire destroyed a supermarket in Jamaica Plain this morning." The audience now has an idea of what happened and is ready to get more details about the story. In the subsequent sentences of the story we get more specific. Our final sentence brings some conclusion to the story.
>   The best advice to someone writing a news story is to "tell" the story just like s/he would tell it to a friend. The first thing you would tell someone about the story is usually your first news writing sentence. Just finish this sentence "Did you hear about . . .?" It works best if you say it out loud.
>   A broadcast news writer must always remember that s/he is writing a story. It must have a beginning, middle, and end. The novice will very often just write a laundry list of facts. One sentence must lead into the next. One idea must lead us to the next.

Dramatic Action

Think of the news as a dramatic action. The story with an obvious conflict (war, a political campaign, a murder trial, a divorce case, the baseball pennant race) attracts immediate attention. Use direct statements rather than questions. Stress the immediacy of the conflict. For example, rather than beginning a story with the question, "Will America ignore world opinion and start a war against Iran?" it is more dramatic to say, "The question in every country in the world tonight is, 'Will American ignore world opinion and start a war against Iran?'" Keep the edge on the currency and excitement of the story. Avoid uninformed presentation of the news, but don't tell the audience you don't know, unless you use it as a tease for a later report that you know is in process. It is better to give whatever details are available without comment than to say, "This is an incomplete story, but . . ."

Technique

Probably the most difficult job for the television or radio news writer is to select out of the myriad details the most salient points and to present them in a very short time. Choose words as carefully as if you were conveying critical information in the limited space of a telegram or on a billboard.

Clarity

Use short, familiar words. You can be artistic without being verbose. Simple, direct language does not have to be dull. Read some works of Ernest Hemingway, who was a reporter before he became a novelist, for examples of such writing. You could begin a news story from South Africa like this:

> The title of a Charles Dickens novel might well be the hallmark of the majority of the Liberian people today as a new dawn blossomed over the long ravished and repressed land. "Great Expectations" surged through the valleys, hills, plains, and urban ghettos as new president Ellen Johnson Sirleaf was inaugurated, indicating a new governmental capacity for the nation's population.

But if you write it the following way for broadcast, you will present more information more clearly in less time:

> Liberia's new president Ellen Johnson Sirleaf took the oath of office today pledging to create what she called a "new" nation. She says she will accommodate all Liberians in the new government.

Non-Technical

Don't be ambiguous. Although you may be an expert in interpreting professional terms, scientific language, or statistics, your audience may not be. For example, if a forest fire destroyed 100 acres of timber, don't say, "One million square feet of wood went up in smoke." Say, "Enough timber went up in smoke to build 40 eight-room houses." Don't explain things in the abstract. Be concrete. Say exactly what you mean. Give specific examples.

Language

Writing should be simple, direct, and understandable. It can be colloquial in form. This does not mean that you should use slang or illiterate expressions, but suggests *informality*. Avoid abstract expressions and words with double meanings. At the same time, don't overdo the simplicity or colloquialisms, or the viewers or listeners will think you're talking down to them.

The writing should be *conversational*. You want to enable the on-air talent to talk to the audience as if they were sitting in the audience's living rooms. *Empathize* with the individual members of your audience. *Personalize* the information. Put yourself in their place. What does the story mean to each of them? As a writer who has put together all the material gathered by the reporters, or perhaps also as a reporter, you know all about the story. Don't forget that for the audience it's brand new!

Use the *present tense*. Don't write, "When we spoke to the holdup victim he said he felt that the people who have been stealing to get drugs have been continuing to do so because there have been too many official coverups of drug-dealing in high places." Write, "The holdup victim blames the continuing rash of drug-related robberies on official coverups of drug-dealing in high places."

Use the *active voice and active verbs*. Don't say, "There were forty people taken to the hospital following a train derailment that occurred early this morning," but, "Forty people are in the hospital as a result of an early morning train accident." Don't say, "The rushing water, churned by the hurricane winds, went over the town's river embankment," but rather, "The hurricane winds churned the water over the town's embankment."

News writer and teacher Dennis White noted,

> When we tell stories we usually use the active voice. But for some unknown reason we often write in the passive voice. (At least that's my experience with writers who are new to broadcast copy.) Keep your copy active. Use simple verbs whenever possible. This helps to keep the copy moving and helps the audience follow the story.

White suggested a key way to determine the impact of the news writer's language on the audience:

> Since the broadcast writer is writing for the ear, s/he should read the story aloud to find out if it really works. You see this in newsrooms across the country: Writers sitting alone at computers reading their copy aloud. They are fine-tuning the sound and feel of the copy. It is the only way to find out how the story works. Does it read well? Does it flow? Is the language simple and clear?

Spell out numbers. Although some writers, especially those with close deadlines, save time by writing "people by the 100s descended on City Hall," it is easier for the on-air reporter to read "people by the hundreds descended on City Hall." Spell out in *phonetics* any uncommon names or pronunciations. Note in the Hurricane Hugo story, "Let's go to Wendy Chee-OH-gee of the Newstar Network live in Savannah." *Identify* all people clearly. If the person in the story is important, identify him or her with a job or title. It means more to the audience to learn that "Elizabeth Miller, Executive Director of the Citizens Committee to Combat Global Warming, today declared her candidacy for Congress," than "Elizabeth Miller, local political activist, today declared her candidacy for Congress."

Use style books. The *Associated Press Stylebook and Libel Manual* and the *United Press International Style Book* are both good sources for standard approaches to punctuation, spelling, use of numerals, use of capitals (upper case versus lower case), abbreviations, and how to state dates, ages, size, and capacity.

Objectivity

The writer, producer, or reporter with integrity aims for fairness and honesty in news reporting. The level of objectivity achieved is ultimately determined by (1) the policy of the station, network, channel, or site owner; (2) the political and social attitudes of the community; (3) pressures from advertisers, including a desire to avoid anything controversial; (4) personal biases of the news director, newswriters, and newscasters; (5) expediency in news reporting; and (6) *infotainment*.

Although the first four factors are determined largely by individual choice, the last two, expediency and infotainment, are part of the media business and are frequently justified as necessary for effective competition. Political campaigns are classic examples of expediency in reporting. By seeking easy coverage, radio and television news too often accept "sound bites" prepared by the candidates and interpretations given by the candidates' "spin doctors," and pay relatively little attention to the candidates' qualifications and the issues. Newswriters' acceptance of the easy-out "sound bites" instead of insistence on meaningful reporting exacerbate the media's inadequacies. A prime example was during the 2008 presidential election in the United States. For the first time, representing one party, either an African-American or a woman would be the nominee for president, and in the other major party, for the first time a woman was the vice-presidential candidate. More attention appeared to be paid by the media to the personal lives of Barack Obama and Sarah Palin than to their qualifications and to the issues. When Palin withdrew from live press interviews after early disasters, the media generally ignored her policies and made her a media star by concentrating on her personality.

Because the news is potentially identical on virtually all broadcast and cable networks and on same-market local broadcast stations, and especially on competing networks' national news shows, increasing emphasis is placed on the entertainment rather than on the news aspects, of the programs. Stations vie not with better-covered news or with news-in-depth, but with personality and shock stories. Increasingly less time is devoted to hard news and more to entertainment features.

Media designation of the private lives of celebrities as "news" appears to change with the times. It does seem to coincide, however, with the increase in advertising and the direct relationship of increased media income to higher numbers of readers, listeners, and viewers. For example, in the 1920s, when one of Presidential-hopeful Warren Harding's several mistresses threatened to blackmail him and hurt his election chances, the Republican National Committee paid the blackmail. The media did not make it a cause célèbre. In the 1960s, when President John Kennedy openly had a steady stream of women, some of them high profile movie stars, visit him in the White House for extramarital sexual affairs, the media turned a blind eye. Three decades later the media made a feeding frenzy out of President Bill Clinton's sexual encounters with a White House intern, not only exacerbating political opportunism for impeachment, but thrusting into the spotlight the intern and several other figures, creating for them the opportunity to make money as media celebrities and appear in more media stories and, coincidentally, generate more audiences and income for the media. More recently the extra-marital affairs of a number of state governors and U.S. senators pushed virtually all other news at the time, including that of critical importance to the lives and futures of Americans and the rest of the world, into secondary consideration and even into media limbo. On a television situation comedy, or sitcom, about a newspaper, an editor says to a reporter: "Please tell me you're working on a story full of mayhem and scandal." Fiction is often a true representation of real life!

Proper and ethical promotion is necessary and expected. Deliberately misleading the public is something else. For example, CBS reporter Martha Teichner was asked to report, on the air, about Somalia during a U.S. action there. She stated in the *Columbia Journalism Review* that although she had done some research on Somalia, she had never been there. "Even if I'm correct and accurate," she said, "I'm superficial." In 2013, in Cleveland, Ohio, a man named Ariel Castro was charged with kidnapping three girls and holding them captive as sex slaves for a decade. The police briefly held and questioned Castro's two brothers as possible participants. The media, in a frenzy to generate viewers, listeners, and readers, prominently showed photos of the brothers along with stories about them, tacitly giving the impression that they were guilty. The fact that it was shortly announced by the authorities that there was no evidence they had been involved in the crime and presumably had no knowledge of what their brother had done did not make up for the notoriety and even death threats they received because of what many considered the unethical conduct of the media. Even CNN, in recent years providing less and less hard news in favor of titillating celebrity and murder and mayhem feature stories, devoted air time over a period of weeks to rehashing every angle and detail it could find on this event. The late Don Hewitt, former executive producer of *60 Minutes*, warned "There is . . . a line that separates show biz from news biz. The trick is to walk up to it, touch it with your toe, but don't cross it." Even local stations devote time to mostly inane banter between news anchors, time that could be used for better presentation of news stories.

"Infotainment" has replaced "information" on many news programs. The Roman writer Horace proclaimed, "Let fiction meant to please be very near the truth." Too many newswriters and producers today seem to have reversed this advice and have attempted to let truth meant to please be very near fiction. Is this approach appropriate for reporting the news, or does it suggest a lessening of responsibility and values that will lead, as it did to the Roman Empire, to the downfall of media news?

Accuracy

Write so that the viewer cannot possibly misunderstand. Even an unintentional careless or vague comment, or the integration of video or audio materials that distort the story because they are incomplete or out of context, can give the audience false impressions or incorrect assumptions concerning a given issue, person, or event. Make certain that the terminology used is correct. For example, don't refer to a figure in a story as a "car thief" if the person has not been convicted but is actually an "alleged car thief."

Be certain that all names are spelled correctly, with phonetic descriptions wherever necessary to guarantee that they are pronounced correctly by the on-air reporter. Be certain that all information about people mentioned in the story, such as age, occupation, and city, is correct.

Quotes are most susceptible to distortion. Using quotes from the people involved—participants, eyewitnesses, or expert analysts—adds considerably to the immediacy of a news program. But any given interview is likely to be considerably longer than can be used on the air. Be careful that the segments you select to be used are not out of context or do not put undue emphasis on an aspect of the story that is, in fact, a minor part of it. One way to be sure that quotes are absolutely accurate is to record them verbatim. Don't allow any distortion of the facts, even if their enhancement makes the story more interesting.

One way to ensure objectivity and accuracy is through *verification* of any and all information gathered. If any segment of the material you are preparing for a script doesn't seem to ring true, double-check it with the reporter. If there is any further doubt, try to reach the original source yourself. If you can't do that, determine with the producer whether or not the material should be used.

Personality

Write the news so that it fits the personality of (1) the network, station, or web site; (2) the particular news program; and (3) the reporters or anchors presenting the news. The network, station, or web site may be promoting a particular image for itself, such as alternative, breezy, serious, or fast and hard-hitting. The station may want to convey a different image for different news slots: the morning news as bright and entertaining, the evening news as world-shaking and in-depth.

Because personalities make the difference in attracting audiences to news programs that are essentially the same in content, write to fit the style of the newscaster(s). The words must be consistent with the vocabulary developed for the given newscaster; the sentence structure must reflect the rhythm and pace appropriate for that newscaster. You may be writing for the image of a dynamic, combative reporter, or a low-key friendly person who stops in to chat about the news, or a father or mother figure who conveys a sense of trustworthiness and authoritativeness. In this respect, the newswriter prepares dialogue the way the playwright does—consistent with the personality of the character who is delivering it while maintaining its accuracy and integrity.

Format

Formats vary from the writing of basic continuity to the more expansive and detailed demands of one- and two-column scriptwriting. In some instances, the writer may do little more than prepare the transitional continuity for the news program. Sometimes the on-air anchors extensively rewrite after the newswriter has done one or more drafts. When the final script reaches the on-air personality just before air time, he or she usually does little more than read through and change words or phrases, but not content, to better fit his or her air style. Some stations have a standard opening and closing for each short news report or break, with the broadcaster filling in the content with material from the wire services.

The final copy is meant to be read live (or recorded for presentation shortly thereafter) and, therefore, must be as clear as possible. It must have no errors. Sometimes the writer should assume that the on-air personality reading the copy is a robot and will read exactly what is written, with no variation from the script. Although good on-air reporters go over every script carefully to be certain that they understand every word, phrase, and meaning, this is not necessarily true of all on-air newscasters. For clarity and ease of reading, several simple rules apply: no hyphenated words at the ends of lines, no split paragraphs (that is, no paragraphs carried over onto a subsequent page), phonetic spelling of words or names that might be difficult to pronounce, and consistent use of upper case or lower case to help the reader to distinguish easily between directions and the material to be read on the air.

Although the script examples in this book are single-spaced to save space, copy should be double-spaced and sometimes even triple-spaced. That makes it much easier to edit and for the announcer or anchor to read.

Formats vary from station to station, but generally each story is given a *slug*—that is, a title. Usually the slug is at the top of the page and contains the title of the story, the date, the program on which it is to be presented, and the writer's name. Alternatively, the slug sometimes is placed in block form at the side of the page. Capitals or lower case can be used, as long as consistency in style is maintained. For example:

COUNCIL IMPEACHMENT—2/16/14—6 p.m. News—J. Carter
or
Council Impeachment
2/16/14
6 P.M. News
J. Carter

Radio Rundowns

The basic radio news format has changed little over the years, except that on most stations the 15-minute news program has become 5 minutes or a 1-minute update. The following is the prepared format for a 10-minute-plus radio newscast.

WBSM NEWS FORMAT

:30 BEFORE THE HOUR:
    ANN: (READ THREE SHORT HEADLINES) THESE STORIES AND MORE AFTER
       ABC REPORTS ON WORLD AND NATIONAL EVENTS. SET YOUR WATCH
       TO WBSM. THE TIME AT THE TONE IS _____ O'CLOCK.

:00 ABC NEWS (NETWORK)
:05 LOCAL NEWS (PLAY NEWS SOUNDER)
    ANN: IT'S _____ DEGREES AT _____(TIME)_____.
       I'M _____, WBSM TOTAL INFORMATION NEWS, BROUGHT TO
       YOU BY ___(READ SPONSOR TAG)___.
:07 ANN: WBSM NEWS TIME _____.
       (PLAY:COMMERCIAL:60)
:08 ANN: (COMPLETE THE NEWS)
:10 ANN: THE NEWS IS BROUGHT TO YOU BY _____(SPONSOR TAG)WBSM NEWS
       TIME _____. NORM MCDONALD'S WEATHER FORECAST IS NEXT.
    (PLAY: 30 WEATHERCAST)
    ANN: IT'S _____ DEGREES IN DOWNTOWN NEW BEDFORD. I'M
       _____, WBSM TOTAL INFORMATION NEWS. OUR NEXT NEWS AT
       _____ O'CLOCK.

    WHEN GIVING TIME, USE "DIGITAL" TIME.
NOTE: EXAMPLE: FIVE MINUTES PAST FIVE IS "FIVE-OH-FIVE."

Courtesy of WBSM, New Bedford, Massachusetts

Some stations use the wire services almost exclusively for their news, adding only key local stories from local sources. Even so, they must have a prepared format containing opening, closing, and transitional lead-ins for specific organizational parts of the newscast, including the commercials. Here is such a format for a five-minute news program.

FIVE MINUTE NEWS FORMAT

OPEN: Good morning (afternoon) (evening)
Welcome to the _____ [time] news.
[Read three wire news stories in order of importance. If no key story, organize by International, national, local.]

ANNCR: More news after this.

COMMERCIAL

ANNCR: In local news _____ [read two stories]

ANNCR: Weather for the local area _____ [current and forecast]

CLOSE: That's the _____ [time] news and weather. I'm _____ [announcer's name]

Television Rundowns

The television news program follows the same basic format approach, except it is more detailed. Television news programs require a *rundown*—a listing of all stories and their sources—in preparation for organizing and writing the script. A network newscast can have several rundowns, beginning early in the day for an evening newscast. A local station may have only one rundown before the actual script is written.

Writing the script that appears over the air is only the final stage of a long, arduous, and frequently complicated process. For a program such as *CBS Evening News,* the planning and development begin early. The first step is the "CBS Program Log," distributed early on the morning of the show, showing all the film pieces used on the CBS morning news, midday news, evening news, and even on the other network news programs from the previous day.

Second, written at about 6 or 7 A.M. and distributed at about 8:30 A.M., is a "CBS News Insights" sheet showing who is assigned to what coverage and what the planned assignments are for the day and containing a domestic and foreign "Who's Where" so that any staff member is reachable at all times.

Third, at about 11 A.M., a "Who Does What" rundown is distributed, showing which associate producers and which reporters are doing what and where.

Fourth, at about 11:15 A.M., a "Morning Line" is issued, with more information on the big stories and who is assigned to them.

Fifth, at about 12:30 or 1 P.M., a "Prelineup" is completed, providing a list of the stories expected to be used on the program.

Sixth, at about 3:30 P.M., the technical "Lineup" comes out, listing the stories that will be on, their sequence, and times.

Seventh, at about 5 P.M., an "Editorial Lineup" lists more exact information on where each story is. Until show time there are "Lineup Revisions" rundowns, incorporating any changes. The final rundown sheet and the final script are completed as close to air time as possible, to incorporate the latest breaking news.

The rundown form varies depending on the approach and organization of the given news department, but it should contain everything pertinent to the show.

A simple rundown would have elements such as the following:

SHOW	DAY	DATE	PRODUCER		PHONE	ANCHOR		
6:00 PM	FRIDAY	09/23	JIM JAMES		X7642	SARAH SMITH		
PG	SLUG			FORM	GRAPHIC		TIME	TOTAL
1	OPEN			OC	EVENING NEWS		:10	:10
2	EGYPT			OC	EGYPT REBELS		:25	:35
	EGYPT—			REM			:20	:55
	AL ALBERT							
	EGYPT—			REM			:25	1:20
	JANE JANES							
3	CONGRESS			OC	BUDGET CUTS		:20	1:40
	HOUSE WHIP			SOT			:15	1:55
	APP. COMM.			SOT			:15	2:10
	CHAIR							
4	BASEBALL			OC	MULTI-MILLION		:30	2:40
				CONTRACT				
	BASEBALL—			SOT			:25	3:05
	JOE BALLPLAYER							

Script Forms

A radio news show has a relatively simple format compared with the television program. Radio news has a studio announcer or newscaster and, depending on the importance of news coverage to the station, will have live or recorded narration, interviews, and voices and sounds of the event. Television news, however, ranges from the sophisticated, using all possible video and audio sources and digital techniques, to the simple "talking head" newscaster reading a script, with no visuals. The television writer must know the capabilities of the station in order to establish a format that will or will not use visuals chroma-keyed or digitally inserted in back of the newscaster, visuals without sound, graphics, SOT, reporter or anchor voice-over (VO), or any of the other techniques discussed in Chapter 2.

The Radio Script. The radio script is usually the one-column form, with remotes, recordings, or other sound sources written in. The first of the following scripts is an example from a half-hourly newsbreak update of radio station WBCN-FM, Boston.

The second script is an example from a local radio station in Boston, Massachusetts, that does not have its own newsgathering service, but can nevertheless provide local as well as national and international news by adapting newswire materials.

Keep in mind that all radio scripts are double-spaced. They are single-spaced here only because of space considerations.

ANNCR: A new term begins for the U.S. Supreme Court . . . and the justices are expected to continue focusing their attention on abortion. Good morning. There are three abortion cases before the court . . . two having to do with parental consent or knowledge—the third an Illinois statute and regulations that required doctors' offices and abortion clinics to be equipped as if they were hospitals. That statute was declared unconstitutional by a federal appeals court.

TAPE: (Tribe: volcanic explosion)

ANNCR: Harvard law professor Lawrence Tribe says other matters before the court deal with the right to privacy and the right to die . . .

TAPE: (Tribe: the States)

ANNCR: The justices will also hear key desegregation cases from Kansas City, Missouri and Yonkers, New York. Carol Williams reports.

TAPE: (Williams)

ANNCR: November seventh is election day and in Cambridge and Brookline the issue on the ballot will be rent control. Patrick Murray has the first of two reports.

TAPE: (Murray)

Courtesy of WBCN-FM Radio, Boston

Good afternoon. I'm Ramona Parks with the 12 o'clock news update.

FOUR PEOPLE ARE DEAD FOLLOWING A HELICOPTER CRASH ALONG MEMORIAL DRIVE IN CAMBRIDGE SHORTLY AFTER 9 THIS MORNING.

A MASSACHUSETTS STATE POLICE HELICOPTER HAS CRASHED ON THE ROOF OF THE HARVARD UNIVERSITY SAILING PAVILION ALONG THE CHARLES RIVER.

AUTHORITIES BELIEVE THE HELICOPTER LEFT FROM THE NASHUA STREET HELIPAD IN BOSTON A SHORT TIME BEFORE IT LOST CONTROL.

POLICE SAY THE PAVILION ON MEMORIAL DRIVE WAS UNOCCUPIED AT THE TIME OF THE CRASH.

NO ONE ON THE GROUND WAS INJURED.

BOTH SIDES OF MEMORIAL DRIVE ARE CLOSED.

TRAFFIC IS BEING DIVERTED THROUGH LONGFELLOW BRIDGE AND DOWN MASS.AVE. IN CAMBRIDGE.

IT IS BEST TO AVOID THIS AREA.

* * *

THE U-S SUPREME COURT WILL DETERMINE WHETHER MASSACHUSETTS COURTS VIOLATED THE CONSTITUTION WHEN RULING THE SAINT PATRICK'S DAY PARADE IS OPEN TO THE PUBLIC.

THE SOUTH BOSTON ALLIED WAR VETERANS ARE TRYING TO BAN GAYS FROM MARCHING IN THE PARADE.

IRISH AMERICANS, LESBIAN, AND BISEXUAL GROUPS OF BOSTON ARE FIGHTING TO MARCH IN THE PARADE.

THE STATE COURTS SIDED WITH THE GAY ACTIVISTS PROMPTING THE SPONSORS TO CANCEL THE EVENT.

THE U-S SUPREME COURT WILL HEAR ORAL DEBATES ON THE ISSUE IN APRIL.

* * *

TURNING TO INTERNATIONAL NEWS . . .

AN ENVIRONMENTAL GROUP SAYS IT WILL SUE SEVERAL COMPANIES FOR TRANSPORTING HIGHLY RADIOACTIVE WASTE.

GREENPEACE IS READY TO FILE SUIT AGAINST FRENCH, BRITISH, AND JAPANESE COMPANIES FOR SHIPPING WASTE THROUGH THE FRENCH CITY OF CHERBOURG (SHEHR BOORG).

THE BRITISH SHIP, PACIFIC PINTAIL, IS LOADED WITH FOURTEEN TONS OF RESIDUE FROM FRENCH REPROCESSING OF SPENT JAPANESE NUCLEAR FUEL.

THE SHIP LEAVES TOMORROW FOR JAPAN.

continued

THE COMPANIES SAY THE SHIPMENT COMPLIES WITH INTERNATIONAL REGULATIONS, HOWEVER ENVIRONMENTALISTS DISAGREE.

THEY SAY THE VESSEL AND CONTAINER ARE NOT SUFFICIENTLY IMMUNE TO COLLISION OR INTENSE HEAT.

* * *

IN SPORTS LAST NIGHT THE CELTICS SHOCKED THE SUNS WITH A VICTORY OF 129 to 121.

IN TODAY'S WEATHER EXPECT A SUNNY BREAK THROUGH THE CLOUDS WITH A HIGH OF 38 degrees.

TONIGHT EXPECT FAIR SKIES WITH A HIGH OF 25.

TOMORROW CLOUDINESS WILL CONTINUE WITH SOME SNOW TURNING TO RAIN, WITH A HIGH OF 42.

RIGHT NOW OUTSIDE OUR BACK BAY STUDIOS IT'S 35 DEGREES.

THANKS FOR JOINING US. I'M RAMONA PARKS.

NOW BACK TO T.J. WITH JAZZ OASIS ON 88.9 WERS BOSTON.

Courtesy of the Associated Press and WERS

The Television Script.   As you've already noted, the television script usually follows the standard two-column format, with the video at the left and the audio at the right, as in the following:

VIDEO	AUDIO
JOE ON CAM	Welcome to KSTZ's 10 o'clock news. Tonight's big story: snow buries the northeast. I'm Joe Rogers.
MARY ON CAM	And I'm Mary Kane. Roads and airports are closed from Delaware to New Hampshire.
VO New York City	In New York City cars are buried and streets are empty of people.

Approach

Each station and each news program aims for a distinctive style. Though the news in any given market may be the same, the ratings race requires the station to find an approach that is different enough from its competitors to draw an acceptable audience.

At the same time, there are still basic approaches common to writing and presenting the news in any medium and any market, necessary for creating a news program of acceptable and, hopefully, high quality. The good writer tries to combine both of these considerations.

What does your station and program aim for? Which audience does it want to capture? Will the approach to news be consistent with the overall station format? Is the content primarily hard news? Soft news? Features? An emphasis on local happenings? Are you competing with other stations by playing up personalities rather than content and format?

Audience demographics are just as important to the news program as to any other broadcast format. The kinds of content and the level of presentation must be understood by and must appeal to the target viewers or listeners. Consider the time of day the broadcast is being presented. Is the audience at the dinner table? Seated comfortably in the living room? Rushing to get to work on time? At a computer in a coffee house?

Suppose you want to establish an informal and friendly relationship with the audience. Obviously, you wouldn't lead off with antagonizing or shocking stories. Do you want to capture the immediate attention of the audience? Try leading off with an item that has personal meaning to the audience, written in dramatic terms.

For example, suppose a news report from Washington, D.C., shows that unemployment nationally rose from 9.5% to 9.8% during the previous month. You could simply give the statistics:

The Department of Labor's monthly report, issued today in Washington, D.C., showed a rise in unemployment figures of three-tenths of a percent in November over October, to nine-point-eight percent from nine-point-five percent.

But a good writer would go further:

Four hundred thousand more people are without jobs this month than last month, according to the latest figures from the Department of Labor. Unemployment in the United States went from nine-point-five percent to nine-point-eight percent—an estimated thirteen million, eight hundred thousand Americans out of work.

A writer sensitive to the local audience might put it this way:

Four thousand more Center City residents are looking for work this month, according to figures released today by the U.S. Department of Labor. While the national rate for unemployment went up to nine-point-eight percent in November compared with nine-point-five percent in October, the rate for Center City went up from nine-point-six percent to ten-point-six percent, a marked increase, resulting in an estimated twenty-four thousand people in our town without jobs. Nationally . . .

The independent television station is likely to emphasize local news because its competitor affiliate stations have access to network feeds and better resources for regional coverage. Can the independent find local news approaches different from those used by the affiliate in its local news segments? A half-hour news show by an affiliate may have only a few minutes of local news. Keep in mind that a half-hour television news program may have only eight or nine minutes of actual hard news, the rest going for sports, weather, features, and commercials.

The local independent, spending less time on national and international reports, might carry a virtually identical lead as the affiliate on the unemployment statistics story, but then could add:

VIDEO	AUDIO
	Harriet Probing took our cameras to the Center City unemployment compensation office on River Street. Harriet:
Harriet:	SOT: 25 secs

Electronic news gathering (ENG) and digital recording permit greater immediacy in local news reporting. Local news has become even more people-oriented, more informal in nature. With a wider range of sources to choose from because of the mobility of the mini-cam and videophone, and even cell phones, small stations do more and faster investigative reports, special reports on controversial issues, and features with good visuals. Small stations can more easily, as in the unemployment office example, localize the news for local audiences. Even a large market affiliate can localize news while stressing international, national, and regional stories.

Newspapers have done this, in reverse, for many years. Except for regional papers (examples are the *New York Times*, the *Washington Post*, the *Los Angeles Times*), newspapers have concentrated on the local news and added wider-ranging stories from various press services. The television affiliate takes the broader news from the network and adds its own local coverage. Some newspapers in some countries—England and Australia are good examples—have attempted to duplicate this approach with national editions that add local news for specific distribution regions. *USA Today*, distributed in the United States and abroad, has done the same. A small newspaper that has local news clones all over the world is the *Metro*.

As electronic media distribution modes increase, news coverage is likely to be oriented to more and more specialized audiences, similar to the approaches used by weekly newspapers and magazines as metropolitan dailies have disappeared. French historian Jacques Ellul, in his book *The Political Illusion*, expressed concern over electronic media approaches to news that stress information and ignore analysis. He argued that a political democracy cannot function effectively without people being able to analyze the errors of the past and to understand the present through that analysis. Ellul wrote, "Current news pre-empts the sense of continuity, prevents the use of memory, and leads to a constant falsification of past events when they are evoked again in the stream of news."

News programs must be careful not to confuse straight news with analysis or personal commentary. Some commentators editorialize in the guise of presenting information. Distortion of stories or emphasis on only one side of a story can change a news report into a commentary. Incomplete statements and the excessive use of color words can do the same thing. For example, using the unemployment figures story:

> Almost a half million additional American workers are unable to feed their families this month. They join over thirteen million other Americans—more people than reside in our entire state—who were already out on the streets last month, as the Department of Labor unemployment statistics showed a whopping increase of over three percent from October to November.

The preceding report is not necessarily false or unjustified. The point is that the audience should know whether it is getting a hard news report or news with even subtle commentary.

Some newscasts sell sensationalism, similar to the magazines at supermarket checkout counters. Remember that the newscaster is coming into audiences' homes as a guest, almost like a personal visitor. The approach should be informal, friendly and, ideally, honest, if the newscaster is to be welcomed again.

The most common type of presentation is straight news, on radio usually in five-minute or one-minute newsbreak segments, on television usually in half-hour programs, and on the Internet in varied time segments. Some news personalities are known for their commentaries, rather than straight news, and the audience expects analysis or personal opinion, not hard news, from them. But sometimes commentaries are integrated into straight news shows. The recent trend has been toward some news analysis and a lot of feature stories and dramatic aspects of individual stories. Occasionally a network or station carries news specials that probe the news.

Following the continuing success of *60 Minutes,* which began in 1965, other networks developed similar news shows, such as *Dateline, 48 Hours,* and *20/20* that tended toward mini-documentaries with more analysis than regular news programs—albeit these programs most often deal with human interest features or trivial subjects rather than with important events or issues.

At the other extreme is the use of *re-creations*—performers acting out a news sequence that the news team was unable to cover live or find **actuality** visuals for. Following criticism from many sources, including the public, networks, at least for now, have discontinued the use of re-creations.

In addition to *general news* programs, there are *straight news* shows devoted to specific topics, such as the international scene, financial reports, garden news, consumer affairs, educational or campus news, and similar areas. The approaches within each specialized category can vary, such as stressing the public service aspects or the human interest elements of the subject.

Although the straight news program is the most often used approach, some news programs provide in-depth reporting and obtain all the information possible on the particular story. In the unemployment figures example, using local interpolations of the statistics, following-up with comments from the workers affected, and interviewing employees and government officials provide an in-depth approach.

A third basic approach is the *interpretive* method, where the basic facts are analyzed for their immediate and future impact on the public through reporter commentary. The writer asks himself or herself: "What does this *really* mean to the audience?" In the unemployment figures story, the writer would include an analysis of the cost of the unemployment to the community, the effect on local and state taxes and services, the expected strength or weakness of the local economy, the effect of the lost income on local businesses, potential changes in school curricula to cope with an anticipated economic depression, possible solutions to the problem, and any other key areas that interpret the report's meaning for the viewers or listeners. Of course, the same interpretive approaches can be applied to reporting the national figures alone, without a local aspect, and international implications can be added.

The fourth basic approach is the kind we see mostly in movies and television shows and read in books about broadcast news, the *investigative* approach. The reporter or writer discovers and even *makes* the news by digging up material not available to the press in general and bringing to the public new and usually exclusive information on the subject. But with over 90% of the U.S. media owned or controlled by politically conservative sources, even investigative reporting has become highly selective in what aspects of a given story to present. For example, the *Washington Post,* highly critical of the Nixon White House, made it possible for its reporters Woodward and Bernstein to do the now-classic story of the Watergate scandal. On the other hand, to this very day most media outlets still perpetuate the fiction that the Bush White House invaded Iraq on the basis of faulty intelligence when, in fact, the intelligence was right on target, with the U.N. and the U.S. weapons inspectors both reporting that there was no evidence that Iraq had weapons of mass destruction and the CIA reporting that there was little or no credible probability that Iraq would attack the U.S. In this the U.S. media, principally conservative, appears to be trying to avoid further criticism of a Republican president. Sometimes the media's ideology rises above party-line support, as in the case of virtually no reportage by the mainstream media of the Obama White House's actions in continuing and even increasing the Bush White House's assault on Americans civil liberties, including Obama's use of drones not only for arbitrarily killing anyone the president designates, but for continuing detailed surveillance over the lives, beliefs, and behavior of all Americans. It was only after whistleblowers Bradley Manning and Edward Snowden, considered traitors by some and patriotic heroes by others, revealed the excesses of government conduct to the Internet world that some of the U.S. media seriously covered the actions and issues. Republican President and former General Dwight Eisenhower warned Americans against the military-industrial complex which, at this juncture, appears to include the media.

Any given news report can be a combination of more than one of the approaches discussed previously. Basic investigation should be a factor in all good news reporting. A mantra that too many journalists—and too many of those who receive the news—ignore is "if you can't trust the source, you can't trust the story."

Without a free, objective, investigative press, there is no public check on corruption and chicanery in the public and private sectors. The recent economic recession, among other things, resulted in investigative reporting in all of the media being downsized. Investigative reporters are leaving the profession. Many of those who investigated government corruption and corporate scandals have been going into corporate promotion and advertising and into government public relations jobs. Who will tell the public? Who will warn the public? Who will protect the public?

Advocacy News

Although news, ideally, should be objective and fair and should avoid any vested political, social, religious, economic, or other point-of-view, too often the news reflects the wishes of the network or station owner, the reporter, the advertiser, outside pressure groups, or other sources that want to mold public opinion. Although the slanting of presumed objective news presents a serious ethical problem, some aspects of news reporting actually take a legitimate advocacy approach.

Editorials and commentaries are direct forms of advocacy news, presenting an overt point-of-view or personal opinion. As previously noted, investigative writing and reporting, however, also frequently become advocacy news. Although few stations present specified editorial comments, many stations include investigative, advocacy news reports as part of their regular news broadcasts or as special reports under the heading of news and public affairs. A principal difference between the advocacy of editorials and the advocacy of investigative reports is that the former usually represents special or vested interest points-of-view whereas the latter frequently represents the interest of the public-at-large—the consumer.

Consumer Reports

A prime example of this kind of advocacy news is the consumer report. Paula Lyons has been one of the country's leading consumer reporters. The purpose of her consumer news reports has been to educate the public by investigating and revealing problems such as deceptive sales approaches, vendor scams, mislabelling and false advertising in the distribution of products and services, obtuse or misleading instructions or requirements from government or quasi-official agencies, and other practices that cheat or delude the consumer or that exploit a segment of the population. The writing for this kind of program should be direct, factual, and serious. That does not mean that humor, sometimes through satirizing the subject, cannot be used as a way of making the report attractive to the audience. The script should expose openly, and in as much detail as can be made clear in the limited air time, the specific ways in which the consumer can be duped and the specific ways in which the consumer can protect himself or herself.

Lyons suggested the following approaches for investigating and writing consumer news reports: The idea for any given report can come from various sources, and one key source is the writer-reporter herself or himself. Others include any information source that will help expose a problem in the marketplace or educate the consumer about something new, including individual consumers, consumer organizations, government agencies, and the media. For example, in the following script, "The Rugmark," the idea for the report came from the National Consumers League.

Once you have the subject, Lyons said, you must do the research. Where possible, travel to the site of the concern. Obtain all audio, video, and print materials available. Radio and television archives are helpful. In "The Rugmark," for example, Lyons incorporated some shots from a CNN documentary, *Faces of Slavery*. Interviewing all parties is important, including consumers, retailers, manufacturers, consumer activists, and experts in the particular field. If the issue covered is controversial, talk with all sides before completing the script.

Lyons stated that one technique for putting an audio consumer report together is to first line up all the best sounds—that is, the materials recorded— and build the script around them. However, for a video program—Lyons's reports aired on radio and television both—you must think visually. The pictures must tell the story, not simply be used as background. Avoid "video wallpaper." At the story beginning "tease" the audience—get its attention. Make the viewers or listeners stop what they are doing and pay attention because they are intrigued by the opening. The opening doesn't always have to be strong and dramatic, however. Lyons advised that a softer approach can be used, as in "The Rugmark," where the opening is on consumers shopping, to create an identification for the audience members with what they themselves have done.

THE RUGMARK

2:34   ANCHOR: LEDE

HAND WOVEN ORIENTAL CARPETS . . . THEY'RE LUXURIOUS AND BEAUTIFUL . . . BUT SOME COME WITH A HIDDEN PRICETAG . . . THE LIVES OF VERY YOUNG CHILDREN.

ILLEGAL CHILD LABOR . . . INDEED BONDED SERVITUDE IS A BIG PROBLEM IN THIS INDUSTRY. HOW CAN YOU AVOID BECOMING A SUPPORTER OF THAT?

CONSUMER EDITOR PAULA LYONS INVESTIGATES A PROGRAM CALLED "THE RUGMARK."

LEDE: PAULA

THE RUGMARK IS A LABEL THAT WILL SOON TURN UP ON SOME ORIENTAL CARPETS. SUPPORTERS SAY IT WILL MEAN THAT THE RUG WAS NOT MADE WITH CHILD LABOR. BUT CAN ANYONE GUARANTEE THAT? THE INDUSTRY HAS ITS DOUBTS.

SONY:

nat: sot 25:23 "Beautiful, beautiful rug, what a combination of colors."

continued

IF YOU'VE EVER SHOPPED FOR AN ORIENTAL RUG, IT IS EASY TO BE DAZZLED BY THEIR BEAUTY, OVERWHELMED BY THE MANY CHOICES, AND STUNNED BY THE COST OF SOME.

NAT: . . . "Do you have anything like this (no) a little less expensive?"

BUT NOW THERE'S SOMETHING ELSE TO WORRY ABOUT . . . WHETHER OR NOT . . . THE RUG WAS MADE LIKE THIS . . . WITH THE LABOR OF CHILDREN.

IN INDIA, PAKISTAN AND NEPAL, SOME ESTIMATES SUGGEST THAT ONE MILLION CHILDREN UNDER 14 YRS. OF AGE, WORK LONG HOURS, IN MISERABLE CONDITIONS, WEAVING ORIENTAL RUGS FOR LITTLE OR NO PAY.

GRINDING POVERTY LITERALLY FORCES MANY FAMILIES TO SELL THEIR CHILDREN TO LOOM OWNERS.

:47–:57
*CG TL
LINDA GOLODNER
Child Labor
Coalition

50:00 "The manufacturers just pay a pittance to the family to take these children away and then the children are fed at the loom, often they sleep at the loom. And it is virtually bonded slavery."

ACTIVISTS IN INDIA WHO HAVE BEEN RESCUING CHILDREN FROM THESE LOOMS HAVE JOINED FORCES WITH UNICEF, THE INTERNATIONAL LABOR ORGANIZATION AND THE CHILD LABOR COALITION HERE IN THE UNITED STATES TO DRAW ATTENTION TO AND APPLY MARKET PRESSURE TO STOP THIS ABUSE OF CHILDREN.

57:52 "What we want to do is educate consumers so that they can make the choice in the market place of choosing a carpet that was not made with child labor."

THEIR SOLUTION? THE RUGMARK . . . A LABEL SOON TO APPEAR ON CARPETS CERTIFYING THAT THE LOOM OR FACTORY WHERE IT WAS MADE HAS BEEN INSPECTED AND FOUND FREE OF CHILD WORKERS.

STAND-UP All agree that the Rugmark is an excellent idea, laudable even. But local retailers are not sure it can really deliver on what it promises.

1:56–2:05

*CG TL
GREGORY HITES
Gregorian Rugs

GREGORY HITES, GREGORIAN RUG 35:35

"You are talking about an industry that is spread out over a very wide geographical area. It will require a tremendous amount of monitoring and also a lot of disciplined monitoring."

continued

2:08–2:15*CG TL
STEPHEN BOODAKIAN
Koko Boodakian & Sons

STEPHEN BOODAKIAN, KOKO BOODAKIAN AND SONS

25:54 "To certify and visit the looms on a regular basis, and to do it and to know that it's being done without corruption, is extremely difficult."

BUT SUPPORTERS OF THE RUGMARK SAY THEY WILL CONTINUE TO PUT PRESSURE ON RETAILERS TO SUPPORT THE PROGRAM. THEY BELIEVE IN THE RUGMARK'S INTEGRITY AND SAY TO DO NOTHING ABOUT CHILD LABOR IN THIS INDUSTRY . . . WOULD BE WORSE.

GOLODNER "There are a lot of people making money on the backs of these children."

SONY 2:34
"backs of these children."

TAG:

IT APPEARS THE SUCCESS OR FAILURE OF THIS EFFORT WILL DEPEND ON BUILDING TRUST. RIGHT NOW, LOCAL RETAILERS SAY THEY ARE MORE COMFORTABLE TRUSTING THEIR OWN SUPPLIERS' ASSURANCES THAT THE RUGS THEY SELL ARE NOT MADE BY CHILDREN, THAN THE ORGANIZERS OF THE RUGMARK WHO ARE UNKNOWN TO THEM.

NEVERTHELESS, THE RUGMARK IS HAVING AN IMPACT. ORGANIZERS SAY IT WILL START TO SHOW UP IN STORES IN THIS COUNTRY PERHAPS AS EARLY AS THIS COMING FALL.

Courtesy of Paula Lyons and WBZ, Boston

Radio: Audio

Radio newswriting is closer to newspaper reporting than is television newswriting. Where the television report can show the event unfolding, the radio report has to include more descriptive writing—particularly verbal descriptions of scenes, people, and actions. The radio writer has to create word pictures, conveying through words clear and striking visual images. In television, the audience sees the events and any persons being interviewed. In radio the voices in such interviews must be clearly identified. It is important in radio to integrate as much audio background as possible—the sounds of the event and people associated with it, live or recorded—into on-the-spot reports.

Television: Visuals

Remember: On television the *picture* is paramount. Don't waste the relatively few precious words you have in the average-length story by saying something the audience can see. In contrast with the radio newswriter, the television writer does not create word pictures, but emphasizes visual pictures. *Show* what is happening; don't *tell* about it.

Don't try to cover too much too quickly in the visuals. Even viewers used to television news's fast pace require some time to absorb the information. Generally, keep any picture on the screen at least three to five seconds—longer, of course, depending on its importance in the story; otherwise the audience gets more of a montage, an impression of a series of quick shots without a content focus. If you want to create a mood rather than to give information, then the montage approach will work.

When you put together the news story, you're working in a chicken-or-egg situation. You know at the outset what the story is from the reporter's written materials, but you can't begin to write the script, either dialogue or narration, without looking first at all the available visuals so you can determine which ones to use. After you've selected the visuals, you can write the narrative around them. Be careful not to use visuals for their own sake. They must be an integral part of the story and in themselves be able to tell the story. You may find some great recorded materials, but if they don't move the story along, don't use them.

Sometimes, especially in small independent stations with limited field resources, you can find yourself short on visuals for a given news show. Try to find additional visuals from some source, if you can't send a reporter out to get more. Stock footage, still pictures from the morgue, graphics created by a staff artist, materials usable from the Internet—all of these are better than a talking-head newscaster. You can write VO narration for such visuals, making sure you clearly identify them for what they are. If you use stock footage of a hurricane, for example, note that the shots of the hurricane are from a previous year in the same area, and that shots of the current hurricane are expected to be available for the next newscast.

Timing is important for the writer. Make sure you have the exact times for all visuals, especially those that are not self-contained. You don't want to write VO narration for a silent segment that runs longer or shorter than the visual itself. If the visual segment is shorter and if the extended narration is an essential part of the story, give the narration to one of the newscasters OC, either as a lead-in to or follow-up of the visual segment. The writer should prepare stories of different time lengths for the final story of the program, in case the program is running short or long. The alternatives may be different lengths for the same story or entirely different stories of different lengths.

Rewriting

One of the newswriter's duties, particularly on the local level, is rewriting. A smaller station without a news-gathering staff sometimes is totally dependent on the newswire. The announcer, given sufficient time and energy, edits those stories that can be adapted appropriately to include a local angle, evaluating the stories impact on the community. In such cases the announcer rewrites the news.

The writer in any size station tries to find a thread or angle that means something special to that station's viewers or listeners. That means rewriting the news that has not been gathered locally. For example, stories dealing with the national or state economy might be rewritten to reflect their relationship to the local economy, business conditions, or labor union concerns.

Probably the most common form of rewriting is updating. An important story doesn't disappear once it is used. Yet, to use exactly the same story in subsequent newscasts throughout the day is likely to turn away audience members who have heard it more than once; they might conclude that the station is carrying stale news.

An example of this was the coverage of the bombings at the Boston Marathon in 2013. The critical importance of the story kept it in the media headlines for days and, in many cases, for weeks afterward. The public was eager for information about what happened and about the search for the perpetrators. In the first few days, despite the lack of new information, in order to satisfy the public interest the networks and stations kept the story on the air, necessarily repeating reports over and over again. For avid viewers, the repetition became a turn-off; for new viewers—although most viewers tuned in/logged on from the beginning—the material was not old hat. Newswriters faced the task of presenting old material in new formats, rewriting the same material into fresh forms.

Look for several major elements when you update news stories. First, determine if there is any further hard news, any factual information to add to the story. Second, if the story is important enough, it is likely that some investigative reporting will have dug up some additional background information, if not new data, that was not available when the story was first aired.

Third, depending on the event's impact upon society, any number of people, from VIPs to ordinary citizens, will have commented since the story's initial release. Include these commentaries, preferably in recorded interviews.

Fourth, a story by its very nature can relate to the day's other events. Your update can include new material showing those relationships.

Fifth, a story should be rewritten for the audience it is reaching. The person preparing for work or listening to radio news during "drive time" on the way to work may have different news interests than the person at home listening a few hours later. The early afternoon news on television reaches different audience interests than does the evening or late night news.

Finally, even if there is no additional information or any other angle that changes the content of the news story, rewrite simply to give it variety, to maintain a fresh news feeling for the station's image.

Following are examples of the same news story on one radio station's update reports.

6:00 A.M. Update: "It's the first Monday of October . . . and that means the U.S. Supreme Court begins a new session. The Court will hear three more cases concerning abortion. Harvard law professor Lawrence Tribe feels the Court may try to dismantle Roe versus Wade piece by piece." (TRIBE: ". . . volcanic eruption.")

7:00 Update: "It's the first Monday of October . . . and the Supreme Court begins its new term. The high court will look at three cases . . . each case is aimed at limiting a woman's right to an abortion." (TRIBE.)

7:30 Update: "A new term begins for the U.S. Supreme Court . . . and the justices are expected to continue focusing their attention on abortion. Good morning. There are three abortion cases before the Court . . . two having to do with parental consent or knowledge . . . the third an Illinois statute and regulations that required doctors' offices and abortion clinics to be equipped as if they were hospitals. That statute was declared unconstitutional by a Federal Appeals Court." (TRIBE.)

8:30 Update: "Abortion. The right to privacy and the right to die. Just three of the matters that go before the United States Supreme Court as it begins its new term. Good morning. Many observers are saying we'll see more of the Court's shifting to a more conservative bent. One of those observers is Harvard law professor Lawrence Tribe." (TRIBE: " . . . this term.") " . . . the Court will also look at the power of judges in desegregation cases. One concerns public housing in Yonkers, New York."

Courtesy of Sherman Whitman, WBCN-FM Radio, Boston

Internet Newswriting

Professor and veteran newspaper and Internet journalist Dr. Bob Stepno, one of the country's experts on writing news for the Internet, offered the following description of web journalism and advice to the student on approaches and techniques for web news writing:

Writers creating material for news, information and entertainment sites on the World Wide Web use the same skills they use writing for other media—skills ranging from the basics—curiosity and love of language, to the other basics—grammar, spelling and punctuation.

The Internet can deliver anything that can be converted to digital form: text, photos, animation, sound and full-motion video, as well as computer programs that let their active audience make choices, send messages, search databases and play games. It's all a matter of "bits," the ones and zeroes of computer code called "binary digits." Those bits, whether they represent sound or color, can flow through the same wires and fiber-optic cables, which means the Internet can and does deliver "media" of all kinds.

A story's opening paragraph and its headline often appear as the index-entry of a Web site's main page, and Web "usability" experts recommend the newspaper conventions of headlines, summaries and the "inverted pyramid" story. They have learned from surveys (and common sense) that readers browse and skim their way around the Web—and may not get past the first paragraph without a clear invitation. Like newspaper page designs that put the most important stories "above the fold," the essential information on a Web page should be visible as soon as the reader arrives, not out of sight at the bottom of a long scrolling window.

Given the discomforts of staring at text on a computer screen, there's a lot to be said for shorter stories and simple structures.

That doesn't mean a writer can't take a more "narrative" or "feature" approach to a story, or that a newspaper feature opening with a scene or anecdote can't be published online. The *Wall Street Journal* does it all the time, to name one home of the "anecdotal lead." Clever and informative headlines, pictures and separate summary paragraphs are among the ways to point readers to a story—and from there a well-written anecdote may be as inviting on the screen as it is in print.

The story or section summaries on that opening page also might be all the reader needs—or wants—to read. For that reason, they should be more than a "tease." Similarly, headings, subheadings, highlighted keywords and bulleted lists can help the rushed reader to get some information and move on, if that's his goal. Even if you have an ulterior motive—such as leading readers into a longer visit so that they will see multiple advertisements from companies that pay your salary—it's a fair bet that empty promises and P.R. puffery may convince them to go elsewhere.

"Choice" is just a mouse-click away, so writing for the Web should offer choices—a choice of short and long versions of a story, a choice of "entry points" or a choice of media. The original concept behind the Web is the word "hypertext," coined in the 1960s by Ted Nelson, a computers-for-the-people evangelist, to describe new non-linear or nonsequential forms of writing that computers would make possible someday. . . . The online reporter (or re-write editor) has more room to work with than her TV or newspaper counterpart. The story could have sidebars about the City Hall maintenance budget, the mayor's past promises to fix the roof, or a link to a story about last year's rainy-season meeting when half the ceiling *did* collapse. In print, the writer might try to weave all of those elements into one piece. Online, they can be written as separate items linked to a central menu, and the reader can choose which to read first, or at all.

The same has been true in newspapers and magazines for years—a complicated story may have to be broken into a series, or shorter "side-bars" may be added to explain points that do not fit the main narrative. On the broad sheets of a newspaper, sidebars, boxes and photos give the eye multiple points to enter the page. On the smaller computer screen, a Web page's menus can do something similar.

If the story itself does not seem to fall into a natural narrative, then there's all the more reason to experiment with "chunking" the information into logical blocks, putting each block on a separate Web page and linking them together. The more complex such a hypertext document becomes, the more the Web developer should compensate by providing overviews, summaries, maps of all the pieces of the puzzle.

In planning a Web publication, the writer also can plan to present information in layers of detail, or in layers of "media richness," to be chosen by visitors whose computer systems or browsing time can handle more pictures, audio or video.

Television and radio writers, even more than newspaper and magazine writers, have to "filter" the news and get to essentials. The audience is presented with an efficient package, but has to take it or leave it. On the Web, planning a story is not only a matter of deciding what to say, but choosing the form—or forms—in which to say it. Writers and producers of online sites get to make their own choices about which medium works best for the story at hand—text, still or moving image, sound or a combination.

Each medium has its strengths. Video captures people, emotion and action. Yes, aim a video camera at the people with tears in their eyes, the touchdown, the charging lion or the burning building. But you may want to use text instead of a reporter's "talking head" if you have to explain what's going on in the picture. Then use the Web's hypertext links to connect to background, more detail, and related stories. And use audio to deliver natural sound and the voices of people telling their own stories, not an announcer reading a script. . . . Web readers do tend to scan, so some of the best opportunities to reach them are in short bursts of writing: Headlines and sub-headings, photo captions, summaries and bulleted lists of key facts.

If readers' main online reading experience is email, that should give you some ideas about style and tone—personal and relaxed are good. However, emulating the grammar, spelling, punctuation and capitalization of casual email writers would not do much for your credibility as a professional communicator. These "new media" really are "new." It is hard to predict how readers preferences and habits will develop, especially as screens get bigger, brighter, flatter and more detailed.

An example of how Internet news is frequently a combination of newspaper and television news writing techniques is a MSNBC story, "G-8 leaders debate deal to limit global warming." Datelined Rome, the lead paragraph states, as would a newspaper story: "World leaders gathered at the Group of Eight summit Wednesday wrestled over a potential landmark agreement on limiting the global rise in temperature, but were expected to emphasize that signs of economic recovery are not yet strong enough to withdraw powerful stimulus measures." Next to the opening paragraph, under a photo of U.S. President Barack Obama and Italian Premier at that time, Silvio Berlusconi, is a "launch" icon for a video of the meeting. The story continues in depth as it would in a newspaper, but with the addition of interactive segments, including a report on Obama's arrival in Italy the previous day, sidebar stories and videos on some of the prominent leaders at the meeting, and related text and video on such topics as "quake aftershocks prompt G-8 airlift plan" and "G-8 cash sought for climate change fund."

Another example, from MSN Music News, "Jackson's kids emerge from behind the veil," dealt with the memorial service for pop music star Michael Jackson. Datelined Los Angeles, the lead paragraph stated: "Michael Jackson's three young children, after a lifetime of fierce protection from the prying eyes of the world, came out into the open Tuesday for the most public and heart-wrenching debut imaginable." The rest of the story, in newspaper fashion, was a combined feature and news report on Jackson's children at the memorial service. But utilizing the Internet's interactive capabilities, the user could access interlaced material such as "Daughter's tearful goodbye," "Watch the entire memorial," "Quotes from the Jackson memorial service," and "Photos: Michael Jackson memorial."

Local station television news is still a staple and one of the few formats originating and produced locally as conglomerates grow larger in the media industries. WINK-TV, in Fort. Myers, Florida, serves several counties as a regional station. Janet Wilson, former executive assistant to the news director, included among her work the rewriting of television news stories for the station's web site. In the list below, she describes some specific techniques and approaches she used in writing news for the Internet, and some key differences between writing for the broadcast media and the Internet:

- *Approach:* TV news is visual. Often times the pictures tell the story. The writing can make it seem more important or less important to the viewer. When writing for the web, it is all about the writing. On many web sites, there are no visuals to enhance the story. The words have to tell the complete story and make it relevant to the reader.

- *Writing technique:* People tend to write in shorter sentences for TV news. Writing for the web is different in that the sentences tend to be longer because they have to be more descriptive. It is a lot like writing for a newspaper or magazine.

- *Language:* Many times alliteration is used in TV news, either in the teases or the copy itself. Alliteration makes the sentences sound catchy or interesting to a listener. The written word on the web page does not benefit from this technique. The web writer has to remember there are different pronunciations for a single word. When a news anchor talks about a "lead investigator," the viewer should automatically know they are referring to the person in charge of an investigation. For the web, this has to be clarified. It is not a person who investigates lead, a type of metal, but the head person in charge of an investigation. The web writer should keep these several pronunciation possibilities in mind.

- *Use of visuals:* The visuals on web sites have to be created with the writing. The newscast is streamlined on the page, so the entire newscast can be viewed. The people who watch the streamlined webcast may not be the same people who read the individual stories on the web.

■ *Length of story:* There is no minimum or maximum, at least on the WINK-TV web site. TV news writing is restricted to about a minute's time. The web story could be endless. Like a newspaper story, it does not have to fit into a particular format or size. The web story's length is as long as needed to tell the story.

■ *Interactive elements for the web:* Web readers can be linked to an endless number of other sites. If the story is about a hurricane, for example, a web reader can be linked to the National Hurricane Center or FEMA (Federal Emergency Management Administration) for more information. News people are not usually experts, but can link the readers to experts.

■ *TV and Internet differences:* In a TV news story a reporter can point to an object and say, "look at this document" or "look at this burned-out home." When writing for the web, the object or event has to be described, if there are no visuals. If the web site is an extension of the TV stations' news department, it is important to remind the audience that it is the TV station delivering the story. Where on the TV newscast the viewer would see a reporter doing an interview, on the web we have to say something like, "a mother tells WINK-TV News her story." In rewriting a story for the web, I change reporters' words if I can think of a more descriptive word to use. I also do not have the same strict time restrictions that a field reporter has and sometimes have a few extra moments to phrase things in a way that tells the story a little better.

A reporter in the field also may write a story in a more relaxed speaking language, such as using contractions. For the web page I like the more formal written language. In addition, field reporters do not always write in complete sentences. It is up to the web writer to change that for the Internet story. Further, field reporters may not focus on correct spelling. Spelling is important on a web page.

In one of the stories I wrote [the 'Pastor' story on the following page, used as an example of a TV story rewritten for the Internet], the story was not posted until the station did a second televised story on the incident. For it to make sense to the readers, additional background information was added to the web story. The web story has to be a different entity from the story that aired on the TV news.

The following is an example of Janet Wilson's adaptation of a TV story for the Internet. What changes do you find between the first script, that of the television broadcast, and the second script, the web presentation?

P-PASTOR FOLO P-PATOR FOLO SHOW DATE SOURCE 6p 7/3 P-PASTOR FOLO 390 07/04 08:44:54 PKG PRODUCTION CUES: SCRIPT:

((CG=PUNTA GORDA/MONDAY))

46-YEAR OLD PASTOR PAUL KING WAS JUST CHARGED WITH AGGRAVATED CHILD ABUSE . . .

BUT ACCORDING TO SHERIFF'S RECORDS . . . IT'S NOT THE FIRST TIME HE'S HAD CHARGES FILED AGAINST HIM.

LAST OCTOBER DOUGLAS POOLE . . . WHO IS A PARENT . . . FILED A BATTERY COMPLAINT AGAINST KING.

KING REPORTEDLY SHOVED POOLE, AFTER POOLE CONFRONTED HIM.

ACCORDING TO THE REPORT, KING ACCUSED POOLE'S CHILD OF CHEATING.

IN 1997 . . . ANOTHER SIMPLE BATTERY CASE WAS FILED AGAINST KING.

THIS TIME BY A MOTHER WHO SAYS SHE HAD TO SPANK HER OWN CHILD OR KING WOULD HAVE DONE IT HIMSELF.

THE WOMAN . . . WHO DOESN'T WANT TO BE IDENTIFIED . . . SAYS SHE TOO HAD TO SIGN A FORM THAT ALLOWS THE SCHOOL TO PUNISH STUDENTS AS SCHOOL OFFICIALS DEEM NECESSARY.

((CG=MOTHER OF FORMER STUDENT))

44:35 We do believe in spanking here. It doesn't happen often but then I found out it happens all the time and it has been unbelievable the abuse that has been reported to me from other parents.

MANY OF THE COMPLAINTS FILED . . . NEVER LED TO CHARGES.

AND THIS MOTHER SAYS . . . MANY PARENTS ARE AFRAID TO COME FORWARD TO BLAME KING.

SHE DOESN'T WANT ANOTHER CHILD HURT.

46:42 How he could even attempt to put his hands on another child even take the risk, that shows me there is a very serious problem.

PASTOR KING TOLD REPORTERS MONDAY . . . HE LOOKS FORWARD TO BEING VINDICATED IN COURT.

((CG=PASTOR PAUL KING/HARBORVIEW CHRISTIAN CHURCH)) 11:13 No. None. I am a man of God and I will not agree to a lie.

Courtesy of Janet Wilson

HOME
NAVIGATE
NEWS
CBS SHOWS
WEATHER
WINK TALENT
SPORTS
PROGRAMMING
CALL FOR
ACTION
LOCAL GUIDE
LINKS
RECIPES
MONEY
HEALTH
CBS KIDSHOW
SHOPPING
PRESS
RELEASES
CONTACT US
JOBS AT WINK
UTILITIES
SITE MAP
FEEDBACK
CHANGE CITY
HELP

navigate   shortcut

HOME   ?

CBS
Online Store

come on down

HOME   CBS

Pastor Accused of Child Abuse

Port Charlotte
Friday, July 13 - 05:43 PM ET

(WINK) WINK News has learned of more allegations of abuse against Port Charlotte pastor Paul King who was arrested and faces charges for paddling an 8-year-old girl with a wooden paddle. **WINK News** also learned that two other organizations, the Association of Christian Schools and the Department of Children and Families, are looking into the pastor's actions.

King was released from jail after posting a $20,000 bond Monday. King is director of Charlotte Regional Christian Academy and is a pastor at Harborview Christian Church.

Tammy Pipkin, the mother of the girl who was punished, says her daughter was severely beaten on May 11th. Pipkin took her daughter out of the school after the punishment.

WINK News also spoke with another parent who claims King abused her daughter and several other children 4 years ago. A search of Charlotte County records verified that the woman did file a report against King, but no charges were ever filed against King for the incident.

The mother, who did not want to be identified, tells **WINK News** she had to sign a form that allows the school to punish students as school officials deem necessary.

The unidentified mother says, **"We do believe in spanking here. It doesn't happen often, but then I found out it happens all the time. And it has been unbelievable the abuse that has has been reported to me from other parents."**

The mother believes many parents are afraid to come forward to say anything against King. **"How he could even attempt to put his hands on another child, even take the risk, shows me there is a very serious problem."**

Charlotte County Sheriff's records show another allegation against King. Last October, Douglas Poole, a parent, filed a battery complaint against the pastor. King reportedly shoved Poole after a confrontation.

King tells **WINK News** that he looks forward to being vindicated in court. **"No plea bargain. None. I am a man of God and I will not agree to lie."**

Justin Herndon, a WINK-TV reporter and writer, described the differences between TV and Internet news stories:

Stories on the website are about as important today as telegrams were in their time. The Internet allows us to disseminate our story instantly and attract viewers who are at work or away from home during the day. That gives us a chance to update our viewers, and the more they know they can depend on us during the day, the more they will choose to watch our newscasts at night. The web story differs from on-air content mainly because it is not always in the present tense and often gets posted after we are off the air. That said, it's probably the most edited of our content because it is like a newspaper that will live in cyberspace for an extended amount of time versus a minute or two on TV. TV scripts are often concise and can be done extemporaneously. Web stories take more time and get strict punctuation. It can also make you better on-air because the more you write properly, the better you will speak.

WINK feature writer and reporter Judd Cribbs stated that "When posting video of my stories to the web, I try to use the accompanying text as a complement to, rather than a copy of, my video. I try to add extra insight or context to the text, or maybe add details that time did not allow in the video. Two things I avoid: 1. Copying and pasting my script into the text box. I am always disappointed when I read a story on the web and then watch the video, and the text is just a word-for-word copy. 2: Writing only a summary paragraph. I think the web copy should have quotes and a narrative, just like the video. I also try to add different quotes to the text to avoid repetition. This might take a little extra time, but I think it's well worth it." Here is an example of one of Cribbs's feature stories, first for television, then for the Internet.

LUPE LOPEZ IS A SPRY AND FRIENDLY FORMER MARINE WHO FOUGHT ON THE FRONT LINES OF WORLD WAR
TWO AND ALSO SERVED IN THE KOREAN WAR.

NOW, AT THE AGE OF 82, HE HAS DISCOVERED A HOBBY WHICH IS UNIQUELY HIS OWN. HE RECENTLY BEGAN MAKING DOLLS OUT OF SOCKS FOR ALL THE DEPARTMENTS AT THE V-A CLINIC WHERE HE VOLUNTEERS. IT BEGAN WHEN THE DOG-LOVING LUPE MADE A SOCK-DOG DOLL FOR HIS DASHBOARD.

"and it wouldn't fit, so I made another one and I give them to the girls and that's really what started me."

THAT LED TO ATTEMPTS AT BIGGER DOLLS

"and the first thing you know, I used a whole sock and my son said, well, Dad, go ahead and make them. And I enjoy it . . ."

HE'S MADE ABOUT 40 NOW . . . ALL MARINES IN CASE YOU HAVEN'T NOTICED.

". . . that's the only thing I know how to make. I don't know how to make anything else."

AT FIRST, LUPE USED WHATEVER MATERIALS WERE NEARBY.

". . . rags, anything. I use my old shirts, shorts, anything I can get my hands on I'll stuff 'em with it. I used my old socks and then I used my son's socks and he said, Dad, we're

continued

running out of socks. So he bought me a package, so I'm making them now out of brand new socks because all the old ones are gone."

NOW HIS PROCESS HAS BEEN STREAMLINED AND THE DOLL-BUILDING TECHNIQUES HAVE BEEN IMPROVED, BUT SINCE LUPE IS ALSO A PATIENT AT THE V- A CLINIC, IT DOESN'T REALLY MATTER HOW LUPE MAKES THE DOLLS. WHAT MATTERS IS WHY LUPE MAKES THE DOLLS.

"I show them I appreciate what they do for us. All the veterans do. But this is my way of thanking them for what they do for me."

Anchor: JUDD

Read rate: 15   LUPE HAD A CAREER AS AN ENGINEER BUT SAYS

THIS IS THE FIRST HOBBY HE'S EVER HAD.

CG: Super/Under—Cribbs' Notes   ROLL CUE: THANKS JUDD

TAKE: OPEN   (OPEN)

Courtesy of Judd Cribbs, producer Jessica Hehir, WINK-TV, Ft. Myers, FL

Judd Cribbs's adaptation of the same story for the Internet:

Lupe Lopez is an energetic former Marine who, at the age of 82, just discovered a new hobby of his own making.

For the past few months the Texas native and Cape Coral resident has been making sock dolls for the different departments at the Fort Myers V.A. Outpatient Clinic where he volunteers.

"This is my way of thanking them for what they do for me," says Lupe. "I show them I appreciate what they do for us. All the Veterans do."

Lupe has made about 40 dolls and began stuffing his old socks in them, but now has to buy packages of new socks for the project. And he only models Marines because he says "that's the only thing I know how to make."

"I enjoy it," he explains. "I've never had a hobby before but I just like to do this."

Professor Jack Lule notes in "The Power and Pitfalls of Journalism in The Hypertext Era," in *The Chronicle of Higher Education*, that "news differs in tone, tenor, depth, and style depending on whether it appears in a newspaper, in a magazine, on the radio, or on television. Online news is different from all of those media, and oddly, embraces them all." He explains that news on the Internet can have the depth that newspapers offer, the approach and orientation of a "smart-mouthed" magazine, talk radio's immediacy and call-in interactivity, and TV's visual impact. Lule gives an example of the Internet newswriter's obligation to "write a tightly woven main story with logical, independent links to other angles and topics." In writing an article about a kidnapping for example, the writer can go far beyond possibilities in any of the older media by including "links to transcripts of the sheriff's press conference, a three-dimensional map of the house, an exhaustive list of evidence, a detailed timeline of events, and profiles of defendants and prosecutors." Lule's example excellently represents the interactive non-linear Internet writing approach. But, Lule cautions, in combining the most effective aspects of all these media into online news that uses the interactive potentials of chat rooms, forums, and email, the newswriter must give priority to ethics. As this book has pointed out in all formats, the writer must know the media and learn effective techniques, but the power of the writer and the media to affect the audiences' thinking and feelings requires a strong commitment to responsible ethical purpose and behavior.

Even with an ostensibly objective format—such as hard news—the writer must be certain that all points of view and interpretations are available. If the older media are skewing the news—as they frequently do because of the advertiser, owner, or, sometimes, producer-writer control—the Internet offers the possibility of implementing the presentation of alternative viewpoints to popular thought and belief otherwise usually unavailable. A person might do extensive web browsing, but the writer can help orient the browser to sites that offset restricted attitudes and information.

Gatekeeping and Alternative Views

Probably the most important difference between news in the traditional media, such as radio and television, and news on the Internet is the issue of gatekeeping. A half-dozen multinational corporations control almost 90% of the international broadcasting and cable distribution and news dissemination. The corporate executives, as was demonstrated in the Worldcom and other media giant scandals in recent years, put their personal profits ahead of service to the public and manipulate and censor the news to serve their personal beliefs and corporate interests. They are the gatekeepers. We get only the news and views that they want us to get. The Internet, however, has challenged the international corporations' control of our information and ideas. Any group or individual can report news and views not found on the older media, without censorship or vested interest control. One such organization is FreeSpeech.org, which also provides a TV news service as Free Speech TV. With sources from all over the world, it provides written and visual coverage of rallies and marches against corporate and governmental behavior. Examples of recent issues and events covered anti-war and anti-racist protests, corporate and wall street actions that plunge millions of families into poverty, union-busting, blockade of humanitarian aid to Palestinian enclaves, torture of political prisoners worldwide, support of regimes that permit rape as a weapon of population control, and similar matters generally ignored by the mainstream, corporate-controlled media in the United States and elsewhere and by government-controlled media in many countries. If your interest is in journalism and you have a strong social and/or political conscience, you may wish to examine the content and structure of such programs on Dish TV, Direc

TV, and the Internet. On pages 189-192 are examples from FreeSpeech.org's Internet news programs of recent years. Note the links to additional material such as its online TV channels and schedules, and videos, interviews, lectures, and other materials related to social and political issues and events.

Special Considerations

A most important concern of people of color, women, ethnic groups, and others not fully integrated into the American broadcasting mainstream is the lack of adequate news coverage pertaining to their special interests and needs. Many of the complaints to the FCC concerning failure of stations to serve community needs relate to both the quantity and quality of news items that affect or are about special groups. Many journalists, in both print and electronic media, say this is because it is difficult for a "non-minority" journalist to completely understand the concerns of people in "minority" groups.

Reporter Martha Bradlee, in an *op ed* piece on "Media's Racial Inequalities" in the *Boston Globe*, suggested that "perhaps in our largely white, middle-class newsrooms we have real empathy only for someone we can closely identify with . . . in my 10 years as a reporter in Boston, I remember only a handful of instances where we in the media have done background pieces of the 'what was he really like' variety on minority victims living in low-income, high-crime areas. We have, however, knocked on countless doors in the suburbs to try to humanize the white victim and show the pain of the victim's family."

Covering a non-majority group requires a special sensitivity and empathy with the history, environment, culture, problems, and aspirations of that group. It has been suggested that being a member of that group is necessary for the understanding that results in the most effective story. Television news executive Robert Reid has been quoted as saying that reporters or writers from the "minority" group make a difference by providing perspectives that "majority" group professionals don't have. "Blacks in television tend to accord a more even treatment," Reid contended. "How often do you see a man-in-the-street interview and no Blacks are interviewed? The Black reporter is more likely to come back with some Blacks among those interviewed." The same has been said about the inclusion of women and other groups in news stories.

Closing this sensitivity gap requires a twofold approach: providing equal opportunity for reporter-writer jobs for all kinds of stories, and recognizing that a member of a particular group is likely to bring a sensitivity and perspective to covering a story relating to that group that non-members might not.

Like the commercial writer, the newswriter must be aware of the needs, attitudes, feelings, and motivations of the group covered, as well as those of the general audience watching or listening. The impact of a particular news event on a special group—and such impact, by the nature of our society, frequently is

FSTV
FREE SPEECH·TV

Your Progressive and Independent
TV AND MULTIMEDIA NETWORK

Home   Subscribe   Get Involved   About   Calendar   TV Channels   FSTV Blog

VIDEOS ON DEMAND   TV SCHEDULE   MEMBERSHIP DRIVE

Search this site

FREE SPEECH BLOG

Categories

Current News and Opinion
Free Speech TV News
Media Consortium
U.S. Social Forum
Detroit 2010

The Media Consortium
Alternet
The New Republic
The Nation
Wikileaks
Afro-Netizen
American Forum
BraveNewFilms
Campus Progress
Chelsea Green

Latest Blog Posts

2011, May 6, 3:15pm
Make Sure Mom Will Have Medicare

While you're thinking of your mother on Mother's Day, think about the health care options your mother should have once she is 65. One of the greatest gifts we can leave for our parents is the defeat of the Medicare privatization plan that conservatives want to foist on the country.

That's why Jewish Funds for Justice has created a Facebook campaign to help send the message that children who love their parents will not want Medicare turned into a private insurance voucher program.

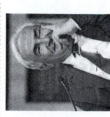

2011, May 6, 3:03pm
The IMF's Switch in Time

The annual spring meeting of the International Monetary Fund was notable in marking the Fund's effort to distance itself from its own long-standing tenets on capital controls and labor-market flexibility. It appears that a new IMF has gradually, and cautiously, emerged under the leadership of Dominique Strauss-Kahn.

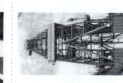

2011, May 6, 9:16am
House Repubs Push to Renew Drilling

House Republicans passed a bill yesterday afternoon that would require the Obama administration to expand offshore oil and gas drilling. As oil prices shoot up, Republicans have pushing for more domestic drilling, even as oil companies report record profits.

2011, May 5, 10:52am
Homeland Security Post bin Laden

Nearly a decade ago, America's War on Terror began as a manhunt for Al Qaeda leader Osama Bin Laden, the mastermind behind the 9/11 terrorist attacks. But over the next nine years, that anti-terrorism effort evolved into a multi-faceted crusade: birthing a new national security agency, blossoming into two bloody wars in Afghanistan and Iraq,

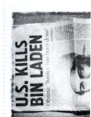

continued

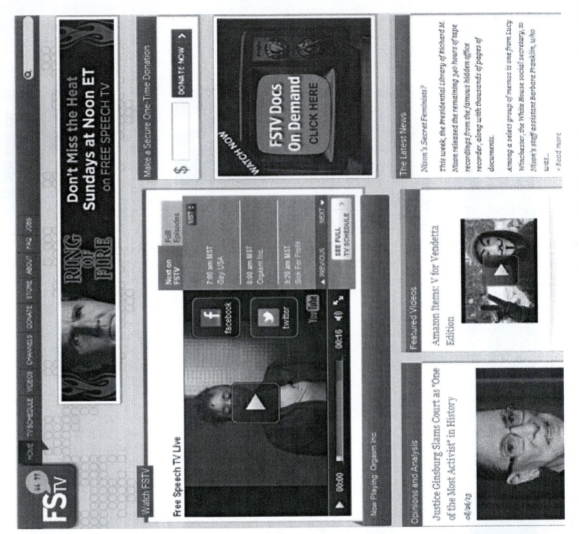

FSTV web site

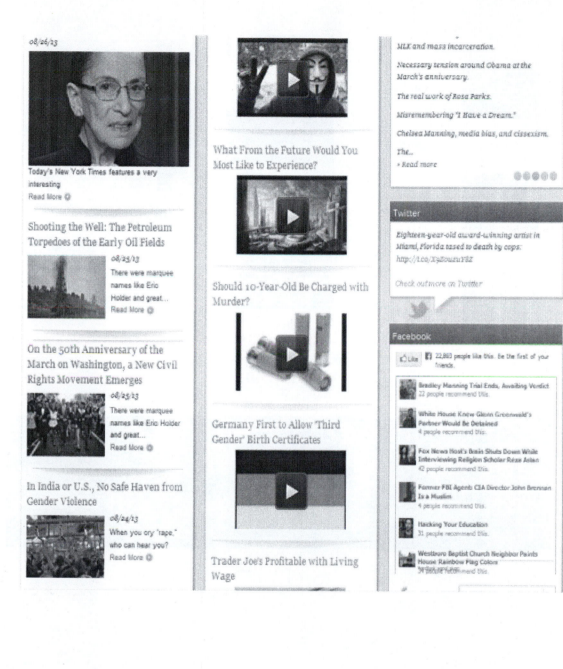

08/26/13

Today's New York Times features a very interesting
Read More ○

Shooting the Well: The Petroleum Torpedoes of the Early Oil Fields

08/25/13
There were marquee names like Eric Holder and great...
Read More ○

On the 50th Anniversary of the March on Washington, a New Civil Rights Movement Emerges

08/25/13
There were marquee names like Eric Holder and great...
Read More ○

In India or U.S., No Safe Haven from Gender Violence

08/24/13
When you cry "rape," who can hear you?
Read More ○

What From the Future Would You Most Like to Experience?

Should 10-Year-Old Be Charged with Murder?

Germany First to Allow 'Third Gender' Birth Certificates

Trader Joe's Profitable with Living Wage

MLK and mass incarceration.

Necessary tension around Obama at the March's anniversary.

The real work of Rosa Parks.

Misremembering "I Have a Dream."

Chelsea Manning, media bias, and cissexism.

The...
» Read more

⬤⬤⬤⬤⬤

Twitter

Eighteen-year-old award-winning artist in Miami, Florida tased to death by cops:
http://t.co/XyDvazuY8Z

Check out more on Twitter

Facebook

👍 Like 📘 22,863 people like this. Be the first of your friends.

Bradley Manning Trial Ends, Awaiting Verdict
22 people recommend this.

White House Knew Glenn Greenwald's Partner Would Be Detained
4 people recommend this.

Fox News Host's Brain Shuts Down While Interviewing Religion Scholar Reza Aslan
42 people recommend this.

Former FBI Agent: CIA Director John Brennan Is a Muslim
4 people recommend this.

Hacking Your Education
31 people recommend this.

Westboro Baptist Church Neighbor Paints House Rainbow Flag Colors
recommend this.

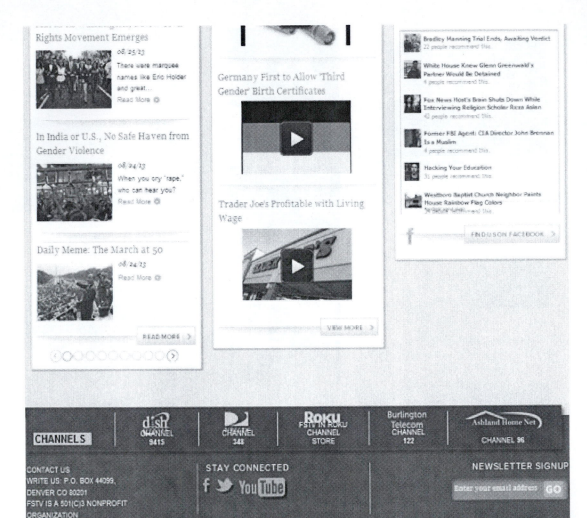

different than it is on the majority population—usually is ignored, except where the happening or issue directly and strongly relates to that specified group. The following example of how a general news story can be written to include or, depending on the audience, to be specifically oriented to a special group, is from the National Black Network (NBN) radio service:

November 5–8 P.M.—King

The administration's attitude toward Black unemployment is "cruel, cynical, and vicious . . ." I'm Ron King with World Wide News from the National Black Network in New York. That biting and descriptive assessment of administration policies toward Black unemployment was given today by Black Maryland Congressman Parren Mitchell. Speaking before the Joint Economic Committee of Congress in Washington, following today's release of new unemployment figures, Mitchell blasted the administration for policies which have increased unemployment. Today's figures show a nationwide jump from 10.12 to 10.4 percent, with Black unemployment remaining at a staggering 20.2 percent. Congressman Mitchell says that's unconscionable.

Courtesy of National Black Network

While it may appear on the surface that discrimination in news coverage may have disappeared, especially after America elected its first African-American president, an article in the *New York Times* by journalist Bob Herbert, entitled "What Color Is That Baby," gives pause for thought. Lamenting the lack of media coverage of the murder of dozens of public school students in the current school year in Chicago, Herbert notes that they were nearly all African-American or Latino. He contrasted that with the enormous coverage given the murder of a white Wesleyan College student and of a white masseuse who had advertised on Craig's list during the same period. Herbert recalls an editor's conference some years earlier, when Herbert was a newspaper reporter, on running a story about a baby that had been killed. The editor asked, "What color is that baby?" Herbert writes that "everyone understood what he meant. If the baby was white, the chances were much better that the story was worth big play . . . the press is still very color conscious in the way it goes about covering murders. Editors may not be asking, 'What color is that victim?' But on some level, they're still thinking it."

Sexism, perhaps inadvertent based on past conditioning, is a factor for consideration. In the 2008 presidential election, for example, media references to the candidate for the Democratic presidential nomination Senator Hillary Rodham Clinton and to the Republican vice-presidential nominee Governor Sarah Palin were frequently "Hillary" and "Sarah." By contrast, Republican presidential nominee John McCain and Democratic presidential nominee Barack Obama were rarely referred to by their first names.

Be sensitive to all races, ethnic groups, nationalities, and others who are the subjects of news accounts, foreign and domestic.

Legal Considerations

Although the Communications Act of 1934, as amended, prohibits the FCC from censoring programs, another clause in the act gives the FCC authority to take action against what it interprets as indecency. Chapter 1 describes the status of this constraint.

The "freedom of the press" provision of the First Amendment applies differently to broadcasting than to print because of the electronic media's special nature. The number of printing presses that can be put into service to publish newspapers is unlimited, but the number of frequencies that can be used to broadcast news is limited. The crowding and chaos on the airwaves were the reasons for the Radio Act of 1927, which provided the first legal basis for airwave regulation.

Though the print media have virtually total freedom under the First Amendment to print what they want, the limited number of broadcast frequencies has resulted in the courts, including the Supreme Court, consistently applying the First Amendment differently to television and radio stations and affirming the regulation of broadcasting in the "public interest, convenience, and necessity" as stated in the Communications Act. Depending on the philosophy of the party in power, the FCC has either strongly enforced rules and concepts it believed best served the consumer—such as the now defunct Fairness Doctrine and Ascertainment of Community Needs—or has trusted the marketplace to decide, and strongly deregulated broadcasting, as was done in the Telecommunications Act of 1996.

Libel

Nevertheless, many aspects of statute law (laws passed by a legislative body) and case law (established through court decisions) apply to both print and air, although sometimes in slightly different ways. One of the most important of these laws that apply to the broadcast writer is defamation.

Defaming a person's character or reputation in writing is called *libel;* when done through the spoken word it is called *slander.* However, the term "libel" applies to broadcasting as well as to print because the courts have stated that television and radio news programs follow written scripts. Court decisions have made it extremely difficult to prove a case of libel. A plaintiff must satisfy five requirements: that he or she has, in fact, been defamed, that the broadcast clearly identified this person as the person being talked about or shown, that the defamatory material was actually broadcast, that the broadcaster stated the false information about the person either through negligence or through malice, and that the plaintiff has suffered actual damages from the broadcast. As you can see, it is extremely difficult for someone to win a case of libel. Nevertheless, it does happen, and the writer should be careful that his or her script does not contain libel. If there is any question, check with the station's legal counsel.

One privilege the reporter in the United States has that is not available to the media in most countries is that of fair comment on public figures, including political leaders. Although a private person might win a libel case by proving negligence, a public figure almost always has to prove deliberate malice. In addition, U.S. journalists can make "fair comment" on any politician, even the president. Fair comment essentially means expressing any opinion about the political figure, no matter how damning or embarrassing—or even vicious. Personal attacks against presidents found in the U.S. media would land the journalists in jail in most other countries.

Privacy

Another area in which to be careful is the invasion of a person's privacy. Although courts usually consider public figures open to virtually any kind of press examination, intrusion on an ordinary citizen's private life by causing embarrassment through revelation of false or highly personal information can be the basis for a lawsuit. The courts have almost always, however, upheld the public interest or newsworthiness factor as a defense against such a suit. The courts do not look kindly, however, on invading a person's material space. Obtrusive spying on a person, unlawfully entering that person's premises, gaining entrance to private property to photograph that person's private behavior, and physical intrusion against that person are some areas in which journalists have been found guilty of invasion of privacy.

A comparable invasion of privacy concern is appropriating a person's likeness or speech for commercial purposes without that person's written permission. Other than in *bona fide* news coverage, make sure you get that consent.

Reporter's Privilege

Most states have what is called a *shield law*, protecting a reporter from having to divulge his or her confidential sources. No national law protects a reporter from having to divulge privileged information and if your script contains material that you obtained by promising your informant that you wouldn't reveal the source, you may find yourself in a court case having to choose between naming the source or being held in contempt, fined, or sent to prison. The judge makes that determination in each individual case, deciding whether the reporter's privilege or the defendant's right to a fair trial is paramount.

A continuing confrontation between the courts and broadcast news reporters and writers is over cameras in the courtroom. Though a growing number of judges and legislators have accorded broadcast news the same privileges as print news, in most courtrooms and legislative assemblies cameras are not allowed, and not even microphones are permitted in many. To the degree that television writers use visual and aural material as part of their scripts, they can be more limited than are their newspaper counterparts in obtaining the news.

In most states, the individual judge in any given trial can decide whether cameras are allowed in his or her courtroom. Determination is made by balancing the media's First Amendment rights against the Sixth Amendment rights of the defendant to a fair trial. Federal courts (but not the Supreme Court) have experimented with courtroom cameras, allowing individual judges to decide.

One of the most restrictive areas for reporters and writers is the federal government. Although 1974 and 1976 amendments to the Freedom of Information Act ostensibly allowed the press to report the government's actions, the Freedom of Information Act has been restricted by many administrations—even aside from national security concerns—preventing journalists from reporting the peoples' business to the public. Material designated as pertaining to national security or to certain internal agency matters are exempt. A document can also be arbitrarily classified as confidential and kept secret on the grounds that it is necessary for law enforcement purposes or investigations.

One more legal issue directly affects your writing—the right to protect your work. You can protect your own scripts by **copyrighting** them (see Chapter 11 for details). Be sure that you don't use anyone else's copyrighted materials, whether words, visuals, music, or anything else in your scripts without obtaining legal permission.

SPORTS

Writing sports is similar to writing news. The basic principles and techniques apply to both. The style, however, is different. If anything, sports broadcasts must be at least as precise and direct as news broadcasts. Peter Lund, when president of CBS Sports, noted the requirement for accuracy in preparing sports material: "Entry level people often are in the position of supplying information to producers and talent. It must be accurate, and available at a moment's notice."

The language of sports is more colloquial, and although technical terms should be avoided so the general audience won't be confused, sports jargon and expressions in common use relating to a specialized area of sports are not only acceptable, but necessary to establish expertise by the sportscaster and empathy between the sportscaster and the audience. The fan is interested in the competitive aspects of sports, in who wins and who loses. Keep in mind the dramatic elements when you write the sports script.

Although sports divisions usually are under news departments, the phenomenal growth of coverage of live athletic contests has resulted in independent status for sports at some networks and larger stations. The smaller the station, the more likely sports will be found under the direction of the news department. Though the newswriter is sometimes required to write the sports sections of the news script, the material usually is gathered and written by the sportscaster. In addition, all-sports cable channels have proliferated, with live coverage, sports news, interview shows, and sports features programs.

Internet Sports

An increasing number of web sites deal with sports: features, history, personalities, and trivia, among other topics. Individual teams have their own web sites, and subscriptions are available to watch games live on the Internet. The unlimited number of sites in cyberspace permits sports fans to find even the narrowest area of interest in any given sport from almost anywhere in the world. As sports begin to stream from broadcast stations and cable systems onto the Internet and as the Internet itself begins to originate the kinds of sports programs now found on the older media, greater opportunities will open for the media sports writer (and researcher, announcer, commentator, director, and producer).

Many of the smaller colleges and universities whose games are rarely or never covered by broadcast and cable channels are increasingly showing their teams contests over the Internet. Ivy League commissioner Jeff Orleans stated that "We can produce our own television and reach, literally, the entire world on the web, without having to go through the issues of, is there cable capability, is there satellite capability, is there advertising support." Commissioner Doug Fullerton said, "This is the future. The fans will decide what they are going to watch and when they are going to watch it." ESPN inaugurated a new online sports contest channel a ago that included some of the top college teams in the country as well as some not ordinarily covered on cable. ESPN vice-president Tanya Van Court stated that this "truly is interactive television."

For the writer, the interactive aspects of the Internet have expanded both the opportunities and requirements. The same principles that apply to cyberspace news writing, as delineated earlier in this chapter, apply to cyberspace sports writing, including the viewer's interactive opportunities such as linking to previous athletic contests or excerpts, athlete interviews and backgrounds, stadium or playing ground views and information, statistics, fan comments, press reports, and virtually any material relating to the sports event or program being presented.

Types of Sports Programs

The *straight sportscast* concentrates on summarizing the results of sports events and on news relating to sports in general. Some sportscasts are oriented solely to summaries of results, which can come from wire service reports or other sources. Material that is obtained from newspaper accounts or the wires should be rewritten to fit the particular program's purpose, the audience's interests, and the sportscaster's personality. Although there are occasional broadcasts of sports roundups of 15 and more minutes in length—usually as part of a network day-long coverage of athletic events or a late night special weekend wrap-up—most straight sports broadcasts are part of the daily evening and nightly news shows. On cable, however, sports programs have proliferated, from ESPN live coverage, news, and feature channels of major sports to channels that cover minor sports such as bowling and even poker tournaments. A sport that had long been considered of relatively minor interest in the U.S., European football—or soccer, as it is called in the U.S.—dominated the U.S. airwaves during the World Cup tournament. Pay and premium channels provide live coverage of virtually every game of virtually every major sport and of some minor sports.

The sports *feature* program can include live or recorded interviews with sports personalities, anecdotes, or dramatizations of happenings in sports, human interest or background stories on personalities or events, or remotes relating to sports but not in themselves an actual athletic contest (for example, the retirement ceremonies for a football coach).

Any sports program can amalgamate several approaches or, as in an after-event critique or summary, concentrate on one type alone. Many sports news shows are combinations of the straight report and the feature.

The most popular sports broadcast is, of course, the live athletic contest.

Organization

Sports broadcast formats parallel those for the regular news show. The most common approach is to give all the results and news of the top sport of the season and work down toward the least important sport. The most important story of the most important sport is given first, unless a special item from another sport overrides it.

Within each sport the general pattern in this organizational approach includes giving the results first, general news (such as a trade or injuries) next, and future events last. If the trade or injury is of a star player or the future event is more than routine, then it becomes the lead story.

The local result or story is usually the lead within the given sports category at the local station, and the local sports scene ordinarily precedes all other sports news.

The News and Feature Program

The sports segment of a typical late evening news show might look something like the following script.

VIDEO	AUDIO
LA DODGERS STADIUM BENNY BIGBAT HITTING	The illegal drug use scandal hit another peak today when the Dodgers' star outfielder, Benny Bigbat, was suspended by baseball Commissioner Timothy Crackdown for 50 games for using one of the banned substances. The commissioner did not reveal which one it was.

continued

VIDEO	AUDIO
	Losing Bigbat, who is leading the Dodgers in average, homers, and RBIs, is a big blow to the team's pennant hopes. Bigbat won't return to playing status until after the All Star game on July 14. He was also fined an undisclosed sum. He's at the top of the Dodgers' payroll, making $12 million plus incentives for this season.
COOPERSTOWN HALL OF FAME ANNCR:	Your favorite baseball cards come to life tomorrow at baseball's Hall of Fame in Cooperstown, New York, as three new diamond immortals are inducted.
	Commissioner I.M. Ownerowned will present the game's highest honor to catcher Roger Stamina who holds the record of 1562 straight games caught without an injury, first baseman Lefty Longarm, who won the Golden Glove award 16 straight times in his 20-year career, averaging only 1.667 errors per year, and outfielder Bill Ballsmasher, whose .324 batting average, average 37 homers per year, and the most doubles ever batting left-handed in rain-delayed night games in July led the Cincinnati Reds to an unprecedented four straight National League World Series titles. Bill Ballsmasher talked to us today about his illustrious career:

[Though numbers are usually spelled out in news reports, their preponderance in sports reports usually results in their use as ordinals.]

BALLSMASHER ANNCR:	The Boston Red Sox are still suffering from the late inning blues. They lost another one today to the Cleveland Indians in the ninth inning, 7-6.
FENWAY ANNCR: VO	Leading 6-1 behind the powerful pitching of Jack Strongarm, the Sox dropped two straight fly balls in left field in the top of the ninth—there's left fielder Joe Weakhand missing the first one, and two pitches later he drops the second one in the same place—then allowed this towering home run over the Green Monster by Indians second baseman Harry Hurryup, then the first base on balls by Strongarm, followed by an error by third baseman Wayne Bobble, and the game-winning homer by Indians pinch-hitter Justin Time. Joe Weakhand tried to make up for his errors by this triple into the right field corner with one out in the last of the ninth, but the next two Sox struck out to end the game. Sox manager Hereford "Sticky" Notlong had this to say about the Sox fifth straight loss.

continued

VIDEO	**AUDIO**
NOTLONG ANNCR: OC	Boston heads for Chicago now, the Sox going foot to foot with the Sox in a marathon of four games in three days, leading off with a twi-night double-header tomorrow.
	In other American League games today:
SCOREBOARD ANNCR: VO	Baltimore 2, Minnesota 0 Detroit 8, Kansas City 4 Toronto 6, Seattle 0
ANNCR: OC	and the Yankees and Texas Rangers play tonight.
VET STADIUM ANNCR: VO	The sparse crowd of 6,149 who showed up at Vet Stadium in Philadelphia were treated to a rarity for Philly fans.
	Veteran pitcher Robin Curve, obtained only last week on waivers from the Atlanta Braves, treated the fans to the first no-hitter at Vet Stadium in 14 years. He won 1–0 over the Arizona Diamondbacks on Mike Hitts 31st homer of the year in the third inning. Meanwhile Curve walked only one and struck out 14, including the last two batters of the game. Watch this strikeout—called—and this final one—swinging.
SCOREBOARD ANNCR: VO	Only two other National League games this afternoon, the New York Mets sinking the Los Angeles Dodgers 12–2 to move into a tie for first place in the East with the Braves, who dropped a squeaker to the San Diego Padres 5–4, in 11 innings.
ANNCR: OC	In golf today, Bernie Ems took an early lead in the Southern Open in Atlanta, birdieing the last three holes to finish with a Flying Hand Country Club course record of 62. Five strokes behind was pre-tournament favorite Panther Forest, whose three bogies on the first nine prevented him from catching up despite a remarkable 32 on the back nine.
COUNTRY CLUB ANNCR: VO	Here's Ems sinking an 18-foot putt on the 18th hole.
DERBY	Sad news today for horse racing fans. Swift Stride, the last triple crown winner, died today at Raceway Farms, Kentucky, at the age of 22. Remember when Swift Stride nosed out Fast Legs to win the Derby?
ANNCR: OC	We'll be back at 11 with late sports.

Commentary and News

Some sports news programs go beyond the basic information and include analysis and commentary. The following excerpts from ESPN's *Sports Center* illustrate this approach. Note how the writing concentrates on short, punchy, fast-paced material, starting with "headlines" and moving into the stories with more detail. The selections below deal with just three sports, but the program itself covers all the pertinent sports, with special attention to baseball, at the time in the middle of its season.

Breaking news into "Sportscenter"

Barry Bonds' attorneys are preparing for him to be indicted on charges of tax evasion and perjury.

The Associated Press reporting Bonds legal team has begun formulating his defense and his lawyers believe the indictment could come as soon as next week.

Big news from the golf course.

Michele Wie forced to withdraw.

This happened about an hour ago.

Suffering from heat exhaustion

The 16-year old struggled with the high temperatures throughout the day.

Would have missed the cut.

Less than three weeks after the Americans were knocked out of the World Cup, Bruce Arena is out as coach.

Arena's contract is not being renewed and a search for his replacement will begin immediately.

With that we welcome you to "Sportscenter."

With Dave Revsine.

I'm Michele Bonner.

* * *

ESPN's legal analyst Roger Cossack is joining us now.

Bonds' legal team thinks he cold be indicted within the next week. What gives them the sense, do you think, that this indictment is imminent?

They have been in contact with the United States attorney's office over the last period of months knowing this is going to happen and working on arrangement to surrender him at the courthouse rather than have him arrested. This is what lawyers for the defense do with prosecutors. They know it is coming, so they say what is the best way to work this out.

continued

What is the threshold it takes to get an indictment? What is the level of evidence needed to get somebody indicted?

Very low. The question the grand jury has asked is not whether Barry Bonds is guilty beyond a reasonable doubt. That is for the jury. They ask if a crime has been committed and probable cause to believe that Barry Bonds is the person who committed it. [The interview continued, detailing the legal process.]

* * *

As we move to golf.

The mighty quad cities, day two of the John Deere classic.

Day one didn't go well for Michele Wie. Plus seven.

Par three, seventh. Grabs her stomach in some discomfort.

She par-ed the hole. Still in some obvious pain.

Very warm in the quad cities.

Wie birdie putt. She drains that. Even par for the round.

She was playing fairly well, but you can see she is over in the woods.

Looking as if she might get sick.

She was advised to stop.

She decided she did want to try to play on.

[The commentary accompanying the visuals continued with the Wie story.]

* * *

Bruce Arena is out after eight years coaching the U.S. soccer team.

Tommy Smith, what is next ? Who will they get to replace him?

A lot of people are saying that Klinsmann is the man who should come in.

Why not?

This is what the next coach of the team is going to have to do—cast his net

very, very wide. He has to find young players.

[The story continued with an analysis of the current team and what needs to be done to improve it.]

Courtesy of ESPN

ESPN's "Pardon the Interruption" program's format is analysis-commentary on the news. Here is the opening excerpt from one of the shows.

> **"Pardon the Interruption" (PTI)**
>
> **PRE-OPEN**
>
> MW: PTI, but I'm Mike Wilbon down in Arizona where in three hours my undefeated Chicago Bears will be right here, bringing the pain.
>
> TK: I'm Tony Kornhauser. I spoke to a lot of Bears yesterday, Mike. They hate you.
>
> **A BLOCK (HEADLINES)**
>
> TK: Welcome to PTI, boys and girls. In today's episode the Saints beat the Eagles, Miami and Florida International beat each other down, and the Tigers look unbeatable.
>
> TK: Saints beat Eagles.
>
> TK: We being today with the New Orleans Saints holding the ball for the last 8 minutes and 26 seconds (notes: roll) against the celebrated Philadelphia Eagles and running the clock down to 3 seconds so John Sarney could kick a 31-yard field goal and make the Saints 5–1. Wilbon, you saw your player Donovan McNabb sitting glumly through that last unrelenting drive. Did the better team win the game?
>
> * * *

Courtesy of ESPN

The Live Contest

Newspaper and magazine cartoons showing a viewer glued to a television set for seven nights of baseball in the summer and seven nights of football, basketball, or hockey in the fall and winter are not exaggerations. The live athletic contest is the most exciting and popular sports program.

Although men traditionally have been the dominant audience for sports contests, the impact of Title IX, providing women in colleges and universities with equal opportunities in athletics, has led to the rise of women's professional sports, with women's teams and individuals getting increasing media coverage and, concomitantly, increasing the number of women watching sports programs.

The writer, as well as the producer and on air talent, should determine at least the audience's general gender demographics for a given event to prepare continuity and filler material that are attractive and understandable to that audience. The importance of sports in television programming is demonstrated by *Monday Night Football* having been the male viewer's number one prime-time program for 36 years—since its inception in 1969 until it was discontinued in 2006. The prime-time sport most attractive to women has been figure-skating. Although advertisers on sports shows seem intent on attracting a young male audience as their primary target, studies show that older males are avid viewers as well, especially of sports that they continue to play, such as golf.

As with non-sports hard news, athletic contests can result in happenings that prompt follow-up with continued news stories and features. In the 2013 NCAA

March Madness basketball tournament, for example, the Eagles of Florida Gulf Coast University made history by defeating second- and seventh-seeded teams to become the first fifteenth-seeded team to reach the "Sweet Sixteen." The Fort Myers, Florida University became the focal point of "Cinderella" stories, with it and its athletic program and students received continuing media attention even after the basketball team was eliminated from the tournament.

Although the jobs of the live event sportscasters differ in radio and television—the former are narrators, describing every detail of the action, whereas the latter are announcers, adding only explanations or color to what is being viewed—the writer's job is the same. The writer principally provides opening, transition, and closing material, plus enough color or filler material to keep every moment occupied. This background material includes information relating to pre-event action and color, statistics, form charts, material about the event's site and history, background about the participants, human interest stories related to the event and to its participants, and recorded or planned live interviews with participants during an appropriate break in the event being aired—anything that either heightens the audience's interest or helps clarify the action to the audience.

This material must be prepared in advance and must be available to the broadcaster for use immediately when needed. The writer's primary function for the live contest, therefore, is that of researcher and outliner. The script can be little more than an outline, a series of statistics, individual short unrelated bits of information, or short paragraphs providing some in-depth background, sometimes pre-game and post-game segments, and opening, closing, and transition materials. Frequently, when the announcers have worked with the format for a while, they provide virtually all the continuity themselves, in many instances not even writing it out. They may work only from a rundown sheet, with a minimum of standard written continuity, as in the following example for a professional basketball game—a composite of rundown sheets from several major market stations.

Giraffes Rundown Sheet		
OPEN & BILLBOARD	STUDIO	1:00
TALENT ON CAMERA	REMOTE	1:20
1ST POSITION	STUDIO	2:00
ANTHEM, PLAYERS & TIPOFF	REMOTE	
START FIRST QUARTER		
2ND POSITION (AUDIO "A")	STUDIO	1:30
3RD POSITION (PROMO DROP #1)	STUDIO	1:30
END FIRST QUARTER		
4TH POSITION	STUDIO	2:00
START SECOND QUARTER		
5TH POSITION (AUDIO "B")	STUDIO	1:30
6TH POSITION (GIRAFFES PROMO #1)	STUDIO	1:30

continued

END SECOND QUARTER

* * *

[Here a standard halftime format would be used, including, in this example, four promos, and a brief news segment. The transition continuity, written out for the talent, would be as follows:]

HALFTIME NEWS INTRO
At the half the score is _____ .
When we come back, Norm Nonjock will be with you with a Channel 84 news update.
  Stay tuned.

* * *

START THIRD QUARTER

11TH POSITION (GIRAFFES PROMO #2)	STUDIO	1:30
12TH POSITION (PROMO DROP #2)	STUDIO	1:30

END THIRD QUARTER

13TH POSITION	STUDIO	1:30

START FOURTH QUARTER

14TH POSITION (AUDIO "C")	STUDIO	1:30
15TH POSITION (PROMO DROP #3)	STUDIO	1:30

END OF GAME

16TH POSITION	STUDIO	1:30

* * *

[Here usually is a promo for the next program on the channel. In this example it is the late news, the scheduled timing of which frequently fits in right after the game The continuity would be as follows:]

End of Game (News promo)

With the final score _____ .

We'll be back to wrap it up, but now let's go to Norm Nonjock and Jacqueline Jurnlist to find out what top stories you'll be seeing in tonight's news.

* * *

WRAP-UP FROM REMOTE

[Here is sample wrap-up continuity, as it would be written for the talent, the producer, and the director:]

TALENT ON CAMERA   AD-LIB RECAP (:30–1:00)

continued

VIDEO	AUDIO
CHYRON NEXT GAME	So that's about it from here. Join us next Thursday night, November 15th at 8 o'clock when the Giraffes will take on the Skywalkers right here in the Bigstore Sports Arena.
CHYRON PRODUCER	Giraffes basketball on channel 84 was produced by Jim Dropshot.
CHYRON FINAL SCORE	Once again, the final score is _____
	This is Sam Slamdunk saying goodnight from the Sports Arena and we invite you to stay tuned for the channel 84 late news, to be followed by the Jay Scribbler Show. Goodnight.

APPLICATION AND REVIEW

1. Using the front page stories from your daily newspaper, write the complete script for a 15-minute radio news program.
2. Take the same news material and write the script for a half-hour television news program, using any visuals you can justify as being appropriate and likely to be available.
3. Rewrite one of the news stories in exercises 1 or 2 for broadcast to a predominantly African-American, Latino, Asian-American, or Native American audience.
4. Rewrite one of the news stories in exercise 1 or 2 for the Internet, with appropriate links.
5. If your college or university has a radio or television station or web site, arrange to write a news story for one of the news programs.
6. Write a news story around the following facts: (a) your college or university has just been purchased by the Toysan Company of Japan, a leading world manufacturer of electronic communication equipment; (b) the purchase price is $100 million if yours is a small institution, over $1 billion if a larger one; (c) the purchase becomes effective on January 1 of the coming year; (d) your institution's president has assured that "the purchase of this institution will not affect the high quality of our curriculum in any way; in fact, it will strengthen it with an immediate infusion of ($20 million if a small school, $100 million if a larger one) for new academic programs and faculty." What additional information and materials do you need to flesh out the story?

7. What athletic contest will take place at your college or university, or in your community, in the near future? Prepare a rundown, opening and closing, and transition continuity for that contest.

8. Prepare a five-minute straight sports summary of your institution's athletic contests, ostensibly for use on your college or university radio or television station, or for a local broadcast station.

9. Rewrite exercise 8 for your institution's web site.

CHAPTER 6

Features, Documentaries, and Reality Programs

Features and documentaries are usually under the direction of the news departments of stations or networks. Features and documentaries deal with news and information and, frequently, opinion. They can relate to current or historical events or ideas. They can be academic, cultural, or even abstract, without apparent connection to any contemporary or major issue or concern.

Some practitioners and critics consider the *documentary* the highest form of the news and information art. Documentaries provide information and present a point of view (**POV**). A good documentary can have a profound influence on social, political, and economic developments and even on legislation in a city, region, or country.

Anything that deals with a nonfiction treatment of a subject in a format that is not straight news or interview or discussion is often called, interchangeably, a feature or a documentary. This book labels as "features" those productions that do not deal with a controversial issue or do not take a point of view toward the subject. Those that do are defined in this book as "documentaries." The writer—and producer—who wants to make a documentary that has substance and meaning should have a "fire in the belly," should be passionate enough about something to try to motivate the viewer or listener to take action on the issue.

The feature, as defined here, is a straightforward report on an event, situation, person, or idea, such as the life of someone in the community. If that person happens to be homeless and if the production makes a strong point about the community's obligation to do more to help homeless people, the piece crosses from feature to documentary. A production about the day-to-day operations of a new local industry is a feature; one that shows corporate executives inflating their companies' profits and then selling their stock options before their companies declare bankruptcy is a documentary. The feature can be simply a travelogue about the autumn leaves in New England, the local zoo, or a new beach resort. The production that stresses acid rain or careless treatment of animals or cancer dangers from sun exposure or ecological dangers from global warming moves into the realm of the documentary. For example, one of the country's most beautiful ecological areas is the southwest Florida coast, especially the barrier islands such as Sanibel and Captiva near Fort Myers. A program showing that area's beaches and flora and fauna nature preserves would be a feature. But if the program shows that millions of gallons of excess water from nearby Lake Okeechobee are polluting the estuaries to these barrier islands, the nutrients killing wildlife and fish, destroying plant life, and harming beaches, then it is a documentary. Both the feature and the documentary can be highly artistic; the purpose of the content is different.

The *special event* sometimes is confused with the feature. Although the feature is a planned, scripted production, especially prepared for the network or station, the special event is part of the stream of life, usually a live happening planned by some source other than the media producer. The special event is closer to straight news than is the feature or documentary and is sometimes unanticipated, whereas the latter is always carefully preplanned.

The special event can be a visit to the city by a head of state, a holiday ceremony in front of city hall, the ground breaking for a housing complex, the local premier of a new film with one or more of its stars present, the opening of a new hospital wing, or even the opening of a new shopping mall. The feature, on the other hand, may deal with the work of a special community service health group such as an AIDS support organization, the operation of the local fire department or school board or of a national association of fire fighters or school boards, a how-to-do-it broadcast such as weatherproofing homes against hurricanes, or a behind-the-scenes story on any subject, from raising chickens to electing public officials. The documentary goes a step further and takes a point of view on the subject.

The late Don Hewitt, former producer of *60 Minutes*, stated, "The key to *60 Minute*'s success is a combination of good old-fashioned reporting and recognizing people who have an ability to tell stories rather than simply reporting an event." Telling a story goes beyond the news report. A good feature or documentary has what a special event does not: drama, depth, and empathy between the audience and the subject.

Special events have no set time limits, although networks and stations try to avoid open-ended coverage so they can preplan program time sales. Features can range from 30 seconds to 30 minutes or even an hour in length.

Continuing special events, such as Thanksgiving Day parades, Fourth of July band concerts, and Labor Day union rallies, many of which follow the same general pattern from year to year, can be pre-planned and scripted, much like a feature. Research is the key. The personalities who report the event need not only the standard intro, outro, and transition material, but require a precise rundown on the order or agenda of what is planned. The material prepared by the writer and organized by the producer and director should be in as much depth as possible, not only for the event itself but for the preliminary commentary that gives the audience the background and history of the event and prepares it for what is to come.

Documentaries are rarely found on radio any more, except on public radio. Because full-length TV documentaries are costly to produce and usually don't draw competitive ratings, they have been made more palatable for television audiences by being presented in shorter or, as they are sometimes called, **mini-documentary** form. *60 Minutes* has been highly successful in popularizing *mini-features* and *mini-docs* of about 12 to 15 minutes in length and prompted mini-feature and mini-doc programs such as CBS's *48 Hours, Dateline NBC,* and ABC's *20/20.* Reflecting the exploitation/scandal mood of the lowest common denominator viewing public, many of the segments of these programs have concentrated on stories revolving around titillation, mayhem, scams, and personalities. Many of you reading this will remember being caught up in what seemed like an unending series of features and documentaries following pop icon Michael Jackson's death, some reviewing his musical contributions, others exploiting his private life and probing for scandals.

Features and documentaries in the traditional informational and educational formats, both video and film, also grew on specialized cable channels such as A&E, Discovery, and the History Channel, frequently a full half-hour or minus hour in length commercial time, of course.

Sometimes a highly dramatic news event can trigger a number of follow-up documentaries in prime time on the major networks and cable channels. For example, the spate of gun violence in the United States in 2012 and 2013, including the murder of 12 people and wounding of 50 at a showing of *The Dark Knight Rises* Batman movie in Colorado, the murder of six Sikhs in their temple in Wisconsin, the murder of 20 elementary school children and six teachers in Connecticut, among other gun-tragedies, sparked a continuing stream of documentaries, not only concerning the people involved, but on the influence of hate groups on the perpetrators, the role of guns and the lack of gun controls resulting in the United States having one of the world's highest death rates from gun violence, the Second Amendment "right to bear arms" provision of the Constitution, the roles of the political parties regarding gun control (Democrats for, Republicans against), the availability of guns and the mental states of people who are allowed to purchase guns, the responsibility of parents in monitoring their children's exposure to and access to guns, and a myriad of other topics relating to guns and killing. Special happenings frequently result in an immediate spate of "while-the-story-is-still-hot" features and documentaries on the given subject. The good writer evaluates all significant news stories and explores in depth those aspects that lend themselves to good and meaningful documentaries.

WRITING TECHNIQUES

Both the feature and the documentary require careful research, analysis, and evaluation of materials. Both can consist of many diverse forms: news, interviews, panel discussions, dramatizations, speeches, and music. Both follow an outline-to-script approach. After deciding on the subject and the approach, the writer outlines as fully as possible, developing a detailed *routine sheet* or *run-down*. After determining which of the anticipated materials—live interviews, stock footage, old recordings, family photographs and diaries, and other materials—are available, a preliminary script can be written. After the research is completed and all the material going into the show has been assembled, a final script is prepared.

Form

Both the feature and the documentary can be dramatic, but not the way a fictional play can. Each should be a faithful representation of a true situation. This is not to say, however, that all such programs are unimpeachably true. Although they contain factual, informational, and educational content, editing and narration can make any series of actual sequences seem other than what they really are.

For example, the pseudo-documentary or fictional documentary, frequently called the *docudrama,* has become relatively popular. It may take authentic characters, but fictionalize the events of their lives; it may present the events accurately but fictionalize the characters; it may take real people or real events and speculate as authentically as possible on what might have occurred to fill information gaps; it may take several situations and characters from life and create a semi-true composite picture.

Although both the feature and documentary deal with issues, people, and events of current, recent, or past times, neither are news stories as such. Both explore behind and beneath the obvious, with the documentary going more in-depth for a defined persuasive purpose. The feature principally should inform; the documentary principally should make the audience think and feel. The documentary explores as much as possible the reasons for what happened, for the attitudes and emotions of the people involved. Comments of experts and the reactions of other people who might be affected are used to assess the implications and significance of the subject for the whole of society.

Whereas the feature is more often oriented toward objectivity, the documentary is oriented toward interpretation and a point of view. A news feature on a murder in a New York City park by a gang of youths may present fully all of the known factual material. A documentary on the same subject covers considerably more in background and character exploration and provides an understanding and an impact that otherwise would be missing.

Although some features and documentaries are prepared in a studio and depend largely on studio interviews and available stock materials, most are produced in the field. *Actualities*—the people and events recorded live—are essential for creating a credible program.

Approach

The feature and especially the documentary contain the real words of real persons (or their writings, published and unpublished, including letters, if they are not living or cannot be reached, or if no recording of their voices is obtainable), the moving pictures of their actions (or photos or drawings if film or video is unavailable or they lived before motion pictures), and available sounds and visuals of the events. These materials, sometimes seemingly unrelated, must be put together into a dramatic, cohesive whole and edited according to the outline and the script.

How do you start? First, the writer must have an idea. The idea for the program frequently comes from the producer rather than from the writer. What subject of public interest is worthy of treatment? The attitudes of the ordinary Israelis and Palestinians toward the struggle that wreaked havoc on them all? The feelings of children, college students, poor people, and elderly about political legislation that threatens their lives and futures? The rampage of AIDS? Political and economic discrimination against people of color? Government corruption? The cover-up of U.S. torture at Guantanamo and other prisons? State laws on gay marriage? Head injuries in professional football? All of these have feature possibilities. By going further with each topic—Have the Western and Middle East powers done everything possible to establish bases for peace in the Middle East? How can election laws be changed to make it possible for candidates to win on credentials and not principally on the largest campaign fund? How can the subjugation and virtual slavery of women in many countries be ended? How does your college administration deal with faculty and staff labor unions on your campus?—you have the makings of documentaries.

Process

First, determine the subject and point of view. Will this be an objective feature or a subjective documentary?

Second, prepare a tentative outline—not a road map, but a general direction.

Third, do thorough research: analyze library and Internet resources, make personal visits to people and places, determine what visual and aural materials are available, and study them.

Fourth, prepare a more definitive outline, a detailed rundown sheet.

Fifth, work closely with the producer and director (in many instances the writer is also the producer and sometimes also the director) to solidify the outline and prepare a full script. During this period the writer may suggest specific materials to be obtained, recommend the orientation of these materials, and even help gather them.

Sixth, prepare lead-ins, lead-outs, and interview background materials and question-and-answer outlines as the actualities are gathered, and other transition material as the script begins to take shape. As the material comes in, the writer continually revises the outline, accommodating new, unexpected material and deleting anticipated material that is not obtainable.

Seventh, when most of the material is in, prepare a full script. Revise this script in conference with the producer and director.

Eighth, after all the material has been gathered, seen, and heard many times by the writer and the rest of the production team, write the final script, sometimes called the *working script*. This final version is used for selecting and organizing the material to be used in the final editing and timing of the program. The final working script and the *transcript*—the program as aired—should be virtually identical, with the transcript containing the actualities, interviews, and other materials that cannot be scripted word for word beforehand. Some producers prepare their working scripts in detailed routine or rundown form, without the actualities. Some include the complete actualities, transcribed from the video or audio materials. Usually, much more material is obtained than can be used.

Sometimes an entire program can be developed from just a few minutes of material available exclusively to one station or producer. The writer might decide that this material would make a unique beginning or ending and might build the remainder of the show around it. For example, a network might have an exclusive recording of a minute's duration of a secret meeting between the heads of two major world powers. From this recording, with the aid of stock footage, interviews, commentary, and further fieldwork not even necessarily directly related to the event, a complete program can be created.

Technique

Endowing a story with human interest is a key to good feature or documentary writing. Even if you want to present only facts, and even if the facts seem stilted and dry, you can make them dramatic. Develop them by embodying traits of the people they represent. Even if the subject is inanimate, such as a new mousetrap, toxic waste, a current fad, or a nuclear warhead, endow it with live attributes. Haven't we all run across machines that seem more alive than some people we have known?

Develop the script according to the same basic principles you use for writing the play and the commercial. Get attention. What is the problem or situation that requires the program to be made? For the documentary, especially, the conflict is important. Explore the people or characters involved with the subject. Develop the theme by revealing more information; in the documentary, build the conflict through the complications until it reaches a crisis point. Although major happenings create dramatic action, the little things, the human elements, are important in establishing empathy and holding the audience's interest.

A narrator almost always is used. But too much narration distracts. Don't let the program look or sound like a series of educational interviews or lectures. A narrator frequently can summarize information that is not obtainable through actualities. Make the points clear and concise, and even if you are propounding one point of view, be certain to include all sides of the issue as the evidence presumably builds to support your position.

The Feature: Application

The feature often is a public service presentation, providing informational and educational content. But it doesn't have to be purely factual or academic in style. A variety show or drama format or elements of entertainment formats can make the feature more interesting to the audience. The feature can be oriented around a person, a thing, a situation, a problem, an idea, or an organization. The feature can be historical or current; it can explore concepts or show how to do something.

The following example deals principally with an organization (the Red Cross), includes a problem (disaster work), a situation (life-saving), and how-to instruction (artificial respiration). This feature was originally produced live by a local commercial station as part of a public service series.

HOW RED CROSS DOES IT

VIDEO	AUDIO
CG TRI-STATE STORY CG RED CROSS EMBLEM	MUSIC: RECORD "RED CROSS SONG" IN AND OUT BEHIND STATION ANNOUNCER: As a public service, WEHT presents TRI-STATE STORY—a half hour prepared through the cooperation of the Springfield Chapter of the American Red Cross. Here to introduce our guests for this evening is Mr. John Smith, Director of Public Relations for the Springfield Red Cross. Mr. Smith:
CAMERA ON SMITH	(MR. SMITH THANKS ANNOUNCER AND INTRODUCES TWO GUESTS, MR. HARVEY AND MR. JONES. THEN ASKS MR. HARVEY TO SPEAK.)
CAMERA ON HARVEY CLOSEUP OF PHOTOS	(MR. HARVEY TELLS OF RECENT DISASTER WORK IN HARRISBURG AREA, SHOWING PHOTOGRAPHS OF SERVICE WORKERS.)
CAMERA ON SMITH AND JONES	(MR. SMITH INTRODUCES MR. JONES. THEY DISCUSS SUMMER SAFETY SCHOOL FOR SWIMMERS. JONES LEADS INTO FILM WITH FOLLOWING CUE): "Now I'd like our viewers to see a film that was made at Lake Roundwood during last year's Summer Safety School."
CAMERA ON JONES	(8:35) (SILENT—JONES LIVE VOICE-OVER) (JONES INTRODUCES ARTIFICIAL RESPIRATION DEMONSTRATION.)
CAMERA ON TWO BOYS CAMERA ON SMITH	(JONES DESCRIBES METHODS OFF CAMERA.) (SMITH THANKS JONES AND HARVEY AND GIVES CONCLUDING REMARKS.)
(CG) TRI-STATE STORY	MUSIC: THEME IN AND UNDER STATION ANNOUNCER: Tri-State Story, a WEHT Public Service Presentation, is on the air each week at this time. Today's program was prepared through the cooperation of the Springfield Chapter of the American Red Cross.

By permission of American National Red Cross

The following working script from CBS Radio's "The American Challenge" series is followed by a transcribed excerpt from that same program. Compare the designations of actuality content and time lengths in the working script with the aired material. A preliminary script would not contain the exact beginnings and ends of the interviewees' quotes and their timing, necessary in subsequent script versions for precise editing, but would indicate the people being interviewed and the anticipated gist of what they would say.

WORKING SCRIPT

THE AMERICAN CHALLENGE

pgm 10   ward   to live free
MUSIC THEME up 3 seconds then under for
          CRONKITE: The American Challenge. Thirty Special Reports this weekend brought to you by

THEME UP TO END AT: 13

CRONKITE: This is Walter Cronkite, CBS News, reporting on the CBS Radio Network. In a time when the relationship between Great Britain and the colonists in America was steadily growing worse, Thomas Jefferson wrote: "The God who gave us life gave us liberty at the same time; the hand of force may destroy, but cannot disjoin them."
That's not true anymore. Drugs, electrical stimulation of the brain, the techniques of behavioral psychology can leave life, while taking liberty. An American Challenge, after this.

(COMMERCIAL INSERT)
Defining freedom is probably a job better left to philosophy students and the people who put dictionaries together. Historian Blanche Cook, a teacher at New York's John Jay College of Criminal Justice, believes it is easier to say what freedom is not.

    In: You start looking at what . . .
  Runs: :30
    Out: . . . and stops this man.
  Behavioral psychologist B.F. Skinner believes that a concern for freedom has outlived its time.
    In: I think you can show . . .
  Runs: :36
    Out: . . . then the behavior will change.
Our very survival, says Dr. Skinner, depends upon controlling people. And the techniques for maintaining that control are available.
    In: I think we have that . . .
  Runs: :16
    Out: . . . to use it.

continued

For historian Cook, the problem is quite different.
    In: We're using this really splendid . . .
   Runs: :25
    Out: . . . which could free us, really.
To find freedom and the limits of freedom. A matter for debate and an American Challenge; to make liberty more than a word stamped on our coins.
This is Walter Cronkite, CBS News.

TRANSCRIBED PROGRAM

#10—TO LIVE FREE
(MUSIC)

WALTER CRONKITE: THE AMERICAN CHALLENGE. Thirty special broadcasts this weekend. This is Walter Cronkite reporting on the CBS Radio Network.

In a time when the relationship between Great Britain and the colonists was steadily growing worse, Thomas Jefferson wrote, "The God who gave us life, gave us liberty at the same time. The hand of force may destroy, but cannot disjoin them."

That's not true anymore. Drugs, electrical stimulation of the brain, the techniques of behavioral psychology can leave life, while taking liberty. An American challenge, after this.

* * *

CRONKITE: Defining freedom is probably a job better left to philosophy students and the people who put dictionaries together. Historian Blanche Cook, a teacher at New York's John Jay College of Criminal Justice, believes it is easier to say what freedom is not.

BLANCHE COOK: You start looking at what the various police departments, for instance, have done with some of the new technology. The most bizarre thing of all is a fancy program: plant an electrode into somebody's brain who steals a lot, let's say, and gets arrested all the time. And he's going downtown to the supermarket, let's say, and all of a sudden the computer picks up that his adrenalin is going fast, and his heartbeat is going fast, and they figure out, well, he's going to steal something. The computer programs a shock, and stops this man.

CRONKITE: Behavioral psychologist B. F. Skinner believes that a concern for freedom has outlived its time.

B. F. SKINNER: I think you can show that we are misguided in our insistence on the right of the individual, for example, to breed as he wants, or to consume more than a reasonable share of the resources of the world, to pollute the environment. These are not real freedoms, they are the products of our present culture. And if we can change that culture, then the behavior will change.

CRONKITE: Our very survival, says Doctor Skinner, depends upon controlling people, and the techniques for maintaining that control are available.

SKINNER: I think we have that. We have the rudiments of it. And we have to change our culture in such a way that we will be permitted to use it.

CRONKITE: For historian Cook, the problem is quite different.

continued

COOK: We're using this really splendid technology, which could be used to feed people, you know, to really make our lives very comfortable, we're using it to control people. I think that's the really big challenge: how do we use the technology that we have, which could free us, really.

CRONKITE: To find freedom, and the limits of freedom, a matter for debate, and an American challenge, to make liberty more than a word stamped on our coins.

This is Walter Cronkite, CBS News.

Courtesy of CBS News

Television

The following excerpts from a television working (or final) script, *Ave Maria: The Story of the Fisherman's Feast*, by Beth Harrington, illustrate many of the key elements that make a high-quality feature. As you read the script, note, in sequence, the following techniques of good writing:

1. The opening clearly establishes the locale. At the same time it obtains attention and interest by comparing and contrasting the old and the new, suggesting a dichotomy of change on one hand and no change on the other. The visuals of Boston Harbor become narrowed to the North End neighborhood, bringing the viewer closer to the action.

2. Although the feature is rooted in a historical event, the viewer can best identify with the current practice. The script makes the connection immediately.

3. As with most features and documentaries, the narrator plays a key role. In television, however, unless the narrator is a personality in his or her own right, he or she should remain in the background and principally be a voice over the visuals. Following the introduction, the narrator's comments in *Ave Maria* are V.O. a montage of historical photos.

4. Actualities are incorporated as soon as feasible, with a fishing captain, Ray Bono, the first key interviewee.

5. Although the interviewee may be telling a story and giving information, the writer does not let him or her become a "talking head" or substitute narrator. Use of visuals located during the research phase is important; for example, newsreel footage of the Boston fishing fleet in 1938 (many decades before the program) is run during the comments of the narrator and Captain Bono.

6. Again, the writer avoids the talking head problem in the Ray Geany interview, with Geany becoming a narrator over appropriate visuals. The same technique is used when the interviewee, band leader Guy Giarrafa, mentions Arthur Fiedler and a visual of Fiedler is inserted.

7. In several places dramatizations are used to enhance the commentary. For example, the feelings and beliefs of the people in the procession are made clearer through the interviews with Fathers #1 and #2 than if those attitudes had simply been described by the narrator. This technique is used again following comments that attendees are North Enders and visitors. Interviews with North Enders and visitors, including children, are developed to enhance human interest and viewer empathy.

8. Though not presenting a political or social point of view as a documentary would, *Ave Maria* nevertheless is sensitive to human aspects of the subject. For example, note Eddie Marino's comment about how the festival helped him overcome alcoholism, and several people telling how participation in the procession affected their personal lives.

9. Although concentrating on the festival's broad aspects, the script does not ignore the religious focus and includes dramatizations to emphasize its importance.

10. The ending is a clear linking, again, of past and present, stressing the event's continuity. We see what is happening, but, most important, we are taken behind the scenes for the human interest factors—a significant component of the good feature.

"AVE MARIA: THE STORY OF THE FISHERMAN'S FEAST"

VIDEO	AUDIO
	(music up and under the following:)
Seagulls in flight, shots of Boston Harbor.	NARRATOR:
Changing face of the North End. Key in titles:	Change?
"The North End, Boston, Massachusetts."	The North End has seen its share. From English colonists to Italian immigrants.
	Big change. It's like they say, the one thing you can count on is change. Pleasure boats crowd out the fishing boats. Tenements become condominiums.
Montage of shots of older North Enders, procession and neighborhood views.	But some things don't change. Like the Italian feasts. Oh sure, they're different now. But they continue. Thanks to a handful of dedicated people, they continue.

continued

VIDEO

Fade to black. Fade up on collage intro of faces of feasts. Title: "Ave Maria: The Story of the Fisherman's Feast."

Montage of historical photos of North End at turn of century, founders of society, etc.

Universal Newsreel footage of Boston fishing docks.

LS of "St. Jude" (fishing boat) going out to sea.

MS of Captain Ray Bono.

AUDIO

There's one feast in particular that's—special.
And this is its story.
(fade music)

(Roma Band: Marcia Reale)

NARRATOR:
At the turn of the century, Italian immigrants, like these men from Sciacca, Sicily, formed mutual aid societies—combination insurance agencies, support groups and social clubs.

The Society of the Madonna del Soccorso took care of members' medical needs, provided for burial, and—most importantly—ran the annual feast in honor of their patroness.

The feast was a tradition dating back to sixteenth century Italy.

But there was a second level of tradition at work here. For generations, the members of the society had been fishermen.

Today, Captain Ray Bono is the grand marshall of the Fisherman's Feast, one of the last in a long line determined to continue the tradition.

RAY BONO:
In my particular family, I'm the only one that's left fishing.
There may have been maybe 150 boats years ago. Now there might be 20 and most of the 150 boats were more or less family boats.
So you were fishing with your cousins, your father, your uncle, your brother, your brother-in-law. Today you haven't got that. Today it's just crews.

continued

VIDEO	AUDIO
	You might have a couple of boats with a brother on board or something like that. But not many of them are related like years ago.
	NARRATOR:
Universal Newsreel footage of Boston fishing boats at sea in winter. Key in title: "Boston Fishing Fleet, 1938"	The fishermen didn't have it easy. Atlantic winters were hard and the good weather was no picnic either. Then and now, these men put their trust in the Madonna. Ray carries a picture of her on board.
	RAY BONO:
Cut back to Ray Bono in MS.	The boat was sinking. We were waiting for the Coast Guard to come and get us. We threw the life raft overboard. And as we threw it overboard, it deflated. Now we were all alone. The closest boat was 12 miles from us. And I turned to that picture and said, "Save us and the boys." And we got hauled off in the helicopter. And that was the most that I really felt . . . felt for her at that time.
	NARRATOR:
North Enders coming out of church.	The descendants of the fishermen have their own reasons for taking part in the feast.
	RAY GEANY:
CU of Ray Geany. Key in name and title: President, Madonna del Soccorso Society.	As a kid, I never missed a feast. Granted, my father wasn't a fisherman. My father wasn't even Sicilian! But we were brought up with a tradition from my mother's family that this was a major event and we grew up in the feast. Every year we'd come and see the feast and we'd be part of it. Whether we were on a float, or carrying a sheet, we were always part of it. Carrying a flag. As soon as you got a little taller and pestered the committee enough, you carried the saint.

continued

VIDEO	AUDIO
Cutaway to statue of the Madonna.	Joining the society once we reached 18 was very important because we were carrying on a tradition. I didn't get very involved personally to the extent my brother did until . . . my grandmother died. One of her wishes was that we continue the feast. That was important to her. On her bedroom walls, she always had a picture of the Madonna with a candle in front of it. She was very devoted. She wanted to see to it that her grandchildren played a role in continuing the society, continuing the feast.
Cut back to CU of Ray Geany.	
	* * *
	NARRATOR:
Shot of Roma Band playing, zoom onto Guy Giarraffa.	What would a North End feast be without music? Tarantellas, marches, hymns? The Roma Band began in 1919 and since then has played at nearly every feast.
	GUY GIARRAFFA:
MS of Guy with name and title: "Guy Giarraffa, Maestro, Roma Band."	The Fisherman's Feast, in my opinion, is Number One, colorful. It's excitement. Why? Because they're Sicilians and I'm Sicilian, too. And we're excited. Some years ago, I remember, I was directing the Roma Band on North Street. Somebody spotted Mr. Arthur Fiedler, the late Arthur Fiedler walking down the street. So they said, "Guy, it's Maestro Arthur Fiedler." And I said, "So what?" (laughs) He said, "Whaddya mean, 'so what!'?" And I said, "Well, whaddya want to do?" "Shall I tell him to come up?" I said, "Go ahead." So this musician goes down and he begs him. He says, "I belong to the union, I can't." We say, "C'mon, forget about the union." So he comes over and he directs a march or two. They took pictures and the next day I understand the picture went all over the world, Hawaii, Europe, everywhere. It was a great honor.
Cut to photo of Arthur Fiedler conducting the Roma Band.	

continued

VIDEO	AUDIO
	NARRATOR:
Shots of procession as it wends its way through the North End.	Sunday's procession is an all-day affair. The statue of the Madonna is carried through the streets of the North End.
	(Music under)
	(Music out)
	FATHER #1:
Three-shot of fathers with super: "Angels' fathers."	I don't count my years by New Year. I'm serious. My year doesn't end or start on New Year's. My year begins and ends with this feast.
	FATHER #2:
CU of second father.	We used to look forward to this the way other kids looked forward to Christmas. And I remember our parents used to go out a couple of months before the feast and buy us new clothes—new shoes, new slacks, new shirts—We all had to look perfect for the feast.
	RAY GEANY:
Montage of money-collecting shots.	The primary purpose of raising money during the feast is to pay for the feast. As far as being money-making, unfortunately, that's the one thing people see. They see money coming out of the windows, and they look at all that money. Well, you can get a lot of one dollar bills, stack 'em up very high and it looks very impressive. But when you count 'em and you have bills totalling anywhere from $25 to $35,000 dollars, you need a lot of one dollar bills to pay for it. If any businesses was run the way the feasts were run, they'd probably go under in a year.

* * *

continued

VIDEO	AUDIO
	(music up and under the following)
	VENDOR:
Montage of shots of vendors, visitors and North Enders.	During the summertime, you don't have to be Italian to be Italian. Everybody can come down here and be Italian.
	VISITOR:
	I'm proud to swap my Galway hat for my lovely Italian hat. And God bless everyone.
	NORTH ENDER:
	It's everyday living. It's just people get together and show their emotions for each other and they're happy.
	NORTH ENDER:
	It's very good. I like it very much.
	NORTH ENDER:
I	I got to dance three times a week. I gonna dance all my life. Some days I no dance, I'm not feelin' good, I feel sick. I dance, I feel alright.
	VISITOR:
	We used to have relatives here. I'm of Italian-American extraction, so we just come down, bring the kids down and try to keep in touch with their heritage. That's basically what it is. You know, you get out to the suburbs, and you become kind of homogenized after a while. You kind of lose some of your ethnic connection, so to speak.
	[INTERVIEWER:
	What do you guys think of it?]

continued

VIDEO	AUDIO
	KID: It's great!
	[What's your favorite part?]
	KIDS: The food!
	VENDOR: We have fried calamari, the onion ring that tastes like a clam. It's delicious. It's nutritious. Who wants some?
	VENDOR: Who wants one here? Do you want one?
	NARRATOR:
Eddie Marino in his stocking feet, followed by Eddie reciting a prayer to the Madonna.	As a devotion, Eddie Marino walks the procession each year in his stocking feet. He says his faith in the Madonna helped him overcome alcoholism.
	EDDIE MARINO (V.O.):
	I was on skid row and I turned to her when she was coming out. I stopped in the street and knelt down in front of her and said, "You make me or you break me." I prayed so much to her I got my wish. (SFX: Eddie's prayer)
	JIMMY GEANY:
Eddie and Jim Geany two-shot, followed by more procession footage of Eddie.	Eddie, here, I guess you could say is our mascot of the Fisherman's Feast. He is our inspirational leader actually. Of course, we're all dedicated, but I don't think there is anyone more emotionally involved with the Blessed Mother and the feast of the Madonna del Soccorso than Eddie right here.

continued

VIDEO	AUDIO
Cut back to Jim Geany interview.	Another favorite part of the feast is the angel, what we call the angel ceremony. That's what sets the Fisherman's Feast apart from the other feasts in the North End. It's something special to all the Sciaccadanis.
	* * *
	[INTERVIEWER:
Cut to interview with North End woman, key in title: "Ex-Angel."	Tell us about the fact that you were an angel? Can you describe it as you remember it?]
	NORTH ENDER:
	Well, I would say it was the biggest thrill of my life. I don't know how else to describe it. Except that it's a big honor and it's been traditional. My daughter has done it, my granddaughter, so have all my relatives, my cousins, nieces and so on.
	ANDREA:
Cut back to interview with first angel.	It's uncomfortable because you're on your stomach and all your weight's on the belt and when you're hanging there it's hard to get enough air to say the speech and then it's like I said, the air's hard to get a lot of air in. And sometimes you have to put all your air in 'til your next line. It's pretty hard.
Shots of angel getting ready for her "flight," followed by street scenes just prior to ceremony.	(Music up and under the sequence, then out.)
	NARRATOR:
Shots of other angels reciting prayers.	The Madonna has arrived. The angel ceremony begins.

continued

VIDEO	AUDIO
Angel "flight" sequence from start to finish.	(Music up and under the sequence.) JIMMY GEANY (V.O.): I guess I do the work I do because I like to think that somewhere up there in heaven my grandfather is looking down at me—who was a fisherman and a charter member of the society—and up there he's smiling somewhere and he's proud.
Fade to black. Credits.	(Music out)

Written by Beth Harrington; courtesy of Ms. Harrington

RADIO

As indicated earlier, although commercial radio has become almost exclusively music, talk, and sports, non-commercial public radio continues to produce high-quality documentary and feature programs. One example is the following news feature, "The Snoezelen Room," written and produced by Amy Tardif, WGCU-FM Station Manager and News Director and winner of many awards for her radio writing and producing. "The Snoezelen Room" added to her collection of regional Edward R. Murrow awards in 2013.

SNOEZELEN ROOM OFFERS STIMULATION FOR DEMENTIA PATIENTS
3/26
Tardif

There's a new adult multi-sensory playroom of sorts at a continuing care facility in Fort Myers. It's where people with Alzheimer's or other forms of dementia go for either stimulation or relaxation. Even its name is playful—the Snoezelen Room. WGCU's Amy Tardif went for a visit and has this report.

Runs: 5:40

This is 79-year-old Lyle Olsen's third visit to the Snoezelen Room at Cypress Cove in Fort Myers.

Lyle "If you wanted to come in here and really unwind and relax this would be the place to do it."

The retired accountant, who, as the CFO for Bloomington, Minnesota helped build the Mall of America, has been experiencing memory problems. So his wife Audrey makes sure he comes here weekly.

Audrey "It was something we can do together. We both felt really good afterwards."

Originally developed in the Netherlands in the 1970s, Snoezelen Rooms—filled with various pieces of sensory equipment—are popping up around the world. They're especially common in Europe. The word *Snoezelen* comes from the Dutch words for snoozing and sniffing. And you can do both in here—a 200 square foot former spa Cypress Cove created in November.

Recreational Therapist Theresa Farrell says it calms the restless and stimulates the passive as she explains the focal point of the room—four acrylic tubes that stretch nearly from floor to ceiling filled with rising bubbles that change color.

Theresa "And I've really noticed that the bubble tubes help to sooth and relax a lot of our agitated residents. A lot of times they like to mimic the motion of the bubbles going up and down. We offer various types of wireless devices where they can actually change the colors if they like. This is a sound activator...."

The tubes are Lyle Olsen's favorite thing in the Snoezelen.

Lyle "Because just whatever it is inside those tubes is relaxing just to look at it and the different colors then to go back and forth again is relaxing."

The colors in the tubes are bold and bright—green, blue, red, and yellow. They might be hard for some of us to look at for more than a few minutes. But Cypress Cove's Healthcare Administrator Jay Groesser says it's just the opposite for Lyle Olsen.

Jay "As we age the ability of the eye to take in light diminishes dramatically from when you're younger. So what may appear to a younger eye to be bright for someone that's aged it's not that bright to them. It does stimulate and help them."

The room is set up the way clients like it. That's called a sensory diet. In Olsen's case for example, if he reacts well to aroma therapy, a spray of his favorite scent may be misted throughout. He can bring his own music or Farrell can choose to play music he likes while he's in the room. And since Olsen used to play the guitar, when she positions his wheelchair in front of the Tonky Honk organ she tries to tune it to something familiar.

Lyle/Theresa "Try it now. Do you play? Literally? Not very well. You go ahead. I'll try. I don't know any songs. Can you help me? No, I can't think of any off hand either. Maybe we'll see if we can find a guitar setting. Yeah! Ooh that's an organ."

The Tonky Honk organ has large flat, round keys. He doesn't have to actually touch them, just place his hand over them to make a note. Farrell says it helps Olsen control his environment and practice reaching out. For people with Alzheimer's, she says it can provide even more stimulation.

Theresa "The average person touches 300 surfaces every 30 minutes and a person who has late stage dementia only touches 1 to 5 surfaces within the same time frame so you can bring an environment to them that provides that stimulation that they aren't receiving on a daily basis."

Jay "It's not invasive and it returns to the patient the control and issues that they're losing and that's causing many times some of the agitation that they're experiencing."

The room also includes things Olsen is encouraged to use to stimulate his hearing and fine motor control such as a rain stick (sound) and a chime xylophone (sound).

Cypress Cove's former Nursing Home administrator had the vision to bring a Snoezelen Room here. It took donations from resident families, literal bake sales and funding from a local foundation to raise the 30,000 dollar cost. Recreational Therapist Theresa Farrell says they're first focusing on residents who show high levels of agitation, behavioral disturbances, depression or apathy.

Theresa "For those who are more socially isolated I really want them to be more engaged in meaningful activities. And for those that are agitated I would love to see results where they can actually engage in the regularly scheduled activities."

Farrell says it works—and behavioral neurology fellow at the University of Florida, Dr. Glen Finney, says although there is very little literature on the Snoezelen room's use in dementia, what there is appears promising.

Finney "It did show some small amount of benefit in those studies for basically helping things like agitation and people's apathy which is a huge symptom of Alzheimer's disease."

Dr. Finney says any stimulus is the key as it encourages the brain to try to heal itself.

Finney "That would be a theoretical model—that the multi-sensory stimulation may help stimulate the strengthening or even formation of connections in the brain. It very well could be a useful thing to study for Alzheimer's and other dementia patients."

The community can use Cypress Cove's new Snoezelen room. Access to others shouldn't be hard to find. A Pennsylvania-based Snoezelen equipment vendor says there are about 500 in Florida and a few thousand installations across the United States in hospitals, rehab centers, hospices and all kinds of other facilities.

Amy Tardif, WGCU news.

Courtesy of Amy Tardif, FM Station Manager and News Director, WGCU Public Media, Ft. Myers/Naples, Florida.

DOCUMENTARIES

Next to the drama, the documentary is said to be the highest form of television and radio art. Many broadcast news personnel say that the documentary, combining as it does news, special events, features, music, and drama, *is* the highest form. At its best the documentary synthesizes the creative arts of the broadcast media and makes a signal contribution to public understanding by interpreting the past, analyzing the present, or anticipating the future. Sometimes this all happens in a single program, in a highly dramatic form that combines intellectual and emotional meaning.

Types

Robert Flaherty is a seminal figure in documentary development. His *Nanook of the North* set a pattern for a special type of documentary film. This type went beneath the exterior of life and carefully selected those elements that dramatized people's relationships to the outer and inner facets of their world. Flaherty started with an attitude toward people: He eulogized their strength and nobility in a hostile or, at the very least, difficult environment.

Pare Lorentz, noted for his productions of *The Plow That Broke the Plains* and *The River* forwarded another type of documentary: Presenting a problem that affects numerous people and the ways in which the problem might be solved. Lorentz's documentary type called for positive action by the viewer to remedy an unfortunate or ugly situation. A third documentary or feature type is exemplified by the British film *Night Mail*, produced by innovator John Grierson. The details of ordinary, everyday existence—in this instance the delivery in Britain of the night mail—are presented in a dramatic but non-sensational manner. In this type we see people or things as they really are; we receive factual information without a special attitude or point of view expressed or stimulated.

These early film types provided the bases for writing the film and video documentary today. The documentary can use one of these approaches or—and this frequently is the case—combine two or more types in varying degrees.

Point of View (POV)

Good documentaries have a point of view. What is the *purpose* of the particular documentary you are preparing? To present an objective, many-sided view of a community's traditions and problems? To present solutions to one or more of those problems? By lack of criticism, to justify violence—war—as a means for international political gain? To show the effects of pollution on our natural environment? To carry it a step further and show how the audience can stop the pollution? To show the courage of a particular group—people of color fighting "profiling," women who want control of their own bodies, victims of AIDS, political opponents being spied on by their own government—in a hostile political or social environment? To show that the only way to find true physical and spiritual rejuvenation is to spend one's vacation time in encounter groups (or health clubs, dude ranches, or hot tubs) in southern California? To what degree will the writer's personal beliefs (or those of the producer, network executive, agency representatives, or sponsor) determine program content and orientation?

A point of view is important, whether the program is prepared by a small production company with little money or by a network with a big budget. A documentary can be produced with a minimum of funds and equipment: mini-cam and access to an editing room for television; or a couple of audio recorders for radio. One such documentary, produced as a course project in a radio class at the

University of North Carolina at Chapel Hill and winner of a national award for public service reporting, illustrates how simple and direct the documentary-making process can be.

First, the class decided on a subject: The problems of the small farmer in North Carolina's Piedmont region (where the university is located) and the possible relationships of these problems to politics.

The three major documentary types were combined in the purpose of the documentary: to present information in a straightforward, unbiased manner; to show by implication the problem that had to be solved and to indicate several possible solutions; and to present the farmer as a persevering person in a difficult economic environment. The class decided that farmers and experts from the university should be interviewed and edited in a counterpoint manner.

Research was the next step, with as much material as could be found on the problem gathered from an examination of all available literature and from preliminary talks with farmers and persons familiar with the farm problem. The subject and purpose were clarified further and, on the basis of the documentary's projected findings, specific interviewees were chosen—farmers for the size, location, and crop of the farms, and experts for their academic departments and special areas of study.

A careful distillation of material already gathered led to a series of pertinent and interrelated questions to be asked of the farmers and the experts. After the interviews were completed, a script containing the narration and a description of the recorded material to be inserted was developed from all the material, including library research and personal interviews. A script analysis indicated places that were weak, some because of the lack of material and others because of excess material. Further field work and the addition and pruning of material resulted in a final script, ready for the editing process.

The following are excerpts from a composite of the script and a verbatim transcript of the program. The final script is shown in capitals; the material in parentheses is that actually recorded and incorporated into the program with the narration. The recordings were done on tape, which has been disappearing in this current digital age. Note here the use of numbers indicating the tape and **cut** to be used, with the first and last words of each cut to help the editor.

One criticism of this script may be that it tries to cover too many subjects. Another may be that it is not sufficiently dramatic. Take the material contained in the script and other material that you can get through your personal research, and rewrite this documentary in outline form, improving it as you think necessary.

	THE PIEDMONT, NORTH CAROLINA FARMER AND POLITICS
OPEN COLD:	TAPE #1, CUT 1, DUPREE SMITH: "I WOULD LIKE VERY MUCH . . . BEST PLACE TO WORK." (I would like very much to spend my entire life here on the farm because I feel like being near the land and being near the soil and seeing the operation of God on this earth is the best place to live and the best place to work.)
MUSIC:	IN, UP, AND UNDER
NARRATOR:	THIS IS THE SMALL FARMER IN THE PIEDMONT OF NORTH CAROLINA.
MUSIC:	UP AND OUT
NARRATOR:	YOU ARE LISTENING TO "THE PIEDMONT, NORTH CAROLINA FARMER AND POLITICS." THE VOICE YOU JUST HEARD WAS THAT OF DUPREE SMITH, A FARMER IN PIEDMONT, NORTH CAROLINA. IN RURAL AMERICA A CENTURY AGO THE FARM PROBLEM WAS AN INDIVIDUAL ONE OF DIGGING A LIVING OUT OF THE LAND. EACH FARMER SOLVED HIS OWN INDIVIDUAL PROBLEMS WITHOUT GOVERNMENT AID. NEARLY EVERYONE FARMED. TODAY, BECAUSE OF INCREASING COST OF MAINTAINING CROPS, LARGER SURPLUSES, HEAVIER STORAGE COSTS AND LOWER FARM INCOME, THE SMALL FARMER IN NORTH CAROLINA, AS WELL AS ACROSS THE NATION, HAS BEEN UNABLE TO DEPEND ON HIS LAND FOR A LIVING. PRODUCTION CONTINUED TO GROW, SURPLUSES MOUNTED. FARM INCOMES FELL AND THE GOVERNMENT SUBSIDIES NECESSARILY GREW.
PROFESSOR KOVENOCK:	TAPE #2, CUT 1: "THE COMMON PROBLEMS . . . ARE THESE." (The common problems shared by almost all national farmers today and, at the same time, most North Carolina farmers, are these.)
NARRATOR:	YOU ARE LISTENING TO PROFESSOR DAVID KOVENOCK OF THE POLITICAL SCIENCE DEPARTMENT OF THE UNIVERSITY OF NORTH CAROLINA.
KOVENOCK:	TAPE #2, CUT 2: "FIRST OF ALL . . . SHELTER FOR HIS FAMILY." (First of all, a decline in the income going to the farmer—a problem of—this is particularly for, let us say, the marginal farmer, the farmer with a small operation in North Carolina and the rest of the country—the problem of obtaining employment off the farm, that is, some relatively attractive alternative to continuing an operation on the farm that is becoming insufficient for feeding, clothing, and buying shelter for his family.)

continued

NARRATOR:	THIS IS DUPREE SMITH'S PROBLEM.
SMITH:	TAPE #1, CUT 2: "YES, THAT WAS MY DESIRE . . . PART TIME AND WORKING." (Yes, that was my desire after returning from service, was to go back to nature and live and raise a family where I felt that I would enjoy living to the fullest. For several years, on this same amount of land, I was able to support my family and myself adequately. For the last year or two, this has been on the decrease. The decline has been to such an extent, that I've had to go into other fields—my wife helping part time and working.)
NARRATOR:	WHAT SPECIFICALLY ARE DUPREE SMITH'S PROBLEMS?
KOVENOCK:	TAPE #2, CUT 3: "THE COMMON PROBLEM . . . OCCUPATIONAL PURSUIT?" (The common problem shared by the North Carolina farmer and by the national farmer would be, first of all, the condition of agriculture, the relationship of the supply of agricultural commodities to the demand and, of course, consequently, the price that the farmer receives which, of course, now is somewhat depressed. The second major problem is the condition of the rest of the economy as a whole—that is, is it sufficiently good so that the farmer has some alternatives to continuing his, currently, rather unsatisfactory occupational pursuit?)
NARRATOR:	FARMERS ARE MARKETING MORE, BUT ARE RECEIVING LOWER PRICES FOR THEIR CROPS AND PRODUCE. DR. PHILLIPS RUSSELL, A FORMER COLLEGE PROFESSOR AND RETIRED FARMER, HAS THIS TO SAY:
PHILLIPS:	TAPE#3, CUT 1: "THE FARMER HAS BEEN LOSING . . . IN AN UNPROTECTED MARKET."
RUSSELL:	(The farmer has been losing out everywhere, because he has to buy the things that he needs in a protected market and he has to sell in an unprotected market.)
NARRATOR:	WHAT IS THE FARMER'S ANSWER TO THIS PROBLEM? FARMING HAS BECOME A BUSINESS INSTEAD OF A WAY OF LIFE. THE FARMER IS FORCED TO CURTAIL HIS ACTIVITIES ON THE FARM IN ORDER TO SUPPORT HIS FAMILY. DR. RUSSELL SAYS:
RUSSELL:	TAPE #3, CUT 2: "THAT'S THE ONLY WAY . . . 24-HOUR FARMER." (That's the only way that a man can continue in farming—is to make some extra money in town to spend it out in the country because he's losing everywhere as a 24-hour farmer.)

continued

NARRATOR:	FARMER HARRY WOODS COMMENTS:
HARRY WOODS:	TAPE #4, CUT 1: "I WOULD HATE . . . AT THIS TIME." (I would hate to have to try—let's put it that way—right at this time.)
INTERVIEWER:	TAPE #1, CUT 1 (CONT.): "WOULD YOU LIKE . . . IT FULL TIME?" (Would you like to be able to work it full time?)
WOODS:	TAPE #4, CUT 1 (CONT.): "WELL, I ENJOY . . . IT'S PRETTY ROUGH." (Well, I enjoy farming. I enjoy it, but as far as actually making a living out of it, I would hate to think that I had to do it, because it's pretty rough.)
NARRATOR:	MANY BELIEVE THAT THE BASIS FOR SOLVING THE PROBLEM LIES AT THE FEDERAL GOVERNMENT LEVEL. HARDEST HIT IS THE FARMER WHO CAN LEAST AFFORD IT, THE SMALL COMMERCIAL FARMERS WORKING INFERIOR LAND. THEY LACK ADEQUATE CAPITAL TO IMPROVE THEIR HOMES. MUCH OF THEIR EFFORT GOES INTO PRODUCING THEIR OWN FOOD. OFTEN THEY DON'T HAVE THE MECHANICAL AIDS TO MAKE THEM MORE EFFICIENT. THEY ALSO GET LITTLE BENEFIT FROM THE SUBSIDIES AND HIGH SUPPORTS BECAUSE THEIR YIELD IS LOW AND THEY CAN'T AFFORD TO STORE UNTIL THE GOVERNMENT MAKES PAYMENT.
RUSSELL:	TAPE #3, CUT 3: "IF FARMING . . . THAT'D BE FATAL." (If farming is to be continued, and the country still has to rely on the farms for three very important things: food, feed, and fiber, and if the farming system collapses, we won't have enough fiber, and in case of war, that'd be fatal.)

* * *

NARRATOR:	BESIDES PRICE SUPPORTS, STORAGE AND SOIL BANKS, THE GOVERNMENT SPENDS SOME TWO AND A HALF BILLION DOLLARS TO OPERATE ITS OTHER FUNCTIONS FOR THE IMPROVEMENT OF FARMING. THERE IS LITTLE AGREEMENT AS TO JUST WHAT ROLE GOVERNMENT SHOULD PLAY IN ASSISTING THE FARMER. FARMER HARRY WOODS HAD THIS TO SAY:
WOODS:	TAPE #4, CUT 2: "THE FARM PROBLEM . . . TO HAVE THEM." (The farm problem has been with us ever since I've known anything about the farm, and there have been both sides in, and it's never been solved yet. Until they really get down to business and want to solve it, why, it never will be. Now, you said something about politics, why, you know, and I think that everybody else realizes that there is politics in the farm program as they are administered. By the time that they go into the Congress and come out, you know what happens, and, it's difficult to ever work out something that, well, that is

continued

workable. But, as far as Republicans or Democrats, why, we've had farm problems under both parties, and I think we'll continue to have them.)

KOVENOCK: TAPE #2, CUT 4: "THERE'S COMMON AGREEMENT . . . THIRTY-EIGHT CENTS."
(There's common agreement, common ground for agreement, that during the last seven or eight years that farm income has gone down roughly twenty-five percent. The farm purchasing power is at the lowest point since sometime during the 1930s. Further, we have relatively great social dislocation among farmers and non-farmers in rural America due to the relative decline of the position of the farmer in the economic sphere. We now have more employees in the Department of Agriculture than we've ever had before, and, of course, they are serving fewer farmers. The size of the surplus is, of course, grounds for common agreement. It's multiplied six or seven times; it's now worth, roughly, seven billion dollars. And, of course, the farmer's share of the dollars that we spend in the grocery store has declined now to a low point of thirty-eight cents.)

* * *

MUSIC: IN AND UNDER

NARRATOR: THESE ARE THE PROBLEMS.

MUSIC: FADE OUT

NARRATOR: THE ANSWERS ARE NOT APPARENT. THE FARM INCOME DILEMMA SPELLS TROUBLE, NOT ONLY FOR THE FARMERS, BUT FOR THE PEOPLE WHO DO BUSINESS WITH THEM, POLITICIANS, GOVERNMENT OFFICIALS AND TAX PAYERS ALIKE. WHAT DOES THE FARMER, AS A MEMBER OF THE AMERICAN SOCIETY, DESERVE? PROFESSOR S. H. HOBBS OF THE SOCIOLOGY DEPARTMENT OF THE UNIVERSITY OF NORTH CAROLINA HAD THIS TO SAY:

HOBBS: TAPE #5, CUT 1: "ONE IS THE PROBLEM . . . ECONOMIC SYSTEM."
(One is the problem of maintaining income adequate to maintain a level of living comparable with other groups. This does not mean that farmers deserve an income equal to that of any other group, but he does deserve to have an income that enables him to live comfortably in the American economic system.)

NARRATOR: IN A REGULATED, PROTECTED, AND PARTIALLY SUBSIDIZED ECONOMY SUCH AS OURS, THE FARMER REQUIRES CONSIDERABLE PROTECTION. THE TASK IS TO DEVISE NEW METHODS WHICH WILL PROVIDE HIM WITH AN ADEQUATE INCOME FOR THE VITAL FOOD WHICH HE PRODUCES.

continued

SMITH:	TAPE #1, CUT 1: "I WOULD LIKE . . . PLACE TO WORK."
	(I would like very much to spend my entire life here on the farm because I feel like being near the land and being near the soil and seeing the operation of God on this earth is the best place to live and the best place to work.)
MUSIC:	IN, UP, HOLD, UNDER.
NARRATOR:	YOU HAVE BEEN LISTENING TO "THE PIEDMONT, NORTH CAROLINA FARMER AND POLITICS." THIS PROGRAM WAS A STUDENT PRODUCTION OF THE RADIO PRODUCTION CLASS IN THE DEPARTMENT OF RADIO, TELEVISION AND MOTION PICTURES OF THE UNIVERSITY OF NORTH CAROLINA. ASSOCIATED WITH THE PRODUCTION WERE BUD CARTER, YOSHI CHINEN, JIM CLARK, WILLIAM GAY, ROGER KOONCE, JOHN MOORE, ANITA ROSEFIELD, ALEX WARREN, ANNE WILLIAMS, STEVE SILVERSTEIN AS ENGINEER, AND WAYNE UPCHURCH, YOUR ANNOUNCER.
MUSIC:	UP AND OUT

Structure

Edward R. Murrow's *Who Killed Michael Farmer?* was one of broadcasting's classic documentaries. Although produced for radio, which now rarely does any documentaries, its approaches and techniques influenced video documentaries. It can serve as a model for documentary writing today. Here are some key structural elements in *Michael Farmer* that apply to video as well as radio:

■ Select carefully from the mass of recorded material several short statements by persons involved and present them immediately to get the audience's attention and interest as well as to tell, sharply and concretely, what the program is about. The stark nature of opening cold—that is, no introduction, no music, simply the statements—can lend force to an opening. Early on let the audience know the approach that the documentary will take. In *Michael Farmer,* the narrator says, "But there is more to be said. More is involved here . . . the roots of this crime go back a long ways." Clearly the event and people will be explored in depth, a problem will be presented, and solutions will be sought.

■ Suspense is an important documentary ingredient. But it is not necessarily only the suspense of finding out what is going to happen. Because the documentary is based on fact, we already know what is going to happen in many cases. The suspense can be in learning the motivations, the inner feelings, and the attitudes of the people involved even as the actual event is retold.

■ Video documentary makers should be familiar with the techniques D. W. Griffith pioneered for film. One important technique that can be applied to video is dynamic cutting: Switching back and forth between two or more settings and two or more persons or groups of people who are following parallel courses in time and in action.

■ Various physical and emotional viewpoints are presented in increasingly dramatic order until a climax is reached—much as in writing a play. All of these elements should relate to each other, build on one another, and concomitantly carry the suspense into an ultimate explosion. The audience should be put into the center of the action, feeling it perhaps even more strongly than if the incident or action were fictionalized.

■ When the script has almost completed telling what happened, don't be tempted to end it there, as if the documentary's purpose has been accomplished. The script should imply, through the interviews and the narrative, that there is more to the story than "who, what, when, and where." The script can begin to explore motivation, to get behind the problem.

■ In getting to the "why," the script can go beyond the actual participants and, where feasible, seek out experts to analyze and comment on the problem.

■ In addition to presenting, where available, the solutions to the problem already tried, the script can suggest solutions that are still to come.

BIOGRAPHIES

The biography is a frequently produced documentary/feature type. This kind of show is sometimes called a "compilation documentary." Nat Segaloff was one of the writers and producers of the A&E cable network's *Biography*. Segaloff described the process of writing and producing for this format:

> Unlike the seminal documentaries of Robert Flaherty and John Grierson, the compilation documentary does not attempt to present reality as much as entertain and, on occasion, editorialize. The discipline is to construct a film almost entirely out of previously existing footage linked with narration and interviews that add resonance. Compilation documentaries can be dry, electric or entertaining, but they all have one thing in common: They couldn't exist if somebody else hadn't made another movie first.
>
> Essentially, the producer of a compilation documentary is stuck with somebody else's footage; the trick is giving it a new twist. Within the constraints of its format, *Biography* had a lot of creative space:

1. Tell a person's story in strict chronology;
2. Narrate it in the past tense (even if the subject is still alive, which can be alternately awkward and ghoulish);
3. Have mostly other people tell the subject's story ("It's called 'Biography,' not 'Autobiography'" is the credo) even if the subject is still alive.

Fortunately for *Stan Lee: The ComiX-MAN* (the network's title, geared to capitalize on the popularity of *The X-Men* TV show), Stan was very much alive and we enjoyed the full support of Marvel Comics, which allowed us rare access to artwork, characters, films and personnel—within the limits, however, of a cable TV budget (roughly one-fourth of a network budget). The complexity of researching, booking, shooting, and editing a one-hour show (actual time without commercials: 43:30) strains that budget.

I like to describe the drill as "an eight-week show that takes 16 weeks to do." Each profile includes between 8 and 12 interviews, 5 to 7 minutes of licensed action material (film clips, music videos, etc.) and between 100 and 200 photographs or supportive action footage (called "B-Roll"). Typically, the interviews are conducted in hotel rooms or private homes. The producer asks the questions, but the subject is directed to give self-contained answers so the producer can be edited out.

The process is to weave a compelling narrative out of these recollections. Sometimes the subjects' stories advance the "plot" of the person's life; other times two, three, or even four people will give separate versions of the same event and the producer and editor must string them together as though they were one continuous tale.

The effect of this interwoven narrative enlivens even the most mundane story—provided it has a good punch line. A voice-over narrator bridges the gaps.

Where TV magazines involve the producer shooting tapes in the field and then throwing them at the editor to finish, *Biography* shows compel the producer to stick with a single story from inception to mix. This is financially inefficient (I don't know of anybody who can do more than four a year), but can be tremendously satisfying work.

The difference is the venue. A&E is enlightened; they recognize that the viewer isn't an idiot. Best of all, since the shows are about real people caught up in real quandaries, it's possible to address complex social and political issues within the framework of a person's personal story.

In an age where documentaries have the reputation of being boring, A&E has the key to making and showing truly subversive television. Don't let this get around.

Getting all viewpoints on all sides and organizing them into a comprehensive whole creates a rounded, complete picture of the person being studied. Segaloff pointed to an example in his biography of *Stan Lee: The ComiX-MAN:* the description of how Stan Lee and his wife, Joan Lee, met. Segaloff noted that the following excerpts from the unedited script "show how editing can intertwine two separate recollections of the same incident into the appearance of a single cohesive story . . . of course, this is planned when we do the interview, but it always works (unless the story tellers have differing memories of the same event)." [Stan Lee produced the blockbuster films of one of his comic book characters, Spider-Man.]

Stan Lee unedited transcript

NS [INTERVIEWER Nat Segaloff]:

I want to ask you about the most animated person in your life, I'm looking for a segue, that is of course, Joan. You married her, but as I understand it according to legend, was that you visualized what she would look like before you even met her?

SL [Stan Lee]:

Well, its a funny thing about how I met my wife. You know, I used to draw cartoons when I was very young, little drawings. Almost everybody who draws, every guy I guess, you, you like to draw girls and you usually draw your idealized girl's face. And it has been the same face that I had been drawing all the time, you know, I, I, big beautiful eyes and a turned up nose, and nice lips and I had gotten real good at drawing this face. And one day, a friend of mine told me that he had arranged this blind date for me, there was a model, at a hat showroom somewhere. In those days, the hat models were the most beautiful girls ever, because they were just taking photos of their faces all the time, for the hats. So I was thrilled about that and I went up the, to this place. Joan opened the door—she was not the girl that I was supposed to meet. She was the head model there and she was one and she opened the door and she's English, so the English accent, you know, may I help you?, and I took one look at her and it was the face I had been drawing all my life. And I think I said something stupid like, I love you, and anyway, that's how we met. I didn't date the other girl, I started dating Joan.

* * *

Interview with Joan Lee

NS:

The classic story of your first meeting with Stan, uh, where you were modeling hats, I'm looking to go back and forth through the stories. You weren't expecting to meet him, as I gather.

JL [Joan Lee]:

No, not at all. We were having a Christmas party, as a matter of fact. A Christmas party, and there was a little girl called Betty Sue—blonde and very pretty. And Stan was supposed to have a date with her. And I remember it very clearly, he came to the door (laughs) and he had his raincoat thrown over his shoulder. It had to be like this, you know, and a scarf or something, like a cravat. And he said press the doorbell and it was on Fifth Avenue and 37th Street and busy (garbled) called Latham hats. Press the door and I opened it and said hello. And he said, hello, I think I'm going to fall

continued

in love with you. And I thought this is one I can't let get away. And I was a terrible flirt in those days, too, so I ushered him in, and talked to—I think he took Betty Sue out that night, that was it. And then I think he called a week later, . . . we had lunch and I think it was then he told me he was a writer. I think he did carry a briefcase too. I remember thinking, well, what are you writing? This is wonderful. This is so romantic. This is divine. I mean, we are both so young. And he said, well, I write—I'm editor for a comic book. And I said, oh, comic books, oh, we don't have comic books in England, we don't read comic books. And then he did all those things and I thought he was the most interesting man I have ever met in my life. So, that was it. I decided, the truth, that I absolutely could not let him go. I think it was 8 weeks longer, I was in Reno and we were married and there you go.

Courtesy of Nat Segaloff

To show how the approaches Segaloff described are implemented, following are excerpts from Acts I and V of the program, *Stan Lee: The ComiX-Man,* (© A&E Television Networks).

"Stan Lee: The ComiX-MAN!"

INTRO—HOST IN STUDIO

HOST

Hello. I'm (Peter Graves) (Jack Perkins) and welcome to "Biography." What do "Spider-Man," "The Incredible Hulk" and "X-Men" have in common? If you said "comic book heroes" you'd be on the right track. If you said "Stan Lee" you probably have a closet full of his work. Stan Lee is the man behind the incredible popularity of Marvel Comics. He virtually re-invented comic books—and his own life story is as iconoclastic as any of the classic super heroes he helped create.

FADEOUT

ACT ONE

FADE IN: Clip: "Spider-Man" (animated)

DISSOLVE TO:

Simmons (3)
04:06:54

GENE SIMMONS

Spider-Man, The Hulk—there's not a, there's not a country
in the world that doesn't know those names.

CUT TO:

Yet more LIGHTNING, then

CUT TO:

Clip: "The Incredible Hulk"

DISSOLVE TO:

Ferrigno (1)
00:08:12

continued

LOU FERRIGNO

When you meet Stan, he to me is the only living Marvel comic hero on earth.

                                                                                    CUT TO:

Clip: "The Fantastic Four"

                                                                                    DISSOLVE TO:

John Semper
01:48:54

JOHN SEMPER

Think about it: this man took, um, a few short years to lay down the
framework for characters and a popular mythology that would last for
thirty years.

                                                                                    CUT TO:

Even more LIGHTNING, then

                                                                                    CUT TO:

Clip: "The X-Men"

                                                                                    DISSOLVE TO:

Ritter (2)
02:26:14

JOHN RITTER

That's something about Stan Lee: you have the feeling
that, uh, he doesn't want to be bored and he doesn't want
to bore you and, consequently, everything is new and exciting.

Music changes to heraldic Wagnerian themes as we

                                                                                    IRIS TO:

Stan's story told in comic book panels that illustrate the narrative that's to come.

NARRATOR (V.O.)

Stanley Martin Lieber—writer—editor. His dream stifled by a boss devoid of
vision. Then, one night, he is seized by all-consuming originality. Forsaking
his job security, he vents his creative spirit—and revolutionizes an industry
to become: Stan Lee: The ComiX-MAN!

                                                                                    END ON:

The comic book closes to reveal the cover: John Romita's caricature of Stan Lee as Spider-Man. We
SUPERIMPOSE the main title:

                            Stan Lee: The ComiX-MAN!

Music change to Jazz-era themes as we

                                                                                    IRIS TO:

continued

Tilt-down a huge collage of comic book covers.

NARRATOR (V.O.)

The life of Stan Lee is really two stories, and it begins—not with Stan Lee—but with comic books.

* * *

Photo of Stan;
Stock shots NYC
and photos

NARRATOR (V.O.)

Stan Lee. He was born in upper Manhattan—Stanley Martin Lieber. The son of Jack and Celia Lieber, Stan was precocious, skipping grades and winning the New York Herald Tribune essay contest three weeks running. Unlike his peers, who devoured comics, young Stan preferred books: the classics of Edgar Rice Burroughs, Mark Twain, Arthur Conan Doyle and more. He also loved movies, and spent his free time at the local theatre, absorbed in their tales of action and adventure.

SEQUENCE of movie swashbucklers, chases, etc.

* * *

NARRATOR (V.O.)

After graduating high school, Stan looked for full-time work. A distant relative, magazine publisher Martin Goodman, needed a helper at one of his companies, Timely Comics. Stan arrived at Timely's cramped Manhattan offices just as editor Joe Simon and art director Jack Kirby were creating Captain America—and preparing to leave.

EVANIER (02:09:00)

[Ah] after ten issues they quit over a financial dispute, ah, starting another precedent in the industry, but by that time an office boy named Stan Lee had been brought in. [edit]

NARRATOR (V.O.)

Not taking comics seriously, Goodman gave his 18-year-old office boy a free hand. This capricious decision would soon change an entire industry: Stan Lee and the history of comics books are one and the same.

EVANIER (02:09:15)

I think Stan's first published story was in Captain America number three, a little text piece on Captain America written by Stan Lee. It's bylined, one of the first bylines in comics.

WAR FOOTAGE—recruits in basic training.

NARRATOR (V.O.)

World War Two interrupted the Golden Age of comics and punctuated the career of Stan Lee, who enlisted. The Army posted him stateside with the unusual classification of "playwright."

continued

NARRATOR (V.O.)

After the war Stan returned to writing and editing comics, which had become an industry without a focus.

EVANIER (08:03:04)

The modus operandi of Marvel Comics, or Timely Comics or Atlas Comics was: find out what other people have got that's selling and strip-mine the market. Put out knockoffs of it.

STAN (04:49:10)

We did war stories, romance stories, humor stories, um, horror stories, monster stories, um, little funny animal, animated comic stories. Whatever was the trend at the moment, that's what we did.

NARRATOR (V.O.)

It was also an industry without prestige.

ELLISON (05:08:30)

When they started out, they were considered for kids because, like all native arts, they're demeaned at the outset, whether it's Grandma Moses's painting or the, or the, or the, or the, ah, ah, banjo, or the mystery stories, all of which are singularly American constructs. There're only, there're only about five real American folk arts and comic books is one of them.

STAN (04:55:15)

In those days comics weren't thought of very highly. And I remember when we would go to parties, people would walk over to me and say, What do you do? And I tried not to say it—Oh, I'm a writer, and walk away. But the person would follow me, Well what do you write? Oh, stories for young people. Walk away further, they'd follow me. What kind of stories? Magazine stories. Well, what magazine? At some point I had to say comic books and the person who had been interrogating me would say, Oh, I see, and turn around and leave me, you know.

NARRATOR (V.O.)

One person he met at a party didn't walk away. She was actress-writer Joan Clayton Boocock. They met by accident, and also by Fate, at a social gathering.

STAN (04:49:41)

Well, it's a funny thing about how I met my wife. You know, I used to draw cartoons when I was very young, little, little drawings. Almost everybody who draws, every guy I guess, you, you like to draw girls and you usually draw your idealized girl's face. And there had been one face that I had been drawing all the time . . .

JOAN (05:44:35)

And I remember it very clearly: he came to the door and he had his raincoat thrown over his shoulder.

STAN (04:50:35)

Joan opened the door. She was not the girl that I was supposed to meet. She was the head model there and she was the one I had been drawing all my life! And I said . . .

JOAN (05:44:58)

—helllllloo. And he said Hello, I think I'm going to fall in love with you—

STAN (04:50:48)

And I took one look at her and it was like the face I had been drawing all my life. And I think I said something stupid like, I love you—

JOAN (05:45:10)

—and I thought this is one I can't let get away.

NARRATOR (V.O.)

Joan and Stan were married in time for Christmas.

* * *

Music transition; Stan signing autographs at ComiCon

NARRATOR (V.O.)

Today, Stan Lee's undiminished energy is focused on expanding the Marvel Universe, including his own label called Excelsior. His future is the uncharted realm of fantasy—explored every time a kid, of any age, finds adventure in the pages of a comic book. And, yes—he finally has respect.

STEWART (06:14:42)

I think Stan's efforts were instrumental in creating something that was very contemporary and something that could be respected as an art form as an entertainment form that allowed more people to enjoy it and that by, in and by itself raised it to the level that it is today.

LIEBER (07:29:50)
NEW BITE

What he did to it is what gave it life. Uh, by putting in humor, by having those characters, by the way he did, by, he just wrote it very well and very personal and it, and it took off, and, um, it just grew from them.

ELLISON (05:29:12)
NEW BITE

In my dealings with him, and I'm not an easy guy as you may gather, Stan Lee has always been absolutely four square. Absolutely straight. He has never lied to me. If he made me a promise, he did it.

ASNER (20:17:26)

He's more youthful now than when he began. Uh, he's to be admired.
And uh—bottom line—he's a terribly decent chap.

JOAN (05:56:17)

And he's healthy and energetic and talented and very happy being Stan Lee.

STAN (21:03:33)

When I was a kid, I used to draw a lot, so I figured, hey, I'm gonna try this for a while. I'll get some experience and then I'll get out into the real world and get a real job. I never thought it would be permanent.

Dissolve to head shot of Stan Lee smiling.

FADEOUT

OUTRO: Host in studio

HOST

Like his super-heroes, Stan Lee is down-to-earth and endearingly human. Hollywood filmmakers court him seeking fresh ideas; he travels the country as Marvel's goodwill ambassador. But, with all his success, he still has the optimism that he started with more than thirty years ago. And he shares it with his readers—of all ages. Now here's a look at our next "Biography"
####

"Stan Lee: The ComiX-MAN," Produced by Nat Segaloff.
© A&E Television Networks. All Rights Reserved. Courtesy of Mr. Segaloff.

MINI-DOCUMENTARIES

The success of *60 Minutes* prompted the growth of the mini-documentary, or mini-feature in a magazine format. The *60 Minutes* hour-length program permits 15 to 20 minutes per segment, but the half-hour length of magazine shows such as the syndicated *Chronicle* series allows segments of only about 7 minutes per story. The writer must be concise, and, because many mini-docs bridge early evening periods between news and entertainment programs, must combine both news and entertainment.

Ron Blau, filmmaker and television writer-producer, has written documentary films, full-length television documentaries, and dozens of mini-documentaries ranging from 4 to 10 minutes each. He believes that the standard documentary and mini-documentary are essentially the same except for the obvious difference: The longer show has more time in which to present information and develop ideas.

Most minidoc writers work through the same chronological process. First is selecting the topic or theme, which can come from any source: the executive producer, the field producer, newspaper stories, and, less frequently, the freelance writer-producer. After the topic is determined, the writer must do appropriate research; some can be done in libraries and online, some on site, and some through interviews.

Following initial research, an outline is prepared, somewhat similar to a rundown sheet. The outline remains flexible because the writer does not yet know who is going to say what or what kinds of visual or aural material will be available. Blau advocates outlining a fairly simple structure because there is not enough time in a minidoc for anything complicated. He explained that there are three principal types of material to look for: voice-over, *bites* or quotes, and what he terms "breathing" visuals—video, film, or stills of background, actions, or persons without voice. Room should be left for music, too. The final outline becomes the basis for shooting.

Following shooting, the screening of all materials permits the writer to prepare the final script. According to Blau, most writers structure the piece from the bites and the voice-overs. He advises that the piece be allowed to breathe: A piece on dance could have dance itself shown without any voice-over, and a piece on housing could have video of the neighborhood or of interiors without voice. The latter approach is sometimes referred to as using the **B roll**, arising from the old practice of putting interview material on one projector and non-interview visuals on a second or B projector.

Most documentary writers practice the basic principles of journalism: start with a strong topic opening giving the essence of the piece, follow immediately with the five Ws, then fill in the details in whatever time is left. Some writers structure the piece around voice-overs and fill in with the bites and breathing shots. Ron Blau's approach is to begin with something attention-getting that is of special interest to the audience, then fill in the basic structure with field materials, and, finally, add the voice-overs.

With the numerous pieces needed for a given program series (sometimes at least three for every half-hour show), and the limited time available to produce them (sometimes less than a week per segment), you need either to have a large staff or to take extra care to see that all the information is accurate. Be careful not to take liberties with the facts if you find that time and staff haven't permitted you to get all pertinent information. Write from what you have. Don't make up facts to fill in. Many minidocs essentially repeat what has been covered in the press, and you may be tempted to embellish to give the story a new look. Where do you draw the line between factual documentary and fictional documentary? *New York Times* critic John J. O'Connor referred to the result of the failure to make the distinction as the "questionable craft of 'docudrama.'" Don't pass off fiction as fact.

Following are excerpts from two short sequences from one of Ron Blau's mini-documentary scripts, Prodigies. *Analyze where and how they follow Blau's writing approach.*

<u>PRODIGIES</u>

<u>Intro</u>

VIDEO	**AUDIO**
KIDS	MUSIC: In, up, and under.
Pix from Josh's nursery school without Josh in shots.	NARRATOR (V.O.): Until now we have been looking at forces which shape a child's mind at close range: like gifts a child is born with . . . and the family's effect.
Exterior with kids.	But some forces are as big as America itself.
	These forces are cultural influences—which push some ethnic groups to the top—which allow more boys than girls to shine in some fields—which limit the progress of other groups.
	America may seem like a great melting pot, but within her borders cultural pressures still encourage some of her people more than others to travel paths of giftedness.
End of Intro	
Exterior: Wei-Jing's school.	MUSIC: Rap music, in and up.
Interior: Hallways.	SFX: Natural sounds. Music out.
	NARRATOR (V.O.): Each year the Westinghouse Science Talent search rewards a few outstanding high school students with the largest no-strings-attached scholarships in the country: up to $20,000! Recently, the top five awards all went to a single ethnic group.
Math Club	SFX: Natural sounds, then V.O.
Wei-Jing at computer	WEI-JING: Normally in class I try to comprehend what's going on. And most of the time I remember everything. And so when a test time comes, it's just like a normal day. And I really look forward to tests since when there's a test that means there's less homework.

continued

VIDEO	AUDIO
Frisbee	NARRATOR (V.O.): Wei-Jing who's a descendent of the first emperor of the Ming Dynasty, is now headed for Harvard.
Wei-Jing	WEI-JING: I'm hardworking in the sense that I am very, very inquisitive and curious about things and like to find out the why's and how's in nature and . . . well . . . I'm just very curious about things. And also I like to find competitions that I can enter. For example, I enter all the math contests.
Benjamin Bloom Japanese file footage. American school.	BLOOM: We study parents in Japan, Hong Kong, and in other countries and ask the parents, "How would you explain your child doing poorly in school?" The Asiatic parents explain it in terms of the amount of effort the child puts in. In the United States, when we ask the parents, for example, "Why is your child doing poorly in arithmetic?" the mother says, "Well, I was never good at arithmetic." They reply that this is an inherited defect.
Japanese file footage.	NARRATOR (V.O.): Asia, of course, is an entire continent, with an enormous density of people. These children are from Tokyo . . . but they share with children in Beijing and Phnom Penh an ancient tradition of discipline, of respect for learning, and of status based on educational achievement.
Wei-Jing	WEI-JING: I guess the major factor is that the Asian people . . . like the families . . . are really hard and demanding in what their sons and daughters achieve. They are expecting very high achievements from their children. And I guess that's the major factor.
End with Frisbee shot. End of Wei-Jing segment.	
Edith doing math at blackboard with friend Carlos.	SFX: Natural sound—conversation—5 seconds.
Edith	EDITH: I think it started when I got into high school and they had a math team and I'd never heard of such a thing. The idea of being able to go out and do math problems for fun and for competition was terrific.

continued

VIDEO	AUDIO
	NARRATOR: The "Math Olympiad" is a competition to find the top eight high school math students in America. In the history of the Olympiad, Harvard student Edith Starr is the only <u>woman</u> ever to win. Altogether, only a small fraction of mathematicians are female.
	Why are women a rarity in some fields? We noticed only three in a chess match we covered with Ilya Gurevich . . . out of a field of 142 players. We were told this is typical.
	It's <u>possible</u> that genes play some part in this imbalance; no one's proved otherwise. But most experts point to <u>cultural</u> forces.
Ruth Feldman	FELDMAN: Even today I think girls grow up thinking that somebody is going to take care of them. That they're going to be wives and mothers and maybe they are going to have careers for a while, but they can always fall back on a man. So I think with gifted girls, particularly, it's important to give them the idea that they really can make their own decisions. They can choose a career if they want to, they can choose home and motherhood if they want to. These options need to be available to girls.
Edith walking.	NARRATOR (V.O.): So, Edith Starr is an exception who can light the way for others. She feels she's successful in math because she was not brought up like most other girls.
Edith	EDITH: My parents encouraged me although they didn't push it on me in any way. But they were always happy when I did well. And I guess they always encouraged mind puzzles, word games. I had a lot of teachers, as well as my parents, who encouraged me in everything I did without pushing me.
Feldman	NARRATOR: Regardless of the field, fewer girls than boys get identified as prodigies. But this imbalance may someday disappear.
End with pix of girls.	FELDMAN: Once the culture begins to entertain the possibility that the same kinds of extraordinary possibilities exist in girls as in boys, you'll start seeing girl prodigies. It's as simple as that.

Courtesy of Ron Blau and WBZ-TV, Boston

The Internet has become a prime avenue for the distribution of mini-documentaries and mini-features, some no more than a minute or two long. The access not only to individual web sites, but to YouTube, Facebook, and other "social" venues enables anyone, professional and amateur alike, to show their creative productions. Keep in mind that your mini-feature or mini-doc should be more than just some snippets or impressions caught with your camera or iPhone. Even for the shortest presentation, your piece should have a beginning, middle, and end, following the principles of good writing that you'd use for a full-length production. Too short a time? As an example of being able to tell a story in such a short time, look at some of the 30-second commercials in Chapter 4.

SPECIAL CONSIDERATIONS

Features and documentaries are especially adaptable to programming for ethnic and racial groups. Some critics have suggested that unless you belong to the group being presented in the feature or documentary, you may not have sufficient firsthand knowledge and emotional understanding of that group to write about it accurately, perceptively, and with depth—even with the best will in the world.

Loraine Misiaszek, who was director of Advocates for Indian Education and a producer of radio and television programs by, about, and for Native Americans, found that non-Indian writers frequently use words such as "squaw" and "breed," not realizing how derogatory they are. She also expressed concern with programs about Native Americans that are "put-downs," that editorialize instead of presenting the facts, and influence listeners into drawing conclusions that judge Native American actions as "bad," whereas an outside objective view might find them to be "good." "Anyone concerned with scriptwriting for radio or television," Misiaszek warned, "ought to be aware of this problem. It is not necessarily intentional, but it happens because of the general conditioning in our society that causes people to think of Indians in terms of stereotypes."

The same viewpoint was expressed by Thomas Crawford, who wrote and produced Native American programs. The writer "must first of all become familiar with idioms, patterns of expression, turns of thought, and pronunciations of the particular Indian community with which one is dealing," Crawford stated. "This kind of background will enable a scriptwriter to deal with the subject in a way that will interest and be appropriate to the people." Crawford stressed the need for personal experience and empathy by the writer. "The complexities of writing a program for or about Native Americans on a national level would be nearly prohibitive for the non-Indian. An Indian writer can present idioms and viewpoints as a valid part of the Native American scene in the United States."

These concepts can be applied to almost every racial, ethnic, and other special group, especially when you are writing a feature or documentary, which requires you to be knowledgeable about the subject.

REALITY PROGRAMS

In the 1990s a new format took hold in U.S. television: the "reality program." The American viewing public is attracted to the format's combination of truth-based events, highly dramatized script interpretations, highly stylized productions, and people in competitive situations ranging from land or sea or air races, to surviving in dangerous places, to nabbing a husband, to winning a talent contest, to police investigations, adventurous rescues, emergency medical activities, and courtroom cases—among other circumstances or predicaments.

Features, documentaries and reality programs ostensibly deal with real events. That is, they in themselves are not fictional creations in the traditional drama sense, but are about something that actually exists or existed. The subject of the documentary may be fictional (for example, a study of the characters in a novelist's works) or may be real (a study of that novelist's writing techniques). The reality program presents or records a factual happening, as differentiated from a scripted fictional piece. *Law and Order* and *CSI* may give the appearance of a real police investigation and may, in fact, be based on real events, but they are not reality shows. They are scripted dramas. *Lost* was a scripted drama of people trying to survive on an island. *Survivor* was a reality show of people actually put in a situation of trying to survive on an island—or in another difficult setting. A documentary could be a program *about* making a television program like *Survivor*.

Some critics see reality shows as an extension of the documentary, with an emphasis on human interest factors that, as Van Gordon Sauter, former president of NBC news, stated, "form an emotional link between . . . stories and . . . audience." Some critics, however, believe that reality programs distort rather than depict reality. They question whether the events as presented are too selectively untypical of what actually happened, and they express concern that some events shown in reality programs are reenactments, with performers and/or performances, rather than actual occurrences. Other critics state that reality programs have an educational value, introducing the public to the work and life of people in key professions, such as safety, health, and law. Some see reality shows solely in terms of their entertainment value, citing the suspense of competition and the presentation of physically attractive people. Both types, entertainment and educational, are discussed below.

Writing Technique

Daniel J. Blau, producer and writer of the latter type, the *America's Next Top Model* program, described in an interview on the web site, "Television Without Pity," some of the writing approaches for this kind of reality show. Blau and other writers work from hundreds of hours of raw footage of the would-be models in their daily lives, such as getting ready for the day, eating breakfast, speaking with friends, and making the professional rounds. Working with an editor, the producer and writers create an hour television program. They start with treatments, choose the talent who will be in the particular episode, refine the "story arcs" and, after the shoots, write the actual script—that is, a "line-by-line beat" of what each contestant does during the day leading to "their challenges and their photo shoots" and ending in judging which contestants will be eliminated. Blau stated that the work is "primarily a post-production job . . . we write everything after the fact." He stressed that although they might write "pickups" for the talent on the set, "we don't feed lines to the girls," and that the things that they are doing in competing with each other, they actually do. While the reality show writer does not write an actual pre-production script, the treatment and post-production script clearly constitutes writing.

Moira Mayer, Director of International Development for MTV Networks, produced and wrote reality shows. She described her work:

> MTV has been at the forefront of creating and pushing the boundaries of reality television. Even before the groundbreaking show *The Osbournes* premiered in 2002 on MTV, the channel had already clocked 10 seasons of the genre-inventing *The Real World*. We now live in a world where everyone thinks their life and experiences would make a good reality show!
>
> Here are a few rules, guidelines and observations I have come up with from developing reality and documentary style shows over the past few years:

- Since reality television captures unscripted real life situations, there is no need for writers and directors in the traditional sense. This role is now played by Field Directors in the field and Story Editors in the edit suite.

- It is really important to have strong Field Directors who can direct the action as it unfolds in real time in a way that makes a stronger scene and helps build the narrative.

- These golden moments and scenes are the fence-posts that will help the Story Editor string the story together in the edit bay.

- For example, we were shooting a young rock band in a hotel room. The guitarist picked up his guitar and started singing in an isolated corner. Later in edit, we needed to build this moment into a scene to fill time and make a story transition. We ended up having to piece together different shots and cheat it to look like the guitarist had a few friends singing along with him. In industry slang, this is known as "Frakenbiting." An experienced field director would have directed the action by suggesting to the band-mates to go join the guitarist and therefore build a more authentic and powerful scene. Who knows if they might have come up with their next hit in that jam session, right while our cameras were rolling!

- Music Supervisors are very important. They usually watch the rough string out of the show and suggest music that would punch up the scenes to add drama or comedy to the unscripted moment.

- A good executive producer will create a general framework for the crew, briefing them on what they think is the best way to capture the subjects, but the crew must be allowed spontaneity in the field and be prepared for everything.

- When you're shooting a reality show, cameras roll continuously, even when the principals are asleep.

■ You must have a crew that can support that much footage gathering. This usually means a minimum of 2 units, with 3 units being a good safe bet.

■ Even when the shoot day is wrapped, you can still assign a camera to film sunsets and sunrises which are vital for showing transitions and the passage of time.

■ Assume that you can never go back in time to get the shots you need. Use the crew to capture absolutely everything in the environment, which can be later used in the edit as cut-aways or frames to accentuate a point.

■ Things said on the fly (OTF in industry slang) often make the best scene enders and are great ways to direct the narrative.

■ Nothing goes to waste . . . what is left on the cutting room floor could become DVD extras or online "after show" material.

Although sometimes using re-creations to depict real events and real people, *America's Most Wanted* is considered to be the longest running reality program in the United States, aired weekly from 1989 to 2011, then as quarterly specials, its final episode on cable in 2013. The show's basic format revolved around wanted criminals, frequently from F.B.I. files. The program reenacted the crime, gave full details about the wanted people, including their criminal acts, their background, where they were last seen, the details of their escape if they had been previously in custody, and what they look like, with special identifying features. The program then provided a phone number so viewers with information about the wanted person could call. Many criminals have been apprehended through information generated by the program.

Philip Lerman, supervising producer of *America's Most Wanted*, advised the would-be writer of reality television that "there are really only two things to remember: One: It's reality. Two: It's television. Unfortunately," Lerman added, "those two don't always go together easily. But they can be made to work together, with a little bit of effort." His advice to the writer begins with the reality part:

Because you're writing about things that really happened—or things that *supposedly* really happened—you have to be very careful. There are only two kinds of "truth" you can report: things you saw happen yourself, and things which a jury decided are true. *Everything else in the world is hearsay,* and you should treat it as such. Watch the careful attribution in good reality programs: it's there for a reason. It's not just a legal dodge to say "police say Shmidlap robbed the bank"; it's a reflection of the reality-writer's world view. You don't *know* anything, other than what you've been told. So be honest about who told you.

Lerman continues his advice with television considerations:

Television dramas can move at a fairly slow pace; there's a belief that the audience is invested in the characters, emotionally tied to them, and will stay with them. Television reality is just the opposite: the belief is that the audience views this programming as "information," of which there is much available in the world—and the moment this information stops being relevant, interesting, or important, the viewer will turn away.

So, when writing for television, you have to be crisp, brief, emotional; your words must be charged, electric, exciting; you must live in fear that at any moment your audience will become bored with you and turn away. There are those who will tell you that this kind of writing reflects a belief that the audience is dumb and has the attention span of a fruit fly. They are wrong. It does not. It reflects just the opposite. The audience you are writing for is entirely too sophisticated to be fooled by flowery writing. They can spot an interesting show, or a boring one, in seconds. They're busy, and they have a lot of choices, and they will watch what they damn well please—and if you want to maintain their interest, you'd better look and sound damn sharp.

Lerman concludes,

So where does that leave us? Writing for reality means being cautious; writing for television means being bold. Reality TV must be circumspect, yet direct; careful, yet carefree; judicious, yet risky; informational, yet entertaining. It is in that careful balance, it is along that edge, that the good reality writer thrives. Tightrope walkers are never clumsy; therefore, the key element to writing for reality television is simply this: a fine sense of balance, a light touch, and a little bit of grace.

America's Most Wanted has been one of the best-written reality programs, combining the various facets noted in producer Lerman's advice. Following are two script excerpts from *America's Most Wanted*, the first illustrating the "documentary approach" and the second (the script's opening few pages) illustrating the inclusion of dramatization and reenactment.

PAUL PLOUFFE	FINAL DRAFT (AS VOICED)	CAMEROTA
	SUGGESTED WALSH INTRO:	
	Before MTV there was a musical tv show that came out of Pittsfield, Massachusetts. In fact, it's still on the air today. 12-year-old clips from that show's archives are our best clue for finding this next guitar-strumming fugitive. Our reporter Alisyn Camerota visited Pittsfield and brings us this report.	
GEORGE MORELL INTRO TO SHOW	"Hello everyone and welcome to our show."	
THE MORELL SHOW	VO #1 The year was 1982. The place Pittsfield, Massachusetts. And every Wednesday night, local music fans would tune into the George Morell show. "We're gonna do a little singing . . ."	
GEORGE MORELL SHOW	VO #2 Part Hee-Haw, part kareokee, the show featured George Morell and his sidekick, singer and guitar player Paul Plouffe.	

continued

PAUL PLOUFFE O/C	"Giddyup, ahumbop, ahumbop, a-mow-mow . . ."
	VO #3
MICHELLE WALKING UP ON STAGE	Plouffe's 15-year-old daughter Michelle was also one of the regulars.
GEORGE MORELL INTRODUCING MICHELLE	"Now here's Michelle. Hi Michelle." (Michelle sings . . .)
MICHELLE PLOUFFEO/C 00 25 50	"Everyone thought we were the typical American family. You know, look at her up there, singing with her parents. I don't think that anyone ever really knew. I don't think anyone ever had an idea what was happening."
	VO #4
MORE GEORGE MORELL SHOW PHOTOS OF MICHELLE AND HER FRIEND AT SEVEN YEARS OLD— 02 05 49	What the audience didn't know was that behind the scenes Michelle was suffering a personal hell. According to police, Plouffe had been beating and molesting Michelle and molesting Michelle's best friend since the girls were seven.
MICHELLE PLOUFFE O/C 00 30 00	"My father's excuse for everything was let me teach you now so that you don't have to experiment when you're older. I don't want you to grow up and to be 16 years old and go in the backseat of a car with someone. So, let me introduce it to you this way.
ALISYN STAND UP IN FRONT OF HIGH SCHOOL 02 07 36	AFTER NINE YEARS OF MOLESTATION, MICHELLE COULDN'T TAKE IT ANYMORE, SO ONE DAY WHEN SHE WAS 16, SHE WORKED UP ENOUGH COURAGE TO TELL HER TEACHER HERE AT HER HIGH SCHOOL. THAT AFTERNOON, MICHELLE WAS PLACED INTO FOSTER CARE . . . AND HER FATHER WENT ON THE RUN.
MICHELLE O/C 01 10 27	"They called me on a Saturday and told me that he had taken off. I was very angry. Very angry."
	VO #5
	Two years passed with no sign of Plouffe. Then Michelle received this audio cassette. It was from her fugitive father. On it, Plouffe makes a frightening request.
PLOUFFE AUDIO OVER FREEZE OF HIS PHOTO	"There's something I want to ask you . . . I'd hate to see myself about to cash in and never have asked you. Would
CUT THIS IN HALF******	you consider the possibility of meeting me somewhere? And before you panic, hear me out. It would not be where I live, I'd travel a long way. I'd just like to eyeball you."

continued

	VO #5
SLOW-MO OF PLOUFFE SINGING CUT TO AMW INTRO JOHN TALKING	Michelle declined the offer, hoping her father would have a rendevouz with the law instead. When that didn't happen, it would take an episode of "America's Most Wanted" to give Michelle her next idea.
****use a different show of Sharon!!	
MICHELLE O/C—01 13 00	"I saw previews of America's Most Wanted and I said to myself, Wow, that looks like Sharon.'"
	VO #6
AMW RECREATION AND PHOTOS OF SHARON BEING ON THE SET WITH JOHN	Sharon Stone was an old high school friend of Michelle's and the two had a lot in common. Sharon's father had also physically and sexually abused her. Like Plouffe, Sharon's father was also a fugitive. And so was Sharon's mother. That is until America's Most Wanted got involved and captured them.
*****add reaction	"Oh my God!!"
MICHELLE PLOUFFE VOICE OVER CAPTURE REPORT OF SHARON'S PARENTS	"I remember she called me and she said, 'They found 'em.' And I thought I would fall on the floor. I really did."
SHARON STONE O/C	"Finally there was an ending to my story and then that's when she got the notion may be I can do something about mine."
MICHELLE O/C	"I pretty much believed that if they could do it for her, they may be able to do it for me."
MICHELLE PLOUFFE V/O OVER HER IN THE YARD PLAYING WITH HER CHILDREN	"I guess you could say that if anything that my father had done for me, he has made me strong and he has made me tough. And I will not allow him to live the rest of his life without doing something about it."
REPRISE SONG AND MUSIC HERE FOR BIG FINISH	(End on song . . .)

WANTED:
Paul Plouffe may be earning a living working in a convenience store and singing on the side. This is how he looked in 1986 when he was arrested for theft in Burlington, Vermont.

Unfortunately, Plouffe was released before he could be extradited back to Pittsfield on the rape charges. If you know where Plouffe and his guitar are tonight, please call 1800 CRIME TV.

KOBIE MOWATT   DRAFT #7 (AS VOICED)

* * *

Kobie Mowatt

PAN of Kennedy Street sign/ MUSIC UNDER scenes of hustlers hanging out on the Kennedy St. corridor	SUGGESTED WALSH INTRO: Here in Washington D-C, [crime statistic]. The gangs here are called "crews." Their violence has forced residents to live hiding behind locked doors. Our first story tonight deals with one of the most dangerous crews. *************************
	*****SOUNDWAVE NOTE: Place VO #1 so word "Capital" lands on the capitol)***
PAN of bus, then to the U.S. Capitol	WALSHVO #1 {ends at 01:00:22} [Read any time] THEY OPERATE IN THE SHADOWS OF THE NATION'S CAPITAL
	********soundwave note: place vo #1a so that words "first and kennedy" land on street sign, "kobie mowatt" lands on mowatt actor********
	WALSH VO #1a (01:00:22) (19 SECS)
crew members selling drugs to drive by cars, playing dice game, exchanging money and crack	THE CREWS CARVE THE NEIGHBORHOOD BLOCKS INTO DRUG TURF THEY VIOLENTLY DEFEND. THEY TAKE THEIR NAMES FROM THE STREET CORNERS THEY CALL THEIR OWN. THIS CREW WAS KNOWN AS THE FIRST AND KENNEDY, OR 100-KENNEDY CREW. POLICE SAY KOBIE
SHOT of street sign on corner of 1st and Kennedy Streets, N.W.	MOWATT WAS THE CREW'S MOST VIOLENT MEMBER.
SHOT of Kobie Mowatt playing dice game	
CUT to William Ragland walking with groceries as he passes crew members playing dice who are blocking the sidewalk	Nats: crowd comments from the dice game
Kobie Mowatt jumps up from the dice game and bumps into Ragland another crew member jumps up Bennie Lee Lawson	RAGLAND: Get out of my way son! KOBIE: You got a pass Pops? BENNIE: Yo man, yo, yo that's Darlene's gramps, he alright Kobie, go on Pops.

William Ragland walks past the crew	WALSH VO #2 (01:00:55) 3 sec TIGHT! [OR MUST LOSE NATS]
	BENNIE LAWSON WAS ANOTHER MEMBER OF THE 100 KENNEDY CREW.
crew members let him proceed, as they watch him walk away CUT to Det. Anthony Brigidini OC.	DET. ANTHONY BRIGIDINI: We always knew Kobie was a killer, and an instigator. Who has absolutely no feeling or worry about the well being of others. He's out for himself, and the members of his crew and that is it.
CUT to shot of crew members gathered together sitting on a couch in a basement apartment, smoking, drinking. Kobie holding and loading a machine gun. CU shot of a member loading a pistol	*****soundwave note: MAKE SURE "KOBIE MOWATT" FALLS ON MOWATT ACTOR [AT 01:01:14] IN FOLLOWING VO *************************
CU of Kobie holding a machine gun in a mirror, pan back to other crew members on the couch still preparing for the drive-by	WALSH VO #3 (01:01:12) 13 sec IN SEPTEMBER OF 1990, KOBIE MOWATT AND SEVERAL OTHER CREW MEMBERS WERE PLANNING A DRIVE-BY HIT ON A RIVAL CREW. BUT ACTING ON A TIP, D-C POLICE STRUCK FIRST.
MCU of Kobie standing up looking at police with machine gun in hand/CU of detective with gun in hand pointing at Kobie/Kobie puts down gun, they both stare at each other in a hateful way	DETECTIVE: Police, everybody hands up! Drop it Kobie, drop it now!

Adapted from the British program, "Dancing With The Stars" has become a premiere reality show on American television. Like other reality programs it does not have a traditional script. But also like the others, it has a rundown. Attesting to the thorough preparation that goes into this highly successful show, the rundown is fully detailed, running over 20 pages for the one-hour program. It indicates the necessary extensive and intensive collaboration among writer, director, and producer. Below are several of the opening and closing pages of the rundown.

DANCING WITH THE STARS
· RUNDOWN ·

LIVE: March 9, - 16:59:55
    ABC
LOC: CBSTV City - Stage 46

Show #801 (13 Couples)
8:00p - 10:02p EST

Item#	Description	Page #	SHOW Seg	SHOW Cum	Notes Notes
ACT 1					
		SHOW START	16:59:55		
1.	**PROFILE: BBC LOGO (SOT)**	(1)	0:00:05	17:00:00	
2.	**HOST WELCOME/INTRO COUPLES** (Tom Bergeron, Samantha Harris) MUSIC: KETTLE DRUM BEATS (APB) APB: ANNOUNCER VO DEKO: "LIVE" BUG LOC: DSR BALCONY	(2)	0:00:36	17:00:36	
3.	**COUPLES ENTRANCE** (11 Couples[22]) MUSIC: "THEME" (LIVE) APB: TOM BERGERON VO APB: SAMANTHA HARRIS VO DEKO: NAMES & PHONE NUMBER STRAP	(4)	0:01:34	17:02:10	
4.	**EXPLAIN FORMAT/** **INTRO COUPLE #1 TRAINING PACKAGE** (Tom Bergeron, Samantha Harris) LOC: HOSTS-UPSTAGE OF JUDGES COUPLES-DANCE FLOOR	(12)	0:01:10	17:03:20	
5.	**PROFILE: COUPLE #1 - LIL' KIM & DEREK** **TRAINING PACKAGE (SOT)**	(15)	0:01:26	17:04:46	
6.	**INTRO COUPLE #1 - LIL' KIM & DEREK** (Lil' Kim, Derek Hough) MUSIC: TENSION BED (APB) APB: ANNOUNCER VO	(16)	0:00:07	17:04:53	
7.	**COUPLE #1 - LIL' KIM & DEREK DANCE** **(CHA CHA CHA)** (Lil' Kim, Derek Hough) LOC: DANCE FLOOR MUSIC: "Nasty" (LIVE) (1:09) DEKO: PHONE NUMBER BUG (1:00)	(17)	0:01:24	17:06:17	

DANCING WITH THE STARS - RUNDOWN

Item#	Description	Page #	SHOW Seg	SHOW Cum	Notes
8.	**COUPLE #1 - LIL' KIM & DEREK** **JUDGES' COMMENTS/CREDENTIALS** (Tom Bergeron, Lil' Kim, Derek Hough, Judges[3]) LOC: UPSTAGE OF JUDGES DEKO: LOWER 1/3 JUDGES' NAMES & CREDENTIALS a. LEN COMMENTS b. BRUNO COMMENTS c. CARRIE ANN COMMENTS DEKO: FULL VOTING PROCEDURES - "GO TO ABC. COM"	(18)	0:01:38	17:07:55	
9.	**COUPLE #1 - LIL' KIM & DEREK** **REVEAL SCORES / REACTIONS** (Samantha, Lil' Kim, Derek, Judges[3]) LOC: SAMAN THA, LIL' KIM, DEREK-B/S, JUDGES - JUDGES' AREA MUSIC: TENSION BED (APB) EFX: 2-WAY DVE BOXES DEKO: JUDGES' RESULTS/SCORES APB: ANNOUNCER VO - JUDGES' NAMES MUSIC: KETTLE DRUM BEATS (APB) DEKO: PHONE NUMBER STRAP	(21)	0:00:48	17:08:43	
10.	**TOSS TO COMMERCIAL/BUMPER OUT** (Tom Bergeron, Shawn, Steve, Lawerence, Belinda & Jonathan) LOC: TOM-UPSTAGE OF JUDGES SHAWN, STEVE, LAWERENCE, BELINDA & JONATHAN-B/S MUSIC: RHYTHM BED/BUMP STING (LIVE)	(24)	0:00:25	17:09:08	
ACT 1 TOTAL TIME				**0:09:13**	
11.	**COMMERCIAL POSITION #1**	(25)	*0:02:41*	17:11:49	
ACT 2					
12.	**BUMPER IN** PROFILE: SHOW LOGO (MOS-OVER LIVE SHOT) MUSIC: "THEME" (LIVE) DEKO: "LIVE" BUG	(26)	0:00:05	17:11:54	
13.	**WELCOME BACK/INTRO COUPLE #2** **BELINDA & JONATHAN TRAINING PACKAGE** (Tom Bergeron, Belinda, Jonathan) LOG: TOM-UPSTAGE CENTER BELINDA, JONATHAN-B/S	(27)	0:00:20	17:12:14	
14.	**PROFILE: COUPLE #2 - BELINDA & JONATHAN** **TRAINING PACKAGE (SOT)**	(28)	0:01:19	17:13:33	

DANCING WITH THE STARS - RUNDOWN

Item#	Description	Page #	SHOW Seg	SHOW Cum	Notes Notes
15.	**INTRO COUPLE #2 - BELINDA & JONATHAN** (Belinda Carlisle, Jonathan Roberts) MUSIC: TENSION BED (APB) APB: ANNOUNCER VO	(29)	0:00:08	17:13:41	
16.	**COUPLE #2 - BELINDA & JONATHAN DANCE (WALTZ)** (Belinda Carlisle, Jonathan Roberts) LOC: DANCE FLOOR MUSIC: "What the World Needs Now" (LIVE) (1:08) DEKO: PHONE NUMBER BUG (1:00)	(30)	0:01:21	17:15:02	
17.	**COUPLE #2 - BELINDA & JONATHAN JUDGES' COMMENTS** (Tom Bergeron, Belinda Carlisle, Jonathan Roberts, Judges[3]) LOC: UPSTAGE OF JUDGES a. BRUNO COMMENTS b. CARRIE ANN COMMENTS c. LEN COMMENTS	(31)	0:01:45	17:16:47	
18.	**COUPLE #2 - BELINDA & JONATHAN REVEAL SCORES / REACTIONS** (Samantha, Belinda, Jonathan, Judges[3]) LOC: SAMANTHA, BELINDA, JONATHAN-B/S, JUDGES - JUDGES' AREA MUSIC: TENSION BED (APB) EFX: 2-WAY DVE BOXES DEKO: JUDGES' RESULTS / SCORES APB: ANNOUNCER VO - JUDGES' NAMES MUSIC: KETTLE DRUM BEATS (APB) DEKO: PHONE NUMBER STRAP	(33)	0:00:54	17:17:41	
19.	**TOSS TO COMMERCIAL / BUMPER OUT** (Tom Bergeron, Lawrence, Edyta) LOC: TOM-UPSTAGE OF JUDGES LAWRENCE, EDYTA-B/S MUSIC: RHYTHM BED / BUMP STING (LIVE)	(36)	0:00:29	17:18:10	
ACT 2 TOTAL TIME				**0:06:21**	
20.	**COMMERCIAL POSITION #2**	(37)	*0:03:52*	17:22:02	
ACT3					
21.	**BUMPER IN** PROFILE: SHOW LOGO (MOS-OVER LIVE SHOT) MUSIC: "EXTENDED THEME" (LIVE) DEKO: "LIVE" BUG	(38)	0:00:10	17:22:12	

DANCING WITH THE STARS - RUNDOWN

Item#	Description	Page #	SHOW Seg	SHOW Cum	Notes Notes
22.	**WELCOME BACK/ INTRO COUPLE #3 LAWRENCE & EDYTA TRAINING PACKAGE** (Tom Bergeron, Lawrence, Edyta) LOC: TOM-UPSTAGE CENTER LAWRENCE, EDYTA-B/S	(39)	0:00:15	17:22:27	
23.	**PROFILE: COUPLE #3 - LAWRENCE & EDYTA TRAINING PACKAGE (SOT)**	(40)	0:01:29	17:23:56	
24.	**INTRO COUPLE #3 - LAWRENCE & EDYTA** (Lawrence Taylor, Edyta Sliwinska) MUSIC: TENSION BED (APB) APB: ANNOUNCER VO	(41)	0:00:07	17:24:03	
25.	**COUPLE #3 - LAWRENCE & EDYTA DANCE (CHA CHA CHA)** (Lawrence Taylor, Edyta Sliwinska) LOC: DANCE FLOOR MUSIC: "25 Miles" (LIVE) (1:09) DEKO: PHONE NUMBER BUG (1:00)	(42)	0:01:23	17:25:26	
26.	**COUPLE #3 - LAWRENCE & EDYTA JUDGES' COMMENTS** (Tom Bergeron, Lawrence Taylor, Edyta Sliwinska, Judges[3]) LOC: UPSTAGE OF JUDGES a. CARRIE ANN COMMENTS b. LEN COMMENTS c. BRUNO COMMENTS	(43)	0:01:00	17:26:26	
27.	**TOSS TO COMMERCIAL/ BUMPER OUT** (Tom Bergeron, Lawrence Taylor, Edyta Sliwinska, Steve-O, Lacey) LOC: TOM, LAWRENCE, EDYTA-UPSTAGE OF JUDGES STEVE-O, LACEY-B/S MUSIC: RHYTHM BED / BUMP STING (LIVE)	(44)	0:00:22	17:26:48	
ACT 3 TOTAL TIME				0:04:46	
28.	**COMMERCIAL POSITION #3**	(45)	*0:02:31*	17:29:19	
ACT 4					
29.	**BUMPER IN** PROFILE: SHOW LOGO (MOS-OVER LIVE SHOT) MUSIC: "THEME" (LIVE) DEKO: "LIVE" BUG	(46)	0:00:08	17:29:27	
30.	**WELCOME BACK/ TOSS TO SCORES** (Tom Bergeron, Lawrence, Edyta) LOC: TOM-UPSTAGE OF JUDGES LAWRENCE, EDYTA-B/S EFX: 2-WAY DVE BOXES	(47)	0:00:13	17:29:40	

* * *

DANCING WITH THE STARS - RUNDOWN

Item#	Description	Page #	SHOW Seg	SHOW Cum	Notes Notes
105.	**COUPLE #12 - DENISE & MAKS** **REVEAL SCORES / REACTIONS** (Samantha, Denise, Maks, Judges[3]) LOC: SAMANTHA, DENISE, MAKS-B/S, JUDGES - JUDGES' AREA MUSIC: TENSION BED (APB) EFX: 2-WAY DVE BOXES DEKO: JUDGES' RESULTS / SCORES APB: ANNOUNCER VO - JUDGES' NAMES MUSIC: KETTLE DRUM BEATS (APB) DEKO: PHONE NUMBER STRAP	(149)	0:01:03	18:50:06	
106.	**TOSS TO COMMERCIAL / BUMPER OUT** (Tom Bergeron, TBD, Tony) LOC: TOM-UPSTAGE OF JUDGES TBD, TONY-B/S MUSIC: RHYTHM BED / BUMP STING (LIVE)	(152)	0:00:21	18:50:27	
ACT 10 TOTAL TIME				**0:06:50**	
107.	**COMMERCIAL POSITION #10**	(153)	*0:03:06*	18:53:33	
ACT 11					
108.	**BUMPER IN** PROFILE: SHOW LOGO (MOS-OVER LIVE SHOT) MUSIC: "THEME" (LIVE) DEKO: "LIVE" BUG	(154)	0:00:06	18:53:39	
109.	**WELCOME BACK/INTRO COUPLE #13** **TBD & TONY** (Tom Bergeron, TBD, Tony Dovoloni) LOC: TOM-DSR TBD & TONY-DANCE FLOOR (poss) PROFILE: CLIPS OF TBD & TONY (SOT) MUSIC: TENSION BED (APB)	(155)	0:00:49	18:54:28	
110.	**COUPLE #13 - TBD & TONY DANCE** **(WALTZ)** (TBD, Tony Dovoloni) LOC: DANCE FLOOR MUSIC: "Moon River" (LIVE) (1:12) DEKO: PHONE NUMBER BUG (1:00)	(156)	0:01:31	18:55:59	
111.	**COUPLE #13 - TBD & TONY JUDGES' COMMENTS** (Tom Bergeron, TBD, Tony Dovoloni, Judges[3]) LOC: UPSTAGE OF JUDGES a. LEN COMMENTS b. BRUNO COMMENTS c. CARRIE ANN COMMENTS	(157)	0:01:56	18:57:55	

DANCING WITH THE STARS - RUNDOWN

Item#	Description	Page #	SHOW Seg	SHOW Cum	Notes
					Notes
112.	**COUPLE #13 - TBD & TONY** **REVEAL SCORES / REACTIONS** (Samantha, TBD, Tony, Judges[3]) LOC: SAMANTHA, TBD, TONY-B/S, JUDGES - JUDGES' AREA MUSIC: TENSION BED (APB) EFX: 2-WAY DVE BOXES DEKO: JUDGES' RESULTS / SCORES APB: ANNOUNCER VO - JUDGES' NAMES MUSIC: KETTLE DRUM BEATS (APB) DEKO: PHONE NUMBER STRAP	(159)	0:01:13	18:59:08	
113.	**INTRO DANCE RECAPS** (Tom Bergeron) LOC: UPSTAGE CENTER	(162)	0:00:12	18:59:20	
114.	**PROFILE: DANCE REMINDERS X 13 (SOT)** DEKO: Couple Names & Number STRAPS *POSITION COUPLES, TOM & SAMANTHA* *IN SEMI-CIRCLE DURING PROFILE*	(163)	0:01:34	19:00:54	1:31 @ : 07 each 1:44 @ :08 each 1:57 @ :09 each 2:10 @ :10 each
115.	**LEADERBOARD/GOODNIGHTS & CREDITS** (Tom Bergeron, Samantha Harris, 13 Couples[26]) DEKO: CREDITS (OVER LIVE SHOT) MUSIC: CLOSING THEME (APB) LOC: SEMI-CIRCLE CS: COUPLES 1-6, TOM, SAMANTHA, COUPLES 7-13	(166)	0:00:59	19:01:53	
	ACT 11 TOTAL TIME			**0:08:20**	out at 19:01:53 PM
116.	**NETWORK BLACK**	(169)	*0:00:02*	19:01:55	

TOTAL RUNNING TIME: **2:02:00**
TOTAL TIME ALLOWED: **2:02:00**
OVER   **00:00**

ACT TIMINGS:
ACT #1   0:09:13
ACT #2   0:06:21
ACT #3   0:04:46
ACT #4   0:08:23
ACT #5   0:06:38
ACT #6   0:13:08
ACT #7   0:11:48
ACT #8   0:06:25
ACT #9   0:08:02
ACT #10   0:06:50
ACT #11   0:08:20
TOTAL PROGRAM TIME: **1:29:54**
TOTAL COMMERCIAL TIME: 0:32:06
TOTAL TIME ALLOWED: **2:02:00**
OVER   0:00:00

Courtesy BBC Worldwide Productions, LLC

Can reality shows have a point of view and not just present reality per se? Absolutely. Certainly, some are banal, exploitative, and repetitious in their format. However, some are artistic and/or educational in their entertainment. In one MTV reality show, *The Buried Life*, four buddies go cross-country in an RV, displaying a lot of adolescent behavior and humor. But on the way they stop to aid people who need help. In another reality show, *T.I.'s Road to Redemption*, a rapper with his own problems tries to keep kids from the kinds of anti-social situations in which he grew up. These and other reality shows convey positive social messages to contrast with the reality programs that are either embarrassing, mundane, oriented to cretins, or revel in indolent and decadent youthful excesses. As reality programs continue to proliferate, hopefully you'll have an opportunity to write for one that provides you and the audience with intellectual and emotional satisfaction.

APPLICATION AND REVIEW

1. Write a routine sheet for a how-to-do-it *radio* feature. The subject should be important to a professional or vocational group in your community.

2. Write a script for a behind-the-scenes human interest *television* feature. The purpose should be to persuade as well as to inform. Try a public health or social welfare subject, or a biography.

3. Write a documentary script for television *or* radio, using one or a combination of the basic documentary types. Choose a subject that is vital to the welfare of humanity and is controversial in your community as well as nationally.

4. Write a documentary script for the medium not used in exercise 3. Choose a subject that is relatively *unimportant* and not of vital interest to humanity. Can you, even so, incorporate a point of view that makes the documentary pertinent to your community?

5. Outline a 15-minute segment that might be appropriate for *60 Minutes* and a 7-minute segment for a TV magazine program.

6. Adapt one of the previous exercises for the Internet.

7. Write a treatment for an episode of your favorite reality show.

8. Write a treatment for a new reality show.

9. Write a one- or two-minute feature or documentary for YouTube or another online venue and arrange with someone in a production class to produce it.

10. Analyze one script you have written for any of the previous exercises. Does it give equal consideration to the status and viewpoints of both genders? If women or racial or ethnic minorities are part of the subject covered, are they presented objectively and honestly?

Interview and Talk Programs

The term "talk programs" encompasses the major program types that are not news, documentaries, drama, music, features, game shows, education and training programs, or commercials. That leaves interviews, discussions, and speeches. In the 1990s the "talk" show phenomenon swept radio and into television. Talk hosts and hostesses dominated non-music radio stations, and even many music stations added talk programs to boost ratings, especially in the evening and late night hours when television rules the airwaves. The tenor of the times and the predominantly conservative media reflected the political conservatism in talk program growth into the new century, with commentators such as Rush Limbaugh becoming broadcast icons; there were—and are—comparatively few liberal commentators. Some talk shows are editorial commentaries; some are interview or discussion programs. A few, like *The Colbert Report* and *The Daily Show,* use comedy and satire to make their points. A guest is either interviewed or engaged in a discussion of specified issues with the program personality. Some formats have call-in lines to permit the public-at-large to participate as discussants and, occasionally, as interviewees. Such political talk shows are principally on radio, but some are found on television and cable.

Purely entertainment talk shows that only sporadically go into the serious political or social sphere also proliferated. Jay Leno and David Letterman have been masters of the interview in this context. Oprah Winfrey's success in airing not only ideas and attitudes, but also emotional and physical—frequently sexual—feelings and experiences led to many similar shows on television and radio. These also are essentially interview shows.

None of these formats require fully prepared scripts. Interview and discussion shows are outlined, either in *rundown* or *routine sheet* form. The principal reason they cannot be fully scripted is that the interplay of ideas and, sometimes, feelings among the participants requires extemporaneity. Another reason is that the participants, excluding the interviewer or moderator, usually are not professionals and cannot memorize or read a prepared script without seeming strained or stilted. Another format, the formal speech, usually by a political candidate, is fully prepared, including the intro and outro.

The writer should complete as much of a script as necessary and possible in all talk formats. Why take a chance with an unprepared question or unanticipated answer or an irrelevant series of comments when the chances of success are better with prepared material? Some talk programs that have long-established formats and experienced questioners or moderators may need only a **rundown sheet**—a detailed list of all program sequences with the elapsed time, if known, for each item.

The more detailed **routine sheet** contains as much of the actual dialogue and action as can be prepared, including remarks that are designed to appear as ad-libs to the audience. The improvised nature of talk shows makes them more open to mistakes, slow action, dullness, and the other afflictions that mark unscripted, unrehearsed programs. Good writers (and producers, directors, and performers) want as much preparation as possible.

Because broadcasting operates on a split-second schedule, the final version of the rundown or routine sheet must be adhered to as meticulously as if it were a fully scripted program that had been rehearsed down to the exact second of playing time. Sometimes alternate endings of different lengths are included so that the director can choose the right one, especially in live shows, to make the program end on time.

THE INTERVIEW

Interviews are used in many programs, especially news, documentaries, features, corporate and educational programs, and, of course, entertainment interview shows. The basic approaches for the interview are essentially the same for all these formats.

Types

The three major interview types are the opinion interview, the information interview, and the personality interview. Any given interview can combine elements of all three.

The Opinion Interview

Any interview that concentrates on the beliefs of an individual can be an opinion interview. Because many of these interviews are with prominent people, usually experts in their fields, such interviews are often information and even personality interviews as well. Even in the completely ad-lib "street" interview, the interviewer should have an introduction, a question, and follow-up questions developed for possible answers. Prospective interviewees can be briefed before the program is recorded or goes on the air live.

The Information Interview

The information interview is usually the public service type. The information can be delivered by a relatively unknown figure or by a prominent person in the field. Because the main objective is the communication of information, sometimes a complete script will be prepared. The interviewee can provide direct factual material, deliver information oriented toward a cause or purpose, or combine information with personal belief. If a script is written, the speaker's personality should be considered. If the interviewee is not likely to be a performer—a good "reader"—then it is better to prepare a detailed outline and to rehearse the program as an extemporaneous presentation.

The Personality Interview

This is the human interest, feature story interview. The program format can be oriented toward one purpose—to probe, embarrass, or flatter—or it can be flexible, combining and interweaving these various facets. The most successful recent personality interview programs seem to be oriented toward a combination of probing for personal attitudes and revelation of personal beliefs and actions. To prepare pertinent questions for the personality interview, obtain full background information on the interviewee. Outline the questions and talk with the interviewee before the program to prepare the in-depth questions and the logical order of questioning.

Preparation

The television or radio interview may be prepared completely, with a finished script for the interviewer and interviewee. It may be oriented around an outline, where the general line of questioning and answering is prepared, but the exact words used are improvised. Or it may be completely unprepared, or ad-lib. A prime example of such a situation occurred when television journalist Katie Couric held a live interview with Alaska Governor Sarah Palin, who had just been nominated as vice-president on the Republican ticket in 2008. Palin's lack of knowledge and information on several basic political and governmental policies and practices proved to be such an embarrassment that her campaign avoided any unprepared live interviews for the rest of the race. Such is the power of the media—and of even a given interview or talk show—that some critics cite the Couric interview as one of the prime reasons for increasing public lack of confidence in Palin's ability to be an effective elected official, impinging on her party's chances to win the election.

Very rarely are interviews either completely scripted or completely ad-lib. The full script usually results in a stilted, monotonous presentation except where both the interviewer and interviewee are skilled performers who can make a written line sound impromptu, a situation that does not often occur. On the other hand, the totally unprepared interview is too risky, with the interviewee likely to be too talkative, embarrassing or embarrassed, or just plain dull, and the interviewer faced with the almost impossible task of organizing and preparing appropriate questions on the spot.

Most interview scripts are written in outline form. First, the producer, interviewer, and writer prepare a broad outline of the purpose and form of questioning. Following intensive and extensive research, they prepare appropriate questions. To be ready to ask meaningful questions in a logical order, the interviewer must have an idea of the possible answers to the major questions already developed. For this purpose, a preliminary conference, or **pre-interview** may be held. The interviewee is briefed, sometimes briefly, sometimes extensively, on the questions to be asked. The interviewee indicates the general line of answering. Then the writer develops follow-up and probe questions and arranges them in the most logical and dramatic order. The rundown or routine sheet lists the actual questions to be asked, the probable answers, and follow-up questions based on those answers.

Sometimes, of course, the interviewee is not available for a pre-interview, and the writer must guess at the probable answers. If the research on the interviewee has been thorough and accurate, a certain consistency can be correctly anticipated. Sometimes the interviewee who can't be pre-interviewed can be persuaded to come to the studio before the program is to be aired or recorded for a brief discussion. In such cases the writer works closely with the producer and interviewer to revise the material already prepared, right up to the last minute. When the interviewee cooperates by permitting both a pre-interview and a pre-show meeting, the writer's opportunity for developing an excellent script is greatly enhanced.

The key to the successful interview is preparation. The writer/researcher must dig deeply, and the interviewer should be equally familiar with the interviewee's background, attitudes, and feelings. We've all seen too many interviewers who are obviously poorly prepared. Michael McLaughlin, author of *Screw*, a controversial book about the prison system, appeared on many talk/interview shows on radio and television and noted that there is a big quality difference in the programs where the interviewer has taken the time and effort to actually read the book: "When the interviewers have done their homework, know the book, have prepared good questions, and can follow-up with an intelligent discussion based on the book, the shows are much livelier and more interesting."

The writer of this text, sometime is along with a frequent co-author, has had the same experience when discussing his books on talk shows or being interviewed as expert an on a given subject. Too often the interviewer or talk show host or the show's writer has either not read the book or skimmed it too quickly, and the prepared questions are relatively trivial or ancillary to the book's purpose or content. Without a pre-interview, the guests on the program may have prepared material more pertinent to the topic and may not be prepared to provide as good an interview for untargeted questions. As a writer or writer/interviewer, you should avoid this possibility. Some interviewers try to aggrandize their own egos by baiting or arguing with the expert guests. Sometimes it works and creates a lively confrontational program even if the content takes a back seat. However, if the guest is not fast and sometimes funny with repartee, it becomes one-sided and boring. Make certain you know enough about your guest before you finalize the show's approach.

Phyllis Haynes, writer, producer, and host of interview shows on national, regional, and local television, has advocated good "homework." Although interviewer approaches vary—Barbara Walters' conversational empathic approach, Oprah Winfrey's enthusiastic probing with questions the average viewer might ask—preparation is the key. "Reading about the guest, reading what the guest has written, preparing questions that reveal a deep level of understanding and concentration," Haynes states, are key ingredients of good interviews.

Arguably the most successful interviewer in television history, Barbara Walters has conducted interviews combining all three interview types: opinion, information, and personality. Recently retired she always came across as confident and comfortable in questioning interviewees in all of these areas and talking in depth with them, often eliciting information and feelings not previously revealed. Some of her interviews with political leaders result in headline-making statements affecting world affairs. How did she do it? Through intensive research and preparation.

Neophyte interviewers and writers who learn that Barbara Walters' shows had no formal prepared scripts sometimes assume that there was no preparation. Actually, the detailed research reports and extensive lists of questions Walters required of her staff frequently entailed more work than the writer might do for many other formats with full scripts. One of Walters' classic interviews was with stage and television star Carol Burnett. Walters worked from a 38-page research report that provided chronological facts about Burnett's life and quotes from various sources about her personal as well as professional background and beliefs. From the research report Walters developed a list of more than 100 probe questions, only a fraction of which could be used in the actual interview.

The categories of questions included:

- a year-by-year chronology of key events in Burnett's life;
- a section on her childhood, family, and education, including her ethnic heritage;
- her early career and efforts to break into the entertainment field;
- her subsequent successes in show business and the media;
- her personal life, including eating habits, non-smoking vegetarian, huge weight loss, relationships to father and mother, self-esteem as a child and adult, accepting care of and responsibility of younger sister, failed marriage, religious beliefs, belief in reincarnation, practice of meditation;
- immediate and long-term career plans.

Research

Research is the key to effective preparation. Find out everything possible about the interviewee (or for a non-interview script, about the subject matter). What has the interviewee written or produced? Are there any biographical materials, either in a book or in magazine articles, such as music, film, theater, art, dance, business, or scandal magazines. The same is true for political figures, business executives, and other professions as well. *Who's Whos* are a good source for initial background information. "Googling" the subject and checking the subject's postings on social media usually provides a lot of information, although the accuracy of some information found on the Internet is questionable.

Sources for information include the Internet, libraries, and the archives and morgues of stations and newspapers. Helpful documents may be on file in government offices if the interviewee (or subject matter) has been in any way connected with the government. A politician or political subject? Talk to political organizations; ask to see available files. Citizen-activist or public interest matters such as pollution, welfare, health care, housing, and similar areas? Try civic associations. Physician? Educator? Attorney? Architect? Psychologist? Professional associations cover virtually every field. An increasing number of celebrities, including political figures, have web pages. Are they on YouTube? Twitter? LinkedIn?

Don't hesitate to contact experts in the field of the interviewee or subject matter. If you dig hard enough you'll find more than one expert familiar with the interviewee or with even the narrowest topic. Become so thoroughly familiar with the person or subject that the questions you prepare are intelligent and meaningful. Don't waste your time and theirs with innocuous questions or ones to which answers are available elsewhere. Make the most of the time you have with the interviewee.

Get the information you need for the interview, the feature, or the news story firsthand. Often you can find secondhand or thirdhand sources that are completely trustworthy. Conversely, the information may already have been distorted when it reached them. Talk first to people who personally know or knew the interviewee, who have worked with the subject or actually participated in the event. Talk with eyewitnesses, with the people directly and actively involved. Only after that should you talk with people who know *about* the person or topic.

Be sure your research is accurate by choosing your sources carefully and correctly and by evaluating what your sources tell you. Be careful of individual points of view. You want the facts first; interpretation comes later. Don't confuse the two. Repeat questions if you are not sure you heard the entire answer or heard it all clearly. Unless you have a photographic memory, don't trust that you will remember everything accurately. Record the information electronically or by the old reportorial method, on a notepad.

Don't forget audience research, which is as essential for the talk show, including the interview, as for any other type of program. How much might the audience already know about the topic and the person being interviewed? What are the audience's likely attitudes toward the topic and the interviewee? You can't prepare the final interview orientation or specific questions until you can anticipate the probable answers.

Format

In all interviews—prepared, extemporaneous, ad-lib—the writer prepares at least the opening and closing continuity, introductory material about the interviewee, and for each section of the program, lead-ins and lead-outs for commercial breaks. And, of course, there are the questions to be asked and, if possible, the probable answers.

The closing continuity should be of varying lengths in case the program runs short or long. Without a script that can be rehearsed for time, such flexibility is necessary.

Each interview program has its own organization, and the writer must write for that particular format. Some interview shows open with an introduction of the program, note the topic or approach, and then introduce the guest. Others open cold, with the interview already under way, to get and hold the audience's attention, and then bring in the standard introductory material.

The following format rundowns from the classic public affairs program *Face the Nation* are simple and clear approaches, illustrating both kinds noted earlier. First, the script for CBS Television features an announcer introducing the show and a follow-up billboard and then the interview, followed by standard closing material. Next, the CBS Radio script opens with the interview in progress, then cuts away for the standard introduction. Following the interview is the standard close.

CBS TELEVISION

Face the Nation

HERMAN TEASE QUESTION _____

SENATOR _____ ANSWERS _____

(ANNCR: V.O.)

FROM CBS NEWS WASHINGTON . . . A SPONTANEOUS AND UNREHEARSED NEWS INTERVIEW ON "FACE THE NATION" WITH SENATOR _____. SENATOR _____ WILL BE QUESTIONED BY CBS NEWS DIPLOMATIC CORRESPONDENT MARVIN KALB, DAVID S. BRODER, NATIONAL POLITICAL CORRESPONDENT FOR THE WASHINGTON POST, AND CBS NEWS CORRESPONDENT GEORGE HERMAN. "FACE THE NATION" IS PRODUCED BY CBS NEWS, WHICH IS SOLELY RESPONSIBLE FOR THE SELECTION OF TODAY'S GUEST AND PANEL.

BILLBOARD _____   10 sec. _____

COMMERCIAL _____   1:40 _____

(HERMAN CLOSING)

I'M SORRY GENTLEMEN, BUT OUR TIME IS UP. THANK YOU VERY MUCH FOR BEING HERE TO "FACE THE NATION."

COMMERCIAL _____   30 SEC. _____

continued

(ANNCR: V.O.)

TODAY ON "FACE THE NATION" SENATOR _____ WAS INTERVIEWED BY CBS NEWS DIPLOMATIC CORRESPONDENT MARVIN KALB, DAVID S. BRODER, NATIONAL POLITICAL CORRESPONDENT FOR THE WASHINGTON POST, AND CBS NEWS CORRESPONDENT GEORGE HERMAN.

BILLBOARD _____   6 SEC. _____

"FACE THE NATION" HAS BEEN SPONSORED BY IBM.

(ANNCR: V.O. CREDITS)

NEXT WEEK ANOTHER PROMINENT FIGURE IN THE NEWS WILL "FACE THE NATION." THIS BROADCAST WAS PRODUCED BY CBS NEWS. "FACE THE NATION" ORIGINATED FROM WASHINGTON, D.C.

Courtesy of CBS News

CBS RADIO

Face the Nation

12:30:00–12:58:55 P.M. _____
                          (Date)

OPENING: Radio takes audio (Herman asks tease question, guest(s) answer(s)). Before TV announcer comes in, Radio cutaway as follows:

SOUND: RADIO "PUBLIC AFFAIRS SOUNDER"

ANNOUNCER: From CBS News, Washington . . . "Face the Nation" . . . on the CBS Radio Network . . . a spontaneous and unrehearsed news interview with Senator _____. Senator _____ will be questioned by CBS News Diplomatic Correspondent Marvin Kalb, David S. Broder, National Political Correspondent for the Washington Post, and by CBS News Correspondent George Herman. We shall resume the interview in a moment. But first, here is George Herman.

(2:00 Herman Tape)

ANNOUNCER: And now, we continue with "Face the Nation."

INTERVIEW

CLOSING: Radio cuts away from TV audio on Herman's cue. (". . . Thank you very much for being here to "Face the Nation." A word about next week's guest in a moment.")

(PAUSE::02 PROMO _____)

continued

ANNOUNCER: Today on "Face the Nation," Senator _____ was interviewed by CBS Diplomatic Correspondent Marvin Kalb, David S. Broder, National Political Correspondent for the Washington Post, and CBS News Correspondent George Herman.

Next week, (another prominent figure in the news), (_____), will "Face the Nation."

Today's broadcast was recorded earlier today in Washington and was produced by Sylvia Westerman and Mary O. Yates. Robert Vitarelli is the director. "Face the Nation" is a production of CBS News.

SOUND: CLOSING "PUBLIC AFFAIRS SOUNDER"

Courtesy of CBS News

Some interviewers want to be certain that full and reasoned information and commentary are presented to the audience, and they prepare clear informational promos for use before the given program and well-researched and well-written extensive *intros*—that is, openings. One program using this approach is "The Connection," a public radio show originating at WBUR-FM, Boston, and heard on a number of stations. Following is the promo and the opening for one of the shows that dealt with a critical public issue.

From WBUR Boston and NPR

I'm Dick Gordon. This is The Connection.

"There are terrorists living among us . . ." so says a coalition of interest groups including loggers, miners, farmers and developers who regularly confront environmental activists. But are they? Are they terrorists? According to new legislation, the brazen confrontations of the suffragists and the principled disobedience of the civil rights movement could all be termed—terrorism. This week in California—the definition will be tested in court. The Star Wars 17, Greenpeace activists facing felony charges for interfering with missile tests, are going to trial—in a nation where the old rules of "what was acceptable" are out—amidst a new atmosphere of "what won't be tolerated." Environmental Protest, the Patriot Act and what, if anything, is still civil in disobedience—next on The Connection. First this news.

* * *

I'm Dick Gordon. This is The Connection.

America has always had a tradition of dissent: The Boston Tea Party is still celebrated, as are the underground railroad and 1950s lunch counter occupations. And protest always involves making noise—whether at Main Street marches or sidewalk sit-ins—ruffling feathers is par for the

continued

course—often essential—in demanding change. But the concept—and maybe even the cache—of civil disobedience is changing in the wake of September 11th. With the birth of the Patriot Act, free speech and political action could be facing higher stakes . . . look at the environmental movement. When eco-tactics go beyond bumper stickers for "saving the whales" and into burning ski resorts, the line between activism and what's called Ecoterrorism blurs. Tomorrow, Greenpeace activists are in court, facing up to six years in prison for protesting the US Missile Defense System. Greenpeace says it's concerned that it may not be possible to have a fair trial amidst America's New War . . . Connection listeners, in the wake of September 11th, how's the debate changing over civil disobedience, saving the forests, freeing the mink, and uprooting experimental crops? When is "Making a point" just making a mess? Call us at 1-800-423-8255, that's 1-800-423-TALK. With me today is Mara Verheyden-Hilliard, attorney and co-founder of Partnership for Civil Justice in Washington, DC; Teresa Platt, Executive Director for Fur Commission USA, and Andrea Durbin, National Campaign Director for Greenpeace. . . .

Courtesy of "The Connection," WBUR-FM, Boston

Program formats frequently develop out of the interviewer's personal approaches and techniques, especially when the interviewer is also the show's writer and producer. Duncan MacDonald was all three for the interview program she conducted on WQXR, New York. After a while she did not need a written opening, closing, and transitions. She concentrated on the content. One of her keys was to be certain that under each major question there were enough follow-up or probe questions so that she was never faced with the possibility of getting single-phrase answers and running out of topics and questions in a short time. The following is a rundown outline she used for one 30-minute interview program.

Today is the anniversary of the signing of the United Nations Charter in San Francisco. In observance of this anniversary our guest today is Dr. Rodolphe L. Coigney, Director of the World Health Organization liaison office with the UN in New York City.

Dr. Coigney was born and educated in Paris. He began his career in international health and became director of health for the International Refugee Organization. In his present post at the UN he represents WHO—the World Health Organization—at Economic and Social council meetings, the Committee of the UN General Assembly, and other bodies of the UN.

continued

1) Dr. Coigney, as one of the 10 specialized agencies of the UN, what is WHO's specific function?

   a) Is it included in the Charter of the UN?
   b) Active/passive purpose?
   c) Is WHO affected by various crises within the UN? Financial/political? Your own crises in health?
   d) Do you have specific long-term goals, or do you respond only to crises in health? Earthquakes/Floods/Epidemics?

2) How does the work of WHO tie in with other UN organizations?
   UNICEF/ILO/Food and Agriculture/UNESCO/International Civil Aviation/International Bank/ Reconstruction and Development/International Monetary Fund/Universal Postal/International Communications/World Meteorological.

3) Background of WHO.

   a) How started? Switzerland?
   b) Headquarters for all international organizations?

4) How much would the work of WHO differ in a country medically advanced, such as Sweden, as opposed to developing countries: Africa, Far East?

   a) Religious or social taboos?
   b) Witch doctors?
   c) Birth control?

5) Can you give an example of a decision made at Headquarters and then carried out in some remote area of the world?

6) What do you consider WHO's greatest success story in fighting a specific disease: malaria, yaws?

   a) Ramifications of disease? Economic/Disability for work?

7) Your secretary mentioned on the phone that you were going to Latin America. What specifically takes you there now?

8) How does a country get WHO assistance?

   a) Invited?
   b) Matching funds?

9) We are aware of the shortage of doctors and nurses in the United States. What is the situation worldwide?

   a) Do you think Public Health is an important career for young people? Now? For the future?

Courtesy of Duncan MacDonald

Structure

The beginning of the interview should clearly establish who the interviewee is. You'd be surprised how many neophyte writers forget that many in the audience may not recognize even the most famous or infamous person. Something as obvious as giving the name of the person is sometimes overlooked.

If the person has a specific profession, title, or accomplishment that warrants the interview, identify what it is immediately, to establish the interviewee's credibility (or reputation) for the interview.

Early on make clear the reason for the interview. What is the purpose? What should the audience be looking for throughout the interview and especially at the end? From a simple personality interview the audience may learn no more than what the interviewee does on his or her vacations. If the interviewee is a movie star or a rock idol, that may be sufficient for much of the audience. Figure out what the audience wants to know and prepare questions to get those answers.

Don't start with hard, controversial questions. That will only put the interviewee on the defensive and could lead to evasion or stonewalling. Begin the interview with background questions that establish the interviewee's expertise and position and set him or her at ease. You can begin with questions of a human interest nature so that the audience gets to know something about the guest's personality before the interview is too far along. Even with a well-known personality, this is desirable in order to give a sense of the real person as differentiated from the public image. In the strictly informational, news-type interview this approach could be distracting, although even in such programs the interviewer sometimes asks personality questions.

Avoid questions that don't go anywhere. They may have some entertainment value, but they tend to slow the entire interview and keep both the interviewer and the interviewee from getting into the interview's purpose.

Remember that it is an interview, not a monologue by either the interviewee or interviewer. How many times have you seen or heard an interview in which the interviewer seems to do most of the talking and sometimes doesn't even give the interviewee an opportunity to finish an answer? Write questions, not commentary, for the interviewer.

Seek depth in the interview. It is not enough to discuss only who, what, where, when, and how; you want to find out why—and that applies to a full-length interview as well as to a news story interview. For example, if you were interviewing a former president about a scandal in the Department of Commerce in his administration, you need to ask not only "*How* did Commerce keep the scandal quiet for so long?" but also "*Why* didn't the White House act on the scandal?"

Be careful of boring or distracting repetition in the questions and in the possible answers. For instance, know enough about the interviewee to avoid asking, "Did you find that making that movie was the most exhilarating artistic experience in your career?" if the answer is likely to be, "Oh, yes, making that movie was the most exhilarating artistic experience of my career." In other words, don't put words in the interviewee's mouth if there is a chance they will come right back at you. Ask questions that will prompt original answers, such as "How do you rate making that movie among your career experiences?" An interview that is too controlled comes across to the audience as stilted or manipulated.

As with any good show, build to a climax—to the most dramatic or confrontational questions.

In all interviews, regardless of the format or orientation, some basic structural standards, if not rules, apply:

1. Establish the purpose of the interview.
2. Establish the type of interview approach to be used.
3. Establish who the interviewee is.
4. Establish the interviewee's background in relation to the particular interview or news story.
5. Establish the setting: the subject's home, a studio, an event such as a new movie opening or an award ceremony, a political meeting, a divorce court.
6. Create a rising action; increase interest after you've got the audience's attention through effective questions and follow-up.
7. Summarize at the end.

Technique

Some key points to remember when working on the final script:

1. Research thoroughly; the writer's most important job for the interview program is research. Get all the background possible on the subject, whether inanimate or a person.
2. Know the probable answers so that you can prepare appropriate probe questions.
3. Double-check all the facts, particularly the interviewer's statements. Nothing is as embarrassing as the interviewee stating on the air that the interviewer has made an incorrect statement and the interviewer has no concrete data to back it up.
4. Write copy that fits the program's style. What is the principal approach: To attack guests? To goad guests? To praise guests? If the latter, is it the back-patting puff-piece kind? Is information, opinion, or personality to be stressed? A combination? Which is dominant? Does the particular interview have a religious orientation? A political orientation? A sexual orientation?
5. Be specific with the questions so that there is no doubt about the information or ideas you are seeking. If you have a generalized or open-ended question, be sure that the interviewee is likely to feel free to talk on the subject.

6. Repeat follow-up, probing questions in different forms if the interviewee tries to evade them. With sufficient research, you will know which questions the interviewee might try to stonewall, and you can prepare additional questions accordingly.

PREPARATION—SCRIPT

Earlier in this chapter the importance of preparation was noted. Preparation applies not only to research on the subject, but preparation of as much of a script as possible. Amy Tardif, FM Station Manager and News Director of WGCU Public Media in Florida, hosts a weekly talk-interview program entitled "Gulf Coast Live Arts Edition." Tardif believes that no matter how expert the program's conductor, there can be distractions, momentary lapses in concentration, disturbances outside the studio, and other factors that break the continuity of thought. Without an immediate script reference, the program can be subject to moments of dead air, irrelevance, or confusion. Here is a sample script for one of Tardif's programs. Note the careful timing and the multiple follow-up questions for each topic and sub-topic—many or most of which may not be used, depending on the length of the guest's responses, but which guarantee a continuous flow for the show. Note, too, how the insertion of audio segments from some of the films under discussion lends variety and enhances audience interest.

Gulf Coast Live Arts Edition Rundown

7/23

2:00 – Billboard

From Southwest Florida public radio this is Gulf Coast Live Arts Edition.

Sanibel author and professor Robert Hilliard is out with a new book in which he asks how often does Hollywood produce protest films? And when the movie industry does address controversial issues do they have an effect on the public? He says they do, to some extent and in his book, titled *Hollywood Speaks Out: Pictures that Dared to Protest Real World Issues* he describes in great detail some of the movies he feels have had a profound effect in motivating reform. We'll explore the gamut today.

Plus the Marco Island Historical Society wants you to vote on which of two paintings—one by Paul Arsenault, the other by Jonathan Green—should become the mural on the outside of the future Marco Island History Museum.

First this news.

continued

2:01 NPR Newscast

2:06:00 Funder/Button

This is Gulf Coast Live Arts Edition, I'm Amy Tardif.

Sanibel resident Robert Hilliard's newest book *Hollywood Speaks Out: Pictures that Dared to Protest Real World Issues* highlights directors, filmmakers and actors who have taken on the social issues of American society such as racism, war, poverty, anti-Semitism and homophobia. But the catch is—these films were rarely produced during the time period the controversy they are exploring occurred. And he asks why not? And can movies made about the depression or about war actually motivate change or create a better world for the people seeing the stories so many years later? He says things may be changing of late—with the time between events and their protest films shrinking.

Robert Hilliard joins us in studio today. He was Chief of the Public Broadcasting Branch of the Federal Communications Commission. He's the author of many books about the media as well as plays, including, in full disclosure, one I produced for him. Hilliard has also taught at a number of universities including a course called "Pictures of Protest" on the issues depicted in his newest book. Thanks so much for coming in today!

If you'd like to join our conversation, call at 1-877-428-8255, that's 1-877-GCU-TALK. You may send email to gulfcoastlive@wgcu.org.

> Why did you decide to teach the course "Pictures of Protest"?

> Where and how long did you teach that course?

> Was there ignorance or a motivation in your students about these films that kept the class going all those years?

> Why did you decide to write this book?

> One of your biggest themes is that protest films just don't happen when they should. Why not?

> But is that changing in the twenty first century?

> That's thanks mainly to independent film makers, not really thanks to Hollywood?

> What tends to happen to those in Hollywood who make pictures of protest?

We're talking with Sanibel resident Robert Hilliard about his newest book today. The book **is** *Hollywood Speaks Out: Pictures that Dared to Protest Real World Issues.* Our phone number is 877-GCU-Talk — that's 877-428-8255. The book categorizes protest films. It begins with the chapter on war. Hilliard writes, "The most effective anti-war movie ever made was produced during a period when no major or international war was going on—between World War I and World War II." It was *All Quiet on the Western Front* in 1930. Here's the trailer:

continued

Clip 1 All Quiet – runs: 1:56

Why was this film so successful?

Yet it still gets boycotted and banned?

You write that some people have compared "Platoon," about the Vietnam War, with the content and impact of "All Quiet on the Western Front." Was "Platoon" considered a protest film?

So were there films about the Iraq war more recently?

Charlie Chaplin first comes up in the chapter about anti-semitism. Hilliard writes Chaplin's film "The Great Dictator" was the only film that even came close to protesting the Nazi's policies toward the Jews.

Clip 2 Dictator – runs: 2:11

You applaud Chaplin often in your book, why?

You say nothing comes close to Chaplin's "The Great Dictator" protesting anti-semitism except perhaps Steven Spielberg's "Munich." What's that about?

We're speaking with author Robert Hilliard. His latest book is about protest films made in Hollywood—often long after the issue they're protesting. Do they make a difference so many years later? You can ask a question by calling us at 1-877-GCU-Talk or by sending email to gulfcoastlive@wgcu.org.

One notable exception to protest films being made at the time of the controversy comes in your chapter on prison and justice systems. You write the seminal prison protest film was produced in 1930—it was called "The Big House". He says another early film—"I Am a Fugitive from a Chain Gang"—had a powerful impact. Here's the orginal trailer from 1932.

Clip 3 Chain gang – runs: 1:24

What kind of impact did that film "I Am a Fugitive from a Chain Gang" have on society?

You ask in the book if perhaps a new film might be appropriate now on the mistreatment of prisoners?

But is it likely?

Why was 1967's "Cool Hand Luke" one of the most effective protest films against the prison system?

How was "Dead Man Walking" effective in motivating new social attitudes toward capital punishment?

Switching now to labor and management issues—what were the most effective pro-labor protest films?

Why is "Salt of the Earth" preserved in the Library of Congress?

continued

Join our conversation about protest films by calling 1-877-GCU-Talk. That's 1-877-428-8255 or email us at gulfcoastlive@wgcu.org. Our guest is Sanibel author Robert Hilliard. The next chapter is about protest films about poverty. The icon for movies about the Great Depression is "The Grapes of Wrath."

Clip 4 grapes runs: :35

That was a clip from the 1940 film "The Grapes of Wrath." Kind of sounds like today huh?

Bob, is it interesting that the Associated Farmers of California called for a boycott of all Twentieth Century-Fox films and the producers of "The Grapes of Wrath"?

What was the Breen Office?

A couple of Charlie Chaplin films come up again in your chapter on poverty. Tell us about them.

Why did it take so long for Hollywood to produce a significant anti-racist protest film?

What's the significance of Spike Lee coming on the scene as an Independent director?

What was the blaxpoitation era?

On to politics—here's a clip from the movie Robert Hilliard calls the seminal Hollywood movie protesting politics as usual—1939's "Mr. Smith Goes to Washington"

Clip 5 smith runs: 1:36

Why do you say "Mr. Smith Goes to Washington" is so important?

Have political protest films had any effect on the current political scene at the time they were made?

Why do you think "Wag the Dog" from 1997 and "Bulworth" from 1998 are still having an impact on young people?

Our guest today is author and professor Robert Hilliard of Sanibel. His latest book is called *Hollywood Speaks Out—pictures that dared to protest real world issues*. Can you think of a protest movie we haven't mentioned? The number is 1-877-428-8255, that's 1-877-GCU-TALK. You may email us at gulfcoastlive@wgcu.org.

In 1993 the film "Philadelphia" protested homophobia but you say it was controversial for more reasons than the obvious. Why?

And 12 years later, in 2005 "Brokeback Mountain" was highly successful but still encountered much resistance.

Moving on to technology, what two things does the movie "The Matrix" protest?

continued

How long did it take before movies began to protest the beliefs that women were dependent on men?

At least one film about terrorism came out since you finished the book. Did "Body of Lies" have any elements of protest?

Have any movies come out since you finished this book that you think have had an effect on the public to motivate change?

You're writing another book on this subject? When do you expect it to come out?

Thanks so much for joining us today Robert Hilliard!

His book is *Hollywood Speaks Out: Pictures that Dared to Protest Real World Issues*. When we come back the Marco Island Historical Society asks for your vote to decide which of two paintings to turn into a mural on the outside of its future museum. You're listening to Gulf Coast Live Arts Edition on Southwest Florida Public Radio.

BREAK Music – "20th century for theme song" :20

Break @ 12:48

Welcome back to Gulf Coast Live Arts Edition. I'm Amy Tardif.

The Marco Island Historical Museum opens to the public next February. It will have what's said to be the largest mural in Southwest Florida gracing one of its exterior walls. The mural will depict the days of the native American Calusa people. But just what image should tell their story? The Marco Island Historical Society wants you to choose. It's narrowed the selection down to two paintings, is putting them on display and is seeking votes. Joining me now by phone to explain the process is President of The Marco Island Historical Society and member of The Museum Capital Campaign Darcie Guerin (Gareinn). Hello!

You can join us too by calling 1-877-428-8255, that's 1-877-GCU-TALK.

So who are the two paintings by?

You can see them on our web site—wgcu dot org, click on programs and today's show and then click on the thumbnail to see each one.

Darcie can you please describe Paul's painting, and now Jonathan's?

Were they narrowed down from many entries?

What will happen to the ones not selected for the mural?

Tell us about each of the artists—Paul Arsenaut and Jonathan Green.

Who will paint the mural—which you say will be 8 by 40 feet?

There's an old saying "a picture can tell a thousand words." Is that what you're seeking to do with the mural?

continued

We're talking about the Marco Island Historical Society's quest to choose a painting for its mural on the outside of its new museum.

> Where will the paintings be on display for people to choose their favorite?
>
> How do people vote?
>
> What stage is the Marco Island Historical Museum's construction in at this point?
>
> When it's finished what will people find there, beside the Calusa mural?

(Calusa close music)

> That's all the time we have today. Thanks so much Darcie Guerin!

The paintings will be on display at the M&I Bank on Marco Island from July 24 to August 14 and in the M&I Bank in Naples from August 17 to September 2. Ballots will be available at each location. They'll also be online at marco news dot com and at naples news do com. The winner will be announced September 7. For a listing of arts events around Southwest Florida, go to wgcu.org and click on community events and the arts calendar. This is WGCU, Fort Myers, 90-point-1 FM / WMKO Marco 91-point 7 FM. I'm Amy Tardif.

Courtesy of Amy Tardif, FM Station Manager and News Director, WGCU
Public Media, Ft. Myers, Florida

FORMAT TIPS

The Entertainment Interview

The entertainment interview has become a staple of the late-night show, exemplified in the *Tonight Show with Jay Leno,* succeeded in 2014 DY Jimmy Fallon, and the *David Letterman* show. Although entertainment and personality revelation, rather than information and opinion, are the key elements in these interviews, the latter frequently emerge. The content varies with the show's orientation and interviewer. The early morning counterpart shows tend more toward news and information interviews, but they have their share of entertainment interviews.

Formats and scripting for such shows are similar. The principal written preparation is the rundown sheet, listing all segments and their running times. Specific dialogue can be prepared by several writers: the personal writers of the show's guests, to be certain that the anecdotes, responses, and ad-libs are in the style and reflect the best image of the given performer; personal writers of the show's star; and writers working for the producer, to provide transitions and shore up any weak material of a guest.

Writers frequently work on extemporaneous and ad-lib dialogue during rehearsals, when they and the producer can judge how well any given segment is shaping up. Sometimes the producer, director, and host do much of the writing themselves, their closeness to the program giving them a special sense of what will and won't work. The rehearsal period offers the show's participants an opportunity to make notes for their own dialogue.

The News Interview

Although news and sports are covered in Chapter 5, the basic concepts of the interview discussed here also apply to those formats. The essential differences between the interview for the interview show and the news or sports program relate to time and condensation.

The broadcast news interview is brief, anywhere from a few seconds to rarely more than a minute. The newspaper or print news story can have several interviews, presenting varied and even contradictory viewpoints, but the broadcast news story does not have time for more than one or two interviews. Those used must be as representative and accurate as possible in conveying the story's essence.

The interviewer has to get the interviewee to make a statement that gets across the idea quickly. The writer's eliciting phrasing of the questions is the key to conveying this effectively. For example, suppose the interview is with a former member of the administration about the Department of Commerce scandal. You could phrase a general question, "What do you think about the Commerce scandal?" and hope for a concrete answer. But no politician from the guilty political party is likely to give one. A more succinct question, perhaps as a follow-up to the first one, is, "Who was responsible for the Commerce scandal?" Even that, however, allows an evasive answer. More specific is the following: "Do you think that the president knew about and condoned the corruption in Commerce?" But that still doesn't require the interviewee to give the specific information you want. You need more than a "yes" or "no" answer.

If the answer is "yes," be prepared with follow-up questions that ask "Why do you think he did nothing about it? Was the White House itself involved in the scandal?" If the answer is "no," be prepared to ask "These were his appointees. Did he not keep tabs on them?" And "He had frequent cabinet meetings with the Secretary of Commerce. Was he deliberately kept in the dark?" And "Why didn't the president comment on the scandal after it broke?" In other words, decide what interview information is essential to the point of the news story and be certain that questions are prepared to elicit that information.

Keep in mind that when interviewing politicians, one of their main purposes is to leave the viewer or listener with an easy-to-remember catch phrase or "sound bite." Try to get the interviewee to go beyond that, with a fuller explanation. Dig deeper!

Give the interviewee the opportunity to say what he or she thinks. Even if the interviewer is the focal point of the show and might even know more about a given subject than the guest, it is important to get the guest to talk as much in depth as possible and to deal directly with controversial issues, with the interviewer hopping in with the next prepared question only if the interviewee moves too far away from the topic or becomes repetitious or boring. For example, on one of his shows dealing with the U.S. bombing of civilians in Iraq and Afghanistan, Larry King had several prominent critics and government officials. The mood of the United States at that time generally was supportive of the bombing. Those who opposed it had their motives and even their loyalty questioned. Venerable video journalist, the late Walter Cronkite, however, was not to be put off and seriously and sharply criticized the media for allowing the military to censor them and for reporting incomplete and even inaccurate information from the war zone. Larry King allowed him to continue his criticism of the military and government for not providing a clear and substantial reason for the bombings and to also note a number of possible self-serving political scenarios. This kind of maverick interviewee commentary, allowed and encouraged, makes for a good interview.

Be accurate and honest. Don't take quotes out of context and don't edit them so that the interviewee's comment is distorted. The same holds true for narration prepared for the on-air reporter. Give full information. It would be false reporting to have the reporter say, "The president told this reporter on the presidential plane today that he is going to immediately end corruption in government," when what should have been written was, "The president told reporters at a press interview today aboard presidential plane *Air Force One* at Andrews Air Force Base—and I quote: Any further revelations of corruption in government will get the immediate attention of the Oval Office.'"

Although the so-called person-in-the-street interview can sometimes provide good feature material, accuracy and meaning in the news story necessitates interviews with people who are (1) experts, (2) observers, or (3) participants, either directly or indirectly, in the news story.

For example, after an apparently accidental plane crash, who would you seek out to interview for your news story? You have many choices of experts, including the plane's crew if available, an aeronautics engineer, the plane's manufacturer, a Federal Aviation Administration official, and an experienced air traffic controller. In addition, see if there were any bystander observers. And, in a time when the government continually warns of terrorist threats, whether real or not, you'd check with the Department of Homeland Security, the FBI, the CIA, and other appropriate agencies.

Observers would include people who saw the plane in trouble, or exploding, or actually crashing. Participants would include, of course, any survivors among the passengers or crew, as well as current air controllers and others involved in monitoring the plane's flight. Be certain that your interviewee does have an actual connection with the plane in the appropriate category and is willing to talk about it.

Especially with non-professionals, be careful of leading the interviewee to give the answers you want, rather than what the interviewee actually knows or thinks. This is important in both the reporter's commentary and the interview questions. As an illustration, if the anchor's script reads, "Joe Eyewitness described the plane crash as a fiery ball dropped from the sky, exploding as it hit the earth," and the interview tape follows with Joe Eyewitness saying, "I saw the plane crash. It was like a fiery ball dropped from the sky, exploding when it hit the earth," then the writer/producer has dropped the ball, too.

And don't forget to identify the interviewee. If the interviewee who saw the plane crash is not identified by name in the news interview itself, put the name, title, position, or reason for being interviewed on the screen—"Joe Eyewitness" or "plane crash eyewitness."

The good interview script, even for the short news-bite, requires extensive research and effective writing. Sometimes, however, especially for the short interview, the writer may provide no more than an intro and outro, with all the rest of the preparation done by the reporter. Of course, in such cases, the reporter must also be an experienced and competent writer.

Most often, news interviews are in the field, and, if not live, the reporter records as much as possible for editing to the time allotted on the newscast. The preparation is similar to that for the longer interview, except that the brief time allowed requires identification of only the most important questions and possible answers before the interview. The following script is an example.

Tuesday, October 27

:30 State housing director E.Z. Skimmer

Grand jury handed up indictment today charging Skimmer with misappropriation of $500,000 of housing funds for his personal use.

Q: Do you intend to resign? (No.)

Q: Are you saying the charges are untrue? Follow-up: ask specific denials to each count of the indictments; misappropriated from Jan. 10–Sept. 25; books show shortages on eight different occasions; deposits in personal bank accounts $400,000 during that period.

Q: If you didn't take the money, who did? Follow-up: Aren't you responsible for continuing audits of the books? Why didn't you know?

Q: How do you account for $400,000 in deposits in your personal bank accounts in eight months on a salary of $100,000 per year?

The Internet

The Internet, increasingly offering all the formats of television and radio, is not, as restricted in content as are broadcast radio and television. Promotions and commercial connections that might be limited in the other media are commonplace on the Internet. The following is the opening segment of an interview on the eBay radio show. Note the generally informal and casualness of the dialogue and the promotion of a good-cause fund-raising.

eBay Radio Show Segment Transcript

Show Date: 9/27

Segment 1 – You Got the Griff – on Sundays too!

Lee: Let Stephen King kill you, Robby's helmet, and reviews all feature in today's eBay Radio news. I'm Lee Mirabal. Fans are willing to spend thousands for the chance to put their name in a famous author's novel. One unnamed winning bidder has paid $25,100 to have his or her name in an upcoming Stephen King book. The listing said, "let Stephen King kill you in his upcoming novel."

Item condition is an important piece of information for buyers and eBay has found that listings with specified conditions are more likely to sell. So, soon they will extend the ability to list your item's condition to more categories across the site. Be looking for it.

Over 70 of America's most famous actors, musicians, athletes, and politicians teamed up to help eliminate illiteracy by donating their doodles to the cause. The celebs allowed their drawings and autographs to be used in designs for envelopes that will be auctioned off on eBay to mark World Literacy Month.

Matt Ackley, senior director of marketing at eBay, has announced an exciting new feature, eBay Reviews and Guides. eBay members have always shared information with each other through discussion forums, groups, and more. Now Reviews and Guides makes that sharing even easier.

Robby Gordon is auctioning the helmet he threw at Michael Waltrip during a NASCAR race. eBay had pulled the auction after someone placed a $10 million bid. The listing is back up after eBay verified some of the bids. That's eBay Radio news. I'm Lee Mirabal. Now back to eBay Radio where you got the Griff.

Griff: A big hello to everyone around the world who listens to eBay Radio. We really appreciate that you tune in to us every week. This segment of eBay Radio is brought to you by SellersVoice. com, making it easy to add your voice to your eBay listings. I was watching that listing about Stephen King.

Lee: Oh really?

Griff: Yeah. There was another author too.

Lee: There are several of them that are going to be doing it. Grisham is doing it as well.

Griff: Right, John Grisham.

Lee: And several other famous ones.

Griff: We'll do anything for immortality.

Lee: Oh yes (laughter). But isn't that funny. "Stephen King will kill you in his next novel."

continued

Griff: Now, you know, there's a whole story to be written about this, which is a fiction about somebody who bids on a listing where you can get your name into a Stephen King novel and then you die.

Lee: It writes itself.

Griff: It writes itself, exactly. What's up with charity and eBay giving and the Katrina and Rita hurricane victims?

Lee: Well, I think we were thinking that maybe people are still…you know, you idea, I keep thinking back and you shamed all of us.

Griff: I did and you know what?

Lee: Because, well let me tell you for those just tuning in that didn't hear you last week or the week before. You have decided to, for a year, give a certain percentage of certain items that you sell to the hurricane survivors.

Griff: That's correct.

Lee: And I've thought about that and thought about it and you're absolutely right. You know, I keep putting money in the supermarket box and all that kind of stuff and I sent a $25 thing in the night I was watching the telethon and all that, but you're right. We need to remember these people for a long time.

Griff: That's right. I think giving has to hurt a little bit.

Lee: Yep.

Griff: So, coining from my lapse Catholic background, it's not too difficult. But I'm going to have something up for the next year that will benefit the victims of both hurricanes. I say this right now, but I just checked my listing and it ended and I've got to get something back up ASAP.

Lee: Well, you know, we also would love to hear during our Open Phones segments from any of you who are giving through eBay to this cause.

Courtesy of Chris Murch, President, WS Radio

DISCUSSION PROGRAMS

Discussion programs are aimed toward an exchange of opinions and information and, to some degree, toward the arriving at solutions, actual or implied, on important questions or problems. They should not be confused with the interview, in which the purpose is to elicit, not to exchange information.

Approach

The discussion program writer has to walk a thin line between too much and not enough preparation. You cannot write a complete script, partially because the participants can't know specifically in advance what their precise attitudes or comments might be before they have heard a given issue or statement that might be brought up in the discussion. On the other hand, a complete lack of preparation would likely result in a program in which the participants would ramble; the moderator would have the impossible task of getting everybody someplace without knowing where they were going. To achieve spontaneity, it is better to plan only an outline, indicating the general form and organization of the discussion. This is, of course, in addition to whatever standard opening, closing, and transitions are used in the program. The outline might include opening and closing statements for the moderator, participant introductions, and general summaries the moderator can use in various places throughout the program.

The discussion outline should be distributed to all participants in advance so that they can plan their own contributions, such as necessary research, in accordance with the general format. The writer should indicate the issues to be discussed, the order in which the discussion will take place, and, where feasible, the time allotted for each point for each participant. If possible, the participants, in consultation with the writer (or producer or director), should prepare brief statements of their general views so that there can be a preprogram exchange of ideas and a coordination of all participants' contributions toward a smooth, well-integrated program. Just as too much preparation can result in a dull program, too little preparation can result in participants being unable to cope with the needs of a spontaneous program. In addition, lack of pre-planning with the participants can cause unnecessary duplication of material. A program in which everyone agrees on everything can become quite boring; pre-planning should ensure, for incorporation in the rundown or routine sheet, that all points of view on the given issue receive adequate representation—unless, of course, the program is deliberately oriented toward a particular, non-objective viewpoint. Some discussion programs deliberately encourage interruptions and spurious, even physical arguments among the participants, aimed not at informing or mentally stimulating, but at "infotaining."

A decision should be made during early planning whether to use a controversial topic, certainly a good way to achieve vitality and excitement in the program, and whether to promote or avoid disagreement among the participants. The topics should be presented as questions, thus provoking investigation and thought. In addition, the topics should be broadly oriented, preferably toward general policy, and should not be so narrow that they can be answered with a yes or no response or with obvious statements of fact.

In the extemporaneous discussion program the same principles apply as in the interview. Opening and closing remarks and introductions should be written out. If possible, general summaries should be prepared for the moderator. In some instances, depending, as in the interview program, on format and approach, a brief outline or routine sheet consisting of a summary of the program's action and a listing of the topics to be covered, or a rundown sheet, may be sufficient.

In television, visual elements should be incorporated. The setting should, if possible, relate to the topic. The visual element can be relatively simple, but should help to convey a feeling of excitement and challenge for the topic under consideration.

Types

The major types of discussion programs are the panel, the symposium, the group discussion, and the debate.

Panel

The panel discussion—not to be confused with the quiz-type or interview-type panel—is the most flexible. Several people in a roundtable situation exchange ideas on some topic of interest. There is no set pattern or time limit on individual contributions and sometimes not even a limitation on the matters to be discussed. The participants usually do not have prepared statements, but have done whatever background preparation each individual has deemed necessary. A moderator, who usually does not participate, attempts to guide the discussion and to see that it does not get out of hand or too far from the topic.

It is important that each person invited to participate on the panel has something special to contribute to both the content and the process. For example, one may be argumentative, another conciliatory; one may quote statistics, another philosophy; one may be humorous, another ironic. Determine how the program should affect the audience and keep its attention.

The approach is generally informal, with the participants offering personal comments and evaluations at will. On occasion the discussion may become heated between two or more participants. The moderator tries to see that the discussion is not dominated by just one or two persons. No solution to the problem being discussed is necessarily reached, although the moderator frequently summarizes to pull the discussion together and to clarify for the audience—and the participants—the point at which the panelists have arrived.

A routine sheet usually consists of the moderator's opening remarks, introduction of the panel members, statement of the problem, flexible outline of subtopics to be discussed under the main topic (the outline should be given to each panel member sometime before the program, preferably in time for them to prepare materials if they wish), and the closing. As you read the following beginning and end of a routine sheet prepared for a panel discussion program, note the careful and liberal insertion of subtopics. The complete script repeats the principal question and the subtopics several times in the one-hour show.

Apply to this script the following questions (which you should apply to any discussion script that you subsequently write): Do you feel that the phrasing of the subtopics provides the essentials for a good discussion? Is the topic development too limited or is there opportunity for the clear presentation of varied opinions, attitudes, and information? Does the program organization seem to move logically toward a climax? Does there seem to be a logical interrelationship among the various parts of the discussion? Are the participants properly introduced? Does the structure permit periodic summarizing? (See exercise 7 in the "Application and Review" section at the end of this chapter.)

WTAK ROUNDTABLE

Palestine

Thursday, 7–8 P.M.

MODERATOR: (OPEN COLD) Palestine—to be or not to be? This question has been reiterated thousands of times throughout the world. A Palestinian state has become a symbol of the political, religious and ideological conflict that has torn apart much of the Mideast.

This is your Moderator, Tom Guide, welcoming you to another "WTAK Roundtable."

All of us by now are fearfully aware of the critical importance of maintaining peace in the mid-east. The Israeli government's invasion of Lebanon and shattering of its infrastructure, its invasion of GAZA with numerous civilian casualties, and ruining of much of its food and water supplies, medical services, education, and transportation routes and its blockade of humanitarian aid have increased the commitment of countries partial to the Palestinian cause to destroy Israel and increased the dedication of more and more individuals to fight Israel through terrorist suicide-bomb attacks. Is there any solution? Would the establishment of a Palestinian state and the restoration of property and homes taken from Palestinians decades ago bring the peace sought by the ordinary citizens on both sides of the conflict? Is there no solution possible, with Arab states unwilling to turn back from the goal of pushing Israel into the sea? Will outside pressure, including United Nations intervention and peacemaking negotiations by the United States, lead to a solution? Are there any areas of compromise that will be satisfactory to all parties?

This evening, with the aid of our guests, we will attempt to seek some answers to these questions.

Dr. Robert Charlton is a professor of political science at Yalvard University and an authority on the mid-east. Dr. Charlton teaches modern political theory. He recently spent several months in the mid-east studying the situation there. Good evening, Dr. Charlton.

CHARLTON: Response

continued

MODERATOR:	Dr. Brno Zdislaw is an associate professor of religion at Missitucky State University. He has written extensively on the rapid expansion of Islam as the state religion in a number of countries and its attitude toward Judaism. He has written on the role of religion as a factor in the mid-east conflict. Good evening, Dr. Zdislaw.
ZDISLAW:	Response
MODERATOR:	Our third panelist is Dr. Beatrice Stone, professor of history and economics at Kings College. She specializes in United States foreign policy and international politics. She has served as cultural attache with the U.S. State Department in embassies in several mid-eastern countries. Good evening, Dr. Stone.
STONE:	Response
MODERATOR:	I'd like to remind our participants and our listeners that questions are encouraged from our listening audience. Anyone having a question for any or all of our panel members is invited to phone the WTAK studios at 555-3296. Your question will be asked directly of the panel, if pertinent to the specific discussion in progress, or taped and played back for our panel to answer at the first appropriate opportunity. That's 555-3296.

In view of the horrors perpetrated by all participants in the conflict, including what some are calling genocidal ethnic cleansing, do you think there is any chance of any peace accord and, if so, would it be likely to last longer than a few weeks or months? Dr. Stone, would you start the discussion on this question?

(BRING IN OTHER PANELISTS ON THIS QUESTION. DETERMINE TENTATIVE AGREEMENT ON SOME AREAS, AS BELOW.)

1. Sharing of territory and political power with degree of sovereignty within the political structure of each group? Including the Palestinians right of return?

2. Establishment of a separate Palestinian state, as often proposed? Role of Jerusalem as a capital?

3. Accommodation of all religions without any one seeking to impose its beliefs and practices on the others?

4. Renouncing of terrorism (suicide bombing) and pledge to withdraw from all Palestinian lands? Would such assurances be kept?

5. United Nations peacekeeping force at imposed borders and economic assistance as a stabilizing factor?

6. Continued U.S. mediation to negotiate continuing problems?

MODERATOR:	(REMINDER TO AUDIENCE ON PHONE CALLS)

* * *

continued

MODERATOR: (IF ABOVE TOPICS NOT CONCLUDED BY 8 MINUTES BEFORE THE END OF THE PROGRAM, SKIP TO FOLLOWING): Of all the possibilities discussed on the program, which, if any, do you think has the most chance of succeeding?

MODERATOR: (SUMMARY AT 8 MINUTE MARK)

1.   Sharing of territory/right of return.

2.   Palestinian state.

3.   Accommodation of all religions.

4.   Renouncing of terrorism, occupation.

5.   U.N. role.

6.   U.S. role.

MODERATOR: (AT 1 MINUTE MARK) Dr. Robert Charlton, Dr. Brno Zdislaw, and Dr. Beatrice Stone, we thank you for being our guests tonight on this WTAK Roundtable discussion on the possible solutions to the Palestine question.

GUESTS: (MASS RESPONSE OF GOOD NIGHT, ETC.)

MODERATOR: We thank you all for listening and invite you to join us next week at this same time when "WTAK Roundtable's" guests, _____ , and _____ will discuss _____ .

This has been a presentation of WTAK, the FM radio station of stimulating talk, New Concord.

Even when a panel discussion program is known for its extemporaneous approach, some key continuity must be prepared. The following script stresses a free-form discussion on headline issues and events with a moderator and several guest "experts," some in the studio and some by remote. Note that the opening includes an introduction, a statement of the topic, and an initial question.

THE WINSTON REPORT

Moderator: Erica Winston

Guests: Cynthia Brand, James Frederick, Hal Jayson, and Rachel Levy

ANNOUNCER: From Washington, D.C., Federated Motors brings you the Winston Report, an unrehearsed discussion presenting opinions on major issues of the day. Here is your moderator, Erica Winston.

continued

WINSTON: Welcome to the Winston Report. Joining us today to talk about the status of President Obama's stimulus plan are Cynthia Brand and James Frederick in the studio with me, in New York Hal Jayson, and in Cleveland Rachel Levy. Given the increasing unemployment figures over the past few months, is President Obama's stimulus plan working?

SOT: OBAMA: It takes time. The deep recession we inherited cannot be erased overnight. We are seeing signs that it is beginning to crack. Patience and determination will get us back on the right track.

WINSTON: The stimulus has some big companies like General Motors pulling out of bankruptcy. Yet, bankruptcies among small businesses throughout the country are increasing. Home foreclosures are growing while executives of bailed out companies like AIG are getting multi-million dollar bonuses. What's happening?

[DISCUSSION]

WINSTON: Thank you all, Cynthia, Jim, Hal and Rachel. Next week: The Media and Pop Icons—the death of Michael Jackson.

ANNOUNCER: Federated Motors is proud to present The Winston Report. We take you where you want to go when you want to go. Good night.

SPEECHES

Most speeches are prepared outside the station, and the staff writer usually has no concern with them except to write the opening and closing material for the station announcer, which can include introductory comments about the speaker, depending on how well known the latter is. It is improper to go beyond: "Ladies and gentlemen, the President of the United States." If the president is speaking at a special occasion or for a special public purpose, however, prespeech commentary would describe the occasion and purpose, with appropriate background material. Commentary and analysis can also follow a speech.

If the speaker is not well known, information about that person's position and qualifications as a spokesperson on the issue should be presented, as well as the reason for his or her appearance. A good rule to remember is that the better known the speaker, the less introduction needed.

In some instances, usually on the local level, speakers unfamiliar with radio and television time requirements may have to be advised how and where to trim their speeches so they are not cut off before they finish. Speakers unfamiliar with television and radio techniques frequently do not realize the need for split-second scheduling and their speeches may run too long or, sometimes, too short, leaving unfilled program time. In other instances it may be necessary to remind (or even help) the speaker to rewrite in order to adhere to legal, FCC, or station policy concerning statements made over the air, including slander (libel) and indecency.

If a speech is prepared by the station's writer, it must, of course, be done in collaboration with the speaker. First, determine the format. Will it be a straight speech? Will a panel or interviewer be included? Will the audience be able to ask questions? At all times the speech must fit the speaker's personality.

Occasionally, the televised speech can be developed into more than simple verbal presentation and can include film, tape, photos, and other visuals. Such speeches are, however, more like illustrated talks or lectures and, if so, would likely be prepared as features.

The following is a simple, basic format, containing intro, outro, and transitions, used for speeches during a political campaign.

ANNCR: To help our listeners in Smith County get more information on the candidates and their issues in the upcoming election, this station is presenting "Election," a series of interviews with the candidates running for county and local offices.

Today's first interview is with _____, candidate for the office of _____.

RECORDING:

ANNCR: You've just heard an interview with _____. Our second interview today is with _____, candidate for the office of _____.

RECORDING:

ANNCR: You've just heard an interview with _____. Tomorrow, for your further information before you vote on November 2, we will interview _____, candidate for _____, and _____, candidate for _____. The views expressed by the candidates are their own and do not necessarily reflect those of this station.

SPECIAL CONSIDERATIONS

Although many talk shows, documentaries, and features deal with people of color, minority ethnic groups, women, and other constituencies that traditionally have been denied equal opportunity in employment and equal dignity (in stereotyped program portrayals), many members of these groups still have a strong perception of insensitivity by the electronic media. The talk program offers a special opportunity to focus on a person, problem, or idea relating to special groups or subjects. The feature and documentary, the commercial, and the play offer excellent opportunities to deal with these special considerations directly and candidly.

Women's Programs

Changes in media programming for women coincided with the feminist movement's initial gains in the 1970s, including its overt efforts to abolish negative images of women in the media. The media not only reinforce and create attitudes toward women, but can also serve as a direct means for women to improve their status in a male-dominated society. Romy Medeiros de Fonseca, an early women's rights movement leader in Brazil, noted that television "is the first means of education from which Brazilian men have not been able to bar women. They stopped them from going to school, stopped them from studying, kept them at home and cut off all contact with the world. But once that television set is turned on there is nothing to stop women from soaking up every piece of information it sends out. They soak it up like a sponge, and they don't need to be able to read a word." The Internet has now opened more information and education channels to millions who previously had no access to such materials and has become a worldwide base for communication to, from, and about segments of populations previously shut out from communication's mainstream. Blogs and twitters alone have made significant differences.

For decades conventional wisdom in the media dictated that women's programs were those that primarily attracted women viewers and listeners because of the times of day they were presented and that carried content traditionally deemed of interest primarily or solely to women. Such programs consisted largely of non-controversial, stereotyped material such as club meeting announcements, advice on interior decorating, cooking hints, information on fashion and make-up, and interviews with local personalities who provided advice, products, or services that presumably met women's homemaker needs.

Most of these programs have evolved into serious considerations of drugs, youth violence, consumer rights, environmental pollution, media impact on children, especially social media, local education problems, and similar subjects. Topics vital to women that affect the entire population and provide women with information and tools for equal rights and opportunities have replaced the cooking- and cosmetic-oriented format.

The effects of nuclear power plants on community health, acid rain, fracking, toxic waste dumping, rape, abortion, birth control, war casualties, job training, financial dependence and independence, and legal discrimination against women and its remedies are some topics one finds today on the so-called woman's show.

Many of these programs serve as consciousness-raising tools for both women and men. Interview shows in particular can provide younger women with role models and younger men with new, positive views of women.

Barbara Walters—a pioneer in establishing the acceptance of a woman interviewer-commentator on talk programs, features, and documentaries—stated that information-education programs that appeal to both women and men should be developed on daytime television. "To say a show is just for women is to put down women," she emphasized.

Writing the woman's program is not appreciably different from writing other program types, as far as the basic form is concerned. But these programs should be sensitive to women's status, contributions, achievements, aspirations, and needs in the same way they are to men's. Sexism that is not deliberate is still sexism, and special sensitivity is required by the writer who has not experienced the discrimination or stereotyping faced by women.

Cable has expanded the programming oriented to women and to other special considerations and groups. Cable channels such as WE, Oxygen, Oprah, and Lifetime program materials that recognize women's needs and views. Talk shows oriented to women's roles and potentials in society are increasing on cable, where the large number of channels and freedom from dependence on individual program ratings (cable systems use cumulative ratings over a given time period) free cable from some of broadcasting's bottom line dictates. The following script is from such a program that has been syndicated on local cable origination channels.

WOMEN ALIVE

Hostess: Ina Young; Guests: Marsha Della-Giustina, freelance news **producer and professor of mass communication, Emerson College, and** Debby Sinay, vice-president of sales, WCVB-TV, Boston.

Feature	Time Segment	Total Time
Introduction by Ina Young	01:00	01:00
Two Commercials (1 minute each)	02:00	03:00
Interview with Marsha Della-Giustina	10:30	13:30
Two Commercials (1 minute each)	02:00	15:30
First Part of Interview with Debby Sinay	05:30	21:00
Two Commercials (1 minute each)	02:00	23:00
Second Part of Sinay Interview	05:00	28:00
Thanks and Outro by Ina Young	01:00	29:00
Credits	01:00	30:00

INTRODUCTION:

INA: This is WOMEN ALIVE and I am your hostess, Ina Young. Television is considered to be a very glamorous, often high-paying profession. One successful series can make instant stars of previous virtual unknowns.

continued

Yet, for every Barbara Walters and Connie Chung there are thousands of women working industriously behind the cameras in television offices and studios.

Today on WOMEN ALIVE we will be looking at "Television Broadcasting from the Woman's Viewpoint" and our two guests are two talented TV women. Marsha Della-Giustina is a freelance news producer and director of broadcast journalism and associate professor at Emerson College, Boston. Debby Sinay is vice president of Channel 5, WCVB-TV, in Needham, Massachusetts. So stay with us here on WOMEN ALIVE and we will be back with a behind-the-scenes look at "Television Broadcasting from the Woman's Viewpoint."

COMMERCIAL BREAK

INA: Today on WOMEN ALIVE we are going to take a look behind the glamour and the glitter of television. We are all familiar with the high-paid, highly visible news anchorperson. But what do we know of the men and women who ferret out the news and prepare it for television delivery? We know the stars of popular series, but are we aware of the television sales staff that keeps each station a productive and flourishing business? Our first guest is Marsha Della-Giustina, freelance news producer and professor at Emerson College. Welcome to WOMEN ALIVE, Marsha.

[The initial questions relate to the process of news gathering, processing, preparation, and reporting, regardless of gender. After the credentials and knowledge of the interviewee are established, again regardless of gender, questions relating to women are introduced, such as the following.]

INA: Marsha, at Channel 5, where you do freelance producing, how big is the news staff? How many men, how many women? What are the approximate ages? Which seem more appreciated by management?

* * *

When a station changes ownership, such as recently happened at Channel 5 when Metromedia purchased it, there is a great turnover, staff leaving, fired or replaced. Is there any pattern now at Channel 5, in relation to women and minorities?

* * *

What kinds of advantages and obstacles can a woman with a career behind the camera in TV broadcasting expect? What do you foresee in the immediate future for women—and men—in this profession?

[The second interview, with Debby Sinay, followed the same format.]

> INA: We are back again with WOMEN ALIVE and our second guest today is Debby Sinay, vice president of sales at Channel 5 in Needham, Massachusetts. I am delighted to have you on the show, Debby.
>
> * * *
>
> As vice-president at a major television station, could you give our viewers an idea of what that entails?
>
> * * *
>
> How big a staff do you have? How many males, how many females? Do females bring different qualities to the job than males? Is one sex better than the other? Which responds better to taking orders from you, a female boss?
>
> * * *
>
> Do you think that being female helped or hindered you in your climb up the corporate ladder?

Written and produced by Ina Young, Essex Video Enterprises, Inc.

Ethnic Programs

The same sensitivity applies to African-American, Latino, Asian-American, and Native American programming, among others. The growth of Black-owned and Black-oriented stations and Spanish-language networks has resulted in talk shows and other programs specifically oriented toward African-American and Latino and Latina audiences. Other racial and ethnic groups have had fewer media outlets oriented toward their concerns. The traditional outlets rarely program for these groups.

In Chapter 6 of this book, "Features, Documentaries, and Reality Programs," some examples of writing for these special audiences are presented. In all cases the questions of language and terminology are important. The special background and history as well as the immediate needs of a particular group help determine the writing approach.

A program designed for listeners or viewers from a special group would be written differently than the same program designed for a white majority audience. The vocabulary or dialogue that refers to sections of a given community or to events frequently has explicit meaning only to the targeted audience.

For example, one program produced on radio by the Chinese Affirmative Action Media Committee in San Francisco combined news, commentary, and satire. The writers were scholars of Chinese-American history and people in the arts, as well as reporters and media experts. The materials reflected perspectives and viewpoints of the Chinese-American not usually heard on the air.

Using the media as an integrating tool is an approach taken by many producers of programs for or about special groups. Dr. Palma Martinez-Knoll wrote and produced a Latino program in Detroit, *Mundo Hispano*, which consisted of a variety of formats including cultural presentations, interviews, different kinds of music, information for women, news, features, documentaries, commercials, and

PSAs—similar to the formats of many other ethnic programs. *Mundo Hispano* also included a weekly editorial. "Like the rest of the program," Martinez-Knoll noted, "the editorial shows that the American Hispanic community is an offshoot of the Spanish-speaking community all over the world. It is not a Chicano here, a Puerto Rican here, but an entire linguistic community who face a common problem. It is the entire community that must communicate with the majority society."

It is important to remember, as discussed in Chapter 6, that within the many subcultures that exist in the United States—and with transportation and communications advances having facilitated migration and global interrelationships in most other countries of the world, as well—certain words, concepts, and practices have become indigenous. Some analysts refer to this as cultural cueing. The writer who is not a member of the sub-culture he or she is writing about must be certain that the material being written accurately reflects the cultural cueing of the specific group. One way to do this is to consult in depth with representatives of that group if you do not happen to be a member of or well-versed in the history and mores of the group.

The Internet, to a large extent through social media but as well in alternative programming not dependent on commercial corporate advertising, has opened new vistas for women, racial, ethnic, lifestyle, and other groups that have been stereotyped and/or denied equal access to represent their views and concerns in the older media.

APPLICATION AND REVIEW

1. Prepare an outline, rundown, and routine sheet for an opinion interview, a personality interview, and an information interview. Each interview should be with a *different person* of local importance.

2. Do the same exercise, using the *same person* as the subject for all three interview types.

3. Prepare an outline, rundown, and routine sheet for a panel discussion program on a highly controversial subject, first for radio, then for television, then for the Internet. What are the differences?

4. You are the writer-interviewer for an interview show. Choose a book written by someone on your college or university faculty. Prepare a script outline, with intro, transitions, outro, appropriate questions, and follow-up questions for a 15-minute interview with the author about the book. If possible, produce the interview in conjunction with a media production course or for your institution's media outlets.

5. Prepare the format for a talk show on your college radio station or a local radio station that is oriented toward African-Americans, Latinos, Asian-Americans, or Native Americans.

6. Develop a format for a television, cable, or Internet women's talk show that provides to both men and women a service not now available.

7. Prepare the outline and continuity (containing at least the intro, transitions, and outro) for a panel discussion program on a topic that is currently in the headlines of your local, regional, or nationally distributed newspaper (e.g. the *New York Times*, *USA Today*). Use the press story as the content focus.

Music, Variety, and Comedy

Although talk and other non-music specialized formats have increased on radio, radio programming today still is principally music. Stations rely primarily on recorded music for content. Those affiliated with one or more of the many radio network services receive news and feature feeds to integrate into an otherwise all-music format.

In the 1930s Martin Block successfully developed the concept of a radio announcer playing records separated by comment and commercials, yet conveying the feeling that the performances were live in the studio. Since then, the disc jockey and deejay shows have become national institutions. Before television drew almost all the major live talent away from radio, live studio musical programs featured symphony orchestras, popular singers, jazz bands, opera stars, dance orchestras, and other musical soloists and groups. Virtually all such programs gradually disappeared from radio; many radio programs with music, particularly comedy and variety shows, made the transition to television.

Over the years a number of television series starring musical personalities, groups, and orchestras were highly successful. Generally, singers have fared better on television with variety formats than with strictly musical ones. A highly successful exception in recent years have been "reality" talent shows such as *American Idol*. Individual musical groups occasionally appear on television in specials or as separate acts on non-musical shows such as *Saturday Night Live*, Conan O'Brien, David Letterman, Jay Leno, and other late-night programs. Continuing music specials have proven popular with some audiences, especially on public broadcasting, including operas and pops concerts, but have not otherwise found broad popular appeal. The advent of MTV in the early 1980s moved television music shows into a new dimension. The growth of cable allowed MTV, the first 24-hour music service, to prosper and spawn other services that feature popular groups whose music and personalities blend into highly visual, often dramatic, energetic formats viewed by a wide audience. The Internet opened a whole new playing field for music, with cyberspace not only providing access to virtually every music source in the world, but enabling anyone to distribute their own music program. Keep in mind, however, the penalties for pirating music, that is, downloading for the purpose of sharing without the payment of specified royalties, if required.

Other than scripting the music video, the scriptwriter's job in music is principally to prepare continuity—intros, outros, and transitions—and the rundown or outline for the show. Very few radio disc jockey shows have prepared scripts anymore. Most often, the deejay works from a playlist and develops his or her own continuity—in script form, in notes, or in his or her head.

A professional never takes a chance on making a mistake if it can be avoided. The top pros have a program's every detail worked out in advance. The deejays who insist that everything they do is ad-lib, with no preparation, are, with few exceptions, either pretending or are amateurs who won't last very long.

Writing the variety show, with the comedy that it requires, is a special talent that cannot be taught—and this book doesn't attempt to do so. This book does present some basic principles for formulating the variety show format and some basic techniques for writing comedy.

MUSIC: RADIO

A music program should have organic continuity: a clear, specified format, a central program idea, a focal point around which all the material is organized and from which the show grows and develops. Although most disc jockeys are spontaneous with their continuity, the music content of most of their programs is carefully planned and organized.

Each program's format preparation reflects the format or image of the station as a whole. Specialization is the cardinal principle of most stations' programming. Some stations combine several programming types—two or more types of music plus news, talks, and features—and are known as **full-service stations**. Originally, FM was equated with "good" music, especially classical music, and had a smaller audience than did AM. In a way, over the years AM programming, especially music, migrated to the better-fidelity FM band. Virtually every format and music type is found on FM, but popular music is the prevailing category. Definitions of types of music are constantly changing and music formats change accordingly. Contemporary music means that of living composers to some programmers, but is limited to current popular hit songs by others.

Irrespective of how *contemporary* or *pop music* is precisely defined, music both reflects culture and builds it. Contemporary music is the dialogue of youth, providing a sense of psychological freedom for the listener and a sense of artistic freedom for the performer. Pop music is a sociological phenomenon, partly because it reflects the flexibility, growth, and change of society, particularly young society. The Beatles changed not only the face of popular music but also the attitudes and behavior of youth. The Beatles motivated an escape from the traditional formulas, and their music was not music alone of bodily rhythm, but music of ideas, communicating unspoken and spoken meanings that were vital and forceful to the young people who eagerly pursued them. The basic concept was not new, but the music was. Combined with the inexpensive availability of the transistor radio receiver, it made radio the link between creative artistry and creative reception as never before. At the beginning of the 21st century new music fads such as "rap," "hip-hop," "fusion," and "alternative" were the popular formats, with music available anywhere and in any format through iPods and other technological devices that permit a listener to virtually program his or her own personal radio station. Recording companies and radio stations believe that recorded music on radio is a democratizing tool, serving the desires of the public. Occasionally the question can arise, of course, whether wants are the same as needs and whether the *democratic denominator* is merely a euphemism for *lowest common denominator (lcd)*. In any event, recording companies and radio stations have found that the terms "democratic" or "lcd" are broad in scope and that a station cannot be all things to all listeners. Thus, the trend toward specialization and development of numerous major formats, with individual stations in individual communities tending to exclusivity within any given type.

Format Types

After World War II radio needed a new approach. Postwar growth in the number of stations was almost completely local, and local revenues began to exceed those of the networks. Music programs on local stations had affinity blocks—15-minute or half-hour segments devoted to a particular band or vocalist. Format was what was decided on each day by the program director, disc jockey, or music librarian; the latter frequently prepared the actual continuity. In many local stations the disc jockey would sign on in the morning with piles of records already waiting, prepared for each show for that day by the music librarian the night before. The disc jockey might not even know what the music for each show was before it was played.

Then came top-40, an attempt to reflect and appeal to the listeners' tastes by choosing records based on popularity as judged by sales charts, juke box surveys, and record store reports. Top-40, at its beginning, was eclectic, with several stations playing the same 40 most popular selections and the disc jockey's personality providing the principal difference between station images. Soon, however, many stations began to seek specialized audiences and concentrated on certain types of top-40 music, such as country and western, rock and roll, and other forms. By the late 1960s many top-40 stations had become almost mechanical, with virtually no disc jockey patter, a playlist of only the most popular records, and quick segues from record to record. From time to time top-40 stations rejuvenated themselves by bringing back emphasis on the disc jockey, providing "warmth" between records and more flexibility in format. When personality becomes important, deejays spend more time on continuity.

In the 1990s adult contemporary stations took over where **MOR** (middle-of-the-road) stations left off in the 1970s. The approach is the same—"adult" music without extremes in volume, timing, rhythm, or technique. The sound and the performers have changed as the tastes in music change from generation to generation. Adult contemporary stations are personality oriented, and announcer-deejays frequently become local and even regional celebrities. As consolidation has increased, however, with conglomerates feeding the same program to a number of distant stations, localism, once on the rise, has now virtually met its demise.

Rock was easy to categorize when it was new. Hard rock, underground rock, acid rock, and other rock offshoots required flexibility in rock station formats. The sociopolitical nature of some 1960s rock lyrics required a soft sound, compared with emphasis on tempo and volume alone. Jazz and folk rock have led many artists into combinations of country and rock. Specialized subtypes of rock emerged, and by the 1990s new evolutions of what the Beatles started dominated the airwaves. As young people in the 1990s began to rebel against the inequities and insensitivities of the 1980s, contemporary music again reflected political overtones, but the sound was louder, harder, and called rap. In the next decade rap gave rise to hip-hop, alternative, and acoustic.

"Easy listening" (formerly called "beautiful music" on many stations and featuring traditional string music of Mantovani, André Kostelanetz, and others) is still a popular format, but today is a mixture of instrumental, specially performed studio versions of popular vocal songs, light jazz, and soft rock vocals. Easy listening music is chosen carefully to fit the moods and tempos of different times of the day.

Country and western music emerged as a major radio format with spectacular growth in the 1970s, capturing surprising success in urban as well as smaller markets. In the 1980s and to an extent 30 years later, revival of jazz and the Big Band sound brought a return of these formats. Most radio stations have narrow-based formats so that they can appeal to a well-defined and loyal audience, such as "nostalgia," "oldies," "classic rock," and "album rock." As you read this, tastes undoubtedly have changed again, by the year or by the month, and some entirely new major format may currently be popular. Even within each format there are many variations and adaptations to the individual station's market and listening audience.

Today, one can listen to virtually any type or subtype of music one wishes—but not necessarily on broadcast radio. Cable, satellite, and the Internet offer literally hundreds of music stations or channels. Competition among music radio stations and channels is so intense that one of the important writing assignments is to create effective promotional continuity. Here is an example of a promo that expresses both the station's image and its availability of music.

106.7 WIZN EXPANSION IMAGING
GRASSO
7/25

LIKE STEVIE RAY VAUGHAN . . . WE'VE GOT DOUBLE TROUBLE!
(Clip) THE WIZARD HAS DOUBLED THE PLAYLIST. THAT MEANS MORE ROCK
AND LESS REPEATS SO YOU CAN KEEP ROCKIN' WITH THE WIZARD ALL DAY
LONG. 106 POINT 7 WIZN—THE WIZARD ROCKS (DOUBLED)

continued

WE'VE GOT DOUBLEVISION. (Clip) THE WIZARD HAS DOUBLED THE PLAYLIST. THAT MEANS LESS REPEATS DURING THE WORK DAY, BIGGER AND BETTER BLOCK PARTY WEEKENDS . . . AND TWICE AS MUCH CLASSIC ROCK THAN ANY OTHER STATION IN BURLINGTON AND PLATTSBURGH. BIGGER IS BETTER, FROM 106 POINT 7 WIZN . . . THE WIZARD ROCKS.

LIKE A FAT GUY AT A BUFFET, WE'VE JUST DOUBLED OUR SIZE! 106 POINT 7, THE WIZARD ROCKS.

WE'VE JUST DOUBLE THE PLAYLIST TO DOUBLE YOUR PLEASURE AND DOUBLE YOUR FUN. THIS IS 106 POINT 7 WIZN, ROCKIN' WITH TWICE AS MUCH CLASSIC ROCK THAN ANY OTHER STATION IN BURLINGTON AND PLATTSBURGH.

IF YOU LOVE CLASSIC ROCK, THEN YOU'LL LOVE THE WIZARD TWICE AS MUCH . . . WE'VE DOUBLED THE PLAYLIST. WIZN IS THE STATION WITH THE BIGGEST CLASSIC ROCK LIBRARY IN BURLINGTON AND PLATTSBURGH, 106 POINT 7 WIZN. THE WIZARD ROCKS.

WE'VE DOUBLED THE PLAYLIST, SO SIT BACK AND ENJOY TWICE AS MUCH CLASSIC ROCK AS EVER BEFORE, FROM 106 POINT 7 WIZN, THE WIZARD ROCKS.

EVERY ONE ELSE IS TRYING TO LOSE WEIGHT SO WE'RE BUCKING THE TREND AND GETTING FATTER . . . WAY FATTER. NOW WITH TWICE THE WAISTLINE AND TWICE THE PLAYLIST, THIS IS 106 POINT 7 WIZ, THE WIZARD ROCKS.

WE'VE DOSED UP ON ROCK AND ROLL VIAGRA! WE'VE DOUBLED OUR PLAYLIST AND NOW IT'S TIME TO GET IT ON! THIS IS 106 POINT 7 WIZN, THE WIZARD ROCKS.

NOW PLAYING TWICE AS MANY SONGS AS BEFORE, THIS IS 106 POINT 7 WIZN, THE WIZARD ROCKS.

Courtesy of Mike Grasso

Theme

Some music programs, in addition to being made cohesive through a type of music, are developed around a central theme: a personality, an event, a locality— anything that can give it unity. The writer—the person who prepares the script or rundown sheet continuity—can find ideas for central themes in many places: special days, national holidays, the anniversary of a composer's birth, a new film by a popular singing star, a national or international event that suggests a certain theme such as love, war, the jungle, adventure, corruption, drugs, and so forth. The musical selections themselves should have a clear relationship to each other, and the non-musical transitions should indicate this relationship.

The following script illustrates continuity for a classical recorded music program built around a theme.

ANNCR:	Today's program, celebrating next Friday's Halloween, features music of the supernatural. One of the best-known examples is from Leo Delibes "Coppelia," the ballet in which an engaged young man, Frantz, falls in love with Coppelia, a mechanical doll that today we might refer to as a humanoid. We will hear several selections from "Coppelia," which was first performed in 1870, in Paris.
MUSIC:	"Coppelia"
ANNCR:	Igor Stravinsky wrote the first act of an unfinished opera, "The Nightingale," which he later used to create a symphonic poem, "Song of the Nightingale." The Emperor of China rejects a live nightingale for a mechanical one. When the Emperor is on his deathbed, the live nightingale returns and sings to him, raising his spirits and his will to live.
MUSIC:	"The Song of the Nightingale"
ANNCR:	The opera "Lorelei" by Catalani is about the mythological female temptresses that live on a Rock in the Rhine River and lure unsuspecting sailors to their doom. Listen to "Dance of the "Water Nymphs" from "Lorelei."
MUSIC:	"Danced of the Water Nymphs."

Organization and Technique

Variety is important in any musical program, which should reflect the elements of any good entertainment program. Open with something that gets the audience's attention, relax a bit, then build to a climax. Offer the listener a change of pace throughout; after each high point give the audience a rest and then move on to a higher point.

The deejay-producer-writer must analyze the potential audience—just as do the producers and writers of commercials. Though the audience is given the music that interests it—the station format and image are created for a particular audience—the program should not play down to the audience or pander to a low level of taste. The deejay-producer-writer, to a great degree, molds and determines the tastes in popular music. No matter what type of music is used, present the best of that type. How do you determine what your audience thinks is best? Check which songs and artists are most popular with that audience. One way is by looking at the charts.

Never forget that the audience tunes in to a program because it likes that particular musical format. Reasons for listening may differ: for relaxing, thinking, learning, dancing, background while working, reinforcement while playing, or many other purposes. This suggests adhering to a single music type. Although there are exceptions, mixing Beethoven with country or rap with string quartets is obviously not an effective way to reach and hold an audience. In addition, the program organization and continuity should fit the performers' personalities, whether a band, a vocalist, or a disc jockey.

Continuity sometimes seems to be limited to orchestras that "render," singers who give "vocal renditions of," pianists who have "impromptu meanderings" and are playing "on the eighty-eight," and songs that are "hot," "cool," "mellow," "explosive," "ever-popular," or "scintillating." The trite joke or play on words for transitions and lead-ins has become an overused device. Phrases such as "For our next number" and "next on tonight's playlist" have long ceased to serve a worthwhile purpose. Perhaps that doesn't leave much choice? If you can't think of something new and fresh and not trite, keep it simple.

The timing of the show has to be exact, with the combination of musical selections, continuity, and commercials coming out to the program length. You do this by outlining all these elements on a rundown sheet. Each record or tape cut has a specific time length indicated. Each commercial is written for a specified time. Don't forget to leave time in between for transitions and lead-ins. Rundown sheets such as the following are frequently used.

THE WILL DOUGLAS SHOW
August 28, 10:00–10:30 A.M.

1.	I Gotta Feeling	The Black Eyed Peas
	LIVE: COMMERCIAL (60)	
2.	Paparazzi	Lady Gaga
	LIVE: COMMERCIAL (30)	
3.	Party in the U.S.A.	Miley Cyrus
	LIVE: PROMO, NEWS (15)	
4.	Run This Town	Jay-Z and Kanye West
	CART: COMMERCIAL (60)	
5.	You Belong with Me	Taylor Swift
	OFFTIME: 29:55	
6.	Use Somebody	Kings of Leon

A rundown or format sheet can be prepared for an entire evening's schedule, containing the timing for each musical piece and the listing of non-musical program segments, as in the following example for a classic pop-rock station.

9:00	Fantasy/Mariah Carey	4:00
	Gangsta's Paradise/Coolio Featuring LV	3:50
	Runaway/Janet Jackson	4:17
	news	2:00
	Kiss From A Rose/Seal	3:07
	You Are Not Alone/Michael Jackson	3:32
	Only Wanna Be With You/Hootie & Blowfish	3:14

continued

9:30	Waterfalls/TLC	4:30
	I'll Be There for You/The Rembrandts	3:45
	As I Lay Me Down/Sophie B. Hawkins	4:39
	Boombastic/Shaggy	4:10
	news	2:00
	Run-Around/Blues Traveler	3:08
	He's Mine/Monkenstef	3:10
10:00	Til You Do Me Right/After 7	3:53
	Tell Me/Groove Theory	3:35
	Roll To Me/Del Amitri	5:04
	news	2:00
	Brokenhearted/Brandy	4:30
	Here Comes Trouble/Small Town No Airport	4:10
	Colors of the Wind/Vanessa Williams	3:02

The Pop Music Program

Although few pop music deejay shows have written continuity, it doesn't mean that no preparation is done. Every show has to have some kind of rundown or outline to make certain that commercials and other announcements are included at appropriate places within the program's specified running time. At the very least, a pop music program will have a playlist from which to work, usually a tabulation of the most popular songs of the past week from which the deejay, traffic manager, or librarian chooses those numbers that fit the musical format of the given show.

Few disc jockeys can come to the studio without any preparation for the specific program and come up with a good, professional show. Some personalities can recall, organize, interrelate, and present ideas correlated with musical numbers with speed and fluency. Unfortunately, too many deejays who think they can, actually can't. Ad-libbing usually becomes boring and repetitious or embarrassing. Successful deejays rarely take a chance with complete ad-libbing. Why be half-safe when you can be more sure with some preparation?

Harold Green, when general manager of WMAL, Washington, D.C., detailed the preparation required for his music programs, including the gathering and development of material to be used as continuity:

The day of the "limited" announcer is about over. Just a beautiful voice, or just a snappy, witty or attractive personality is not enough for today's successful radio station. All the tricks, gimmicks, formats, points of view have been tried in one form or another. Some are quite successful in a limited way. The danger that the individual suffers is the strong possibility that he will remain submerged or anonymous. This is particularly true in a station that depends strongly on a particular "format." We feel that the stations that matter in the community don't limit themselves to a format or other gimmick. The key is community involvement—information with a purpose—and a continuity of sound (in music and personality) that will continually serve, and please, the audience that particular station has cultivated.

Our announcers go on the air each day with a thick folder of clippings, personal observations, letters from listeners, and reports from all the news and sports sources. By the time our announcers go on the air each day, they are fully briefed on all that is happening that is significant in the news, in sports, special events in the community, special broadcasts of more than routine interest scheduled for that day and week, or anything else that amounts to information *with a purpose*. Generally, each day's music preparation time amounts to approximately 50% of air time. A four-hour program requires about two hours to prepare musically. This is because the music list must reflect variety and balance: up-tempo music, boy vocal, lush orchestral, girl vocal, combo or variety, group vocal, and back around again. Specialty, novelty, or other types that break the pattern must be showcased by the D.J. There must be a reason for playing these "extras," and it must be explained.

It is safe to say that when a person does a smooth, informative, professional four-hour show—and one that teased the imagination and piqued the curiosity—he or she did an equal four hours of preparation. If they don't, they'll know it in about an hour. I'll know it in about an hour and a half, and the listener will know it before noon the next day.

Without preparation, background, genuine interest in the world, and diligent attention to getting informed and staying informed, broadcasters sink instantly into mediocrity. They are then relying on tricks. . . . They are ordinary. . . . They are short-changing the audience.

They won't last long.

In specific pop music forms the deejay is expected to be highly knowledgeable. Standard selection sources for pop music programs are trade magazines. *Radio and Records, Cash Box, Billboard,* and *Variety* provide information about the best-sellers, including rank in sales and type of music. In addition, these publications frequently give background information and carry news and features about the artists. For a top-40 show, the ranking list is indispensable. But for all formats the information obtained from the trade journals makes it possible to organize a program and, where feasible, to write meaningful continuity.

Michael C. Keith, longtime radio programmer, professor, and author of many books on the medium, describes three principal copy types for the pop music show, besides commercial and PSA scripting: "liners," "positioners," and "promos."

Liners are specific statements that announcers or deejays make about the programming.

For example:

> KISS 108 ACCUTIME . . .
> MORE Q-ROCK POWER HITS . . .
> A LITE 92 FM MUSIC SWEEP . . .

Positioners tell the listener exactly what the station is all about—its place on the radio dial. For example:

> BOSTON'S BEST MODERN ROCK STATION . . .
> THE EASIEST SOUND IN THE BAY CITY . . .

Promos are just that. They promote the station. For example:

> HITS 96 GIVES YOU 96 DOLLARS EVERY 96 MINUTES . . .
> EVERY NITE AT 9 THE BEST IN SPORTS TALK ON AM 1080 . . .

Keith stresses that economy is very important in writing this kind of continuity. The writer must consider time and space limits. The writer should create simple, declarative statements, no more than a sentence for each, that should be pertinent and direct. These statements are used between program elements and are called "drop-ins." The deejay will talk until the lead or post (the beginning) of a song and read a liner right until that point. Highly formatted and planned shows, Keith notes, have no ad-libbing, no extemporaneous material. The deejay must read the liners as they are written and where they are placed, with no deviation. The continuity writer, therefore, is a very important part of the pop music program.

Chad Rufer, when program director of WINK-FM, Ft. Myers, Florida, wanted written continuity from "newbies"—the on-air people who have come without much experience in the field. He found that experienced deejays know the music, procedure, and audiences so well that they can work from personal notes. All programs, however, need a "show prep" form and music log. The days are long gone when a deejay can walk into a studio and organize a show as it goes along. Rufer presented the following examples of the minimum preparation necessary, a rundown or outline of one afternoon's programs, and the rundown or music log of one show.

Afternoon Show

HOT LIST • HOT LIST • HOT LIST •

| The Show | | The Best Of The Rest |

The Show

OPEN	
3:05	Surf and Song Festival This WINKEND
3:15	Elvis Duran Roller Coaster Tour
3:25	Lady Gaga wearing Kermit the frog . . . pics @ winkfm.com
3:35	Phrase That Pays, tease Miley Cyrus (dumped Jonas Bro Boyfriend details on Twitter)
3:40	Follow us on Twitter win txts to Green Day
3:50	Colbie's new album "breakthrough" tease Sleaze at 4:15
4.05	Phoner Request
4:15	Tease Top Sleaze Stories
4:20	Danielle Sleaze Report/Traffic
4:30	Kelly Clarkson Tour Dates announced . . . Yes, FL! WINKFM.com
4:35	Green Day Concert next week, set up phone topic
4:40	Phone Topic Caller #1
4:50	Phone Topic Caller #2 Tease Katy Perry MTV VMA's/Traffic

The Best Of The Rest

Top News Stories

WINK NEWS SKYTRACKER
Meteorologist Jim Farrell
Today-

Ton-

Tom

Pier at Ft. Myers Beach
Edison Home
Centennial Park
FGCU
Edison
SunSplash in Cape Coral
Caribbean Garden in Naples
Naples Pier
5th Ave
Miramar Outlets

WINK 96.9

3   P   Monday   07-27

CUT# TITLE	ARTIST	ARTIST 2	SONG NOTES	CAT TMP	INTRO L	END

00:00   , , SW2, VO0002, "Generic Liner", " ", 00:10,
0:10
DA8440 0:13.00Not Meant To Be   Theory of A Deadm
A   MS   13.0/   3:25/   F

TALK BREAK
                                                    0:10
DA4103 0:09. 00Hey There Delilah   Plain White T's
R   MS   09.0/   3:44/   F
07:29   , ,SW2, VO0018, "LSR LINERS", " ", 00:10,
0:10
DA0138 0:07.00You Belong With Me   Taylor Swift
B   MS   07.0/   3:43/   F

TALK BREAK

0:10
DA4258 0:10.00Everything You Want   Vertical Horizon
N   MS   10.0/   3:51/   F
15:23   , ,SW2,DA0008, "PHRASE PROMOS", " ", 00:10,
0:10
15:33   , ,COM, DALIVE, "18:00 SPOTBREAK", " ", 05:20 , , L,
5:20
20:53   , ,SW2, VO0004, "Wink 96.9 MSXIMAGE", " ",00:15,
0:15
DA5133   0:14.00I Don't Want To Be   Gavin DeGraw
P   FS   14.0/   3:27/   F

TALK BREAK

 0:10
DA3214 0:06.00Just Dance   Lady Gaga
D   FS   06.0/   3:16/   C
28:01   , ,SW2,VO0999, "WMS DAILY 10", " ", 00:10,
0:10
DA0156 0:13.00Second Chance   Shinedown
B   MS   13:0/   3:38/   F

continued

TALK BREAK

0:10
31:59   , ,SW2, DA0007, "Wink 96.9 Promo", " ", 00:30,
0:30
32:29   , ,COM, DALIVE, "33:00 SPOTBREAK", " ", 05:10, ,L,
5:10
37:39   , ,SW2, VO0002, "Generic Liner", " ", 00:10,
0:10
DA0669 0:06.00The Climb   Miley Cyrus
A   MS   06.0/   3:41/   F

TALK BREAK

0:10
DA6045 0:08.00Better Than Me   Hinder
R   MS   08.0/   3:27/   F
45:07   , ,SW2, VO9908, "NEW Fallin for You/Colbie", " ", 00:10,
0:10
DA0140 0:18.00Fallin For You   Colbie Colliet
C   FS   18.0/   3:29/   F

TALK BREAK

0:30
49:16   , ,SW2, DA9900, "STACKER PROMO OPEN", " ", 00:10,
0:10
49:26   , ,SW2, DA9923, "Gotta Be Somebody/Nickelback", " ", 00:10,
0:10
49:36   , ,SW2, DA9985, "Please Don't Leave Me/P!NK", " ", 00:10,
0:10
49:46   , ,SW2, DA9997, "Light On/David Cook", " ", 00:10
0:10
49:56   , ,SW2, DA9999, "Legal I.D.", " ", 00:10,
0:10
50:06   , ,COM, DALIVE, "48:00 SPOTBREAK", " ", 07:15, , L,
7:15
57:21   , ,SW2, VO0004, "Wink 96.9 MSXIMAGE", " ", 00:15,
0:15
DA3001   0:13. 00Beautiful Day   U2
P   MS   13.0/   3:56/   F
61:32   , ,SW2, VO0018, "LSR LINERS", " ", 00:10,

continued

```
0:10
DA8396   0:11.00Gotta Be Somebody                Nickelback
D     MS        11.0/     3:54/      F
65:36               , ,SW2, VO0002, "Generic Liner", " ", 00:10,
0:10
DA6093   0:00.00Black Horse  &   The Cherry TrKT Tunstall
R     MS        00.0/     2:54/      C

68:40          59:50, * , , . . . , "Top of Hour Reset", " ", 00:00, , M,
0:00
DROP SONGS ARE E AND F.   CIRCLE THOSE SONGS NOT PLAYED.   MUSIC Tot. 70:45
```

Courtesy of Chad Rufer, Program Director, WINK-FM

MUSIC VIDEOS

Music television networks vied for places on the cable dial. Like radio, many music television networks tended toward specialization to reach specific demographic audiences. Although most maintain a mix of music, some feature one music type more than others, and some networks are principally or exclusively oriented to a given music, such as jazz, country, MOR, rock, pop, alternative, rap, metal, and reggae. Some orient their non-music materials to a specific topic, such as sports, drugs, health, and dating. Some, such as the Spanish Language Network and the Christian Music Network, aim at designated audiences. New technology has fostered new competition. The "Radio and Internet Newsletter" (RAIN) reported that "Once upon a time, MTV was a thorn in the side of major media outlets, bringing maverick programming and unique content that shook up the entertainment media landscape for good. Now . . . MTV is facing the kind of competition in the digital world that it used to represent to the media giants." It's digital and it's cyberspace!.

Without visual action and attractiveness, the music video program might just as well be listened to on radio. Although the music must be the audience's primary focal point, the visuals must be integrated effectively enough to hold the audience's attention and interest. The success of music videos illustrates the importance of visual action.

The first thing the writer must ask is, "What will the picture add to the sound?" Gimmicks, strange angles, and bizarre shots are not justified for their own sakes; they must have an integral relationship with the music and the performer. You can discover ideas in a locale related to the musical number, the mood expressed by the song, the idea or story presented in the lyrics, and the origin or image of the performing group, among other things.

For many years simplicity was the key: visual concentration on different sections or members of the orchestra, on the rock performer's body gyrations, on the ballad singer's facial expressions. This worked well to a point, but for a performance lasting longer than one or two numbers the visual coverage became repetitious and boring. Music videos broke the mold, incorporating abstracts, free forms, dramatic situations, drawings and paintings, architectural compositions, combinations of colors and angles, and a kaleidoscope of digital effects.

Other art forms, such as pantomime and dance, can provide interpretive visualizations of the music. Inanimate objects and forms can illustrate realistic and non-realistic content and feeling. Landscapes, people, places, actions, and events can indicate various environmental, fantasy, and psychological meanings and moods for the music.

According to Patrick Kriwanek, a music video producer and teacher, experienced producers do not need to submit scripts or storyboards, but operate from ideas created from the essence of the musical number to be videoed. Established directors "wing it from the edge of a martini glass," noted Kriwanek.

Although the young, beginning writer-producer may be asked to follow a proposal acceptance with a script or storyboard, the key is the proposal—that is, the *treatment*. Producer Joel D. Hinman, of Scorched Earth Productions, advised that in his "long experience the more successful treatments have relied on visually specific language. An artist, for instance, will want to know what they are wearing. If you have a choice, be specific."

Music video writer Ernie Fritz advised the beginning writer to determine first what the recording company's purpose is for the video. "If the song is already getting air play," Fritz said, "they're not looking for innovative video art. They want the video for support. Sometimes, however, they want you to make the video predominant because the song isn't getting much air play and they want the video to generate it." For writing technique, Fritz stressed the importance of listening to the song very carefully before preparing a video treatment. "Understand it emotionally as well as intellectually, what the music says as well as what the lyrics say," Fritz stated. "Sometimes the music is going in a different direction than the lyrical content. Capture the feeling as well as the narrative of both the music and lyrics."

Rik Cordero is a leading contemporary music and music video writer and producer. He offers the following advice on approaches and techniques for music video writers.

> Writing for music videos is a creative process that exists somewhere between commercial and narrative writing. It's important to discuss any existing ideas with the artist and record label before you begin. However, you must discover your own original voice and make that stand out amongst the elaborate descriptions of locations or sweeping camera moves.
>
> If you are chosen to write for a music video, chances are that the artist saw some of your past work and wants to implement some of that style or tone into their video. Having a conversation with the artist is a great way to discover their inspirations and personality traits which will have a strong impact on the end product. It's important to gain their trust but never become a pushover. Your job is to create a concept that enlightens and excites them. Including stock images or photos is also a great way to draw the artist or label commissioner to your words.

I like to excite artists by coming up with visual metaphors for their lyrics. For example in the Kid Sister "Big N Bad" treatment she has a line that says "rep yo click, rep your spot". In the song she's speaking to her listeners who are proud of where they live. In the video it's an interior shot of Hot Dougs, a famous Chicago landmark with Kid Sister and various customers and workers raising plastic cups into the air like a toast. To me, it was a fun way to show Kid Sister acknowledging where she came from without standing in front of a "Welcome To Chicago" sign.

Writing a captivating music treatment takes time and it's usually best to practice with musician friends or independent artists who are looking to shoot a low budget music video. This exercise forces you to come up with creative ideas because you can't throw money into glitzy performance shots or special effects. Sometimes a label will pass if your treatment sounds too over the top or expensive.

A well-written music video treatment has a distinct voice and immediately makes the reader believe that no one else understands the song as much as you do.

The following is an example of a music video pitch treatment by Rik Cordero.

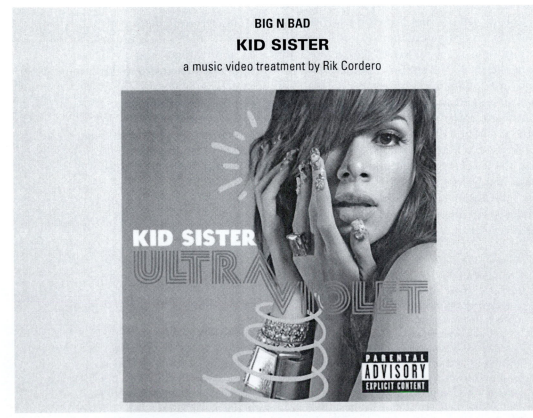

BIG N BAD

KID SISTER

a music video treatment by Rik Cordero

continued

"Big N Bad" is an incredible record for Kid Sister, a hard hitting, epic track that invokes the edgy and innovative Fool's Gold aesthetic. Naturally, the video for this electrifying track has to be an equally euphoric and powerful *visual* experience. I'm genuinely inspired by the frantic energy of the lyrics as much as I am by the hook-laden production and the infectious melody and chorus. I want to avoid all of the music videos clichés of the pop/dance genre and instead focus on the gritty and authentic urban backdrop of Chicago. From beginning to end, Kid Sister will capture our imagination while showing us a day in the life scene from an around-the-way girl straight out of Chi-Town.

We open on Kid Sister draped in high fashion walking with a few friends into Hot Dougs. The camera, on steadicam will track them in slow motion as we cut to inserts of Kid Sister spitting the first verse inside of the restaurant while her friends are ordering in the background. We'll cut between interior and exterior shots at Hot Dougs as the urban atmosphere and landmarks will distinguish the authenticity of actually being in Chicago. Slow motion scenes will also paint the atmosphere with different angles and images that tie into the lyrics: Kid Sister making a crazy Chicago style hot dog ("ain't nobody makin' shit quite like me, quite like this"), Cook in the back, grilling dogs, sweatin from the heat ("grab a towel throw it in, throw it up"), couple of kids at a table raising their paper plates in the air while chillin with the owner ("rep yo click, rep your spot"), etc. Kid Sister's performance for the remainder of each verse will cut between shots in front of the Hot Dougs as well as shots walking down the block, showcasing the architecture of the neighborhood along with slow motion inserts and cutaways and her reactions.

Cut to the first chorus with Kid Sister and a whole bunch of Extras now crowded inside of Hot Dougs. Sweeping camera angles inside the spot will suggest a strong sense of camaraderie and community. The continuous movement of the camera will keep the momentum of the video energetic as we focus on the natural quirkiness and charisma of Kid Sister. As we approach the 2nd verse, we see Kid Sister pull up in her car by her neighborhood in the South Side of Chicago.

Kid Sister begins the 2nd verse as she continues walking through the street block. The energy and culture of the neighborhood is an important character in this video. As Kid Sister continues to flow through her verse, we'll feature a crowd of extras behind her, rockin to the beat. The energy is on full blast at this point as the camera tracks them fluidly down the block. These shots will be intercut with Kid Sister's performance in front of Hot Dougs along with any additional slow motion camera shots like shots of her family chillin in front of a house, etc. Cut back to the second chorus with the Extras all packed into Hot Dougs.

As Kid Sister begins the final verse and chorus we track her walking alone into the back of a local Hip Hop open mic type of spot, real small and dilapidated like The Shelter in "8 Mile". She's got the hoodie on and walks onstage spitting the final verses as the crowd throws their hands in the air. The energy is even more energetic as we continue cutting to slow motion inserts and cutaways of the crowd as well as Kid Sister's reaction shots. All of this will be very dark and shadowy and most of all real!

This one of a kind music video will be shot on RED Digital fitted with 35mm lenses to accomplish a unique, gritty and cinematic look that jumps off the screen with energetic images. In essence, this video will represent my vision of BIG N BAD. I sincerely love this song and I will exceed even ***my own*** highest expectations to create a video that combines passion, technical skill, a dark action driven storyline, and captivating artist-driven performances. I'm looking forward to any additional input you may have. Thank you.

Copyright by and Courtesy of Rik Cordero

MUSIC ON THE INTERNET

Music on the Internet has led to laws and litigation reminiscent of the early 1920s when the American Society of Authors, Composers and Publishers (ASCAP) won a court case against the nascent radio stations, litigation that affirmed ASCAP members' ownership of music they had copyrighted. The radio stations played records and used sheet music for live shows that had been copyrighted by members of ASCAP without getting permission or paying any fees. In other words, they pirated the intellectual property of others. Suppose production companies produced a script you wrote without paying you for it or getting your okay to do so? Since then ASCAP and Broadcast Music, Inc. (BMI) periodically negotiate a contract with the National Association of Broadcasters (NAB) in which each station pays a statutory fee (a fixed amount based on the station's market) for unlimited use of ASCAP's and BMI's music inventory.

In the past decade, various web sites on the Internet have moved from pirating to ethical use of copyrighted music after losing a number of lawsuits. Napster's file-sharing system had permitted Internet users to create MP3s, a digital form of audio recording, which allow storage of music on hard drives. Users could exchange copies of their MP3s. The problem was that Napster did this without paying fees, thus turning all its users into pirates as well. Napster was successfully sued for copyright infringement. Before you use any music on the Internet, be sure you are ethically and legally clean and get proper clearances. A new copyright royalty fee to record companies as well as to songwriter organizations caused hundreds of Internet "pirate" radio stations to close. Online music services such as Listen, Pressplay, and RealOneMusicPass began to grow by paying legal fees to artists for their music. As critic Jefferson Graham wrote in *USA Today*, these services are among those "in the race to become the great celestial jukebox that could someday make the universe of music available anywhere, anytime, at the click of a mouse." In a few short years that has come to pass.

The growth of Internet radio stations along with the economic recession of the latter part of the 2000 decade, pushed terrestrial and cable radio into near-crisis situations. The merger of Sirius and XM satellite radio further changed the playing field for traditional music radio. Shortly after their merger, SiriusXM reported over a million downloads of its iPhone and iPod touch applications. Interactive sidebars in Internet radio have created new audiences for the audio and music industries. Listeners can select specific artists or music styles at any time and can establish their own playlists for as many selections and as long a time as they want. The Internet also permits less restrictive music formats, enabling receptors to go to sites with background information on artists, reviews of albums, history of the type of music, and similar data previously not easily available. With listeners able to respond directly and in-depth to the deejay or program producer, Internet radio stations can more accurately serve audience needs than can traditional radio stations, including those that stream their signal onto the Internet. The ultimate flexibility is the music radio Internet service with multiple channels or the service with multiple links and sites that lets the listener set up his or her own personal radio station. The writer can set up interactive choices that give the listeners complete control over what they hear, including the type of musical style, choice of artist, and specific musical numbers. Some audio programmers have taken music on the Internet a step further and have integrated the music with graphics.

VARIETY AND COMEDY

Reading a chapter of a book or reading a dozen books will not give a writer the talent or skills of the great comedy writers, but the writer can learn some basic approaches to organizing the variety program and writing humor—including elements of drama and music as well as comedy.

Program Types

By the 1980s variety shows had all but disappeared from television. What were once among the most popular shows were reduced to occasional specials. Elements of the variety show are still found in late evening entertainment programs such as the *Tonight Show with Jay Leno,* the *David Letterman Show* and other late-night shows. Whether variety shows will resurge in the near future is anybody's guess—but the broadcast writer should be prepared.

The term "variety" implies a combination of two or more elements of entertainment and art: singer, dancer, stand-up comic, comedy skit, Shakespearean actor, puppeteer, ventriloquist, pianist, rock group. Depending on the program's principal figure, several of these elements would be incorporated in a manner that shows off the star to the best advantage. Catchall, non-star variety shows are rare.

The basic variety show types are the vaudeville show, the music hall variety, the revue, the comic-dominated show, the personality (usually singer or dancer) program with guests, the musical comedy approach, and the solo performance. Although all of these forms have been on television from time to time over the years, they have varied in popularity.

The variety show is not a haphazard conglomeration of different acts. Even the vaudeville show—exemplified in television history by the *Ed Sullivan Show*— carefully integrates and relates its various acts and frequently focuses on a clear central theme. Vaudeville and music hall variety are basically the same, oriented around specialty acts of different kinds. The revue is organized primarily around music and dance, with comedians frequently providing the continuity and transitions between musical numbers.

The comic-dominated show can consist of a comedian as the central performer, with various guests or standard acts. A singing personality can mix his or her songs with participation in comic skits, with contributions from guests, creating what is in essence a revue centered on one performer. When such shows have a thread of continuity, no matter how thin, they become musical revues. The thread can be any kind of theme: the songs of one composer, a national holiday, a historical happening, the biography of a famous entertainer, a locale—almost anything can serve.

An adaptation of the vaudeville variety show has been successful on American television, substituting a host or hostess who rarely participates in the overt performing and who introduces and interviews various guest entertainers. Because much of the program is banter between host and guest (and in these segments the host or hostess is a principal entertainer), these are frequently called talk or interview shows, most notably exemplified by the late-night programs already noted. There can, of course, be combinations of various performance types and variety forms on any given program. Some of these programs have become even more sophisticated through the Internet, where viewers can click on icons for background information on guests and other materials.

Approach and Organization

The most important thing for the variety show writer to remember is that there must be a peg on which to hang a show. You must develop a clear central theme, capable of being organized into a sound structure, with a unity that holds all the parts of the program together. Otherwise, each number will be a number in itself, and unless the audience knows what the next act is and especially wants to watch it, the audience feels free at any time to go to another station, channel, or web site. The theme could be a distinct one or the continuity factor could simply be the personality of the host, comedian, or singer. An exception is the vaudeville or music hall type of presentation. In these shows the audience is held by frequent reminders of the special act still to come.

Within each separate variety show type, distinct orientations must be determined by the writer. Will the musical portions stress popular or novelty numbers? Will the dances be classical in style? Modern? Presentational? Representational? Interpretive? The comedy must be written to fit the comic's personality and must contain a sufficient amount of what appears to be ad-lib material to enhance the public concept of the comic's spontaneous talents. What kind of comedy will be emphasized? Simple good humor? Wit? Satire? Slapstick? Will it combine elements of several types? Will it go into special areas of farce, sophisticated humor, irrelevancy, or irreverence? Does the comedian's style require material oriented toward broad, physical gags, or an intellectual approach?

When planning a variety show, consider the intrinsic meaning of the term "variety." You must differentiate between each successive number and among the various program segments. Contrast is important—not so much that the viewers become distracted, but enough so that there is no feeling of sameness or repetition, a feeling too easily transferred into boredom. Musical number should not follow musical number, comedy routine should not follow comedy routine. Even in a show featuring a popular singer, the continuity is broken up with an occasional skit or a guest performer. The suspense created by a juggler who balances an unbelievable number of fiery hoops on the end of his or her nose should not be followed directly by the similar suspense of acrobats balancing one another on each other's noses.

Comedy

Although many books contain hundreds of comedy situations and thousands of one-liners, few books do more than give you ideas for comedy or overviews of comedy approaches. You can't learn to be a comedy writer from a book. Each comedian has his or her own "shtick." You can learn individual techniques by watching them. And some books delve into principles of comedy writing that you may be able to apply, depending on your own type of humor.

Comedy writer Hal Rothberg, writing in *Audio-Visual Communications*, advised that "to write funny, you have to think funny." He offered several guidelines for the comedy writer:

1. "Understand your audience." Are audience members the type who will laugh at slapstick or prefer more sophisticated humor? Situation comedy or one-liners?

2. "Make the humor spring from the characters or situation." As with writing any action, the characters and the situation must first be believable to the audience before you can move into comedy, satire, or farce.

3. "Use all your tools." Don't forget that humor can be presented both aurally and visually. For video, you can use films, cartoons, and other visuals alone or with live performers. For audio, sound effects have always been useful tools.

4. "Watch the budget." Neophyte writers sometimes think that far-out situations that are expensive to produce automatically will be funny. A relatively low-budget show like *Saturday Night Live* demonstrates how creativity is more effective than costliness alone.

5. "Keep it clean." In some situations blue humor may fit, but on television one must be careful while being clever. Too many nightclub stand-up comedians resort to sophomoric bathroom humor and four-letter words as substitutes for comic ideas. Too many young comedy writers substitute shock for stimulation.

6. "Don't beat a joke to death." Except for the running gag, don't repeat something, even if you think it's good. It works only once.

7. "Mix 'em up." Use a variety of ways to get laughs. Surprise your audience. Varying camera perspective or the music mood can be just as effective as a punch line.

8. "Keep it fun." In most situations, the audience wants to see only the bright side of life. Heavy humor is risky for the mass audience. That doesn't mean meaningful humor will not work. Mark Twain and Will Rogers were superb satirists of society. Jerry Seinfeld made gentle humor and commentary on everyday foibles work on television.

9. "Try it out, but don't be discouraged." Before you sell or give it to your agent or client, try it out on friends, strangers, anyone from whom you can get a reaction; then cut, fix, and rewrite.

10. "Don't expect to be loved." The people you sell your comedy writing to are likely to be skeptical; until your material is getting laughs from an audience, don't expect much applause.

11. "Read a little." To write humor, you have to keep up with what is happening to people and the world. Find out what other comedy writers are producing and what is working.

12. "Are you communicating?" What is the purpose of your humor? Is there a goal besides simply making people laugh?

As Rothberg said, "First and foremost, communicate."

APPLICATION AND REVIEW

1. Prepare rundown sheets for three different local disc jockey pop music radio shows, each with a different music format.

2. Select one of the music formats discussed in this chapter and write a script including home page, rundown, and continuity for an Internet music radio station.

3. Write the complete script for a half-hour radio classical music show, to be distributed on a national basis to local stations.

4. With other members of a writing team (for example, several other members of your class) prepare the rundown and continuity for an hour special featuring the pop music group or personality currently at the top of the sales charts.

5. As part of a writing team, write a treatment for a five-minute music video. Write one alone.

Corporate, Educational, and Children's Programs

According to *Writer's Market*, corporate and educational media, including advertising, informational, and training programs, have been a bigger business than Hollywood. The Internet has added considerably to this field. Corporate media programming—or, as it is still sometimes called, industrial programming—includes virtually all the formats covered thus far in this book.

Examples of corporate media programming include "talk" programs that feature managers or subject area experts discussing new sales approaches, manufacturing processes, or organizational changes, among other topics; **teleconferencing,** small or large meetings connecting two or more sites via cyberspace; executives giving speeches to employees or to the public at large; company leadership being interviewed for internal or external distribution; and formal education and training programs.

Feature and documentary formats provide historical, scientific, public service, operational, or other background regarding the company to enhance its institutional image. News formats convey information about the company on a periodic, sometimes daily, basis.

All companies use commercials and/or announcements. News, features, and commercials have been merged into a format that has grown in recent years, sometimes called infomercials. These range from short commercial spots, usually about 30 seconds, that combine public service information, such as consumer data, with a commercial message, to 15- and 30-minute and sometimes even longer programs that sell a product or service. Pop-ups and other ads on the Internet have expanded this outreach.

The feature/documentary and commercial have been united for public relations programs. For example, if the company wanted to expand onto some property that was going to be used for low-income housing, a feature-type commercial showing how the company's expansion will provide jobs for low-income families, below market-rate loans for worker home-ownership, and another equivalent suitable site for housing could defuse opposition to expansion and gain increased support for the company and its products.

Perhaps the most widely served corporate purpose is education and training. Video training programs are produced internally by many companies. Some have highly sophisticated production centers and a staff of producers and writers (usually, the producer and writer are the same person—an important consideration for students who are studying production but neglecting writing courses). Training videos are produced for all corporate levels and for all purposes. Programs run the gamut from introducing the physical surroundings in which new employees will work, to more sophisticated requirements such as filing procedures for entry-level office personnel, to more complex procedures such as operating a given mass production machine, to an even higher level such as introducing the development of a new company product based on a recently invented scientific process.

Videos and computer programs can teach new clerks grammar skills and vice-presidents how to make speeches to employee groups. Programs are produced to introduce new products, new selling techniques for old products, new operational systems, new reporting procedures, and new budget and financial processes to a relatively few or a few hundred people at one site, or to literally thousands of employees scattered all over the world for a multinational corporation.

Another area of corporate media is the *point-of-purchase (POP)* presentations. These are monitors at retail outlets where the presentation is designed to influence undecided customers to purchase a given product. The writer orients these programs principally to the customer, but many stores find a secondary use for them: to inform employees about the products and to train employees how to sell products most effectively. Some stores contract the presentations for the latter purpose only. This means the writer must creatively combine commercial and training objectives.

Although writing any format is essentially the same for all media distribution situations, corporate media's bottom line may not relate directly to selling the product. The company's purpose with any given video, audio, or computer program can vary greatly: to enhance employee morale, obtain good public relations, sell, persuade colleagues, or educate and train. The writer must determine the company's specific purpose for any given corporate media program. All of these corporate purposes were for many years served by video, audio, and film distribution. Computers are now essential in corporate use and the Internet is the key medium.

Corporate media writing is not confined to industry but refers as well to media use by government offices, educational systems and institutions, and professional and citizen associations and organizations—in other words, by any group that wants to inform, persuade, or educate, internally and externally.

Corporate Programs

PROCEDURE OBJECTIVES

To develop an idea for a program, the writer must know the program's purpose. Usually, there are two major objectives: that of the client or management and that of the target audience. It generally is easier to determine the purposes of an in-house production because management usually is precise about what it wants the media program to accomplish.

The writer must determine, as well, the purposes of the audience. If a training program is aimed at company employees, as most corporate media programs are, how is the intended audience going to be motivated to watch and pay attention to the program and to actually learn from it and follow through on the management goals inherent in it?

Demographics are important here for two major reasons. The first and perhaps most obvious reason is the same as that for writing commercials: Determine what kinds of program materials will appeal to the viewers or listeners, get their attention, keep their interest, and persuade them to do whatever it is management wants them to do. The second relates to motivation: Determine why the viewer or listener should take the program seriously. Every member of the audience must be made aware of what is in it for him or her. Will learning the new production technique and using it successfully earn a raise or a promotion? Is proper use of the new computer system necessary for keeping one's job? Will expanded sales of the new product result in escalated commissions? Does learning how to make good speeches in order to increase participation as a middle manager in community affairs result in higher bonuses? If the production is for public consumption, such as an institutional feature or an infomercial, the writer uses the public demographics of the target community.

An old but classic example of combining management's purpose with motivating the audience both to watch and learn is "The Hantel Advantage" script later in this chapter. Writer-producer Frank R. King knew what management wanted: increased productivity through faster interoffice communications. The employees scheduled to see the video at regional conferences were forced, however, to take time from their commission-earning routes to attend the meeting and had to get up early in the morning to watch the program.

King used two key motivations in the script. First, he tried to convince the employees that by using the new Hantel computer system they would require less time for any given client transaction, thus saving them hours per week in which they could sell more insurance and make more money or, if they wished, have more leisure time. Second, so the employees would not ignore the video because they were both tired and angry from having to get up early to see it, he included broad, almost farcical humor in an attempt to motivate a happy attitude toward the video, as well as to the workshop that followed. Entertainment became an integral part of learning motivation.

Roger Sullivan, when director of education for the Commercial Union Assurance Companies, offered the following advice for developing effective corporate video scripts:

> It is very important that business program writers understand the objectives of the particular program being produced. For example, when we develop a program for the business adult education community, we have, in truth, two audiences: the organization for which the program is being developed, which wants a program that provides employees with the practical knowledge and skills they need to carry out successfully one or more particular predefined performance functions on the job; and the employee, who seeks personal growth and the ability to carry out a performance function as confidently and competently as possible. Both audiences want to have the learning completed in as short a time as possible and within reasonable cost limits. The production begins with a detailed agreement about the objectives, the performance which the employee can be expected to demonstrate as a result of the learning. The complete scenario is a series of interrelated modules of skills or knowledge leading to the final ability to perform the objectives. The most effective visual presentation for each module is developed. The emphasis is on the practical—how to do it. The theoretical—why—is secondary. Once your audience and objectives are well-defined and the modular building blocks assembled, then the scenario may be fleshed out.

Client/Management Conferences

If you are an out-of-house writer, that is, an independent writer or writer-producer, it will take longer to determine management purposes and target audience demographics and motivations. Although no rule-of-thumb works in all cases, many independent production organizations allocate about two-thirds of the total production schedule to writing the script and one-third to actual production. The more complete the preparatory work, including finalizing the script, the less production time is needed. If the entire production is in-house, the same time ratios generally are true, except the total time allotted to the project may be far shorter. Management often forgets that creativity takes time and expects its media unit to produce a product as quickly as it expects its accountant to provide last week's sales figures.

Whether working within a long or short time frame, the writer must meet with management and with target audience employees. Frequently, the program is produced in-house but is scripted by a freelance writer. That situation calls for the writer to consult with the in-house producer as well as with other offices and personnel in the company who may be affected by the program's purpose or content. During the initial meeting between writer and client (or if in-house, writer and management), clear agreement should be reached about the program's purpose and form.

Budget and Resources

As soon as possible the writer must gain a clear understanding of budget limitations. If, as is frequently the case, the writer is also the producer, a budget should be determined with the client/management at the first meeting. A client may have in mind a program that, from the writer-producer's expert viewpoint, requires a budget of $150,000. The client, on the other hand, may have allocated a budget of $50,000 for that particular project. Make clear immediately the kind of program that can be prepared with the available budget to avoid not only wasted time and resources, but also misunderstanding and recrimination.

When initially discussing the project, the writer must determine whether its purposes can be accomplished in one program and, if so, the optimum program length, whether several shows will be required, or whether a lengthy series is necessary. The purposes, budget, and resources also determine the media form. Video? Audio alone? PowerPoint? In-house computer network?

If you are employed in-house or by an independent production company, you already know the production resources. If, however, you are employed on a freelance basis to write that particular script, you must determine the company's production capabilities or those of the outside organization the company will hire, before preparing an outline.

Treatment or Outline

The treatment is important as the next step in maintaining agreement between writer and client/management during the preparation and production period. It might well cost the writer time and money, and perhaps even the job itself, for the client/management to look at a script several weeks after the beginning of the process and object that it is not at all what the client had in mind, wanted, or expected to get. Therefore, soon after the initial meeting, the writer should prepare an outline and get client/management approval before beginning a detailed treatment, which in turn needs approval before the preliminary script is written. That, as well, should be approved before the final script is prepared. In other words, the writer should be certain that his or her work is on target during every phase of the project.

There are exceptions. Some in-house and independent writers have worked sufficiently long and successfully for the company that their judgment and proficiency are trusted. These writers may be given the project purpose at an initial meeting and told to come back with a completed script in a specified time period. Experienced writers-producers such as Ralph De Jong, one of whose scripts is used as an illustration of good writing later in this chapter, are frequently in that position. As you read De Jong's advice to young writers, below, under *Evaluation*, note that despite his prerogatives he takes the steps necessary to be certain that both he and the client agree all the way.

Research

In most cases research takes the longest time, unless the writer happens to be an expert in the subject being scripted. Although the program should be entertaining as well as educational, it is not an entertainment program. Its purpose is to convey specific ideas and information. It must be totally accurate. To make it interesting, the writer must become familiar with all aspects of the subject, whether the company history or the technical operation of a scientific process. Only then can the writer have enough material to choose the options that will result in the most effective script. Depending on the subject, the writer will do library research, research on the Internet, pick the brains of experts, and talk with the employees who are the targets of the program and with the management officials who decided on the objectives. Roger Sullivan advised the writer to "work closely with subject matter experts and rely on their comments, as well as on your own imagination."

When possible, the writer seeks real-life experience with the subject, such as going into the field with an insurance salesperson and applying the new method promoted in the program, working on the assembly line with the new machine, or accompanying the vice-presidents who are promoting the company's image at community affairs.

Production

When the final script is prepared and approved, production starts. In the corporate situation, unlike many public media circumstances, the writer's job usually does not end with the completed script, but can continue through the editing and screening or webcasting process. There is always the chance that the company president, seeing for the first time a program that has been approved every step of the way by a cadre of vice-presidents, will ask for some changes before the program is used.

Evaluation

A final step that takes place after the program is used is evaluation. Has the program been effective? Did it accomplish management's purposes? Were the audience's needs satisfied? The writer should participate in measuring the program's effects, usually through traditional educational tools of testing and interviewing, to know how to write the next program or series, or new version of that program or series, more effectively.

Ralph De Jong summarized some of these procedures from his own experience writing and producing award-winning programs for government and industry:

> Industrial or corporate films offer the writer an opportunity to bring into play any one or a combination of several conventional storytelling approaches and techniques. But unlike the typical entertainment show, the corporate program demands that the writer be acutely aware of the relationships between people, procedures, processes, equipment and institutional philosophies and goals.

Most corporate programs are relatively short, running anywhere between 10 and 30 minutes, with an average running time of 15 minutes. Since corporate programs are proprietary, the scriptwriter needs to determine a client's objectives and purpose and then conduct sufficient research on the subject so that the final product will convey its message succinctly and with authority, credibility, and integrity.

In addition to running-time constraints, most corporate programs have tight budgets and protracted deadlines. Since the scriptwriter is very often the first person to be involved with a project, it is essential that he or she has a thorough understanding of production techniques in the basic formats. Armed with this knowledge the scriptwriter can utilize various aspects of these formats to create a production that can be completed within budget and on time while meeting its objectives in an interesting, informative, and entertaining way. Where the typical entertainment program is geared for a general audience, most corporate programs are designed for a specific viewership. To ensure that the program meets its objectives, the scriptwriter must identify the target audience and develop a profile of its interests and familiarity with the subject matter so that the program will satisfy both the needs of the audience and the client.

WRITING TECHNIQUES

Donald S. Schaal, as television producer-director for Control Data Corporation Television Communications Services, observed in *Educational and Industrial Television* that "when you come to grips with scripting for industrial programs, for the most part you might just as well throw all your preconceived ideas about creative/dramatic and technical writing in the circular file." Schaal recalled that his initial attempts to transfer the classroom teacher to electronic media failed and that "unfamiliarity with what media could or could not do . . . resulted in a product which left just about everything to be desired. It lacked organization, continuity, a smooth succession of transitions and, in many cases, many of the pertinent details. . . . Since we think so-called 'training' programs should *augment* classroom material and not supplant it, we soon realized that we could gain little but could lose everything by merely turning an instructor loose to do exactly what he does in person in the classroom. . . . The media production he needs for his classroom *must* provide something he cannot conveniently offer his students in person."

Schaal's solution to the problem was to use professionals to do the voice tracks describing electromechanical and electronic equipment. He found, however, that this created a further problem: Although the teacher who knows the equipment doesn't necessarily know how to present it effectively on media, the professional performer who can make a good presentation doesn't usually know much about the equipment. Schaal said that "the solution, of course, is the professional must *sound* as though he invented every part of the machine and painstakingly handtooled it out of solid gold. To accomplish this effect, you must contrive what I like to call a 'shadow' script."

The shadow script, according to Schaal, is a transcription of the classroom teacher's presentation of a particular subject and a minimum rewriting of the transcription for smoother continuity and subsequent voice-over recording by a professional. Schaal encountered two distinct difficulties because the classroom instructor tended to reflect the classroom teaching approach: a lack of concise, clear continuity and the accidental omission of pertinent material. Schaal was forced to reevaluate his procedure.

Now an instructor who comes into our shop to make such a program arrives with at least a very detailed, topical outline prepared with the specific medium—for example, video—in mind. In many cases, he is actually provided with a detailed rough shooting script from which he reads for the benefit of the audio track. These outlines and scripts are provided by the curriculum people of the school and tend to confine the instructor to an orderly and complete description of the equipment . . .

Had we gone the route of preparing formal scripts in the technical writing style (which would have been the most appropriate in this case), dropped the instructor out of the loop completely by telling him he was a clod on video and showing him the door, and refused to cooperate with the curriculum people because they didn't think in terms of video at first, we not only would have alienated a lot of people, but also I doubt if we would have produced a completely usable product . . .

The moral, as I see it, is that corporate media scripts must be tailored to meet the situation. I have talked of only one aspect of industrial scripting—the description of equipment for training people on how to use and maintain it. For this type of script, I feel it is very important to retain the credibility of the person who knows the equipment the best, even though his voice does not appear on the finished product.

For this reason, I confine my rewrites to removing bad grammar and clarifying hazy or badly worded description. I make no attempt at restructuring mainly because the pictures are already there. If I do see continuity problems, however, I call them to the attention of the curriculum people involved and let them make the decisions. I do make every attempt to keep the narrative as conversational as possible without lapsing into the creative/dramatic vein. All such scripts must be straightforward, sound natural, and contain a minimum of slang. Rarely is anything flippant allowed to survive the waste basket. Cliches and stylized narrative are avoided like the plague.

Many corporate scripts use the drama format, creating suspense that holds the audience and a conflict whose solution achieves the presentation's objective. Corporate film writer-director Richard Bruner, who effectively used dramatic dialogue and action rather than the voice-over narration and lecture-type dialogue that dominate many corporate scripts, offered some advice in an article in *Audio-Visual Communications* by Thomas C. Hunter. Bruner explained that when the purpose of the program is simply conveying expository information, narration can do a good job. But "for a program to have dramatic impact," he advised a dramatic format. "The audience must be convinced that something important is at stake. The protagonist must have a stake in the out-come of the conflict."

Bruner warned, however, that clients sometimes get uneasy with the dra-matic approach "because to have a conflict, everything can't be rosy." The writer must remember that the corporate client, by nature, tends to be conservative. That attitude applies to the artistic as well as content elements of a script. Even a mildly different creative approach might give the impression of rocking the boat. The writer sometimes has to convince the client that without the creative factors necessary to make the script entertaining enough to be watched or heard, the program could turn out to be dull and boring and not fulfill the corporate objectives. Bruner cautioned, however, that creativity for its own sake can be overworked and that the writer must avoid a profusion of special effects and "razzle-dazzle."

The "talking head" and "straight sell narrative" rarely work well in the corporate training script and are to be avoided in most situations. How then does the writer convey the system, routine, procedure, or ideas that result in effective learning? Corporate training scripts rely largely on two major approaches: the right-way–wrong-way demonstration and the step-by-step demonstration.

In the right-way–wrong-way demonstration, a character uses the system or product or machine incorrectly, with unwanted and unhappy consequences. This is followed by a character doing it the right way. The process can be shown step-by-step, if desired, so that every stage is absolutely clear. For example, a restau-rant chain may contract for a video that teaches new personnel how to serve wine. In one sequence the novice manages to push the cork *into* the bottle, put a *red* wine bottle into an ice bucket, pour the wine without showing the wine label, offer-ing the cork for odor, or providing a preliminary taste, fill each glass to the top, and then, of course, spill the wine onto the table cloth and the customers' clothes. Treated with humor, and followed by a demonstration of how to serve wine correctly, the sequences show the correct procedure and the common mistakes to avoid.

Humor is an effective device for most script formats; it's risky, however, in the corporate script. Many writers have found that a sense of humor often is not appreciated. Some corporate executives seem to equate humor in the script with making fun or light of their product or service. Further, comedy writing is extremely difficult. Many writers *think* they are funny, but often they are guilty of sopho-moric humor. Corporate producers will tell you that they've rarely seen humor work in corporate scripts.

A second major approach for effective learning in the training script is step-by-step demonstration. The expert, office manager, or production unit chief can demonstrate point-by-point how to do the particular task. The demonstration can be reinforced by slow-motion, close-ups, repetition, and key scripted ques-tions from the character or characters playing the learning-employee roles. When the demonstration is completed, the person playing the learner may then be asked to go over the process point-by-point. Internet interactive elements greatly enhance this approach.

Reinforcement and repetition are extremely important. Tell the audience what you are going to tell them, tell them, and then tell them what you've told them. Sum up after each learning module and sum up at the end of the program. Complex processes should be repeated slowly enough for each aspect to be made clear. Visual action, voice and sound effects, music, written words—usually in large block letters—and diagrams—in color where possible and always clear and precise—are good supports.

Because the corporate script is more formal than most entertainment scripts, it is especially important to apply the principles in the style section in Chapter 3, "Format and Style." Several key points are the following:

1. *Use the active voice instead of the passive whenever possible.* Many writers tend to use the words "there are"—the passive voice—rather than stating the facts or ideas directly and actively; for example, don't write "There are eleven chapters contained in this book" instead of "This book contains eleven chapters."

2. *Use simple, colloquial language, suited to the level of the audience.* You are not writing print literature, but visual and aural presentations. Conform the rhythm and pace of the language in the script to the subject matter and temper of the program. Keep sentences short, especially with how-to demonstrations. Don't try to cram too many ideas into a short time period. A principal drawback in most neophyte scripts is the overload of information, making it difficult for the audience to keep up with, much less remember, everything presented.

3. *Be exact. Be precise.* The audience should have no doubt about what is being said or shown, or what it should be learning. Don't assume that all the audience members understand all the technical language just because the audience is an employee group. Explain and define all technical terms. On the other hand, you should determine what specialized words or terms are common knowledge for that audience and include them as a means of establishing empathy with the audience and, where appropriate, in place of more formal terms that might need more explanation.

4. *Use the right word and spell it correctly.* Just as you should do for all writing in any situation, don't hesitate to use your dictionary and thesaurus.

5. *Be direct in training programs.* For example, when instructing the audience about how to use a new machine, don't have the demonstrator say, "Next, you should release the thingamabob, and then you should spin it through the fragamaran . . ."; simply write: "Next, release the thingamabob and spin it through the fragamaran . . ."

6. *Think visually, write visually, and revise visually.* Most corporate scripts are visual. Many writers have a tendency to think of instructional writing as print writing because most of their experience with such learning is with textbooks.

7. *Be neat.* Neatness counts. Make a good impression with what you submit. If your script looks sloppy, the people deciding whether to hire you may assume that your work in general is sloppy. The corporate world has little patience with artistic bohemianism.

APPLICATION: VIDEO—INTERNAL TRAINING

Frank R. King, when director of video training for the John Hancock Mutual Life Insurance Company, was asked to produce a video program to introduce agents in 430 locations throughout the country to a new companywide computer system, HANcock TELecommunications. The video was to lead off day-long meetings in which agents were to learn about HANTEL. The script objectives were to (1) kick off each regional meeting with a positive feeling, (2) convince managers that if they did not use the new computer system the company wouldn't save the money that prompted its installation, and (3) make clear the personal benefits of the system to each individual manager and agent.

King chose a dramatic format that would lend itself more easily to humor than would a narrative or discussion format. He had to motivate the audience to accept the content and to pay attention to the video at an early morning hour. King condensed the informational or specific learning objectives to four that would show as well as tell managers how and why HANTEL should be used: (1) to train agents, (2) to facilitate sales, (3) to create a more efficient sales proposal system, and (4) to strengthen administrative processes. He titled the script "The Hantel Advantage." As producer as well as writer, King hired professional talent for some of the lead roles and used selected John Hancock employees in minor parts.

As you read the first part of "The Hantel Advantage" script, which follows, note how it reflects some of the techniques discussed earlier, including the right-way–wrong-way approach, as shown in the comparison of the fictional insurance company without a computer and the John Hancock Company with HANTEL. King stays with the play format, concentrating on motivating dialogue rather than on expository monologue. The contrasts between the old and the new are exaggerated sufficiently to provide visual humor and entertainment for the viewer.

THE HANTEL ADVANTAGE

AUDIO	VIDEO
	JHVN LOGO
	Fade up: Opening Title:
	THE HANTEL ADVANTAGE
	Fade to Black
NARRATOR: (Music under):	Fade up on: LS
	Aerial photo, small town.
Our story takes place in a small town. Like any other American town, there are a number of businesses here, including two life insurance companies.	Slow zoom in.
Now, most people think that life insurance companies are all the same. But there's one person in this town who knows better. That's Bob Shields. Bob's brother is an insurance agent himself, and now Bob's decided to become an agent too. He's made plans today to learn a little bit about how the 2 companies in town operate.	Dissolve to: Exteriors: Olde Fashioned Life and John Hancock, with signs. The first is old, decrepit; JH is modern, clean.
	Cut to: Pan and follow one pedestrian, Bob Shields, walking through light crowd. Late 20s, well-dressed, whistling tune.
(MUSIC OUT)	
	Bob walks into door of Olde Fashioned Life.
	Zoom into sign.
BOB: Er . . . excuse me . . .	Interior, reception area. Receptionist is sleeping in her chair.
	She is snoring.
Uh . . . miss . . .	Bob tries waking her, getting louder and louder, finally succeeds with a shout.
HELLO?!!?	
RECEPTIONIST: (Waking suddenly) OH! What . . . what is it? (She looks around anxiously) (Sees Bob. Angrily:) Who are you? What do you want, anyway?	
BOB: Sorry, miss. My name is Bob Shields, and . . .	

continued

AUDIO	VIDEO
RECEPTIONIST: (Interrupts) Well, Bob Shields, do you always shout at people? Can't you see this is a place of business?	Bob peers over her shoulder into clerical area. We see several clerks, all sleeping in their seats.
BOB: Well, I'm really very sorry. I have a 10:00 appointment with Mr. Hindenburg.	
RECEPTIONIST: Well, just find a seat over there and he'll be with you soon.	
	Bob finds waiting area, sits down. Looks around for reading material. Finds old magazines with 1970s dates. Reacts with surprise. Starts to read.
	A kindly, frail woman about 40 enters office and goes to receptionist. Bob watches . . .
RECEPTIONIST: (Gruff tone) Yeah!	
WOMAN: (Taken aback slightly) Uh . . . How do you do? I wonder if someone can help me?	
RECEPTIONIST: Could be. What's your problem, honey?	
WOMAN: Well, my husband and I just moved here a few weeks ago from Minnesota . . . You see, our moving expenses were a bit higher than we expected, and we were hoping we might be able to get some money out of an Olde Fashioned policy my husband bought in 1989?	
RECEPTIONIST: Well, it's not that easy, you know. We can't do that *here*. First, you've got to fill out these change of address forms. (She slaps on the counter a pile of papers.) Then you've got to complete these "Intent to Raid the Nonforfeiture Value" forms (more papers). After that, there's this one: "Declaration of Anticipated Financial Status for the Next 35 Years" (more papers). And if the amount you want is over $15, we need your fingerprints, passport information, police record, and grammar school history on these (a last huge bunch of papers).	From receptionist's viewpoint: only the very top of woman's head now shows above the huge pile of papers.

continued

AUDIO	VIDEO
WOMAN: Thank you. How soon will I get my money?	
RECEPTIONIST: (Looking at calendar) Well, this is November . . . with any luck around Easter.	
WOMAN: THANK YOU.	As she struggles to take the papers off the counter, dropping many . . .
Fade to Black	
(MUSIC UNDER)	TITLE: That afternoon . . .
	Wipe to: Bob enters *JH* office. Goes to receptionist. Office is bright, neat, receptionist is attractive young woman.
(MUSIC OUT)	
RECEPTIONIST: Hello, may I help you?	
BOB: Yes, thanks. My name is Bob Shields. I have a 2 o'clock appointment with Mr. Davis.	
RECEPTIONIST: Oh yes, Mr. Shields. Mr. Davis is expecting you. If you'll have a seat I'll tell him you're here.	
	BOB sits, notices a small sign on end table or wall that reads:
	ASK US ABOUT THE HANTEL ADVANTAGE!
	Same woman enters office, goes to receptionist. She looks haggard from her ordeal that morning.
RECEPTIONIST: Yes, Ma'am. What can I do for you?	
WOMAN: I *hope* you can help me. It's about a John Hancock insurance policy my husband has. I'd like to get a loan through the policy . . . if that's not asking too much?	
RECEPTIONIST: I'm sure we can help. Let me get one of our representatives to take care of you.	
DAVIS: Mr. Shields?	DAVIS enters waiting area. Walks over to Bob.

continued

AUDIO	VIDEO
SHIELDS: Yes.	
DAVIS: I'm Herb Davis. Glad you could make it today.	
SHIELDS: It's nice to meet you, Mr. Davis. I appreciate your taking the time for me today.	
DAVIS: My pleasure.	
SHIELDS: I've got a lot of questions—but first of all, tell me—what's this (pointing to sign) about a HANTEL advantage?	
DAVIS: Well, before we talk about your aptitude test or anything else—that's a pretty good place to start, because HANTEL has really become the *heart* of our agency. If you'll come with me, I think I can *show* you what HANTEL's all about.	DAVIS & BOB peer into agent's office. We see AGENT, about 45, with WOMAN.
AGENT: Mrs. Bingham, by any chance do you know the number of the policy?	
WOMAN: No, I'm afraid not—but I think I have the last bill John Hancock sent me. Would that help? (Goes into purse.)	
AGENT: Yes, that'll give me just what I need.	
WOMAN: (Hands bill to agent)	
AGENT: (Writing it down) OK. Now the 1st thing we should do is make sure we get that new address.	
WOMAN: Oh, yes. It's 506 Whitman Rd.	
AGENT: Fine (writing). Now if you'll be kind enough to wait here for just a moment I'll be right back.	Agent exits, DAVIS & BOB watch him go.
DAVIS: You see, Bob, HANTEL stands for *HANCOCK*TELECOMMUNICATIONS. Right here in this office, we have a direct link to the computer system in our Boston Home Office. It's really a whole new way of doing business in the insurance industry.	

continued

AUDIO	**VIDEO**
DAVIS: (V/O)	AGENT arrives at clerical window . . . Gives request, info to HANTEL operator . . .
For example, Bob, with HANTEL our agents have instant access to a wide range of information contained in literally millions of John Hancock policies. We can do a lot of things in just seconds now that used to take us days through the mail. We can make necessary changes in policy information . . . and we can find out policy values that are up-to-the-minute!	HANTEL operator, on terminal: changes address to 506 Whitman Road. Calls up value screen and points to Cash Value, Accumulated Dividends figure and writes these down. Gives to Office Manager. CU: Check being written by OM (young male).
DAVIS: The machinery is something, Bob, but I'll tell you—Hantel's *real* value is the better service our clients get—and it sure helps the agents sell!	
	DAVIS & BOB
	AGENT'S OFFICE. Agent returns.
AGENT: OK, Mrs. Bingham, here's that money you needed (hands her check). We took it out of your dividends. You had plenty to spare.	
WOMAN: So soon? That's marvelous! *Thank* you *very* much!	
AGENT: Not at all. We're happy to help. While you're here, Mrs. Bingham, tell me about this new house of yours. Have you and your husband taken any steps to protect your mortgage?	
WOMAN: Well, I don't think we've done anything about that, no.	
AGENT: The biggest single investment most people make is in a home. Don't you agree?	
WOMAN: Oh, definitely.	
AGENT (V/O): Your home is important to your husband and yourself. I'd like the chance to talk to both of you together about making sure your options are left open . . .	CU, BOB, nodding in appreciation at this scene.
(fade out)	

continued

AUDIO

WIPE TO:
(FAST-MOVING SCENE)
<u>HINDENBURG:</u> SHIELDS?
<u>BOB:</u> Uh—yes.

<u>HINDENBURG:</u> Harry Hindenburg's the name—
insurance is my game! How
ya doin!

<u>BOB:</u> Pretty good, thank you . . .

<u>HINDENBURG:</u> (Slaps Bob on back, knocking him
over) That's great! Glad to hear it! You wanna be
an agent with us, right!

<u>BOB:</u> Well, I'd like to become an agent, yes, but I
haven't decided which company to go with quite
yet.

<u>HINDENBURG:</u> (Blowing smoke in Bob's face
as he talks) Oh, a comparison shopper eh? Very
smart, kid. I like your style.

<u>BOB:</u> (Coughing) Um . . . thanks. Where do you
think we should start?

<u>HINDENBURG:</u> Well . . . (thinking; suddenly, he
grabs Bob's shoulder, startling him). Come with
me! We've got the very latest in *communications!*
State-of-the-art stuff, you know what I mean?
Josephine, would you send that letter I gave you
to the Home Office now?

<u>JOSEPHINE:</u> Sure, Mr. H.

<u>HINDENBURG:</u> (to Bob): Our company uses
only the fastest birds.

<u>BOB:</u> Oh. where's your Home Office?

<u>HINDENBURG:</u> Ottawa.

VIDEO

Waiting room of Olde Fashioned Life. Bob
reading magazine. Hindenburg enters. He is
about 45 or older, short, rotund, smokes cigar,
conservatively dressed, looks old-fashioned:
belt and suspenders, hair parted down center &
slicked back, handle-bar moustache, early 20th
century look.

Josephine takes letter on her desk, folds it into tiny
square, opens bottom drawer of
desk, removes carrier pigeon, attaches letter
to leg, and throws bird out window.

continued

AUDIO	VIDEO
BOB: How long will it be before you get an answer?	
HINDENBURG: Well, usually about two months, but this is the mating season. Might take a little longer.	
WIPE TO:	Clerical area, JH. Bob & Davis talking. Davis holds folder.
DAVIS: You know, Bob, we try to organize our office to accomplish two things: to help our agents sell insurance, and to give our clients the quickest, most courteous service possible. Believe me, HANTEL has really made that easy.	

[The end of the program describes the actual working of HANTEL as it relates to specific insurance operations and procedures.]

"The Hantel Advantage" written by Frank King, Director, John Hancock Video Network, John Hancock Companies

APPLICATION: POWERPOINT AND AUDIO— INTERNAL TRAINING

Slide presentations that were once key approaches for corporate educational and training programs morphed into PowerPoint presentations. At certain levels of learning, visual motion is unnecessary and still pictures can be highly effective. The following PowerPoint presentation illustrates the how-to approach with narration. The program objective is to help employees learn why and how to use charts and graphs. The use of charts and graphs—still pictures—to teach the information is, therefore, especially appropriate.

The format of the script on the following pages, "Data Analysis and Display," written by David Brandt for use in manufacturing training by Avco Systems TEXTRON, has the visual information on the left, audio narration on the right. This script also contains an "instructional design" or "I.D." column—illustrations of the learning cues. Analyze the script for these cues, noting the sequence of modules relating to the presentation and reinforcement of information, including repetition, simplicity, and clarity. What elements do you find that motivate the employee to learn the material presented?

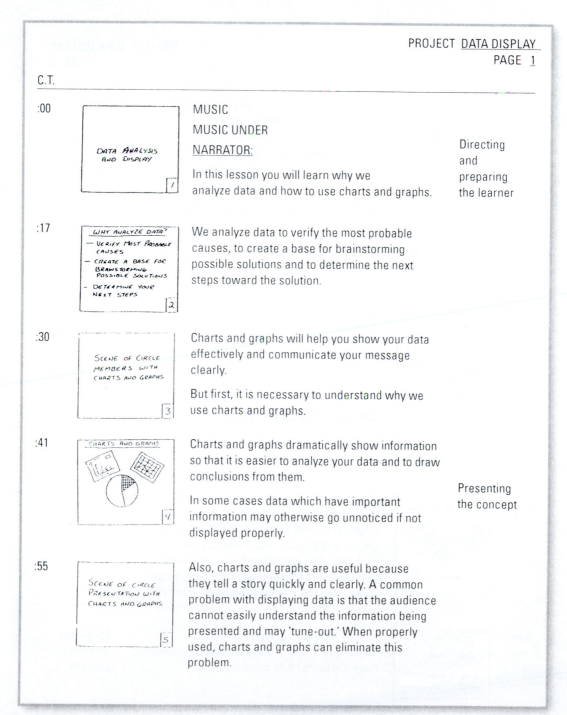

PROJECT <u>DATA DISPLAY</u>
PAGE <u>1</u>

C.T.

:00

DATA ANALYSIS
AND DISPLAY

1

MUSIC

MUSIC UNDER

<u>NARRATOR:</u>

In this lesson you will learn why we
analyze data and how to use charts and graphs.

Directing
and
preparing
the learner

:17

WHY ANALYZE DATA?
— VERIFY MOST PROBABLE
  CAUSES
— CREATE A BASE FOR
  BRAINSTORMING
  POSSIBLE SOLUTIONS
— DETERMINE YOUR
  NEXT STEPS

2

We analyze data to verify the most probable
causes, to create a base for brainstorming
possible solutions and to determine the next
steps toward the solution.

:30

SCENE OF CIRCLE
MEMBERS WITH
CHARTS AND GRAPHS

3

Charts and graphs will help you show your data
effectively and communicate your message
clearly.

But first, it is necessary to understand why we
use charts and graphs.

:41

CHARTS AND GRAPHS

4

Charts and graphs dramatically show information
so that it is easier to analyze your data and to draw
conclusions from them.

In some cases data which have important
information may otherwise go unnoticed if not
displayed properly.

Presenting
the concept

:55

SCENE OF CIRCLE
PRESENTATION WITH
CHARTS AND GRAPHS

5

Also, charts and graphs are useful because
they tell a story quickly and clearly. A common
problem with displaying data is that the audience
cannot easily understand the information being
presented and may 'tune-out.' When properly
used, charts and graphs can eliminate this
problem.

continued

1:13   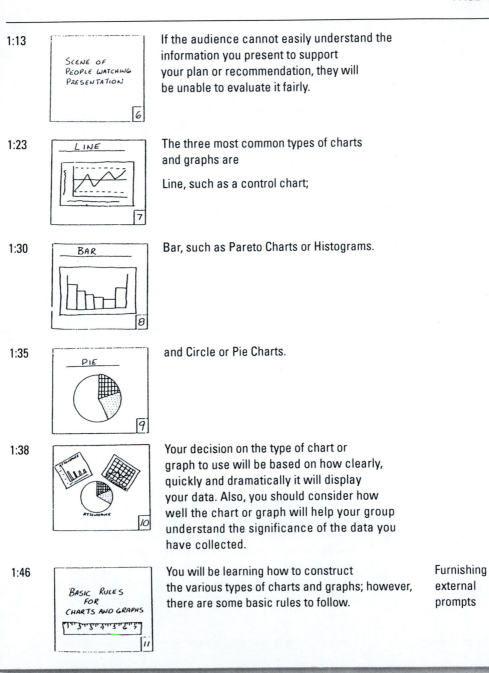   If the audience cannot easily understand the
information you present to support
your plan or recommendation, they will
be unable to evaluate it fairly.

1:23   The three most common types of charts
and graphs are

Line, such as a control chart;

1:30   Bar, such as Pareto Charts or Histograms.

1:35   and Circle or Pie Charts.

1:38   Your decision on the type of chart or
graph to use will be based on how clearly,
quickly and dramatically it will display
your data. Also, you should consider how
well the chart or graph will help your group
understand the significance of the data you
have collected.

1:46   You will be learning how to construct   Furnishing
the various types of charts and graphs; however,   external
there are some basic rules to follow.   prompts

continued

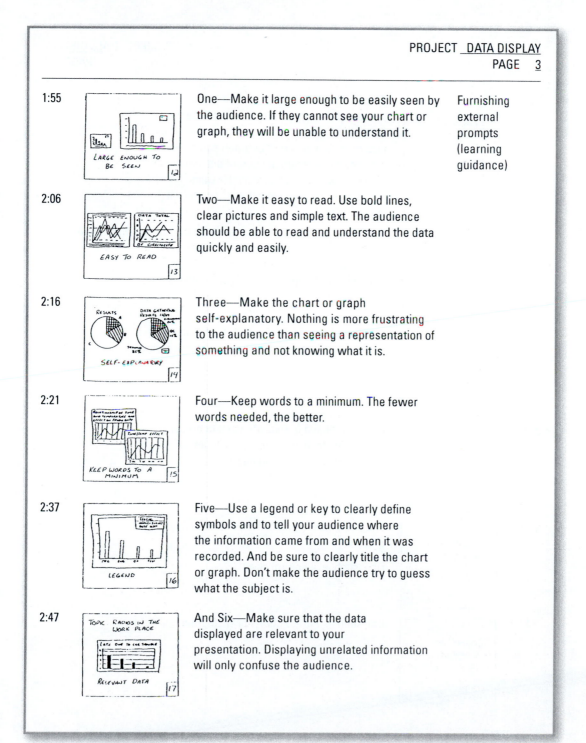

1:55	One—Make it large enough to be easily seen by the audience. If they cannot see your chart or graph, they will be unable to understand it.	Furnishing external prompts (learning guidance)
2:06	Two—Make it easy to read. Use bold lines, clear pictures and simple text. The audience should be able to read and understand the data quickly and easily.	
2:16	Three—Make the chart or graph self-explanatory. Nothing is more frustrating to the audience than seeing a representation of something and not knowing what it is.	
2:21	Four—Keep words to a minimum. The fewer words needed, the better.	
2:37	Five—Use a legend or key to clearly define symbols and to tell your audience where the information came from and when it was recorded. And be sure to clearly title the chart or graph. Don't make the audience try to guess what the subject is.	
2:47	And Six—Make sure that the data displayed are relevant to your presentation. Displaying unrelated information will only confuse the audience.	

continued

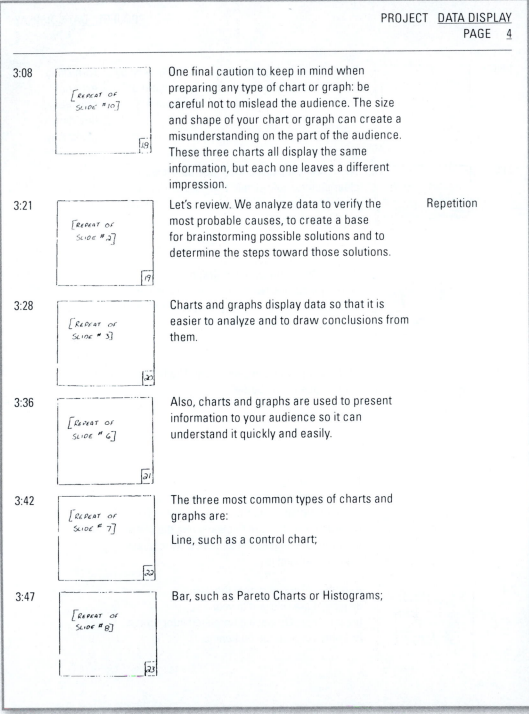

3:08

[REPEAT OF SLIDE #10]

19

One final caution to keep in mind when preparing any type of chart or graph: be careful not to mislead the audience. The size and shape of your chart or graph can create a misunderstanding on the part of the audience. These three charts all display the same information, but each one leaves a different impression.

3:21

[REPEAT OF SLIDE #2]

19

Let's review. We analyze data to verify the most probable causes, to create a base for brainstorming possible solutions and to determine the steps toward those solutions.

Repetition

3:28

[REPEAT OF SLIDE #3]

20

Charts and graphs display data so that it is easier to analyze and to draw conclusions from them.

3:36

[REPEAT OF SLIDE #6]

21

Also, charts and graphs are used to present information to your audience so it can understand it quickly and easily.

3:42

[REPEAT OF SLIDE #7]

22

The three most common types of charts and graphs are:

Line, such as a control chart;

3:47

[REPEAT OF SLIDE #8]

23

Bar, such as Pareto Charts or Histograms;

continued

PROJECT   <u>DATA DISPLAY</u>

PAGE   <u>5</u>

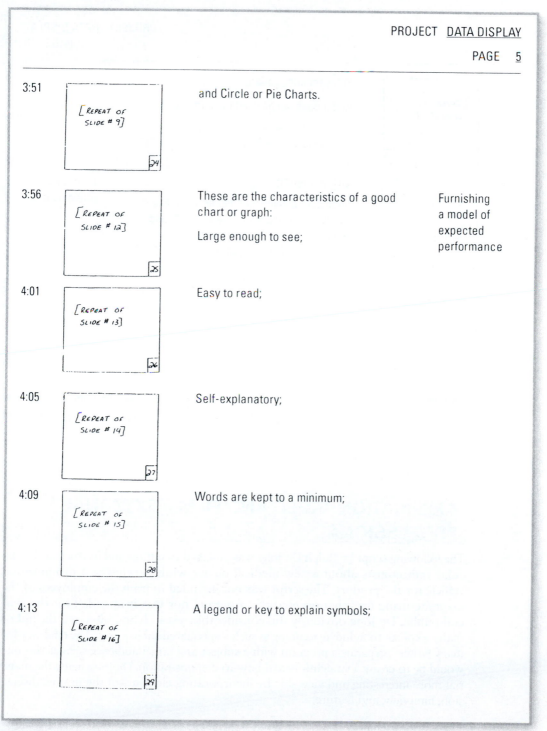

3:51   [REPEAT OF SLIDE # 9] |24|

and Circle or Pie Charts.

3:56   [REPEAT OF SLIDE # 12] |25|

These are the characteristics of a good chart or graph:

Large enough to see;

Furnishing a model of expected performance

4:01   [REPEAT OF SLIDE # 13] |26|

Easy to read;

4:05   [REPEAT OF SLIDE # 14] |27|

Self-explanatory;

4:09   [REPEAT OF SLIDE # 15] |28|

Words are kept to a minimum;

4:13   [REPEAT OF SLIDE # 16] |29|

A legend or key to explain symbols;

continued

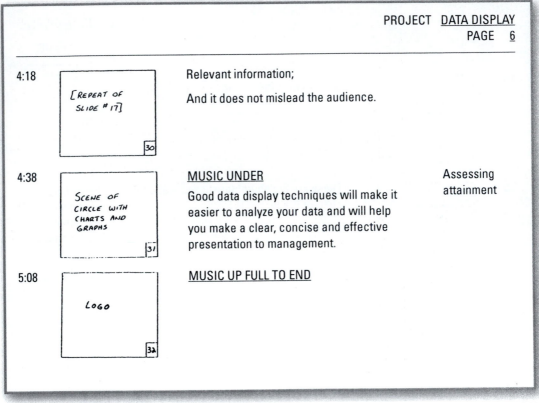

PROJECT <u>DATA DISPLAY</u>
PAGE <u>6</u>

4:18

[REPEAT OF
SLIDE #17]

30

Relevant information;

And it does not mislead the audience.

4:38

SCENE OF
CIRCLE WITH
CHARTS AND
GRAPHS

31

<u>MUSIC UNDER</u>
Good data display techniques will make it
easier to analyze your data and will help
you make a clear, concise and effective
presentation to management.

Assessing
attainment

5:08

LOGO

32

<u>MUSIC UP FULL TO END</u>

Written by David Brandt for Avco Systems TEXTRON

APPLICATION: VIDEO AND FILM—EXTERNAL PROFESSIONAL

The following script by Ralph De Jong was designed to inform and instruct cardiovascular radiologists about a new medical device while serving as a promotional vehicle for the product. The script was not intended to train the employees of the manufacturing firm that ordered the program, nor was it intended for the general public. De Jong obviously did considerable research and obtained the aid of many experts to achieve accuracy in such a specialized subject area. The tendency for many writers preparing a program with a subject and target audience such as this one would be to create a straightforward how-to demonstration. De Jong made the material more interesting and viewable by incorporating elements of the drama, discussion, interview, and feature.

What principal differences and similarities do you find in technique between this script and the John Hancock and Avco Systems scripts? "An idea I had," writer-producer De Jong stated, "was to include a 3-minute segment that could be lifted in toto and put into a continuous loop for screening in a convention display booth." Do you find this loop complete in itself? Does it maintain the continuity of the larger script? Though not designed for a retail store, it serves the same purpose as POP (point-of-purchase) videos by attempting to convince buyers seeing the product at professional convention sales booths to order it.

THE MINI-BALLOON APPROACH TO INTRAVASCULAR OCCLUSION

VISUAL	AUDIO
<u>TEASE</u>	
Angiography—Catheter Lab area: Johns Hopkins Hospital, Baltimore.	(SFX: AMBIENT SOUNDS/VOICES.)
LS: Personnel coming and going through double entry doors. A patient or two being wheeled in/out of lab area. Elevator to right in middle distance.	
Elevator doors open and several passengers emerge. Among them are a man and a woman. (Man is patient coming in for a varicocele procedure using the B-D MINI-BALLOON.)	
Man and woman take a few steps and encounter Robert White, MD, who has entered scene walking from behind camera-left. White is dressed in surgical gown, mask loose around neck. He is on his way to cat lab.	(SFX: WHITE, PATIENT, WOMAN EXCHANGE A FEW WORDS OF GREETING. WHITE ASKS PATIENT HOW HE FEELS, ETC. WHITE TELLS PATIENT HE WILL SEE HIM SHORTLY.)
Patient and woman walk off-camera. White heads for cat lab.	
Camera follows as White passes through entry doors. White full frame.	
White joins several other MDs who are examining radiographs depicting a pulmonary arteriovenous fistula	

continued

VISUAL

malformation or other condition suitable for MINI-BALLOON occlusion.

Close in slowly on MD group.

Continue moving in, focusing on pulmonary AVM radiograph displayed on light box.

Begin series of cuts of diagnostic radiographs, matched to narrative.

Carotid cavernous fistula.

Bronchial pulmonary artery fistula.

Hemobilia.

Renal traumatic aneurysm.

Varicocele.

Show two or three other conditions suitable for MINI-BALLOON occlusion; i.e., vascular head and neck neoplasm/hepatic artery branch/ traumatic fistula or aneurysms of non-essential branch/or dry field surgery. Shots should be tight enough and on long enough for relatively experienced eye to identify problem.

Final diagnostic radiograph serves as freeze-frame which becomes live-action cine of MINI-BALLOON procedure in progress: dye being injected and balloon catheter coming on-screen—for positioning.

[LOOP SECTION BEGINS]

AUDIO

(SFX: CONVERSATION AMONG MDs IS HEARD MOMENTARILY AS THEY DISCUSS MEDICAL PROBLEM SEEN, THEN FADES UNDER AS NARRATOR SPEAKS.)

NARRATOR V/O
These radiologists are discussing a nonsurgical technique for occluding blood vessels—a technique that can be performed with local anesthesia—and, generally, with less patient risk than that associated with the injection of particulate embolic material.

The procedure about to be performed on this patient is also suitable as the therapy of choice for other vascular conditions that may exist in various parts of the body . . .

. . . carotid cavernous fistula . . .

. . . bronchial pulmonary artery fistula . . .

. . . hemobilia . . .

. . . renal traumatic aneurysm . . .

. . . varicocele . . .

. . . and others . . .

(NO COMMENTARY)

(SFX: FADE IN MUSIC LOW, THEN UNDER.)

NARRATOR V/O

This is balloon embolotherapy—a proven technique for transcatheter vascular occlusion. The procedure seen here centers on the use of a detachable balloon

continued

VISUAL	AUDIO
Cine continues: MINI-BALLOON seen being reversed, positioned, inflated and detached as Main Title crawls.	system—a system that provides control, reversibility and precise placement at the desired point of occlusion.

VISUAL

Cine continues: MINI-BALLOON seen being reversed, positioned, inflated and detached as Main Title crawls.

MAIN TITLE

THE MINI-BALLOON
APPROACH TO
INTRAVASCULAR
OCCLUSION
Presented by
BECTON-DICKINSON AND COMPANY

Cine continues briefly after titles, then go to brief lap dissolve of slightly elevated, moderate wide angle pull-back revealing preceding cine on portable viewer screen: angled OTS of radiologist's POV. (RADIOLOGY LIBRARY) Radiologist seen at portable viewer, looking at screen.

Continue pull-back to reveal radiologist and narrator in library.

During pull-back, narrator, with medical journal in hand, walks from bookstacks to portable viewer, glances at screen, then speaks on-camera. (Narrator dressed in casual attire: somewhat tweedy jacket, tie, etc.)

MS.

MCU.

AUDIO

system—a system that provides control, reversibility and precise placement at the desired point of occlusion.

(SFX: CROSSFADE TO RADIOLOGY LIBRARY AMBIENCE.)

NARRATOR (ON-CAMERA)

Until the 1930s, surgical ligation was the only technique available for occluding a specific blood vessel.

Then, in that year, a minute particle of muscle tissue was implanted percutaneously to embolize a carotid cavernous fistula.

While the procedure was successful, it was not until the early 1960s that advances in medical technology made it possible for intravascular occlusion techniques to be explored and developed more extensively.

continued

VISUAL

Camera follows as narrator walks to library table.

Cut to CU L-R pan: assorted embolic/occlusion materials and devices, ending with B-D MINI-BALLOON system.

Cut to table-top MS: Narrator in background, half-seated at end of library table top. Embolic/occluding devices in foreground. MINI-BALLOON system closest to narrator. Narrator gestures toward materials while speaking.

Move slowly over devices toward narrator, stopping as narrator picks up MINI-BALLOON catheter.

Cut to OTS: MINI-BALLOON catheter in narrator's hands.

Slow zoom toward MINI-BALLOON, going to out-of-focus and dissolving to:

ANIMATION: Flow-direction feature of MINI-BALLOON.

ANIMATION: Positioning of MINI-BALLOON in vessel.

ANIMATION: MINI-BALLOON inflation and detachment.

ANIMATION: hold momentarily on detached balloon in vessel.

[LOOP SECTION ENDS]

AUDIO

Since then different types of particulate material and mechanical devices have been injected—by way of a catheter—to promote vascular occlusion.

(NO COMMENTARY THROUGH PAN.)

Today, each of these is used for intravascular occlusion. When they are used and how they are used depends on the medical problem involved, the condition of the patient, and the skill and experience of the physician.

Of these, only one provides permanent vessel occlusion where you want it—when you want it.

NARRATOR (ON-CAMERA)

This is the Becton-Dickinson detachable MINI-BALLOON system.

When the MINI-BALLOON is injected into a vessel by way of a catheter . . . it becomes flow-directed.

(SFX: FADE OUT LIBRARY AMBIENCE TO DEAD AIR.)

And, because it is tethered, the MINI-BALLOON is completely controllable—it can be guided forward or backward so that it can be placed precisely at the desired point of occlusion.

Once in position, the MINI-BALLOON is inflated . . . and detached.

continued

VISUAL

Dissolve to MLS: cat lab corridor.

Move in to MS, then to MCU of White and two other physicians seen at left studying radiographs of varicocele.

XCU: Syringe in hand, smooth injection.

Dissolve to cine: balloon injection.

<u>NOTE:</u> From here, visuals are combo of live action and cine. Included are: balloon positioning, flow-directability, reversibility, inflation, deflation to reposition, re-inflation and final positioning, detachment and catheter removal. During this sequence, use modified split-screen with circular cine inserted with live action.

AUDIO

(SFX: FADE IN CAT LAB AREA AMBIENCE.)

<u>WHITE AND COLLEAGUES</u>

(PICK UP BRIEFLY ON CONVERSATION AMONG WHITE AND COLLEAGUES DISCUSSING

VARICOCELE CONDITION SEEN ON RADIOGRAPH. COMMENTS CENTERING ON PROBLEM AND WHAT NEEDS TO BE DONE.)

* * *

<u>WHITE</u>

Once you have blood back and a good seal, then we simply give a nice smooth injection . . . until the balloon catheter is well beyond where you want to send it.

(PAUSE)

(<u>NOTE:</u> WHITE'S COMMENTS FROM HERE TO INCLUDE BALLOON MANIPULATION, FLOW DIRECTION, REVERSIBILITY, INFLATION, DEFLATION TO REPOSITION, RE-INFLATION AND FINAL POSITIONING, BALLOON DETACHMENT AND CATHETER REMOVAL. ALSO INCLUDE TEST INJECTION TO SEE BRIDGING COLLATERALS.)

continued

VISUAL

Final cat lab sequence: circular cine inserted with live action. Cine shows balloon in position. Slowly expand cine insert to full-screen, then slowly dissolve to CU of White removing catheter and begin lazy pull-back to MLS of procedure wrap-up. White, tech(s) and patient; then patient being wheeled out of lab. White and tech(s) having conversation, relaxed.

MLS: White and tech(s) talking, patient being wheeled out of cat lab.

Insert dissolve cuts: reprise of opening diagnostic radiographs.

Dissolve in complete ANIMATION sequence.

Dissolve to full-screen cine: reprise of footage appearing behind Main Title as end credits crawl.

AUDIO

WHITE

(AFTER FINAL COMMENTS REGARDING PROCEDURE, TALKS BRIEFLY CITING PERSONAL EXPERIENCE WITH MINIBALLOON PROCEDURE (STRAIGHT, NO HARD SELL) AND THE TECHNIQUE, GIVING SUGGESTION ON APPROPRIATE MEDICAL CONDITIONS TO BEGIN WITH AND SOME TO WORK UP TO, THEN SHIFTS TO BRIEF CHAT WITH PATIENT, WITH PATIENT RESPONDING.)

(CONVERSATION WITH TECH(S) UP MOMENTARILY, THEN SLOWLY CROSS FADING TO MUSIC LOW AND UNDER, COMING IN WITH RADIOGRAPH REPRISE.)

NARRATOR V/O

MINI-BALLOON embolotherapy—a nonsurgical approach to intravascular occlusion.

A proven technique suitable as the therapy of choice for a wide range of vascular conditions . . .

. . . a procedure that centers on the use of a detachable balloon system—a system that provides control . . . reversibility . . . and precise placement at the desired point of occlusion.

(SFX: MUSIC UP THEN FADE OUT.)

Courtesy of Ralph J. De Jong, President, WORDSYNC, Harpers Ferry, W. Va.

APPLICATION: VIDEO—EXTERNAL INFORMATION AND PUBLIC RELATIONS

Well Aware was a video series written, produced, and directed by Barbara Allen for Memorial Hospital in York, Pennsylvania. Shown principally on cable, the series had several objectives: To inform the public about common medical problems; to teach the public how to deal with those problems—in some instances through personal treatment, exercise, diet, and similar approaches not requiring medical supervision and in other instances by consulting a physician; and to create positive feelings about Memorial Hospital through this public service program.

Using her background as a documentary writer-producer for broadcast and non-broadcast television, Allen incorporated several techniques, including interviews, demonstration, and feature material. Though informational, this program has a lighter approach than the training program. Because it seeks a general audience in the community, it must be entertaining as well as informative to attract and keep the viewer.

The following description and analysis of her work as a writer for the series was especially prepared by Allen for this book.

What does a writer have to know when he or she also wears the hats of director, co-host, and, sometimes, editor? This is how it works for me.

Well Aware is produced entirely on location, of necessity. The hospital is not equipped with a video studio. A professional videographer and grip, or sound person, are hired. The hospital's PR manager and executive producer of *Well Aware*, Sheryl Randol, serves as co-host. The budget is a very modest one, and recording is limited to one-and-a-half to two days.

It's important for the writer to be "well aware" of all of these factors in order to

1. Limit locations to fit into the time schedule and budget, while seeking the most varied backgrounds within each location. It's amazing what you can do with a few plants, some colored gels, a different angle and some well chosen wall hangings.

2. Be prepared to switch to a pre-arranged indoor location for a scheduled outdoor shoot cancelled by rain or snow.

To accomplish these, the writer must have a thorough knowledge of production techniques. It also helps to be patient, very flexible, and have a great sense of humor.

The producer of *Well Aware* makes all arrangements for crew, participants, and locations. Therefore, I must tell her what categories of people or experts are needed, what kinds of locations, the activities to be recorded at those locations and any special equipment or props that might not ordinarily be available at those locations. All of this information saves time and money. I prepare a very specific, second-to-second editing script, with all shot selections shown, as well as dissolves, fades, pushes, music selections and other special instructions.

Then my job is done . . . until the next program . . . and the videographer/editor prepares the master tape.

Following is the first segment of the script of one half-hour Well Aware *program. It is followed by the final minutes of the program, in which the institutional public relations aspect is included. Note the listing of the address of Memorial Hospital for obtaining written material on the program's subject, and the lines "Memorial Hospital wants you well . . . and well aware of everything that affects your health. Won't you tell your neighbors and friends about us?" At the beginning of the script is a needs-assessment list prepared by the writer for the producer. At the end is a sample list of questions prepared by the writer for one of the interviews.*

The finished working script is reproduced here with the writer-director's notes and check marks included.

WELL AWARE   LOW BACK PAIN

PEOPLE	PLACES	ACTIVITIES	EQUIP/PROPS
TEASE			
Person #1	Outside, driveway,	Lifting grocery bags out of trunk	Car, 2 brown bags with stuffing; some groceries on top
Person #2	Doorway, PR house	Bending to pick up newspaper	Newspaper
Person #3	At window, PR house	Washing window	Bucket, water, long handled squeegee, ladder
OPEN AND CLOSE	Children's playground	Comments	
BA			
SEGMENT #1			
Reporter #1	Empty room for demos.	Demos.	See script, Pg. 3,4
Orthopod	Clinical setting	Interview	Skeleton, part of spine from PT, poss. slides
SEGMENT #2			
BA			
Orthopod	Different clinical setting; office?	Interview	
Gloria Miller, PT	PT dept.	Interview and demos. hot pack, ultra sound, massage, Back Trac etc.	Those needed for activities
2 real patients, if poss.	.		
SEGMENT #3			
Sheryl	Empty room	Demo. exercises and tips	See script, pg. 7,8
Gloria			
2 people to demonstrate			

NOTE: PERSONS IN TEASE AND PEOPLE TO DEMONSTRATE MAY BE SAME PEOPLE

continued

<u>Well Aware</u>   LOW BACK PAIN   **Page 1**

TEASE

VIDEO	AUDIO
	MUSIC UNDER SILENT ACTION
PERSON LIFTING GROCERY BAGS FROM CAR TRUNK.. PAINED!	
PERSON REACHING DOWN TO PICK UP NEWSPAPER AT DOOR...PAIN!	
PERSON ON LADDER STRETCHING DOWN, THEN UP TO WASH WINDOW...PAIN!	
	BA- Ohhh...their aching backs! If back pain has you in a bind, we have some help for you. Coming up next...on Well Aware.
GENERIC OPEN	GENERIC OPEN

continued

Well Aware   LOW BACK PAIN   Page   2

VIDEO	AUDIO
	OPEN
WS BA AT SWINGS *or other playground equip.*	✓ BA- Welcome to Well Aware, Memorial Hospital's monthly program devoted to you, your family and your health.
	I'm Barbara Allen, host for this month, and I have a confession to make. Today's topic is really close to my...back. Remember when we were little and used to flip and twist and hang and swing on equipment like this? Not anymore.
MS ANOTHER ANGLE	My back problems started over 25 years ago when I helped a friend lift and pull a heavy steamer trunk up a long flight of concrete steps and into a house.
	It was a stupid thing to do, but I felt invulnerable then. Now.... after years of recurring back problems, I don't feel invulnerable anymore.

continued

VIDEO	AUDIO

Well Aware   LOW BACK PAIN   Page ___3___

VIDEO

CU   BA

MCU JOANNE IN DR. N's OFFICE ✔

✔DEMOS

JOANNE

2 SHOT

AUDIO

Today we're going to be looking at some of the causes of low back pain...why it happens, how to treat it, and, perhaps most important, how to prevent it from happening again. Joanne Reeser gets us started.

JOANNE- Here's a quick test for you on the causes of back pain. Which of the following are true?

Back pain can be caused by:
1) lifting heavy boxes without bending your knees;
2) turning on a lamp
3) pulling your boots off
4) sneezing

If you said TRUE to the first two, you're right. If you also said TRUE to 3 and 4, you are 100% right.

Dr. Dean Nachtigall specializes in orthopedics, or the skeletal and muscular structure of your body.

continued

VIDEO	AUDIO
	Dr. Nachtigall, I read that back pain strikes 60-80% of us and that low back pain is the price we pay for upright posture. Is that true? ...Why?
	Let's go back to some of the causes in our true-false test.
REPEAT DEMOS	Heavy lifting without bending the knees is clearly a cause, but turning on a lamp?...and pulling your boots off?.... *What happened to that flexible little body that used to swing on jungle gyms?*
VARY 2 SHOT AND CUs	What is it about our spine that makes us so vulnerable to injury and pain?(slipped or bulging disc?)
	Getting back to our true/false test, why can sneezing be bad?...
REpEAT DEMO	What are some of the other common causes?(high-heeled shoes, restrictive clothing, drafts, dampness, low calcium levels, lack of exercise, kidney infections, psychological tension)
	Can we inherit the tendency to back problems?(arthritis, osteo-porosis, structural problems, muscle weakness)

continued

Well Aware   LOW BACK PAIN   Page 5

VIDEO   AUDIO

CU JOANNE   JOANNE- Whatever the cause, when
                                   you injure your back, the odds
                                   are the pain won't go away by itself.
                                        What can you do at home, and
                                   where do you go from there to
                                   get relief?
                                        Coming up next...with Barbara
                                   Allen, right after this message
LOGO   from Memorial Hospital, sponsor
                                   of Well Aware.

                                              SEGMENT #3

GLORIA AND SHERYL DO   *Mention giving address for*
EXERCISES AND GIVE   *exercises + tips at end of*
TIPS   *program.*
DEMOS on all tips   (AT END OF SEGMENT)
                                   Sheryl- Have you been listening,
                                   Barbara?

continued

Well Aware   LOW BACK PAIN   Page 10

VIDEO	AUDIO
BA AT TOP OF CHILD'S SLIDE ON PLAYGROUND BUT YOU CAN'T SEE SLIDE ADDRESS ON CHAR. GEN.	BA- You bet I have Sheryl. And here's how YOU can get copies of these exercises as well as the tips. Write to: Well Aware- Low back pain Public Relations Department Memorial Hospital P.O. Box M-118 York, PA 17405 I'll repeat that in a moment. I can remember a college health teacher who, in teaching good posture, would parade us around in a circle while she proclaimed, "Hitch your sternum to a star." It was funny then....It's not funny anymore. She was right! As simple a thing as standing and sitting properly can help keep back problems away for years to come. If I had to give one piece of advice to people who have never had back problems, it would be..

continued

| Well Aware | LOW BACK PAIN | Page ___11___ |

VIDEO

AUDIO

CHAR. GEN.

Repeat

BA- Don't press your luck.

Once they start, it seems they can be with you, off and on, for the rest of your life.

SO...here's that address again for the exercises and tips.

Remember...what's important before you begin any exercise program, be sure to check with your doctor first.

Memorial Hospital wants you well... and wellaware of everything that affects your health. *Won't you tell your neighbors and friends about us?*

Until next time, I'm Barbara Allen wishing you the very BEST of health!

Maybe just once?

SLOW ZOOM OUT TO SHOW
BA STANDING AT TOP OF
CHILDREN'S SLIDE

SHE BENDS, AND PUTS ONE LEG
STRAIGHT OUT AS IF TO
SLIDE DOWN

FADE TO BLUE

CREDITS

CLOSING MUSIC

Written by Barbara Allen. Courtesy of Ms. Allen and Memorial Hospital, York, PA.

THE INTERNET

One of the leaders in producing and writing corporate materials for the Internet is the Pangaea Multimedia Communications Corporation. (See the extensive article on media technology by Pangaea's president, Eric Johnston, in Chapter 2) Pangaea writes and produces corporate materials ranging from training programs to public relations presentations to informational projects to conferences on the Internet. One such production, entitled "Interactive Streaming Video for the Web," written by Steve LaRochelle, is an example of a corporate script for the Internet and a seminar on writing and creating an interactive web site. As you read it, the "Notes" column will give you additional explanations of writing and producing purposes and techniques. When you have finished studying this script, check the Pangaea web site for sample templates used for Internet scripts, at www.pmcc.com/templates.

INTERACTIVE STREAMING VIDEO FOR THE WEB

Seminar on Demand
Post on web target: January 15

AUDIO	VIDEO	GRAPHICS URL FLIPS	NOTES
WORKFLOW **Workflow.mov** SL-OC: Welcome to the Interactive Streaming Seminar on Demand. My name is Steve. And my name is Tara. We are going to give a behind-the-scene look at what it takes to create an interactive Web site using video to drive all the interactivity.	MS: Informal shot... Tara and Steve sitting on couch. Rich blue light in background.... 20/20 look	none	We will want to keep the files sizes small to improve online performance. Video will automatically play.
TB-OC: Just click on the word "Introduction" to start the seminar.	Video fades to black		All video will only fade to black at the end. NO fade up from black.

continued

AUDIO	VIDEO	GRAPHICS URL FLIPS	NOTES
INTRODUCTION **Introduction.mov**			Have to click on "Site Overview" to start video.
TB-OC: The video you are watching now will *automatically* open different graphics and flash animations in the frame below. And any time you see a glow around an object, such as the one you see over my shoulder, you can click on it for more information.	MS: Informal shot . . . Tara and Steve sitting on couch. Rich blue light in background. . . . 20/20 look	Graphic—Company Inc. EStream Technology Graphic hotspot—camcorder Graphic: Freeze frame of Ski Site	
SL-OC: After you watch this seminar, you'll have a good idea of what it takes to put together an interactive Web site. We are going to use a *waterskiing* Web site that we produced to demonstrate some of the interactivity. To see the waterskiing Web site at any time, click on the link "example site" located in the top left corner of the sliding menu.			
TB: At this point please go to the water ski site and check out some of the interactivity, then come back here learn how we put the site together.			
TB & SL: See you in a few minutes.			
CAPTURE—Viewer has to click on Design, Shoot or Capture to start the video.			
Design: Design.mov	Video fades to black		
SL-VO: The first thing we did was come up with a objective for the site. In our case this waterskiing club wanted to document the season finals. Our objective was to create an interactive site that allows *individual*	Misc shot of event	Graphic: freeze frame of skier	

continued

AUDIO	VIDEO	GRAPHICS URL FLIPS	NOTES
skiers to see specific runs without having to look at a very long videotape.			
TB-VO: Steve and I had to figure out how we were going to show the skiers and add interactivity. So we started to *sketch* out the design of the Web site. A little later in the workflow you will see why planning the functionality of the site is very important to work out early in the process.	SL and TB in edit suite with pad of paper sketching design . . . use CU and MS shots	Graphic: sketches from paper Frame set sample	Need to videotape paper—use as graphic
Shoot: shoot.mov			
SL-VO: We used *three* cameras for the shoot, one on the beach, one from the edge of the woods on the lake, and one in a boat. You'll get the best results for your Web video if you use a tripod and turn off the auto focus control.	Footage from beach, shore, boat. Same shot . . . End with 3 cameras in video. USE PAUSE EVENT. Glow around each camera. Click on:	Graphic: Diagram of lake. Cameras in position . . . shore, woods, boat Graphic: Camera on tripod, text—"Auto focus—off"	
TEXT—**XL 1**—Steve says, "This is an excellent 3 chip camera. The size of the camera makes it easy to balance on your shoulder."	XL1—see URL flip	Graphic—XL1 with text comment & specs	
Elura—Tara notes, "I can't believe the quality of video you can get with a video camera that fits in the palm of your hand."	Elura—see URL flip	Graphic—Elura with text comment & specs	
Optura—Steve says, "The flip out screen is great for review of your shots." Tara says, "With the easy to use menu I could quickly adjust for different exposures and fast action."	Optura—see URL flip	Graphic—Optura with text comment & specs	

continued

AUDIO	VIDEO	GRAPHICS URL FLIPS	NOTES
Capture: capture.mov TB-VO: With all the planning and taping complete, we need to *capture* our video. In our case we used Company connected to a DV deck with an SDI option. With Company products, Mac or *Windows* based, you have the flexibility to capture your video via analog or digital connectors.	TB capturing video. Insert tape, control deck with app, insert another tape, move mouse, etc . . . PAUSE COMMAND AT END OF VIDEO Have a Cleaner 5 box in the shot . . . Have glow around box. (Box is hot spot.) GO TO COMMAND on hot spot	Graphic: Junction box, computer and deck connected to MAC Graphic: Same as above but iFinish	Hot spot on the C5 box
GO TO . . . SL-OC—You found the hot spot. You can capture directly to Cleaner as long as your Mac or PC has a Firewire connector. Cleaner 5 used MotoDV software for capturing video	SL on camera. Video fades to black	Hot spot trigger. Cleaner 5 application Show capture menu item. Graphic of deck connected to PC or Mac	
Edit: must click Company I or iFinish 4 to start video **Company i: editm100.mov** TB-OC: For the waterski site we used Company i to edit the video together. Once we had the video on the hard drive, we could see picture icons of the media in the bin window. We would trim the *video* in the edit suite and then bring the *video* to the program time line. While using the timeline, we *matched* the action between the three different cameras. We also decided to strip the natural sound and add music. If you are new to video editing, you'll find the interface very intuitive and the system very responsive.	TB—Talking to camera sitting in front of Mac system in edit suite.	Flash— **editm100.swf** Start with WS of bin, edit suite & program. Enlarge & shrink bin shot. Enlarge & shrink Edit suite. Enlarge time line. Slide timeline down & shrink. Add three clips. Open slip window. Video in slip window will	

continued

AUDIO	VIDEO	GRAPHICS URL FLIPS	NOTES
		show matched action between different camera angles. **Pop on text** ... match action with "Slip and Slide"	
iFinish 4: editfinish.mov SL: The video you are *watching* now was edited using iFinish 4. This, too, was shot in the DV format. iFinish 4 has the same interface as Company i. One additional feature in iFinish 4 is the ability to *master* to MPEG right from the timeline. You can bring these MPEG files right into an DVD authoring package such as Sonic Solutions DVDit! PE for creating interactive DVDs.		Flash— **editfinish.swf** WS of interface. Master to MPEG selection MPEG mastering window **Pop on text ...** MPEG 1, MPEG 2, system, program and elementary streams Data rates up to 50 megabits, 4:2:1 I Frame	Note: This could be graphic url flips instead of flash
Effects—must click compositing to start video **Compositing: composite.mov** SL-VO: The waterski *site* does not have any layers of video or composite effects. However, if we wanted to *create* some special effects we could use the componsite feature found in Company i or iFinish 4. The composition clip will automatically access Boris FX. Here you have direct access to your bins and unlimited layers. When your composite is complete, you'll notice you take up only one layer in your timeline. This feature gives you the	MS—over the shoulder of Steve. Glow around Boris box. Cut to composite examples created in Boris FX (or composited waterski clip.) End with over the shoulder shot. In each shot put glow around Boris document box.	Graphic: **composite.swf** Timeline with comp clip being stretched out. Boris window comes out of comp clip. Bin pops open. Close bin. Dissolve on many layers. Close Boris. Show timeline with comp clip.	Could use a Boris demo here or create a composite of water ski stuff. If create new piece, then make link from Ossipee main title to the

continued

AUDIO	VIDEO	GRAPHICS URL FLIPS	NOTES
power to create what you think and keep your timeline organized.	Fade to black		newly created composited piece.
GO TO on Boris Box Music under video	Go To video More "Boris" examples	**Hotspot Graphic: borisbox.gif** Boris Box and text with some features, functions and benefits	
Character Generation: cg.mov TB-VO: In the waterskiing video we created three buttons using the character generator. Just create the length of your title in the graphics track, then access the character generator. In this part of the application it's easy to create button with text over the top. You also have the ability to animate these titles and create 3D text. Company i uses Graffiti and iFinish 4 uses Inscriber.	Water ski video with buttons. Dip to black. Show water ski video again, but buttons with text tumble on. Dip to black. Buttons tumble on, then 3D text tumbles on.	Graphic: **cg.swf** Timeline stretch out graphic. Boris interface flies out of graphic clip. Cut to completed "text over video" In Graffiti window. Dissolve off Boris window dissolve on Inscriber window. . . . iFinish 4 text on screen.	

Test Your Knowledge: tyn.mov TB-VO: When creating an interactive video, what is the first task you should do?
    A. Shoot the video
    B. Edit the video
    C. Design the interactivity
    D. Order a pizza
  "GO TO VIDEO. . . .
    A. This is not correct. How do you know what to shoot if you don't know what you are creating? Go back and try again.
	Graphic Video with hot spot on answers. See audio for text applied to screen.
	
	TB on-camera: "Questions" hot spot Back button on video.
	
	Read answer. Fade to black		

continued

AUDIO	VIDEO	GRAPHICS URL FLIPS	NOTES
B. Edit the video? You need to shoot it first. Go back and try again.	Read answer. Fade to black		
C. You are correct. It's always a good idea to sketch out your ideas before you start spending money on tape stock and hiring any production personnel.	Read answer. And so on . . .	1. no url flip 2. no url flip 3. url flip—ideas, design, write, shoot, edit, author, encode, post	
D. Eating pizza can foster new ideas, but it is not necessarily the first thing you want to do. Go back and try again.		4. no url flip	

Author
HTML: authorhtml.mov

TB & SL—OC—When Steve and I produced the waterski site we started by creating an html document which was a frame set. The key element for us at this point is to name our frames . . . these are called "Target names."	TB & SL OC—. . . next to system—edit suite. GoLive and Dream-weaver box in background, but no glow.	Graphics— **authorhtml.swf** Show Dream- weaver and GoLive box. Text—"Drag and drop HTML editors." Dissolve on frame set graphic. Point out target name. Three little "html docs." Slide docs, one at a time, into a frame. Text at top of frame "Content."	This will be the most compli-cated flash animation of the entire project. Good luck.
SL—Individual graphic, text and movie html documents are created. When the video plays, our embedded triggers will call up the appropriate html document. Then open it in the proper frame.			
TB—For example, let's say we wanted a graphic to open in the frame below us. And that frame is called "Content." First we would open a blank html document. Then we would drop a graphic plug-in on that document. Next we would link a document or piece of media to that plug-in. Finally, we would save that html document in a folder called pages. When the video plays it will		Blank html doc & Palette. Animate plug-in to html doc Show Frame Inspector. Pop on file name.	

continued

AUDIO	VIDEO	GRAPHICS URL FLIPS	NOTES
look to the Pages folder. Find the html document. Then open that document in the Content frame below us.		Have that page push back into a "Pages" folder.	
		Graphic of Company logo opens in content frame.	
SL—The graphic you are looking at right now was triggered by this video. To keep all of our files organized, we put all of our media in a folder called Media and all of our html documents in a folder called Pages. If you click on one of these objects that glow, you'll see a hotspot trigger. Check out the eStream section for more details.	Two hot spots appear— GoLive and Dreamweaver boxes have glow. Action is URL flip of each package	**HOT SPOT GRAPHIC:** Dreamweaver— **Dream.html—box with features, function benefits in text**	
		GoLive— **Golive.html** GoLive box with feature, function, benefit in text.	
EStream: authorstream.mov SL—OC—To create the triggers you saw in the water ski video, we'll focus on one water skier, Stephanie Krebs. If you click on her you will see the ski she is using and the wet suit that she is wearing. To create the hot spot we used the following steps.	Fade to black Next video will cut between SL and TB. SL—OC	Graphic— **authors.swf** Freeze frame of Stephaine	
TB—If you look at the skier you'll notice that she stays in a certain area of the screen for almost the entire video. So we placed an event mark near the beginning of the video. We defined the event as hot spot. Next we created the area which remains hot. We also defined the duration of that hot spot.		Fade on timeline EStream window shot hot spot area	
SL—Now we need to define the action of the hot spot. So we type in the location of the graphic file we		Action window show URL and target	

continued

AUDIO	VIDEO	GRAPHICS URL FLIPS	NOTES
wanted triggered and the target frame. In this case the target frame is called Leftcontent.			
TB—The next step is to encode the video using Cleaner 5. We cover the details in the Encode section of this seminar.	Fade to black		

Written by Steve LaRochelle for Pangaea Multimedia Communications Corporation, Arlington, Massachusetts, USA www.pmcc.com.

Formal Education Programs

The formal lesson designed for classroom use has provided students in many schools with subject matter not available in those particular schools. The formal lesson, as well as the informal lesson or material resource, makes it possible for experts in any given area to reach virtually any classroom anywhere either through pre-produced videos or live via the Internet. Sometimes the student receiving instruction via media, either briefly or extensively, is experiencing and where possible participating in an established class either in another school or from a central site. More effective, however, is the media course or subject matter carefully planned and targeted toward a particular student demographic, including age, class level, geographic area, cultural and/or ethnic background, economic status, and all the other factors that indicate the student group's and hopefully the individual student's readiness and motivation to learn the specified educational material.

The formal instructional program writer is, to a great degree, a planner. Writing the program begins with the cooperative planning of the curriculum coordinator, the studio teacher, the classroom teacher, the educational administrator, the producer, the media specialist, and the writer. The writer must accept from the educational experts the purposes and contents of each program. However, she or he should stand firm on the manner of presentation. Many educators are prone to use the media as a classroom extension, incorporating into the programs techniques that might work well in the classroom but are ineffective for the media.

Most important, the writer should avoid the "talking head"—presenting the learning materials the same way it is done by the teacher in the classroom. The media should be used to do what renowned educator John Dewey advocated as a key to good education: Bring the classroom to the world and the world to the classroom.

Approach

First, the writer must determine the learning goals and contents and the lengths of the individual programs. After that he or she can begin outlining each segment.

The outline should carefully follow the lesson plan for each unit as developed by the educational experts. Stress important topics; play down unimportant ones. Some instructional programs are not fully scripted, but are produced from detailed outlines or rundowns. Script preparation is similar to that done for the comparable feature, interview, or corporate program.

Most instructional programs have studio teachers—teachers who conduct the media lesson. Some excellent classroom teachers are poor on camera; and some teachers who do not come across well in the classroom are excellent on camera. Sometimes a professional performer is hired to play the role of the teacher. The detail in the script can vary depending on the competence of the on-camera instructor.

Even in the outline stage the writer should explore the given medium's special qualities that can present the content more effectively than in the classroom. Infuse creativity and entertainment into the learning materials. The instructional writer needs to stimulate the viewer-learner and relate the material to the student's real-life experiences.

Use humor, drama, and suspense, borrowing liberally from the most effective aspects of entertainment programs. *Sesame Street*, though not a formal instructional program, is used in many classrooms and combines excellent techniques and forms, from animation to commercials.

Don't be afraid of a liberal infusion of visuals and sounds. Good use of visual writing permits more concrete explanation of what is presented than in the traditional classroom. You can show the real person, place, thing, or event being studied.

Immediate feedback from the classroom to the media teacher, if the lesson is live, is important. Internet use permits this in an unlimited number of classrooms. Controlled use of Internet lessons, including number of sites and carefully planned interactive materials, offers the optimum possibilities.

Discussions can take place among several classes taking the same subject at the same time. Evaluation, or testing, can be done during the live media lesson through "talkback." The media teacher and the instructional team planning the lessons know what kinds of questions the students will ask and should build in information on those questions and appropriate times during the lesson for questions and answers. Commercial broadcasters have an inordinate fear of dead air time, but good instructional programs build in such time for the classroom teacher to review what the teacher has presented and to establish appropriate interaction among the students and the classroom teacher as well as with the media teacher. With the use of the Internet for formal instruction, interactive teaching and learning is built in, with all of the above possible on an international level—essentially, any group of students anywhere in the world can interact with any other group of students anywhere. Similarly, any student anywhere can theoretically avail herself or himself of any teacher or learning resources anywhere in the world.

Classroom teachers do not work in a vacuum. Every instructional series should have a written teacher's guide that details the purposes, level, content, and evaluation for each media lesson. The guide includes preparatory and follow-up recommendations. Sometimes the guide is prepared after the series is completed; sometimes it is written as the series develops, in which case the guide provides the writer with an excellent outline base for each script.

Techniques

1. *Follow a logical sequence in every script.* Begin with a review and preparation for the day's materials and conclude with classroom follow-up materials such as research, field projects, and individual study.

2. *Motivate the learner with stimulating material.* Make the learning experience exciting for the child in the elementary grade, the adult in the professional school, the employee in the workplace, or the learner at home. Include imaginative visual or aural stimuli and attention-getting material that will retain the viewer's interest.

3. *Target the script to the specific audience.* Determine whether the program is designed for one school, a school system, an entire state, or for national or international distribution. Determine the backgrounds and interests of the students who will be watching the program.

4. *Write at the appropriate level.* Determine, with the help of the educational experts, the desired complexity of the material based on how much the students are likely to know already and the language level the students in that grade level require for optimum comprehension.

5. *Encourage students to create new ideas through their own thinking.*

6. *Follow the principles of good commercial writing.* Get the students' attention, keep their interest, impart information, plant an idea, and get them to take action by evaluating and following-up on what they have learned.

7. *Follow the principles of good playwriting.* Begin with background or exposition; follow with conflict and suspense about what will happen to the idea, characters, or situation; incorporate as complications the problems or methods of what is being learned; move the students toward reaching a climax through their findings. (See playwriting principles in Chapter 10.) Most effective learning takes place when the student is given alternatives and reaches a solution through his or her own thinking. Drama is an excellent technique to use in teaching. For instance, many critics and researchers believe that the dramatists have educated us with deeper insights and feelings about the relationships among people and between people and their environment than have historians or social scientists. As an example, Shakespeare's plays give us more understanding of the motivations and interpersonal relationships of England's kings than do most history books.

8. *Be creative.* Do not simply present information. Make the form of presentation interesting. For example, one of the most effective devices for teaching history is the "You Are There" approach that was popular on commercial television and radio for many years. The script is written as though a team of on-the-spot reporters were at the historical place and time bringing the audience the news through narrative pictures, sounds, words, interviews with the historical figures involved, and comments on the significance of what is occurring. Of course, the settings and the performers' costumes

should be as accurate as possible. The content is factual, but the form generates the interest of the historical drama.

Another often-used approach, especially in science programs, is costumed performers playing the inanimate subjects being studied. For example, an AIDS antibody can be the guide on a tour of how the AIDS virus enters and destroys the body. Although such imaginative approaches are highly learning-effective, the more complex the program, the higher the cost.

One of the simplest and most popular formats is directly presenting views and sounds of people, places, and things that otherwise would not be available in the traditional classroom. Science experiments, biographical interviews, artistic performances, and geographical information are among the areas that fall into this category. The television program using this approach can resemble a travelogue, with the television teacher providing voice-over commentary. An example of this kind of script is the following beginning and ending of one lesson of a series designed for fourth-grade social studies. As you read this script, think about how you would adapt it for interactive presentation on the Internet.

LANDS AND PEOPLE OF OUR WORLD

Lesson Number: 29   Lesson Title: Japan

FILM—1 min.

MUSIC—1 min.

CG—"Lands and People of Our World"

CG—Donna Matson

Legend says that the Sun Goddess founded the islands of Japan, and for many years only tribespeople inhabited the land of the rising sun. Then Chinese traders and other foreigners began visiting Japan; they brought new ideas and culture. But the rulers of Japan didn't want any changes, so they closed their gates, allowing no one to enter and no one to leave. For nearly 200 years Japan and her people remained isolated from the outside world.

Then, in 1853, Commodore Perry of the United States Navy sailed his warships into Tokyo Bay and persuaded the Japanese to open two of their ports to U.S. Trade.

The Japanese quickly learned the ways of the modern world, and today they are one of the greatest industrial nations in the world.

continued

ON DONNA	Hello, boys and girls. Our lesson today is about Japan, one of the most amazing countries in the world today.
PIX #1 MAP—ASIA	Japan is a group of islands, located in Asia, off the East Coasts of Russia, Korea and China, in the Western part of the Pacific Ocean.
	Japan consists of four main islands: Hokkaido, Honshu, Kyushu, and Shikoku, plus about 3,000 smaller islands. All together they about equal the size of the State of California. The islands of Japan stretch from North to Southwest for a distance of about 1200 miles.
FILM—3 min. MUSIC	Mount Fujiyama, a volcanic mountain, over 12,000 feet high, is the highest point in Japan. The islands of Japan are actually the tops of mountains which are still growing.
	Japan is located in the Pacific Great Circle of Fire, and has about 1500 earthquakes each year, but most of them cause little damage.
	Japan has a wide variety of climates ranging from tropical on the southern islands to cool summers and snowy winters on the northern islands.
Tokyo	More than 120 million people live on the islands of Japan, and two out of three live in cities.
	Tokyo, Japan's capital city, is one of the largest cities in the world, with a population of more than 12 million people. Osaka, Kyoto, and Yokohama are also large cities, with populations of more than two million each.
	The city of Tokyo has been rebuilt twice in the last century, once after an earthquake, and again after the air raids of World War II.
	Today it is very much like an American city, with wide paved streets, tall modern buildings, and heavy traffic. Tokyo has been able to grow so fast mainly because of its very modern railroads that carry more than one million people into work each day.
	Most Japanese homes are made of wood panels and sliding doors. They withstand earthquakes well, but not fires. Many homes have beautiful gardens. The floors of the homes are like thick cushions and the Japanese people kneel on the floor while eating off low tables. They sleep on the soft floors in comforters and blankets that they roll up during the day. And to keep these floors clean, they always remove their shoes before entering their houses. The Japanese are some of the cleanest people I've ever met in the world.
Students	In Japan, all boys and girls must go to school for nine years. That's grade one to nine. And they have at least two hours of homework each night, and homework assignments all summer long. All students in Japan are required to study English. There are more than 60 universities and colleges in Tokyo.

continued

Mother and Child	Japanese children are very respectful and polite to their parents and grandparents, and try very hard never to bring shame to their family in any way.
Harbor	Japan is an island nation, and island nations need ships. Japan is a leader in the world in ship building, plastics, electronics, and auto making. Japan imports much steel from us, manufactures trucks, autos and machinery, and exports it to the United States and other countries.
	People travel mainly on electric trains and buses. There just wouldn't be enough room if many people had cars. Space is a problem. . . .
	Japan is also the world's largest exporter of ceramic tableware, cameras, lenses, electronic equipment and automobiles.
Film Ends (3 min.) ON DONNA FILM—7½ min.	As a matter of fact, here are some of the things I own that are manufactured in Japan. My camera, tape recorder, ceramic tableware and car.
	The textile industry is another important industry in Japan. Japan produces more than half the world's supply of raw silk. Silk, remember, comes from cocoons of the silkworms.
Fishing	Japan is one of the world's greatest fishing countries. It has over 400,000 fishing boats. That's more than any other nation.
	* * *
FILM	For over 1,000 years Japan was ruled by an Emperor who had great powers over the people. Today his duties are mainly ceremonial. Here we see the Emperor of Japan greeting his people on New Year's Day at the Imperial Palace Grounds in Tokyo.
	After World War II, the United States helped Japan set up a democratic form of government, and the head of their government is the Prime Minister, who is chosen by the Diet. The Diet is like our Congress, with a House of Representatives and a House of Councilors who are elected by the people of Japan.
	Hibachi, food, toys, dolls, kite.
	Closing
ON DONNA MUSIC—15 sec. ON KITE CG—Consultant CG—Western ITV	

Courtesy of Western Instructional Television

Children's Programs

INFORMAL EDUCATIONAL PROGRAMS

Informal educational programs include those for children. At one time a number of television programs combined information, ideas, morals, and entertainment for young viewers, just as radio did in a previous era. Today, however, with the exception of cartoons, few children's programs remain on television. Networks occasionally do children's specials, several individual stations produce local programs for children, and public television and some commercial stations carry *Sesame Street*. But the day of non-exploitative drama for children is past. Cartoons may have dramatic plots or sequences, but they are by and large written on a very low level, filled with violence and sexism, and in many cases are merely program-length commercials, some with the entire cartoon centered around the toy that the advertiser is trying to sell to the children. Younger and younger children are accessing programs online and using social sites such as Facebook and YouTube.

Some basic principles and techniques apply to writing for children. The foremost principle is to remember the effect television has on the vulnerable minds and emotions of young viewers. One hopes that writers of children's programs will exercise their consciences and discuss new program ideas with child experts and child advocates before writing scripts that may prove harmful to youngsters.

Approach

Imagination is the key to preparing and writing programs for children. The imaginations of children are broad, exciting, and stimulating. Only when we are forced into the conformity of the formal educational system and, later on, when we near adulthood, do our thoughts and imaginations become restricted. Children can release themselves to be led into almost any fantasy, *provided a valid, believable base exists*. The same principle applies to adult farce or comedy. As long as the characters, situation, and environment are believable and the plot is developed logically, the actions and events will be accepted.

Format

Certain age levels respond best to certain kinds of content. The child in the early elementary grades can relate to material containing beginning elements of logical thinking. Sketches with simple plots and fairy tales are appealing. Activities the child can get involved in, if not too complicated, are effective. The child older than eight or nine can respond to accounts of the outside world. Drama is effective, especially stories of adventure

So, follow the charter from 1 to 8
TWO is INTERCONNECTED it's never too late!
Earth and Rosie will take you there,
The Little Earth Charter's a treasure to share!

Planet earth speech:
You know me, Planet Earth!
Life on me comes in so many forms, it's a rich variety of living beings.
They are a big part of my vitality and my beauty. And absolutely every
one of them is interconnected and connected to you!

So, follow the charter from 1 to 8
TWO is INTERCONNECTED it's never too late!
Earth and Rosie will take you there,
The Little Earth Charter's a treasure to share!
For INTERCONNECTED . . . we'll care.
(SONG ENDS)

PART 4 – The Pledge

Finn VO: The Interconnected Web is very delicate so we have to take care of it. Because we are all interconnected, everything we do can have an effect on the web.

Rosie: Yah! And we need the web!

Finn VO: Absolutely! If one part of the web gets hurt, it will affect all of us!

Rosie: OH NO!

Finn VO: So do you pledge to uphold the Interconnected Principle?

Rosie: Yes! Come on, kids, stand up and take the pledge with me!

Finn VO: Then put your hand on your heart and repeat after me:
"I pledge . . . to respect and understand . . . that everything on earth is interconnected . . . and is somehow connected to me."

Rosie: I pledge . . . (repeats pledge line by line)

Finn VO: That's the Little Earth Charter . . . principle number 2!

Rosie: For Interconnected, we *will* care!

(END CREDITS)

Courtesy of Rosie Emery and JC Little

Another example of Rosie Emery's writing for children, a written-out script, is from her "Curious Kids" series for public media WGCU, Fort Myers, Florida. This segment, "Krik Krak," is part of a series on healthy eating aimed at the Haitian community. "Krik, Krak" is a standard way of beginning a story in Haiti.

Krik, Krak

Writer: Rosie Emery
"Curious Kids"
WGCU Public Media, Fort Myers, Florida

Peter: Krik

Justin: Krak

Lori: Someone has a story to tell!

Logan: Once upon a time, there was a boy . . .

Peter: Who didn't like to eat his vegetables, so one day . . .

Justin: His Maman made him some bon bouillon!

Logan: Bouillon is a soup that has all kinds of vegetables in it, like spinach, cabbage and string beans.

Lori: When his Maman wasn't looking, the boy tried to pour his soup away!

Logan: But she caught him just in time!

Lori: She said, if you want to grow big and strong, il faut bien manger!

Justin: Fruits and vegetables keep us healthy. So eat as many as you can!

Courtesy of Rosie Emery

Rosie Emery's notes on writing for children provides some approaches that may be of special value to those planning to go into this field. She states:

We are all storytellers; we may not recognize this in ourselves, and yet who amongst us has not at some time had a story to tell? Stories and myths help us to find our place in the universe, to connect to our cosmology. Creatively, I am first and foremost a singer. songwriter and storyteller; from these aspects of myself I draw the inspiration that shapes and forms the work that I write and develop for children. While I grew up in a world filled with space, nature and plenty of time for reflection and imagination, children today live in one that is increasingly interactive, not to mention creamed with rapid-fire images and sound-bytes. So as I write for new media and television in the present, I seek to find a balance between the past and the future; and while story and song have evolved over the centuries into movie, television, and You Tube, their basic premise remains the same; it is only the delivery mechanism that has changed. I have found that songs and stories are a wonderful way to connect with children. Not lonely do they captivate and entertain them, but used as educational tools they also reinforce and enhance what has been learned. Rather than trying to fit into someone else's model of what is "hip" or "current," I endeavor to be aware of modern technologies and trends, incorporating them when relevant while maintaining my own authenticity. After all, we can surely learn from the past and the present as we imagine and create the future. When I write a new song or script, I begin with the story. How can I tell it in such a way that it conveys the information in a fun, intelligent, and memorable way? Metaphor and imagery spark the imagination and linger on long after information has dwindled. Interactive media provide exciting mechanisms for storytelling and songwriting—a writer can provide a beginning, middle, and allow the participant to create the end, vice-versa.

Video Games

The computer has opened up more than one new way of learning. In addition to the Internet, the computer (and consoles) has made video games a potential key aspect of children's education. While many if not most video games promote physical and psychological violence, in the past few years more and more video games are teaching positive learning skills. For example, Age of Empires and Empire Earth reenacted historical events. Wiz World taught children to speak and understand English by putting the learner into a virtual situation where use of the English language is necessary for success or even survival. Situations vary from dodging flying monsters to buying fruit in a supermarket. Venture capitalists are betting that the fundamental education models are changing and will be transformed by the Internet, and thus they are investing in online educational video games. This is another new frontier for the writer.

APPLICATION AND REVIEW

1. Choose a business or industry in your area that is large enough to benefit from a media training program. Discuss with its training, sales, or human resources director some of its current needs and prepare a half-hour video script designed to solve a specific problem.

2. Discuss with the director of your college or university's public information office some of the current promotion campaigns of the institution and prepare a 15-minute PowerPoint script that can be used for the general public or for prospective students and their parents. Adapt this script for the institution's web site.

3. Prepare a 10-minute script, either video or audio, that can be used to orient new members of a campus organization of which you are a member.

4. Prepare a treatment for the pilot of a half hour "quality" children's program that you will try to get produced by a local television or radio station or cable system or web site.

5. Using as a base the template found on www.pmcc.com/templates, adapt one of the previous exercises for the Internet.

CHAPTER 10

The Play

Writing the play is generally considered to be the most difficult endeavor as well as the highest achievement in the performing arts. Creating the video or film play is the culmination of learning how to write for the media and the basis for all other formats. Whether a 30-second commercial or a two-hour documentary, the script structure depends on the elements of the play: exposition, conflict, complication, climax, and resolution.

Take the commercial, for example. In addition to those commercials that literally are mini-dramas (one or more characters in a situation that involves the sponsor's product or service), all commercials present a problem (a conflict), show how a life situation is difficult or unfulfilled (complication), and how the problem is solved and life becomes better when the sponsor's product or service is purchased (the climax and resolution). All documentaries depend on dramatic action involving the person, persons, or events being shown in a condensation of the real-life occurrences. Even a disc jockey program that is well planned achieves a rising level of interest that gains and holds the audience's attention.

The play is the staple of television, whether in sitcom, action adventure, or serious drama form, despite the proliferation in recent years of the reality format. Even the generally unrehearsed and unscripted show follows the organization of the play. The conflict, complications, rising suspense action, and climax need to be planned well enough to hold the audience's interest and increase it to a peak as the particular event or contest nears its end. Daytime television relies heavily on the play, usually sitcoms, but also on whatever other genre happens to be popular enough to draw good ratings and is available in syndication. Soap opera plays are among the most popular television programs, both day and evening.

If you learn the elements that go into writing a good play, even if you never discover within you the motivation or talent to actually write a play, you will be better able to write other video and audio formats effectively.

Brander Matthews, one of the theater's all-time leading critics and teachers, wrote in his book *The Development of Drama*, "Dramaturgic principles are not mere rules laid down by theoretical critics, who have rarely any acquaintance with the actual theater; they are laws, inherent in the nature of the art itself, standing eternal, as immitigable today as when Sophocles was alive, or Shakespeare, or Molière."

The rules of playwriting are universal. They apply generally to the structure of the play written for the stage, film, television, and in most countries, radio. The rules are modified in their specific applications by the particular medium's special requirements.

Don't assume, merely because there are rules, that great playwriting can be taught. Genius and inspiration cannot be taught, and playwriting is an art on a plane of creativity far above the mechanical facets of some phases of continuity writing. America's first and foremost playwriting teacher, George Pierce Baker, stated that what can be done, however, is to show the potential playwright how to apply whatever genius and dramatic insight he or she may have, through an understanding of the basic rules of dramaturgy.

Yet, even this much cannot be taught in one chapter or in several chapters. Any full discussion of playwriting technique requires at least a complete book, several courses, and endless practice. What will be presented here is a summary of the rules of playwriting and some new concepts of playwriting for the special needs of the media. If you seriously want to write drama for the electronic media, first explore as thoroughly as possible the techniques of writing the play for the stage. Only then will you have a sound basis for the video or film play.

Remember that a play is a play is a play. Whether presented over the airwaves (broadcasting) or through cable, satellite or cyberspace, the play is the same—a dramatic presentation reaching people seated in front of an oblong box with a relatively small (compared to a movie theater) screen and increasingly for smaller three-, four-, and seven-inch screens on iPhone and iPads. Sixty-inch and larger high definition digital flat screens taking up half of a living room wall have begun to change some of the restrictive concepts applied to writing the television play, such as the number of characters and the size of the setting. In addition, aside from made-for-TV movies, which may cover two or more hours of air time, most television dramas and sitcoms limit scripts to 21 minutes, including intro and outro, for the half-hour time period and 42 minutes for the hour program. The remaining 9 and 18 minutes, respectively, are devoted to commercials. The limited time concomitantly limits the characters and plot lines, with the exception of the serials where a given plot line, like those of soap operas, may continue for weeks or even years. There are key differences between plays written for television and screenplays written for theatrical release. While some observers believe that in not too many years many homes will have entire walls used to display computer-relayed programs, making video shows more comparable with theatrical films, this is not yet the case, and potential TV playwrights still need to heed television's artistic restrictions.

SOURCES

Before the actual techniques of writing can be applied, the writer must be able to recognize and exploit the sources out of which the ideas for the play can be developed.

The writer can find the motivating ingredient for the play in an event or happening, a theme, a character or characters, or a background.

Many times a playwright has witnessed or experienced an incident or a series of incidents that contain the fundamentals for good drama. From this event or happening the playwright can build character, situation, theme, and background. Remember, however, that what is exciting in life is not necessarily good drama. Drama is heightened life. Drama compresses a situation's most important elements and requires a rearrangement, revision, and condensation of life to make it dramatic rather than merely human interest reporting. The beginning playwright may have difficulty understanding this, particularly when he or she has participated in or observed an interesting life situation. What seems to be the most tragic, most humorous, most exciting thing that has ever happened to the writer can actually be hackneyed, dull, and undramatic in play form.

Because something seems dramatic in real life does not mean that it will be dramatic if put into a play. Such transposition requires imagination, skill, and, to no small degree, the indefinable genius of playwriting. For example, many of us have seen a situation where a destitute maiden aunt has come to live with a sister and brother-in-law, and in her psychological need has become a disturbing factor in the marriage. To the participants, or even to a close observer, such a situation might have provocative and electrifying undertones. To someone not connected with the situation, it appears, and understandably so, dull and uninspiring. To the imaginative playwright, in this case Tennessee Williams, it became one of America's all-time great plays, *A Streetcar Named Desire*.

The writer can initiate the preliminary thinking about the play from a theme or an idea. Although censorship often hampers the media playwright, the writer can find basic concepts such as loyalty, independence, and self-realization as motivating factors upon which to develop a drama. The theme must be translated into specific and full-blown people and concrete situations. The theme of loyalty, for example, might include the son who won't marry because of his psychologically motivated belief that he cannot leave his mother. Independence covers many variations of the story of the wife who leaves her husband because she is not accorded the freedom or respect she feels she needs. Self-realization covers an endless supply of potential plays oriented around the artist who prefers living on bread and beans in a cold-water flat rather than accepting a lucrative advertising agency job. The writer must be wary of attempting to develop a play around a theme alone. The theme serves merely as the germ of the idea for the play.

Another source for the play can lie in a background. The backgrounds of war, of high society, of a drug environment, and of the business world have provided the settings and motivations for many plays. The college student could do worse than to use the campus as a background for the play.

A final source for the play can come from a character or several characters, either as a group or rolled into one. In modern dramaturgy, character motivates action; that is, the plot develops from the characters. For this reason, the choice of character as a source provides a potentially stronger play foundation than do the other sources. The writer must be cautious, however, in using this source independently of the others; it is difficult to build a play solely around a character or combination of characters taken from real life. For example, how trite is the idea of a salesman getting fired from a job because he is getting old and cannot make as many sales as he once did. Even if his character is enlarged by adding pride, self-deception, and despondency leading to suicide, the dramatic potential is not yet fully realized. But work on the character, develop his many facets, beliefs, psychological needs, physical capabilities, and relationships to other people, clarify a theme and background, and you might eventually get to Willy Loman of one of America's greatest plays, Arthur Miller's *Death of a Salesman*.

In a *New York Times Magazine* article, Charles McGrath described the work of the staff writers for the crime-and-punishment television drama *Law & Order*. He noted that the program's scripts are developed in numerous ways, including looking at newspaper headlines for crimes and for legal issues, such as New York State's instituting the death penalty—an issue that actually became the basis for *Law & Order* episodes. Sometimes ideas are hard to come by. McGrath quoted executive producer and head writer Michael Chernuchin as saying that at times "we have no idea what we're doing and we just sit around and toss things around."

The sources of the play—situation, theme, background, and character—are individually only germs of ideas. Explore, expand, and revise these elements to determine if they have any dramatic value. If they have, then the playwright can take the next step. Inexperienced writers—and lazy ones—sometimes believe that all they have to do is have an idea and a pretty good notion of where they are going with it, and then sit down and write the play. Unfortunately, this is not the case. The actual writing is the dessert of the playwright's menu. The hard work is devoted to planning the play and, later, to revising the manuscript. After deciding on the source or basis for a play, clarify in your mind and on paper the various elements that develop from the base. For example, if you choose to work from a background, determine the characters, situation, and theme that go with the background.

Ideally, you should write out of personal experience or knowledge to give the play a valid foundation. If you are too close, either emotionally or in terms of time, to the life-ingredients of the play, however, it will be difficult to heighten and condense and dramatize the material; you will tend to be a reporter rather than a dramatist. The playwright should never be part of the play, but should be able to write it objectively. Feel and understand every moment of what you write, but try to do so as a third person. Don't use the play as personal therapy. If you are tempted to do so—some playwrights have done so successfully—at least be sure that the character who represents you is not so internalized as to be without foibles or otherwise unbelievable. It usually is a good idea to be several calendar years and several emotional light years away from the real-life events and characters when you start to write the play.

STRUCTURE

Until the 18th century, with the exception of works by a few playwrights (notably Shakespeare), plot or action was the dominant element in the play. The plot line was the most important factor, and the characters and dialogue were fitted into the movement of the action. Modern drama has emphasized character as most important. The actions that determine the plot are those the characters *must* take because of their particular personalities and psychological motivations. The dialogue is that which the characters *must* speak for the same reasons.

The three major elements in the play structure—character, plot, and dialogue—all must be coordinated into a consistent and clear theme. This coordination of all elements toward a common end results in the unity of the piece, a unity of impression. The characters' actions and the events must not be arbitrary. Prepare the audience for these actions and events in a logical and valid manner; this is called *preparation*. Give the audience the background of the situation and of the characters; this is the *exposition*. In addition, consider the *setting*, to create a valid physical background and environment for the characters.

After you are certain that you understand and can be objective about the characters, theme, situation, and background, you can begin to create each in depth. Do as much research as possible, to acquaint yourself fully with the potentials of your play.

Each character should be analyzed. Write it out so that you have the characters' complete histories and motivations in front of you at all times. Develop a background for each character, for not only the duration of the action, but also before the play's opening (even going back to ancestors who do not appear in the play but who would have had some influence on the character's personality). A complete analysis of a character also provides an indication of the kind and form of dialogue the character would use. Test the dialogue on paper, putting the character into hypothetical situations with other characters. Remember, the dialogue is not an approximation of real-life speech; it must be heightened and condensed from that of real life.

After the characters have been created, you are ready to create the situation, or plot line. Do this in skeletonized form. You need, first, a **conflict**. The conflict is between the **protagonist** of the play and some other character or force. A conflict can be between two individuals, an individual and a group, two groups, an individual or individuals and nature, an individual or individuals and some unknown force, or an individual and his or her inner self. (Note how many of these describe the format of a TV *reality* program.) For the play, the nature of the conflict is determined largely by the kinds of characters involved.

After the conflict has been decided upon, the plot moves inexorably toward a climax, the point at which one of the forces in conflict wins out over the other. The play reaches the climax through a series of complications. Each complication is, in itself, a small conflict and climax. Each succeeding complication complicates the situation to a greater and greater degree until the final complication makes it impossible for the struggle to be heightened any longer. Something has to give. The climax must occur. The complications are not arbitrary. The characters themselves determine the events and the complications because the actions they take are those, and only those, they must take because of their individual motivations and personalities.

George Pierce Baker wrote in *Dramatic Technique* that the "situation exists because one is what he is and so has inner conflict, or clashes, with another person, or with his environment. Change his character a little and the situation must change. Involve more people in it, and immediately their very presence, affecting the people originally in the scene, will change the situation."

British playwright Terence Rattigan wrote similarly in a *Theatre Arts* article, "The Characters Make the Play":

> A play is born—for me, at any rate—in a character, in a background or setting, in a period or in a theme, never in a plot. I believe that in the process of a play's preliminary construction during that long and difficult period of gestation before a line is put on paper, the plot is the last of the vital organs to take shape.
>
> If the characters are correctly fashioned—by which I do not mean accurately representing living people but correctly conceived in their relationship to each other—the play will grow out of them. A number of firmly and definitely imagined characters will act—must act—in a firm and definite way. This gives you your plot. If it does not, your characters are wrongly conceived and you must start again.

A medium interprets for the audience what we have written. Writing for films is different than writing for the stage, just as writing for radio is different than writing for previous media, just as writing for television is different than writing for radio, just as writing for the Internet is different than writing for all of the other media. If we take the same basic script elements—plot, characters, setting and dialogue—we would write them to fit the aesthetic and technical requirements and potentials of the given medium.

Once the preliminary planning, gestation, research, and analysis are completed, the writer is ready. But not for writing the play. Not yet. Next comes the scenario or treatment or detailed outline. The writer who has been conscientious up to this point learns from these devices whether he or she has a potentially good play—if any play at all. Through careful construction and analysis of this pre-script material, the writer can eliminate the bad points and strengthen the good points before the play is written.

Before even writing the scenario, treatment, or outline, however, the writer should have a knowledge of the concepts of dramaturgy—of the basic rules for the play regardless of the medium, and of the modified rules for the film or video play, as determined by the special characteristics of these media.

CONCEPTS OF PLAYWRITING

The special characteristics of the television audience and of the medium itself require special approaches by the television playwright, as discussed in Chapters 1 and 2. You can combine the viewer's subjective relationship to the television screen with the electronic potentials of the medium to direct the audience's attention purposefully. Direct the audience to the impact of the critical events in the character's life and to even the character's smallest, subjective experience. Bring the audience close to the innermost feelings and thoughts of the character. The medium's intimate nature makes this possible.

Although radio drama has virtually disappeared in the United States, the radio medium has rightly been called the "theater of the imagination." The only limitations in radio are those of the human imagination. There are no restrictions on place, setting, number of characters, kinds of actions, or movement of time. The radio writer can take the audience anywhere and have the characters do anything. Radio can create mental images of infinite variety. Writing the radio drama is good training for the person who may one day be writing commercials or other **continuity** for the audio medium.

The classic components of play structure include (1) unity, (2) plot, (3) character, (4) dialogue, (5) exposition, (6) preparation, and (7) setting. The basic principles of each apply to all plays, regardless of the medium for which they are written. The special characteristics that apply to video and audio are noted under each of these principles.

Unity

All elements in a play should relate in a thorough and consistent fashion to all the other elements, all moving toward realizing the playwright's purpose. This is the unity of action or impression. No single extraneous element should detract from the unified total impression the audience receives.

Video

The unities of time and place are completely loose and fluid in television, film, and online. Television can present many settings of any kind in minutes and even seconds. Television has been able to achieve what playwright August Strindberg, in his "Author's Note" to *A Dream Play*, hoped for in the theater: a situation where "anything may happen: everything is possible and probable." Strindberg advocated plays where "time and space do not exist," where "imagination spins and weaves new patterns: a mixture of memories, experience, unfettered fancies, absurdities, and improvisations." Some writers, producers, and directors in commercial television see the medium as more than a marketplace and are incorporating video art into their dramatic productions, ranging from music videos to commercials.

The unity of action or impression, however, is as vital to the television play as to the most traditional of stage plays, and the television writer should be certain that this important unity is present. Each sequence must be integrated thoroughly with every other sequence, all contributing to the total effect the play is designed to create.

Audio

Radio has no unities of time and place. Radio can take us 20,000 years into the future and transport us 20,000 years into the past. Radio can take a character—and us along with the character—to the North Pole, the moon, a battlefield in a jungle, or the depths of Hades, creating without restriction the settings for our imaginations. Unlike television and the film, radio is not limited by what we can see or believe visually.

No matter how loose the unities of time and place, however, radio, like video, must have a unity of action. The script must maintain a consistency and wholeness of purpose and development.

Plot

The play's plot structure is based on a complication arising from the individual's or group's relationship to some other force. This is the conflict, the point when the two or more forces come into opposition. The conflict must be presented as soon as possible in the play, for the rest of the play structure follows and is built upon this element. Next come a series of complications or **crises**, each one creating further difficulty relating to the major conflict, and each building in a rising crescendo so that the entire play moves toward a final crisis or climax. The climax occurs at the instant the conflicting forces meet head on and a change occurs to or in at least one of them. This is the turning point. One force wins and the other loses. The play can end at this moment. There can, however, be a final clarification of what happens, as a result of the climax, to the characters or forces involved. This remaining plot structure is called the *resolution*. (Note, again, how reality shows follow this pattern.)

The elementary plot structure of the play can be diagrammed as follows:

Video

The plot of the television play follows the structure in the diagram. For the video play a half-hour or an hour in length, the time restrictions require a tight plot line and a condensation of movement from sequence to sequence. In brief minutes we must present what life might have played out in hours, days, or years. Real life is un-emphatic, whereas drama must be emphatic. The short time allowed for most television plays requires that the plot contain only the essence of the characters' experiences—the heightened extremes of life. Aim for the short, terse scene.

In a continuing series, such as day time soap operas, the plot is deliberately stretched out. Although in each episode some climax(es) must occur to avoid frustrating the audience, the final climax of the continuing basic conflict of some characters may never come—the episode merely moves with new complications from week to week.

How do you effectively condense real life to drama? Consider some approaches presented by George Pierce Baker in his noted book on playwriting, *Dramatic Technique*. First, the dramatist can "bring together at one place what really happened at the same time, but to other people in another place." Second, events happening to a person in the same setting, but at different times can be brought together. Third, events that have "happened to two people in the same place, but at different times may . . . be made to happen to one person." Finally, "what happened to another person at another time, and at another place may at times be arranged so that it will happen to any desired figure." Baker concluded, "The essential point in all this compacting is: when cumbered with more scenes than you wish to use, determine first which scenes contain indispensable action, and must be kept as settings; then consider which of the other scenes may by ingenuity be combined with them."

Unless you are writing a two-hour or longer TV special or a made-for-TV movie, the program time length requires that the conflict come as soon as possible. Although the stage play can take almost a full act to present background through exposition, the television play may even open with the conflict. A major reason for this, aside from the time limitation, is the need to get and hold the audience's attention. Unlike theater and movie audiences, which have paid a fee and feel a compunction to stay, television and iPhone audience members who are not caught by the play in the opening seconds can press a remote button or icon to take them instantly to another channel.

The point of attack—conflict—in the video play should come quickly and bring with it the first important moment of pressure. That requires bringing in the background, or exposition, even as the conflict is being presented. Through the character's dialogue and actions, you have to tell who they are, show where they are, place the time of the story, and reveal what actions or events have led up to the conflict.

Because of the aforementioned time and space restrictions, a conflict between individuals, or between an individual and himself or herself, usually is more effective than are conflicts between groups or any large bodies or forces. One trend in television drama and sitcoms is to have a number of different individuals in conflict or competing with each other. (This, too, is the essence of most reality shows.)

Don't forget the complications. Although the time length of a single episode limits the number of complications, you must have enough to validate and build the actions of the major characters. You can't just have the characters do anything to move the plot along. All their actions have to be done because they are responding to a complication that causes them to behave in such a way that is consistent with the kinds of people they are. Each complication moves the characters and the action closer to a climax.

The time limitation often forces television to dispense with the resolution entirely, unless some doubt remains about some moral principle involved. Sometimes the resolution can be incorporated as part of the climax. On some shows the play ends with the climax, is followed by a final commercial, and then returns to the playscript for a brief resolution or epilogue.

Audio

The radio play follows the same plot structure as the television play—exposition, a conflict, complications, a climax, and if necessary, a resolution. A rising action must create suspense and hold the audience. Because the conflict can come at the very beginning of the play, exposition is revealed as the action is progressing. A major difference from the video plot line is that the radio writer must concentrate on one or two simple plot lines or conflicts, avoiding too many subplots. This is because the radio audience cannot see and differentiate among characters as easily as in the visual medium.

Character

Character, plot, and dialogue are the three primary ingredients of a play. All must be completely and consistently integrated. Character is the prime mover of the action and determines plot and dialogue. Too frequently the beginning writer or the writer who takes the easy way out tries to conform the characters to a plot structure. Most of the time it doesn't work; the characters appear artificial and sometimes even confusing to the audience.

Not only do the qualities of the characters determine the action, but also character is revealed through the action. This is done not through what is said about a character, but through what a character himself or herself says or does in the play in coping with the conflict and responding to the complications.

Character is delineated most effectively by what the person does at moments of crises. This includes inner or psychological action, as well as physical action. A character must be consistent throughout the play in everything said and done and must be plausible. This does not mean that the characters are copies of real-life persons; they must be dramatically heightened interpretations of reality. In reality shows the characters are, indeed, real-life people, albeit carefully selected and briefed in order to guarantee, as much as is possible, conflicts and competition among them.

Video

The video writer knows that time restrictions do not allow a character in the play to be the same person you see in life. The playwright cannot validate a character's actions by saying, "But that's what he (or she) did in real life!" Constantly emphasize "heightened life" and "moments of crisis" in creating your characters. Concentrate on the actions that strikingly reveal the individual character. Concentrate on the few characters whose actions strikingly reveal the purpose of the play. Don't use unneeded people. A character who does not contribute to the main conflict and the unified plot line does not belong in the play. If a character is essential, by all means include him or her. But if there are too many essential characters, rethink the entire approach to the play. This principle does not apply, of course, to the continuing series, where the continuity of characters over many weeks or months permits many featured characters and greater time and opportunity to develop characters.

Television's mechanical, electronic, and digital devices permit a physical closeness and empathy between the characters and the audience, facilitating the presentation in depth of the intimate, inner beings of the characters. The television writer, through the director, can direct the audience's attention to details that project the characters' most personal feelings, conveying details about the characters that otherwise might have to be explained verbally.

The continuing television series, whether hour dramas or half-hour sitcoms, begins with clearly conceived characters in defined ongoing conflicts. With the characters, dialogue, and basic plot structure in place, and developed over time, each week's episode becomes essentially the presentation of a further complication, showing how a character reacts to and copes with it. The climax in each episode relates to that complication, and the basic conflict continues into the following week. What we have, then, is a concentration by the writer each week on a new plot element, not on new characters (except for those who are introduced relative to the specific complication or, sometimes, as part of the overall continuing plot).

The good writer does not forget that the relationships among the characters are paramount: byplay between character and plot, with character determining incident and vice versa. Think about any critically acclaimed television series you have watched. The characters rather than the plot principally drive the play. Concentrate on weaving a subjective, intimate portrayal, while applying the basic dramaturgical rules for television, and your characters will emerge as the motivating force in your video play.

Audio

The lack of visual perception in radio might be expected to change the revelation of character from what he or she says and does—as in television—to solely what is said. This is not so. Character in any medium is revealed through what the character does. The difference between radio and television is that in radio what the character does is not shown visually, but is presented through sound and dialogue.

Otherwise the same principles apply: The characters must be consistent with themselves, motivate the plot, be heightened from real life, and interact with each other. Because of the lack of visual identification, however, too many voices can become confusing to the radio audience, and the number of roles in the play and in any one scene should be limited.

Dialogue

Because the play (but not necessarily the reality show) does not duplicate real people or real life, as the documentary does, but heightens and condenses them, the dialogue also has to be heightened and condensed rather than duplicated. Real-life dialogue is sometimes colorful and dramatic, but mostly is slow, plodding, and uninspiring. Just as you can't legitimately say, "Oh, but that's what the character did in real life," you can't say, "Oh, but that's what the character *said* in real life." If you do, you've written a documentary script—or a bad play. In the reality program, editing tries to take care of that problem.

The dialogue must conform to the character's personality. Be consistent with the character throughout the entire play, forward the plot line, and reveal the character. If you have several characters in the play, each will speak differently, depending on their personalities and backgrounds. If you find you can interchange dialogue among characters, you're in trouble.

Video

Video can substitute visual action for dialogue in forwarding the situation and providing exposition. Establishing shots and closeups eliminate time-consuming dialogue in which the character describes places or things or even feelings. Remember the anecdote in Chapter 1 about the film producer cutting the Broadway playwright's first act screen treatment of 30 minutes of dialogue to one minute of visual action? Concentrate on action and reaction, keeping the dialogue to a minimum and the picture the primary object of attention. But be careful not to go too far. Close-ups can become awkward and melodramatic if used too much.

Dialogue should be written so that the purpose of every exchange of speeches is clear to the audience and carries the plot forward. It is difficult to work exposition into the heightened and condensed dialogue of a show's beginning, when the conflict is grabbing the audience's attention, but you must present the necessary background even while presenting the continuing action. Take a cue from the most successful dramatic programs: Keep the dialogue terse and avoid repetition.

Audio

Even more than in television or on the screen, dialogue in radio serves to forward the situation, reveal character, uncover the plot line, and convey the setting and action to the audience. Everything on radio is conveyed through dialogue, sound effects, music, or silence. Because you can't show things visually, dialogue (and sound and music) must clearly introduce the characters, tell who they are, describe them, tell something about them, and even describe where they are and their actions. But it must not be done in an obvious manner. For example, it would be trite to have a character say, "Now, if you'll excuse me, I'll push back this gold-trimmed Louis the Fourteenth chair I'm sitting in, take my tan cashmere overcoat hanging on the brass clothes tree right inside your front door, and go." Or, "Now that we're here in my sixth-floor bachelor apartment with the etchings on the wall, the stereo speakers in the corners by the windows, and the waterbed on the red plush carpet in the center of the room . . ." All that should come out naturally in the dialogue between the characters involved.

Exposition

Exposition reveals the background of the characters and the situation and clarifies the present circumstances. It must not be done obviously or come through some arbitrary device, such as a telephone conversation, a servant, or the next-door neighbor. It must come out as the play unfolds and be a natural and logical part of the action. Exposition must be presented as early as possible, to make the characters, plot, and conflict understandable to the audience. The reality show sometimes uses an emcee, a narrator, or even voice-over to set the scene or recap the action.

Video

The short time allotted to the one-time video play permits only a minimum of exposition. The need to get right into the conflict requires the exposition to be highly condensed and presented as soon as possible. In the continuing video series, where most of the audience already know the characters, plot, and setting, the only exposition usually necessary is for the complications that forward the plot line in that particular episode.

Audio

Exposition is difficult with audio because it must be presented solely through dialogue and sound. Because the audience can't see the characters or the setting, the writer must present the exposition clarifying those elements as early as possible. There is a tendency in radio writing to give exposition through verbal description; as in any good play, however, it should be presented through the action. To solve the problem, radio sometimes employs a technique rarely used in other media, the narrator. The narrator can be part of the action (for example, a character talking to the audience about what's happening), or be divorced entirely from the drama.

Preparation

Preparation, or foreshadowing, is the unobtrusive planting, through action and dialogue, of material that prepares the audience for subsequent events, making their occurrence seem logical and not arbitrary. Proper preparation validates the actions of the characters. How many times have you watched the end of a play and said, "Oh, that character wouldn't have done that," or "That's too pat an ending"? Always keep in mind that when you have a character take an action that precipitates the climax or resolves the play, that action should develop from the kind of person the character is and should be something that the character *had* to do. It should not be something that you had the character do to complete your plot line. The audience members should never be able to say, "Oh, how surprising!" but should always say, even if they didn't expect it, "Why, of course!" In the reality show the aim is to keep the audience guessing until the final denouement.

Video

The writer should prepare the audience in a subtle and gradual manner for the subsequent actions of the characters and events of the play. Nothing should come as a complete surprise. The audience should be able to look back, after some action has taken place, and know that the action was inevitable because of the personality of the character who performed the action, or because all of the circumstances leading to the event made it unavoidable. The short time for the video drama means you must condense the clues of preparation and integrate them early in the script.

Audio

Because the radio writer cannot present the preparation visually, with all its subtle nuances (for example, a close-up showing a character carrying a gun, when otherwise the character seems to be a nonviolent, peaceful person), you must be certain that just because *you* know what the character's motivations are, you do not fail to let the audience know. If anything, radio requires an overabundance of preparation.

Setting

Setting is determined by the play's form and by the character's physical environment. The setting reflects the type of play: reality, farce, fantasy. As well as presenting locale, background, and environment, the setting serves the psychological and aesthetic purposes of the play and the author, creating an overall mood for the audience and the performers. All settings are designed to show the actions of the characters most effectively and must be integrated with the play's forward movement.

Video

Video drama essentially conforms to the play of selective realism, in both content and purpose, and realistic settings usually are required. The medium's electronic advantages make it possible, however, to create any kind of setting at any time, from the fantasy set of a dream sequence or flashback to the non-realistic setting of science fiction. Music videos have influenced the aesthetics of setting and direction in commercials and even in dramas.

Audio

Radio settings are limited by the need to present them through dialogue and sound, but otherwise the presentation is limited only by the imaginations of the writer and audience. You can put the audience into any setting you wish, far beyond that available to the video writer, even with the most sophisticated special visual effects. Although you are not likely to write a play in commercial radio, you may create settings for radio commercials and features.

Movement from setting to setting can be accomplished through silence, fading, narration, a music bridge, or sound effects. Note in Chapter 2 the example of the audience being with the character in a car about to go over a cliff, and the writer's option of keeping the audience at the cliff top watching the car fall into the chasm or going down with the driver.

Don't skimp on sound. The sound effects accompanying the character's actions clarify the setting. Exits and entrances of characters must be made clear through sound. Music establishes the mood and atmosphere of a setting. Sound and music provide transitions of time and place.

DEVELOPING THE SCRIPT

Now you know the principles of good playwriting! That doesn't guarantee that you can write a good play. You need inspiration and talent as well. Suppose you have them. You're still not ready to write the play. First comes the *scenario* or the *treatment, outline,* or *summary.* Except for the occasional acceptance of a completed script from a known and experienced writer, a story editor first wants to see a treatment.

The Treatment, Scenario, or Outline

The definitions for scenario, treatment, summary, and outline vary. Sometimes the terms are used interchangeably. Sometimes, as in this book, summary and outline refer to a short, preliminary overview of the proposed script, perhaps only a few pages in length, and scenario and treatment refer to a longer presentation, ranging from a fifth to a third or more of the length of the projected final script. The Writers Guild of America, East, advises, in its booklet *Professional Writer's Teleplay/ Screenplay Format,* "Nearly every teleplay/screenplay begins with an outline which in more detailed form is called a treatment. It is a scene-by-scene narrative description of your story, including word sketches of your principal characters. A treatment might also include a few key camera shots and a sprinkling of dialogue." The Guild suggests the following length guidelines for outlines/ treatments: 10–15 pages for a half-hour teleplay, 15–25 pages for one hour, 25–40 pages for 90 minutes, and 40–60 pages for the two-hour play.

The treatment/scenario or summary/outline gives the story editor and the producer a narrative idea of what the play is about. It tells them whether the proposed script fits the needs of their particular program. It's a waste of the writer's time to prepare a full script if the play, no matter how good, does not conform to the formula of the specific show.

Some producers and story editors want to see a short outline or summary first, to determine if the overall idea is on the right track. If they like the summary, they then ask for and evaluate the scenario or treatment. And, finally, if the treatment is approved, they will ask for a complete script.

The outline/treatment helps the prospective buyer and can be of immeasurable help to the writer as well. It can tell you whether or not you've got a good play. Careful development and analysis of the treatment can help you eliminate weak points and strengthen good ones. The treatment provides a continuing series of checkpoints in the construction of your play, which can save you exhausting work and valuable time by catching problems before they are written into the script. This avoids complete rewrites later to eliminate them.

Before you create the "public" treatment for submission, you should prepare a detailed working treatment designed to help you construct the play. Your working treatment should contain the play's purpose, theme, background, characters, basic plot line, and type of dialogue. You should include case histories for all of your characters. Prepare plot summaries for each projected scene in chronological order. Write down the elements of exposition and preparation. As you develop the plot sequences and think about the character's actions, insert important or representative lines of dialogue consistent with what a given character would say and the manner in which he or she would say it. Even in its simplest form, this kind of working treatment will help you clarify all the basic structural elements before you begin writing the play.

Although this suggested working treatment can be as long as or longer than the final manuscript, the treatment prepared for submission is shorter because it concentrates on a narrative of the plot, character descriptions and actions.

In Chapter 3 you read a sample outline and a sample treatment, preceding the format examples for the Gladys-Reginald beach scene. The outline and treatment were very short because they referred to only one page of script. The Writers Guild sample formats in Chapter 3 are a bit longer and are represented in treatment form by the following beginning of an outline.

"The Lost Men"

An Outline for a 1-Hour Teleplay

by

Billy Bard

ACT ONE

The scene is a typical suburban railroad station. It is evening, and commuters are pouring out of the station into wife-chauffeured cars. Among them we see JACK DOBBS, a balding but powerfully built businessman of 40. His friend, FRED McALLISTER, offers him a lift, but Jack says he will wait for his wife. After several minutes of waiting, Jack decides to flag the station taxi instead.

A few minutes later, the taxi pulls up to a lovely colonial house. Jack pays the driver, and gets out. Then he looks very puzzled by what he sees. The grass on the lawn is overgrown, and an elderly white-haired WORKMAN is nailing wooden boards across the windows. Jack asks the Workman what is going on, but the Workman ignores him. Jack becomes angry. He demands an answer, pointing out that he lives here. The Workman replies that he must be mistaken; that no one has lived in this house for the past five years! On Jack's bewilderment and anxiety, we fade to black.

We are in the office of DR. HARRY WESTON, psychiatrist, who is listening to the tale of his patient, Jack Dobbs. Etc., etc.

From Professional Writer's Teleplay/Screenplay Format,
written by Jerome Coopersmith

Following the first working treatment—and as many subsequent ones as necessary to make your preparation as complete as possible—you'll arrive at the point where you feel ready and confident to flesh out the play. This is where the pleasure of accomplishment comes in, for most playwrights the most enjoyable part of writing. If you've planned well, the play will virtually write itself. If you find that some radical departures from the treatment are needed, then your preparation was not as good as it could or should have been. Go back to the treatment and shore it up, even if you have to start all over. Otherwise, you'll find that although you might complete most or all of the first draft of the play, you'll need many more extra drafts to repair all the holes, in the long run requiring much more time and effort than you would have needed with proper preparation.

HIGH CONCEPT

If you are writing a screenplay, you will need to sell the *concept*, that is, the basic premise of your script. Studios and producers frequently use the term *high concept* to describe a story idea that is not only producible but is likely to sell. Some of the things they look for are a story that is unique, one that will appeal to a wide audience, and one that you can describe in one sentence from which they can encompass the entire movie. In short, when you pitch your idea, you have to convince them that it is marketable. On its web site, *www.scriptforsale.com*, ScriptForSale presents the following example: The basic idea of the film is for the authorities to try to use one criminal to catch another, specifically enlarging on that concept to make both criminals serial killers, the one not already in prison killing and skinning kidnapped women. A special relationship is developed between the FBI agent assigned to catch the killer and a psychiatrist who turns out to be cannibalistic. The concept that is considered especially marketable is the psychiatrist being able to play psychotic games inside the head of the FBI agent. In case you've not already guessed, that was the high concept for the movie, "The Silence of the Lambs."

The high concept script usually commands a higher fee than that for the traditional script. In addition, a high concept script will often get a reading by a production company that otherwise might not even look at your unsolicited proposal. The same applies to agents who may be too busy to consider your script, but when they hear a high concept, summarized in just a few sentences, that has the stamp of marketability, they frequently change their minds.

PLAY ANALYSIS

When non-news television production moved to Hollywood from New York, film soon replaced tape in the recording of programs. Film has now been replaced by digital recording. The basic approaches used with film are still the same, adapted to digital.

The "Filmed" Play

The digitally recorded film play sometimes is more the director's creation than the writer's. The director can virtually rewrite the play in the editing room. Between film sequences the director can change sets, costumes, makeup, reset lights and camera, and even reorient the performers.

In addition, the filmed play is not shot in chronological order. All the sequences taking place on a particular set or location are shot during the same period of time, no matter where they appear chronologically in the script. It is difficult to achieve clear continuity of performance, mood, or rhythm. Editing, therefore, is most critical in pulling together seemingly unrelated sequences and even individual shots into a smooth whole.

Screenwriter William Goldman, in a dialogue with Mal Karman in *Filmmaker's Newsletter,* described screenwriting as a craft. "It's carpentry. I don't mean that denigratingly. Except in the case of Ingmar Bergman, it's not an art." He added that "a screenwriter's most important contribution to film is not dialogue, but structure . . . you try to find something cogent that will make it play as a story; that will take us from A to Z." As a novelist, Goldman found the screenplay form "short, the cameras insist that you hurry, you have little time for detail . . . it's a craft of pacing and structure."

Screenwriter and professor Jean Stawarz tells how to write the made-for-television movie as differentiated from the theatrical film:

> It would be too simplistic to state that storytelling is storytelling, no matter what form is used to tell the story. Movies that are made for television versus films that are made for a theatrical release are vastly different. Both are accepted forms of storytelling; both adhere to the chosen genre and follow it; both have plot, characters, dialogue, and denouement. They are stories told in acts with beginnings, middles, and ends. But yet there are significant differences between the theatrical feature film and the made-for-television movie that any writer who wishes to write long form scripts must consider.
>
> **Budget Considerations**   In the world of television movies, decisions are more likely to be financial than artistic. This is not to say that made-for-television movies lack artistry, but more to suggest that the primary motivation for decision making in television movies is budget.
>
> Made-for-television movies are usually produced on a budget that, when compared to the average Hollywood feature film, is scaled down. . . . This decrease in budget imposes restrictions on the made-for-television movie. Movies made for television tend to keep the locations simple, have minimal special effects, and plots that are less complex. A television movie often only employs just one subplot whereas a feature film can have many subplots.
>
> **Structure**   When a writer sits down to create a screenplay for a feature, her or his structural options regarding the number of acts and the flow of the narrative are limited only by imagination. Film screenwriters have no obligation to tell a story in three acts, or to use a linear structure. But the structure of a

television movie script differs from that of a theatrical film script largely due to the insertion of commercial breaks into the story. Made-for-television movies might go so far as to utilize devices such as flashbacks or flash forwards, but typically a made-for-television movie has seven acts and follows a linear narrative.

The reason for this has to do with the insertion of commercial breaks into the movie. Because many commercial breaks disrupt the narrative flow, the writer needs to be concerned with act breaks that will keep the audience engaged enough to continue watching after a three- to five-minute commercial break.

As in a feature film, the made-for-television movie structures each act so that there is a mini plot point, a turning point, or a moment where the tension or conflict escalates at the end of the act. However, in feature screenplays this device is used to create rising action, but in television scripts it is used essentially to keep the audience watching.

Commercials also determine the length of each TV movie act that decreases as the story progresses. The first act is the longest, and each subsequent act becomes progressively shorter. In addition, the first act break almost never comes on the hour or the half hour. The rationale for this is twofold. First, there is the need to "hook" the viewer with a long first act. Once viewers are engaged with the film, they will be less likely to turn it off or switch channels during the commercials. Second, by avoiding placement of the act breaks on the hour or half hour, the viewer will be less likely to flip through channels throughout the commercial breaks and come upon another program or show that looks more interesting.

Length A feature film typically runs anywhere from 90–120 pages. And as a general rule of thumb, one page of a properly formatted feature film screenplay equals one minute of screen time. Hence, a 120-page feature would equal approximately 120 minutes, or two hours.

The time allotted for made-for-television movies is also 120 minutes; however, the average television movie only runs about 95 minutes. The other 25 minutes are filled with commercials and network promos. If a writer were to submit a script for a television movie, it would be expected that the script would run about 95 pages.

Content Another consideration for writing long form scripts is content. Language, nudity, and violence have far greater restrictions for television than they do for feature films. The content of a theatrical film can go as far as the studios and distributors wish to take it, depending on what rating they desire for the film's release. However, theatrical feature films that hope to one day be aired on network television must endure nudity, sexual content, and violence being edited for a television audience. But with language, which is more difficult to edit, feature film directors are careful to shoot television versions, asking actors to replace unacceptable expletives for words or phrases that are acceptable for TV.

When it was aired on network prime time, the film *Thelma and Louise* replaced the theatrical film version of the line, "I shoulda gone ahead and *fucked* her . . ." with the acceptable television version, "I shoulda gone ahead and *touched* her . . ." The television line had a vastly different meaning and was unlikely to be something that the character would have said considering that he had just attempted rape. However, that change in dialogue, along with some judicious editing, allowed the network to air that particular scene.

While standards for television content have changed, and will most likely continue to change, aspiring television movie writers should be aware of what is considered to be acceptable content for a television audience.

Format Screenplays are written in their own unique format. Software programs help make the writer's job easier by providing standard screenplay format. While the difference between writing a script for a television situation comedy differs from the format for a theatrical feature script, the television movie does not have its own unique format. Writers can use the same format for feature films that they would use for a made-for-television movie. All the elements of the screenplay form—scene headings, character names, parentheticals, dialogue, shots, and transitions—are all placed in the same location on the page. The only difference that the writer needs to consider is that scripts for television movies tend to label the beginning and the end of each act, with a page break at the end of each act. Feature films do not call out act breaks on the page, but instead allow the story to flow scene by scene from beginning to end.

Getting Started The best advice for writers wishing to write made-for-television movies would be to watch these movies and to learn understand the differences between plot and structure for television movies and theatrical features. While there are visible differences between writing a made-for-television movie and a theatrical feature film script, in the end what producers ultimately want is a well-written and compelling story.

Professor Stawarz offers examples of the theatrical film script and the made-for-TV film script. The first is an excerpt from the shooting draft for "The Powwow Highway," written by Stawarz and Janet Haney, produced by Handmade Films and released by Warner Brothers.

Note how the descriptions of the settings and characters combine with the dialogue to create atmosphere and introduce attitudes.

POWWOW HIGHWAY

EXT. VILLAGE—DUSK

ON SCREEN TITLE: NORTHERN CHEYENNE RESERVATION—LAME DEER, MONTANA

The Montana sky is glutted with grey winter clouds. Rundown buildings line the dirt streets of Lame Deer.

EXT. JIMTOWN BAR—DUSK

Muted laughter and country music waft from a rusty Quonset hut. A faded sign: JIMTOWN.

continued

INT. JIMTOWN BAR—DUSK

Indians crowd the lively hangout, gossiping and trading bawdy jokes. A Skin in a cowboy hat plucks a six string and sings country tunes. Just a pool table, but it's the social backbone of the rez.

INT. AT THE POOL TABLE—NIGHT

An eager crowd is mesmerized by a handsome Cheyenne who dominates the match. Chalking his cue, BUDDY RED BIRD leans across the table. He's lanky and strong, with an intense face.

Buddy SHOOTS, sinking the ball with startling force. BUFFALO HORNS, a pimply rube, pipes up.

> **BUFFALO HORNS**
> Who's head just rolled down that pocket, Buddy?

> **BUDDY**
> (grins)
> Looked a lot like Sandy Youngblood to me.

He takes aim and the eight ball ricochets off the side, spinning into the far pocket.

> **BUDDY**
> And that's the man in the White House.

Buddy's opponent, LOUIE SHORT HAIR, is an energetic hothead with the battle scars to prove it.

> **LOUIE SHORT HAIR**
> (irked)
> Hey, Red Bird, am I gonna get a shot off, or what?

WHAM! Down goes the six ball.

> **BUDDY**
> That was the coal mine at Big Mountain.

He angles on the two.

> **BUDDY**
> . . . Here's the Swinomish pipeline—

The two clacks into the four. Both vanish.

> **BUDDY**
> And that fuckin' monstrosity out on Route 314!

A stunning bank shot CLEARS the table. Buddy sets down his cue to a round of CHEERS.

> **OLD LADY**
> Teach ya ta play like that in college, Buddy Red Bird?

continued

LOUIE SHORT HAIR
Let's go, smartass. I'll whip your butt this time.

Louis puts the cue stick in Buddy's hand, but he gives it back.

BUDDY
Naw, I gotta go.

He heads out, to a chorus of protests. As Buddy reaches for the knob, the door CRASHES open.

ANGLE ON DOOR

Two hundred and fifty pounds of flab fill the doorway. Buddy has to struggle to squeeze by. The crowd howls with laughter.

A mammoth Cheyenne bumbles in, six foot four, with a long, greasy braid dangling, PHILBERT BONO would be terrifying, if he didn't have the face of an angel.

VOICES
Hey, fat Philbert!! Speaking'a Big Mountain—

Philbert lumbers toward the bar, ignoring the wisecracks. Someone tosses a lariat around his massive waist. He shimmies out of it, spilling drinks on the surrounding tables. The JEERING escalates.

Philbert commandeers two stools. MANNY sets him up with three cold beers. The fat man goes right down the line, draining them. Manny keeps it coming: chips, pretzels, beef jerky. Three more cold drafts.

MANNY
Okay, Phil?

Mouth fill, Philbert nods. Unwrapping a linty roll of quarters, he settles in front of the droning television.

INSERT—TV COMMERCIAL

A CAL WORTHINGTON-TYPE launches into his spiel. Ridiculous in a polyester suit and Indian headdress, the salesman sits atop a blue Pinto.

SALESMAN (V.O.)
(obnoxious)

How folks! Come down off the ranch or the rez and pick your pony! We got pintos, we got mustangs, we got Broncos, hot to trot and ready to roll. No money down, easy credit, ride one away today.

BACK TO SCENE

Manny picks up the change on the bar.

continued

> MANNY
> You borrowin' Louie's pick-up for the powwow?

Philbert chews, transfixed by the salesman's babble.

> MANNY
> You got a ride? Philbert?

The annoying car lot jingle simpers in the background.

> CUSTOMER (O.S.)
> Hey Manny! Where's them onion rings?

Manny moves off.

INSERT—TV COMMERCIAL

The giddy Salesman spurs the Pinto. It rolls forward through the car lot.

BEGIN PHILBERT'S VISION #1

A brave riding a spirited paint among a herd of wild horses.

CUT TO:

EXT. DESERT HIGHWAY—DAY

ON SCREEN TITLE: SANTA FE, NEW MEXICO

A yellow Volvo skims past the sage and cactus.

INT. VOLVO—DAY

The driver's window is down, and her long hair whips in the breeze, a glistening banner. BONNIE RED BIRD has the classic fine features of the Cheyenne.

Bonnie's children have inherited her looks: SKY, eight years old, sitting beside her, and seven year old, JANE, reading MAD magazine in the back seat.

There's a carefree feeling about this early morning ride. None of the Red Birds notice a POLICE CRUISER waiting in the brush.

INT. CRUISER—DAY

The OFFICER behind the wheel starts his engine.

> COP 1
> That's her. Let's go.

INT. VOLVO—DAY

Bonnie sees the flashing blue light in her rear view mirror.

continued

                                    BONNIE

   (startled)

   I'm not speeding!

                                    JANE

   You still gotta stop.

Bonnie turns onto the shoulder. The police car follows.

                                    SKY

   What did we do, Mom?

"The Powwow Highway," written by Stawarz and Janet Haney, produced by Handmade Films and released by Warner Brothers.

The following is from the TV screenplay for a CBC/BBC/PBS movie entitled *Napi's Rope*, written by Jean Stawarz and aired under the title *Spirit Rider*. Although the excerpt is too short to analyze content, it is a good example of script form and transitions.

                                    ACT TWO

INT. CABIN—NIGHT

Setting his things down, Jesse sneaks a look around. Not much in the way of furniture, but the place is clean and organized.

In one corner is a bed with a faded quilt. On the opposite wall, a rusty army cot is freshly made up with new sheets and a blanket. Offering the only privacy, a sheet hangs on a string between the beds.

                                    NINA

   I just need your signature here . . .

The old man stares at the papers spread out on the table, then slowly slides a drawer in the table open. He takes out a pen and signs his name with a flourish.

He carefully recaps the pen and puts it away.

                                NINA (CONT'D)

   Well, then I guess that's it. Unless you have questions . . .

                                    JOE

   No.

Shuffling to the stove, he inspects the contents of a boiling pot.

Nina snaps her brief case shut.

continued

NINA

> Here's my card. you can call if—

She glances at Jesse.

NINA

> If anything comes up.

The old man nods. Laying her business card on the table, Nina heads for the door.

Jesse follows her outside.

EXT. CABIN—NIGHT

An old, three ton Fargo is parked next to the Ford. Thick dew covers both vehicles. Jesse shivers involuntarily.

JESSE

> Hey, uh . . .

Nina turns as she opens the car door.

JESSE (CONT'D)

> (faltering)
> You taking off?

Every chink in his bravado facade shows.

NINA

> Don't worry. It'll be fine.

Instantly, Jesse regrets his weakness.

JESSE

> (snapping)
> Who said I was worried? He don't bother me.

Nina smiles.

NINA

> Go easy on him, Jesse. He's an elder.

She gets in her car, starts the engine and drives off, leaving Jesse alone, shivering in the cold.

END OF ACT TWO

ACT THREE

INT. CABIN—NIGHT

Joe's eating supper when Jesse comes back in. There's an empty plate on the table. Nervous, Jesse pulls a chair up to it.

Reprinted by permission of Jean Stawarz.

The Sitcom Model

One of the most successful television series of all time was *The Cosby Show,* which was taped before a live audience, usually in an hour and a half for each half-hour episode. The following is the first act (5 scenes) from a two-act, 15-scene episode, "Vanessa's Bad Grade." It is presented here as a model for writing sitcom scripts. Included is a listing of characters and scenes, usually provided by the writer to the director in the final draft of the script.

Most sitcoms tend to be played for one-liners or visual gags, with considerable stress on either double-entendres or slapstick. *The Cosby Show* found its humor in the characters' personalities, reflecting the gentler nature of a family household, while using for its weekly complication(s) realistic situations that confront many families and with which many viewers identified. It was one of the most honored and consistently high-rated programs in TV history. Many critics consider it a model for subsequent family comedies.

As you read "Vanessa's Bad Grade," note how the writer first establishes the atmosphere of the household and the feelings and personalities of the characters in relation to each other. The exposition comes out of the situation: Those who might not have watched *The Cosby Show* previously quickly learn that Cliff and Clair have found little time to go out by themselves and, in discussing their plans, they reveal that Cliff is a physician. The humor comes out of the situation: Cliff has little opportunity to go to a movie because he may be called upon to deliver a baby at any time. In determining whether Friday night is a possibility, he reads the weather forecast—"Friday's forecast: clear and warmer. No babies." It is not a gag that the writer has thrown in. It is what Cliff would logically say, given his personality.

The conflict, Vanessa wanting a new sweater, is presented immediately. It's certainly not an earth-shaking conflict, but one that is common to the homes of many viewers. Will she get the sweater? Most important, given the background of the characters, what conflicts will her efforts to get the sweater engender between Vanessa and her parents? Scene 3, between Cliff and Theo, and later with the Huxtable children, is humorous, developing out of what the characters would naturally do and say. Scene 4, in addition, pushes along the plot line, emphasizing Vanessa's continuing attempts to get the sweater. In scene 5, the conflict is heightened—it is the rising action in the play structure chart presented earlier in this chapter. Vanessa's bad grade, which she received after ostensibly studying with her boyfriend, Robert—she wanted the sweater in order to look nice when she went to the dance with him—complicates the situation.

The remainder of the play, not presented here because of space limitations, provides several positive guidelines for family and friends interrelationships: the impropriety of taking clothes without permission, the difference between serious studying and just socializing, and the need for everyone to take personal responsibilities seriously (Cliff and Clair say they'd like to play more, too, but have to work: "We have bills to pay and allowances to give out").

An overview shows the plot to be rather modest. But when combined with the depth of the characters who have been developed over a period of time, the excellent use of humor stemming from their interpersonal relationships, and a situation with which a substantial part of the audience—adults and children—can identify, we have an excellent script meeting the formula for the sitcom.

THE COSBY SHOW
"Vanessa's Bad Grade"
SHOW #0212–13

CAST

Cliff Huxtable	Bill Cosby
Clair Huxtable	Phylicia Ayers-Allen
Denise Huxtable	Lisa Bonet
Theo Huxtable	Malcolm-Jamal Warner
Vanessa Huxtable	Tempestt Bledsoe
Rudy Huxtable	Keshia Knight Pulliam
Robert	Dondre Whitfield
Announcer (V.O.)	TBA

SET

ACT ONE   PAGE
Scene 1:   INT. KITCHEN—MORNING (DAY 1)   (1)
Scene 2:   INT. LIVING ROOM—THAT AFTERNOON (DAY 1)   (7)
Scene 3:   INT. KITCHEN—CONTINUOUS ACTION (DAY 1)   (9)
Scene 4:   INT. LIVING ROOM—TWO DAYS LATER—AFTERNOON (DAY 2)   (15)
Scene 5:   INT. RUDY & VANESSA'S ROOM—CONTINUOUS ACTION (DAY 2)   (19)

ACT TWO
Scene 1:   INT. RUDY & VANESSA'S ROOM/HALLWAY—THAT NIGHT (DAY 2)   (21)
Scene 2:   INT. LIVING ROOM—LATER THAT NIGHT (DAY 2)   (23)
Scene 3:   INT. HALLWAY/RUDY & VANESSA'S ROOM—CONTINUOUS ACTION (DAY 2)   (26)
Scene 4:   INT. LIVING ROOM—CONTINUOUS ACTION (DAY 2)   (28)
Scene 5:   INT. DENISE'S ROOM—CONTINUOUS ACTION (DAY 2)   (32)
Scene 6:   INT. HALLWAY—CONTINUOUS ACTION (DAY 2)   (34)
Scene 7:   INT. DENISE'S ROOM—CONTINUOUS ACTION (DAY 2)   (35)
Scene 8:   INT. RUDY & VANESSA'S ROOM—CONTINUOUS ACTION (DAY 2)   (41)
Scene 9:   INT. KITCHEN—CONTINUOUS ACTION (DAY 2)   (44)
Scene 10:   INT. DENISE'S ROOM—A LITTLE LATER THAT NIGHT (DAY 2)   (50)

continued

ACT ONE
Scene 1

FADE IN:

INT. KITCHEN—MORNING (DAY 1)
(Cliff, Clair, Denise, Vanessa, Rudy)

(RUDY SITS AT THE TABLE BLOWING BUBBLES IN HER GLASS OF MILK. CLAIR ENTERS)

CLAIR

Rudy, don't blow bubbles with your straw.

RUDY

Okay.

(RUDY SUCKS MILK INTO THE STRAW, PUTS IT IN HER BOWL)

CLAIR

Rudy, put the straw down and drink your milk.

(RUDY DRINKS THE MILK OUT OF THE BOWL)

CLAIR (CONT'D)

All right, that's enough. Breakfast is over. Go brush your teeth and get ready for school.

(CLIFF ENTERS)

CLIFF

Hey, Pud.

RUDY

Hi, Daddy. Don't play with the straw.

(RUDY EXITS)

CLAIR

How are you feeling?

CLIFF

Hmmm.

CLAIR

When did you get in?

CLIFF

Hmmm.

CLAIR

Poor baby. That's the third time this week.

continued

CLIFF

Clair, I would say that during my career, I've delivered about three thousand babies. Somehow, almost all of them decided to be born between two and five A.M. on the coldest winter nights of the year. There must be an all-weather radio station just for babies. When they hear, 'It's two A.M. Heavy snows and arctic winds,' they shoot for daylight.

CLAIR

Maybe we should forget about the movie tonight.

CLIFF

No, no. We're going.

CLAIR

You're too tired.

CLIFF

I'll be fine.

CLAIR

That's what you always say. Then as soon as the lights go out, so do you. Why don't we go Friday night?

(CLIFF PICKS UP THE NEWSPAPER)

CLIFF

Listen to this, Clair. 'Friday's forecast: clear and warmer.' No babies.

CLAIR

Then Friday it is.

(VANESSA ENTERS)

VANESSA

Mom?

CLAIR

Yes?

VANESSA

Can we go shopping? I need a new sweater.

CLAIR

Vanessa, you just got some new sweaters for Christmas.

VANESSA

I know, but Robert's seen me in all those.

CLIFF

You could wear them inside out.

continued

VANESSA

But Robert's taking me to the school dance on Friday and I really want to wear a new sweater. I've even got one picked out.

CLAIR

Oh?

VANESSA

I want one exactly like the one Denise got.

CLAIR

Why don't you ask Denise if you can borrow hers?

VANESSA

Mom, she's not going to let me have her sweater.

CLAIR

She might. Why don't you tell her why you want it and ask her nicely? You may be surprised.

VANESSA

All right. I'll try. Denise . . .

(SHE EXITS)

CLIFF

You want to take any bets on this one?

CLAIR

It could happen. Denise has been in that position with Sondra, so she might be understanding.

CLIFF

Okay. A jumbo box of popcorn at the movie says Vanessa doesn't get the sweater.

CLAIR

I'll take that bet.

DENISE

Ha! Are you kidding? No way. You're not getting it.

(DENISE AND VANESSA ENTER)

VANESSA

But, Denise, I asked nicely.

DENISE

I don't care.

continued

VANESSA

But it's for the dance. Robert is taking me.

DENISE

I haven't even worn that sweater yet. Bye, Dad.

VANESSA

Why don't you wear it today, and then you've worn it. Bye, Dad.

(DENISE AND VANESSA EXIT)

DENISE

No.

VANESSA

But—

DENISE

No.

CLIFF

I like it buttered, no salt.

CUT TO: WARDROBE CHANGE
(Cliff)

ACT ONE
Scene 2

INT. LIVING ROOM—THAT AFTERNOON (DAY 1)
(Cliff, Theo)

(CLIFF IS ASLEEP ON THE COUCH. THEO ENTERS, SLAMS THE DOOR, REALIZES CLIFF IS THERE, RECLOSES THE DOOR QUIETLY. AS HE PASSES CLIFF REACHES UP WITHOUT OPENING HIS EYES AND GRABS THEO)

CLIFF

You slammed the door.

THEO

Sorry, Dad. I didn't know you were sleeping. But you tell us all the time to make sure the door is closed.

CLIFF

Sit down. Sometimes you slam the door so hard it sucks the air out of the house. That's why I always keep a window open, so the walls won't buckle.

THEO

Got it, Dad. Sorry I woke you.

continued

                              CLIFF
It's okay, Son. I've been trying to take a nap ever since Sondra was born. It's been twenty years. By now I'm so tired that if I ever do take that nap, I may never wake up.

                              THEO
Dad, that's a sad story.

<u>CUT TO:</u>

                          <u>**ACT ONE**</u>
                           <u>Scene 3</u>

<u>**INT. KITCHEN—CONTINUOUS ACTION (DAY 1)**</u>
(Theo, Vanessa, Robert, Denise)

(VANESSA AND ROBERT ARE AT THE TABLE)

                           VANESSA
I really love it when we study together.

                           ROBERT
Me, too.

                           VANESSA
I wish we had all our classes together.

                           ROBERT
Me, too.

(THEO ENTERS)

                            THEO
Hey, Robert.

                           ROBERT
Hey, Theo.

(THEO STARTS RUMMAGING THROUGH THE REFRIGERATOR)

                           VANESSA
Sshhh.

                            THEO
What?

                           VANESSA
Please keep it quiet. We're trying to study. We have a big history test tomorrow.

                            THEO
Okay. I was just looking for some juice.

continued

(THEO EXITS)

> **VANESSA**
> Did you hear who's playing at the dance Friday?

> **ROBERT**
> No.

> **VANESSA**
> The Spikes.

> **ROBERT**
> Wow. They've got saxophones.

> **VANESSA**
> And did you hear who's in charge of decorations?

> **ROBERT**
> Who?

(THEO ENTERS)

> **THEO**
> What are you guys studying?

> **VANESSA**
> The War of 1912.

> **ROBERT**
> Vanessa, 1812.

> **VANESSA**
> Right.

> **THEO**
> Well, I don't want to bother you because I know a lot happened in that war. I'll be done in a minute.

(DENISE ENTERS FROM THE LIVING ROOM)

> **DENISE**
> Hi Robert, Vanessa.

(AS SHE CROSSES TO THE PHONE)

> **DENISE (CONT'D)**
> Everyone stay out of the living room. I just woke Dad up, and he's real cranky.

(SHE PICKS UP THE PHONE AND STARTS TO DIAL)

> **VANESSA**
> Excuse me. We're studying in here.

continued

DENISE

I told Monica I'd call her.

VANESSA

Use the phone upstairs.

DENISE

Hey, I'm here.

VANESSA

But we're studying.

THEO

They're having a big test on the War of 1912.

DENISE

Vanessa, you can take a break for a minute so I can make one phone call.

VANESSA

We can't. We have to study.

DENISE

Come on, Vanessa.

VANESSA

Okay, I'll consider taking a break if you let me borrow that certain item of clothing I asked for earlier.

DENISE

I don't have to lend you something that belongs to me to use something that belongs to all of us.

SFX: PHONE RINGS
(THEO ANSWERS IT)

THEO

Huxtable residence. Hi, Janet. Just a second. Vanessa, should I tell her to call back?

VANESSA

No. Let's take a break.

ROBERT

Okay.

DENISE

Hey, wait a minute. You told me you couldn't take a break.

VANESSA

But it's for me.

continued

DENISE

Theo, don't give her the phone.

VANESSA

Give me the phone.

DENISE

Theo.

VANESSA

Theo.

THEO

Hey, I'm out of this.

(THEO PLACES THE PHONE ON THE REFRIGERATOR
(VANESSA SNATCHES IT)

VANESSA

Hi, Janet . . . She is? When did you find this out? . . . She must be doing this because she found out I was going to wear a red skirt . . .

DENISE

Thanks a lot, Theo.

(DENISE EXITS)

THEO

Do you have sisters, Robert?

ROBERT

No.

THEO

Go home tonight and thank your parents.

DISSOLVE TO: WARDROBE CHANGE
                                                       (Vanessa)

ACT ONE
Scene 4

INT. LIVING ROOM—TWO DAYS LATER—AFTERNOON (DAY 2)
(Cliff, Rudy, Clair, Vanessa, Announcer (V.O.))

(THE LIVING ROOM IS EMPTY. BOBO AND A COUPLE OF OTHER DOLLS ARE SITTING ON THE COUCH, FACING THE TELEVISION)

SFX: AEROBICS EXERCISE SHOW WITH COOL MUSIC

(CLIFF ENTERS)

continued

ANNOUNCER (V.O.)
This is the exercise class for the cool people. We are the people who believe you don't need pain to have gain. I'm going to tell you what you can do, but you do what you feel like doing. Just be cool about it. First, let's loosen up that neck. Take your head and just kind of roll it around. If you don't feel like it, that's cool.

(RUDY ENTERS)

RUDY
Hi, Daddy.

CLIFF
Whoa, Rudy, Aren't these your friends?

RUDY
They wanted to watch TV.

CLIFF
Are they trying to get in shape?

RUDY
Yes.

CLIFF
They don't look like they're really into it. Why don't you take them upstairs and read to them.

RUDY
Okay.

(CLIFF LOADS RUDY UP WITH THE DOLLS)

ANNOUNCER (V.O.)
Now, let's stretch out that lower back. Raise your arms. If you want to, raise them high above your head. If not, that's cool. Now bend over and touch your palms to your toes. That's all right. This time we're going to try it with your knees straight. Be cool about it. And remember, if you don't attack your heart, your heart won't attack you.

(CLIFF TURNS OFF THE TELEVISION)

(CLAIR ENTERS)

CLAIR
Hi, Cliff.

CLIFF
Hi.

CLAIR

continued

How are you feeling?

CLIFF
Great. I'm all ready for the movie tonight.

CLAIR
Are you sure you're not too tired?

CLIFF
No. I've gotten lots of sleep the last two days, and I just finished my exercises.

CLAIR
Good. This is supposed to be a fabulous movie. Carla told me at work today that this film has won major awards throughout Europe.

CLIFF
The thing that I'm really looking forward to about this movie, is the box of popcorn you owe me.

CLAIR
Cliff, you'll get your popcorn.

CLIFF
Not a regular now, Clair. A jumbo. Big. The giant tub. The size where you have to climb in with the popcorn and eat your way out.

CLAIR
You'll get it.

(VANESSA ENTERS)

VANESSA
Hi.

CLAIR
Hi, Vanessa.

VANESSA
When are we eating?

CLIFF
I'm not. I'm saving room for popcorn.

CLAIR
Vanessa, we're going to eat early.

VANESSA
Good. Because I want to have time to get ready for the dance tonight.

continued

(VANESSA EXITS)

CLIFF

And by the way, I also want the jumbo size soda.

CLAIR

That wasn't part of the bet.

CLIFF

Well, buy me the soda and I'll let you climb into my tub of jumbo popcorn.

<u>**CUT TO:**</u>

<u>**ACT ONE**</u>
<u>**Scene 5**</u>

<u>**INT. RUDY & VANESSA'S ROOM—CONTINUOUS ACTION (DAY 2)**</u>
(Theo, Vanessa)

(VANESSA IS SEATED ON THE BED)

THEO

Hey, Vanessa.

VANESSA

Theo, can I talk to you for a moment?

(THEO ENTERS)

THEO

What's wrong?

VANESSA

I got my history test back.

(VANESSA HANDS HIM THE TEST PAPER)

THEO

Whoa, this is a 'D.'

VANESSA

I know. I've never gotten a 'D' before. I've seen them, but never next to my name.

THEO

And this one's in red. That's the worst kind to get.

VANESSA

I don't know how it happened. Robert and I studied for this.

continued

THEO
Yeah, I saw that.

VANESSA
When do you think I should tell Mom and Dad?

THEO
The sooner the better.

VANESSA
But if I tell them now, they might not let me go to the dance with Robert.

THEO
Vanessa, there's a chance you may never dance again.

VANESSA
But how can they get mad? I've been getting 'A's' all along. This is just one little 'D.'

THEO
When it comes to Mom and Dad, there are no little 'D's.' Vanessa got a 'D.'

(THEO EXITS. ON VANESSA'S REACTION WE)

FADE OUT

END OF ACT ONE

From "Vanessa's Bad Grade," The Cosby Show, written by Ross Brown. Courtesy of The Cosby Show

SPECIAL PLAY FORMS

The "Premium" Play

Non-broadcast material, such as that on cable networks and over the Internet, are not yet subject—at this writing—to FCC regulation of indecency or profanity, although most cable nets are careful not to present content that is likely to lead to such regulation. Premium channels (or "pay" channels, as they are often called) have more leeway insofar as a viewer must especially opt to receive them. HBO (Home Box Office) has been remarkably successful in producing high-quality drama. One of its most acclaimed series, along with *The Sopranos*, was *Six Feet Under*. The following are excerpts from one of its programs, "The Rainbow of Her Reasons." The first excerpt is the initial scene, which introduces the characters and sets the theme and highlights the continuing dramatic device of the program—someone is dead before the first fade. The second excerpt illustrates the greater freedom premium cable shows generally have. The series freely deals with politics and religion, frequently with humor and satire, and does not shy away from profanity. The writer of this episode, Jill Soloway, is known for her irreverence and sharp humor.

EXT. POINT DUMB CLIFF - DAY

Sarah and Fiona, in hippie-hiking-wear, traverse a rocky path overlooking the ocean. Sarah brandishes an African walking stick, her breathing as clear as Nordic wind. Fiona grunts as she goes.

SARAH

Here, take this.

Sarah hands Fiona the walking stick, then picks up speed and gets a few feet ahead.

FIONA

You know, you were right? It is good I
got out, I was starting to feel depressed,
you know? Just the inside
of my house and all those kiln fumes.
And that morose NPR.
> (exhales)

Yes!

SARAH

You know I've seen a whale every time
I've been up here this month!

FIONA

You promised me whales!

Sarah makes her way around an outcropping where the path narrows like a ledge. The WIND WHIPS UP.

SARAH

> (not heard by Fiona)

Careful through here.

FIONA

Is that a whale or a wave!

Fiona looks out toward the sea, shading her eyes. instead of looking at the path ahead. Her next step puts her onto an unsteady piece of powdery sandstone that crumbles a little.

FIONA (CONT'D)

Oopsie.

SARAH

> (still walking, oblivious)

Foster told me they were sperm whales,
but I've seen pilot whales as well! Not that
I know the difference! He can tell by the
kind of patterns they make in the water!

continued

CLOSE ON FIONA'S FEET, which slip.

Sarah hears a ROCK tumbling, then turns to look. As she comes back around, she can't see much, just the walking stick doing cartwheels in the air as it bumps off the bluff.

                          FIONA
Sarah!?

Sarah comes back to the SOUND OF more FALLING ROCKS:

                          SARAH
You runnin' out of breath, pokey?

But it's too late. Fiona is nowhere to be found. The flurry of movement—leftover rock and leftover Fiona spirit—communicate something. Sarah whips around, looks out to sea, just in time to catch a distant glimpse of FIONA'S BODY HITTING THE WATER. Sarah stares at the water for a sign of Fiona. Nothing. Her jaw slacks open, as she goes into shock.

FADE TO WHITE.

A TITLE CARD FADES IN AND OUT, in BLACK LETTERING:

                 FIONA LENOMS KLEINSCHMIDT
                          1952–2005

INT. FUNERAL HOME—KITCHEN

Dregs of wine and food are left. Bettina and Ruth are exhausted, Sarah's in a drunken rage, her teeth stained red.

                          SARAH
I killed her! I killed my best friend!

                         BETTINA
Honey, you didn't kill her.

                          RUTH
Of course you didn't. You always tell
me everything happens for a reason.

                          SARAH
Oh, fuck off! Just fuck that one to
the ground, 'everything happens for a
reason,' what a crock!

                         (MORE)

                     SARAH (CONT'D)
You say there's a reason Grandma lost
her legs and there's a reason there's

continued

war and tsunamis and George Bush got
re-elected and they stopped
manufacturing Quaaludes?

                    BETTINA

Remember ludes? God, I remember
'ludes.

                    SARAH

Shit goes wrong because there's
fucking evil in the world like George W.
Bush and me! I'm evil!

                    RUTH

Sarah, no.

                    BETTINA
          (relishing this)

Let her go.

                    SARAH

It was my idea to go get her to go on
the walk, she didn't want to! I
dragged her, she turned me down twice!

                    BETTINA

Twice, huh? You left that part out.

                    SARAH

Who am I, the Antichrist? Someone
should lock me up and keep me in a
cage, someone should dig a hole and
throw me in it, not let me out—

Sarah slumps into her chair and SOBS LIKE A BABY. Bettina raises an eyebrow.

                    BETTINA
          (mouthing to Ruth only)

Twice?

FADE TO WHITE.

Courtesy of Jill Soloway

Content Drama

TV critic Tom Shales wrote in the *Washington Post* that, put together, all the media, including social networking "and its elevation of the trifling, the quotidian and the banal" have become "a passive sensory environment . . . standards seem to have been not so much lowered as eliminated." Shales concludes that "content" has replaced "substance." Yet, every once in a while television drama speaks out bravely and deals with key moral and ethical issues in society, revealing and discussing inequities in political, social, economic, and other spheres. The writer, usually limited to easy-laugh sitcoms (with laugh tracks) and non-controversial drama, occasionally has a chance to say something of importance. In earlier days of television, in the 1950s and 1960s, before the control of the media fell into fewer and fewer hands through multiple ownership and consolidation authorized by Congress and implemented by the Federal Communications Commission, a number of drama series dealt with critical issues in society. A prime example, since seen in continuing reruns, was "M*A*S*H," a brilliantly entertaining condemnation of war. In more recent years, real world issues were presented on every episode of "The West Wing" series. Arguably the most significant current writer and producer of content drama has been David E. Kelley, using a variety of settings in series such as "LA Law," "Picket Fences," "Chicago Hope," "The Practice," "Ally McBeal," "Boston Public," and, more recently, "Boston Legal." Steven Coe has written in *Broadcasting and Cable* that Kelley's writing approach is inimical in the world of computers: He writes his first drafts with a pen on a legal pad. His plots and frequent subplots maintain continuity from one episode to the next. "Hot button" issues come through the professions of the characters, from hospitals to courtrooms, and from their personal relationships and travails. Coe quotes Kelley as stating that when he writes he keeps in mind that the audience wants to be entertained and "that doesn't mean you can't provoke them and antagonize them and challenge them in the course of the entertainment as long as you keep the entertainment part of the equation alive." Following is an excerpt from a episode of "Boston Legal" entitled "Stick It," in which a court case includes what some critics believe has been the strongest condemnation of America's invasion of Iraq presented on television.

INT. JUDGE SANDERS' COURTROOM-DAY

(SHAPIRO MAKES HIS CLOSING STATEMENT)

SHAPIRO: Clearly she committed a crime. She didn't pay her taxes. The only question is will you (os) hold her accountable? (on camera) Now no doubt, Mr. Shore will try to paint her as (os) some kind of activist hero. (on camera) But she is no hero, folks. At a time when freedom has never been more (os) precarious in this country, for her to refuse her (on camera) civic and legal duty to pay her taxes, while we have soldiers dying over there, (os) this woman's (on camera) deliberate action is as unpatriotic, as un-American, as it is illegal. This is the cut and run behavior of a coward. (os) Don't you (on camera) dare declare her a hero.

continued

(SHAPIRO SITS DOWN; ALAN CONSIDERS A MOMENT AND THEN STANDS)

ALAN: (clears his throat) When the weapons of mass destruction thing turned out not to be true, I expected the American people to rise up. (laugh) They didn't. (os) Then when the (on camera) Abu Grab torture thing surfaced and it was revealed that our government participated in "rendition," (os) a practice where we kidnap people and turn them over (on camera) to regimes who specialize in torture, I was sure then the American people would be heard from. We stood mute. (os) Then came the news that we jailed (on camera) thousands of so-called terrorist suspects, locked them up without the right to a trial, or even the right to confront their accusers, certainly we would never stand for that. We did. (os) And now it's been discovered the executive branch has been conducting (on camera) massive illegal domestic surveillance on its own citizens, you and me. And I at least consoled myself that finally, finally the American people will have had enough. Evidently we haven't. (os) In fact, if the people of this country have spoken, (on camera) the message is we're okay with it all. Torture, warrantless search and seizures, illegal wiretappings, prison without a fair trial, or any trial, war on false pretenses, we as a citizenry are apparently not offended. There are no demonstrations on college campuses. In fact, there's no clear indication that young people even seem to notice. Well, Melissa Hughes noticed. Now you might think instead of withholding her taxes, she could've protested the old fashioned way. Made a placard and demonstrated at a presidential or vice-presidential appearance. But we've lost the right to that as well. The Secret Service can now declare free speech zones to contain, control, and in effect criminalize protest. Stop for a second and try to fathom that. (os) At a presidential (on camera) rally, parade, or appearance, if you have on a supportive t-shirt, you can be there. (os) If you're wearing or carrying something (on camera) in protest, you can be removed. This in the United States of America! This in the United States of America! Is Melissa Hughes the only one embarrassed?!

(ALAN SITS DOWN ON THE WITNESS STAND)

ALAN (CONT'D): (sigh)

SANDERS: Mr. Shore, that's a chair for witnesses only.

ALAN: (os) Really long speeches make me (on camera) so tired sometimes.

SANDERS: (os) Please get out of (on camera) the chair.

ALAN: Actually, I'm sick and tired.

continued

SANDERS: Get out of the chair.

ALAN: But what I'm most . . .

(ALAN STANDS)

ALAN (CONT'D):   . . . sick and tired of is how every time somebody disagrees with how the government is running things, he or she is labeled un-American.

(SHAPIRO STANDS)

SHAPIRO: Evidently It's speech time.

ALAN: And speech in this country is free, you hack. (os) Free for me, (on camera) free for you, free for Melissa Hughes to stand up to her government and say, "Stick it."

SHAPIRO: Objection!

ALAN: I object to government abusing its power to squash the Constitutional (os) freedoms of its citizenry. And (on camera) God forbid anybody challenge it. They're smeared as being a heretic. Melissa Hughes is an American. Melissa Hughes (os) is an American. (on camera) Melissa Hughes is an American!

SANDERS: Mr. Shore, (os) unless you have (on camera) anything new and fresh to say, please sit down. (os) You've breached the decorum (on camera) of my courtroom with all this hooting.

ALAN: Last night, I went to bed with a book. Not as much fun as a 29 year old, (os) but the book contained a speech by Adlai Stevenson. (on camera) The year was 1952. He said, "The tragedy of our day is the climate of fear in which we live. And fear breeds repression. Too often sinister threats to the Bill of Rights, to freedom of the mind, are concealed under the patriotic cloak of anti-Communism." Today, it's the cloak of anti-terrorism. (os) Stevenson also (on camera) remarked it's far easier to fight for principles than to live up to them. I know we are all afraid. But the Bill of Rights, we have to live up to that. We simply must. (os) That's all Melissa Hughes was trying to say. She was (on camera) speaking for you. I would ask you now to go back to that room and speak for her.

END ACT FOUR

Courtesy of David E. Kelley

The Soap Opera

The daytime adult dramatic serial, or soap opera, was described by critic Gilbert Seldes in *The Great Audience* as "the great invention of radio, its single notable contribution to the art of fiction." Although the radio soap opera is no longer with us, the television soap opera has become at least its equivalent in art, interest, and impact. Fergus Bordewich wrote in the *New York Times*:

> Although soap opera aficionados would seem to be a minority among college students, there are nonetheless thousands of young people around the country who daily put aside their Sartre, Machiavelli and Freud . . . to watch the moiling passions of middle-class America as portrayed on daytime TV. What is it about these slow-moving melodramas with their elasticized emotions that today's college students find so engrossing? . . . The fact is that in recent years the subject matter of daytime TV has changed and become much more relevant to the interests of young viewers . . . the "generation gap," abortion, obscenity, narcotics and political protest are now commonly discussed and dealt with on the soap operas of TV.

Prime-time soap operas have become among the highest rated shows on television, here and abroad. To avoid a confusion of terms, we refer to prime-time soaps as the continuing dramas with a set of continuing characters and continuing plot lines.

Most soap opera viewers seek a vicarious excitement that they do not ordinarily experience. Seeing people with problems at least as bad as the viewers' own makes their lives a little more tolerable. Soaps provide information, education, and emotional relief. Some hospitals' group therapy sessions use soap operas as models, where patients relate the characters' problems to their own. Some viewers identify so strongly that they call or write in to the network or station as if the soap characters were real, sympathizing with them, and asking for the names and addresses of the psychotherapist, abortion clinic, or drug rehabilitation center used in the show by the fictional characters so that they can seek the same help.

Like life, soap operas just seem to go on and on with no endings in sight, just a series of continuing complications. Sometimes soaps seem a little too clear cut—good is good and bad is bad. The writer should find appropriate median areas. Keep in mind that soaps offer the audience identification and diversion at the same time. This means that the plot lines and characters have to be flexible, meeting the audience's needs and reflecting the changes in society.

Technique

The setting should be familiar—the household, doctor's office, school, police station, fire station, small town, or large city—presented so viewers anywhere can identify in some way with the background and environment.

The characters, likewise, should be familiar, not necessarily in a detailed way, but in the kinds of persons they are and the problems they encounter. Every viewer should be able to say, "That person is like Uncle Mike, or Cousin Amy, or the plumber, or—even—like me." That means developing the characters on simple and obvious levels, with clear, direct motivations.

Most important, the characters should be provided with the opportunity to get into infinite amounts of trouble. They must face problems that are basically real, but that can hold the audience with their melodrama. Sometimes the characters must face insurmountable odds, yet somehow overcome them, unless a performer is leaving the show and you have to kill off or otherwise get rid of his or her character. To create vicarious adventure for the audience, the characters should do things the viewers would like to do, but probably never will.

Because the soap opera's principal purpose is to create viewer empathy and identification with the characters, the characters must be the motivating factors when you create the scripts. The plot should contain a number of subplots to accommodate the many characters. Though bearing on the main conflict, the subplots should complicate each character's life, sometimes almost beyond endurance.

Because the soap must continue year after year, and because some viewers cannot watch each episode, the plot usually moves very slowly, with one minor event at a time. Naturally, on the weekly soaps, each episode must have a sharp plot, involving many characters in moments of crisis. An unexpected knock at the door can be built into a complication lasting for weeks or months on the daily soaps. Daily soap opera dialogue is much like that of real life, slow and undramatic. Listen to the people talk on subways, street corners, and in supermarkets. The dialogue on the weekly soaps, however, usually reflects their hyperaction.

Start each episode at a peak—the crisis of what seems to be a complication. In each program that complication should be solved, or take another turn and level off. Before the program is over a new complication should be introduced, making it necessary for the audience to tune in the next episode to find out what will happen.

In all soaps, daily or weekly, you need a **lead-in**—a summary of the basic situation and the previous episode. You also need a **lead-out**—the new complication, the cliff-hanger that brings the audience back.

The Miniseries

The miniseries enables the writer to bypass the usual time restrictions of television. With four, six, or even more hours, the writer can include a great many characters and subplots. Exposition can be presented slowly and carefully. Characters can be explored in depth. You have time to adequately prepare and clearly delineate the socio-psychological as well as physical setting. Sometimes the longer length lures a writer into the soap opera syndrome: a slow, literal pace. The miniseries is not a soap opera, to be carried through dozens and even hundreds of hours. It is a complete play that should hold the audience for the several episodes that it is on the air. Like any good play, the miniseries needs a tight, consistently developing rising action.

Even though the miniseries usually is produced as a made-for-television movie, don't lose sight of the television medium's special qualities. Regardless of length, don't succumb to the temptation to pad; if the going gets boring, the audience will switch to another channel.

Many miniseries are based on history. Be accurate. While fictionalizing characters and enhancing events, don't misrepresent the facts or the course of history. A highly lauded miniseries, *John Adams*, had excellent production qualities and performances. Unfortunately, it had historical inaccuracies that were ignored to enhance the dramatic aspects. Always keep in mind that a play is heightened life, and though you should avoid melodrama, you need to make history dramatic and accurate at the same time.

The Adaptation

Some miniseries are taken from novels or nonfiction works. The adapter's biggest problem is getting away from the original work. Avoid slavishly following the original's action sequence and dialogue. Compared with a play, those elements in a prose work can be undramatic, repetitious, and introspective. The author of a novel or a history can describe people, explain their feelings, clarify situations and motivations, and even present the characters' innermost thoughts without the characters themselves uttering a word. In the play you can *explain nothing;* you must *show everything.*

Get away from the craft of the original work and create a new work, using as a base the theme, background, characters, and plot. A sense of the original dialogue is important, but non-dramatic dialogue from a book frequently sounds ludicrous when read aloud. Become thoroughly familiar with the original work, then lay it aside and develop your play structure from the elements you have.

Retain the author's intent, but don't be literal. You are adapting, not copying. Where necessary, delete and add scenes and characters, combine characters, change characterizations, add action sequences. Writer-adaptor Irving Elman analyzed some pitfalls as well as advantages of two approaches to adaptation.

> The tendency with the first type is for the writer's creative urge, with no outlet through original creation of his own, to use the material he is adapting merely as a point of takeoff, from which he attempts to soar to heights of his own. If he happens to be a genius like Shakespeare those heights can be very high indeed. But if he is not a genius, or even as talented as the writer whose work he is adapting, instead of soaring to heights, the adaptation may sink to depths below the level of the material he "adapted." The second writer, with sufficient outlet for his creativity through his own writing, is less tempted (except by his ego!) to

show up the writer whose work he is adapting, proving by his "improvements" on the other writer's material how much better a writer he is. But if he genuinely likes and respects the material he is adapting, he will restrain himself to the proper business of an adaptor: translating a work from one medium to another with as much fidelity to the original as possible, making only those changes called for by the requirements of the second medium, trying in the process not to impair or violate the artistry of the original.

The Sitcom

Good comedy doesn't only make people laugh; it makes them think and feel at the same time. At an early age some of us are instilled with wit, outrageousness, sensitivity, absurdity, incongruity, incisiveness, and a few other attributes that constitute humor. When we combine these talents with an irreverent look at the sacred cows of the society in which we live, and then learn the techniques of how to express them dramatically, we have the tools for comedy writing.

Good comedy has always been born out of contemplating the seriousness of life. Next time you watch a sitcom on television, see if it leaves you laughing, thoughtful, and stimulated, or whether it narcotizes your brain and your feelings. Too many of the latter type are poorly written sophomoric farces, satisfied with surface characterizations and trite situations. Good sitcoms are good plays. You can create characters with comic flaws or, if you're not careful, you can create comic stereotypes. Once the characters have been established, the dialogue and plot emanating from them are clear, and your principal writing job is to find something new or different for them to deal with each week.

The Cartoon

Although the animated cartoon is associated with children's programming and, when written for a children's audience, follows the principles that apply to writing children's scripts, several series have established the viability of the television animated program for adults. Animated characters have one advantage over "live" characters in television plays. They can do and say things that are consistent with their cartoon characters that the audience of a real-character program would not accept. The animated program can satirize behavior, ideas, institutions, and even contemporary figures in a way that the regular drama or sitcom usually does not. The shock of the satirical edge in the animated program is blunted by an unspoken perception that, after all, it's not real but a cartoon, whereas in a "real people" program, similar satire of people or institutions might be seen as a personal attack on one's self, heroes, or ideology. The "toon" children in *South Park* express adult ideas that would be considered outrageous if expressed by "real" people.

Whether animated or real, good satire requires consistency in the characters and their motivations. The principles of writing the good play—relating to character, plot, dialogue, exposition, preparation, and setting—apply as much to writing the animated adult cartoon as to writing the non-animated adult drama or sitcom. *The Simpsons*, for example, represent reality as much as the characters do in a non-animated drama—the working-class families of the real world, creating empathy between themselves and their audience. As Charles McGrath wrote in an article entitled "The Triumph of the Prime Novel" in the *New York Times Magazine*, "The most realistic TV family of all . . . is Homer and Marge and the gang . . ."

SPECIAL CONSIDERATIONS

As noted in the genres discussed in previous chapters, the writer should consider the orientations of certain audiences.

The Children's Program

Three major types of children's shows dominate television: the educational program; the serious drama; and the equivalent of the lowest-common-denominator sitcoms for adults, the Saturday morning children's cartoons. This section deals only with the programs that are in play form—including cartoons. Saturday "kidvid" has always been to some degree exploitative of children, stressing violence and product advertising. Some children's shows have become program-length commercials, making the product the actual content of the script.

If you are going to write plays for children, you are likely to be faced with the kind of ethical dilemma discussed in Chapter 1. Certainly, your conscience tells you not to create a program that can be psychologically harmful to children, but your checkbook tells you that you need money to pay the rent. Nevertheless, we can hope that the writer, first and foremost, would think about the program's effect on the vulnerable minds and emotions of young viewers. Even *unintended* violence and prejudice are inexcusable. If you have any qualms of conscience, try out new program ideas on child experts and advocates before writing the treatment of a script that might prove harmful to children.

For the writer of the children's program, imagination is the key. Some advertisers, producers, and writers think that children will believe anything. Actually, children's imaginations are so sharp that they are sometimes more critical than adults. Children will believe a fantasy, if it has a valid, believable base to begin with. If characters, situation, and environment are established logically in terms of the characters' motivations, the subsequent events and actions will be accepted. The best format is that which respects the child who is watching.

Read the approaches and techniques for writing children's programs in Chapter 9.

Women

The negative images of women in television and radio are legion. Commercials, dramas, and sitcoms frequently stereotype female characters as either incompetent or overbearing. Studies of Saturday morning cartoons show that even children's programs have few females who are principal characters and most are used to support males in their tasks. Females are usually subservient or submissive and are usually the victims of actions initiated by male characters. Even where a female is a leading character, she frequently encounters a problem that can be solved only by a male.

However, adult female representations have changed considerably in recent years, reflecting the impact of the feminist movement and the work of organizations such as the National Organization for Women. Women characters in TV have increasingly been written as professionals in prestigious fields, including government leaders and judges, and in other roles formerly reserved for males, including physicians and police officers. Television writers have given girls and young women new role models on which to pattern their own future careers.

Racial and Ethnic Stereotyping

The principal problems racial and ethnic minorities have with the media are similar to the traditional roles of women: denigrating, stereotyping, or unrealistically sympathetic or condescending portrayals. Rarely is this because of conscious racism, but rather because of insensitivity. Unless you have been part of the group in the portrayal, you will have difficulty understanding the special experiences of members of that group in society.

Writer Donald Bogle stated that "the television industry protects itself by putting in a double consciousness . . . [it takes] authentic issues in the black community and distorts them." *Washington Post* critic Joel Dreyfuss reviewed a new television series about a black family, advising that if the producer "gets some black input into the writing end of the program, it might move away from the brink of absurdity and develop into a pretty good television program."

Lorraine Misiaszek, as director of Advocates for Indian Education and producer of television and radio programs, stated her concern about language and terminology as conveyors of stereotypes. "Anyone concerned with script writing," she said, "ought to be aware of this problem. It is not necessarily intentional, but it happens because of the general conditioning in our society that causes people to think of Native Americans in terms of stereotypes." Thomas Crawford, writer-producer of Native American-oriented programs, advised that "in writing scripts with, for, or about Native Americans, one must first of all become familiar with the idioms, patterns of expression, turns of thought, and pronunciations of the Indian community with which one is dealing." Russ Lowe, as a producer of a weekly radio program for the Chinese Affirmative Action Media Committee, stressed the necessity of getting an accurate understanding of the perspectives and viewpoints of the Chinese-American that are not otherwise usually presented on the air. Dr. Palma Martinez-Knoll, who produced the Project Latino series in Detroit, stated that "too many writers, because of lack of understanding, are either prejudicial or condescending. When writing about Latinos, or creating Latino characters, make them part of everyday society, not an excluded group." She urged the writer to show the Latino and Latina as responsible persons who are integral parts of the community.

Even long established subgroups of the white majority are subject to stereotyping. How many gangster characters do you see in television dramas who have a last name ending in "a" or "o"? New immigrant groups are particular targets, and Southeast Asians have joined blacks and Latinos as television's stereotypes of drug pushers. As a result of the "9-11" attack, Arab-Americans and American Muslims are frequently portrayed as terrorists, although the most outrageous domestic terrorist act, the bombing of the Murrah Federal Building in Oklahoma City, was committed by white Christian Americans. Groups such as the aged and the mentally and physically handicapped are other minorities who have been largely neglected or stereotyped by the media. The key for the writer is sensitivity to people's needs as a whole and an understanding of and empathy with the specific person or group being portrayed.

INTERNET CONSIDERATIONS

The availability of links within the context of a play presented on the Internet—whether drama, sitcom, soap, or any other dramatic genre—enhances the real life approximation of the material. Most of the material on television and virtually all the material in feature films is in play form. In real life, the audience has an infinite number of choices in any given situation, depending on the audience's personal interests and the play's characters' personal traits. As noted earlier in this chapter, the characters write the play. Any given character says and does only what that character must do and say under the given circumstances.

Life is not one-dimensional and neither are people; thus, the existence of choices. In creating empathy between each individual member of the audience and the characters or personalities the writer creates, the writer needs to provide opportunities for the viewers to choose those variables that bring him or her closer to any given character, even to the extent of interactively changing the plot line of the play, inasmuch as in a good play the characters determine the action and complications of the plot, not the other way around. Therefore, the writer can offer multiple exposition possibilities, a variety of possible plot complications to move along the rising action, and even a selection of climaxes or endings, including different resolutions. The viewer can become more immersed, more a part of the Internet presentation than with other media. The writer should be sure, no matter how many linkage variables, that a consistency of character and dialogue is maintained in any combination of whatever links, sidebars or choices are available.

Let's say you have a drama scene in which the husband and wife are arguing about a particular vacation they took. In the room is a photo album. Although neither the husband nor the wife wishes to risk being wrong by getting out the photo album to verify where the vacation was, the writer can, during the argument, focus a shot on the album and let the audience know that by clicking the computer cursor on the album it will automatically open, giving the audience an opportunity—if they want to take it—to determine who is right or wrong about the vacation site. The argument might even concern which music they danced to on that vacation; similarly, the writer can enable the audience to click on a designated CD in the music cabinet in the couple's living room and listen to the specific selection. Another example: the couple is being nostalgic about a safari they took in Kenya's Masai Mara game preserve; the viewer can click on an icon for an interactive film and take a similar trip—even a virtual reality trip—on that safari route. Just imagine the kinds of sci-fi virtual reality experiences you, as the writer, can provide, enabling the audience to explore a myriad of choices and experiences—even, perhaps, being eaten by a lion!

Episodic Review, an online magazine "devoted to original Web-based entertainment" such as Web soap operas, comedy and drama series, serial novels, Internet cartoons, and online journals, listed the following qualifications for a Web program:

1. High quality writing.
2. Superior editing, with few, if any, grammar errors or misspellings.
3. Accessibility; regardless of special effects, add-ons, or other technology used, the site has to be available to a majority of browsers. If, for example, the web site can be seen only by Netscape 6.0 users with Flash and high speed access, it is too limited.
4. Good design. The site must be easily navigated, with few if any broken links or images.
5. A special or unique quality that differentiates it from other similar sites.

Cypher Films of New York has for several years made short films for the Internet. Executive officer and writer-producer Franklyn Strachan offered some advice to online writers, stating that writing and shooting for online distribution clearly is different than doing it for other media, principally because "you are usually dealing with limited time and a limited screen. There is less time to tell a story and less space to compose a screen shot. Your thinking has to get smaller and be faster paced." Whether one is creating a one-minute or a one-hour presentation, he urges the writer to make sure that it's a concept he or she has a passion for, that offers feelings or ideas that are important. He suggests not only creating an outline, but early on a storyboard to provide an understanding of what the characters look like and what they wear. Strachan stated that one must be aware of time limits. "In a short online video, a scene to which you want to add tension may be only ten seconds long, but if all your other scenes are five seconds long, you have tension." He adds that "lighting has to be brighter than normal for Internet videos," and that one must tell stories "in a much shorter time frame." "Mainly you are composing for a tiny screen and computer speakers," he stated. Strachan advises that even when one makes videos of live, unpredictable events, having a narrative is still essential, to separate the videos from those of "tourists taking random pictures."

The Internet imposes its own restrictions. The size of a computer monitor and an iPhone or iPad makes a significant difference to a viewer's perception of the image displayed. Majestic scenery and big scale events lose in size and thereby impact. The experience becomes more intimate and less awe-inspiring. The limited size also restricts the amount of information that can be shown to the viewer at any one time. Objects that stand on the movie screen or TV monitor may disappear into the background.

To improve image quality, one should minimize the amount of unneeded detail in the picture. Keeping backgrounds simple and using even lighting makes the image easier to compress. Big action sequences, subtle references through details, and set design might be lost.

Because the Internet reaches a worldwide audience, high concept projects are better than more complex narratives with strong national or cultural references and ties. In general, high concept films have wider audience appeal, driven by simple plots and developments easily translated to different languages and cultures. The marketing potential of reaching a global audience also makes the Internet a potential gold mine for merchandising, sequels, and spin-offs.

The distinguishing trait of the Internet as opposed to other media is its potential for interaction. The creation of an interactive script involves a great deal more work in its creation than a conventional script. First, for the audience to be able to make its own choices and "create" its own adventures, the writer must exhaust all possible outcomes and developments of the story while still working toward one or several different resolutions that stay true to the story's internal logic and character development. This constitutes one of the main challenges for interactive writers, developing their vision of an ambiguous text to engage their audiences into propelling the narrative in a certain direction.

PROBLEMS AND POTENTIALS

You may believe you have written an excellent play, and then find that the final version of your manuscript has little relationship to the subsequent production or shooting script. The production script contains all the revisions, plus technical information, put in by the producer and director. Unless the writer's contract includes the right to approve of any further revisions, the writer may find changes in content, form, and style about which he or she has not even been informed.

After a script has run the gamut of script editor, producer screening, agency or network approval, production planning, rehearsal, and final editing for performance, the writer might have difficulty recognizing it. As a writer, all you can do is offer a script of the highest artistic merit of which you are capable, and then fight to keep it that way. At worst you can always request that your name be taken off the credits.

Rod Serling, one of television's most articulate as well as prolific writers (many college students know only his work as creator and principal writer of *The Twilight Zone*), called television a medium of compromise for writers. In an article by D. B. Cohen in the *Washington Post,* Serling criticized television for "its fear of taking on major issues in realistic terms. Drama on television must walk tiptoe and in agony lest it offend some cereal buyer." Serling also was concerned about commercial intrusion into the artistic integrity of television plays. "How," he asked, "do you put on a meaningful drama or documentary that is adult, incisive, probing when every 15 minutes the proceedings are interrupted by 12 dancing rabbits with toilet paper?"

Through his *Twilight Zone* series and in many of his other TV plays, Serling dealt with social issues such as prejudice, racism, individual liberties, and nuclear war that were otherwise considered too controversial by most networks and sponsors. Despite the restrictions he encountered, shortly before Serling died he said that television had developed to a point where, at least sometimes, "you can write pretty meaningful, pretty adult, pretty incisive pieces of drama."

So, despite the networks *and* sponsors *and* ad agencies *and* story editors *and* producers *and* directors, whether you write something of importance and value depends mostly on you. You can find comfort because your script is still the prime mover, the one element upon which all other elements of the production stand or fall. Without your script, there is no program. With a script of high quality, with writing of ethical and artistic merit, you can at least take pride in knowing that you have made a significant effort to enlighten as well as to entertain, to stimulate as well as to satiate, and to fulfill some of the mass media's infinite potentials.

APPLICATION AND REVIEW

1. Write an episode of your favorite television sitcom or drama. (Depending on time or instructional circumstances, you may wish to limit it to a 15-minute script.)
2. Adapt the script written for exercise 1 to the Internet.
3. Write an original play for the medium of your choice.

CHAPTER 11

Professional Opportunities

"So you want to write for the media!" could be an advertisement heading to entice glamour-struck young people into schools, correspondence courses, books, or computer software all but guaranteed to make them next year's Emmy or Oscar winners.

I am convinced—after many years of teaching television and radio writing, of writing for television and radio, and of knowing television, radio, screen, and Internet writers— that creative writing of the highest quality can rarely be taught. It requires that amorphous gift called talent.

Putting together words or visual images that conform to specified formats can be taught. In that sense, many people can learn to write rundown sheets, routine sheets, and even very good scripts for the media.

That's not a bad thing. If one accepts a certain format and approach as ethical and contributory to a positive effect upon the viewers, then nothing is wrong with being a competent draftsperson of scripts. You can attain great success in this role of interpretive writer—taking a format already created by someone else and putting it into a form that best presents it to the audience. Like an actor, a dancer, a musician.

Writing in its highest sense, however, is not copying or interpreting. Writing is *creating*. The writer's ultimate aim is to be creative—as the composer, the painter, the choreographer is creative.

Creativity cannot be taught in a classroom but comes from a combination of motivated talent and experience. Certain forms, techniques, and approaches can and should be learned. Just as the painter must learn what is possible with color, form, line, and texture, so the writer must learn what is possible with the tools available to him or her. That is what this book tries to do.

The *creative* art of writing requires more, however. Creative writing is a synthesis of one's total psychological, philosophical, and physical background, heightened into expressiveness through knowledge of form, technique, and approach. I have rarely found a person in any of the classes I have taught who was not able to write an acceptable rundown, routine sheet, or script in each media program genre. But too infrequently have I found a person who could go beyond a basic format and create a script that truly fulfilled the potentials of the media in affecting—in a humanistic, positive manner—the minds and emotions of the audience.

But if you have the talent and learn the technique, that Emmy or Oscar might well be within reach.

Beyond skills and talent, you need dedication. You need even more: passion.

Jill Soloway, whose writing credits include HBO's acclaimed series *Six Feet Under*, describes in her book, *Tiny Ladies in Shiny Pants*, the need for passion in writing. "It wasn't until I actually got excited about writing, real writing, that I had samples worth sharing," she states. She adds this practical approach: "Whether you have the passion or are faking it, you should be open to what the exec wants. But not too open." Soloway emphasizes that there is no such thing as a "Cinderella Story" when it comes to writing. Write and keep writing. You need experience. "When you think you can jump in without doing the work, it's an insult."

I hope that you who are reading this and contemplating a career in writing for the media are capable of the highest level of creative writing. But even if you are not, career opportunities exist. Indeed, sometimes the creative writer has less opportunity for gainful employment because of difficulty in lowering his or her artistic plane of writing to conform with the formulas of the particular programs or script types.

In presenting some views on careers and the opportunities for writers in various areas of the media, I am making no judgment about what you should accept for your particular talents, skills, and ambitions. How far you should go or how limited you should let yourself be only you can decide. But know your capabilities and what satisfies you. Set some goals.

The combinations of potential and restriction, of opportunity and responsibility, of creativity and compromise pertain to virtually all writing jobs for all levels and types and for all broadcast stations and other media-producing organizations. A flyer announcing a Humanitas Prize for television writing by the Lilly Endowment, Inc., expressed it this way:

> The writer of American television is a person of great influence, for the values projected on the TV screen begin in his or her mind, heart, and psyche. Few educators, churchmen or politicians possess the moral influence of a TV writer. This entails an awesome responsibility for the TV writer. But it also provides a tremendous opportunity to enrich his or her fellow citizens. How? By illuminating the human situation, by challenging human freedom, by working to unify the human family. In short, by communicating those values which most fully enrich the human person.

Whether the professional media writer is always or ever permitted to do this is another story. Barbara Douglas, whose executive position at Universal Studios included finding scripts, packages, and properties for film and television, acknowledged the frustrations of the writer within the commercial requirements of broadcasting, but believed that there is hope for creative, talented people who can write alternative scripts that large companies could produce. She affirmed, in *Media Report to Women*, that integrity can be retained within an area of compromise, in which a script has mass commercial value but is not a sellout. "It's this fairly narrow area of quality which I wish our promising young people would consider, instead of either leaping to low-grade imitations of what appears to be a way to turn a fast dollar, or alternatively coming from a place that's so far from the mass mind that the script turns the studio people off before they get to page five."

Barbara Allen, writer, producer, and teacher of television and radio, offered some additional basic considerations for those who want to write successfully for the broadcast media. She suggested that you should be

- Creative enough to turn out bright ideas fast
- Self-disciplined enough to watch others "improve" on them
- Organized enough to lay out a concise production script
- Unstructured enough to adjust to last-minute deviations
- Persistent enough to be able to research any subject thoroughly
- Flexible enough to be able to present it as a one-hour documentary or a 30-second spot
- Imaginative enough to write a script that can be produced at a nominal cost
- Practical enough to have a second plan for doing it at half that cost
- P.S. It also helps if you can spell, punctuate, and type

Where are the jobs in broadcast writing? Allen described the categories as follows:

- *Network radio:* news, editorials, features
- *Network television:* soap operas, game shows, stunts for quizzes, comedy writing, preprogram interviews, research, children's programs, series writing, news, promotion, continuity—including all program genres and formats
- *Local radio and television:* news, promotion, continuity, documentaries, special programs
- *Related areas:* cable systems, independent film production and syndication companies, advertising agencies, freelance commercials, department stores, national and state service groups, safety councils and charity

enterprises, utility companies, farm organizations, religious organizations, government agencies, educational institutions and organizations, other corporate business and industry

Other writing positions include:

- ▪ Advertising sales reps at radio stations that prepare copy for their advertisers
- ▪ Radio deejays and program directors who write promos and station IDs
- ▪ Freelance producers and personnel of production houses who may write a variety of scripts

And, as stressed in this 11th edition of this book, convergence has created a new and all-encompassing playing field for the media writer: the Internet.

Most writers need to know how to write in a number of media forms. The more, the better the job opportunities.

Although regular staff jobs with stations, corporate organizations, and other entities are salaried, a great many writers are freelancers; they write scripts on a per assignment basis, negotiating a fee per script with the media outlet, producer, or corporate organization, subject to the minimum compensation standards established for those adhering to the Writers Guild of America contractual requirements.

Sometimes the writer works alone on a script; sometimes the producer assigns the writer to a team of writers. In still other circumstances, a salaried or freelance writer finds that after a first rewrite the script is turned over to someone else for completion.

Be prepared for frustration and even unfairness. As with anyone else entering any phase of the visual or audio fields, you must be willing to break in with a low-level job, usually in a small market or in a junior position on a corporate team.

Writer's Digest, which provides continuing analyses of markets for writers in the various electronic media as well as in print, summarized opportunities in broadcasting (and cable) as follows:

> Opportunities at local stations and networks include news writing, editing, continuity writing, commercial and promotion writing, and script and special feature writing.
>
> News writers and editors collect local news and select stories from the wire services, often editing and rewriting them for local audiences. News persons may also serve as reporters, covering local stories and interviews along with a cameraperson. Continuity writers develop commercials for sponsors that don't have advertising agencies, write station promotional and public service announcements, and occasionally program material. Both news and continuity writers are able to get across the essentials of a story in simple, concise language. Most script work is done on a contract or freelance basis, but some staff writers are

employed. Special feature subjects are generally sports and news stories, usually written by a staff writer in one of these areas. However, stations are always eager to listen to new feature ideas from staff writers or outside writers.

Good broadcast writers have all the basic writing skills at their command and, since they frequently don't have time to rewrite, develop speed and accuracy. A college education in liberal arts or journalism is desirable, but a good writer who has other talents such as announcing is also well-qualified. The writer with talent and original ideas will get the job.

It is best to approach a broadcast company through an employment agency. If you prefer not to do this, submit a resume with some of your best writing samples to the station or personnel manager and ask for an interview. Apply first at a small station and get that priceless experience that you can list on your work record, then contact the larger organization.

Apply the preceding information to the Internet, too.

Staff jobs fall into many categories: news, advertising spots, continuity—all of the format genres and, in addition, administrative areas such as promotion and research that require writing skills. Further, the station that cannot afford to hire a line of writers usually seeks a producer, director, or talent with writing skills. A look at the "help wanted" columns in professional journals reveals ads such as these:

- Morning Show Prep Writers: Do you write comedy for a successful morning show? ABC Radio Networks is looking for full-time writers to expand its Morning Show Prep Service.
- Tease Writer: King 5 Television in Seattle, Washington, has an immediate opening for a Tease Writer to join our award-winning news team. This position is responsible for writing and producing all teases and bumpers during 5–7 P.M. news block, hourly updates, and news cut-ins during programming.
- Producer: Hard working top-rated news shop needs producer dedicated to putting out a quality show. Good writer, copy editor. . . .
- Writer/producer: Chicago's fastest growing TV independent seeks hands-on promotion writer/producer. . . .
- Promotion writer/producer: . . . creation and execution of on-air news promotion, including but not limited to breaking news coverage, miniseries, talent showcasing . . . person will write copy for print advertising. . . .
- TV producer/director: . . . research, write, edit, and coordinate programs.
- Producer: . . . good writer, copy editor. . . .
- Associate Producer: For top news operation. Major market news producing and writing experience essential.
- Promotion writer/producer: . . . enthusiastic, talented, and creative promotion writer/producer to create on-air promotions. . . .

■ Radio Newscaster: . . . on-air experience required, college optional, excellent writing skills mandatory.

Virtually all ads for news producers include requirements such as "must have excellent writing skills," "must have strong writing skills," and "strong hard-hitting writing skills a must."

Writing the play is essentially a freelance occupation, although many successful freelancers find themselves part of the writing stable of successful individual programs or production companies, earning a regular salary well above the minimums specified by the Writers Guild of America. Because the stipend for writing the play is relatively high, enabling a writer to live comfortably by selling only a few screenplays or several half-hour and hour dramas each year, the competition is tough.

PLAYWRITING

"Breaking into television is more difficult than for any other writing field," according to former television writer and vice-president of RKO Radio, Art Mandelbaum. "It requires plotting a game plan at least as intricate as plotting the structure of a story or teleplot." Mandelbaum suggested several guidelines for those who want to write for sitcoms or continuing television series:

1. Study very carefully the particular series you want to write for and analyze every major character.

2. Simultaneously find out, if possible, the series rating to determine if it will still be on the air the following year. All series shows are assigned to writers by the producer before the season starts so that even if your script is read and bought, it won't be seen, probably, for about a year-and-a-half. For this reason, too, don't write anything too timely that might be out-of-date by the time the program is aired.

3. Find out the demographics of each show; contact the networks and learn who watches, where the heaviest audience is.

4. You must obtain an agent in Hollywood. It is a waste of time to send material directly to a producer. An agent can provide you with fact sheets provided to writers on every show. The fact sheets brief writers on formats, requirements, and taboos. The Writers Guild sends out information on all shows to its members.

5. After studying a particular show, provide your agent with a great many ideas for that show. Don't lock yourself into one show idea. If you come up with 50 one-paragraph thumbnail sketches, your agent will have enough to present to the producer even if the first few are immediately shot down.

6. If your agent sells a show idea, then you can get a contract for a treatment—and you can break into the Writers Guild.

7. Make sure you are grounded in the classics. Basic themes and plots are modifiable and, if you study television shows, you'll note that they are constantly used.

8. Don't let all your friends read your work. By the time their critical appraisals are finished you'll find that your head is spinning or you'll be revising your scripts into something you didn't intend to say in the first place.

9. If an agent offers suggestions that conflict with your ideas concerning a particular show, follow the agent's advice. As a beginner, trying to break in, you are totally dependent on an agent.

10. Television writing is a continuing compromise. The first thing you're pushing is the detergent; the second thing is the content.

Mandelbaum's practical approach combines a range of attitudes: Some writers and producers are extremely optimistic about the extent of artistic creativity and social impact possible for the drama writer, others are extremely pessimistic and cynical. All agree, however, that you must have the talent to write plays, must write drama that fits the needs and format of the program series (including the dramatic specials that are not continuing-character series) or whatever the current trend in Hollywood for feature or made-for-TV movies happens to be.

The editors of *Writer's Digest* analyzed the television play market in a pamphlet entitled *Jobs and Opportunities for Writers*:

> Television has to fill at least 18 hours every day with fresh, appealing material. This necessity makes it one of the best markets for freelancers. It's one of the highest paying, and producers are constantly looking for new ideas and new scripts. Most new show ideas come from freelancers and many of the subsequent scripts are written by other freelancers. Good dialogue writers will find TV a highly rewarding market. . . . TV producers usually accept scripts only through agents, which means that writers cannot submit work directly to them. But writers can keep themselves informed on the current market picture through *Writer's Digest*, whose issues publish information on new TV shows along with practical articles on TV script writing. The annual *Writer's Market* contains a detailed list of agents' names and addresses.

Television and film writer Alfred Brenner stated in *Writer's Digest* that the technological revolution in communications has created a world of expanding markets. He advised the writer that "the only way to break in is by writing a professional script." It must be noted, however, that more than one playwright has been quoted anonymously about what happens to a writer in Hollywood: "They ruin your stories. They butcher your ideas. They prostitute your art. They trample your pride. And what do you get for it? A fortune!"

The fee is higher for theatrical screenplays than for television plays. The Writers Guild basic agreement sets fees for all forms and lengths of screen and broadcast writing. Fees are also set for non-dramatic programs such as comedy and variety shows, audience participation programs, documentaries, children's programs, and others. The "schedule of minimums" theatrical and television basic agreement is available on the Writers Guild East and Writers Guild West web sites, www.wgae.org and www.wga.org. Minimum fee schedules for radio are in a separate agreement that can be obtained from the Guild.

It is to a writer's advantage to join the Writers Guild. Not only does the Guild provide minimum fee protection, but it also offers a pension plan, a health fund, and other union benefits. The Guild also offers advice on legal matters, agent contacts, and a substitute *copyright* system, among other things. The writer who sells a first screenplay or teleplay to a company working under a Guild contract will be required to join.

As emphasized by Art Mandelbaum and *Writer's Digest*, having an agent is important. To get one you need examples of your writing that will convince the agent that you've got the ability to write scripts that sell and the potential to make money not only for yourself, but also for the agency. Use your writing class and production outlet opportunities in college to write as well as you possibly can, and develop a saleable portfolio.

The best way to find an agent is through some personal contact, usually a writer friend who puts you in touch with his or her agent. If you have no such contact, you can approach an agent with an inquiry citing your past credits, if any, and a brief description of the project(s) you currently have completed or on which you are working. *Guide to Literary Agents* is a good compendium of agents' names and addresses and lists agents under various categories.

The annual *Writer's Market* also contains a list of agents' names and addresses. The Writers Guild of America provides a list of agents, designating those willing to look at the work of new writers. Before submitting a script to an agency, however, send a summary, and the agency will send you a release form if it is interested in seeing the full script or treatment.

COMMERCIALS AND COPYWRITING

The three areas that provide leading opportunities—that is, where a large number of writers are employed—are commercials, news, and drama. Extend your reach to the Internet. Kirk Polking, when director of *Writer's Digest* School, analyzed careers for copywriters for a *Writer's Digest* article, "The TV Copywriter":

> Of all the writing jobs today, the network television commercial copywriter probably gets paid more, for less actual *writing*, than any other writer. Charles Moss, whose copy jobs include the American Motors account and others handled by the Wells, Rich, Greene agency, pointed out that he might spend

only 15 minutes a week writing, he stated that 'Much of the rest of my time is spent sitting around this table with art directors and account executives analyzing a client's product and trying to find the right idea to sell it in one minute.' *Idea* is the key word here and many top agency copy chiefs say they're looking for "concept creators," not writers. '*Writers* we can always hire,' says one creative supervisor. 'What's harder to find is someone with a new idea, a fresh approach—someone who can create the theme for a brilliant, visual short story, with a sales message, in 60 seconds.' Ron Rosenfeld, when copy chief at the Doyle Dane Bernbach advertising agency, said, 'We're not necessarily looking for copywriters as such. We want people who have a great sense of the graphic and are good at thinking in pictures.'

. . . The commercial copywriter has to sell the client first before he can sell his idea to the public. How does he do this? . . . A client says, 'Too many young copywriters come in with only one idea and can't do a good job of showing why it will effectively sell the product. They're too jealous of their own idea—maybe they're afraid they'll never get another. A real professional can lay aside an idea you don't like, and come up with five others and show you 11 good reasons why each one would be effective.'

. . . 'There's a screaming need for good commercial copywriters,' said Ed Carder, as Director of the Radio and TV Department of the Ralph Jones agency, 'but the writer has to have a thorough basic understanding of the English language, how the media work and the discipline to work within time and space limitations.'

. . . What about freelancing in this field? It usually takes the form of moonlighting. A small agency will go to a copywriter at a leading agency whose style they like and ask him to do a job on the side. Mostly the agencies work with their own staff people and know fairly well what their next year's needs are going to be in the way of personnel based on their client list. Rarely has an agency bought a commercial idea submitted by a writer through the mail. Some of the larger clients and agencies have a form rejecting all such submissions automatically to protect themselves from claims of plagiarism. A writer who has what he or she thinks are some new, fresh approaches to the commercial might do best to work with local agencies first, contacting them with a resume of his or her professional experience and asking for an appointment to present several specific commercial ideas for specific clients of the agency. If they're good, they'll get a chance.

. . . Most agencies agree that a good liberal arts background is essential for any copy-writing job.

Several Doyle Dane Bernbach copywriters discussed in *DDB News* how they judge other copywriters, and offered some advice to the person seeking to break into the field. In describing what she seeks in going over someone's portfolio, Sue Brock stated, "The first thing I look for is whether there is an ad there that I would have okayed. And then, if there are none like that, whether there is the germ of a good idea that perhaps was goofed up in the execution. Then, after you've decided that there is something there that is fresh or exciting, you call the person in, and at that point you are influenced by the person's personality. If she sits there hostile and full of anxieties, you lose interest, because this is very much team work, and all the little belles and stars have a very rough time." Judy Protas warned that "in this business, where criticism is very much the order of the day, a writer whose personality can't stand up to criticism would fall apart at the seams." Brock added that "you have to have a pretty good opinion of yourself or you won't survive. You have to have a pretty strong ego, because everyone here is willing to criticize—traffic, the messengers, everyone. And if it happens to be your boss who's criticizing, you're going to have to change your copy." Protas concluded that "you have to know when to stop discussion. You're expected to fight for your opinion, but not start whining and arguing defensively over something in which only your ego is involved."

Eric Schultz, as president and general manager of stations WRKO and WROR in Boston, looked for three principal attributes in copywriters: (1) creativity—the ability to dream up new and exciting approaches to selling the product or service; (2) good listening skills—the ability to hear what the client is saying, what the client wants to sell, and how the client wants to sell it; and (3) excellent writing skills.

Promotion writers, sometimes attached to sales or commercial writing offices in smaller stations, need to go beyond just a knowledge of broadcast writing, according to Schultz. They need broad-based skills, not only the ability to prepare promos in the medium itself, but to write for all other media, from newspaper releases to billboards to bumper stickers.

George Gray, former president and general manager of WBSM-Southern Massachusetts Broadcasting Company, offered this advice for the person who wants to obtain a job writing commercial copy: "Learn to write a simple, declarative sentence." He believes experienced and inexperienced applicants both should have the ability to write "simple, clear, short sentences, using a lot of nouns and verbs, a limited number of adjectives, and very few adverbs." He advised writers to learn to "express a thought in the simplest terms. Nothing loses a listener more quickly than high-flown imagery. My advice to my own writers is: Tell them, tell them what you told them, then tell them again." Gray stated that although managers seek to hire people who have had experience in the real world and who understand the client's business goals and the purposes of the commercials they write, paramount are "the techniques of thinking, habits of study, organization of time and energy, and self-discipline that people who have a college education presumably have learned, and which are all essential for one to be a successful professional broadcast writer."

NEWS

Consolidation and economic conditions have virtually eliminated news programs—and writing—at local radio stations. Jobs for news reporters-writers at local television stations and cable networks are still available. Alternative news sites on the Internet have opened up new opportunities. Desired preparation for a career in varies with the station, network, and site. In some instances a pure journalistic background is preferred; in others, specialization in television, online or radio techniques is wanted; in still other cases judgment and news sense is subjectively evaluated, with training a secondary consideration. Stanley S. Hubbard, as president and general manager of Hubbard Broadcasting, Inc., described in *Television/Radio Age* what he looks for:

> What is a news person? Is a news person qualified because he has a degree from a university which says he graduated in journalism? Or is a news person qualified because he has held a job someplace as a news person? I think not. I think that a news person, in order to really be considered capable, has to prove that he or she has news ability and 'news sense.' The time restrictions involved in producing television news require that in order to be successful, a television news person has to have genuine news sense. It is not possible, insofar as my experience has indicated, for a person to learn news sense in a journalism school. . . . Journalism schools can prepare you very adequately to go to work in a news room and learn how to successfully fit into the mechanism, but just because a person successfully fits into the mechanism, it is a mistake to think that a person necessarily has news sense or the judgment required of a licensee in the discharge of his public responsibilities.

Background, formal or informal, is required, of course. Because of the attention being directed to local and regional events on local stations, Barbara Allen recommended that, as a potential local reporter-writer,

> (1) you need to be familiar with every aspect of city government, the people who make up the power structure in your community, the business and industries that support your area's economy, your schools, colleges and local personalities, (2) the breadth and depth of your knowledge about people and government and art and politics and education, science and social and economic problems will be the underpinnings of your value as a journalist, and (3) your function and responsibility is to see what seem to be isolated events against the background of the forces which cause those events.

Teresa McAlpine, former managing editor of a news radio station in Boston, looked for some experiential background when interviewing potential beginning newswriters. She first determined whether the applicants had some experience in writing broadcast news, "which requires different skills than writing for newspapers. Our beginning writers write news for broadcast from many sources, including personally conducted telephone interviews from which they prepare stories. Previous news writing is essential. It can have been with a college station or a non-paying internship somewhere . . . as long as it's media writing."

The same requirement is beneficial for online news writing.

The second thing McAlpine looked for was the applicant's ability to write simple sentences in conversational style. She expected the writer to have a sense of news judgment, and she tested applicants by giving them print stories to rewrite for radio, judging whether the writer found the proper lead for radio, and presented it in a "catchy, conversational style." Finally, she looked for speed.

Fast-breaking radio news stories frequently have to be written very quickly. "To the good newswriter," she stated, "all of this comes naturally."

As for education, McAlpine stated that a liberal arts background is the best preparation, coupled with a continuing knowledge of world events from assiduous reading of newspapers and magazines and listening and watching broadcast news (and online news). If the applicants have little or no previous experience in broadcast news writing, they can balance that by having a communications major or degree. She also said that courses in media writing will have taught the applicants the essential forms and techniques and that "this is a definite plus."

Irving Fang, in his book *Television News,* listed the behavioral attitudes a journalist should have, according to the American Council on Education for Journalism:

1. Ability to write news copy
2. Judgment and good taste in selecting news items
3. Ability to edit copy of others
4. Knowledge of the law especially applicable to media
5. Knowledge of general station or site operation
6. Understanding of the mechanical problems of the specific medium
7. Appreciation of the media's responsibility to the public, particularly in its handling of news
8. Ability to work under pressure
9. Ability to make decisions quickly
10. Speed in production
11. Familiarity with the various techniques of news presentation (including first-person reporting, recordings, interviews, remotes)
12. Knowledge of newscast production
13. Ability to gather news
14. Ability to read news copy with acceptable voice quality, diction, and so on
15. Ability to find local angles in national or other stories
16. Quickness to see feature angles in routine assignments
17. Ability to simplify complex matters and make them meaningful to the listener or viewer

Where do you look for a job as a newswriter? Everywhere and anywhere. If you're breaking into the field, try the small stations first, where you can gain experience doing all kinds of writing, including news. If you want or need to live and work where there are predominantly large stations, be prepared to start as a copy person or in another entry position. Be aware, however, that it is extremely difficult to advance in a network or similar large operation, and the lack of experience and competitive structure can keep you on a rung of the ladder quite removed from news writing for a long time. Most experienced newswriters and managers recommend the small station route as the one with the better chance. If you are studying in a journalism, communications, broadcasting, or similar department, your professors already will have contact with stations in your state or region and usually will recommend capable graduating students for jobs. You can, of course, contact stations anywhere in the country yourself; ask your professors for help in preparing your resume, and don't forget the experience you obtained, it is hoped, with the university's non-commercial station or with a local commercial station while working toward your degree. Your professors can also refer you to national organizations and associations that have placement services.

The relatively few freelance newswriters-producers usually are people who have achieved sufficient recognition to be able to name their own spots and terms. For the less experienced, however, local stations do provide some outlets. If you are a writer and have a camera that you can use well or a recorder with which you can be creative, you can frequently provide special features on local events. Local history, geography, civic affairs, local and state holidays, and unusual happenings and personalities offer a plethora of possibilities. This might be worth trying on your own time on a part-time basis. Some larger stations employ students as news stringers to cover campus news, particularly athletics. Internships provide experience, as well as contacts. And if you've had the foresight to take courses on writing and producing for the Internet, you should look at the growing number of news web sites. Writing is the key to news, no matter what position you hold. Jim Boyd, a newscaster for television station WCVB, Boston, gave credit for his success as a disciplined writer to his early education's emphasis on grammar: "There is nothing more important in the business I'm in—that is, being a newscaster—than writing."

CORPORATE MEDIA

Writer's Market reported that "business and educational films are much bigger business than Hollywood." Business and industry require a great variety of formats and types, including advertising, informational and training films and, increasingly, online materials.

Many companies have in-house media centers, with the salaries for writers-producers varying just as greatly as in stations and networks. Freelance corporate writing and producing is a big business. Even many companies with their own production units frequently hire outside talent and consultants.

Approach a company whose products or services you already know something about. Prepare yourself well so that if you obtain an interview with the media center director, personnel chief, or another officer of the company, you can talk as if you not only are an expert in writing and producing corporate media, but an expert in the company's field, as well.

If you make a good impression, you may be asked to submit a proposal on a specific subject. If the proposal is satisfactory, you'll be asked to submit an outline or treatment. Negotiate a contract before you start writing, including a fair fee, a schedule, and a clear statement of what the script's content and purpose are expected to be.

Frank R. King, former director of video training for the John Hancock Mutual Life Insurance Company, advised that if you are planning to enter the corporate video field, you should "pick an industry you think you might enjoy." Students should prepare themselves by learning the content areas of the specific industries in which they are interested. However, more important for the writer than knowing the industry or video techniques, King said, is the ability to write creatively, to use language correctly, including the basics, and to work with people. He advocated conscientious study in scriptwriting courses. He further advised people applying for jobs in corporate video to bring, if at all possible, a demo with a clearly labeled indication of what the applicant did in the production. If the applicant can afford it, demos should be left for review by additional persons. If that is not possible, the applicant should bring and leave some sample scripts.

Scott Carlberg, writing in *Video Management*, recommended several guidelines for freelancers to protect their integrity as writers and their status in the field. He suggested that a freelancer must be kept informed at all times of the job particulars, must have direct access to the key people involved in the production, and should meet personally with the client, if necessary, to be certain what the need is for the media project and what objectives should be used in the script to solve the problems. Establish one reliable contact in the company as the internal project coordinator, Carlberg advised, and do not be manipulated into promising or doing work of a superhuman or unreasonable nature. Finally, he warned freelancers about the internal politics found in any organization and the need to avoid being used as "a pawn in internal corporate political games."

Dr. Jeffrey Lukowsky, when communication consultant for Digital Equipment Corporation, confirmed that opportunities exist in corporate media as a whole if you are a writer. Many companies spend huge sums of money on external writers, many have writers-producers on their staff payrolls, and many use both in-house and out-of-house writers, Lukowsky said. Corporate media writers should be skilled in both print- and scriptwriting, he advised. Among the types of writing required, he listed dramatic simulations such as duplicating customer environments to train people in sales techniques, news about the company's product or service, product technology information and training, and productions enhancing the company image. "If you've written drama," Lukowsky said, "you'll have a better opportunity to break in. Often a writer is asked to take product information and turn it into a case study or role play for training purposes."

Try first to get a job with one of the smaller corporations, doing whatever job might be available, whether production assistant or assistant script editor,

Lukowsky advised the newcomer. After a period of preparation and experience, then you might seek a position with one of the larger *Fortune 500* companies. Other ways of breaking in, Lukowsky suggested, are through corporate media production agencies, which contract with companies for writing and production personnel, and with individual production houses, the so-called vendors contracted with by corporations to produce media programs. In every situation, Lukowsky recommended, come with a portfolio, showing some of the work you have written, and prove your ability to do the work required.

Writer's Market annual yearbook lists key production companies for business and education writing.

THE INTERNET

With more and more entertainment and news programs streaming onto the Internet and the probability that soon virtually everything now found on television, radio, and cable will be found on the Internet, the current generation of college students seeking to break into media writing has an opportunity to get in on the ground floor of this expanding communications phenomenon. One important area of writing jobs for the Internet is with the traditional media themselves. More and more television and radio stations and cable networks are adapting their programs before releasing them into cyberspace so that they can take advantage of the Internet's interactive potentials. This is true, as well, for commercials. Use of attractive and seductive links pulls the potential customer further into the advertising pitch, sometimes making it seem impossible for him or her to leave until a product or service is purchased. Advertising agencies will be fertile fields for new writers who know how to write for the Internet.

The increasing use of the Internet by corporate media portends an expansion of corporate writing and production, both in-house and through outside producers who provide multimedia services. One such company is the Pangaea Multimedia Communications Corporation, discussed in Chapter 9. Eric Johnston, founder, president, and CEO of Pangaea, offers the following advice for those who want to break into multimedia, including Internet writing and production.

> As an employer in the world of new media, including the Internet, we are constantly looking for talented individuals ranging from those with skills in video production to those skilled in the many aspects of computer technology. There is a great deal of competition. Recent graduates have to compete not only with their peers, but also with those working in the hundreds of new small businesses and, as well, with seasoned professionals.
>
> Writing skills are vital—no matter what your specialty is. If you are able to organize and articulate a thought clearly in the correct medium for your target audience, you will have a greater impact and you will quickly become a critical player. As an employer, our first judgment of an applicant's writing skill is to review her or his cover letter and resume. A potential employer needs

to understand your level of experience, and it can be advantageous to clearly state your specific roles, responsibilities, and the skills or understanding you ultimately gained from that experience.

The characteristics of an ideal employee should include a set of attitudes as well as technical skills essential to success. One's writing is not simply a placement of words, but must reflect an understanding of these attitudes and technical skills. The excitement and enthusiasm of recent graduates must be accompanied by the commitment, dedication, and understanding of reality. Simply having taken courses in a particular area and doing class projects qualify only as exposure. If the colleges and universities have done their jobs, their graduates should have solid understanding of their areas of study; but the job applicant who stands out is the one who has applied her or his knowledge to the real world. Work experience gained through internships and entry level work prior to graduation enable the job applicant to integrate theory and practice. For example, those who have only studied and never practiced often don't fully understand some very important aspects of effective work: attention to details, process, procedure, and protocol. They sometimes fail to understand the key elements of commitment, deadlines, and follow-through.

Some employers have observed that too many graduates seem to be focused principally on short-term gain, disregarding higher values such as ethics, standards, and potential long-term benefits. How that person presents subject matter may be drastically different from the way a person who truly believes in their work and the impact of that work writes. When recruiting, we look for long-term commitment and genuine interest and enthusiasm, and we attempt to match individual direction with that of the projects and the company. All of these things are reflected in one's writing and work habits.

Communication is critical. Understanding the proper channel and medium of communication is useless if it is not used. The individual must understand who the players are, how to gain access to them, and how to write in ways that communicate effectively to them. An employee needs to apply this communication skill both to clients' projects and internally with co-workers. I have seen too many situations where lack of communication skill caused a loss of productivity, time, or goodwill. If an individual has something of value to add, but is unhappy and doesn't communicate it, or has not thought through who should be included in the communication loop, it can result in a loss for the company.

Writing in the new media environment is fast-paced. There is no time to revise or rethink whether or not the communication has been handled correctly. Work must be completed at a high standard of excellence on a tight timeline. The successful employee must understand that missing deadlines can impact not only the next task or project, but also compensation and even employment.

Writing for new media has some unique characteristics. The product is often structured differently than that of traditional writing. There's less space for meandering. The key point must be made clearly and succinctly at the beginning. Content and examples or explanations must be organized differently than with traditional writing. Each point must be written as a clear "stand-alone" item that the reader can either choose to explore or to overlook. The reader may not follow the same sequence or logic that the writer uses in traditional writing. Therefore, every point must retain its meaning when read in any imaginable order.

Writing for the Internet is a challenge for the employee because, at this point in time, he or she is a key actor in what is still a relatively new field where experimentation is still rewarded. The best of new media writing is still ahead.

THE PROPOSAL

For long formats, including plays and corporate scripts, you need a proposal. The proposal must be accepted before you get the go-ahead to prepare a treatment, which, in turn, is a prerequisite to getting a contract to write the complete script. As a writer you need a proposal for the producer or the station or the advertising agency—for any person or office that must pass initial judgment on the project. The producer who wants to sell a project to a network must first present a proposal.

The proposal tells what the script is about and frequently also covers the logistics necessary for the script's profitable production, including budget, potential distribution, promotion, and other areas. The proposal must sell the idea of the project—its feasibility and the availability of sources for research and development and other resources necessary to the project's completion. Be practical. More than one neophyte who might have been an excellent TV writer has been told by a producer that the proposal simply isn't financially feasible, citing as an example the naive writer's prototype "most expensive line": "The Romans sacked the city." With a video drama show's usual budget, they certainly did not! With Hollywood's film budgets, they might have!

The proposal is, in effect, a sales tool with which you convince your script's prospective purchaser why that script will result in monetary gain and prestige for the buyer. Your proposal should include the following: (1) an assessment of need—why the prospective purchaser needs that script; (2) the goals to be achieved by that script—Is it a corporate script to train? A sitcom to entertain?; (3) a summary of the idea and the script; (4) the potential audience; (5) the feasibility of the script—Can a series be written? Are materials available and clearable for the proposed single or multiple program production? Is talent available? Are necessary writing and production resources obtainable?; and, if you are a producer or a production company, (6) anticipated budget, including above- and below-the-line costs; and (7) placement or distribution—its place on the schedule, ratings potential, syndication expectations, corporate limits.

Don't allow all of your planning and hard work to go to waste; remember: *Neatness counts*. In an article, "Scriptwriting," in *Writer's Market*, Michael Singh reminded writers that "a page's appearance and readability—format, type size, neatness—are important assets . . . first impressions play a large role in determining whether or not a reader will continue beyond the first 20 or so pages."

PROGRAM PITCH

The usual way to sell a program idea is through the *program pitch*. Networks and independent producing companies seek new program ideas, and select those considered promising out of hundreds submitted every week. That is, the idea's creator is allowed to present the proposal in person to one or more program development executives representing the network or production company. The presentation is called a program pitch or sometimes, within the industry, *spitballing*. Although you can submit your idea and request a program pitch on a freelance basis, you have a much better chance if you use an agent.

The purpose of your program pitch is to convince the potential producer or distributor that the series (or one-shot program such as a documentary, TV movie, or music special) is going to attract a sufficient audience and make money for the company. Therefore, you present more than just the program content. Describe the characters or performers, the detailed format (including plot and character relationships if it is a sitcom or drama), the setting, and any special attributes that make the content different from similar concepts. In addition, it can be helpful to present a realistic anticipated budget, some preliminary demographics of potential viewers, the kinds of advertisers the program format and viewer demos are likely to attract, your program's counter-programming value (that is, in competition with other networks or distributors), likely market clearances, and promotion potentials.

In other words, if appropriate, you try to present a bottom-line plan of production, distribution, and potential sales as well as a detailed program description. If your characters or other program elements lend themselves to ancillary income (such as animal soft toys, character T-shirts, posters, theme recordings, or comedy routines on videos), mention that too.

The pitch should be done clearly, cleanly, and quickly. It must be complete and simple enough that the executive will remember it and be able to repeat it in condensed form to other program development personnel. Above all, don't be boring. The most successful pitches are more than just verbal presentations. You should always include a handout—that is, something to later remind the executive of what she or he heard and saw; an outline or, preferably, a program treatment; an outline if it is a series and an outline or a treatment of at least one episode, plus an outline or overview of several subsequent episodes; a clear list and description of the major characters, plot lines, and settings; an emphasis on any unique program characteristics that make it especially competitive (such as realistic scenes of the Los Angeles Police Department activities or a well-known standup comic, assuming you already have legal commitment from such a person); sample sequences with characters and dialogue; special effects or music that give the program a special flavor.

Use whatever other materials enhance your presentation: video, audio, PowerPoint, photos, charts, and even puppets of your principal characters.

Keep in mind that you may have only a few minutes to make your pitch. You've got to sell the concept with the fewest possible words. As described in Chapter 10, go for the "high concept."

Your aim is to convince the program development people that your idea is worth taking a chance on and to give you an advance to write one or more complete scripts. If you already have a completed script, make sure it is a good one. If they like it, you may get a contract for more scripts and possibly even money for a pilot if you are part of a production outfit as well as a scriptwriter.

If the powers-that-be don't like your proposal, you'll receive a rejection letter in a short time. If they do like it, your agent (or you, if you don't have an agent) will get a call in a short time. If you hear nothing for a while, don't hesitate to ask your agent to check on your proposal's status; if you don't have an agent, after a respectable time—several weeks—call the network or production company yourself and ask where it stands.

COPYRIGHT

You can't copyright an idea. If you are creative, you will find that some time, some place, one or more of your ideas will be appropriated without compensation or credit to you. It's happened to all of us; series formats, script outlines, and concepts for various kinds of programs have from time to time been adapted or even wholly used by unscrupulous producers. On the other hand, many ideas, script concepts, and formats can be thought up by more than one person at virtually the same time, and when you see or hear under someone else's name a creation that you had submitted to a network or station or agency, it might not be a rip-off at all. Because networks, stations, production companies, and agencies require you to sign a release for the purpose of protecting themselves in instances where your submission was not original or the first one received, you can never quite be sure!

To protect yourself, copyright your work. Unfortunately, not everything that the writer creates for video or audio is copyrightable. Ideas for and titles of programs cannot be copyrighted. According to the U.S. Copyright Office, narrative outlines, formats, plot summaries of plays and motion pictures, skeletal librettos, and other synopses and outlines cannot be registered for copyright in unpublished form. Copyright will protect the literary or dramatic expression of an author's ideas, but not the ideas themselves. If you want to copyright a script, it has to be more than an outline or synopsis. It should be ready for performance so that a program could actually be produced from the script. The Copyright Office defines materials not eligible for copyright:

> Works that have not been fixed in a tangible form of expression. For example: choreographic works which have not been notated or recorded, or improvisational speeches or performances that have not been written or recorded. Titles,

names, short phrases, and slogans; familiar symbols or designs; mere listings of ingredients or contents. Ideas, procedures, methods, systems, processes, concepts, principles, discoveries, or devices, as distinguished from a description, explanation, or illustration. Works consisting entirely of information that is common property and containing no original authorship.

Unpublished scripts in complete form or a group of related scripts for a series may be copyrighted. If a script is a play, musical, comedy, shooting script for a film, or a similar dramatic work, it can be copyrighted. The Copyright Office describes these works as including "published and unpublished works prepared for the purpose of being 'performed' directly before an audience or indirectly 'by means of any device or process.' Examples of works of the performing arts are music works, including any accompanying words; dramatic works, including any accompanying music; pantomimes and choreographic works; and motion pictures and other audiovisual works." Registering a particular script protects that script only and does not give protection to future scripts arising out of it or to a series as a whole. Sound recordings may also be copyrighted.

You can obtain copyright forms and detailed explanations of how to determine what is copyrightable as well as the procedures for obtaining a copyright from the Copyright Office, Library of Congress, Washington, D.C. 20559 or through www.copyright.gov. The copyright protects a work for the life of the author plus 70 years. In late 2009 the Copyright Office instituted a new procedure for registering works, electronic online filing that is quicker, more efficient and cheaper than the old method of filing paper forms in the standard categories of TX (literary works), VA (visual arts), PA (performing arts), and SR (sound recordings). You may still do the latter with a fee of $65 per submission. However, under the eCO—electronic copyright office—you may register the work online and submit the material online or, after online registering and paying a fee of $35, send a hard copy to the copyright office.

Another form of script protection, if you don't want to apply for a copyright, is the Script Registration Service of the Writers Guild of America (WGA), which is available to non-members as well as members for a modest fee. Screenplays and other written material may be registered through the WGA/West and WGA/East web sites. The oft-used self-addressed registered or certified mail approach can have some value in any future litigation, but more formal registration is advised for better protection.

COLLEGE PREPARATION

Most station managers say that there is no substitute for experience. And many add that colleges are not adequately preparing students for a media career. Part of their concern is that many people entering the field directly from college do not understand the commercial field. Conversely, station managers are concerned, as well, that students do not get a proper blend of social sciences and humanities along with hands-on training, but tend to go too much in one direction or the other.

Courses in writing for the media are necessary to help you master the basic techniques and formats. If you are planning to go into a particular aspect of writing, such as copywriting or playwriting, take advanced courses in those areas. Make certain that you've taken the basic courses that give you a grounding in the essentials of grammar, punctuation, spelling, and clear, direct expression of ideas. Be sure, as well, that you take social and political science courses that give you the background for thinking, reasoning, and understanding, whether used to create characters and plot lines for a screenplay, a sitcom, a 30-second commercial spot, a blog, or to write news and documentaries. Media managers will tell you that they look at your transcript for such courses as history, psychology, political science, and sociology. They want courses that make you a full, rounded person, not a narrow-area specialist whose use to the station or company is limited. If you want to move to supervisory writing positions, you need to understand financing and budgeting. Include one or more business courses in your curriculum. If you expect to be a writer-producer, be sure your interpersonal, presentational, and people skills, oral as well as written, are good. If you've had a course in negotiations, you'll do better for yourself when arranging contracts.

Chad Rufer, former program director of WINK-FM, Ft. Myers, Florida, advises those who want to work in radio to learn all aspects of radio station operations, not only the area in which they want to concentrate. Take courses that will prepare you for radio production, sales, marketing, on-air work, and the Internet. Rufer advises: "Hard work will pay off in the end."

Dr. W. Joseph Oliver, professor of communication at Stephen F. Austin State University, conducted a study of top-level broadcast executives' recommendations for academic preparation for broadcasting careers. Practical, applied media courses and business-oriented courses were highly favored, with liberal arts courses receiving strong support.

The managers stressed the importance of solid writing skills for all potential employees. Dr. Jeffrey Lukowsky, professional communication consultant and a former professor of mass communication, recommended that the student who wants to be a corporate media writer take a variety of courses in both print and script writing, including writing for video, audio, magazines, and short story writing. The latter two are essential preparation for writing the frequent case study scenarios, in both print and dramatic form. Lukowsky also advised getting production as well as writing experience in college, in both audio and video. "There is more audio work in corporate media than most newcomers think."

And it goes without saying that you should take as many courses in new media writing, programming, and producing as you can fit into your schedule. Include those Internet courses that stress visual creation and graphics development, and especially those that concentrate on using the Internet's interactive capabilities.

Most important, don't restrict your future professional opportunities by concentrating on too narrow an area. Your college education should go beyond either theory or technical skills alone, and be the best "hands-on/heads-on" learning combination possible.

Entering the Field

Now that you know everything there is to know about writing for the media; have had courses or internships in which you've written award-winning-quality scripts; become fully knowledgeable about television, radio, cable, and the Internet; and have ordered your cap and gown for graduation, you're about to get to the hard part: getting a job.

Hopefully, through internships, part-time or summer jobs, or your institution's career placement office—or relatives with media contacts—you've got a position already lined up. If not, your next step is to target job opportunities and prepare a resume and letters of application.

Where do you find out about jobs? Through many sources, including a college's career office, your professors, friends and relatives, and fairly easy personal research. If your Internet is principally in broadcasting, the *Gale Directory of Publications and Broadcast Media* lists all the stations in the country. Check the "positions available" sections of publications such as *Broadcasting & Cable*, *Variety*, and other professional and academic journals (which you should have been reading as part of your course work). For media positions in academia, look at *The Chronicle of Higher Education*. Go online to Craig's List. Read newspaper want ads. Check the personnel or human resources departments of networks, stations, production companies, and ad agencies, almost all of which can be found online. Try social networking sites such as Facebook and MySpace, and professional sites such as LinkedIn. Employment agencies can be helpful, but be careful of those that charge exorbitant fees, some up front and others upon placement. Some are illegitimate. Once you've located the one—or dozen—ideal job openings, start applying. You need a resume and a letter of application. Because the letter of application is usually the first contact the potential employer has with you, it has got to reflect your ability and the kind of person the employer is looking for.

Social Media

The Internet has become a principle venue for finding and applying for jobs, not only in the media, but in other professions, as well. Social media sites have become key marketplaces for making contacts, obtaining information about openings, learning about prospective companies, and obtaining recommendations. The competition in using those sites for job purposes is fierce and even in the relatively short time that social media have become vital in job-seeking a number of principles and techniques for using them to your greatest advantage have developed.

Personnel directors and others doing hiring are increasingly researching and evaluating job candidates on social media. That means being sure your profile and postings on whatever social media you are active are professionally impressive. That means that any postings, including personal comments or photos on sites such as Facebook should be free of any suggestions that you are immature, frivolous, or otherwise a possible risky choice for a responsible future in a given organization. Control your social image by checking the privacy settings on all your social sites. Make sure that any photos of you are totally professional and that if the potential hirer calls you in for an interview, he or she will recognize you from the photo or photos. Make sure, as well, that information about you, including and especially your resume, also stresses professionalism, in form as well as in content. Juvenile writing, incorrect grammar, sloppy spelling or punctuation—and you are wasting your time expecting to be seriously considered for any position. Make very clear what you are looking for in a career and what your qualifications and experience are for that particular career and/or job. Post information that's pertinent. For example, if you had a summer job at McDonald's or at Macy's it should be listed only if pertinent to the job you are seeking—such as dealing with customers for a media company or selling time for a radio or television station.

Determine which social sites will serve your best. While you may get some personal leads from Facebook, your major professional contacts may come from LinkedIn. Interacting with people in the media industries might be most effective through Twitter. You don't need to use a shotgun approach, that is, posting everyplace you can. Making too many contacts, especially with people you don't know well, can be a disadvantage. Be sure that whatever you post, including resumes, on any site shows you off to the best advantage. The personal profile you present is your selling point. The better and more complete your profile, the greater the chances are of your making the contacts and generating the offers you want. Mitt Ray, CEO of Social Marketing Writing, recommends seven key elements necessary for a good profile.

*Have a good profile picture. It should reflect a happy, positive, capable person.

*Have a good headline. Feature your important positions, present and past.

*Add web sites. (LinkedIn, for example, permits a maximum of three.)

*Fill in your experience. In addition to your position and role in the organization, note how you helped the company.

*Good recommendations build credibility. Get as many good ones as you can. If your recommenders have profiles on social media such as LinkedIn, they will also be looked.

*LinkedIn allows you to add one of your Twitter accounts, expanding the information presented about you.

*Display your blogs—if they are appropriate and helpful. You can do this with the WordPress and Blog Link tool applications.

For Mitt Ray's examples pertaining to each of the seven keys, see http://social-marketingwriting.com/7-ways-to-get-the-best-out-of-your-linkedin-profile/?pf

Letter of Application

Here are some suggestions for preparing a basis letter of application. The cover letter should be short, no more than one page, if possible. For the reader who is going through dozens or even hundreds of letters, time is of the essence. Include only the most pertinent and necessary information. The opening paragraph should explain why you are writing. Did you see the job advertised or listed or are you writing cold? If the latter, note that you are inquiring about current *and* future opportunities. Find the name of the person in charge of the office to which you are applying and spell their name and title correctly. A general "to whom it may concern" or "Director of Personnel" heading indicates a lack of personal enterprise. Following the introduction, clearly show how your credentials specifically fit the specific job for which you are applying. Present a strong summary of your skills and experience. Summarize your background and highlight any special achievements that will make you especially valuable to the employer in that particular job and to the company as a whole. Refer to your enclosed resume. The final paragraph of your letter should seek some action, such as an interview or more information about the company (presuming you have specific questions that have not been answered through what should have been your already exhaustive research about the company), and should contain full information of how and where you can be reached: Email address, home phone, cell phone, fax. Have someone who is a good critic—presumably your media professor—check the letter for you. Proofread carefully, then proofread again before you send it. Because you need to tailor your cover letter and resume to a particular position in a particular company, be prepared to amend both every time you apply for a job.

If you are applying online, be certain that your grammar, spelling, and punctuation are perfect and that your spacing is proper. If your letter of application is being sent by post, add to the above neatness and cleanliness in whatever the hiring officer receives. Any indication that you are careless or sloppy will disqualify you before your credentials are even read.

Sample Letter of Application

22 Any Street
Mytown, MA 02345
June 1, 2014

Ms. Alice B. Stein
Director of Human Resources
United Broadcasting Company
1236 West 58th Street
New York, NY 10069

Dear Ms. Stein:

I am writing to apply for the position of Assistant to the Producer of Reality Programs, as listed on the United Broadcasting Company's web site. Enclosed, as requested, is my resume and three letters of recommendation.

While earning my Bachelor of Arts degree in Mass Communications at Ivy College, I concentrated on television programming and production, took advanced courses in computer technology, and interned as an assistant to the director of programming at Boston television station WMBC, an affiliate of UBS. I also served for two years as an on-air personality with my college's noncommercial radio station, WZZZ.

In addition, I took elective courses to develop my writing skills and in business management, political science, and psychology. As my references note, I am dependable, prompt, and dedicated in my work.

I would appreciate the opportunity to meet with you for an interview. I may be reached at any time on my cell phone, 617-555-1111, and at lwannabee@worldlink.net.

Sincerely,

Leslie Wannabee

The Resume

A **resume** should succinctly present all of your pertinent attributes related to the specific job for which you are applying. Your name and contact information should be at the top. The first heading should be "Objective," oriented with each application to the specified position. The next heading should be "Education and Training." Present everything that adds to your qualifications for the position, but avoid items that are so petty that it appears you have to pad your credentials. Follow that with "Experience" or "Employment." Include internships in the field and part-time jobs that are pertinent. Working as an assistant to the manager of a retail store one summer, or doing market research field surveys that required interviewing people, or selling video and audio equipment at a department store is relevant, but flipping hamburgers at Mickey D's would appear irrelevant to working in television production. A further heading would be "Special Skills." Do you have expertise with some computer programs? Have you organized and led work or discussion groups? Have you achieved certain ranks or successes in organizations, such as a Scout group or your college's student assembly or clubs? As with your cover letter, work with your institution's career services office in the preparation of your resume.

Sample Resume

LESLIE WANNABEE

22 Any Street – Mytown, MA 02345 — (617) 555-1111 — lwannabee@worldlink.net

OBJECTIVE
Entry Position in Television Production

EDUCATION AND TRAINING

B.A. in Mass Communications, Ivy College, 2014.
  Major areas: television programming and production, computer technology.
  Other concentrations: business writing and management, political science,
  psychology.

EXPERIENCE

Internship: Assistant to Director of Programming, WMBC-TV, Boston, Summer,
  2013.
Producer and Director, Ivy College Annual Student TV Productions Awards
  (Ivy College closed-circuit TV streamed to Internet), 2013.
Producer and Deejay, "Music in the Morning," WZZZ-FM (Ivy College),
  2011–2014.
Counselor, Camp Muckabout, Northwoods, Maine, Summer, 2010.

SPECIAL SKILLS

Computers: Internet Technology
Leadership and Interpersonal Relationships: Junior Class Vice-president,
  2011–2012.

PERSONAL

Sports: Golf (Ivy College tourneys, 2011–2013); Tennis (High School Varsity).
Professional and Social: LinkedIn, Facebook.

* * *

Because you are competing with many others for any given job, your resume
has got to immediately grab the attention of the prospective employer. The person reading it is likely to have an overflow of applications and will skim through
each letter of application and resume. The key aspects of the job in question must
be prominent in your resume. Use words from the job description in describing
your goals and experience. Include links to your social media sites, a personal
web site if you have one, and your portfolio if it can be accessed online.

But be sure that your portfolio, whether viewed online or otherwise, is of at
least satisfactory quality. Your senior television or film production project may
have earned an "A" and may be excellent in comparison to other student projects.
But is it of professional quality? A prospective employer is quickly turned off by
an applicant whose best submission is clearly not close to professional standards

and who, by submitting it, clearly has little concept of such standards. Just as you should have your cover letter and resume checked by someone in the field before you submit them, you should have examples in your portfolio similarly checked before submitting them.

Be sure that your resume (and cover letter) stress not what you want from the company, but what you can do for the company. Jenny Foss, of JobJenny .com, advises that "this is your first work sample . . . your first opportunity to showcase your business writing skills and your eye for detail. Don't squander it." Therefore, she says, flawless spelling and grammar are essential. She also advises that you customize your resume, to tailor it to the details of each separate position you apply for, "regardless of how similar the positions are to each other."

The Interview

If you are fortunate enough to be asked to a personal interview, be aware that although you've got your foot in the door, it's up to you to get your entire self inside the company. Be prepared for the interview by extensive research. While you already know something about the specific organization, having prepared a targeted application and resume, you now need to know everything you can learn about the company. You need to impress the interviewer with your knowledge as though you already are working there. Learn about the company's history and its goals. Find out about its achievements and problems. Determine what its current priorities are. A key interview question is why you are interested in working for that particular company. Saying that it's because you need a job will certainly not get you a job. Talk about the company and its officers in terms of how your goals coincide with theirs, how your attributes and attitudes match both the private and public profile of the company. Another standard interview approach is the interviewer asking you to talk about yourself. Prepare to talk about those aspects of your life and behavior and thinking that fit into the company's aims and reputation. Find similarities, without being obvious about it, between yourself and the founder and/or officers of the company—who you have researched before going to the interview. Be sure to dress appropriately for the interview. Find out how formal or casual the company's policies are. Near the end of the interview, you will be asked if you have any questions. Have some prepared that indicate your interest in the goals and success of the company. Ask about your own future in the company, other than personal benefits, about how you can help it grow. Susan Ricker of CareerBuilder.com advises ". . . turn off your cell phone and come ready with your enthusiasm and expertise. Present yourself as a true professional and you're sure to ace the interview."

Finally, don't forget to thank the interviewer at the end of the interview for his or her time and repeat your interest in the company and the position. And don't forget to send a thank you note no later than the next day, either by email or letter. It should be more than a pro-forma thank you, and should reflect what you would say if you were seeing the interviewer again in person. Susan Ricker says "highlight the best points of the interview . . . confirm that you're still interested in the job and that you look forward to hearing back from the company." If you don't hear back in couple of weeks, call and ask politely what the status is in filling the position.

* * *

As you finish reading this textbook and complete your course in writing for the media, note the four attributes writer Debbie Macomber suggests, in *Writer's Digest*, that will serve you well in your quest for writing success: Purpose, Patience, Passion, and Persistence. She states: "Believe in your project, believe in yourself and in the power of your dream."

GLOSSARY

A/B roll A/B/C/D rolls are used in linear postproduction; two or more videotapes run in synchronization to create dissolves or special effects.

Actuality The news event heard or seen as it is actually occurring; a sound or video clip from a news event.

American Research Bureau (ARB) Market research company that conducts surveys.

Analog Nondigital recording of material in radio and TV. See **Digital**.

Aperture The diameter of a camera lens opening, also called an iris opening, that controls the amount of light permitted to reach the film.

Applet A small *java* program that can be embedded in an *HTML* page. Applets differ from full-fledged java applications in that they are not allowed to access certain resources on the local computer, such as files and serial devices (modems, printers, etc.), and are prohibited from communicating with most other computers across a network. The common rule is that an applet can only make an Internet connection to the computer from which the applet was sent. See **HTML, Java**.

Application Server *Server* software that manages one or more other pieces of software in a way that makes the managed software available over a network, usually to a *web* server. By having a piece of software manage other software packages, it is possible to use resources like memory and database access more efficiently than if each of the managed packages responded directly to requests.

Ascertainment primer Former FCC requirement that a station applying for a license or for renewal must survey community problems and show how programming has dealt and would deal with these problems.

Associated Press (AP) Preeminent among the wire services used by news programs in the United States.

Atom An evolving protocol for syndication and sharing of content. Atom is being developed as a successor to and improvement over *RSS* and is more complex than RSS while offering support for additional features such as digital signatures, geographic location of author, possibly security/encryption, licensing, etc. Like RSS, atom is an *XML*-based specification.

ATR Audiotape recorder.

Attribution Stating the source of the information or the quote in a news story.

Automation Use of computers to control some media equipment and to perform some duties otherwise required of personnel. The term is also used in television to pick up satellite feeds and to start videotape cassette commercials and prerecorded programs.

Back-timing Applying the time left in the program to the remaining script segments, frequently requiring alternative script endings to fit different time lengths.

Bandwidth Range of signal frequencies, or amount of data, a carrier can handle.

BBC See British Broadcasting Corporation.

BBS (Bulletin Board System) A computerized meeting and announcement system that allows people to carry on discussions, upload and download files, and make announcements without being connected to the computer at the same time. In the early 1990s there were many thousands of BBS's around the world. Most were very small, running on a single IBM clone PC with one or two phone lines. Some were very large and the line between a BBS and a system like AOL gets crossed at some point, but it is not clearly drawn.

Bed A music base.

Binary Information consisting entirely of ones and zeros. Also, commonly used to refer to files that are not simply text files, such as images.

BING Windows and MSN search engine for information on people and topics.

Bite A recorded quote, used in documentaries and news programs.

BlackBerry A hand-held device that includes a phone, fax, email, text messaging, video receiver, Internet browsing, time and calendar organizer, corporate data access, paging, and other elements—in effect, a mini-computer.

Blending Sometimes used in radio to denote combining and sending out over the air two or more different sounds at the same time.

Blog (weB LOG) A blog is basically a journal that is available on the *web*. The activity of updating a blog is "blogging" and someone who keeps a blog is a "blogger." Blogs are typically updated daily using software that allows people with little or no technical background to update and maintain the blog. Postings on a blog are almost always arranged in chronological order with the most recent additions featured most prominently. It is common for blogs to be available as *RSS* feeds. See **Blogosphere** or **Blogsphere, RSS**.

Blogosphere or Blogsphere The current state of all information available on *blogs* and/or the sub-culture of those who create and use *blogs*. See **Blog**.

Blu-ray The name blu-ray disc is derived from the blue-violet laser used to read and write this type of disc. It is owned by Sony, the makers of Betamax. Because of this shorter wavelength (405 nm), substantially more data can be stored on a blu-ray disc than on the common DVD format, which uses a red, 650 nm laser. Blu-ray discs can store 25 GB on each layer, as opposed to a DVD's 4.7 GB. Several manufacturers have released single layer and dual layer (50 GB) recordable BDs and rewritable discs. All supporting studios have either already released or have announced release of movies on 50 GB discs.

Boom A crane, a pole, or other device used in television that holds a microphone or camera at the end, allowing it to follow or move closer to the performers.

bps (bits-per-second) A measurement of how fast data is moved from one place to another. A 56 K *modem* can move about 57,000 bits per second. See **Bandwidth, Bit**.

Bridge A sound, usually music, connecting two consecutive segments of a radio program.

British Broadcasting Corporation (BBC) The non-commercial public broadcasting system in the United Kingdom.

Broadband High-speed, high-capacity transmission carried on coaxial or fiber-optic cable.

B roll Visuals without voice on a second source in documentary or news features production.

Browser A computer software program that allows a user to find and access documents from various sources on the Internet. Also, a user engaged in the act of browsing. See **Client, Server, URL, WWW**.

Bumper Material added to the beginning or end of the principal part of a commercial or to the end of a program that is coming up short.

Byte A set of bits that represent a single character. Usually there are 8 bits in a byte, sometimes more, depending on how the measurement is being made.

Cable Wired, as differentiated from over-the-air or broadcast, television transmission. See **Coaxial cable**.

Cable News Network (CNN) A 24-hour news and talk conglomerate of several different channels.

Camcorder A compact combined camera and videocassette recorder.

Cart Audio cartridge; old radio scripts usually specify a cart number, which designates the segment to be inserted at a given place in a program; some scripts use the term *cut* with a number referring to the segment on audiotape. Now rarely used.

Cassette Old container/playing device for either an audio or videotape. Now rarely used.

CD Compact disk; a 4.5-inch diameter disk containing digital audio or digital computer information that is read by a laser-equipped player. An international format for delivering high-fidelity audio.

CD-ROM Compact disc read-only memory; a form of optical storage used as a central medium for distribution of multimedia applications.

Chain break Network break for national or local ads.

Character generator (CG) Electronic device that cuts letters into background pictures.

Chroma key Electronic effect that can cut a given color out of a picture and replace it with another visual.

Chyron The brand name of an electronic character generator, sometimes used generically, but in error, for all electronic character generators. See **Character generator**.

Client A software program that is used to contact and obtain data from a *server* software program on another computer, often across a great distance. Each *client* program is designed to work with one or more specific kinds of *server* programs, and each *server* requires a specific kind of *client*. A web *browser* is a specific kind of *client*. See **Browser, Client, Server**.

Close-up Filling the television screen with a close view of the subject. As with other shot designations, it has various gradations (e.g., medium close-up) and abbreviations.

CNN Cable News Network

Coaxial cable Metallic conductors that carry a large bandwidth and many channels; wired television.

Co-location Most often used to refer to having a *server* that belongs to one person or group physically located on an *Internet-connected network* that belongs to another person or group. Usually this is done because the server owner wants their machine to be on a high-speed Internet connection and/or they do not want the security risks of having the server on their own network. See **Internet (Upper case I), Network, Server**.

Computer An electronic system that manipulates information in digital form and controls external devices. A storage and retrieval machine that can be used by the writer as a word processor or with a television, radio, or film format program.

Conflict In a drama, the two or more forces that are opposed, creating the suspense for the play.

Continuity The generic term applied to the radio and television written copy.

Control board Instruments that regulate the output volume of all radio input sources and can blend the sounds from two or more sources. Sometimes referred to as a switcher.

Convergence Blending of various media, including Internet, radio, television, print, and educational and entertainment software. Interlinking of computer and information technology, media, and communication networks performing similar tasks. At this stage of convergence, the epitome of multi-media coordination, trending toward one encompassing system.

Cookie The most common meaning of "cookie" on the Internet refers to a piece of information sent by a web *server* to a web *browser* that the browser software is expected to save and to send back to the server whenever the browser makes additional requests from the server. Depending on the type of cookie used, and the browsers' settings, the browser may accept or not accept the cookie, and may save the cookie for either a short time or a long time. Cookies might contain information such as login or registration information, online "shopping cart" information, user preferences, etc. See **Browser, Server**.

Co-op announcement Multiple sponsors on a network commercial; individual messages locally spotted.

Copyright Legal establishment of the author's right to his or her work, protecting it from use without the author's permission.

Copywriter The person who writes broadcast continuity; frequently applied to commercial writers only.

Crane shot A camera shot achieved by use of a crane, usually enabling movement. See **Boom**.

Crawl Movement of titles on screen.

Credits The list of performers, production personnel, and other people responsible for the program, usually run at the end of the program, but frequently run partly at the beginning.

Crisis In the play, when the conflict reaches its zenith and something has to happen that causes one force to win and the other to lose.

Cross-fade Dissolving from one sound to another.

Cross plug An announcement for one of the station's programs or the advertiser's other products.

CS Close shot; frequently used for CU.

CU Close-up.

Cursor The marker (or light) on the computer screen that indicates your position.

Cut In film, instantaneous switch from one picture to another, created in film editing room; also used to designate end of a shooting sequence. In television, instantaneous switch from one camera to another.

Cutting Moving abruptly from one sound or picture to another.

Cyberspace Where all media converge: audio, video, telephone, television, wire, and satellite. Term was originated by author William Gibson in his novel *Neuromancer*. The word *cyberspace* is currently used to describe the whole range of information resources available through computer networks. Frequently used interchangeably with the term *Internet*.

DAD (Digital Audio Delivery) A computerized version of the cart machine.

DAT Digital Audio Tape.

Database A structured collection of information organized so it can be retrieved through a computer system.

DBS See **Direct broadcast satellite**.

Demographics Analysis of audience characteristics.

Detail set A constructed detail of the set to augment close-ups.

Digerati The digital version of literati, it is a reference to a vague cloud of people seen to be knowledgeable, hip, or otherwise in-the-know in regards to the digital revolution.

Digital Use of digits 0 and 1 to represent data; the code that instructs a computer to read, store, and operate on that data.

Direct broadcast satellite (DBS) Permits an individual with receiving dish to pick up designated satellite signals; sometimes called satellite-to-home transmission.

Dissolve Fading from one picture into another. DISS frequently used.

Dolly A carriage with three or four wheels on which a microphone or camera is mounted. Also, the movement of the carriage with the camera toward or away from the subject.

Domain name The unique name that identifies an Internet site. Domain names always have two or more parts, separated by dots. The part on the left is the most specific, and the part on the right is the most general. A given machine may have more than one domain name, but a given domain name points to only one machine. See **IP Number, TLD**.

Download Transferring data (usually a file) from another computer to the computer you are using. The opposite of *upload*. See **Upload**.

Drive time Automobile commuter hours, important in determining radio programming formats and placement of commercials.

DSL (Digital Subscriber Line) A method for moving data over regular phone lines. A DSL circuit is much faster than a regular phone connection, and the wires coming into the subscriber's premises are the same (copper) wires used for regular phone service. A DSL circuit must be configured to connect two specific locations, similar to a leased line (however a DSL circuit is not a *leased line*. A common configuration of DSL allows downloads at speeds of up to 1.544 megabits per second, and uploads at speeds of 128 kilobits per second. This arrangement is called *ADSL*: Asymmetric Digital Subscriber Line. Another common configuration is symmetrical: 384 kilobits per second in both directions. In theory ADSL allows download speeds of up to 9 megabits per second and upload speeds of up to 640 kilobits per second. DSL is now a popular alternative to leased lines and ISDN, being faster than ISDN and less costly than traditional leased lines.

DV Digital video.

DVD Digital videodisc; can contain a full-length movie on one disc.

ECU Extreme close-up.

EFFX Effects; usually simply FX.

EFP Electronic field production; the use of minicam equipment to produce commercials and other non-news materials away from the studio.

Electronic synthesizer An electronic device that can create and process sound, from silence into music and other complex sounds.

Email Electronic mail; a message, typically text, sent from one computer to another.

Empathy The identification of the audience with the emotions and problems or joys of one or more characters in the program.

ENG Electronic news gathering; the use of mini-cam equipment to cover news stories.

Equal Time Rule Congressional and FCC rule that bona fide candidates for the same political office be given the opportunity to purchase equal time for radio and television ads.

Establishing shot Usually a wide-angle shot to open the program or sequence, establishing the physical environment.

ET Electronic transcription; old method used with a number (such as ET #6), refers to a segment on a record to be used in a program. Preceded the use of tapes ("cut #6") and cartridges ("cart #6").

Ethernet A very common method of networking computers in a *LAN*. There is more than one type of Ethernet. By 2001 the standard type was "100-BaseT," which can handle up to about 100,000,000 bits-per-second and can be used with almost any kind of computer. See **Bandwidth, LAN.**

ECU Extreme close-up.

EXT Exterior; designates setting in a film script.

Extranet An *intranet* that is accessible to computers that are not physically part of a company's own private *network*, but that is not accessible to the general public, for example to allow vendors and business partners to access a company web site. Often an intranet will make use of a Virtual Private Network (*VPN*). See **Intranet, Network, VPN.**

Facebook An Internet social network originally for college students, now open to users 13 and older. Customized personal profiles with photos, videos, and other information. "Friends" can write in "friends" pages. Anything posted on anyone's "wall" is open for everyone to see.

Fade, fade in, fade out Gradual appearance or disappearance of sound (in radio) or picture (in television).

Fairness Doctrine Former FCC requirement that if only one side of an issue that is controversial for a given community is presented by a radio or television station in that community, comparable time must be provided for the other viewpoints.

FAQ (Frequently Asked Questions) FAQs are documents that list and answer the most common questions on a particular subject. There are hundreds of FAQs on subjects as diverse as pet grooming and cryptography. FAQs are usually written by people who have tired of answering the same question over and over.

Fax Facsimile; the transmission of written material or pictures through wire or radio.

Federal Communications Commission (FCC) Government agency regulating the use of the air waves.

Federal Trade Commission (FTC) Governmental agency with some regulatory power over advertising.

Feed Transmission from a remote site. Also from a network.

FF Full figure shot.

Fiber optic cable A cable carrying laser light encoded with digital signals; capable of reliably transmitting billions of bits of data per second.

File Generic for almost anything composed on a computer, including documents, graphics, and databases. The storage and retrieval area and list.

Filmed teleplay A drama or comedy produced on film for presentation on television or cable.

Finger An Internet software tool for locating people on other Internet sites. Finger is also sometimes used to give access to non-personal information, but the most common use is to see if a person has an account at a particular Internet site. Many sites do not allow incoming finger requests, but many do.

Firewire Data transfer format that allows direct feeding of a video signal into a computer.

Flame Originally, "flame" meant to carry forth in a passionate manner in the spirit of honorable debate. Flames most often involved the use of flowery language and flaming well was an art form. More recently flame has come to refer to any kind of derogatory comment no matter how witless or crude. See **Flame War.**

Flame War When an online discussion degenerates into a series of personal attacks against the debaters, rather than discussion of their positions. A heated exchange. See **Flame.**

Flash A software program used for authoring multimedia.

Focal length Relates to the distance between a lens and the imaging device (i.e., film).

Follow shot Movement of carriage and camera alongside of or with subject.

Format The physical layout and placement of content for a given program. Also the instructions telling a computer to set up for a certain script type.

Frame One individual visual picture; usually applied to the commercial storyboard. Also used to denote an individual complete picture of a video or motion picture film.

Freeze-frame Stopping the action and holding on a single frame.

FS Full shot.

FTP (File Transfer Protocol) A very common method of moving files between two Internet sites. FTP is a way to *login* to another Internet site for the purposes of retrieving and/or sending files. There are many Internet sites that have established publicly accessible repositories of material that can be obtained using FTP, by logging in using the account name "anonymous," thus these sites are called "anonymous ftp servers." FTP was invented and in wide use long before the advent of the *World Wide Web* and originally was always used from a text-only interface. See **Login, WWW**.

Full-service station A radio station with two or more formats; music, news, talk, features, and so on, as differentiated from a specialized station providing predominantly one service (or one form of music or format).

Gamma correction Adjustment of contrast in a film negative. Also used in video to denote the midrange of the luminance signal.

Gateway The technical meaning is a hardware or software set-up that translates between two dissimilar protocols; for example, America Online has a gateway that translates between its internal, proprietary email format and Internet email format. Another, sloppier meaning of gateway is to describe any mechanism for providing access to another system; for example, AOL might be called a gateway to the Internet.

GIF (Graphic Interchange Format) A common format for image files, especially suitable for images containing large areas of the same color. GIF format files of simple images are often smaller than the same file would be if stored in *JPEG* format, but GIF format does not store photographic images as well as JPEG. See **JPEG, PNG**.

Gigabyte 1000 or 1024 *megabytes*, depending on who is measuring. See **Byte**.

Google Internet search engine for information on people and topics.

Graphics The visual materials (except the taped or live action) used in a program.

Hard drive A computer's main storage area.

Hard news/hard lead The concrete facts about the story. See **Soft news/soft lead**.

HDTV (High Definition TV) An increased number of lines in a picture (1150 scan lines), giving it much better resolution than current systems, especially the U.S. N.T.S.C. standard of 525 lines, plus a widescreen (16×9) format, better color, and 4-channel digital sound.

Hertz The measure of each frequency unit, 1 Hertz (Hz) equaling one cycle per second.

Hit As used in reference to the World Wide Web, hit means a single request from a web *browser* for a single item from a web *server*; thus in order for a web browser to display a page that contains three graphics, four hits would occur at the server: one for the *HTML* page, and one for each of the three graphics. See **Browser, HTML, Server**.

Home page An Internet web site's opening page, which may have links to other pages. Originally, the *web* page that your *browser* is set to use when it starts up. The more common meaning refers to the main web page for a business, organization, person, or simply the main page out of a collection of web pages, for example, "Check out so-and-so's new home page."

Host Any computer on a *network* that is a repository for services available to other computers on the *network*. It is quite common to have one host machine provide several services, such as *SMTP* (email) and *HTTP* (web). See **Network, SMTP**.

HTML (Hypertext Markup Language) The coding language used to create *hypertext* documents for use on the World Wide Web. HTML looks a lot like old-fashioned typesetting code, where you surround a block of text with codes that indicate how it should appear. The "hyper" in hypertext comes from the fact that in HTML you can specify that a block of text, or an image, is linked to another file on the Internet. HTML files are meant to be viewed using a "web browser." HTML is loosely based on a more comprehensive system for markup called *SGML*, and is expected to eventually be replaced by *XML*-based *XHTML* standards. See **Browser, Hypertext, WWW**.

HTTP Hypertext transport protocol, providing connections for the World Wide Web.

Hypertext Method of organizing information retrieval that brings together related material and through links allows a shift to other documents in other hosts. Generally, any text that contains links to other documents—words or phrases in the document that can be chosen by a reader and which cause another document to be retrieved and displayed. See **HTML, HTTP**.

Icon A small picture or symbol representing a computer program, file, or feature.

ID Station identification.

Infotainment Making the news entertaining to draw more viewers, often at the expense of the informational content.

Instant replay Playback of a videotape even as it is recorded, used frequently in live sports events.

INT Interior; designates setting in a film script.

Interactive Two-way communication, usually through computer or cable for information retrieval or instruction response; computers, games, multimedia systems, and other hardware that respond to the actions of the user.

internet (Lower case i) Any time you connect two or more *networks* together, you have an internet—as in international or inter-state. See **Internet (Upper case I), Network**.

Internet (Upper case I) The vast collection of interconnected networks that are connected using the *TCP/IP* protocols and that evolved from the *ARPANET of* the late 1960s and early 1970s. The Internet connects tens of thousands of independent networks into a vast global *internet* and is probably the largest *Wide Area Network* in the world. See **internet (Lower case i), Network**.

Intro Standard material used to introduce every program or designated segments within a program in a series; also called stock opening.

iPhone Small hand-held device combination of cell phone, iPod, camera, text messaging, email, Web browser, music, videos, photos, and other applications.

iPod Portable music player. iTunes software organizes and transfers songs and playlists to iPod in a variety of formats.

IP Number (Internet Protocol Number) Sometimes called a dotted quad. A unique number consisting of four parts separated by dots, for example, 165.113.245.2. Every machine that is on the Internet has a unique IP number—if a machine does not have an IP number, it is not really on the Internet. Many machines (especially servers) also have one or more domain names that are easier for people to remember.

IRC (Internet Relay Chat) Basically a huge multi-use live chat facility. There are a number of major IRC *servers* around the world which are linked to each other. Anyone can create a channel and anything that anyone types in a given channel is seen by all others in the channel. Private channels can (and are) created for multi-person conference calls. See **Server**.

ISDN (Integrated Services Digital Network) Basically a way to move more data over existing regular phone lines. ISDN is available to much of the USA and in most markets it is priced very comparably to standard analog phone circuits. It can provide speeds of roughly 128,000 bits-per-second over regular phone lines. In practice, most people will be limited to 56,000 or 64,000 bits-per-second. Unlike *DSL*, ISDN can be used to connect to many different locations, one at a time, just like a regular telephone call, as long as the other location also has ISDN. See **DSL**.

ISP (Internet Service Provider) A company that sets up a computer network that enables its customers to get online.

ITFS Instructional Television Fixed Service; a relatively inexpensive microwave system that permits point-to-point transmission of instructional, professional, and other materials.

ITV Instructional television.

Java Java is a network-friendly programming language invented by Sun Microsystems. Java is often used to build large, complex systems that involve several different computers interacting across networks, for example transaction processing systems. Java is also used to create software with graphical user interfaces such as editors, audio players, web browsers, etc. Java is also popular for creating programs that run in small electronic devices, such as mobile telephones. Using small java programs (called *Applets)*, web pages can include functions such as animations, calculators, and other fancy tricks. See **Applet**.

JavaScript JavaScript is a programming language that is mostly used in web pages, usually to add features that make the web page more interactive. When javascript is included in an *HTML* file it relies upon the browser to interpret the javascript.

JPEG (Joint Photographic Experts Group) JPEG is most commonly mentioned as a format for image files. JPEG format is preferred to the *GIF* format for photographic images as opposed to line art or simple logo art. See **GIF**.

Key A special effect combining two or more video sources, cutting a foreground into a background.

Kilobyte A thousand bytes; actually, usually 1024 (2^{10}) bytes. See **Byte**.

Kine, kinescope The early television picture tube and, before videotape, the term for recording a television program by filming it off the kinescope through a monitor.

LA Live action.

Laser Acronym for *light amplification through stimulated emission of radiation*; a developing technique for multichannel and multidimensional television transmission.

LCU Large close-up.

Lead The first paragraph of a news story, usually containing the 5 Ws.

Lead-in, lead-out The material introducing the substance of a program, such as a recap preceding the daily episode of a soap opera, and the material at the end of a program preparing the audience for the next program.

Limbo Performer, through lighting and position of camera, stands out from a seemingly black or nonexistent background.

Linear Information presented in a set order, from beginning to end.

Linear editing Refers to accessing pre-recorded analog information on a linear tape for assembling into a new video program and can be time consuming. Nonlinear editing refers to randomly accessed digital information for assembling or constructing a new video program.

Lineup List of stories for a news program, in their order of presentation. See **Rundown** sheet and **Routine** sheet.

Link The means of connecting different materials or documents on a computer web site.

LinkdIn A business/professional Internet social network for connection on jobs, and contacts in various professions and industries.

Live-type taped Television directorial technique that used the continuous-action procedures of the live show. Also called "live on tape"; from the early days of videotape when editing was done by physically cutting the tape—the more put on the tape at the time of recording, the less cutting had to be done later.

Login Noun or a verb. Noun: the account name used to gain access to a computer system, not a secret (contrast with *password*). Verb: the act of connecting to a computer system by giving your credentials (usually your "username" and "password"). Also called logon. See **Password**.

Logo Visual identification symbol of a station, company, or product.

LS Long shot.

M2S Medium 2-shot.

Magazine format A program format with a number of different segments not necessarily related in content.

Magnetic tape A tape coated with magnetic particles; was used in television for recording, storage, and playback of programs or other materials.

Mashup A web page or site made by automatically combining content from other sources, usually by using material available via *RSS* feeds and/or *REST* interfaces. See **RSS**.

Matte A process by which two different visual sources are combined to appear to be one setting, such as placing a performer on one camera into a setting on another; same as **key**, but can add color to the image. Also spelled *mat* or *matt*.

MCU Medium close-up.

Medium shot A wider shot than a CU or MCU, but not as wide as a 3/4 shot or full shot. Usually cuts at about the waist.

Megabyte Technically speaking, a million bytes. In many cases the term means 1024 kilobytes, which is more than an even million. See **Byte, Kilobyte**.

Memory The storage capacity of the computer.

Mic Microphone.

Microwave Transmission on a frequency 1000 MHz and over (not receivable by ordinary home receiver); used for special point-to-point materials.

Miniature A setting used to simulate one that can't be economically built or located live.

Minicam Lightweight, easily portable camera and tape system that facilitates highly mobile news gathering and remote coverage. See **EFP, ENG**.

Minidocumentary A short documentary feature most often used in magazine-type television programs.

Mix In film, rerecording of sounds to blend them together; in radio, combining several sound elements onto a single tape or track; in television, the point in a dissolve when the two images pass each other (the term is sometimes used in place of dissolve).

Modem (MOdulator, DEModulator) A device that connects a computer to a phone line. A telephone for a computer. A modem allows a computer to talk to other computers through the phone system. Basically, modems do for computers what a telephone does for humans. The maximum practical *bandwidth* using a modem over regular telephone lines is currently around 57,000 *bps*. See **Bandwidth**.

Monitor Television-like device on which your computer displays information.

Montage Blending of two or more sounds or series of visuals.

MOR Middle-of-the-road; a radio format combining popular and standard music.

Mortise A cutout area of a picture where other material can be inserted.

Mouse Device for controlling the cursor on a personal computer's screen.

MS Medium shot.

MU Music.

Multiplex In radio, transmitting more than one signal over the same frequency channel, the additional signals referred to as being transmitted on sub carriers; in television, feeding the signals from two or more sources into one camera.

MySpace An Internet interactive social network with users' selected "friends." Contains personal profiles, photos, music, blogs, and other information.

Narrowcasting With the growth of multiple transmission-reception technologies, more and more programming can be aimed at specialized audiences.

National Association of Broadcasters (NAB) A voluntary association of television and radio stations. Until their abolition in 1983, the NAB's Radio and Television Codes of Good Practice served as self regulatory guides for much of broadcasting.

Netiquette The etiquette on the *Internet*.

Netizen Derived from the term *citizen*, referring to a citizen of the *Internet*, or someone who uses networked resources. The term connotes civic responsibility and participation.

Network Any time you connect two or more computers together so that they can share resources, you have a computer network. Connect two or more networks together and you have an *internet*. See **internet** (**Lower case i**).

Newsgroup The name for discussion groups on USENET. See **USENET**.

Node Any single computer connected to a network. See **Network**.

Nonlinear A format that allows users to read and access information in any order they choose.

OC, O/C Off-camera.

Online Being connected to another computer via a telecommunications link.

On mic Microphone position in which the speaker is right at the microphone; this is the position used if no other is indicated.

Open Source Software Open Source Software is software for which the underlying programming code is available to the users so that they may read it, make changes to it, and build new versions of the software incorporating their changes. There are many types of Open Source Software, mainly differing in the licensing term under which (altered) copies of the source code may be (or must be) redistributed.

OS Off-screen sound effects.

Outline An early step in the process of selling a script or program concept; essentially a narrative of the characters and plot; also called a **treatment**.

Outro Standard material used at the end of every program or of designated segments in a program in a continuing series; also called *stock close*.

Outtake Material that has been recorded in the preparation of the show, but is deleted in the completed tape or film.

Pan Lateral movement of the camera in a fixed position.

Participating announcement The commercials of several advertisers who share the cost of a program.

Password A code used to gain access *(login)* to a locked system. Good passwords contain letters and non-letters and are not simple combinations such as *virtue7*.

PB Pull back; referring to camera movement or action of zoom lens.

PC Short for personal computer; a reference to IBM-type computers as differentiated from Apple Macintosh computers.

PDF (Portable Document Format) A file format designed to enable printing and viewing of documents with all their formatting (typefaces, images, layout, etc.) appearing the same regardless of what operating system is used, so a PDF document should look the same on Windows, Macintosh, Linux, OS/2, etc. The PDF format is based on the widely used Postscript document-description language. Both PDF and Postscript were developed by the Adobe Corporation.

People meter An audience measurement device that requires the viewers to participate, ostensibly resulting in more accurate figures.

Permalink A "permanent link" to a particular posting in a *blog*. A permalink is a *URL* that points to a specific blog posting, rather than to the page in which the posting original occurred (which may no longer contain the posting.) See **Blog, URL**.

Pic The individual still picture, designated on the script. The plural is *pix*.

Ping To check if a server is running. From the sound that a sonar system makes in movies, you know, when they are searching for a submarine.

Plug-in A (usually small) piece of software that adds features to a larger piece of software. Common examples are plug-ins for the Netscape® *browser* and web *server*. Adobe Photoshop also uses plug-ins. See **Browser, Server**.

Podcasting or Pod-casting A form of audio broadcasting using the Internet, podcasting takes its name from a combination of iPod and broadcasting. iPod is the immensely popular digital audio player made by Apple computer, but podcasting does not actually require the use of an iPod. Podcasting involves making one or more audio files available as "enclosures" in an *RSS* feed. A pod-caster creates a list of music, and/or other sound files (such as recorded poetry, or "talk radio" material) and makes that list available in the *RSS* 2.0 format. The list can then be obtained by other people using various podcast "retriever" software that read the feed and make the audio files available to digital audio devices (including, but not limited to iPods) where users may then listen to them at their convenience. See **RSS**.

Port First and most generally, a place where information goes into or out of a computer, or both. For example, the serial port on a personal computer is where a *modem* would be connected. On the Internet port often refers to a number that is part of a URL, appearing after a colon (:) right after the domain name. Every service on an Internet server listens on a particular port number on that server. Most services have standard port numbers, for example, web servers normally listen on port 80. Services can also listen on non-standard ports, in which case the port number must be specified in a URL when accessing the server. Finally, port also refers to translating a piece of software to bring it from one type of computer system to another, for example, to translate a Windows program so that is will run on a Macintosh. See **URL**.

Portal Usually used as a marketing term to describe a web site that is, or is intended to be, the first place people see when using the web. Typically a "portal site" has a catalog of web sites, a search engine, or both. A portal site may also offer email and other service to entice people to use that site as their main "point of entry" (hence "portal") to the web.

POV Point of view; applied to programs, usually documentaries, that present a clear and specific point of view. Also used to describe a particular shot, specifying the character's visual point of view, such as "Jack's POV—panning shot of railroad station parking lot."

Pre-interview Establishment of general areas of questions and answers with an interviewee before the taping or live interview.

Prime-Time Rule PTAR; FCC requirement that television stations allocate at least 1 hour during prime time to non-network programming was discontinued in 1996.

Promo Promotional announcement. See **Cross plug.**

Protagonist The principal character(s) in the play, who move(s) the plot forward.

Protocol On the Internet "protocol" usually refers to a set of rules that define an exact format for communication between systems. For example the *HTTP* protocol defines the format for communication between web browsers and web servers, the *IMAP* protocol defines the format for communication between IMAP email servers and clients, and the *SSL* protocol defines a format for encrypted communications over the Internet.

PSA Public service announcement.

Psychographics Audience analysis that goes deeper than demographics and includes attitudes, beliefs, and behavior.

PTV Usually means public television, sometimes used to mean pay television.

Quadruplex The use of four overlapping heads on a videotape recorder to produce tapes of almost-live quality; the first commercial magnetic video recording system, from Ampex. Was used to play back the 2-inch quad tape-recorded from 1956 until the type 1-inch C format was introduced.

RAM A computer's memory capacity, or random access memory.

Rating The percentage of all television homes tuned in to a given program. See **Share.**

Remote Program or materials, usually live coverage, produced at a site away from the studio.

Reuters A worldwide news agency.

Rewrite Writing the story a second (or even a third) time, to add new information or to make it more interesting to the audience who has seen or heard it before.

Router A special-purpose computer (or software package) that handles the connection between two or more packet-switched *networks.* Routers spend all their time looking at the source and destination addresses of the *packets* passing through them and deciding which route to send them on. See **Network.**

Routine sheet A detailed outline of the segments of a program, frequently including designation of the routines or subject matter, performers, site if remote, time, and so on.

RSS (Rich Site Summary or RDF Site Summary or Real Simple Syndication) A commonly used protocol for syndication and sharing of content, originally developed to facilitate the syndication of news articles, now widely used to share the contents of *blogs. Mashups* are often made using RSS feeds. RSS is an *XML*-based summary of a web site, usually used for syndication and other kinds of content-sharing. There are RSS "feeds" that are sources of RSS information about web sites, and RSS "readers" that read RSS feeds and display their content to users. RSS is being overtaken by a newer, more complex protocol called *Atom.*

RT Reel type.

RTSP (Real Time Streaming Protocol) RTSP is an official Internet standard *(RFC 2326)* for delivering and receiving streams of data such as audio and video. The standard allows for both real-time ("live") streams of data and streams from stored data.

Rundown sheet Sometimes used interchangeably with routine sheet, but generally not as detailed.

Scenario Film script outline.

Screen grabs Conversion of an image on a computer monitor (such as that from a film, video, or photo) into a graphics file.

Scroll Moving the computer screen up or down. At one time it was used to list credits on a television show, and sometimes still is where state-of-the-art equipment is unavailable.

SE Sound effects.

Search Engine A (usually web-based) system for searching the information available on the *web.* Some search engines work by automatically searching the contents of other systems and creating a database of the results. Other search engines contain only material manually approved for inclusion in a database, and some combine the two approaches. See **WWW.**

Security Certificate A chunk of information (often stored as a text file) that is used by the SSL protocol to establish a secure connection.

Segue Transition from one radio sound source to another.

Server A computer, or a software package, that provides a specific kind of service to *client* software running on other computers. The term can refer to a particular piece of software, such as a *WWW* server, or to the machine on which the software is running, for example, "Our mail server is down today, that's why email isn't getting out." A single server machine can (and often does) have several different server software packages running on it, thus providing many different servers to *clients* on the *network*. Sometimes server software is designed so that additional capabilities can be added to the main program by adding small programs known as *servlets*. See Client, Network, Servlet.

Service announcement Short informational announcement, not necessarily completely of a public service nature but similar in form to the PSA.

Servlet A small computer program designed to add capabilities to a larger piece of *server* software. Common examples are "java servlets," which are small programs written in the *java* language and which are added to a *web* server. Typically a web server that uses java servlets will have many of them, each one designed to handle a very specific situation, for example one servlet will handle adding items to a "shopping cart," while a different servlet will handle deleting items from the "shopping cart." See Java, Server, Web.

SFX Sound effects.

Share The percentage of all television sets actually on at a given time that are tuned to a given program. See Rating.

Sitcom Television situation comedy; a staple of television programming since the 1950s.

SL Studio location.

Slide An individual picture that was often used in broadcast news and very frequently in corporate video, with a complete presentation in the latter consisting of slides and voice-over narration. Was usually 35 mm format, sometimes larger.

SOF Sound-on-film.

Soft news/soft lead Presentation of the feature aspects, such as human interest, rather than the hard facts of the news story. See Hard news/hard lead.

Software Instructions telling a computer what operations to perform.

SOT Sound-on-(video)tape.

Spam (or Spamming) An inappropriate attempt to use a *mailing list*, or *USENET*, or other networked communications facility as if it was a broadcast medium (which it is not) by sending the same message to a large number of people who didn't ask for it. The term probably comes from a famous Monty Python skit that featured the word "spam" repeated over and over. The term may also have come from someone's low opinion of the food product with the same name, which is generally perceived as a generic content-free waste of resources. (Spam is a registered trademark of Hormel Corporation, for its processed meat product.)

Split screen Two or more separate pictures on the same television screen.

Spyware A somewhat vague term generally referring to software that is secretly installed on a users computer and that monitors use of the computer in some way without the users' knowledge or consent. Most spyware tries to get the user to view advertising and/or particular *web pages*. Some spyware also sends information about the user to another machine over the Internet. Spyware is usually installed without a users' knowledge as part of the installation of other software, especially software such as music sharing software obtained via *download*.

Stock Film or tape footage previously recorded.

Storyboard Frame-by-frame drawings showing a program's video and audio sequences in chronological order; essential in preparing and selling commercial announcements and sometimes required in showing development of a film story.

STV Subscription or pay television.

Summary An overview of a proposed script, summarizing the idea and content for a prospective producer.

Super Superimposition of one picture over another in television.

Switching See Cutting.

Synthesizer See Electronic synthesizer.

T-1 A leased-line connection capable of carrying data at 1,544,000 *bits*-per-second. At maximum theoretical capacity, a T-1 line could move a *megabyte* in less than 10 seconds. That is still not fast enough for full-screen, full-motion video, for which you need at least 10,000,000 bits-per-second. T-1 lines are commonly used to connect large *LANs* to the Internet. See **Bit, Megabyte.**

T-3 A leased-line connection capable of carrying data at 44,736,000 bits-per-second. This is more than enough to do full-screen, full-motion video.

Tag The term "tag" can be used as a noun or verb. As a noun, a tag is a basic element of the languages used to create web pages *(HTML)* and similar languages such as *XML.* Another, more recent meaning of tag is related to reader-created tags where blogs and other content (such as photos, music, etc.) may be "tagged," which means to assign a keyword, such as "politics" or "gardening," this enables searches for "all the blog postings in the past week that are tagged 'prenatal care'." See **Blog, HTML, XML.**

Talk The term applied to a program that concentrates on interviews, conversations, and other forms of talk.

TCP/IP (Transmission Control Protocol/ Internet Protocol) This is the suite of protocols that defines the *Internet.* Originally designed for the *UNIX* operating system, TCP/IP software is now included with every major kind of computer operating system. To be truly on the Internet, your computer must have TCP/IP software.

Tease A program segment, announcement, intro, or other device to get the attention and interest of the audience.

Teleconference An important aspect of corporate video, it enables individuals or groups to hold meetings and conferences although separated by distances.

Terabyte 1000 gigabytes. See **Gigabyte.**

Terminal A device that allows you to send commands to a computer somewhere else. At a minimum, this usually means a keyboard and a display screen and some simple circuitry. Usually you will use terminal software in a personal computer—the software pretends to be (emulates) a physical terminal and allows you to type commands to a computer somewhere else.

Tilt Vertical movement of the camera from a fixed position.

Titles Credits and other printed information on the television screen.

Track, track up Following a subject with a camera (see Follow shot); raising the intensity of the sound. Used in video as a cue from the director to bring up the pre-recorded audio on a tape that will be currently on line: The director might say, "Roll VTR #1 and track it," meaning that both the video and the audio will be on line.

Travel shot Lateral movement of the dolly and camera. Also called a **truck shot.**

Treatment See Scenario.

Trojan Horse A computer program is either hidden inside another program or that masquerades as something it is not in order to trick potential users into running it. For example a program that appears to be a game or image file but in reality performs some other function. The term "Trojan Horse" comes from a possibly mythical ruse of war used by the Greeks sometime between 1500 and 1200 B.C. A Trojan Horse computer program may spread itself by sending copies of itself from the host computer to other computers, but unlike a *virus* it will (usually) not infect other programs. See **Virus, Worm.**

Truck shot Lateral movement of the dolly and camera. Also called a **travel shot.**

Twitter An Internet social network with microblogging with a limit of 140 characters. Messages are called "tweets."

2S Two-shot; the inclusion of two performers in the picture.

United Press International (UPI) One of the wire services used extensively by news programs.

Upload Transferring data (usually a file) from the computer you are using to another computer. The opposite of *download.* See **Download.**

URL Universal Resource Locator; an Internet address.

URN (Uniform Resource Name) A URL that is supposed to be available for a long time. For an address to be a URN some institution is supposed to make a commitment to keep the resource available at that address. See **URL.**

USENET A world-wide system of discussion groups, with comments passed among hundreds of thousands of machines. Not all USENET machines are on the *Internet*. USENET is completely decentralized, with over 10,000 discussion areas, called *newsgroups*. See **Newsgroup**.

VCR Videocassette or video cartridge recorder.

VDT Video Display Terminal; the computer screen.

Verification Double-checking the sources of a story to be certain that it is accurate.

Videodisc Successor to videotape; looks and plays like a record and carries large amounts of easily recoverable video information.

Videotape Magnetic tape used for recording, storage, and playback of segments of or an entire television program.

Video compression Reducing the quantity of data required to present digital video images. Reduces the bandwidth necessary to transmit video, allowing as much as 15 to 30 times more data to be stored with little loss of video quality.

Vidifont See **Character generator**.

Virus A chunk of computer programming code that makes copies of itself without any conscious human intervention. Some viruses do more than simply replicate themselves, they might display messages, install other software or files, delete software of files, etc. A virus requires the presence of some other program to replicate itself. Typically viruses spread by attaching themselves to programs and in some cases files, for example the file formats for Microsoft word processor and spreadsheet programs allow the inclusion of programs called "macros."

Vlog A blog with video material. which can in some cases be a breeding ground for viruses. See **Trojan Horse, Worm**.

VO, V.O. Voice-over; the narrator or performer is not seen.

VPN (Virtual Private Network) Usually refers to a *network* in which some of the parts are connected using the public *Internet*, but the data sent across the Internet is encrypted, so the entire network is "virtually" private.

VTR Videotape recorder.

WAN (Wide Area Network) Any *Internet* or *network* that covers an area larger than a single building or campus.

Web Short for "World Wide Web."

Web page A document designed for viewing in a web browser. Typically written in HTML. A web site is made of one or more web pages. See **Browser, HTML, Web, web site**.

Webcasting Programs on the Internet.

Web site The entire collection of *web pages* and other information (such as images, sound, and video files, etc.) that are made available through what appears to users as a single web server. Typically all the of pages in a web site share the same basic *URL*. The term has a somewhat informal nature since a large organization might have separate "web sites" for each division, but someone might talk informally about the organizations' "web site" when speaking of all of them.

Wide angle lens A lens of short focal length that encompasses more of the subject area in the picture.

Wide shot (WS) Another term for the long shot or establishing shot.

WiFi (Wireless Fidelity) A popular term for a form of wireless data communication, basically WiFi is "Wireless Ethernet." See **Ethernet**.

Windows The operating system used in most computers, frequently updated, requiring purchase of a new Windows system.

Wipe A picture beginning at one end of the screen that moves horizontally, vertically, or diagonally, pushing or wiping the previous picture off the screen.

Wirephoto Photo transmitted through telephone for use in news broadcasts.

World Wide Web, WWW Frequently referred to as the "web," an Internet client-server hypertext distributed information retrieval system; the global interconnected computer networks. Access is through a universal HTML entry code, followed by "www" and the Internet address.

Worldwide Television News (WTN) Provides services to radio, television, and cable.

Worm A worm is a *virus* that does not infect other programs. It makes copies of itself, and infects additional computers (typically by making use of network connections) but does not attach itself to additional programs; however a worm might alter, install, or destroy files and programs. See **Trojan Horse**, Virus.

Wrap, wrap-up The closing for a news program.

WS Wide shot.

WTN Worldwide Television News.

XCU Extreme close-up.

XHTML (eXtensible HyperText Markup Language) Basically *HTML* expressed as valid *XML*. XHTML is intended to be used in the same places you would use HTML (creating web pages) but is much more strictly defined, which makes it a lot easier to create software that can read it, edit it, check it for errors, etc. XHTML is expected to eventually replace HTML. See **HTML, XML.**

XLS Extreme long shot.

XML (eXtensible Markup Language) A widely used system for defining data formats. XML provides a very rich system to define complex documents and data structures such as invoices, molecular data, news feeds, glossaries, inventory descriptions, real estate properties, etc. As long as a programmer has the XML definition for a collection of data (often called a "schema") then they can create a program to reliably process any data formatted according to those rules. XML is a subset of the older *SGML* specification—the definition of XML is SGML minus a couple of dozen items.

YouTube An Internet social network through which users can share videos.

ZO Zoom.

Zoom Changing the variable focal length of a lens during a shot to make it appear as if the shot were moving toward or away from the viewer.

INDEX

CPSIA information can be obtained
at www.ICGtesting.com
Printed in the USA
FFOW03n0838060815
15819FF